BING CROSBY

Bing Crosby about 1950.

BING CROSBY
A Bio-Bibliography

J. ROGER OSTERHOLM

Bio-Bibliographies in the Performing Arts, Number 58
James Robert Parish, Series Adviser

GREENWOOD PRESS
Westport, Connecticut • London

Library of Congress Cataloging-in-Publication Data

Osterholm, J. Roger.
    Bing Crosby : a bio-bibliography / J. Roger Osterholm.
       p. cm.—(Bio-bibliographies in the performing arts, ISSN
0892–5550 ; no. 58)
      Includes discography (p.), filmography (p.), radiography (p.),
videography (p.), bibliography (p.), and index.
     ISBN 0–313–27726–5 (alk. paper)
     1. Crosby, Bing, 1904–1977—Bibliography. 2. Crosby, Bing,
1904–1977—Discography. 3. Crosby, Bing, 1904–1977—Film catalogs.
4. Crosby, Bing, 1904–1977—Video catalogs. I. Title. II. Series.
ML134.5.C76O87   1994
782.42164′092—dc20
[B]   94–28690

British Library Cataloguing in Publication Data is available.

Library of Congress Catalog Card Number: 94–28690
ISBN: 0–313–27726–5
ISSN: 0892–5550

First published in 1994

Greenwood Press, 88 Post Road West, Westport, CT 06881
An imprint of Greenwood Publishing Group, Inc.

Printed in the United States of America

The paper used in this book complies with the
Permanent Paper Standard issued by the National
Information Standards Organization (Z39.48–1984).

10 9 8 7 6 5 4 3 2 1

To my loving wife, Diane, and our children,
Crosby fans all, and my much older brother, Donald,
who caught the Crosby bug and infected me.
The volume is also dedicated
to lovers of music and Bing Crosby,
old and new and those to come, everywhere.

Contents

Preface

If Bob Hope, the great comedian, actor, golfer, writer, and humanitarian, is the Mount McKinley of entertainment, then Bing Crosby, as singer, comedian, actor, sportsman (horses, golf, baseball, boxing, fishing, hunting), songwriter, raconteur, entrepreneur, and philanthropist all combined under one skin and hairpiece, is the Mount Everest. Bing always called himself lucky and lazy, but he worked overtime in activities he liked, not thinking that work, and his worldly luck was that people admired whatever he did. In the late '20s Bing earned money comparable to his talents and spirit, but the Bing of the mid-'30s, now with money equal to his talents, bridled his spirit so that his innate decency overshadowed his fun, and that Crosby is the one who remained at the top of popular entertainment, continuously innovating and challenging new material with that warmth in his voice and respectfulness in his heart until his death on a golf course in Spain October 14, 1977, when his passing was mourned by the whole world.

Everyone is still charmed by his "White Christmas," his Irish lullabies and St. Patrick's Day ditties, his French ballads, his Hawaiian and cowboy songs, his jazz recordings, and his tender crooning of perennial love songs. Single-handedly he increased Hawaiian tourism. The major holidays, not only Christmas, still belong musically to Bing, and the world will always pay him fealty. By 1934 he even taught the world how to relax, in a decade of poverty in which "getting and spending" was replaced by a need to belong and to play. If Bob Hope is like everyone's favorite visiting uncle, Bing became a member of the family.

Of recent performers with youthful indiscretions, only time will tell if they have the wisdom and inner-strength of a Crosby, who never intentionally hurt anyone, to succeed and endure nearly as well and as long. Bing's humble origins lent him a natural sympathy for people, even to siding with the underdog, and for a wholesome life. Crosby was popular for fifty-two years, since 1926 in California, and remains a towering and durable figure today. Bing's first four sons could not manage such a conversion or maintain such popularity, and neither did Elvis Presley, who died from drugs at age forty-two in 1977, two months before

Crosby's death, when the rock 'n' roll star was no longer
popular and having inflamed teenage hearts for fifteen
years, or even twenty-three to his death. Similar comparisons could be made to the Beatles and the Rolling Stones;
only Frank Sinatra has approached Bing in popularity and
durability in singing popular music.

Bing is unique, but being at the top for so long, he
was also the target of a few hostile critics, erstwhile
friends, and a resentful son, and with much less reason than
some who attack others. The most recent, if oblique, attack, too late for further inclusion, is <u>The Secret Life of
Bob Hope</u> by Arthur Marx, son of Groucho, which alleges that
Hope kept a stable of women, whom he shared with Bing.

Bing had an inimitable decency, playfulness, and voice.
His fans would never make the spectacle over a house and
belongings that some Presley fans do. More than Elvis, who
earned more money in the three years after his death than he
had through his whole career, Bing lives in what counts
most, his films and recordings, his annual charity golf
tournament and other charities, and many warm memories.
Along with Kathryn Crosby, Bob Hope is the credible inter-
preter of the real Bing Crosby, and Hope's respect and
admiration for the Mount Everest of our popular culture has
never waned or even wavered since they first met in 1932.

In the 1980s Bing's popularity waned, as was to be
expected after his death. A cloud had surrounded the peak
of Everest. But lately the mists have parted and a noticeable revival of great interest has appeared. His films are
shown more often on television, and his records play more
often on easy-listening radio stations. No doubt Crosby's
popularity will wax and wane, but forever. The spate of
recent detractors will recede into perspective. Perhaps his
fame will rise and fall with the cultural rhythm of civility
and wholesome values against the counterpoint of license and
irresponsibility and of a musical voice against bizarre
video antics.

As a twenty-year-old drummer and singer just learning
his craft in amateur bands in Spokane, Washington, Bing
Crosby absorbed the techniques of several bands, like the
Memphis Five, McKinney's Cotton Pickers, the Original Dixieland Jazz Band, Jack Chapman's, Dwight "Spike" Johnson's,
Jay Eslick's, Vic Meyers', George Olsen's, Jackie Souders',
Cab Calloway's, Paul Whiteman's, and the Mound City Blues
Blowers; of instrumentalists like Rudy Wiedoeft, Ross Gor-
man, Bix Beiderbecke, Jack Teagarden, Tommy and Jimmy Dor-
sey, Joe Venuti, and Eddie Lang; and of several singers,
like Savoy and Brennan, Al Jolson, Eddie Cantor, Gallagher
and Shean, Willie and Eugene Howard, Margaret Illington,
Mildred Bailey, Louis Armstrong, Billie Holiday, Jelly Roll
Morton, Ethel Waters, Nick Lucas, the Mills Brothers, and
Rudy Vallee.

Bing Crosby early defined his code of piety, patriotism, manliness, and fun--financed through song. He was as
deficient in ambition as he was blessed with talent, and
only through the drive of his brother Everett did he go from
a relaxed team-player to an outstanding single, who then
made memorable teams with such stars as Louis Armstrong, Bob
Hope, Dorothy Lamour, Mary Martin, Fred Astaire, the Andrews
Sisters, Rosemary Clooney, and Grace Kelly. He discovered

Victor Borge in 1940, saved the life of Mildred Bailey in 1949, saved the career of Judy Garland in 1950, and revived the career of Rosemary Clooney in 1975.

The various sections trace Bing Crosby from his break with the European style of singing to his own contributions to jazz and romantic ballads; from two-reel musical comedies to major comedies, musicals, and dramatic feature films, for which he maintained the position as the most popular film star for an unequaled five years, from 1944 to 1948; from relying on partners to performing solo; and, inspired by Kate Smith, Vallee, and Whiteman, from daily singing radio programs to major weekly series that dominated the airwaves for years, guided musically by Eddie Lang, Lennie Hayton, Jimmy Dorsey, and John Scott Trotter; then, on television, Bing Crosby was nearly as prominent for another twenty-four years. Russ Columbo, most black singers since 1932, Tony Martin, Frank Sinatra, Perry Como, Dean Martin, Tony Bennett, and even Elvis Presley said they learned the basics of their craft from Bing, who mastered vocal hot-licks and invented the techniques of singing to a microphone.

Each section of the book is organized chronologically. Following a detailed Biography and Chronology, separate series of recordings, films, radio programs, television shows (and home videos), and bibliography have idividually numbered entries. The Index lists the series numbers rather than page numbers, although the Biography and Chronology are indexed by page numbers. Recordings have D numbers; films, F numbers; radio programs, R numbers; television shows, V numbers; and the bibliography, B numbers. In a few cases a late entry is listed with a letter added to the number, like D2539A, to include it without having to renumber the whole series when a further item was discovered. Thus, some late finds have been included rather than silently omitted.

The Biography and Chronology include material gathered especially from sources listed in the Bibliography, though many facts are documented in the text. The Biography includes Bing's family, friends, homes, vacations, and his participation in golf, horse racing and breeding, hunting and fishing, and ranching. Besides providing details of his enormously busy and complex life, it also indicates his innovations and status in music, films, radio, and television. An Epilogue surveys recent opinions of his career and character. The Chronology lists the highlights of Bing's life and career and opens with a list of economic and population comparisons that help in relating earnings and sales from one period to another.

Some new material includes an explanation of a Federal Bureau of Investigation report that Bing paid $10,000 to an extortionist in 1937, a clarification of Bing's actual date of birth, a comprehensive list of each time the Kid from Spokane spent time in jail, his association with Machine Gun Jack McGurn, Dixie Lee's large consumption of brandy while pregnant, more films and cartoons that depict Bing, and a review of recent Crosby detractors.

The Discography lists each commercial and most private recording, the dates, the names of songwriters, orchestras, accompanists, and record labels, and matrix numbers up to 1957. A thorough list of LP albums and compact discs that include more than one song by Bing is at the end of the

Discography. Lists of Bing's gold records, Oscar-nominated songs, and the songs Bing wrote or co-wrote complete the Discography.

The Filmography lists studios, directors, producers, writers, other significant personnel, and the cast. A thorough summary of each film, extensive notes on the production, and usually important passages from two or three major contemporary reviews are included for each Crosby film. An extensive list of films that have Bing in cameo appearances and others that include interesting comments on Bing are also included.

The separate Radiography and Videography are the most complete lists of Bing's radio and television appearances. The major radio series identify the producers, writers, and musicians, and extensively list many of the guest performers as well. The Videography does the same, but with each program listed individually, identifying the known dates, networks, sponsors, and lengths. Then comes an extensive list of home videos that include Bing, usually of his films and television appearances.

The Bibliography is the most extensive listing of books and articles on Bing Crosby that exists. Most sources are briefly annotated, to suggest their value. The only reason the Bibliography could not be truly definitive is that Bing is mentioned in nearly every book and most articles on the art forms he participated in and in many others on history and biography, and that would quadruple the listings with little further advantage in information. The Bibliography concludes with a complete listing of world-wide Bing Crosby clubs.

The volume is designed to serve as the primary reference to the whole career of Bing Crosby. In the three years of research I even learned much about popular culture. A scholar once said that if you study a subject deeply enough, it will relate to everything else, and in my case, with special interests in cultural history and unallied fields like aviation, journalism, and literature, the truism proved true once again.

Fred Reynolds is completing a massive four-volume discography titled The Crosby Collection: A Review of the Commercial Recordings. Too late for reference is the negative 1993 "Biography" hour "Bing Crosby: America's Crooner" on the Arts and Entertainment network. Also too late for the text, MCA produced Bing: His Legendary Years, a 1993 video hosted by Dennis Miller, who calls Bing the "coolest" man, who had forty number-one records, a total of 340 on the Hit Parade, sold a billion discs, and made twenty-nine top-grossing films. In the middle of 1993 even a "minor planet," asteroid 2825-1938 SD, was named Crosby for Bing, underscoring that the crooner continues to swing on a star.

This volume provides the facts of America's and the world's most popular and best-loved singer and celebrity of the twentieth century. Bing Crosby did so much in so many ways that it is easy to overlook many of his great achievements. Here virtually all of them are listed together--lest we forget.

Acknowledgments

Some of the people and institutions that assisted me are John Illiff, Chuck Potter, and the rest of the staff at the John M. Hunt Memorial Library of Embry-Riddle Aeronautical University, Daytona Beach; the library of the University of Central Florida, Orlando, and the Stozier Library and the Music Library at Florida State University, Tallahassee; the Music Library of Stetson University; Bob Hope's North Hollywood office; Reinhold Schlieper, for his computer expertise; Kim Heidt, for help in laser printing; Elinor Miller, for special encouragement and help with French; Roger Beaulieu of Atlantic Camera, and Monk Noell and Brad Disch of Billy's Tap Room, Ormond Beach, Florida; Dan Sullivan, a cousin in Worcester, Massachusetts; Norman Skog, Daytona Beach, another cousin and a noted musician billed as Sonny Houston; my sister Nancy and her husband, Dick Hogan, Northborough, Massachusetts; Allan Gustavson of Worcester, another brother-in-law and locally noted musician; Daniel P. Lenz and Judy Reynolds, Front Royal, Virginia; Hank Mautner, a professor and musician of Ohio; Paul Edson; Stas Makrush; Paul Carpenella, Sr., on boxers; Paul Braim; Kaj Tuunanen; Robert F. McKeon, another cousin. My debts go on.

Help from Britain came from Fred Reynolds; Ken W. Crossland; Michael D. Crampton; John Joyce; R. Baverstock-Bosley; Stanley White; Malcolm Macfarlane, especially on the Videography; James Cassidy; and Bert Minister of Stockport, Cheshire, for the eight issues of <u>Bing Pictorial</u>.

The late Ken Twiss, president of the former Bing Crosby Historical Society, Tacoma, who sent me much material, including clippings on Bing's birth, and copies of some rare Crosby recordings; Vernon Wesley Taylor; F.B. "Wig" Wiggins; Charles D. Baillie; Father Robert Murphy, St. Joseph, Missouri; Bob Lundberg; Ernest H. Sutkowski; Wayne L. Martin; Priscilla J. Koernig; James Robert Parish, who helped greatly with the editing, information, and reliable advice; Michael Pitts and Joe Pike, who provided information for the discography after 1955; Ann V. McKee, Minneapolis, for help with the short subjects.

Glenn Gutmacher, an expert on radio history; Chris Lembesis of Palm Springs for his expertise on radio history; Jean-Paul Frereault, Montreal's greatest Crosbyite and endless helper; and various editors at Greenwood: Mary Blair, Lynn Taylor, and Dr. George Butler. The oldtimer manning Grandpa's Depot store at Denver's Union Station, who clarified railroad routes and stations of the 1930s; Shiv Aggarwal of Embry-Riddle, who corrected some of my mathematics; the teenager across the street who regularly volunteered me to hear his favorite "music" by the likes of the Grateful Dead and Mötley Crüe, renewing my respect for melody and the comparative civility of even the "hottest" jazz; the folks at Grace Lutheran Church, Ormond Beach, who occasionally let me sing a solo and talk about Bing; neighbors Fred Sanford and Fred Betts; Luther W. Davidson; and especially my wife, Diane, who not only encouraged me and abided in good humor my busy hours but typed much of the discography and helped proofread the manuscript. Of course, any errors are mine alone.

BING CROSBY

Bing Crosby: A Biography

PART ONE

CENTER FIELD TO JAZZ: 1903-1925

Harry Lillis Crosby, soon to be called Bing, was born on May 3, 1903, although he always thought he was born on May 2, 1904. His baptism certificate was discovered soon after his death, dating the christening as May 31, 1903; moreover, his sister Catherine was born October 3, 1904. The Tacoma News Tribune, October 16, 1977, gives the story, and the Tacoma newspapers listed the birth on May 6 and May 7, 1903. Lillis comes from his maternal side.

Bing's mother had seven children and was secretive about her own birthdate, even tearing out the page of records from the family Bible. The parish priest in 1977 explained, "Maybe the Crosby family was one of those families that didn't celebrate birthdates."

Bing's father, Harry Lowe Crosby, built a home in Tacoma, Washington, at the end of 1902 at 1112 North J Street. The father was born in 1871 and was a bookkeeper for the county treasurer. He married Catherine Harrigan in 1894. Always called Kate, she was born in 1873 in Stillwater, Minnesota, of devout Irish Catholic parents. Harry, a descendant of New England Pilgrims and the grandson of a famed sea captain from Worcester, Massachusetts, converted for her sake.

When Bing was born they already had three sons. Laurence was eight, Everett was seven, and Edward (Ted) was nearly three. Catherine was born the following year, and Mary Rose was born in May 1906, when the Crosbys considered moving. Harry had lost his job through a change in political parties. Diminutive Kate had her only vacations when she stayed in bed for two weeks after each birth. Harry later found a job as a bookkeeper in a Spokane brewery and reunited the family in July 1906. They lived in a rented house on Sinto Avenue. The family finances were extremely tight, but he bought an Edison gramophone and spent $15 to transport Kate's mother's piano from Tacoma over Kate's objections. They both loved to sing, and Harry played the mandolin. It was then that they discovered that Harry

Lillis was partially colorblind.

Kate lent her superb contralto voice to the church choir, and her brother George was an amateur tenor in many musicals. He was Bing's first idol. Brother Larry was studious and, like Dad, wore glasses. Ev was muscular and boisterous, but Ted was even quieter than Larry.

Harry Lillis entered Webster School in the fall of 1909, and when he was about seven he delighted in the "Bingville Bugle," a full-page comic in the Sunday Spokesman-Review. A playmate named Hobart Valentine thought Harry looked like a character in the strip and began calling him Bingo. Others picked it up and shortened it to Bing, but his mother abhorred the nickname for her favorite child, the most religious of her sons and probably the one who might become a priest.

For now his main problems were eating, earning money, and staying out of trouble. He was the brightest and the laziest of the Crosby boys and was sometimes whipped at school for his free spirit. He sometimes played hooky to fish or swim, smoke cornsilk behind MacGowan's and Buck Williams's barns, or sled in the winter down Ligerwood Hill. More than once Kate promised the truant officer that little Harry would mend his ways. In the summer of 1912 Bing with brother Ted was caught swimming in the Spokane River, a forbidden activity, and Kate demanded that Harry whip them soundly despite their severe sunburns.

Bing sang two solos in September 1913 in the parish hall and whistled one verse. He also served as an altar boy. He sang "One Fleeting Hour" at another function and was stunned by the audience's lack of enthusiasm. Years passed before he sang again in public. Kate sent him briefly to a singing teacher, but the professor's insistence that he practice scales and discipline his voice in the reigning European manner drove him away. His father claimed that he also sent his son to a singing teacher, with the same result. Bing also discovered he had little success dancing but was very good in sports and in classroom singing.

When he wasn't chewing a pencil he was jawing large wads of gum, preferably peppermint. His teachers at the Webster School remembered him 25 years later as unimpressive. One remembered him fondly as a disheveled lad with a good voice. Another--who did not like crooning--said, "We liked his singing as a youngster much better than we've liked it since." Bing was in a few plays, once playing a jumping block in the fifth grade.

Meanwhile, Harry built a two-story house on East Sharp Street. The family moved there in July 1913, and August 25 the seventh and last child was born, baptized George Robert on September 7. This boy became famous as Bob Crosby, but he was named for George Harrigan. Larry had completed his freshman year at Gonzaga College, where all the Crosby boys would go, but only Larry would leave with an earned degree. There were music sessions at home, especially on a cold winter evening following a football game. Bing hated his household chores, especially carrying in wood, and he had a favorite German shepherd named Shep, a shaggy canine.

In 1915 the school principal continued to complain of Bing's behavior, but the boy also began a morning newspaper route that he had for years. He raided a pastry wagon in

1916 with a few friends and spent the night in jail--which was Kate's idea in order to teach him a lesson. Bing would see the inside of a jail cell four times--and nearly a fifth time in 1950--as he coordinated the facets of his personality to produce his unique style of fun and dignity. Kate was usually left with the job of disciplining the children, applying a wooden hairbrush or a strap as Dad sneaked away.

Bing's first schoolboy crush involved Gladys Lemmon, but after dressing up to attend her birthday party, he gave up on girls and went back to song and sports. He won medals in swimming in June 1916 at a Mission Park meet, which he joined when Kate excused him from his chores. He was first in most of the events and second in the others, earning seven medals. Al Rinker saw Bing at Mission Park, a tanned swimming star, sometimes playing handball, popular with his friends, a boy with a quick wit and a quicker tongue.

Bing played third base for Webster and center field for a sandlot team called the Sinto Athletic Club. When he enrolled in the high school section of Gonzaga College as a "commuter" in 1917, he played center field. From the age of three to 22 he lived in the same neighborhood with the same friends. Uncle George taught him how to box, and he attended several matches, but Bing had only two street fights. One was defending the honor of Mary Rose in 1915 against the slander of an older boy who called her fat. Bing fought the boy after school and sent him home with bruises and a bloody nose compared to Bing's merely soiled gray flannel shirt. The other boy could have "killed" Bing had he known how to box. Bing narrowly avoided having to defend his "title" against another boy named Jimmy Cottrell, who later defeated the same traducer and became the Northwest middleweight champion.

In high school he frequently entered elocution contests, reciting popular poems and regularly winning. This practice in precise diction and meaningful phrasing, which continued through college, became useful. Phrasing became one of the techniques Bing mastered better than any other popular singer. He formed the Dirty Six Party at Gonzaga and possibly the Loyal Opposition that was known briefly as the Bolsheviks.

At Gonzaga Bing's curriculum was demanding. Father Shepsey inspired in him a love of English literature. His lack of motivation was met by Father Kennelly, "Big Jim" to the students. The 280-pound priest often sent students to a room called "the Jug," which was very familiar to Bing. The lad excelled in Latin, Greek, and history. His failing was mathematics, for he always had trouble with long division. He composed an essay titled "Why Algebra and Geometry Are Unnecessary in the Modern High School Curriculum" and he retained a lifelong aversion to mathematics. Kate's new hopes that Bing might become an accountant faded.

Bing played center for Gonzaga's Junior Yard Association's football squad--for boys 16 and younger--and later played on the school's baseball and other teams. He was too slow for basketball but excelled at swimming and baseball. His interest in entertainment waned with his part of Marcus Antony in the high school production of <u>Julius Caesar</u>, for a pole fell and flattened him as he read Caesar's will. The audience howled for five minutes, and Bing took bows until he realized the laugh was on him.

In 1918 Bing and his buddies raided a girl's house for the refreshments meant for a dance. They were caught and Big Jim punished them. Bing promised Kate he would join the debating team as soon as baseball season and his stance at third base ended. He did enter the Senior Oratorical Contest against his friend Francis Corkery and won. Other times he regularly became a finalist.

Bing had a morning paper route for the Spokesman-Review, waiting at 4 a.m. four blocks from home for the paper car. In freezing mornings he hauled his papers on a sled. One summer he "thinned apples" near the towns of Wenatchee and Yakima. One winter he dropped his route to be a janitor at the workingmen's Everyman's Club, arriving at 5:30 a.m. to clean up after the loggers. He credits this winter job, his paper route, and rising at six for Mass at Gonzaga with making him a perpetual early riser.

Bing also held many other part-time jobs, like usher at boxing matches, elevator operator, handbill passer, garage roustabout, lifeguard, song plugger at a music store, and locker boy and caddy at the golf course. In December 1917 he lugged sacks in the post office. He never received any money as a song plugger, for he worked for only a few days and quit when the owner, who also owned the Liberty Theatre, would not specify his pay. His favorite job was as a prop assistant in 1922 at the Auditorium Theatre, where entertainers would perform one day on the way to Seattle. Bing took in Savoy and Brennan, George White's Scandals, Willie and Eugene Howard's productions, and especially Al Jolson. Jolson played in Sinbad and Bombo. The Crosbys had all of Jolson's records, which Bing imitated.

So far Bing had virtually no license to party, a freedom he yearned for most of all. Larry and Ev returned from the Army at the end of 1918, the former as a teacher at Gonzaga High School and the latter, when Prohibition became law in January 1919, many say as a bootlegger in Seattle.

Bing organized a quartet that sang lunchtime at the school and joined a band, playing trap drums to accompany six other boys in the Juicy Seven. He "borrowed" the Gonzaga drums and spent hours at Buck Williams' house with the latest records. Yet, he did not want to play drums as much as he wanted the free entry to varsity football games that it allowed. Promising his mother that drumming was a mere diversion that would not affect his studies, Bing invested in a mail-order set in 1922, garish drums with an oriental sunset painted on the bass, which was illuminated inside.

The 1920s were years of radical change, a time called the Decade of Bad Manners, the Jazz Age, and the Lost Generation. Boys wore 'coonskin coats and carried flasks; the girls were braless flappers with thin, short dresses and short hair, and uninhibited sexuality (Allen 61-85). A male band singer in those days was of suspect manhood.

When Bing graduated he merely asked for $2 for a new bathing suit. In September 1921 he entered the college division of Gonzaga, not required to declare a major until his junior year. He made the college baseball team but, standing five-feet-nine and weighing 155 pounds, he was too slight for football. Instead, he became the assistant cheerleader and attended all the games. His hair was already thinning, and Father Gilmore, the chemistry teacher, gave Bing some of his hair restorative, which Bing only pretended to use.

He played semi-professional baseball for the Ideal Laundry and ran away with a classmate named Paul Teeters in the summer of 1922 from a job on a distant farm to play Triple-A baseball in the Pacific League, but he hitchhiked only into Northern California, where hunger drove him back to Portland. He got into a serious scrape there when, visiting Everett, he and Paul were arrested for leaving a Chinese restaurant without paying for their meals. They both spent time in jail. Uncle George Harrigan found him a job with a cousin at a logging camp, but Bing seriously injured his knees with his axe while scouting for logging roads and sluices. His cousin sent him home for his own safety, and Bing, laid up for three weeks, had to give up baseball and football.

Bing's friend Francis Corkery left college for the priesthood in 1923. That summer Bing worked in the shipping room of the Inland Brewery and spent hours at Benny Stubeck's Cigar Store and Luncheonette and Saturday nights at the Garden listening to music by Vic Meyers, George Olsen, and other bandleaders. As a junior he declared himself a pre-law student and worked afternoons for Colonel Charles S. Albert, a lawyer for the Great Northern Railway, for $30 a month. Bing recorded garnishments and occasionally wrote briefs. The only satisfaction he found was in warning a friend to take his pay before a judgment was served. The Juicy Seven added a fifth tune to its repertoire and played for three high school dances over Christmas. Bing was nervous when he sang a solo of "The Bells Are Ringing for Me and My Gal." Then he quit the band.

Al Rinker, still in high school, had a band with a poor drummer and heard of Bing's set of drums. Bing auditioned and was hired about January 1924. The band was impressed with Bing's beat and his good voice. Its repertoire was seven tunes. The bandleader was born Alton Rinker on December 20, 1907, and he had a sister, Mildred Bailey, six years older than Al and four years younger than Bing, singing in Los Angeles. Al played the piano and brother Miles played the clarinet and alto sax, and with Clare "Fats" Pritchard on banjo and Bob Pritchard on a C-melody saxophone they formed the Musicaladers (the "musical aiders"). Edgie Hogle, the manager of the Auditorium Theatre, was their booker, demanding $15 a night for the group, $3 each. Al was the only one who could read music at all, but Bing was soon singing all the vocals at many high school dances.

Bing and Al went to the Bailey Music Company to listen to the latest blues and jazz recordings, then ran home and picked out the parts on his piano, spoonfeeding them to the others. One of their favorites was the syncopation of Dwight "Spike" Johnson's band. Their first job was playing at the Manito Park Social Club, where Bing nervously sang a solo of "For Me and My Gal" with a megaphone. He forgot some lyrics and improvised with "ba-ba-ba-boo." The band stretched its repertoire by playing one tune several times in different tempos. The boys added a sixth member, Jimmy Heaton on the coronet, a musician who became notable with the Goldwyn Studio. They bought a 1916 Model-T Ford for $24

and added the message "Eight million miles, and still en-
thusiastic" painted on the back. Their next major booking
was playing for three months for Frank Finney's variety show
at the Auditorium.

Their agent, Edgie Hogle, vainly implored Bing to join
the musician's union, but Bing could not play a roll and
always declined the test. Edgie also worked in a haberdash-
ery store and began golfing with Bing at the Downriver Golf
Course. On the links they would cavort in a foreshadowing,
according to Bing's father later, of the team of Crosby and
Hope to come. Bing and Al bought used golf clubs and cheap
balls and spent days at the course learning the game. Like
most young men during Prohibition, Bing also bought moon-
shine that lumberjacks would not touch.

The band played a week at the seamy Casino Theatre and
amazed the musicians from the Davenport Hotel. Their rates
increased to $7.50 a night each for the rest of the spring
at the upscale Pekin, a Chinese restaurant favored by drinking high schoolers. They had red and white striped blazers
for a uniform. Over July 6 to 7, 1924, the six boys rented
two cottages at Newman Lake; the second was for six girls.
Then the band went for $25 each for three performances a
week to Lareida's Dance Pavilion, which just opened in
Dishman, ten miles from town. There they had musical effects designed to lure the college crowd away from the
Pekin. Using a megaphone, Bing had an early and expressive
solo of "I Wonder What's Become of Sally." He also had a
fistfight with a boy who brought a girl Bing liked and who
called the singer a "pansy" from the dance floor. At a
break the boys went outside and started swinging, but
friends promptly intervened. One Sunday at Liberty Lake,
bandleader Jay Eslick invited Bing onto the stage to sing a
solo with the band. Members of Johnson's band sometimes
dropped in to hear the group and admired their music.

That September Bing became a college senior. Then Bing
learned he was already earning more money than the assistant
lawyer. Bing said, "Ma, I'd rather sing than eat" and he
left college about January 1925. The job at Lareida's
continued through the summer of 1925, but by September the
Musicaladers disbanded. Three members left for college and
Heaton went to Los Angeles to join his cousin's band.

Bing and Al formed a duet for parties, with Al on the
piano singing harmony to Bing's lead. Roy Boomer hired Bing
to join a quartet for a stage show between films at the
plush Clemmer Theater, with Al accompanying from the pit.
Bing remained as the soloist when the quartet ended, and he
suggested he sing the likes of "Five Foot Two" and "Paddlin'
Madeline Home" sitting at the edge of the stage near the
piano. Thus, he and Al began singing professionally together. They earned $30 weekly each, but in October 1925 Boomer
dropped the show.

Bing agreed to try Los Angeles and visit Al's sister,
who was singing in speakeasies. They paid $8 for the Model-
T and had about $20 between them. Al drove the flivver to
the Crosby house at 9 a.m. on Thursday, October 15. Bing
slept soundly, but he soon appeared with his suitcase,
drums, and golf clubs. After two days they arrived in
Seattle at 9 p.m. The next morning they met Vic Meyers, a
bandleader and future lieutenant governor, and Jackie Soud-

ers and his Orchestra at the Butler Hotel. Souders allowed
the boys to perform for free in front of a more sophisticated audience that included university students. Bing and Al
were sensational. They performed a few more nights with
pay, but they rejected Souders' offer to stay longer.
Meanwhile, Kate was saying prayers for Bing's safety and
success and requested a Novena at the Poor Clares Monastery.

They coaxed the flivver south about ten days before
arriving at the home of Mildred Bailey about November 10.
Bing found her a portly, dark, round-faced brunette who sang
at a posh speakeasy called The Swede's. Bing never played
his drums again except for one of the small cymbals. Mildred's husband was a gentle bootlegger named Benny Stafford.
They let the boys stay in the spare bedroom as long as they
needed it, which was about three weeks.

Two weeks later they had an audition with Mike Lyman at
the Tent Cafe. The nervous boys sang two or three songs
while Bing tapped his cymbal, Bing in his brother Everett's
tuxedo. They became "Crosby and Rinker, Two Boys with a
Piano" at the Lafayette Cafe, where Harry Owens led the
orchestra. By December they were hired by Rube Wolf and
Marco, who were with the Fanchon and Marco Time organization, for The Syncopation Idea, a new musical with 16 female
dancers called the Tiller Girls. They played for five weeks
at the Boulevard Theatre, where Bing featured "All Alone,"
and 13 on the Loew's circuit. Bing continued scat singing
and played a kazoo with a coffee can for a trombone effect.
They earned the $75 they were each paid a week. After hours
the boys chased girls, drank in speakeasies, and enjoyed
their popularity. After these successful weeks they left
Sacramento for Los Angeles and rented an apartment.

In a few days, by April 1926, Bing and Al auditioned at
the Majestic Theatre downtown for Will Morrissey's variety
show with music by Arthur Freed. They were hired at $65
weekly each and were billed as "Two Boys and a Piano--Sing-
ing Songs Their Own Way" when Will Morrissey's Music Hall
Revue opened at the Metropolitan Theater (now the
Paramount). They rehearsed long and Morrissey renamed the
theater the Orange Grove for the duration, about six to
eight weeks. According to Variety, the boys were hits in a
flop show, and on May 3 they performed at a private party
for the stellar cast that opened the El Capitan Theatre.
The revue hung on, however, for two months.

PART TWO

THE JAZZ SINGER: 1926-1929

Bing had long since defined his personal code that
involved piety, patriotism, manliness, fun, simplicity,
friendliness, generosity, and song. His "masculine" traits
included excelling at sports and other outdoor activities,
avoiding signs of effeminacy, stifling emotions, understat-
ing praise, and enjoying the company of attractive women.
His bent towards partying stressed being charming, applying
his intelligence to tell amusing anecdotes, and being "one
of the boys." He wanted life to be easy, fun, and decent,
and his manliness and love of jazz were part of the age.

Bing and Al were hits at the Orange Grove, with demands for encores. Henry Pleasants, a music historian, states that Bing's heritage was the "jaunty, debonair" defiance of a generation with "loud clothes, hip flasks, a slangy vocabulary, cheek-to-cheek dancing, rumble-seat cuddling, flivvers, jalopies--and jazz" against an earlier generation that seemed too serious and too concerned with propriety (Great [B24] 129). Bing was not so original as he was "tentative," "unconsciously assimilative," "adaptive," and "reflected or embodied, both in his singing and his person, his own social and musical environment" (pp. 128, 132). Pleasants adds that Bing's best range in the 1930s was in the octave B flat to B flat and his voice was "one of the loveliest I have heard in 45 years of listening to baritones."

The duo hired Vladimus Goldfarb for two years, who placed them with the Paramount-Publix theater chain at $300 a week each to perform alternately at the Granada in San Francisco and the Metropolitan in Los Angeles, with name talent. They were billed as "Two Boys and a Piano--Singing Songs Their Own Way." At the Metropolitan, a theater seating 2500 people, they sang "In a Little Spanish Town." Their fears vanished as the audiences exploded into applause. Often the audience would not permit the emcee to announce the next act until Bing and Al returned for an encore or two--or four. They played four weeks just as well at the Granada in San Francisco in October, earning the spot as the penultimate act. Here Bing met Peggy Bernier, whom he would meet again.

A 13-year-old girl named Sylvia Picker met Bing in Los Angeles, said she was San Diego's Fairest Rosebud, and hoped to persuade Bing to buy her an ice cream soda. At the Capitol in San Francisco for another six weeks the duo added a mildly risque midnight show that pleased the university crowd. A fraternity led by Randolph Hearst at the University of California at Berkeley invited Bing, Al, and the dancing girls to the frat house for an impromptu performance. A solitary orange floated in a tub full of gin. The girls drank too much, the cast became loud, and the faculty became upset, suspending some students. The show closed in Santa Barbara by July 1926, not always meeting the payroll. The most romantic film star of the day, Rudolph Valentino, died at 31 and was given a funeral in New York on August 23.

Bing states, "Even at this point I'd worked up a way of singing that people were calling 'individual,'" and the "boo-boo-boo stuff started with humming," trying "to do something at the first part of the second chorus to make it a little different from the first chorus, such as humming or whistling." The boo-boo-boo was his imitation of "the kind of saxophone solo Rudy Wiedoeft or Ross Gorman produced when they played their ballad-type numbers. My notion was to make a sound which resembled the human voice with a bubble in it" (Call Me Lucky 78, 80). In 1932 the Mills Brothers were also imitating musical instruments.

Bing had earned, at age 23, his license to party.

With Al, he was intuitively rewriting the jazz scene of the generation, conceiving a brilliant harmony, practicing a living rhythm, and propagating a joyous lesson. Bing would also trill some notes (technically called upper mordents) so slowly and warmly that listeners called his voice "golden."

Their zeal and inventiveness were infectious--a unique style that hailed jazz and frequently assumed unheard heights. Youths adopted their enthusiasm, unleashed rhythms, and elaborate harmonies.

Bing's luckiest break came when Paul Whiteman brought his orchestra to Los Angeles. Whiteman sent musicians Matty Malneck and Ray Turner to evaluate the duo, and soon Jimmy Gillespie, the manager, called them to Whiteman's dressing room. Whiteman, the King of Jazz, had a small piano handy, and the boys auditioned there, before the perfumed, rotund jazz master in a silk dressing gown and eating caviar from a large bowl attended by a silver cooler of champagne. He hired them at $150 a week each for five years, beginning in December in Chicago after their current booking expired.

Don Clarke asked them to record a song for the Columbia label. It was recorded October 18 on actual wax, so there was no flip side. It was "I've Got the Girl"--their first--recorded in three takes in the ballroom with primitive equipment and Clarke's arrangement stifling their style. The record was a flop, and Bing recalled that the recording occurred in a corrugated steel warehouse.

In November they went to Spokane and performed at the Liberty Theatre for five days, earning $200 each, but someone stole $400 from their dressing room while they were on stage. They celebrated Thanksgiving and impressed their friends, Al staying with the Crosbys. Then they went to Chicago. They arrived early at the Tivoli and met the whole troupe, with whom they performed four shows a day. Pops Whiteman gave them a pep talk that helped their nerves. Soon Pops strolled center stage and announced, "I want to introduce two young fellas who are joining my band. I picked them up in an ice cream parlor in a little town called Walla Walla, Washington. I thought they were too good for Walla Walla, and that's why I brought them here. I want you to meet them--Crosby and Rinker!" They pushed an upright piano on stage and settled down after four bars of their first number of their novelty routine. After loud applause they sang their second number and finished to a thunderous ovation and shouts of "Encore!" Al was excited, but Bing remained calm, merely pleased.

They sat in the orchestra, Bing with a peck horn and soon with a dummy mouthpiece, while Al held a guitar with rubber strings. Bing ended up with a prop violin. Pops arranged their second recording session. The boys sang "Wistful and Blue" with the arrangement by Matty Malneck, the featured violinist. They discovered Louis Armstrong playing at the Sunset Cafe, and Whiteman took them to many important parties. A few times Bing was late to rehearsals and performances, but their popularity satisfied Whiteman. Like Pops himself, Bing was propagating jazz.

At a private performance in Cicero, Illinois, Bix Beiderbecke threatened to punch an annoying member of the audience, a well-dressed man who became quiet after the threat. After the show, guitarist Eddie Condon informed Bix that the man he admonished was Ralph "Bottles" Capone, who owned the Montmartre Cafe, and was the brother of the head mobster, and the man who inherited the crime empire in 1932 when Al Capone went to prison.

They performed on the way East and opened at the 4500-

seat Paramount in New York in January 1927. But after the
introduction and pushing the piano downstage, Bing and Al
bombed. Everyone was puzzled, and then the theater's manager ordered them out of the show. They were reduced to performing in the lobby to the overflow crowd. Bing drank
heavily, which Mize attributes to the hedonism of the times
and to the fashion of "campus cutups" (p. 28). Meanwhile,
Whiteman used Bing, Al, and three other singers for his
recording of "Shanghai Dream Man" on February 10.
     The Paul Whiteman Club opened February 18 with the boys
pulling the curtains and pounding with hammers on chimes as
sound effects for "The 1812 Overture" and "The Marseilles."
In their frustration they also kicked chairs and knocked
bells over. Bing and Al sang unnoticed during the intermission. The problem was that New Yorkers did not like their
expansive jazz and intimate crooning. Bing never understood
their failure. Pleasants states that in Bing's early records "he often barely made" the highest notes, "but, more
importantly, . . . his voice then lost its characteristic
timbre" (Great 133). After their work, Bing and Al went to
Harlem for fun at the Cotton Club.
     Bing and Al sang for more recordings, and in Philadel-
phia Pops put them in the show again, and Bing recorded
effective backgrounds with Al and solos in Camden. But Bing
had lost his confidence. When he had drunk his fill, he
would lie down and sleep, sometimes missing a rehearsal or
even a performance.
     Matty Malneck suggested that Harry Barris join Bing and
Al. Barris, the father of a baby girl, was an unappreciated
composer and pianist who could not read music. He was born
in New York in November 1905 and moved to Denver about 1919,
where he studied music in high school under Whiteman's
father, Wilberforce Whiteman. He was short, a natty dresser, a cocky entertainer, drank a little all the time, and
had a loud singing voice that threatened to drown out his
loud piano. Al, however, was quiet, dark, and curly haired.
The desperate trio worked on "Mississippi Mud," Barris's
tune with James Cavanaugh's lyrics, and "Ain't She Sweet"
until they forged a new style, lively but not "intimate."
Pops approved, and they sang at two pianos with Bing between
with a hand-held cymbal. Whiteman put them on at his club
and again they found success--and relief.
     On March 22 Whiteman opened his musical Lucky, written
by Jerome Kern and others, at the New Amsterdam Theatre.
Bob Hope was playing across the street with second billing
on his inaugural Orpheum tour. April 29, listed as the
Rhythm Boys on a record for the first time, the trio sang
for a "Victor test medley." For every record Bing was now
either the lead vocalist or the soloist.
     Bix roomed with Bing, both sharing many of the same
sleepless and carousing traits. Bing bordered on insomnia
his whole life. Bix drank frequently, never exercised, and
died in 1931. Bing's talks on music with him, Jimmy Dorsey,
and others educated him. The singing trio drank heavily,
playing for late private parties. They were paid well but
attracted little notice in the din of the affairs.
     Soon after the musical closed by July 1927, Whiteman
sent the Rhythm Boys out by themselves for awhile, still
recording with the Whiteman Orchestra; sometimes Bing sang

without Barris, sometimes in another chorus without Al and Barris. Whiteman used them as vocalists in many recordings, many featuring Bix Beiderbecke. In August the Rhythm Boys were on the Keith-Albee-Orpheum vaudeville circuit, where they performed twice a day for ten months, while Pops took his orchestra on a tour of England. They included a parody of a mind-reading act and were generally successful through the Midwest. Bing went to football games, and they all partied overtime. Bing was now earning $300 a week.

Bing met Jane Rankin, an attractive woman in Akron, Ohio, but when she intimated that he abandon show business for her millions, he fled. He went through speakeasies, and Bing suggests that it may have been then that he found two interesting men at a Chicago bar--both golfers and one with an Irish brogue. Bing drank brandy for the first and virtually last time and awakened in a hotel room two days later with a hangover among mobsters on the lam, including one of his "buddies"--Machine Gun Jack McGurn. This was a professional boxer and golfer and notorious mobster with the Capone gang, which ran Chicago's South Side. Sicilian born with the name Vincent Gebardi, McGurn sent three thugs on November 9, 1927, to slit the throat and crush the skull of a singer named Joe Lewis for daring to leave the Green Mill club for another. This incident is explained in a biography The Joker Is Wild by Art Cohn (1955) and dramatized in the film (1957), which stars Frank Sinatra.

One man told Bing he would have to stay while things cooled off. While he retreated to the bathroom, police officers shot their way in against machine gun fire and subdued the gangsters. Bing heard strange voices and "large, flat footsteps" approaching. As a man opened the door Bing said he was with Whiteman and had stepped into the room when he heard the shooting. A quick-witted boy had stepped into the room as well, and Bing pretended they had arrived together. The police let him go, but he had missed two days of performances. About February 1929 and September 1932 Bing was again golfing with McGurn around Chicago.

Barris wrote "From Monday On" with Bing, and Malneck arranged to record it with the Rhythm Boys, backed by Bix Beiderbecke, Tommy Dorsey, and Jimmy Dorsey in a trumpet chorus. Mize states that the Rhythm Boys were "the pioneering Swing Style vocal trio" and that Bing furnished "many improvised 'hot licks' and some fetching scat singing" (pp. 28n, 29). They were fired at one theater for not singing enough.

While singing at Chicago's Orpheum Theater, Bing met Peggy Bernier, the star of the touring Broadway musical Good News. Bing fawned on her, but she did not reciprocate. In the end, she left him heartbroken. Her understudy in the musical was Dixie Carrol, who became Dixie Lee. The next day, Bing did not arrive on time at the theater in Rockford, so Al and Barris went on alone. Bing arrived that morning, but he was so drunk that the Rockford police put him in jail for the day. Although Bing and Al never had so much as a disagreement, Al and Barris were furious. They hired an actor to play the outraged manager and tormented Bing for failing to appear. Billboard found the trio in New York on August 9, 1928, at Keith's 81st Street Theater, applauding the comedy and "the art of rhythm perfected to a stellar degree. . . . An Act worthy of big-time booking . . ." (Aug. 18; qtd. Bing 103: 48).

The Kid from Spokane was in Chicago in February 1929 and met Machine Gun Jack McGurn, perhaps for the first time. McGurn was one of Capone's gunners that executed the infamous St. Valentine's Day Massacre that month, attempting to liquidate Bugs Moran's North Side gang. The Dorsey brothers left Whiteman by March, when Bing cut two songs, "My Kinda Love" and "Till We Meet," for his first record as an independent artist. Bing refused an offer to become a solo. Whiteman's whole orchestra left New York on May 26 to film The King of Jazz for Universal, and the radio sponsor leased an entire gold-colored train draped with banners. Whiteman offered free concerts for two hours at 16 cities on the 12-day journey.

The train arrived in Los Angeles, and the next four weeks the musicians went to the Paramount in San Francisco and back to Los Angeles at the Paramount there. Filming waited for a script for the extravaganza, costing $2 million, to be in Technicolor. Bing and two violinists rented a house, and Bing hired Edward Small as an agent. A Ford dealer offered them all new Model A's at discount prices, and Bing bought a convertible. Bing and others joined the nearby Lakeside Golf Club, where Bing worked his handicap down from eight to four.

In September Eddie Lang and Joe Venuti joined the orchestra, both becoming close Crosby friends. Quiet Eddie Lang (born Salvatore Mazarro) accompanied Bing's solos and relaxed as a pool hustler and card sharp. Venuti was called the Fabulous Fiddler and could be violent. The Whiteman radio program continued from Los Angeles, for which Pops demanded religious devotion to perfection. Near the end of July Bing placed his car in storage as the leader took his group East, playing for a Pontiac car convention in Detroit and then for six weeks at the Pavilion Royale on Long Island. In October Bing cut eight records in New York, but on October 31 he was in Hollywood singing solo for Whiteman.

Filming began on November 1, and Bing, now earning $400 a week, roomed with Kurt Dieterle. Bing's salary was $20,800 a year, when the federal agents with Eliot Ness pursued Al Capone for $2800 a year. After one week Bing met a girl at the studio party and drove her home to the Roosevelt Hotel, where a car crashed into the little convertible, throwing the girl onto the pavement. Bing carried the girl into the lobby. She was not seriously injured, but a policeman arrested him.

He was charged with "reckless driving and suspicion of drinking" and attended his hearing a week later after a round of golf, dressed in loud clothes. The judge said, "There'll be no fine. Just 60 days." Bing was transferred to the Hollywood Division jail, but Pops had given his featured solo of "Song of the Dawn" to John Boles. Bing was released under police escort for filming and returned behind bars at night. The sentence was commuted after 40 days. The filming ended in March 1930, and although Bing was featured in the film, John Boles received more notice. The film, like Whoopee! (1930) produced by Florenz Ziegfeld and Samuel Goldwyn with Eddie Cantor, was in two-color Technicolor.

PART THREE

THE SUCCESSFUL CROONER: 1930-1933

On tour heading East Bing refused to pay the band's bootlegger for a bottle of scotch he never received. Pops paid the bill and deducted it from Bing's salary, which led to an argument. In Portland they agreed to part and the trio returned to Hollywood. Like others with natural talent, Bing had little faith in himself to succeed as a solo.

The trio took a week's booking at the Montmartre Cafe, where they became a sensation. Earning $200 a week, Bing met Dixie first at the Cocoanut Grove, when she was more interested in him. A Protestant, she went out with Bing every night, but her friends Sue Carol and Sylvia Picker advised against it. On their own again, the trio sang for 13 weeks   on a local radio program. Then Bing had small parts in two Pathe two-reelers, Ripstitch the Tailor, which was never released, and Two Plus Fours. Ripstitch, produced by Ray McCarey to showcase Bing, was mined for scenes for the other.

In the spring of 1929 the William Fox Film Corporation had hired 17-year-old Dixie Carrol. She was five-foot-three and a beautiful actress, singer, and dancer with bleached platinum-blonde hair.   Nearsighted and shy, she was blunt, yet friendly. She was born Wilma Winifred Wyatt on November 4, 1911, in Harriman, Tennessee. She grew up in New Orleans, which gave her a love for jazz, moved with her family to Chicago, and entered show business at the College Inn after winning a contest for singing most like Ruth Etting.

After only seven weeks of starring on Broadway she was called to Hollywood with a three-year contract. While filming Fox Movietone Follies of 1929 she befriended 16-year-old Sylvia Picker and Sue Carol. She appeared in six more films in about a year and hated each one. Harry Barris was now divorced and threw himself into composing.

The trio recorded "Three Little Words" with the Duke Ellington Cotton Club Orchestra. Duke and his Orchestra were also in the RKO film Check and Double Check, for which the Rhythm Boys dubbed the vocal of "Three Little Words" mouthed by the musicians in the edited film. The Rhythm Boys sang "Just One More Chance" without a credit in Paramount's Confessions of a Co-ed, released the next year, but in another Bing had a brief line, "Hi, gang," and a featured one-chorus solo of "When the Folks High Up Do the Mean Low Down" in Reaching for the Moon.

About August Abe Frank, the manager of the Cocoanut Grove, offered them an underpaid engagement. Gus Arnheim's Orchestra was featured and the Grove broadcast nightly from a studio upstairs on a West Coast network. Here Bing first met Gary Cooper and partied with him and Richard Arlen, often taking them sailing. Bing soloed on two or three broadcasts a week. Bing developed his unique "Crosby Cry," that expressive catch and deep glow in his voice, which contributed to the first mastery of the microphone.

A noted music historian later thought the music Crosby was inventing as "wonderfully relaxed, intimate vocal communication, a feeling for rhythm, phrase and line rarely matched by classical singers, and a smooth, often lovely,

almost always pleasing vocal tone, unblemished by forcing or
by conspicuous differences in character and color between
one register and another, not to speak of what is accomplished in the handling of text" (Pleasants, <u>Great</u> [B24]
127). Pleasants notes that Crosby, in fact, "synthesized"
the styles of Al Jolson, Bessie Smith, and Ethel Waters with
the microphone into a new style that he "passed on to all
who came after him" (p. 127).

Bing had an unsuccessful interview at Paramount-Publix
and a screen test at Fox, but was rejected as a prospect
because of his big ears. Bing and Dixie often attended the
Cotton Club to catch Louis Armstrong, even if it meant
missing his own performance. Rumors circulated that Bing
was often dead drunk. With Sundays and Mondays off, Bing
neglected more rehearsals to party in Palm Springs or attend
Agua Caliente, a large gambling complex at Ensenada, Mexico.
Johnny Burke told him he had met 120 taxi drivers who said
they had assisted an inebriated Bing out of the Cocoanut
Grove, and that a larger "club" was composed of people "who
saw a slightly tipsy Crosby fall through a drum."

The affair with Dixie became serious, and he pledged to
stop drinking. Bing and Dixie married on September 29,
1930, in an informal ceremony at a church on Sunset Boulevard. She agreed to raise children as Catholics but never
would accompany Bing to his church. She was much better
known than Bing, who was called "Bing Croveny" in one paper,
and the Associated Press wrote, "Dixie Lee, film actress,
today married Murray Crosey, orchestra leader, at a simple
church ceremony." They lived for weeks at Sue Carol's
house, when Sue was married to Nick Stuart. Dixie devoted
herself to straightening Bing out, turning him into a sober
performer and mate. She broke his gin bottles and sent him
to a Turkish bath every time she thought it wise. She
upheld strict rules and was a stern disciplinarian whenever
Bing broke them.

Bing's singing gradually changed from a precise and
lyrical tenor to a totally new effect with rich range and
phrasing, strong intonation yet casual finesse, and impecca-
ble rhythm and relaxed syncopation. He stopped straining
for the high notes and relaxed with the more comfortable
lower range that he made popular. Even his whistling excelled in tough competition. Bing recorded "I Surrender
Dear" on January 19, 1931, a song by Barris and Gordon
Clifford and arranged by Jimmie Grier. It became Bing's
first solo hit. His development as a soloist created cracks
in the solidarity of the trio, which corroded further as he
sang all the new songs. Barris concentrated on composing,
with Bing adding some lyrics for verses sung only on records, and Al had interests in producing.

In March Dixie fled to Ensenada for a divorce, but Bing
flew to her side and they reconciled. He acknowledged that
he had been drinking and playing too hard and resolved to
become responsible. Gin had threatened his career five
times, and he was too strong to let it happen again. He
began reading more at night, and for a year or more he did
not have a drop of liquor. Ever after he kept drinking
under strict control. On March 30 Bing cut his next records, singing solo under his own contract with Brunswick
and its young chief, Jack Kapp. Bing and Kapp highly es-

teemed each other and made each other rich.

At the Lakeside Golf Club he met Sennett, who suggested a short musical comedy. Bing filmed one for $600, with an option for three others. The film featured Barris's song "I Surrender Dear," sung twice, which also give the film its title. Bing sang two other songs, including "Out of Nowhere" and often wore a straw hat, the type dubbed "a 98-cent skimmer." Sennett knew immediately that the film would be a hit, and Bing discovered Frank had docked him a day's pay for absences.

Bing hired his brother Ev as his agent for ten percent, and he, a tough negotiator, became the main force behind Bing's uncertain ambition. At the Grove Bing demanded the promised bonuses and an overdue pay raise, which Frank refused. Bing then convinced Al and Barris to walk out with him about the end of May. In retaliation Frank had them blacklisted and the trio dissolved.

Bing met Leo Lynn, a Gonzaga classmate, and convinced him to become his chauffeur. Lynn remained with Bing for years, serving as his movie stand-in and a family intimate. Sennett began paying Bing $750 each for three more shorts, at a time Warner Brothers hired James Cagney at $400 a week for five years, though the contract soon changed. Bing was back at the Educational Studios filming One More Chance, Dream House, and then Billboard Girl. He also filmed Blue of the Night and Sing, Bing, Sing.

Ev sent a copy of "I Surrender Dear" and "Just One More Chance" to NBC and CBS. On an ocean liner William S. Paley saw the glee of teenage girls listening to the songs and wired, "Hire him." Bing visited several clubs in New York, singing for fun, and recorded three songs August 19. Frank relented on the blacklisting in arbitration, and CBS paid Bing $600 for five 15-minute shows a week. The premiere, scheduled for 11 p.m. on Monday, August 31, did not air, but not because he was drunk. Bing had become hoarse rehearsing in an air-conditioned room. The debut aired two days later, after a second postponement, with Eddie Lang playing guitar beside Bing, who sang "Just One More Chance" and "I'm Through with Love." Bing thought his debut a failure, but thousands of fans called and wrote so that the show was extended to six nights a week. The six two-reelers he had filmed soon showed around town, and Cremo Cigars of the American Tobacco Company became the sponsor of the program broadcast at 7:15 six nights a week.

Dixie became close to Lang's wife. Bing had many more recording sessions, including one on November 23, when he sang his theme song, "Where the Blue of the Night Meets the Gold of the Day," written by Roy Turk, Bing, and Fred E. Ahlert. Russ Columbo recorded the chorus five days earlier, but without the verse that Bing wrote. Bing sang on radio some now-forgotten songs he helped write, including "You're Just a Beautiful Melody of Love." Columbo engaged in the "Battle of the Baritones" when NBC hired him to try to steal Bing's thunder. Columbo's theme song, "You Call It Madness But I Call It Love," had been written by Bing and Con Conrad months earlier at the Cocoanut Grove, and Bing never recorded it. The contest lasted only a few months, when Columbo lost the battle.

Bing's sponsored program began October 28, and November

8 he began a ten-week engagement for $2500 a week at the Paramount Theater. This time Bing was a smash hit, extended to a record 20 weeks, when most shows were booked for only two to four weeks. Bing, Carpozi, and others write that the booking lasted 29 weeks. In 1931 Bing became famous. It is his voice that haunts many of songs he recorded. Bing focused on New York nearly two years and befriended a New Jersey boxer named Hank Sinatra, who had a 15-year-old son.

Bing's second ten-week contract at Paramount was at $4000 weekly while he continued to earn $600 a week for his radio program. One week he doubled at the New York and Brooklyn Paramount theaters. That week he did eight stage shows a day in addition to his nightly broadcast, and Ev insured Bing's voice for $100,000. With recordings Bing was earning $7000 a week.

Adolph Zukor asked Bing to star in a picture first called The Crooner for Paramount-Publix. Ev arranged a contract for a flat $35,000 a week for Bing, who also insisted on co-stars in order to share both the credit and any blame. Paramount had decided to hire the singer who was keeping their audiences at home at their radios, for radio and the Depression caused losses at the box office. Fox and Jack Warner had offered Bing more money, but for only a single picture (Swindell 156), and Paramount agreed to more films if the first succeeded. Bing signed on June 4, 1932. He later signed a contract for five films over three years for $300,000. In 1933 Babe Ruth earned $52,000, and he had to settle for $35,000 for 1934. Most sources indicate that Ev was soon arranging for three-film packages for $300,000 every two years.

Duke Ellington invited Bing to record "St. Louis Blues" impromptu. Bing began broadcasting for Chesterfield Cigarettes five nights a week, which wound down to only Mondays and Wednesdays, and he selected Lennie Hayton to conduct the studio orchestra with Eddie Lang on guitar behind him at the microphone. The radio program featured songs and banter, scripted and ad-libbed, which produced one of the most popular programs and a format Bing would repeat.

He was singing up to 16 hours a day and over-stressed his voice. He went to an eminent specialist, Dr. Simon L. Ruskin, who explained that his vocal cords had developed nodes. They could be excised, but no one knew what his voice might sound like. The physician suggested complete rest for two weeks, and Bing gradually recovered his voice, though it returned mellower and two tones lower.

In Baltimore he entered an amateur contest as Charlie Senevsky, sang two songs, and lost to a Bing Crosby imitator. When the Chesterfield program ended by July, Bing was in Hollywood for the film. Dixie, now pregnant, had already gone to a house Bing rented. With ears held back by spirit gum, he began filming The Big Broadcast. Meanwhile, CBS was trying to sign Bing for another radio season, but Ev demanded more money and artistic control. Bing recorded songs feverishly and went on a nation-wide tour for Paramount. At San Francisco the receipts for one performance amounted to $40,000, a new record that topped Al Jolson's draw by $6000.

Bing was singing at the Oriental in Chicago in September and again golfed mornings with Jack McGurn. The master of the Thompson machine gun had access to the best golf courses, which Bing enjoyed. He had dinner once with the mobster and his blonde girlfriend, Louise Rolfe, who gave McGurn his alibi for the St. Valentine's Day Massacre and later married him. But Bing soon felt the social embarrassment and dropped the association. Al Capone began serving an 11-year prison sentence on May 3, 1932, by which time Eliot Ness, the famous G-Man, listed McGurn as one of the remaining major public enemies. He was machine-gunned to death in Chicago on St. Valentine's Day, 1936.

December 2, 1932, Bing began a week accompanied by Lang at M-G-M's Capitol Theater in New York, where Bob Hope was the emcee. Bing had met him weeks earlier at the Friars Club and both met Dorothy Lamour singing at a New York club. Bing and Hope joked with each other at O'Reilly's Bar, across the street from the theater. The extraordinary song-and-dance man and the witty crooner ignited a congenial rivalry on stage. They worked out routines like two businessmen meeting on the street and reaching into each other's pockets, developing a camaraderie with their improvisations, unsure which was the comic and which the straightman. With the engagement over, Bing accepted a CBS contract for a program to air Wednesdays and Saturdays for Chesterfield Cigarettes, opening January 1933 with the same theme song, "Where the Blue of the Night."

Bing had earned a major license to party, at a time when the Great Depression had hit the bottom of national despair. Nearly 13 million people, or 25 percent of the workforce, were unemployed in 1932, and even "rich" men were walking away from their families. The economy only gradually improved until 1941, by which time the materialism of the '20s had been transformed into a need to "belong" and for leisure, both values embodied in the Kid from Spokane.

In Manhattan, two songwriters sued Bing and M-G-M over the song "At Your Command," which Bing sang at the Capitol. Later in Hollywood, Edward Small sued for $20,000 over his 1930 deal for ten percent of Bing's earnings for two years. Eddie Lang's chronic sore throat worsened in New York in late March 1933, when Bing convinced him to visit a doctor. Lang had a tonsillectomy from which he did not recover. Bing sorely missed his friend but hardly expressed his grief. Perry Botkin became the new guitarist, and Bing attended Lang's funeral in Philadelphia. Bing remained in New York three more weeks for Chesterfield as Kitty Lang joined Dixie in Hollywood.

Bing returned to Hollywood and made <u>College Humor</u>. Bing and Dixie also built their first home, on Foreman Avenue in Toluca Lake near the Lakeside Golf Course. Dixie liked Gary Cooper, who sometimes served as the couple's marriage counselor. Bing appeared in a Paramount short and went on tour again. Paramount-Publix rewrote a sequel to a film, added a large part for Bing, and produced the hit with <u>Too Much Harmony</u>. Bing was now a film star as well as a radio and stage crooner. Paramount made a short titled <u>Hollywood on Parade</u>, starring Bing and others, and Mack Sennett spliced his footage together for a three-reeler titled <u>Bring on Bing</u>. Bing wrote a column for a series of articles by movie stars, syndicated by the Newspaper Enterprise Association Service in 1933. He suggested that "in my own estimation, I'm not yet successful" (Carpozi 34). Gary

Evan, named for Gary Cooper and Dixie's father, was born June 27, 1933, weighing nearly eight pounds. Three months later the cameras were turned on again at a double christening ceremony, for Ricky, the son of Richard and Jobyna Arlen had also been born. Cooper became Gary's godfather.

Bing's feature film was such a success that he became one of the princes of the studio. He was given a studio bungalow, one of the dozen lined up on the largest, which was Cooper's. In July Marion Davies obtained Bing for a Cosmopolitan-M-G-M film, Going Hollywood, produced by William Randolph Hearst, the fading actress's lover. Ev arranged $2000 weekly for Bing, and Marion's slow pace and the director's leisureliness consumed six months of filming at barely one scene a day until Hearst demanded more. Bing introduced "Temptation," his first dramatic song. The film's success forced Paramount to yield to Ev's demands for a three-picture contract for $200,000, later $300,000 with a bonus when Bing made the top ten in the Box Office Poll.

In October 1933 he was broadcasting from New York Mondays for Woodbury Soap. Frank Sinatra, age 17, met Bing backstage in Newark in 1933 and became determined to emulate his master. In November, however, Bing was on Catalina Island filming We're Not Dressing with Carole Lombard, who swore like a workman, which to Bing was "clean and lusty."

PART FOUR

THE STAR: 1934-1940

Bing invested $7500 in a boxer and tripled his money. He had the Mills Brothers on his radio show New Year's Day 1934, and they remained through March. Dixie signed in January to co-star with Lanny Ross in Melody in Spring, but in April Dixie discovered she was pregnant with twins that interfered with her kidneys. Unable to keep food down, Dixie resorted to a diet dominated by brandy to manage a difficult pregnancy.

Police informed Bing of a kidnap threat to Gary in April. Bing spoke to reporters and advised friends to publicize such threats. Private guards were hired to protect the home night and day for a month, and for years after the boys were never told why they had to be accounted for at all times. Threats surfaced periodically, sometimes with Dixie uninformed while Bing took safety precautions. Besides the notorious kidnapping of the Lindbergh baby in 1932, Lita Gray, the former wife of Charlie Chaplin, had been kidnapped in 1931, making threats palpable.

Bing first made the list of the top ten most popular movie stars in 1934, ranking seventh. Meanwhile, Bing took the lead in Here Is My Heart, a remake of an old silent film The Grand Duchess and the Waiter. For She Loves Me Not Miriam Hopkins had a better role, but Bing applied his light charm in the male lead and nearly stole the film. Bing introduced "Love Is Just Around the Corner" and "June in January" in one and "Love in Bloom" in the latter. He crooned in one more short musical, Just an Echo for Paramount in 1934. While filming She Loves Me Not he refused to have his ears glued back, as the glue continually failed

under the hot klieg lights. He often had to wear a toupee,
but he constantly attempted scenes wearing a hat.   Jack
Oakie, filming <u>Mississippi</u> with Bing, called him "the Robot
of the Romance" for his girdle and toupee. Record sales in
1934 were one-tenth that of 1929, but Bing increased his
share of the weak market.

Bing reorganized as he outgrew the space at Paramount.
He hired brother Larry for public relations and kept John
O'Melveny as a legal adviser.   He bought a home in Toluca
Lake for his parents, and Dad became the chief bookkeeper
and treasurer.   Bing began making astute investments.
Crosby's headquarters went to 9028 Sunset Boulevard, and the
business was reorganized in 1936 as Bing Crosby Limited,
Incorporated.

On July 13, 1934, Dixie gave birth to twin boys, Philip
Lang, named after Eddie Lang, and Dennis Michael, named
after Bing's maternal grandfather, Dennis Harrigan.   The
twins were vastly underweight.   But Dixie soon signed with
Monogram studio to film <u>Manhattan Love Song</u> as Bing invested
in the new Santa Anita race track in Arcadia in 1934, putting up $10,000 to obtain a box seat at the finish line.
After the track opened in December Bing began buying horses.
He invested about $2000 with a friend for Black Forest, an
unpromising four-year-old that won several races.   Elsewhere, in Tupelo, Mississippi, on January 8, 1935, a baby
named Elvis Presley was born.

Bing returned to radio in New York, now on Tuesdays,
and the Boswell Sisters and then the Mills Brothers became
regulars, and in June 1935 he had his last show for CBS and
Woodbury Soap. In mid-August Bing and Dixie went to Saratoga Springs in upstate New York, where illegal gambling
prospered in nearby Lake Saratoga.   On August 16, the news
arrived of the deaths of Will Rogers and Wiley Post in a
plane crash, and a hastily assembled network memorial was
broadcast, with Bing singing "Home on the Range" with a
catch in his throat.   Later the couple arrived in New York
in time for the premiere on August 30 of <u>Two for Tonight</u>.
The price for a ticket at most movie houses was ten cents.

Bing observed that his finances did not improve much
with his increased earnings and considered retiring from
radio and films, not recordings. He was the first artist
signed by the Decca Record Company, the new enterprise of
Jack Kapp, who sold records for 35 cents instead of 50.
Bing received higher than normal royalties for each record
and first sang for Decca in Los Angeles on August 8, 1934.
Kapp soon prevailed on Bing to sing more ballads than the
hot jazz the singer preferred, and Crosby credited Kapp with
stretching his range and repertoire. Bing Crosby did not
"just experiment with different genres, he created them,"
writes Will Friedwald in his 1992 book on jazz. He adds,
"'San Antonio Rose' launched the country record industry."

Beginning December 5, 1935, Bing was on radio Thursday
nights on the hour-long Kraft Music Hall on NBC, broadcast
from Los Angeles. Bing inherited comic Bob Burns, "The
Arkansas Traveler" who invented the instrument called the
bazooka. His announcer was Don Wilson and Jimmy Dorsey led
the orchestra. Bing credited Caroll Carroll, his writer,
with capturing his way of talking and for encouragement in
ad-libbing. Bing soon earned $5000 a week for the famous

radio series. He shunned a studio audience (so he would not
have to wear his toupee) and hoped to refrain from talking
on the shows, but Cal Kuhl and Carroll wrote such wild lines
for the guests that he had to respond. His wit flourished
and his confidence prospered. Ken Carpenter became the new
announcer as John Scott Trotter replaced Jimmy Dorsey.

Kapp convinced Bing to record "Adeste Fideles" and
"Silent Night" commercially in November 1935, overcoming the
singer's objection that they were not his style by arranging
to have all his royalties sent to charities--more than three
dozen from nearly two million pressings just to 1946 (Mize
71). These 1935 versions are preferred by many listeners to
later renderings. Bing had previously recorded both carols
in late 1934 as a charity for the soundtrack of a missionary
film on China for the St. Columban Missionary Society. The
subsequent commercial master, again in Bing's typical style
but with a "fuller orchestral backing," pleased all religious groups but angered some music critics and teachers who
sent him their objections. For years the royalties amounted
to $50,000 annually, all assigned in perpetuum to charities
of all denominations. The Internal Revenue Service ruled
the charitable arrangement illegal around 1950 and required
personal income tax be assessed before any charitable allo-
cation, reducing the annual "profit" to $5000, but by then
$250,000 had been donated.

Early in 1935 Dixie filmed Love in Bloom with George
Burns and Gracie Allen at Paramount. She waxed a record for
Decca in March. In July she had her hair dyed and went to
Twentieth Century-Fox to film Redheads on Parade, playing
opposite John Boles. On her new film career, Dixie told
reporters she would rather be Bing's wife. Bing brought the
three boys to the set, where Gary thought his mother's love
scene curious and he interrupted the filming. The reviews
were also cool, and Dixie decided to quit for good after
this, her tenth film. Meanwhile, Dixie was named as Bing's
co-star in Anything Goes, but Paramount later announced that
Ethel Merman would reprise her Broadway role in the film.

Bing continued filming three features a year for 1935,
when he starred in Mississippi with W.C. Fields and Joan
Bennett, Two for Tonight with Joan Bennett, and sang a song
in a vignette for The Big Broadcast of 1936. Three more
were released in 1936: Anything Goes, Rhythm on the Range,
and, for Columbia Pictures, Pennies from Heaven. He bought
a 65-acre spread called Rancho Santa Fe north of San Diego.
Bob Crosby and his Bob Cats were touring the South and ran
out of money. Bob phoned Bing for help, who seemed uncon-
cerned, although behind the scenes he arranged to have a New
York music publisher pay Bob $1000 to arrange some music,
enough for the band to recover.

After strenuous pleading by Bing, Dixie recorded two
songs for Decca in July 1936, and in August she sang for her
last recording, a duet with Bing for a disc of "A Fine
Romance" and "The Way You Look Tonight." They moved into a
larger home, a two-story colonial house of 26 rooms, a
tennis court, and a swimming pool on a six-acre lot on
Camarillo Street in Toluca Lake, nearer the Lakeside Golf
Course in North Hollywood. He sold his former Hollywood
house to Al Jolson and Ruby Keeler.

Bing tried to open his golf tournament at Del Mar in

January 1936, but rain delayed the initial Clambake until 1937. It was an affair that occurred six times until the war intervened, and he revived it in 1947 at Pebble Beach. Bing appeared in Swing with Bing, a three-reel film on his first golf tournament. He personally selected the amateur participants to team with top professional golfers, the primary criterion being the ability to have fun, not an obsession with victory cups. Bing's handprints and boot-prints were embedded in a red-tinted cement square at Grau-man's Chinese Theatre on April 8, 1936. For the thirtieth such ceremony Bing dressed in the cowboy clothes he wore in Rhythm on the Range. This was when one could stand across the street and see the Hollywood Hills in the background.

Bing went with Dixie to Hawaii in 1936 and discovered Harry Owens' Orchestra playing an original song, "Sweet Leilani," which Bing wanted for Waikiki Wedding. He had to convince Owens to release it by establishing a trust fund for his daughter Leilani, and the record sold 850,000 copies in 1937, the best of the year (Mize 119). It was Bing's third song to win an Academy Award nomination, the first to win the Oscar, and his first gold record. The film also popularized Hawaii despite the Depression.

"Adeste Fideles" opened the radio program December 24, 1936, and towards the end of the show, after singing "Pen-nies from Heaven," he sang "Silent Night." Bing had begun yet another tradition. Listeners sent "thousands of en-thusiastic letters," and "Silent Night" remained on the Christmas show ever since.

In early 1937 Bing brought Gary to visit his godfather on the set for his Souls at Sea, where the four-year-old said that at home his father called him Bucket Britches. Bing had stronger names for his overweight son and resorted to them when the attempts at dieting failed. The National Father's Day Committee honored Bing as "Hollywood's Most Typical Father for 1937." On June 20 the New York Times ran an article opposed to crooning as popular music. The F.B.I. reported on June 21 that Crosby apparently paid $10,000 to a blackmailer, probably a "procurer," but a year earlier Bugsy Siegel, of the Mafia, had begun extorting that amount from major film stars to ensure that stage hands he controlled would not delay production. Siegel was earning $400,000 a year and bought a mansion near Crosby in Holmby Hills.

Bing invested up to $500,000 to build the Del Mar Turf Club north of San Diego. Bing and Pat O'Brien had to dip into their life insurance as building expenses mounted. Spending more than others, Bing became the president and chairman of the board. Brother Ev, Oliver Hardy, Joe E. Brown, and Gary Cooper were on the executive committee. As part of the opening day, July 3, 1937, Bing had several orphans to his ranch and staged an elaborate show at the track. His horse High Strike won the first race. Kraft sponsored a half hour radio program that morning on NBC, and did so on Saturdays during the 32-racing-day seasons for years. Bing and Ken Carpenter chatted with guests and Bing sang at the Jockey Club, backed by Perry Botkin's guitar. Dixie became noticeably intoxicated that opening day as she had begun drinking heavily (Gary 78). The attendance was regularly star-studded but it was usually low until 1941.

Bob Hope challenged Bing to a golf match on October 15,

1937, with the loser to appear for free in the other's current film. Bing, paired with Ed Sullivan, won with a score of 72 to Hope's 84. Hope made a brief appearance in Doctor Rhythm, beginning another tradition. Bing reciprocated five years later in Hope's My Favorite Blonde (1942) and later in others. The radio feud between them began in the spring of 1938 when Bing made fun of Hope in the latter's first appearance on the show, just as he did at Del Mar. Hope's show began in September 1938, when he made fun of Bing's horses, and each came up with derogatory epithets. Hope frequently attended Del Mar Saturday nights with Bing.

Bob Hope would joke about Bing's wealth, and Bing retaliated with, "Hope doesn't come up with much money. He's a fast man with a squaw but a slow man with a buck." Hope retaliated with a name a caddy coined, calling Bing "the Groaner." The caddy noticed Bing's groan as he swung and especially when he missed a putt. Tommy Dorsey then called Bing "the Old Groaner."

Bing led his radio team to Spokane for a special broadcast at his alma mater in October 1937. Gonzaga University bestowed on him an honorary doctor of philosophy degree on October 21, which they later exchanged for a legitimate degree of Doctor of Music--the only degree he would ever accept. His films for 1937 were Waikiki Wedding and Double or Nothing. In 1938 Bing starred in Doctor Rhythm and Sing, You Sinners, which premiered at Del Mar on the track's opening day in August. That was also the premiere of Johnny Burke's and James Monaco's song "Where the Turf Meets the Surf," sung live by Bing. The next year the song was recorded and is still played at the opening and close of each racing day. Bob Hope appeared at the 1938 Crosby Pro-Am tournament and in a short film titled Don't Hook Now.

Bing founded the Binglin Breeding Stables with Lindsay Howard at Rancho Santa Fe. Bing owned 21 racehorses here and abroad, up to 75 later. Bing and Lin Howard bought Preceptor in Argentina and won several races, including one at Narragansett, Rhode Island, called the Blackstone Valley Handicap.

The fourth Crosby son, Lindsay Harry, was born on January 5, 1938. He was named for Lindsay Howard, for Bing's father, and for Bing, and was the only Crosby with brown eyes. Bing now filmed East Side of Heaven with Jimmy Cottrell, the Spokane boxer, hired as the prop man. Gary, nearly six, pestered Bing so much about singing "Little Sir Echo" that he recorded it with the Music Maids and sang it on the radio, making it so popular it made the Hit Parade.

Dixie starred in the first of her three performances produced by the Westwood Marching and Chowder Club at Del Mar on April 16. It was called the Midji Minstrels, directed by Dave Butler and included Johnny Burke. The newsreels captured Bing and Dixie attending the premiere in Hollywood of Kentucky, a film directed by David Butler and starring Loretta Young, Richard Greene, and Walter Brennan.

A $1600 organ was installed at the St. Charles Church in North Hollywood for Easter, donated by Bing Crosby. To dedicate the grand instrument, Bing sang a sacred concert. He was becoming the most generous philanthropist in Hollywood. On the horses, one famous race at Del Mar was between Seabiscuit and Ligaroti in August 1938 for $25,000. The

horses crossed the finish line in a dead heat, breaking track records. The photo showed Seabiscuit ahead by a whisker, but Bing felt that the picture was read wrong.
     The professional song pluggers voted Bing "Number One Crooner of the United States" for 1938, explaining that he sold more sheet music than anyone else. After Bing sang a song on radio, sales increased 10,000 each day, 50,000 for the week. The other singers were, in descending order, Dick Powell, Tony Martin, Ozzie Nelson, Rudy Vallee, Buddy Clark, Kenny Baker, Benny Fields, Frank Parker, and Bob Hope. The nation was treated to a special 15-minute broadcast on NBC on Christmas morning 1938 as Bing distributed gifts at home to his three older sons. Bing's films for 1939 were <u>Paris Honeymoon</u>, <u>East Side of Heaven</u>, and <u>The Star Maker</u>, the last a loose version of the career of Gus Edwards.
     By 1939 Bing's boys, whom he called the Irishers, summered at Rancho Santa Fe. This was the time that the twins, against Gary's advice, sneaked into their mother's bedroom one night and killed her canary. One by one, the trio felt Bing's strong hand under Dixie's supervision, but the sons wore matching outfits and a requisite smile whenever a photographer snapped the family. Bing's reading included detective stories by Dashiell Hammett and novels by Somerset Maugham, William McFee, and Joseph Conrad. Universal won the rights on May 25, 1940, to distribute Bing's 30-minute musical golfing short titled <u>Swing with Bing</u>.
     Bing joined Harvey Shaeffer in buying a horse named Dreamboat. Despite his poor appearance the horse won many races for a few years. Popular wisdom was that Bing's horses were dogs, and Lindsay Howard complained that Bing's and Hope's jokes hurt their market in selling colts. Sue Carol, Dixie's close friend, became an agent, married Alan Ladd, and made him a star in 1942. Sue was very assertive and had a song written for her in 1928. Then Frank Butler and Don Hartman adapted a tale into a vehicle called "The Road to Mandalay" for Fred MacMurray and Jack Oakie, but they rejected it, and Burns and Allen were unavailable to star with Bing, so it was rewritten for Bing and Hope. Dorothy Lamour claims credit for the idea, and that she was to join the cast wearing her sarong became a hot item.
     Victor Schertzinger, the gentle director of musicals, was bewildered as Bing and Bob Hope ignored the script, but he let the comics proceed. Barney Dean, an old vaudevillian, appeared and remained to suggest jokes. Carroll Carroll wrote some jokes, and Dean and Monty Brice contributed sight gags and lines that helped launch Bing and Bob into their own <u>ad libitum</u> orbit that bewildered earthbound Lamour and angered the scriptwriters, Hartman and Butler. Hartman was on the set when Hope yelled, "If you recognize anything of yours, yell 'Bingo.'" The film opened in New York in April 1940 as <u>Road to Singapore</u>, and one of the great cinematic traditions was born.
     Then Bing filmed <u>Rhythm on the River</u>, a festival of jazz and romance. With Europe at war, Johnny Burke met the challenge in 1940 to write a song for <u>Road to Zanzibar</u> in the language of the fictitious country without upsetting anyone: he wrote, according to Crosby, in Esperanto. Cheerful Johnny Burke and morose bachelor Jimmy Van Heusen teamed up to write Crosby songs. Connie Boswell became a

regular on the radio program when it returned November 1940 and remained a regular through the next year. In a few years she changed the spelling to "Connee." The Music Maids were on even longer, from December 1938 to October 1944.

Bing's diving prowess was tested in Billy Rose's Aqua-cade Review of the 1939-1940 New York World's Fair. Harvey Shaeffer dared Bing to dive from the high board for $100. Bing bounded off the board, but as he went over he worried what his pipe might do to his mouth, so he recovered and splashed down feet first, losing his pipe. Harvey paid only $65, explaining that falling feet first was not a dive.

Bing supported the candidacy of Wendell Willkie against President Roosevelt. He spoke briefly on radio on November 6, the night before the election, stating that he liked what Wilkie had said in his address. A few days later, however, when Roosevelt had won, Bing announced on radio that he hoped the nation would unite behind Roosevelt (Ulanov 240). Never again did Bing endorse a politician.

Another film starring Bing in 1940 was If I Had My Way. By this time Bing had adopted an expression he took from director Lloyd Bacon: "It's Aloha with a steel guitar." The filming of The Birth of the Blues occurred in New Orleans. Bing enjoyed the experience of loosely recreating the story of the Original Dixieland Band. For the third time, Bing made the 1940 Quigley list of the ten most powerful box-office attractions. He ranked seventh. He also recorded his second gold record, "San Antonio Rose." Frank Sinatra had his first hit record in 1939, singing "All or Nothing at All" with Harry James' Orchestra, and soon sang for $125 a week ($6500 a year) with Tommy Dorsey. By comparison, Joe E. Lewis recently hit the big time in Chicago at $2000 a week, $104,000 if he worked a full year.

In 1940 Bing earned $77,000 from Decca, $175,000 from Paramount, $7500 a week from his radio program, and paid $377,000 in taxes. This income alone adds up to more than $625,000 for the year (Current Biography 1941), irrespective of Del Mar, his horses, prize fighters, a gold mine, an employment agency, a real estate project, music publishing, and a girls' baseball team. Bing's total annual income amounted to about $750,000.

PART FIVE

THE SUPERSTAR: 1941-1945

In the summer of 1941 Bing sailed from New York to South America, acting as the altar boy in the ship's chapel, and bought horses and a stable in Argentina. Bing's sarto-rial preferences were already notorious. He explained that he wore loose sweaters to be able to practice golf whenever he wished with the bag of balls he always carried around.

The second Road picture, Road to Zanzibar, was re-leased. Schertzinger, the director, realized that the chemistry between Bing and Hope worked best with Bing as the conniver who wins the girl and Hope as the victim with false bravado. The zaniness on the set continued, frustrating Lamour and producer Paul Jones.

Bing had snatched an unlimited license to party. His

freedom now involved more golf, horses, gambling, hunting and fishing, houses and ranches, a wide array of invest- ments, and complete personal control whenever he wanted it, even as he continued on radio, in films, and on records.

His next film release was <u>Birth of the Blues</u>. He wanted Gary to play him as a child in the prologue to the film, but his screen test was a failure. Discipline ruled at home. Dixie sometimes spanked the sons before breakfast and their father sometimes repeated the discipline in the evening. However, one nurse held their heads under water until Dixie saw it and fired her. The boys preferred week- ends with Dixie's parents, who lived in San Fernando Valley. Dixie's father was an ardent socialist and egalitarian.

Amid America's gloom after the Japanese attack on Pearl Harbor, on Christmas Day 1941 Bing introduced "White Christ- mas" on radio. The song became Bing's third gold record, selling a million 40 times over. Bing's earnings for 1941 amounted to more than $600,000, including $300,000 from Paramount and $100,640 from Decca. Bob Hope's total earn- ings were $464,161.78 in 1940 and about $575,000 in 1941. Paramount paid Fred MacMurray $290,333 and Bob Hope $294,106 in 1941, while Louis B. Mayer received $704,426 as the production manager of Loew's, Inc. Hope worried about kidnappers eyeing his two children for ransom. Gary Cooper, like Bing, also had a realistic fear of kidnapping.

The Crosby Clambake was held for the last time at Rancho Santa Fe in January 1942 while soldiers bunked at the Del Mar Turf Club. When the invasion hysteria subsided, the Marine Corps commandeered Del Mar in the summer of 1942. <u>Holiday Inn</u> was released and became the biggest grossing musical up to then. This was the film in which Bing sang "White Christmas." He sang the title song in <u>Angels of Mercy</u>, a short for the American Red Cross. He also discov- ered Victor Borge for American audiences, adding him to the radio show in December 1941 and keeping him on for 56 weeks. Borge was famous in his native Denmark since 1931, but he had fled from Europe and the Nazis in April 1940.

Sent by short wave, Bing beamed his radio show of January 29, 1942, directly to General MacArthur's belea- guered soldiers of Corregidor. He opened the show singing "The Caissons Go Rolling Along," the song of the Field Artillery and adopted by the whole Army. He starred in <u>Star Spangled Rhythm</u>, and Gary had two appearances in the film. Then Bing made his first cameo appearance in a Bob Hope film, <u>My Favorite Blonde</u>. The crooner was nearly injured filming <u>Road to Morocco</u> when he barely jumped into a doorway out of the way of charging horses. Overhearing Bing tell Dorothy Lamour that "moonlight becomes you," Burke and Van Heusen composed "Moonlight Becomes You" for the film, a song that became very popular in 1942 and Bing's signature song years later for his final daily radio programs.

When Bing was at Paramount, the front door of his bungalow was always wide open. He was friendly with every- one, including the grips and workmen, and they would often step in for a minute or two of wisecracks. Bing would plead with Wally Westmore to omit the "scalp doily" for the next scene, hoping to wear a hat, and would conduct an enormous amount of business while chatting with others, even on the set. But Gary thought he changed when he entered the house, especially when Dixie was drinking.

Bing just could not sing on key for "Sunday, Monday or Always" while recording it at the studio for Dixie, but when Y. Frank Freeman agreed to let Burke and Van Heusen open their own music publishing company, Bing hit the notes and introduced another gold record. Bing had four more gold records in scarcely one year: "Silent Night," "I'll Be Home for Christmas," "Pistol Packin' Mama," and "Jingle Bells." Now he had eight. For the war effort, Bing, Pat O'Brien, Johnny Mercer, Johnny Burke, Jimmy Van Heusen, and others formed the North Hollywood Marching and Chowder Club and Clambake, a group that sponsored a troupe to entertain soldiers and produce an annual minstrel show. The troupe traveled throughout the Southwest, from Oklahoma to California, and entertained more than a million service people, giving shows to 1200 to 32,000 people at a time.

Bing Crosby joined the Hollywood Victory Caravan, a war-bond tour. For two weeks he went to New York, Boston, Houston, and many other cities. At many of the cities he and Hope played exhibition golf matches to sell bonds. Then Bing and Hope would often play weekend golf benefits for the war-relief efforts of the Professional Golfers Association. The Crosby Research Foundation, established in late 1940, had engineers evaluate inventions for the war effort. The War Department would reveal military needs to the Foundation, which would then work with inventors. The Foundation made no charges and took only a portion of the royalties awarded the successful inventors. By this date, however, the royalties were overwhelmed by the expenses.

Road to Morocco premiered at the Paramount in New York in November 1942. The billing set new attendance records. A month later Frank Sinatra made his famous appearance at the same theater. Bing's previous big grossers included The Big Broadcast (1932), Double or Nothing (1937), The Star Maker (1939), and the first Road film.

Bing's home in North Hollywood burned down on January 2, 1943, when a short circuit caused the Christmas tree to burst into flames. Johnny Burke located Bing by telephone at the Brown Derby and finally convinced Bing the fire was true, but Bing refused to abandon his dinner. He drove home later to retrieve $1500 from a shoe. The money was for the horses the next day. The Crosbys lived at the Beverly Hills Hotel before renting one of Marion Davies' houses again in Beverly Hills. Bing had lost his collection of Louis Armstrong records, which Louie replaced, including valuable collectors' discs (Mize 89n). Bing replaced the house with an 18-room Colonial-style house on South Mapleton Drive, Holmby Hills, overlooking the Los Angeles Country Club. Because the club would not permit an actor to join, Bing's father joined and permitted Bing as his guest. On March 4, 1943, "White Christmas" was awarded the Oscar as the best film song of the previous year.

Bing was often away, and Dixie's drinking increased. They had a serious quarrel, which they never explained (Shepherd and Slatzer 243; S&S hereafter). Bing slept in the servant's quarters above the garage for weeks and after that they slept in different rooms. Gary recalls an incident in which Dixie, without warning, savagely attacked the boys until Bing ran to their rescue, picked Dixie up in his

arms, and carried her away (p. 71).   Bing accused Sylvia
Picker, now named McGraw, of being a bad influence.
     The three older boys attended Catholic schools, except
for a year at the Black Foxe Military Academy.   Dixie explained to her sons that they were not special just because
their father was famous.   Sometimes the boys, especially
Gary, had to wear the "Crosby lavalier" about their necks,
which was a shirt or a pair of shoes they failed to put
away.   The house rules were firm.   Dixie hired Georgina
Hardwicke in 1941 to run the house, and she soon became the
boys' nurse, hitting them if they spoke before rising.
"Georgie," as they called the nurse, "quickly became the
lord high executioner of all [their] mother's rules" (Gary
76).   She policed the kitchen and the boys' bedroom, demanding they stay out of the one and quiet in the other.
     Bing attempted to cure Denny's lefthandedness by making
him keep the offensive hand in his pocket.   Denny had an
open personality, but Bing sometimes called him stupid.
More often Bing called him Dude and Handsome, for he would
study himself in a mirror.   Young Linny was quiet.   Bing
called him Head, for his head was large for his body.   Bing
was casual, although his home was formal.   He often lounged
wearing shorts, white socks, and moccasins to read the
Racing Form.   Bing and his boys had already begun their
Christmas Eve tradition of caroling through their neighborhood and singing "Silent Night" and "Adeste Fideles" at the
early Christmas Mass at their Beverly Hills parish.
     In January 1943 Bing's radio program was reduced to a
half hour, and its slate of disparate guests became reduced.
Leo McCarey also had a script for Bing playing a priest.
Paramount's production head, Buddy DeSylva, helped McCarey
sell the idea.   In March Johnny Burke dined at the Crosbys
and composed the song "Swinging on a Star," which became one
of the great hits the next year.   Like Going My Way, the
song won an Oscar and became Bing's ninth gold record.
     Bing waxed only one record from August 1942 to August
1943 because of a musician strike.   Bing's songs were
"Sunday, Monday or Always" and "If You Please."   And Bing
was fourth on the Box Office Poll of 1943, his fourth time
on the list.   The strike resulted in V-Disks, which allowed
records for the military.   For the Fourth of July Bing re-
joined Barris and Rinker for a reunion of the Rhythm Boys
for Whiteman's summer radio program celebrating Pop's 50
years in show business.   When Decca began recording again in
August 1943, Bing recorded two hits from Oklahoma and then,
on September 27, four hits with the Andrews Sisters, including "Jingle Bells" and "Santa Claus Is Comin' to Town."
     When the Marines left the Del Mar Turf Club, Bing and
the directors invested another $200,000 to form the Aircraft
Division, which made small parts for airplanes until Douglas
Aircraft gave them a large contract for wing units for the
Boeing B-17 bombers they produced at Long Beach.   Bing's
1943 earnings approached $1 million ($19,230 a week), at a
time when oxford shoes were $3.79 a pair; a man's all-wool
suit cost $29.95; a loaf of bread, 8 cents; sirloin steak
and lamb chops, 39 cents a pound; Idaho potatoes, 5 cents a
pound; coffee, 19.5 cents a pound; and a carton of cigarettes had risen 40 cents to $1.50.
     Bing sang the title song in The Road to Victory (1943),

a 12-minute short for Warner Bros. for the Fifth War Loan
Drive.   Bing filmed <u>Dixie</u> as his first feature film in
color, and soon he was filming <u>Road to Utopia</u>, when he hurt
his back in a fall in one scene and Hope required medical
attention after a live bear rolled on his hand as it lay
down beside him and Bing. The next day that bear tore its
trainer's arm off.
    Kapp extended Bing's recording contract through 1955 as
serious competition arose when a singer with Tommy Dorsey
sang a song that remained at the top of the Hit Parade for
two months.   The singer was Frank Sinatra, the song was
"I'll Never Smile Again."   The <u>Downbeat</u> poll listed Sinatra
as the most popular male vocalist for 1943, shading out
Bing, Perry Como, and Bob Eberly.   Dorsey had sold Sinatra's
contract for $1, reputedly at the point of a gun held by a
mobster, according to <u>The Mafia Is Not an Equal Opportunity
Employer</u> (1971) by Nicholas Gage (91).
    <u>Going My Way</u> was released in 1944 and grossed nearly $8
million at the box office.   Paramount signed Bing to a ten-
year contract.   Many people in Latin America objected to
Bing's role as a humanized Father O'Malley in a sweatshirt,
but the film made moviegoers out of many Bible Belt Chris-
tians.   Pope Pius XII wrote of his approval, and for the
first time Bing was identified with a character.   Bing and
Sinatra offered to sing a duet for anyone who would buy a
$10,000 war bond, and when it sold they sang the duet,
probably on February 1 for the Hollywood Victory Caravan's
shortwave broadcast to America's armed forces.
    Bing remained a moral beacon in March as Charlie Chap-
lin was accused of "white slavery" with a starlet, a charge
he was acquitted of.   Dixie, however, virtually stopped
going out as her drinking had become chronic. Bing and the
boys knew that each knew, although they did not discuss it.
Bing engaged a psychoanalyst, Dr. Anthony Sturdevant, to go
to the house to help her, and she sometimes stopped drinking
for months.   But the dry periods inevitably ended.   Dr.
Sturdevant looked out one day in 1944 or 1945 from Dixie's
window and saw Gary so enraged that the physician thought
him capable of murder and invited him to talk (Gary 193).
    Beautiful Marilyn Maxwell became a regular on the radio
show in 1944, and Bing sang Cole Porter's "Don't Fence Me
In" in March for the short titled <u>Swingtime with the Stars</u>.
He again demonstrated that he was a "quick study" as he
recorded the song in a complex arrangement with the Andrews
Sisters in one take after a 30-minute rehearsal in July.
Trotter once advised a colleague, "Only play it once.... He
learns so quickly that the second time through he starts
improvising" (Mize 24).   "Swinging on a Star" was on the Hit
Parade for 20 weeks, replaced by the Crosby-Andrews Sisters
"There'll Be a Hot Time in the Town of Berlin" for another
six weeks.   "Don't Fence Me In" then hit the tops in jukebox
selections for eight more weeks.
    Bing bought an 8700-acre working ranch near Elko,
Nevada, in 1944 and a much larger one near Tuscarora in the
fall of 1945.   Gary spent the next summers working hard as a
cowhand.   The first ranch was called the Cross-B, and the
foreman was Johnny Eacret.   Bing spent his days hunting,
fishing, and dictating letters.   In the afternoons he rode
the range, occasionally riding into Gary.   Bing replaced the

Cross-B with a ranch about 50 miles to the north with about
19,000 acres and 3500 head of cattle.   Gary spent the next
nine summers but one working at the ranch, usually ending by
August.   His brothers began working there in 1945, and Gary
was amazed that they seemed to enjoy it.   Dixie went to the
ranch only for a summer or two before she quit.

Bing could not attend the launching in the summer in
Oregon of a Liberty ship named the U.S.S. <u>Nathaniel Crosby</u>,
for Bing's great grandfather.   Then the United Service
Organization, the U.S.O., agreed to send Bing overseas,
perhaps to the Pacific.   The single most rewarding experience of his life occurred in 1944, sailing aboard the <u>Ile de
France</u> to England and France to entertain the soldiers.   On
August 25 the ship reached Greenock, Scotland, where Bing
met Fred Astaire, and together they headed for London via
Glasgow, where thousands of people came to greet them.   He
was the surprise guest at a club in London the next day.
That night at Kettner's Restaurant in Soho a throng demanded
he sing "Pennies from Heaven" <u>a capella</u> from a ledge.   The
people returned and Bing sang eight more songs in the glow
of flashlights from the street.   A reporter wrote that
Bing's performance "did more for transatlantic relationship
than a hundred speeches.   Thanks, Bing."

His troupe included comic Joe De Rita (who later became
one of the Three Stooges), singer Jean Darrell, dancer Dar-
lene Garner, guitarist Buck Harris, and accordionist Earl
Baxter.   Bing toured air bases and a hospital where badly
burned children lay after a B-24 crashed into their school.
As "Der Bingle" the crooner broadcast recorded messages and
songs from a phonetic script into Germany and Norway for the
Office of War Information, from a studio at London.   The
United Press called Bing "a new secret weapon."

He made several records and greeted Glenn Miller when
he arrived the next day.   He sang with Glenn Miller's band,
songs that were transcribed and broadcast later for security
reasons.   That night Bing and Miller recorded "I'll Be
Seeing You," "Swinging on a Star," and "With a Song in My
Heart" live at a theater.   After more recordings the next
day, they went to the opening of the Stage Door Canteen,
where Bing sang. Bing's troupe flew on September 1 to Cherbourg and followed the troops to Paris, giving three shows a
day.   Bing's "barracks" one night were beside a bridge, so
he moved to a far hill.   That night the bridge was shelled,
destroying the building he had evacuated.

A few days later, after Mass, Bing rode to the front in
a jeep with a lieutenant when the telephone wires disap-
peared.   Bing suggested a hasty retreat.   That night at
General Bradley's headquarters Bing explained that he had
reached a distant town.   The general looked puzzled and
said, "We haven't taken that town yet."   Bing replied, "We
had it for a little while this afternoon."   At the end of
the tour Bing visited General Eisenhower and had the use of
the general's car and driver for four days to visit Paris.

Bing returned a changed and more sober person.   He had
sung 2500 songs to audiences both very large and very small,
sometimes only 1000 yards from the active front.   The night
he docked in New York he returned to his radio program.   He
went with Frank Sinatra to Toots Shor's restaurant, where
they received a standing ovation.   The next day Bing left

for the Coast, angry that the Hollywood for Dewey Committee had listed him without authorization as one of the supporters of Thomas Dewey, the Republican Presidential challenger.

Crosby and Sinatra became friends and kidded each other on their radio shows, making occasional appearances. Sometimes they teamed up for bond rallies. Sinatra was on Bing's show in November, singing remote from New York, and Bing appeared as a guest in Bob Hope's The Princess and the Pirate. Then he starred in a role that parodied Frank Sinatra in Here Come the Waves. On Christmas Eve 1944 Bing sang at the midnight Mass at an Army hospital.

For The Bells of St. Mary's, a film for which Sinatra was first considered to play the priest, Jimmy Cottrell had the task of instructing Ingrid Bergman how to box so that she could demonstrate it to a boy in the film. Bob Hope joked about Bing's weight almost as much as Bing concerned himself with Gary's. When Gary reached 10 or 11, Bing would weigh him each Tuesday and belt his bare bottom in his home office for any excess. Bing's was dispassionate as he lectured and then out came the studded belt and a dozen or so reluctant whacks until he drew blood. Yet Gary could not stop eating sweets. Dixie whipped the bare bottoms of the boys for violations in deportment, using a switch they had to cut from a backyard tree to meet her standards. Gary's repressed anger grew as he felt trapped in a life of endless discipline that Bing and Dixie thought necessary.

For the Academy Awards for 1944, in front of a crowd of 5000 people, the largest in five years, Bing arrived with Dixie on his arm. Hope was the emcee, and Gary Cooper announced the nominees for Best Actor. Without his toupee but wearing a dinner jacket, Bing asked, "Are you talking about me?" "Yup," said Cooper. Bing climbed to the stage and uttered, "All I can say is that it sure goes to show what a great and democratic world we live in, when a broken-down crooner like myself can walk away with this hunk of crockery. I was just lucky enough to have Leo McCarey take me by the hand and lead me through a picture like this one. Now if he can find me a horse to win the Kentucky Derby."

McCarey accomplished a first, winning two Oscars as director and as the writer of Going My Way. Fitzgerald won as the Supporting Actor, and "Swinging on a Star" won as the Best Original Song. The film also won the vote of the New York Film Critics as the best of 1944.

Bing never quite believed he was a celebrity and, as Gary explains, "He had a certain ironic detachment that kept him from taking it all that seriously. I remember him joking that he expected to hear a knock at the door one day and there would stand the man in the suit, who would tell him, 'Okay, Bing, the game is up. We found you out, and you have to give it back'" (p. 87).

Bing's first film effort for 1945 (shot in October 1944) was dubbing the singing as a parody of Sinatra for Eddie Bracken in Out of This World. Bing received $26,000 for his singing but no credit in the titles. The money went to his four sons, who were in the film. Duffy's Tavern followed, in which Bing sings a parody of "Swinging on a Star." Bing's sons, ranging in age from 12 to 7, appeared in this film as well.

When it was time to sing on radio, Bing shifted his gum

to one cheek, his pipe to his rear molars, and produced the reliable warm tones and flawless phrasing of the master. Bing was dressed casually for the live broadcasts, which nearly every singer and bandleader in the country waited for in order to revise their own repertoires. Only Bing could utter his polysyllabic lexicon on popular radio and later on television without seeming boorish. A major radio event was a special Command Performance starring Bing, Hope, Sinatra, and many others March 12 in a broadcast of a spoof on the Dick Tracy character. Hope was Flattop and Sinatra played Shaky. Of course, Bing played Tracy, and both CBS and NBC aired the transcribed show with a cast the networks could not otherwise have afforded.

Bing sought to extricate himself from his radio con- tract, returning to the airwaves only once in 1945 after May 17, and then not again until February 7 the next year. McCarey's Rainbow-RKO film, The Bells of St. Mary's, was released and became the biggest money-maker of 1945. Bing introduced the song "Aren't You Glad You're You." The crooner also sang "Buy Bonds" in Twentieth Century-Fox's All Star Bond Rally. Hollywood Victory Caravan was another short released in 1945 in which Bing sang "We've Got Another Bond to Buy." He received a "Page One Award" from the New York Newspaper Guild on December 6 at Madison Square Garden. Through the war he sold Victory Bonds worth more than $14.5 million, and in 1945 Bing was rated the top film star for the second consecutive year.

In June the National Father's Day Committee named Bing the "Number One Screen Father of 1945." An anti-Semitic smear appeared against Bing in 1945. Barry Ulanov tells the story, clearing Bing and acquitting Frank Sinatra of the accusation made by his friends (p. 242). In the summer of 1947 the smear was repeated in a New York party attended by many Sinatra friends, Ulanov, a comedian, and some songwrit- ers, and was repeated elsewhere under some people's breath.

In a 1945 Yank magazine poll, G.I.'s voted Crosby the person who had done most for their morale overseas. By this time his "Silent Night/Adeste Fideles" record that supported charities had reached 1,500,000 sales. "Too-ra-loo-ra-loo- ral," "Don't Fence Me In," and "I Can't Begin to Tell You" ran Bing's gold records to an even dozen, when gold records were rare. The Motion Picture Herald and Radio Daily voted him the most profitable star for the second consecutive year. Box-Office Magazine named him "the year's Top All- American Male Star," while "The International British Poll" placed him as "the Top International Star" and another voted him "Britain's Most Popular Star of 1945." He was voted the "Top Radio Master of Ceremonies" for the fourth consecutive year and "Top Male Vocalist" for the ninth consecutive year in The Motion Picture Daily Fame Poll. Billboard's poll of Army camps gave Bing many more votes than the combined tallies of Sinatra, Perry Como, and Dick Haymes.

Paramount was no doubt paying Bing far more now than the $300,000 it paid him in 1941, and for comparison, Louis B. Mayer paid Elizabeth Taylor a $15,000 bonus and $750 a week ($39,000 a year) after she became a child star in National Velvet (M-G-M, 1944). In 1944 Bing's record royal- ties totaled $250,000; in 1945 the royalties were more than $400,000 on more than eight million discs, up from $77,000 for 1940 (Mize 77n; Barnett). "White Christmas" had already sold two million copies, "Silent Night/<u>Adeste Fidelis</u>" 1.8 million, "Don't Fence Me In" 1.25 million, "Sunday, Monday or Always" one million, and "Sweet Leilani" 850,000 (Mize 76) and reached a million in 1946. Bing earned a total of more than $1.5 million, possibly $2 million, in 1946. Bob Hope earned $1.25 million, not counting $500,000 from his newspaper column and more from products and investments (<u>Newsweek</u>, May 6, 1946).

Bing's properties included several prize fighters, several music publishing companies, a fish packing concern, and other real estate and securities. Bing Crosby Productions, Inc., formed in 1944, produced films, first <u>The Great John L</u> (1945), the touring Water Follies, a girl's baseball team, and other shows. His second film production, <u>Abie's Irish Rose</u> (1946), was a "bomb." He hired Basil Grillo to organize Bing Crosby Productions, and the manager reorganized all of Bing's enterprises. At year's end Bing also learned he was nominated for an Academy Award for his reprise of Father Chuck O'Malley.

PART SIX

THE STORIED CROSBY: 1946-1950

In the summer of 1946 Bing succeeded in breaking his contract with Kraft, and he signed with the Philco Radio Corporation. He had to appear on 13 more KMH shows, to May 9, and make some guest appearances, but otherwise he could go to Philco and ABC. ABC had offered Bing $25,000 a week and stock. The total came to $30,000, of which $7500 was for Bing and the rest for the transcribed production (<u>Bing</u> 103: 48). About 400 independent stations also offered him $100 per broadcast per station, or another $40,000 a week. Each show appeared on three discs, and the network touted Wednesday as "Bingsday."

The film releases in 1946 included <u>Road to Utopia</u>, a pastiche of four old Sennett shorts titled <u>Road to Hollywood</u>, a re-release of <u>If I Had My Way</u>, and <u>Blue Skies</u>, a songfest with story and songs by Irving Berlin. <u>Blue Skies</u> was released October 16, the date of Bing's premiere radio show for Philco, with opening-day receipts assigned to the Sister Kenny Foundation. Both Bing and Ingrid Bergman were nominated by the Academy of Motion Picture Arts and Sciences for their work in <u>The Bells of St. Mary's</u>, but this time the Oscar winners were Ray Milland and Joan Crawford.

Philco allowed Bing to transcribe "The Crosby Show" so long as audience ratings remained up. Now Bing could put three or four shows "in the can" in a few days. Other stars soon did likewise. Bing sold his one-third interest in the Del Mar Turf Club in April 1946 to Arnold M. Grant, a Beverly Hills lawyer, sold some horses, and joined three others to buy 70 percent of the Pittsburgh Pirates (20 percent for himself). Soon he sold the property at Rancho Santa Fe and the stables, disappointed that horse racing had become big business, and again halfheartedly considered retiring. He donated $2500, nearly a fourth of the receipts, for a benefit baseball game played July 1 for nine members of the

Spokane Indians team who died June 30 in a bus crash.   In
August he informally adopted a Belgian girl whose father had
been killed by the Nazis.
     It was a busy time.   Joan Caulfield, a current co-star,
had romantic interests in Bing and expressed regret that he
would not divorce Dixie (Bing 99, Dec. 1991: 23).   He sent a
telegram also signed by Bob Hope and Frank Sinatra to Congress in April, denouncing a bill designed to restrict James
C. Petrillo of the American Federation of Musicians.   They
said it would restrict "the labor rights of all radio workers."   About this time Bing may have suggested a story on an
alcoholic woman (like Dixie) to Frank Cavett, the co-writer
of Going My Way, who contributed the idea to the 1947 film
Smash-Up (Bing 103, Apr. 1993: 13).   Bing's neighbor, Bugsy
Siegel, finally opened the Flamingo in Las Vegas on December
26, 1946, but he was killed by his Mafia associates in
Beverly Hills on June 20, 1947.
     For the new radio show Bing retained Trotter and Ken
Carpenter and replaced Carroll Carroll with Bill Morrow.   He
also added a pianist named Lyle Cedric Henderson, whom he
promptly named "Skitch."   The ratings became weak after a
month.   The Hooper Rating for the first show was enormous,
with Bob Hope as a guest, but for the fourth show it
dropped.   Then it recovered and overall ratings were very
high.   Nevertheless, John Crosby, the radio critic of the
New York Herald-Tribune wrote of the fifth show that Bing's
voice was flat and the show seemed hasty.
     The associate editor of The Musical Digest estimated
that Bing's records filled more than half of the 80,000
weekly hours allotted to recorded radio music, that his
radio show was heard by 25 million listeners weekly, and
that each film was seen by 250 million viewers (Mize 74).
Women's Home Companion voted Bing the leading film star, an
honor repeated the next four years.   Author Ring Lardner
hated crooners but included two Crosby records in his
"perfect radio program" (Mize 75).   Bing's name appeared as
the throwaway line in many films, including The Bamboo
Blonde (RKO, 1946).   In Billy Rose's Diamond Horseshoe (20th
Century-Fox, 1945), the film that introduced "The More I See
You" (which Crosby recorded in 1976), Betty Grable sings,
"I'd love a double order of Bing," and her replacement in
the film calls William Gaxton, "You Civil War Bing Crosby."
     Musicologist J.T.H. Mize describes Crosby's singing
style: he might melt a tone away, glide it into a "downward
portamento" into a lower harmonic, scoop it "flat and slid-
ing up to the eventual pitch" as a "glissando,"   sometimes
"sting a note 'right on the button,'" take diphthongs for
"long musical rides," and "some of his prettiest tones are
heard on ng's" (pp. 77-88).   Mize notes his rare "interpo-
lating pianissimo whistling variations," sometimes "arpeg-
gic," "tremolo," sometimes "trilling," laments that Bing
hardly scatted in public anymore, and offers Patricia McKinney's detailed analysis of the style of "Where the Blue of
the Night" (pp. 26, 53-54, 82-84, 87).   Bing's taste raised
the standards of American popular music, and he sang not so
much personal favorites--mainly jazz--but what the people
liked, despite whatever his publishers offered.   Nearly
everyone admired his voice.   His recording of "Silent Night"
had sold 5 million copies, providing $250,000 for charity.

Prior to 1934 he sometimes displayed the brassiness of Jolson, Cantor, and Ted Lewis--Mize declares--and by 1946 those old-fashioned "plaques" still occasionally crept in (p. 86n). Henry Pleasants thinks Bing's best range was G to G or even lower and that only about this time was he able "slowly to sort out what worked on the microphone and to eliminate what was superficial or incompatible" (Great 132, 138). Still, Bing's voice was incomparable, which Charles Henderson called "phonogenic" and Pleasants "microgenic." His early upper mordents, light and fast, produced a "slight catch, or choke, or sob which was to remain one of the most attractive of his vocal devices," according to Pleasants.

Bing filmed The Emperor Waltz in Canada's Jasper National Park in 1946, where diminutive Barney Dean was as terrified of the bears as of composing an off-color joke. Bing drove his own car to have the freedom to hunt and play golf as he wished. He revived his annual professional-amateur golf tournament in 1947 at Pebble Beach, California, for his seventh annual Clambake, a three-day charitable event on three separate courses each January for which he personally paid all expenses. The links were Spyglass Hill, Cypress Point, and Pebble Beach Golf Club, with the final play occurring at Pebble Beach, a public course. In the first six years at Pebble Beach the Crosby National Pro-Am raised about $150,000 for charity.

Bing received a letter he treasured from his son Linny. After a few brief comments, the boy closed, "Your friend, Lin." Bing was so touched that Gary soon used a similar ending on his own weekly letters whenever Bing was away. Bing would update children's stories for his sons, giving Little Red Riding Hood a scooter in the woods at Pebble Beach, a basket full of candy bars, and the wolf a fancy automobile. Don Quixote became a taller Gary Cooper.

The radio show recorded for January 29, 1947, included Bob Hope and Dorothy Lamour, as they were filming Road to Rio. The most famous songs of the most famous album of all time were re-recorded on March 19, 1947. Bing Crosby and the Ken Darby Singers recorded "White Christmas" and "Silent Night," the two most popular songs of the Merry Christmas album of four 78 r.p.m. records. The album appeared first in 1945, but the 1947 version became the standard, which competed a year later with another called Christmas Greetings by Bing and the Andrews Sisters. In 1948 the four 78's (Album 550) sold for $3.89 and the long-playing record (DL-5019) for $2.85.

In 1947 Bing and Bob Hope filmed a golfing skit in Variety Girl. Bing appeared in a concluding cameo in Bob Hope's My Favorite Brunette and starred in Welcome Stranger. Bing returned to Jasper Park to enter a tournament, go moosehunting, and begin filming A Connecticut Yankee. Bill Morrow filmed the Totem Pole Tournament in September 1947, but disturbed Bing when the camera shutter buzzed. Bing flinched enough that the ball flew far to the right. Bing won the tournament and Morrow had his camera repaired.

Al Jolson left retirement by January 15, 1947, to join Bing on the radio show. The first transcribed program for the fall of 1947 led John Crosby to decide that Bing's voice was no longer excellent, but "the Crosby personality has waxed until now it's the brightest attraction." As a musi-

cians' strike was scheduled for 1948, the end of 1947 found
Bing with a heavy recording schedule.   By 1948 <u>The Motion
Picture Herald</u> named Bing the most popular star of 1947 (for
the fourth consecutive year), and he was also named the most
popular star in England.   By the middle of 1948 he had
recorded 700 songs and appeared in 37 feature films (before
<u>The Emperor Waltz</u> and <u>A Connecticut Yankee</u> were released).

Bing bought a house at Pebble Beach, a two-story modern
California type overlooking the Pacific from the thirteenth
fairway.   Dixie and Bing, well aware of the difficulty of
raising four normal boys when their father was the best
loved entertainer in the land, instilled proper values in
them.   Gary thought he heard racist comments by his father
and friends when Lennie Hayton married Lena Horne (p. 240),
but the regrets were obviously about Hayton's being blacklisted because Miss Horne had associated closely with Paul
Robeson, an outspoken advocate of Soviet Communism at the
height of the Cold War and the beginnings of McCarthyism.

Michael Wilding wrote that it was in 1948 that he
encountered a very drunk Dixie Lee begging for another drink
in the Polo Lounge of the Beverly Hills Hotel.   When he
drove her home, she told him that she was dying of cancer
and could not tell her husband, although Bing dates his and
Dixie's first awareness of her cancer as mid-1952.   Wilding
later learned, he wrote, that she and Bing had become closer
than ever.   Kathryn Crosby also writes that Dixie knew about
1948 that she was terminally ill (<u>My Life</u> 37).

Bing had now sold more than 80 million records, and
Paramount released <u>The Emperor Waltz</u> (1948).   General Eisenhower telephoned Bing to send his boys to visit him at his
hotel, but, "I've seen enough of you," he added.   Bing was
the subject of the "Crosby Cavalcade" of the May 1948 issue
of <u>Photoplay</u> for winning his fourth consecutive <u>Photoplay</u>
Gold Medal as "America's favorite movie star."

On the 222-yard sixteenth hole at Cypress Point, near
Pebble Beach in Del Monte, California, Bing faced the
"toughest par three hole in the world."   It took a 205-yard
drive just to carry over the hazards.   It was February 15,
1948, as the three-handicapper swung into the sun and made a
hole-in-one, the second ace of his life.   Only one other
golfer had ever aced that hole, which is now redesigned.
Bing's first hole-in-one was in 1946.

Frozen orange juice concentrate, a new product, became
interesting to Bing in the spring of 1948, when John Hay
"Jock" Whitney told him on a golf course of the Minute Maid
product of Vacuum Foods Corp.   In the late '50s Whitney was
the U.S. Ambassador to England.   Bing bought 20,000 shares
at 10 cents each, became a director, and agreed to serve as
the company spokesman.   Philco allowed Bing to transcribe a
15-minute daily program of chatter and song to plug the
juice provided he also said a kind word for Philco.   Crosby
Enterprises had produced several popular products and financed the Ampex Company to design a tape recording system
with Bing's Electronics Division in San Calow, California.
Bing also donned a clown suit and makeup for a benefit
performance in Los Angeles on September 27, 1948.   <u>Life</u>
photographer Allan Grant took several photos before Bob Hope
revealed to Grant that he was capturing Bing.

The four sons first joined Bing on radio April 28,

1948, with Clifton Webb as another guest. Gary was on with his three brothers four times and appeared alone or with one of them another 15 times, up to May 30, 1954, when the prime-time weekly show ended. Their money went into their trust funds as Gary began drinking heavily. Dixie welcomed Gary's girlfriends; Bing, however, was suspicious of any girl the boys dated, wondering if their mothers were instructing them in how to trap a Crosby.

The Motion Picture Herald pronounced that Bing won the top honor for the fifth year in a row as the most popular film star of 1948. Betty Grable was once more the runner-up. The editors declared, "As a result of having won it that many times, Mr. Crosby is entitled to the all-time boxoffice championship." British distributors again named Bing the most popular international star. But his radio program was losing its mass appeal. In November Bing made eight appearances on the stage of the vast Empress Hall in London for $400,000.

For A Connecticut Yankee in King Arthur's Court critics lavished high praise on the duet of Bing and Rhonda Fleming on "Once and for Always." The film cost more than $3 million to produce and earned only $3 million in America during the first year. Also in 1949 Bing starred in Top o' the Morning, and for Walt Disney-RKO Radio Pictures he narrated and sang for the first part of The Adventures of Ichabod and Mr. Toad; Basil Rathbone and Phil Harris narrated the tale of Mr. Toad. Bing appeared in another rip-off, Down Memory Lane, with footage from two Sennett shorts. Two albums that stores emphasized in May were Crosby, Danny Kaye, Evelyn Knight, and Ella Fitzgerald on songs from South Pacific from Decca and the album of A Connecticut Yankee.

Then Bing and Hope each invested $50,000 in oil wells in North Snyder, Scurry County, West Texas. Bing convinced Hope to invest another $50,000 each, and that August 9, 1949, they hit a gusher that produced 100 barrels an hour. They would earn $3.5 million each (Time, Oct. 10, 1949). Bing also bought, like Hope, ten percent of the Los Angeles Rams football team on December 13.

Judy Garland had become an unreliable actress by 1949, but Bing remained loyal. After singing duets with him for one record in 1944 and for another in 1945, she appeared on the radio show only once a year from 1946 to 1949, but she was a guest three times at the end of 1950, five times in 1951 (four shows straight in March), and four times in 1952, even serving as the guest hostess two days prior to Dixie's death. Judy considered the female lead in Just for You but backed out in 1951 for stage commitments.

Bing's last performance on ABC for Philco occurred June 1, 1949. The stars returning to the weakening radio air-waves in mid-September included Bing (Wednesdays on CBS at 9:30), Hope (Tuesdays on NBC at 9), Milton Berle (Tuesdays on NBC-TV a 8), Phil Harris and Alice Faye (Sundays on NBC at 7:30), and, following Bing, George Burns and Gracie Allen (Wednesdays on CBS at 10).

Across the Atlantic, in Communist Czechoslovakia, an overflow crowd assembled in October in a theater in Prague to hear Crosby records. Ignoring the hostile announcer, they applauded the scratchy records. The Downbeat poll of 1949 placed Bing in a tie for third with Mel Torme as favorite male vocalists of the year, topped by Billy Eckstine and Frankie Laine. Loud was fashionable. Having been the top film star for five years in a row since 1944, Bing slipped into second place for 1949, behind Bob Hope. Hope became number one for his first time, and Bing said, "So long as it's Bob who leads me I'm not worried. He can't stay there too long because he has acrophobia."

The Golf Writers of America awarded Bing the Richardson Trophy on January 9, 1950, for the year's outstanding contribution to golf. Bing starred in Frank Capra's Riding High and Richard Haydn's Mr. Music. One scene in the latter was filmed at a Hollywood golf course as the director ordered Bing to hit the ball straight and far. Accounting for the wind, Bing swung and admired his drive so much that he followed the ball for an hour and 40 minutes to finish a full game while the crew waited.

On March 13 Bing had an appendectomy and recovered well. On April 1 he attended the world premiere of Riding High at Front Royal, Virginia, which gained $15,000 for the Bing Crosby Stadium there. Bing had heard of their need for a ballfield from state senator Raymond R. Guest, a golfing buddy Bing stayed with that night. Bing had written a check for $1000 on April 30, 1948, for the ballpark. The charitable New York Herald-Tribune Fresh Air Fund participated because Front Royal had been declared one of the leading Friendly Towns the previous year, when it hosted New York youngsters sponsored by the Fresh Air Fund. Front Royal marked Bing Crosby Day on the first of April for five years.

Meanwhile, Bing Crosby Productions entered television with determination, filming at the Hal Roach Studios the first ten of 26-minute films for Proctor & Gamble for a weekly series called The Fireside Theater. The tales included versions of The Canterville Ghost, The Man Without a Country, and eight original scripts. Another 24 shows were soon produced.

After a Hollywood farewell party in March that Dixie did not attend, Bing and Bill Morrow arrived in New York a week before sailing. After attending the New York premiere of Riding High, Bing sailed with Bill Morrow, John Mullin, and Morrow's secretary, arriving at Cherbourg April 14. Mullin was the ex-serviceman who had brought examples of German recording tape and equipment to America. Staying at the Hotel Lancaster in Paris, Bing golfed. Amid rumors that his marriage was breaking up, he attended the races May 8 at the Longchamp track in Paris with the Count and Countess of Segonzac and a nightclub singer named Marilyn Gerson.

The Los Angeles Times reported May 9 that O'Melveny and Larry admitted that the Crosbys "had a serious quarrel," and the lawyer added that they had "strained relations," but brother Larry said he hoped for a separation and knew nothing about a divorce (S&S 252-53). The next day Dixie denied stories of a separation. While in Paris, Bing narrowly avoided a fifth stay in jail, this time for violating the grass near the Champs Elysees one morning while awaiting a luncheon appointment. Meanwhile, Women's Home Companion named Bing the most popular male star for the fifth consecutive year in the magazine's annual poll.

Bing entered the 65th British Amateur Open Golf Tournament at St. Andrews on May 22, where he played to a record

gallery of 4000 fans, all following him, and he scored well
in terrible weather but was eliminated in the first round.
In New York in June, Bing rebuked reporters obsessed with a
separation.   Asked who his tailor was, he replied, "The
Rainbow Division."   He attended a ballgame in Brooklyn with
Groucho Marx and took a train to Pasadena, where Leo Lynn,
not Dixie, met him.   Back in Beverly Hills the home scene
returned to normal (Gary 136).
     Making up for lost time, Bing recorded eight songs and
the next day he and Gary recorded "Sam's Song" and "Play a
Simple Melody."   Gary states that Bing was such a "strong
singer" that he became infectious and got the most out of
Gary, who, in turn, seemed to inspire further heights in his
father.   In singing they were feeding off each other, a jazz
singer's delight.   As Bing feared, the 45 r.p.m. record,
billed by Decca as "Gary Crosby and Friend," became a big
hit and Gary soon became even more independent.
     The Crosbys usually arrived at the ranch in early June
without Dixie to cut out cows and calves and drive steers up
to the summer range, followed by two days of branding.
Later the boys treated fence posts by dipping them in a
large tub of creosote, a dirty chore, and stacked them; then
there was opening hay bins and haying for fifty hands for
two months, with the sons earning $9 a day in 1952 if they
also stacked the hay.   Every year the boys yearned for
August at Hayden Lake, where they swam, water-skied, golfed,
and attended beach parties.   Each son earned $500 for each
radio appearance, which went into their trusts, unknown to
them.   Most of their spending money came from their wages
for six or seven weeks of work on the ranch.
     Bing completed filming <u>Mr. Music</u>, a title he thought
presumptuous.   In August Dixie visited friends in West End,
New Jersey.   Gary was dropped from the academy's team and
became the coach of the "130-pound team," on which Denny
played halfback and Phil a guard.   Phil was small but gutsy,
Denny was a natural, and Gary drank more beer and had more
fights on weekends.   Bing's father died October 5, 1950, and
<u>Mr. Music</u> premiered in New York at the end of the year.
When the next Christmas show arrived, Dixie allowed Bing to
persuade her to join it, for the first and last time.   At
the end of the show Ken Carpenter recommended the latest
issue of <u>Quick Magazine</u>, which featured a picture on Bing on
the cover and the caption, "Bing Plays Poppa Santa."
     From 1946 to 1950 Bing had nine more records that "went
gold."   To the previous dozen he added "McNamara's Band,"
"South America, Take It Away," the <u>Merry Christmas</u> album,
"Alexander's Ragtime Band," "The Whiffenpoof Song," "Now Is
the Hour," "Galway Bay," "Dear Hearts and Gentle People,"
and "Sam's Song," the duet with Gary.

     PART SEVEN

     THE LEGEND: 1951-1955

     Now Bing also had a national ice cream company, a
merchandising unit called Bing's Things, a partnership with
Bob Hope and Monty Moncrief for drilling and leasing oil
wells, and a partnership with Pat Doheny.   About 1950 he

sold his interest in the Decca Company for a $200,000 loss, ending his main adventure in the stock market.

John O'Melveny, the guardian of the sons' estates, argued in Hollywood before Superior Court Judge Newcomb Condes for a contract for the sons with Decca Records in which they would receive three cents for each <u>Crosby Christmas</u> album sold. The crooner's second appearance on television was on February 27, 1951, when he sang a few songs on CBS and "The Red Cross Program." His first appearance had occurred December 19, 1948, when he sang in "A Christmas Carol" on NBC. Dixie flew to New York on March 12 and boarded a Pan-American airliner for a "three-month pleasure tour of Europe." She stayed abroad long enough to celebrate Bing's "fiftieth" birthday in southern France.

Bing underwent surgery for a kidney stone on March 21, 1951, in Santa Monica, and drove in April to recuperate in Vancouver, fishing with Bill Morrow. After weeks in the woods they went to a hotel, where a clerk insultingly refused them a room because they were unshaven, but the manager soon provided rooms. The press often garbling who had insulted whom. Bob Hope hired the night clerk for a movie appearance, explaining that the clerk should be rewarded for his ability "to recognize a bum when he sees one." Bing attended the world premiere of <u>Here Comes the Groom</u> at Elko, Nevada, on July 30, and in September had a cameo appearance in <u>Angels in the Outfield</u>, a baseball movie filmed at Forbes Field, the Pittsburgh Pirates ballpark.

Bing whipped Gary for the last time. Gary turned around, grabbed the cane, broke it over his knee, and shouted that if Bing ever hit him again he would kill him. They parted without another word (Gary 152). In June Bing and Dixie went to Bellarmine for Gary's graduation and gave him an automobile, but Bing soon regretted it as "the biggest mistake I've ever made," for come fall Gary earned poor grades at Stanford. Gary did not have to go to the ranch that summer because he had corrective surgery on his left shoulder for an old football injury, and spent the time at Lake Tahoe with Dixie, but in December Bing took his automobile away. Bing turned down film offers for Gary so that the boy could pursue his studies. Gary was boiling inside, however. With his hostile attitude, if Gary had jumped out a tenth-floor window he would curse his evil fate for falling. Gary was insecure, feared dating, and found courage in the whiskey bottle (Gary 285), but he recorded "Moonlight Bay" and "When You and I Were Young Maggie Blues" with Bing, who also added him to the radio show in San Francisco.

Bing filmed <u>Just for You</u> in 1951. Ethel Barrymore, his co-star, often discussed sports. <u>Here Comes the Groom</u>, one of Capra's last films, was released in 1951. Bing felt that Capra's production of "In the Cool, Cool, Cool of the Evening" was done exceptionally well and contributed to its winning an Oscar for the best film song of the year. On September 29, 1951, Bing and Dixie celebrated their twenty-first wedding anniversary by attending the Cocoanut Grove, where they met and romanced in 1930. Columnist Earl Wilson observed that the "marriage now appears unbreakable and unshakable." Later, the Hollywood Women's Press Club invited Bing to play Santa Claus at their December affair.

In 1952 Bing had a cameo appearance in Hope's film

Son of Paleface. Bing appeared for the third time on television on June 21, 1952, joining Bob Hope and Dorothy Lamour
in a telethon to help finance the American Olympic team.
Reviewers liked the Bing they saw, but he explained that he
preferred radio and had many other things to do.   Then he
admitted, "Sure, I'll get into television eventually, when I
find the right format. But I don't think radio is dead--nor
ever will be."
     Bing signed a radio contract with General Electric for
$16,000 a week (including staff and guests) with a clause
that he would receive about $50,000 as a package for a
television program.   He appeared briefly with Bob Hope in
DeMille's The Greatest Show on Earth and in the Dean Martin
and Jerry Lewis film Scared Stiff. Road to Bali, financed
equally by Bing, Hope, and Paramount, commenced.   Because
the crooner would be home for his birthday celebration May
2, 1952, plans for a party advanced as he worked at the
studio. When Bing returned at seven that evening the home
had been converted "into a veritable tropical garden." When
Dixie rushed to him and hugged him, his eyes watered.
     In June Rosemary Clooney had her first radio date with
Bing, and Dixie consulted a physician for a pain in her
abdomen.   On June 18 Dixie had exploratory surgery, and the
pathologist discovered terminal ovarian cancer, but, according to Bing, he never told her or the sons the seriousness
of her condition.   Dixie went home from the hospital June
25, coincidentally the date of Bing's final radio show for
Wednesdays and Chesterfield cigarettes.   Dixie spoke with
few friends except Georgina Hardwicke, Kitty Lang Good
(former wife of Eddie Lang), Sue Carol Ladd in England, and
Sylvia Picker McGraw. Bing sat for hours with Dixie on his
lap in her bedroom, and she insisted that Bing travel to
France for his next film. Bing completed filming Road to
Bali in August, and Dixie flew with Bing in a chartered
aircraft to Hayden Lake. That September Philip and Dennis
enrolled at Washington State College.
     Bing sailed to England, arriving at Plymouth on Septem-
ber 18. He played golf, including a charity round with Bob
Hope at the Temple Golf Club, Maidenhead, which raised
?7,600 for the English Playing Fields Fund. That night Bob
Hope gave a benefit for the same charity at London's Stoll
Theatre, and Bing sang several songs. He flew to Paris
September 22 for filming.   For a serious scene of Bing
walking the orphan to the railroad station in Little Boy
Lost, George Seaton, the director, told Bing to look sad.
Just before filming, Bing received a letter from Dixie's
doctor informing him that she was dying, and the sadness
that appeared in the take was not acting.
     Bing returned home October 4, and Dixie had daily blood
transfusions for the strength to meet Bing at the Union
Station, as she regularly did. Dixie had a relapse the next
morning, as Bing commenced his new radio program for General Electric with the same staff, first broadcast on October
9, now on Thursdays. Dixie was baptized at home into the
Roman Catholic Church on October 25 and slipped into a coma
three days later, never regaining consciousness. She died
October 31, 1952, at 9:50 a.m. and was buried November 3,
the day before she would have turned 41. Gary describes the
funeral as "a three-ring circus" and "the media event of the

season" (p. 175). Reporters outnumbered the many mourners
and got in everyone's way.

For two weeks Judy Garland and Jimmy Stewart were guest
hosts for the radio show as Bing went into private mourning.
He recorded and fished with Phil Harris and a few other
friends, and continued to criticize Gary for his weight,
drinking, and poor grades. Gary, Philip, and Dennis were
all drinking heavily. Lindsay remained with Bing, and Kate
moved into the house. Bing wrote a seven-page chapter
titled "What a Lady" for his book to memorialize Dixie as
much as he would publicly.

Magnetic video tape was demonstrated to the press on
December 30 as an interim report from Bing Crosby Enterprises. Bing was unable on January 12 to perform at his own
golf tournament but soon returned to Paramount to complete
interior scenes for <u>Little Boy Lost</u>. Bing stood in the
doorway of his studio bungalow as Kathryn Grandstaff ambled
by. Bing said, "Hi'ya, Tex." The 19-year-old hopeful
stepped into the bungalow for tea and joined Barney Dean,
but the starlet did not return. The Friars Club honored Bob
Hope on February 27, 1953, in a banquet with 1500 people
attending, but without Bing. He hated big dinners. A few
days later son Lin shamed Bing into making a lame apology
that Hope accepted, saving their friendship.

Bing dated Mary Murphy, a Paramount starlet, and Mona
Freeman, who had recently been divorced. Mona explained
that they were not romancing. Gossip states that Bing was
also dating Grace Kelly, even in mid-1952 (Spada 77), but
that is a year or two too early. Bing appeared on a Bob
Hope TV show on April 1, 1953, and almost hoped he could
retire to become Gary's agent, but he explained that he was
on TV because "I want to keep in touch with the public and
if you're not on TV it appears you're out of touch."

In mourning, he took Lindsay to Palm Springs. Lin had
not yet completed high school, but they sailed on the <u>Queen
Elizabeth</u> to Europe for seven weeks with Venuti, Trotter,
and Carpenter. Bing played in the British Amateur Golf
Championship at Hoylake from May 25 to 30. With the publication of his autobiography in June 1953, Bing revealed the
trust funds of each son, for as the three older boys approached the age of majority, Bing thought it time they gave
their future serious thought. Reviewers generally applauded
the book, although Orville Prescott missed factual and
serious substance in its pages.

Bing and Lindsay returned from Europe by July. Dixie's
will was probated at a value of $1,332,571.36, but worth
only $550,616.96 after taxes. Bing sent his sons to the
ranch and began to struggle with the tax problem. He had to
pay taxes on the half of his property that Dixie had left
him, for her life insurance was small. He sold 68 horses
for $96,000, giving Lin Howard half the money. Only seven
horses remained. That was the last summer Gary worked at
the ranch. When asked again about the interests of his
sons, Bing was blunt. "Gary shows a real interest in show
business, but he's getting so fat he'll only be able to
qualify for Andy Devine roles." Bing assumed that weight
was a matter of personal discipline.

Bing began filming <u>White Christmas</u> in late August and
<u>The Country Girl</u> in October. Bing had rejected Jennifer

Jones as the female lead in <u>Country Girl</u>, and it was only a week into the production that he agreed that Grace Kelly was the right choice. George Seaton, Bing's new director, was completely satisfied with Bing's performance as a drunken singer, thinking it more remarkable than the standard excellence of Marlon Brando.

He revealed an interest in Rhonda Fleming, but now she was involved with someone else. Bing also dated Audrey Hepburn and Margot James. His new radio season began on Sundays on September 27 without the theme song to make room for discussions on economics by Bing and Carpenter, for Bing felt a patriotic drive to brighten the nation's morale, albeit with G.E.'s wisdom.

Gary, his allowance raised to $60 a month, was off the football team in his junior year, began drinking steadily, and even stole an occasional $20 bill from his father's wallet (Gary 183). Weighing 225 pounds, he took diet pills, "uppers," from several doctors and became addicted (Gary 188). Bing paid the bills, unaware that diet pills could be harmful. Gary took "downers" to sleep and only rarely went to class, except for two weeks before final examinations. The three boys at home had their 10:30 curfews, midnights on Fridays and Saturdays, so they had to drink fast.

Bing invited Kathryn Grandstaff and two sorority friends to the set, and Kathryn sat next to Bing as the others stood behind them. Bing liked Kathryn, but she would turn 20 at the end of November, five months after Gary did, while Bing was nearly 51. Several days after meeting Bing again, she asked to interview him for her Dallas and Houston newspaper column. He was a cooperative subject that fall on the set of <u>White Christmas</u> as she took a greater interest in him and his blue eyes. At the end of the interview Bing asked her to dinner, but that date was delayed a few months.

Bing took Mona Freeman to a party October 10, drove her home, and had an accident at 5:30 a.m. Two of the three people in the other car were seriously injured, and the front end of Bing's Mercedes-Benz was flattened. Bing was laid up for days with a sprained vertebra, which forced Paramount to delay the final scenes of <u>White Christmas</u> (Carpozi 128). Four weeks later the injured people sued him for $1,051,400. The Highway Patrol, however, testified that there was no traffic violation and no evidence of intoxication. The suit was settled for $100,000.

In December Bing and Dolores Hope sent affidavits to a New York hearing on the National Kids Day Foundation, which had raised nearly $3 million in 1952. Bing and Dolores tried to disassociate their names from the charity after they discovered that it spent 90 percent of the money on "administration" costs.

The "Bing Crosby Show," filmed in December, aired on CBS-TV January 3, 1954, with guests Jack Benny and Sheree North. Bing sang several songs and Miss North dropped Benny's arm and her gown to perform a hot dance number. The reviews for Bing's first TV special were cool and Bing seemed to exert minimum effort, according to Jack Gould of the <u>Times</u>. Gould ended his review: "Bing could be a natural for TV and will be when he takes a great interest in the medium's requirements."

Off again to the Crosby Clambake. The tourney raised

$50,000 for charity, $8000 more than in 1953. The affair at Pebble Beach since 1947 had now raised $220,377 for charity. One rainy evening, January 24, Kathryn had her first date with Bing. On the way home he sang "You'd Be So Easy to Love." Her toes went numb; they never had before. Frank Sinatra was the radio guest March 21 and sang "Young at Heart" and duets with Bing of "Among My Souvenirs," "September Song," and "As Time Goes By," while Bing sang three solos. Sinatra returned the next week.

When Bing brought Kathryn to Holmby Hills to meet his sons, Gary thought her a little bothered by them but also a "bright, energetic, positive human being" (Gary 252). Bing took time from filming Country Girl to produce his second TV special, which aired for a half hour in April 1954. Bing announced, "I just finished filming my second TV show, and it's my last. Why do I do it? I don't need it. I won't do TV again, not unless I lose my job in the movies."

Bing was evicted from his Paramount bungalow on April 9, and after cleaning it out he went to Kathryn's for a party. Paramount reclaimed the dressing room because Bing was working too much for other studios. Bob Hope suffered the same fate. On May 2 Bing celebrated his birthday quietly at Kathryn's.

Rosemary Clooney appeared on the May 23 radio show, the penultimate program of Bing Crosby's 25 years on prime-time radio. His final radio show for General Electric occurred May 30, 1954, with his guests Gary and Lindsay. It was in the fall that TV's popularity forced radio to turn to musical programs. Gary had an automobile accident on May 24 in which a Mexican laborer was killed. The Mexicans sued Bing for $65,000, as Gary was a minor. Gary took over the radio show for the summer, and in the fall Bing produced daily 15-minute shows with the Buddy Cole Trio and Ken Carpenter, which aired to 1962 on CBS.

A new Bing, a serious non-singing actor, was born in 1954. George Seaton observed, "Bing is an excellent actor, much better than people realize. It wouldn't surprise me to see him tackle Hamlet someday." Decca reported that Bing had sold 40 million records, and that his three most popular discs accounted for half the total. Those three were "White Christmas" at nine million, "Silent Night" at six million, and "Jingle Bells" at five million. He received a large plaque with 19 gold records on it. Decca began assembling a special album of 89 songs, many re-recorded by Bing and all with Bing's recorded comments. It was expensive for the times, but as "a musical autobiography" it included most of Bing's best songs over the years and a 24-page illustrated biography and discography. Decca hoped to sell 500 albums in Britain and had sold 11,000 there by 1974. Although Britains scorned America in 1954 over McCarthyism, even hooting Martin and Lewis off the Palladium stage, Bing remained popular overseas.

Bing composed a guest column for John Crosby of the New York Herald-Tribune, writing, "I have been pretty busy for about 26 years. I don't want to appear modest or coy, but I have a gnawing fear of being 'on' too long, of having someone say: 'Oh, no--not him again!'" His arithmetic showed that for nine TV shows in nine weeks he would earn only $90,000. After taxes a film yielded $20,000 and the TV

shows only $9,000. He noted, "It certainly gives one pause
to think. There is lots of golfing, fishing, traveling to
be done while I have the desire and am still able to do
these things. And I have four teenage boys, all with the
usual built-in problems, some of them of major dimensions."
He was also dating Grace Kelly and several other actresses,
sometimes taking them swimming at the Ladd's.

Announcing that his sons had serious problems, he
mentioned the difficulties of trying to keep them straight.
When Gary turned 21 on June 25, he took his trust fund,
which amounted to about $220,000. Kathryn became a contract
player for Columbia Pictures and was named Kathryn Grant by
Harry Cohn, the studio head. Bing wrote another article,
this one titled "My Four Sons--and Me," for the October
issue of McCalls. He credited Dixie with courage and with
molding their "four healthy, normal young boys."

Soon Bing appeared at Kathryn's apartment for dinner
cooked by her. White Christmas was released in October,
along with previews of The Country Girl. The premiere was
at the Radio City Music Hall, featuring Paramount's new
VistaVision screen. Bing first proposed marriage to Kathryn
on October 30, a Saturday, as Kathryn and her roommate-
cousin were visiting Bing for the weekend at Palm Springs.
The wedding date was set for February 7, 1955, near Pebble
Beach.

Bing commented negatively on a new sound he was hearing
in an article he wrote for the November 2, 1954, issue of
Look.   Gary, who liked the musicians his father idolized,
also liked just as much "the rhythm and blues shouters and
down home country wailers" he had been listening to for a
few years (Gary 180). Titling his essay "I Never Had to
Scream," Bing stated that music had changed, "but not all
for the better, by any fair means or foul." Elvis Presley
had not yet been heard from. In December Kathryn went on a
U.S.O. tour of Europe, and during a Mass at the cathedral of
Paris she decided to convert to Roman Catholicism. Meanwhile, Bing was interviewed on television by Edward R.
Murrow on his "Person to Person" program. The Country Girl
was released December 16 and became another big hit, and the
American National Board of Review of Motion Pictures voted
Bing the Actor of the Year. Fans, however, wrote Paramount,
stating they still wanted Crosby to sing.

The Kid from Spokane remained a considerable movie
attraction through 1954, although his annual rating slipped
into the eighth spot. He ranked second in 1949, third in
1950, fifth in 1951, and fourth in 1952. He had surgery
again on January 18, 1955, for a second kidney stone. He
had four such operations in the 1950s. He recuperated in
semi-isolation and the February wedding date was postponed
until May 2. The Academy Awards were staged March 30, 1955,
and Bing was nominated for Best Actor. Bing escorted Kathryn to the dinner, where Marlon Brando won the Oscar, and
later to a party at Romanoff's.

In January, as a failing senior, Gary called it quits
at Stanford. He attended college for three and one-half
years, like his father, but with much less success. Soon
the twins dropped out of Washington State, before they
became seniors. Lindsay went to Williams College for less
than a semester in 1953. Bing was stunned and angry with

Gary and did not speak to him for months. Gary went to Bing's agent, George Rosenberg, who signed him with CBS for guest spots. With Bing now doing a 15-minute daily radio program, Gary replaced him once more for the summer, with the show now called "The Gary Crosby Show." The music was arranged and conducted by Buddy Bregman. When Gary began singing in various clubs he began drinking more heavily.

Bing was filming Anything Goes in April 1955, his last film under his ten-year contract with Paramount. Bing also appeared in two shorts: Bing Presents Oreste and Hollywood Fathers. Getting cold feet and with the excuse of film commitments, Bing told Kathryn the second wedding date had to be postponed to September 10 at Hayden Lake.

Jeanmaire, the shapely dancer and Bing's co-star in Anything Goes, was the crooner's guest at Palm Springs to celebrate his birthday in May 1955 (Carpozi 146). When the twins turned 21 they took their trust funds. They received more than $200,000 each and still received income from Dixie's trusts. Gary played with Louis Armstrong in Chicago in June and soon recorded with him and followed him on tour to Australia and elsewhere.

Kathryn flew into Spokane September 3. Bing took her on a tour, but at Hayden Lake Kathryn developed cold feet of her own and flew back to Los Angeles on September 6. After writing her that there were impediments, in October Bing confessed a romance with a "regal blonde" (probably Grace Kelly) and that she had become hysterical and threatened suicide on learning of Bing's engagement to Kathryn (Kathryn, My Life 65). Kathryn forgave him and by December she joined her parents and Aunt Frances in Seattle, where Bing joined them and set September 10, 1956, for the fourth wedding date.

Bing gave a party for the Notre Dame football team on November 26, but the Catholic bishops criticized the moral laxity of films like Guys and Dolls, the Goldwyn film Bing wanted to show and in which Frank Sinatra had third billing behind Marlon Brando and Jean Simmons. Bing instead showed them a Danny Kaye film, The Court Jester, before it was released. Then Bing filmed Maxwell Anderson's "High Tor," his first television film. Bing's songs for the film marked his 21-year association with Decca Records.

Bing hosted a live Christmas Eve radio program, "A Christmas Sing with Bing Crosby," from Grand Central Terminal, New York, including the Norman Luboff Choir and Paul Weston's Orchestra. Bing may have done his part remote from California while Kathryn vacationed in Texas. On December 31, however, he took her to a party at David O. Selznick's and again offered to marry her, now the following St. Patrick's Day.

PART EIGHT

THE EPICAL CROSBY: 1956-1959

Each jukebox in America offered at least four Crosby songs. In January Bing recorded four Cole Porter songs for High Society: three with Louis Armstrong, one with Sinatra, and "True Love" with Grace Kelly. Metro-Goldwyn-Mayer did

not want Grace Kelly singing on the last one, but Bing
insisted and got his way. The record sold over a million
copies and gave Kelly her only gold record, although it was
Bing's twenty-second. "True Love" also became Bing's twen-
ty-third and Grace's second, for it sold as a single and
more than another million in an album. The next month Bing
began filming High Society, with Sinatra, Kelly, and Armstrong. Cole Porter wrote the score after a ten-year absence from Hollywood. "High Tor" was televised March 10,
earning cool reviews but raves over the music.

The year began bad, however, for Dennis was arrested in
the early hours of January 2 for being a drunken passenger
in a car driven wildly by a Stanford student. Dennis was
released from jail hours later when his bail of $20 was
paid. Philip, now a private in the Army, was arrested in
Tacoma on a charge of drunken driving, but evidence showed
he had only two beers. His car had hit a 79-year-old woman.
Philip was then sent to join Dennis in the Army in Schwein-
furt, Germany.

The first new stock of 1956 on the New York Stock
Exchange was Minute Maid. Bing bought the first hundred
shares at $19 as a donation to the Gonzaga University Li-
brary that Bing was endowing. Bing had become the president
of the Bing Crosby-Minute Maid Corporation, the West Coast
distributor of all products of Vacuum Foods, including the
recently purchased Snow Crop line.

Two weeks later Bing had surgery for more kidney stones
and convalesced for three weeks, listening to many radio
shows he had pre-recorded. Then he had minor eye surgery.
The new radio format of song and interesting discussions was
a winner. One critic called it "a pleasant and thoughtful
15-minute show and if you can get the dust off the radio
set, you might try listening some time. You'll dig a brand
new Crosby." And a surprising number of listeners did.

After recuperating at Palm Springs, Bing returned to
the Paramount lot to film Anything Goes with Mitzi Gaynor
and Donald O'Connor. This was Bing's last film for Paramount. The wedding scheduled for March had to wait again.
After filming it Bing said, "Well, if someone came up with a
great musical, maybe I'd do it. But as far as I know, this
is the last musical for me." He was looking for a "good
romantic comedy. . . . Or stories with kids. . . . I feel
I've done everything I can with musicals. I'll never be a
dancer at my age."

Then he learned he was nominated again for Best Actor,
this time for Country Girl. Some Catholic periodicals
denounced Bing for taking the role, but Bing was fascinated
with the character's attempt to overcome his insecurities,
and the actor finally won everyone over to his view. He
dated Grace Kelly, among other actresses, but she became the
Princess of Monaco on April 19, 1956. High Society was her
last film.

Gary was handed his draft notice in May 1956. The Army
sent him to Frankfurt in October, and Bing wrote him promptly on hearing that he was mouthing off about his dislike of
his father. Dennis and Philip had finished their Army
service, passed through Frankfurt, and the three brothers
met and "hit every soldier bar in town." Gary admits that
during his time in the Army he "turned into a full-fledged

alcoholic" (p. 240).

Then Bing made a brief trip to England. "Is Bing
Crosby Going Out--Or Has He Gone?" read a headline in the
London Express newspaper. Bing commented that he no longer
had the feel for a song but still hoped for 20 gold records.
The gold soon came. On his return he went live on the "Ed
Sullivan Show" July 15 and sang "True Love." Then he spent
an evening escorting 23-year-old Mary Ellen Terry, a dancer
and actress. Back in Nevada he dated a dancer named Pat
Sheehan.

Reporters heard in July 1956 that Kathryn had bought a
wedding gown for a September marriage. When word reached
Bing, he said, "I wish her good luck. I hope she has a
chance to wear it." On hindsight, the comment is an exqui-
site equivocation.

High Society, billed as the "Battle of the Baritones,"
was released August 9, and even critics who preferred Sinatra admitted that Crosby won the contest. Louis Armstrong
joined Bing in lively jazz in the film. Bing also donated
another $160,000 to the Gonzaga Library, which the universi-
ty was going to name after its most illustrious alumnus.
Bing gave most of the total of $400,000 that had been col-
lected so far, and he joined a syndicate of ten people who
bought the Detroit Tigers for $5.5 million.

The fourth wedding date approached, and Kathryn flew to
Spokane, now for a secret wedding. The secret got out,
however, and an army of reporters scared Bing away again.
Dorothy Kilgallen leaked the story on September 7, and the
next day Parsons confirmed the story. Hoping to marry
quietly somewhere, they drove into Northern California, to a
ranch he recently bought. A string of press cars trailing
behind, Bing led them near his Rising River Ranch, where he
gave a hospital benefit. Bing retreated to his Pebble Beach
home and filmed a television show. The next morning Kathryn
decided to return to Los Angeles, and Bing agreed. Bing
recorded "Around the World" in October, and fans were disappointed when the B-side of the 78 was merely the orchestral
version by Victor Young, who composed the melody for the
1957 film of the same title.

While Kathryn went on her third U.S.O. tour to Korea,
Bing and Phil Harris toured the South in December 1956,
traveling from New Orleans to Kentucky and points beyond.
As they drove at night in Tennessee past the Jack Daniels
distillery, Bing observed, "See there, Phil. They're making
that stuff faster than you can drink it." "Yeah," Phil
agreed, "but I got 'em workin' nights." The radio contract
with CBS ended on December 28, 1956, and Bing began negoti-
ating with ABC and NBC. CBS, however, offered him a new
five-year contract the next fall that included television.
His daily 15-minute radio show hardly missed a beat until it
stopped in 1962, although his sponsor went from General
Electric to Ford.

Bing visited Kathryn in January 1957 and invited her
out to dinner, but she refused. Later he sent a special
messenger with a note saying that he missed her. She did
not hear again from Bing until July, when he pretended to
being sued and needing her deposition. Obtaining her phone
number, he agreed to wait until she returned from filming in
Spain. By this time she had also entered the nursing pro-

48   Bing Crosby

gram at Queen of Angels Hospital, Los Angeles. Bing filmed
Man on Fire for Metro-Goldwyn-Mayer. It was Bing's first
non-singing film role. He told Pete Martin that the rock
and roll of the day was "really a new name for an old music
medium" that used to be called "race records," which merely
meant the blues. It went from "rhythm and blues" to "rock
and roll," and Bing added, "The beat's old too." Elvis
Presley had his first hit, "Heartbreak Hotel," in 1956,
which he sang on "The Jackie Gleason Show" in March; he sang
others on "The Ed Sullivan Show" in September and October.
     Bing recorded his first rock and roll song, "Seven
Nights a Week," in January (perhaps March) 1957, a record
that fans called "ill advised." There is a parallel between
Bing and Elvis: both preferred guitar accompaniment, a hot
rhythm, were denounced by priests at the outset, excelled
with religious music, and were privately respectful. Of
course, Elvis was also a reckless womanizer and addict and
ended up more a "glam rocker" than a serious singer.
     Music publishing and disc jockeys were scrutinized by
the Senate Commerce Committee. Bing wrote the committee a
letter in which he said, "It galls me exceedingly to see so
much trash on our airlanes and TV screens while the work of
the talented and dedicated songwriters is crowded out of the
picture." Bing charged that the music on radio was the
result of pressure by Broadcast Music, Inc. When one recalls how promoters made an instant success of songs sung by
Del Shannon and Fabian, Bing's complaint seems plausible.
Yet, dozens of singers disagreed with him.
     Disc jockeys also denied undue influence from B.M.I.
Nevertheless, Ella Fitzgerald, Teresa Brewer, Pearl Bailey,
the Four Lads, Frankie Laine, Nat King Cole, Guy Mitchell,
Patti Page, Peggy Lee, Mel Torme, Eddie Fisher, and other
singers were eclipsed by lesser talent. Bing, Sinatra, Dean
Martin, Tony Bennett, Rosemary Clooney, Dinah Shore, Andy
Williams, and Perry Como barely held on while Elvis Presley,
Johnny Ray, Little Richard, Pat Boone, Frankie Avalon, Paul
Anka, and Bobby Darin, along with Ricky Valens, Bryan High-
land, Donovan, Rhinoceros, Noel Harrison, Bobby Rydell,
Troggs, Gary Crosby, and Frankie Vaughan, found fame with
excitable teenagers. Thus were 1931 and 1942 revisited.
     Bing built a new home at Palm Desert next door to Jimmy
Van Heusen. It was Bing's seventh house, and he had designed four of them. He also bought stations KFOX AM and FM
of Long Beach, California, and KPTV, Portland, Oregon. In
May Bing again entered the British Open golf tournament but
failed to qualify. In June he went to France and won a
championship tournament.
     Newsweek praised _Man on Fire_ on July 8, 1957, calling
it "a rather superior 'domestic drama.'" An interview
followed the review, noting Bing's current concerns with
generosity and philanthropy and reason for doing the film:
"he thought it might give pause to parents considering
divorce." He said he had "no personal life to speak of any
more," and he was considering a little television work and a
movie. He said, "I know I can't get by any longer
singing. . . . I know I'm not singing as well as I used to.
Why, I go four of five months without turning on a note."
     In late July and early August Bing recorded 13 songs
with Rosemary Clooney for the album _Fancy Meeting You Here_

(LPM 1854), "a vocal tour of the globe." Bing had been off the air for nine months, since the beginning of 1957, but now he and CBS had concluded a new contract for more daily 15-minute programs. On his first day at the CBS studio he transcribed 11 songs from 10 a.m to 1 p.m. One of the sound engineers said, "Even Elvis Presley can't knock out 11 songs in three hours." He did not know that Bing often recorded many more songs in a session.

Kathryn returned home in September but would not see Bing. He hosted "The Edsel Show," an hour-long TV special on CBS with Frank Sinatra, Rosemary Clooney, Louis Armstrong, and son Lindsay. The critics loved it. Kathryn went to a hairdressers' show October 13 and saw the program on television. She began to cry, a breakdown reported the next day in the Daily Variety. Bing immediately wrote her, but she again ignored him. In desperation, he wrote the next day a tender note: "I'll marry you--any time, any place you wish."

Kathryn's Aunt Mary negotiated terms and that afternoon they flew to Las Vegas. The next morning, October 24, Bing and Kathryn were wed at St. Anne's Church. From there they boarded a plane for Palm Springs. Two days later Kathryn witnessed a forceful vein in Bing as a disturbed woman cursed him after Mass and screamed at him for desecrating Dixie's memory. Bing became heated until others intervened.

Kathryn went to the Holmby Hills home alone while Bing had a golf game, but he arrived in a few days. Gary was entertaining in a border town in East Germany when reporters caught up with him. He denied snubbing his father, saying that he sent wedding congratulations. Kate soon put Dixie's monogrammed blankets and personal effects away. It was about this time that Gary drank too much and doctors also found that he had epilepsy.

Then Bing bought 5.5 percent interest in the Detroit Tigers. He, Kathryn, Kate, Dennis, and Philip attended the dedication of the Crosby Library at Gonzaga University on November 4. A week later Bing canceled a CBS-TV show, chartered a plane, and took Kathryn November 7 for three days to visit her family in Texas. Kathryn maintained a good relationship with Bing's sons, who were nearly her own age, but they sometimes felt she was trying to act like their mother. Then Bing appeared on Frank Sinatra's Christmas television show, a program that critics panned as "sloppy" and poor. The first Christmas of Bing and Kathryn in Holmby Hills upset the boys when they realized that Dixie's decorations had been stored in the garage.

In January 1958 the Clambake became televised, but Kathryn appalled Bing when, as the commentator, she called the eighteenth green of Pebble Beach the seventeenth tee. Bing took over the microphone that Sunday to avoid any further embarrassment. Billy Casper won the contest for his first time. It was also about January 1958 that Bing invited Moe Dalitz, a dentist, and a few business associates to a deer hunt at the Elko ranch, the problem being that Dalitz was a "Top Hoodlum," according to a program J. Edgar Hoover initiated in 1957 ("The Secret Files of J. Edgar Hoover" and "Frontline: The Secret File on J. Edgar Hoover"). Dalitz, a Jewish member of the Mafia with nearly the reputation of Meyer Lansky, came from the Cleveland Syndicate and Detroit but was now one of the heads of the Las Vegas mob. The current owners of Del Mar, two wealthy Texas oilmen named Clint Murchison and Sid Richardson, who bought the track in June 1954, were extending their largesse every August to Director Hoover, but this had nothing to do with Bing.

Dennis married Pat Sheehan, a divorced dancer in Las Vegas that Bing had dated. The wedding occurred in May 1958 in a Protestant church, and the next day a woman named Scott slapped Denny with a paternity suit. Suddenly Bing was a grandfather twice over, for Dennis's wife had a six-year-old son. The illegitimate girl became a non-story when Bing established a trust fund for her, probably worth $100,000. Gary was discharged from the Army in May and soon took an apartment in Hollywood. Dennis and Philip were discharged, but now Lindsay had been drafted. George Rosenberg, Bing's agent, signed Gary with Twentieth Century-Fox in a two-year contract at $50,000 a film and for a tour of nightclubs.

ABC-TV signed Bing to a five-year contract in June 1958 for about $2 million. He agreed to star in two one-hour shows a year and to produce another ten on film over the term. Bing also began another daily 15-minute radio pro- gram, "The Ford Radio Show," with Rosemary Clooney, a CBS radio show that aired to 1962. Look magazine (May 13, 1958) asked Bing to elaborate on a comment he had made recently on "The Perry Como Look Awards" show that his retirement was imminent. He explained, "I mean that it's likely to come any day, any time. . . . I'm just standing by. . . . After all, the public is getting very selective."

Kathryn tried to awaken Gary on August 8, and after suffering his verbal abuse she rode with Bing to the hospi- tal, where she gave birth, expecting a daughter. A boy was born, however, weighing seven pounds nine ounces. He was two months premature. For a name, Kathryn's mother selected Harry Lillis III. A month later Philip married Las Vegas showgirl Sandra Drummond. Bing was happier, however, as the wedding occurred in a Roman Catholic church. Phil cut a couple of records with Bing in attendance and invested in a chain of taco stands, while Denny was a disc jockey with an afternoon show in Los Angeles.

Kathryn released Georgina Hardwicke. Gary was upset and hired her as his housekeeper, but soon he accused her of spying on him for Bing and fired her himself. Bing fre- quently dropped by Gary's to discuss his heavy drinking and the steady flow of girls in and out of the bachelor's "pad," and Gary supposed that Georgie had given Bing all the de- tails. Gary's film career lasted two years, and he was worse in the nightclubs. While Kathryn studied chemistry at the studio, Bing bought land at Rancho Las Cruces on a hill beside the water just east of the tip of Baja in the Sea of Cortez (the Gulf of California), but building the house was a trial. While this proceeded Bing suffered another kidney stone and had more surgery.

Bing's ABC-TV special in October 1958 was a sensation. His guests included Dean Martin, Mahalia Jackson, and Patti Page. Time magazine of October 13 said, "Bing Crosby's topnotch ABC special last week swayed along with rocking- chair ease; its spare (but expensive) sets and casual tone made the usual frenetic TV variety shows look sick by com- parison." Time quoted Bing as saying, "I know I can't get by much longer singing," and concluded, "Many who heard him last week will howl in disagreement."

Disappointed that his sons did not want the Nevada ranch, he sold it and its cattle for more than $1 million in November. He also sold his interest in tape recording to the Minnesota Mining and Manufacturing Company. Bing invited Lindsay home for Thanksgiving Day 1958, but the son went to Gary's instead. Bing took this as a personal affront, and for Christmas he returned Lindsay's gift. Bing began filming Say One for Me in December, playing another priest, now one on Broadway. He produced the film, which took four months. Kathryn was pregnant again. And Lindsay took his trust fund, receiving $227,000.

Kathryn rehearsed for The Big Circus, taking trapeze lessons from the great Barbette of the Ringling Brothers and Barnum & Bailey Circus. Despite the pregnancy she performed her own aerial stunts. That done, she filmed Anatomy of a Murder with James Stewart and Lee Remick (a 1959 release). She was unaware that she had made her final feature film.

Harriet Van Horne reviewed Bing's latest TV show on March 2, 1959. She began, "In terms of style, grace, warmth, wit and charm--charm that would melt a stone idol--no man in showbusiness comes even close to Bing Crosby. He's the blithest, the smoothest and the most durable of them all." Critics were not so kind to Say One for Me.

To communicate with his sons, by the end of March 1959 Bing gave an interview with Joe Hyams of the Associated Press. In a two-part series headlined "How Bing Crosby 'Failed' His Four Sons," Bing said, "I guess I didn't do very well bringing my boys up. I think I failed them by giving them too much work and discipline, too much money, and too little time and attention. But I did my best and so did their mother." The three loyal sons, not Gary, jumped to his defense. Philip said, "None of us feels the way Dad does about it. Sure, we had a few problems. Any family runs into that," and, "I feel Dad did a wonderful job." Dennis thought Hyams made the interview sound worse than what Bing actually said and, "So far as being strict is concerned, I remember we used to get a few cuffs now and then, but everybody gets those. I don't recall any lickings." Lindsay was near tears as he told Louella Parsons, "Pop's been just a great parent, no matter what he thinks."

Gary was stunned at Bing's candid public disclosure, which Gary considered an apology, but Bing and Gary never discussed it. Similar stories appeared under such headlines as, "Bing Calls Self a Flop as Father" and "Crisis for the Crosbys: What's Bothering Bing's Boys--A Report on an American Family That Might Have Done Better by America."

By now Lindsay had his Army discharge papers and moved in with Gary. As his brothers seemed undirected, Gary proposed a quartet, and Rosenberg agreed to promote it. Bing's agent arranged the tour for the Crosby Boys and negotiated for $25,000 a week at the Sahara. The quartet opened in June in Tucson, Arizona. They went to Chicago, Cleveland, and Washington, D.C., and opened at the Sahara in Las Vegas in July. The act had been a huge success until the Sahara. Gary clowned around too much for his brothers and often ignored the script. Gary suffered from hoarseness and fatigue and had to leave early on the opening show.

Reporters asked why Bing did not attend, and Phil read them an encouraging telegram Bing wired from Alaska. Then Gary said that he and his father did not get along and that Bing had done things that "were far from right." Headlines touted the exposed rift and the show was canceled after several nights. The report was that Gary had a virus; the "word" was that he drank heavily, passed out backstage, and threatened to beat up hecklers. Bing was fishing with Phil Harris and Bill Morrow on the yacht <u>Campana</u> off Vancouver, and soon Bing was recording for three days in Europe.

Kathryn gave birth on September 14, 1959, to Bing's first and only daughter, Mary Frances, who weighed six pounds three ounces. When the Crosby Boys played the Moulin Rouge in Hollywood in October, Bing and Rosenberg caught their act three weeks after they opened. Bing went backstage after the show and hugged each son, especially Gary. The boys began fighting at their engagement in Pittsburgh, and in their dressing room in Montreal, while the twins held Gary's arms, Lindsay smashed him in the face. This signaled the end of the Crosby Boys. Duration: six months. A "blood feud" developed between Gary and Philip. Reports of a rift between Gary and Bing, however, were silenced.

Before the year was up, Bing swung his driver for his fourth hole-in-one. This one was at the Phoenix Open Golf Tournament at the Arizona Country Club. Because of the danger to the children from the ocean, he sold the house at Pebble Beach.

PART NINE

THE LEISURELY CROSBY: 1960-1969

The Crosby Clambake featured a $50,000 purse, and it had become a major international event. About 300 golfers, half of them amateurs, participated, playing on three courses over three days. Prompted by a column by Jackie Robinson, the baseball legend, Bing discovered explicit racial discrimination in the Professional Golfers Association and had them nullified for his contest.

Lindsay married a showgirl, Barbara Frederickson, on February 6, 1960, and Bing gave the wedding reception at Holmby Hills. Lindsay invited Georgina Hardwicke, however, and Kathryn remained upstairs, which offended the sons. Kathryn organized Bing's mother's birthday party (she was 90 but thought she was 93) on February 7 and invited brother Ted, who had been a blacksheep since the father died.

Then the Groaner began filming <u>High Time</u>. The film featured the song "The Second Time Around," which earned an Oscar nomination. The cast included Tuesday Weld and Fabian, as Bing continued to surround himself with current talent. Bing substituted for Gary on Bing's television show. Gary insisted he had a sore throat. The day earlier the Bing Crosby-Rosemary Clooney daily radio program commenced on CBS. The Kid from Spokane appeared in New York for the March 16 Perry Como's "Kraft Music Hall" show on NBC. He brought Kathryn to Jamaica, where he almost bought several house lots. The suicide of a cuckolded husband caused him to pick up and flee to Aiken, South Carolina, for the Master's Golf Tournament.   Then he discovered he had bursitis in both shoulders.

The Crosby Boys disbanded and Gary went·solo.   Lindsay and the twins worked as a trio in May, but they played hardly two months.   Dennis opened a sound-equipment store. Gary had heart trouble at the end of May, but his doctor said he could play the Sahara if he stopped drinking and rested.   In June he met a dancer named Barbara Consentino, whom he married two months later.

Bing relented once to dress in drag for a film when he donned an eighteenth-century gown for fraternity hazing, and he was careful to bring Kathryn to the set to watch.   When filming for High Time ended on June 15, Bing set a curious record: completing three films in one day.   He completed cameo roles in both Let's Make Love and Pepe.   The reviews of High Time were mild, noting that Bing looked tired and strained as a jaunty old college student.

A platinum record of "White Christmas" was given Bing on June 9 by the Hollywood Chamber of Commerce.   The plaque states that Bing had sold more than 200 million records and led the whole recording industry into prominence and prof-itability.   Variety wrote that royalty records indicated that "Silent Night" may have outsold "White Christmas." After 200 million sales, record totals become confusing.

Bing rode in the parade of the Calgary Stampede, Alber-ta, Canada, as the Grand Marshal in July.   He and Kathryn arrived in London in August and went to the Olympic Summer Games in Rome.   Bing had his first audience with the Pope, John XXIII, who also blessed Kate and her seven children. The crooner heard a haunting melody and wrote English lyrics for "Domenica"; later he won the Invitational Golf Tourna-ment at Mittersill, Austria, before going to Paris.   In the City of Lights Bing caused a small fire at the Trianon Palace, where they stayed.   Songs for the album Holiday in Europe were recorded in London October 15 at the Decca studio, but the songs were redone in May 1961 in Hollywood. Back home in late December Bing recorded 101 songs in eight marathon sessions.

Gary borrowed money from his father to buy a house in San Fernando Valley but soon found himself carted off to St. John's Hospital as his drinking drove him into delirium. Three days later he was discharged, but he would return. Bing visited Gary and denied to Barbara that Gary had a drinking problem, but when he saw his drunken son he left. Gary beat up a one-armed man and later Barbara caught him in Chicago in bed with another woman.   Then Gary promised to go to a sanatorium in Connecticut, paid for by Bing, to recov-er.   Gary stopped drinking and did not join Alcoholics Anonymous for 19 years, but his singing career was over.

Kathryn insisted on accompanying Bing on a trip Febru-ary 19, 1961, to Argentina, whether for a show or for sports, but Bing did not want her to leave the children and decided to stay home.   On March 2 Kathryn campaigned for her father in Texas to Bing's disapproval.   Her father sought the seat in the U.S. Senate, but John Tower became the ultimate winner.   Carol Lawrence appeared on a Bing Crosby special on ABC in March.   Then Bing went golfing at the Palm Beach Country Club, where he found John F. Kennedy a for-midable opponent.   Playing with the President, Joe, the

Kennedy patriarch, and Chris Dunphy, Bing won with a 77, but
the President's score was only five over par at 78. As Gary
Cooper lay dying of cancer, Bing attended the Academy Awards
Ceremony in April. Asked how Cooper was, Bing said, "He may
see his sixtieth birthday." Cooper turned 60 on May 7 and
died a week later. Then Bing decided to build a home and
buy another to serve as an orphanage at Las Cruces, near the
southern tip of Baja California.

Louis Armstrong raised the specter of racism in a 1961
article in Ebony. Bing was saddened when he read ten years
later of Satchmo's regrets that he had never been invited to
the Crosbys, after the jazz master died in 1971. Bing was
one of the pallbearers. He said, "I was with him a lot when
we worked but he was always so busy. I never went home then
either, probably. I wish I had read that. I would have had
him to my house in the morning. I love him. He's a great
man. I wish I hadn't been so neglectful. It was neglectful. That's all it was. There are white people I've never
had to my home, either--because I'm not very thoughtful. If
they went to fish or play golf or something, I'd probably
have them along, but we entertain very little."

Bing proposed his epitaph: "He was an average guy who
could carry a tune." On August 2 Bing, Hope, and Joan
Collins began filming Road to Hong Kong near London. Mel
Frank located an English estate called Cranbourne, which the
Crosbys shared with Bob Hope his family for $1100 (£400) a
week. Bing took a weekend to relax on the Riviera and
golfed with Joe Kennedy, the President's father. The next
day he was back at the studio, filming the scene in which he
and Hope replaced monkeys in a space capsule. Collins
mentions the filming in her autobiography Past Imperfect,
with uncomplimentary remarks on working with Bing, opinions
that appear in only the British edition (Bing 103: 14).

Bing and Bob golfed every day. After hiring a butler
and an Irish nanny, Kathryn and Harry flew home; three weeks
later Kathryn gave birth to Bing's seventh child, on October
29, 1961. The boy, named Nathaniel Patrick after Bing's
paternal grandfather, weighed nine pounds, two and one-half
ounces. In two weeks Bing returned home. The couple went
fishing and visited San Francisco, where they met Abigail
Folger at her coming-out party given by Phyllis Tucker.
Miss Folger was one of the people killed by the Manson gang
in 1969, which added to Bing's need for home security.

His next TV special on ABC, one taped in England with
British talent, seemed "thin" to the critics. That Christmas Day Bing suffered a serious case of stomach influenza
that required hospitalization. Ten days later Bing had
surgery for the third time for kidney stones. He sent
Kathryn with Mary Morrow to fly in his new Aero Commander to
furnish the Mexican home, which she did so well she actually
broke the family budget for months. Everett retired as
Bing's manager and went to Connecticut with vain hopes of
establishing an independent film company.

The Crosbys went to Palm Desert on February 1 and soon
learned that Lindsay's wife tried to commit suicide, losing
her eight-month-old fetus. Lindsay felt guilty, and Bing
retreated to Las Cruces, where he learned of Kathryn's bad
checks. Kathryn, meanwhile, went to Palm Desert to prepare
the home for the visit of President Kennedy and returned to

Holmby Hills. President John F. Kennedy vacationed at Bing's Palm Desert home for three days at the end of March, spurning Sinatra's invitation. To compound Sinatra's embarrassment, Kennedy later stayed another week at Bing's Palm Desert home. The government explained that security was the primary criterion.

The Road to Hong Kong was released in Britain April 3 and became the fifth most popular film of the year. It opened in America June 27, yielding a $2 million profit for each of the three partners. "DuPont Show of the Week" on NBC aired "Biography of a Movie," which chronicled shortly before the movie was released all aspects of filming the final Road film. The program helped make the movie a financial bonanza.

In May 1961 Bing invited Rosemary Clooney to Las Cruces for a vacation and to record their radio program. Rosemary had a happy day, but a serious injury to Harry, age three, caused Kathryn and Rosemary to fly with him to Santa Monica, California, for better medical care. Bing's Renault beach buggy had run over the son's arm and also injured an eye. Harry was hospitalized until May 30. The Crosbys were regularly occupying the Mexican home, now, from January to June each year. Bing installed a putting green, but there was no network radio reception and mail arrived weeks late.

Bing took his family to Kauai, Hawaii, in late June, where he introduced Kathryn's mother to John Wayne. Bing refused on the telephone to commit Lindsay for psychiatric observation in July and soon went alone to Biarritz, where Kathryn and the children joined him a week later. Bing tried to hire a 21-year-old French airline stewardess named Janine as a governess, but she soon tired of trying to control the children. The couple went to Barcelona for the bull fights, where Bing tried unsuccessfully to hire a Spanish governess. The excursion included a few days in Monaco with Prince Rainier and Princess Grace, where Kathryn thought Bing and the princess too intimate. The royal couple treated the Crosbys to a hamburger cookout. Mary and Harry Crosby bullied the two royal children, and the prince beat Bing at golf. Later Bing sent Kathryn home alone while he sojourned in Paris. The recorded daily radio program ended on September 28.

When Bing returned home October 1 he found a fashion show staged by Kathryn. He still gave her a jade necklace, which was stolen in London in 1977. Princess Grace promptly sent a governess named Marielle, but she lasted only a fortnight of chasing the children. Bing was in the hospital again on October 14, suffering with more kidney stones, this time blamed on the French bottled water Bing had thought pure. The couple went shooting at Weiser, Idaho, on October 27 with 30 others, many of whom proved dangerous. The couple retired with Trader Vic and his wife Helen to Kona Farm in the Sacramento Valley. Harry Barris died at age 57 in Burbank on December 13. Bing did not attend the funeral, as he continued to suffer from kidney stones.

Gary found a few roles on television. Bob Hope was the featured guest on Bing's next TV special, and Gary appeared on the next. Bing and Gary sang "Won't You Play a Simple Melody" as Bing worked at soothing his son. Der Bingle's new Christmas special was broadcast December 24 as ABC-TV's first program in color.

For his golf tournament of January 1963 Bing engaged Harry James and Maurine Barris, Harry Barris's daughter, to entertain. On January 29 Bing was back in the hospital for more surgery for kidney stones. Bing was now planning to sell the Holmby Hills house, but Kathryn quietly resisted leaving Hollywood. She did, however, talk Kate into accepting a move. Then Bing learned that the little hospital he had earned so much money for at Falls Church in Northern California had become an abortion ring. Bing golfed at Palm Springs and in the Hawaiian Open, and did a TV special with Mary Martin, in which they sang "Wait Till the Sun Shines, Nellie."

Philip had several affairs and moved in with Lindsay, who drank excessively. In February Philip committed Lindsay during his manic phase for psychiatric observation while Phil's wife was in Las Vegas partying with gangsters, and Bing fled to Las Cruces after Gary tried to explain the concept of mental problems to him. Gary adopted Steve, his step-son, and laid down strict rules, realizing "that some of it was necessary," "that there had to be limits, rules, and some form of punishment when they were broken" (Gary 287). Bing admired the boy. Kathryn continually invited Gary to Hillsborough, but he refused. Finally Barbara had Bing over to a surprise dinner and he enjoyed himself. Gary began to realize that for years he had been maintaining the hostilities all by himself.

On March 22 Kathryn and the children joined Bing at Las Cruces. Bing bought a new 60-foot fishing cruiser he christened <u>True Love</u>, and the couple began an annual ritual of cleaning the local church before Easter. Bing and Bud Boyd flew to Iceland in July for Atlantic salmon fishing for "The American Sportsman." In his conservation efforts, especially with Ducks Unlimited and Trout Unlimited, Bing campaigned to save the Atlantic salmon. Denmark, Bing's ancestral Viking homeland, was the worst offender and retaliated by banning his records.

Bing had several recording sessions in 1963, beginning July 29 with two duets with Frank Sinatra. Bing was in St. Paul, Minnesota, on August 24, promoting his "Beat Bing Golf Contest," when people came from Stillwater with a copy of his mother's baptismal certificate, showing she was born in 1873 and was only 90. He went to Ohio to watch his wife perform in a play and arranged to sell the Hollywood home for $250,000. Bing and Kathryn attended a dinner at the home of Sammy Davis, Jr., and Mai Britt on December 23, but Davis was disappointed that Frank Sinatra and Dean Martin failed to show up.

Bing had seven other busy recording dates that year, including recording a dozen country songs in Nashville, Tennessee, in October. The next year Bing sang six songs with Sinatra, two for a movie they were in; two duets were Christmas songs. That fall Kate suffered a severe stroke and soon suffered more strokes. In November, as another film had been canceled, Bing was filming <u>Robin and the Seven Hoods</u> at Warner Bros. with Frank Sinatra, Dean Martin, Sammy Davis, Jr., and Peter Falk. Philip had a small role.

Having joined three different classes over three years, Kathryn graduated as a registered nurse in mid-

December 1963. After Bing said he thought she would be
"rusty" for the state exam, Kathryn proposed a bet, a trip
to Tierra del Fuego against "a chunk of Faberge. A flower,
maybe," from Bing. They agreed. Bing's mother went into a
coma in late December and died on January 7, 1964. Nearly
every Crosby attended but Everett, who was hospitalized.
Meanwhile Bing hosted the filmed premiere of "The Hollywood
Palace" television variety show, which was televised on
January 4, and did so every few weeks until the final production in February 1970, when he turned into a state of
semi-retirement.

Bing recorded a patriotic album with Frank Sinatra and
Fred Waring in February 1964, and in June the trio returned
for a Christmas album. The Crosbys bought a 25-room home in
Hillsborough, a house Kathryn called "the Tudor monstrosi-
ty," and nine months later exchanged that for a 14-room
Tudor-style mansion on three acres in the same city, about
20 miles south of the Golden Gate Bridge. The household
staff included Alan Fisher, his wife, an Irish cook, and a
nurse for the children. Bing bought his permanent home from
the estate of the late Phoebe Carter Alexander, and the
house used to belong to Lindsay Howard. The Crosbys moved
north in May and into the other house in December.

Before the move, Kathryn took the two-day state nursing
examination, learning at Las Cruces two weeks later that she
passed with distinction, the tops in her class and the
fourth in California. Because she passed magna cum laude,
Bing presented her with four vitrines sparkling with Faberge
flowers. Soon she and Trader Vic established an eye clinic
at Las Cruces, where she volunteered much of her time and
talents, and expanded to hunt down cases of tuberculosis.
She volunteered to work at hospitals near San Francisco and
served as a director of the Eisenhower Medical Center,
nominated for that post by Bing. She tutored local children
in Las Cruces when she received her California teaching
certificate.

Robin and the Seven Hoods was released in August 1964
as Bing was filming his only television series, "The Bing
Crosby Show," which aired on ABC-TV in the 1964-65 season.
Co-stars were Beverly Garland as his wife and Frank McHugh
as the live-in handyman. Bob Williams, a critic with the
New York Post, liked the first show. Other critics felt the
same, but their evaluation went south as the season wore on.

In March Bing hosted "The Grand Award of Sports" live
from the New York City Theater in Flushing Meadow, during
the 1964-1965 World's Fair. Kathryn's tour in Sabrina Fair
ended in Holyoke, Massachusetts, in August, and Bing was in
the audience after a harrowing airplane landing. Afterwards, Kathryn's mother returned to Texas, the children went
home, and Bing and Kathryn visited brother Everett in Salis-
bury, Connecticut, and then went to New York. There Kathryn
showed Bing Faberge flowers she admired, which were like the
four Bing soon gave her for passing the nursing test so
well. The presentation of the flowers occurred October 23
before Kathryn dragged Bing off again to the opera. He also
gave her a dog named Buzz, but he proved to be afraid of
hunting and went back to its trainer.

In December 1964, while Kathryn worked on an episode of
the "Bing Crosby Show," Bing sent her home for a day, accus-

ing her of flirting on the set.   They both appeared on Bob Hope's Christmas special.   That Christmas Eve Kathryn cooked pheasant for 45 guests and later Bing took his guests caroling and then singing for the staff.   Merle Oberon entertained the Crosby's on January 2, 1965, and Kathryn caught Bing ogling the actress's prominent cleavage.   Soon the Crosbys entertained President Eisenhower at home.   Bing made lists of chores for the children, but he left most of the disciplining to their mother.

That spring Kathryn insisted that Abelardo Rodriguez, the virtual owner of Las Cruces, provide a schoolhouse for the local children.   The Mexican relented under protest, and the philanthropy backfired when it proved more than the workers and children could handle.   It caused such local turmoil that Rodriguez had to expel the workers to La Paz and the Crosbys were unwelcome for weeks.   Then Bing and Harry both had tonsillectomies.   Bing hunted for marlin pancreases for an experimental drug for a man named Bill Brady, ignoring Kathryn's tonsillitis until it became serious, and recalling the case of Eddie Lang, he flew to her side.   He also went on safari with Phil Harris and John Connally, the governor of Texas, for ABC's "American Sportsman" (one of several shows Bing appeared in) and hunted and fished in Alabama, Canada, and elsewhere.

Bing went alone to England to watch his horse, Meadow Court, race.   Bing was well tanned when it won the Irish Sweepstakes Derby at The Curragh on June 26, 1965.   The winnings were $221,536, but Bing had to sing "When Irish Eyes Are Smiling" before he was given the winner's cup.   He remained out of touch for four days.   Bing owned the horse with two Canadian partners.

The Old Groaner began filming another non-singing role in July 1965 for a remake of Stagecoach, the 1939 masterpiece.   Bing brought Harry with him on location near Boulder, Colorado.   Bing played the drunken doctor previously played for an Academy Award by Thomas Mitchell.   When asked how he would compare to Mitchell, he said he did not know and would do the role his own way.   Bing's performance was excellent.   Many people thought he might win a second Oscar, but he was not even nominated.   The title song was sung by Wayne Newton.   At first he thought Ann-Margret difficult, but he realized her contract provided minimal compensation, and he was soon riding with her on her motorcycle.

During one hiatus of filming, Bing brought Harry to Chicago, where Kathryn was performing in George Bernard Shaw's Arms and the Man at the Drury Lane Theater.   He left Harry when he returned and took Mary with him.   In early August, as he flew to Kathryn from location with Mary Frances, he realized that his daughter had learned how to read. He was unable to take Kathryn a few weeks later for another race by Meadow Court because of another attack of a kidney stone.   After surgery Bing watched the films showing the horse coming in second at St. Leger in Doncaster.   After filming another "Hollywood Palace" on September 13, Bing had more surgery, which was unsuccessful.

Two weeks later, however, Bing and Kathryn were in France for a race in which the horse came in seventh and, as it proved later, it had been "nobbled" by French attendants. Bing shot partridge in Burgos, Spain, and met a famous

matador at the Ritz Hotel bar. It's a small world, for the
bullfighter wore a small cross Bing had given Kathryn as a
baptismal gift. Bing chased the man down the street, but it
turned out that Kathryn had thrown the cross to him years
earlier as he dedicated a bull to her, and it was all she
had to respond with. On the next day Bing went hunting and
a drunken companion nearly blew his foot off. In Ireland
Bing confirmed that Meadow Court had been nobbled, badly
shorn, in France, probably on purpose. Bing took Kathryn to
the Abbey Theatre and later arrived at Galway Bay at sundown
for a romantic view.

Son Harry appeared on the next TV Christmas show. The
appearance of a noted portrait painter provided a glimpse of
Bing's life over several months, revealed in an insightful
article in Good Housekeeping in May 1966. Through most of
1965 and much of 1966 Barnaby Conrad painted Bing and Kathryn and found that, unlike many entertainers, Bing was as
warm and lovable as he seemed to the public.

These were Bing's golden years, which he continued to
live without flamboyance. He traveled often, but now took
his family with him in the spirit of togetherness. He was
still a strict parent but thought Kathryn too severe. She
tanned bottoms with a tortoise hairbrush, although Bing
sometimes amused Alan Fisher, the butler, by trying to
appear severe himself, running after the children with a
rolled-up newspaper and shouting, "This has got to stop!"

Gary was at Hillsborough when Bing said, "Why don't we
take a walk?" Bing escorted Gary around the garden for a
walk that took barely a half hour, yet Gary sensed that
their relationship had totally changed (Gary 292). As they
walked up the driveway, Gary put his arm around his father's
shoulder. On reevaluating his father, recalling all his
charities and benefits, Gary concluded that "he was a damn
good guy, really a good man, a straight dude. . . . He
wasn't any tougher than a lot of fathers of his generation.
And a lot of kids can handle that kind of upbringing without
any difficulty" (p. 293).

Bing had only three recording sessions in 1965. Harry
III, at age 7, joined Bing on his annual Christmas show for
"Hollywood Palace." Harry sang "Oh, Come Little Children,"
while Kathryn and Mary Frances had roles in a San Francisco
production of Peter Pan. Bing's TV series foundered, but he
took another serious role for a special on Danny Thomas's
show for October 1967, playing an aging singer who fears
losing his voice. Mary Frances, age 9, had a role in the
play called "Demon Under the Bed," and the reviews were
favorable, some extravagant.

He recorded only two songs in 1966. Bing's brother
Everett died July 13 at age 70 in Connecticut of throat
cancer, and Bing and others attended the funeral in New
England. Bing and Kathryn traveled to England in September,
leaving Mary Frances behind. They visited Greystoke in
Cumberland with the Howards and Lady Lonsdale. Bing fished
for salmon in the River Derwent, Cokermouth, for "The American Sportsman." For his daughter's birthday, he telephoned
her school and sang "Happy Birthday" to her.

Stagecoach lacked the impact of the 1939 original, but
Bing was masterful with his role. He said, "I'd like to get
another part like Doc Boone--something that fits my age

bracket. But only in a good picture, something of stature and importance. I'd like to become a serious character actor." He met Julia Rinker Miller, the daughter of Al Rinker, early in 1967 when she sang backup in many shows, including Bing's. She thought Bing very pleasant and one who "had outgrown his past and was very much in the present, without need of dwelling on the past, as some people do" (S&S 344). The implication on Al Rinker's hostility is telling.

Bing's world of the 1920s was a minor version of the 1960s. He was eminently adaptable, but in 1967, at age 64, he was hard pressed to understand riots and gratuitous violence. The violence of Chicago in the '20s, when mobsters killed mobsters, became in the '60s national and fatal to quiet citizens; gin became mind-altering drugs; the college-age rebellion became high school turmoil; flappers and razzmatazz turned into free love; jazz became heavy rock; speakeasies became street-corner exhibitionism; cynicism became disrespectfulness; partying became egomania; demonstrating headed toward suicide. The Decade of Bad Manners became the Score of Years of Fatal Manners. Polite society languished at the periphery of an underground "alternate culture" that was socialistic and "free," the counter-culture of communes, the hippies, and yippies.

Cox Broadcasting Corporation bought Bing Crosby Productions in September 1967 for $2 million in stock, and Basil Grillo remained as the president. Bing had only one recording session in 1967, singing "Step to the Rear" and "What Do We Do with the World?" on October 31. He appeared in only two or three television shows a year from 1965 through 1969 besides his regular stints as a host for "The Hollywood Palace." Paul Whiteman died in Doylestown, Pennsylvania, on December 29, 1967. Alan Fisher and his wife, Norma, left the Crosbys for a few months in 1968, tired of the dull routine that had settled in. Bing had seven recording sessions in 1968 for 41 songs. The Golf Writers of America bestowed their Golden Tee Award on him in New York in February 1969, in honor of his tournament and charitable efforts.

Religion had become even more important to the Old Groaner. Bing and Kathryn donated $1 million to the now-defunct Immaculate Heart College in Hollywood in 1969; some said Kathryn had done this on her own. Bing sold off most of his holdings but bought another bank. He sold his Sunset Boulevard building and moved his scaled-down office to North Robertson Boulevard, Beverly Hills. He joined Kathryn, Mary Frances, and Nathaniel in a partially animated television production of "Goldilocks" in June 1969, for which Bing sang two solos and accompanied the others in another song. These were Bing's only recordings that year. His recordings remained minimal for 1970 and 1971 as well. He also recorded few songs from 1972 through 1974.

PART TEN

ETERNALLY BING CROSBY: 1970-1977

Bing hosted the final "Hollywood Palace" in February 1970. Of the 190 shows over seven years, Bing had hosted at least 32 of them, including the first, the final, and the Christmas shows. Other hosts included Frank Sinatra and Dean Martin. An hour special called "The Best of the Holly-wood Palace," aired 22 years later hosted by Suzanne Somers on ABC November 25, 1992, slighting Bing's contributions. Somers had declared two months earlier on ABC that Gary had told her that Bing was a sadist.

Nine days after the finale of "The Hollywood Palace," Bing was on "The Bob Hope Show," a 90-minute benefit for the Eisenhower Medical Center being built at Palm Springs. The benefit was held at the Waldorf Astoria in New York on January 27, for which Bing and Hope performed songs from the Road films. The dinner took in $2 million from 1500 guests. Bing had his own hour variety show on April 1, a program highlighting humorous aspects of leisure. Decca Records presented Bing with a platinum record of "Silent Night" on September 15, with the plaque noting his sales of more than 300,650,000 records. Bing made a surprise appearance while Bob Hope was interviewed November 17 in England on the BBC version of "This Is Your Life." Bing said, "I'd be delight-ed to lend my stature to assist this--unknown. Exactly what is it that this--Bob Hope--does? What is his talent?"

He recorded four songs, all carols, on November 16, for his only recordings for 1970. Bing's Christmas show was televised on December 16. While Bing spent more time at home now than did Kathryn, he filmed another non-singing lead for television. This color movie, titled "Dr. Cook's Garden," aired in January 1971 and is the only film in which Bing plays a villain. The same week it aired Bing also appeared on Pearl Bailey's first TV show.

The thirty-first Crosby National Pro-Am began Friday, January 14, 1971, with freezing winds and a $160,000 purse for the professionals in the three-day Clambake. The amount of money raised for charity rose to a total of more than $2 million. As the Vietnam nightmare intensified, Bing quietly joined four others in March to offer millions of dollars in ransom money for American prisoners. The group was called The Prisoners of War Rescue Mission and had the endorsement of the U.S. Department of State. Bing must have shaken his head as he learned that radicals from Brandeis University robbed a bank in 1970 to finance their revolution, machine gunning a Boston police officer to death.

Bing sold his interest in Minute Maid, although he and his family continued to appear in their commercials. "We need the money," Bing joked. Saving the Atlantic salmon continued in 1971, as Bing joined the Boston Red Sox Hall of Famer Ted Williams in a banquet for that benefit. Williams held a poster that read, "Going My Way," beside Bing holding another that added, "To Save the Atlantic Salmon." Bing became a pallbearer on July 6, 1971, at the funeral of Louis Armstrong.

While Bing did little but play golf and film Minute Maid commercials, in which his family was included to add to the children's college fund, he sold the Palm Desert home and enjoyed life. In mid-1971 Kathryn got the idea to improve the fashions of women in the gallery at the Crosby, hoping to inspire better fashion among lady golfers. Bing's sponsorship of professional golf tournaments expanded, for he bought an estate in Mexico, invested in development, and sponsored a women's golf tournament, all in Guadalajara. Called the Bing Crosby International Classic under the auspices of the Ladies Professional Golf Association, it occurred two years, March 15-17, 1974, and March 21-23, 1975, at the San Isidro Country Club. The total purse was $30,000 the first year and $45,000 the second. He was unsuccessful in August 1974 of persuading the PGA to permit women to play in the January Clambakes.

In January 1972 Bing served as the national chairman of the fund drive for the Arthritis Foundation. Bing recorded a dozen songs in February 1972, including those for Flip Wilson's show, and had a guest role in Bob Hope's film Cancel My Reservation, which was released that September. Bing explained that he had not really retired; he just could not find a suitable role. The ones he found were "dirty or pornographic." He lamented that many current films and television programs were not good for young people and that the "profound influence" of films was wasted in "selling, furiously, moral irresponsibility." He detected a trend that only intensified into the 1990s.

On May 2, 1972, Bing and Kathryn were "stocking up with jam and cookies in London" on the way to Bing's eighth safari. Bing went with his family on his eighth and ninth safaris in Kenya in 1972. Mary Frances bagged a man-eating crocodile, while Bing explained that he was merely shooting photographs, reported in the New York Times on August 26. His eleventh safari was in the fall of 1973. Back home some critics like John J. O'Connor thought Bing's TV Christmas show in December 1972 generally uninteresting, except for Bing singing "White Christmas." His only recordings for 1973 occurred on June 8. At home he spent Wednesday afternoons golfing with Harry and Nathaniel at the course near the house and the public school.

He starred in a stunning television program broadcast December 9, 1973. It was called "Bing Crosby's Sun Valley Christmas Show," attracting a record audience of 49,270,000 viewers. This was also the time someone stopped him in a corridor of the NBC building and asked, "Didn't you used to be Bing Crosby?" He decided to become busier, but he had to wait awhile. His brother Ted died in Spokane on December 10, 1973, at age 73, and soon his sister Catherine also died. Dixie's father died on Christmas Day, but Bing was too ill to attend the funeral. New Year's Day, 1974, Kathryn drove him to a hospital near Hillsborough, where doctor's discovered a rapidly growing cyst in his left lung.

Bing underwent critical surgery for three and one-half hours on January 13, 1974. Nearly half his left lung was removed and he had a scar 35 inches long on his back. The cyst was not malignant; it was a rare fungal infection he had contracted in Africa. Bing went home January 26 to recuperate and missed his Pro-Am tournament for the only time, and the weather was particularly nasty. He also quit smoking. His fears for his children increased in February when Patricia Hearst, whose father lived in Hillsborough, was kidnapped by a small group that called itself the Symbionese Liberation Army. Bing had an eight-foot-high ornamental iron fence installed around his Hillsborough property. The fence included sensors, an electrically controlled gate, and two-way speakers. The infamous Manson murders had

occurred in Hollywood in August 1969, and Bing had met one
of the gang's victims in November 1961. Bing also learned
of a kidnap threat against Kathryn.

The Old Groaner tested his voice found it had mellowed
even more.   Once again he made entertainment plans; now
under the aspect of mortality, he did so with a vengeance.
When Duke Ellington died on May 24, 1974, Bing paid tribute
by saying, "Duke Ellington and Louis Armstrong were the
greatest jazz musicians of all time." In Hillsborough Ken
Barnes of England suggested in September a new album that
might be called "Bing--Back on the Ball."   In early October
Bing, Barnes, and Pete Moore agreed in discussions at Bing's
home on the songs for two albums. Bing agreed to record 26
songs, and United Artists of England paid Bing the most
money any single artist received for a package deal (Thompson 226). Bing recorded two songs, one with Johnny Mercer,
for the albums on October 17, delaying the session at the
last moment for some reason from the agreed on date of
October 14. These were Bing's only recordings for the year.
Days later he learned that Mercer had terminal cancer.

Kathryn had a weekday morning television talk show in
San Francisco, which lasted a year and a half (1974-75).
Kathryn interviewed Bing and Phil Harris on October 25,
1974, and later Bing taped his next Christmas special,
"Christmas with the Bing Crosbys." After six years of few
recording dates, he had 16 in 1975; many of the songs were
duets with Fred Astaire. Mel Torme and his family were
house guests at Hillsborough that New Year's Eve. He hosted
his Clambake in January and in February he resisted, like
Bob Hope, the attempt by the PGA to take some of the revenue
for themselves.

Bing flew to London in February 1975 for sessions for
Barnes on an album called That's What Life Is All About.
Bing was again delayed, this time for the death of his
brother Larry. He recorded from February 18 to February 26
and attended a horse race at Doncaster at which a priest won
by betting on the Crosby Dawn. Bing earned £200 ($430) for
appearing on BBC-TV's "Grandstand" and bet £5 on a horse
named Uncle Bing, which also won.

On April 14 he wrote a long letter to Modern Maturity,
summarizing his activities as bird hunting in Texas, Alabama, Georgia, Canada, California, and Mexico in the previous year and that Harry was training five Labrador retriev-
ers. He went to the Mills Brothers Charity Show, a telethon
broadcast from August 21 through the next day. Bing produced and sang for a three-hour taped jazz session accompanied by a piano. Jazz remained his forte. He assembled a
road show, Bing Crosby and Friends, with Kathryn, Rosemary
Clooney, and the Joe Bushkin Trio, which traveled for the
next two years, gaining more performers on the way. Bing
was responsible for reviving Clooney's career. In July Bing
and Fred Astaire taped a dozen songs for the A Couple of
Song and Dance Men album, and Bing appeared as a guest of
Dame Vera Lynn on her London TV show. John Scott Trotter
died of cancer in October. The 1975 TV Christmas special
was called "Merry Christmas, Fred, from the Crosbys." The
main guest was Astaire, and Bob Hope, Joe Bushkin, and the
Young Americans were included. It was on NBC on December 3.

Bing encountered a blizzard of recording dates in 1976

and made many television appearances, including co-hosting
"The Bell Telephone Jubilee" with Liza Minnelli on March 21.
Bing, the authorized biography by Charles Thompson, went on
sale in Britain and then in the United States as Bing continued on tour. He joined Bob Hope for "The Bob Hope Special from Montreal," which aired on NBC April 21. The show
was a benefit for the Olympics and raised $90,000. They
sold out the Forum, near where the Olympiad would be staged
that year. In May he was hospitalized in Columbus, Ohio,
after nearly choking to death in a restaurant, forcing him
to withdraw from a golf tournament. Meanwhile, Mary Frances
moved to Malibu for her career and personal freedom.

     A very successful two-week engagement that June at
London's Palladium was captured for Bing's only live album.
It was here that Bing astounded Rosemary Clooney by confess-
ing to his audience at his final curtain call, "I love you."
While in England he also taped many TV shows, and he and
Rosemary Clooney were guests at Buckingham Palace, receiving
the personal gratitude of Prince Philip for their support of
British charities. Uncle Sam sans whiskers celebrated
America's Bicentennial with a special performance on July 4
for Americans in London, the last date at the Palladium.
From there he toured Gaiety Theatre, Dublin, and Usher Hall,
Edinburgh. Bing, Hope, and Lamour were the honored guests
at a charity ball given in Los Angeles by the Thalians that
fall. The trio was eager to report that they were committed
to another Road film called Road to Tomorrow, to be filmed
in mid-1977. Hope preferred the title Road to the Fountain
of Youth, and Bing suggested, "We've got to get more lunacy
into that script, Rob. When you've got two old guys you've
got to do something wild." Lamour was skeptical.

     Bing gave a special concert at New York's Avery Fisher
Hall on December 6, 1976, as a benefit for Fordham Preparatory School, a Roman Catholic boys' school. Bing Crosby on
Broadway opened the next night for a two-week run at the
Uris Theater, concluding on December 18, and the house was
packed after first few nights. At the end of each performance he introduced a song he said reflected his current
feelings, although he disowned "ever holding anything as
profound as a philosophy of life." That song was "That's
What Life Is All About." He continued to close to standing
ovations by saying with a damp eye and a catch in his
throat, "I love you."

     Clive Barnes, the demanding theater critic of the New
York Times, gave the Broadway show a rave. In my review of
the show, I wrote, "Bing Crosby proves with little apparent
effort that his baritone voice has gained far more in richness than the little steadiness it has lost in the highest
register," and, "Bing's voice is still very strong, and he
can turn up a lot of volume when he wishes. He still has a
respectably high range, stopping at one high note to state
that he had just invaded the territory of Andy Williams"
("The Groaner Is Alive . . . ").

     The prize money for the professionals at the Crosby
Clambake went over $200,000. After videotaping a three-hour
musical performance on March 3, 1977, Bing had a serious
fall. The show was a tribute to his 50 years in show business, although he had been a headliner nearly 52 years. Bob
Hope presented him with a statuette he called the "Crummy

Award." At the Ambassador Auditorium in Pasadena, California, he stepped back from his final bow to a tremendous
ovation and fell into an orchestra pit, which had been
lowered 20 feet. He broke his fall only a little by grasp-
ing a curtain, but that might have saved his life. He cut
his forehead, and a myelogram revealed a ruptured spinal
disc. After three weeks at the hospital in Pasadena, he was
flown to a hospital near Hillsborough. There he spent 11
more nights. While recuperating he drafted his final will,
and he was released from the hospital on April 5. This was,
ironically, the same date Elvis Presley, the erstwhile king
of popular music, was released from a Memphis Hospital, and
Elvis died 11 days later of a drug-overdose while crawling
on his bathroom tile floor. Of the musical troika of Crosby, Sinatra, and Presley, only two remained.

Bing was playing some golf by mid-April and recorded
"Don't Get Around Much Anymore" for an album called <u>A Tribute to Duke Ellington</u>, a benefit for the Duke Ellington
Cancer Center. This was the last song Bing recorded in this
country. In late May he gave Barbara Walters a televised
interview. He became serious as he said that if any children of his lived with someone out of wedlock he would
virtually disown them. He said, "I wouldn't speak to them
ever again. . . . Aloha with a steel guitar." Nathaniel,
age 15, picked up the golfing mantle to become the champion
of his home club, and four years later he would win the
Eighty-first U.S. Amateur Golf Championship in San Francisco
by sinking a 15-foot putt on an extra hole.

Bing established the Harry L. Crosby Trust on June 27
and filed his last will in San Mateo County. He bequeathed
$410,000, with the homes and remaining funds to be deposited
in a new "living trust." He left $150,000, all his personal
effects, and house furnishings to Kathryn, $50,000 each to
Gonzaga High School and Gonzaga University, and more to
friends and family. Kathryn also received a large annual
amount from the private trust. Interest on Gary's royalties
was payable annually with the principal sum due Gary on
reaching 65 (in 1998), the same year he would collect the
principal from Bing's trust. Bing's other children received
their inheritances from Bing at the same age; the older sons
were receiving income from Dixie's estate.

Bing performed with his family at Concord, California,
on August 16 as a trial run for a tour of Norway, Sweden,
and England, and it was a complete sell-out. The Crosbys,
minus Mary and Nathaniel, flew on the Concorde to Oslo's
Fornebu Airport on August 25 to perform at Momarkedet
(Mysen) for a benefit for the Norwegian Red Cross. Bing
taped his last Christmas special, his forty-second, in
London in September. His primary guest was David Bowie, as
Bing was alert to new talent and styles. Working again with
Ken Barnes, he also recorded his last album. Called <u>Sea-
sons</u>, it became Bing's twenty-fourth and final gold record.
His traveling show opened in Preston on September 22, to
good reviews that remarked that his voice was "still
strong." The concert appeared in Manchester September 23.

Three days later a successful engagement began at the
Palladium. He appeared there another two weeks. Mike
Wallace of the CBS "Sixty Minutes" program caught up with
Bing and discussed the problem with a Crosby impersonator

who performed in commercials. Bing's lawyers were charging the impersonator with misrepresentation. With Sunday off, he performed at Brighton October 10.

Bing recorded his last two songs on October 4 with the Joe Bushkin Quartet, singing "Now You Has Jazz" and "Sail Away from Norway." Bing rewrote some of the lyrics of the latter. In Davenport, Iowa, Bing was inducted into the Dancer's Big Band Hall of Fame. The day after the Brighton show, he discovered their London rooms had been burglarized, with the loss of much jewelry. He recorded eight songs for a BBC radio program and was photographed for his final album. On October 13 Bing flew to Spain for hunting and golf. Jazz, romance, family, and sports to the end.

On October 14, 1977, after lunch at the La Moraleja Club course near Madrid, Bing golfed that Friday afternoon, challenging Valentin Barrios, the former Spanish champion, and Cesar de Zulueta, president of the club. Teamed with Manuel Pinero, the Spanish champion, Bing was in fine spirits, humming, singing, and whistling over the links, and his team won the match by one stroke. A few people on the veranda applauded his final putt as Bing carded a respectable 85. Bing bowed and was walking away from the final green, saying, "It was a great game," when he collapsed. Bing succumbed without regaining consciousness in the ambulance speeding to the Red Cross Hospital in Madrid.

Bing's license to party was revoked. Now Bing, too, belongs to the ages. He died, as he lived, in the sunshine, and only Sinatra remained of the most popular singers of the century.

All Spanish television stations interrupted their programs with the sad news. The American ambassador to Spain immediately telephoned Kathryn at Hillsborough, and she began telephoning a long list of friends. Rosemary Clooney flew to Kathryn and the children. Kathryn was shown on television saying, "I can't think of any better way for a golfer who sings for a living to finish the round."

Bing had arranged in his recent will to avoid the horrors of Dixie's funeral. That night Kathryn, Nathaniel, Mary Frances, one of Kathryn's aunts (Mrs. Leonard Meyer), and Basil Grillo attended a Mass in Hillsborough. Gary was playing tennis when he heard of his father's death, and he resumed playing, saying he was not going to act now like he loved or would miss him. He thought, however, that Bing's life and death were perfect, even to dying "doing what he loved most, doing it successfully, taking a bow, knowing he was in good shape with his Church and his God and his fellow man. How many guys get to die like that? What an ending" (p. 298).

Bob Hope was at the Waldorf Towers in New York scheduled for a benefit in Morristown, New Jersey, which became his first cancellation of his long career. He said, "I still don't believe it. I'm absolutely numb." Bing was scheduled to introduce Hope's next TV show, and Hope returned to Hollywood in dejection. Dorothy Lamour said, "I hope the road to heaven is as wonderful as the Roads we traveled together." "For all the roads he traveled in his memorable career," eulogized President Carter from the White House, "Bing Crosby remained a gentleman, proof that a great talent can be a good man despite the pressures of showbusi-

ness. He lived a life his fans around the world felt was
typically American: successful, yet modest; casual, but
elegant." Frank Sinatra was near tears as he said, "Bing's
death is almost more than I can take. He was the father of
my career, the idol of my youth, and a dear friend of my
maturity. His passing leaves a gaping hole in our music and
in the lives of everybody who ever loved him. And that's
just about everybody. Thank God we have his films and his
records providing us with his warmth and talent forever."
George Burns, William S. Paley, Milton Berle, Irving Berlin,
and hundreds of others expressed their grief.

Harry and Alan Fisher left for Spain on October 16 to
accompany the body home while Bing's remains were embalmed
at the Forensic Institute. The next day they claimed the
body and Bing's favorite golf clubs and returned. The torch
at the Los Angeles Coliseum was lighted that night as a
tribute as the casket arrived by airplane. Memorial services were held in several cities around the world. St.
Patrick's Cathedral in New York was jammed with 3000 mourners and 2000 gathered at the Westminster Cathedral in London
for a Memorial Mass. Dennis was grateful for the world's
sympathy, saying, "It was a very fine present. I think my
dad died a fulfilled man. He accomplished everything he set
out to do but he had a lot more to give. We lost him
early."

That night an old-fashioned wake was held at a Los
Angeles hotel. Kathryn said, "He hated funerals. I'm sure
he didn't plan to come to this one." Before dawn that
overcast Tuesday, October 18, a simple and private Requiem
Mass was held at the rectory chapel of St. Paul the Apostle
Church in Westwood. Kathryn had invited 35 of Bing's closest friends and family, including Bob and Dolores Hope, Phil
Harris and Alice Faye, and Rosemary Clooney. Bing's will
specifically requested the presence of Hope. Two reporters
from the National Enquirer wormed their way in as priests
and hunted a story while pretending to comfort mourners.
With sons Gary and Harry III among the pallbearers, Bing was
laid to rest beside Dixie's remains at the Holy Cross Cemetery in Inglewood. His casket was buried extra deep to
leave room for Kathryn's above it.

"Bing Crosby's Merrie Olde Christmas," his last Christmas special, was broadcast on CBS on November 30, 1977. It
drew a large audience. It was Bing's forty-second consecutive Christmas show. Bing and David Bowie sang duets of
"Little Drummer Boy" and "Peace on Earth."

EPILOGUE: The Crosby Legacy in Perspective

The granite gravestone that was placed, like others in
the cemetery, flush with the ground, notes Bing's years as
he knew them: "Bing / Crosby / 1904-1977." That he was
mistaken on the year, and even on the date, of his birth on
May 3, 1903, is trivial; his talent and style are his legacy
and the numbers, though interesting, are insignificant.

Conceding for a moment that Elvis Presley, who died two
months before Bing, sold 500 million records since 1954, and
that Bing sold only 400 million since 1926, we could,
for a simple method, compare relative sales in relation to

population by comparing the nation's population at the midpoints of their careers. Adjusting Presley's sales by the audience in Crosby's time, it would be about 365 million. Crosby's sales would be 508 million in Presley's time. Moreover, in the 1930s, when Bing was first popular, record sales were very low because of the Depression, and many people also maintain that Bing has actually sold more than 500 million records. Bing remained on records and on television consistently until his death, even after his death. Still, on the fifteenth anniversary of Elvis's death it was reported that he had earned 110 gold and platinum records, more than twice as many as the Beatles.

Bing's numbers suffer only from selling records much earlier to a smaller population, and The Guinness Book of World Records used to attribute Bing with selling a thousand million records (a billion). If we take this as an exaggeration, we might settle on a compromise, say, 600 million Crosby discs, certainly 500 million (Bing 103: 7). Bing's "White Christmas" alone had sold 100 million records just in North America by 1987. One Bing follower estimates that Bing sang 3500 songs (including on radio, etc.) and 12,000 counting reprises (Bing 103: 7-8). When Elvis died at age 42 his estate had diminished to $5 million, but it grew, managed by Elvis's wife, to $100 million by the time his daughter, Lisa Marie, inherited it on reaching age 25 in 1993. Bing's fortune was worth three times that back in 1977, and he endowed the world with so much more.

The Bing Crosby National Pro-Am Golf Tournament played on schedule on February 1, 1979, at Pebble Beach with Nathaniel, then 17, as the host and director. The tournament went on as usual until AT&T took it over in 1986, and Kathryn relocated the Crosby Clambake to Bermuda Run at Winston-Salem, North Carolina, where it continues to this day as an amateur event with all earnings devoted to charity. To 1992, in its first seven years there, it raised $9 million more for charity. By August 1978 Kathryn placed the 1,067-acre Rising River Ranch for sale.

Bob Hope unveiled a lifesize high-relief bust of Bing Crosby in March 1979 as a special plaque at London's Palladium. As Gary began his autobiography, Philip promptly phoned James Bacon to say that he, Dennis, and Lindsay thought Bing a good father, strict but not cruel. He said, "He just reared us the way Grandma Kate Harrigan brought him up." He added that Gary was in Las Vegas seeking a divorce. In the fall of 1981 Gary had triple-bypass heart surgery, and Kathryn nursed him back to health.

Gary thought long about his many summers working at the Elko ranch "and realized they could have been a lovely experience." He loved the foreman and the hands and arising early for outdoor work, "wrangling horses and punching cattle," but he would not allow himself to enjoy the experiences; in fact, he hated them simply "because I had to be there" (p. 99). He was now happily married to a woman named Andrea.

Back in 1949 and in his quiet way, Bing supported Mildred Bailey financially when he learned she had diabetes and a heart attack, with a mortgage and hospital and doctor bills she could not pay. This good deed went unnoted until Jimmy Van Heusen revealed it in 1978. The crooner moved her to Santa Monica for treatments that saved her life and placed her in "a cute little house" in Toluca Lake. Donald Shepherd and Robert Slatzer told the tale in February 1980 to Al Rinker, who was recovering from a heart attack, and he explained that he could not have helped her and charged that Bing helped her only to take her jewelry and paintings. He said that afterwards Mildred left Los Angeles to live on her own with friends in the East (S&S 347). She had a brief revival in 1950 and died in Poughkeepsie in December 1951. Rinker knew half the story and refused to believe the other half. This meeting, however, inspired Shepherd and Slatzer to elicit more hostile reminiscences of a soured and dying Rinker, and, after assembling as much negative material as they could, they published <u>Bing Crosby: The Hollow Man</u> in 1981. Rinker died in June 1982.

In 1983 Gary published <u>Going My Own Way</u>, his autobiography that furnishes ambiguous material that could turn Bing into a heartless and cruel father. Gary admitted that his publisher insisted on more tales on his father than he had at first included. Bob Crosby was astonished at Gary's book and said, "I never remember anyone being physically touched in any way." Phil Harris stated that he never saw Bing beat the boys and that someone who was loved so long by so many people could not "be too bad." Harris added, "I love all [the four sons] dearly, but I don't know a one of them who works." At the least, the observation written on Bing in 1948 by his father applies: "As long as his is the 'voice of the people,' Bing's books will more than balance in this life."

Joan Rivers' and "A Current Affair" programs of 1991 are clear examples of unfair innuendo against Bing Crosby, inspired mainly by exaggerating statements by Gary. The Joan Rivers morning talk show was titled "Hollywood Kids in Hell" and was broadcast in September. The investigative show "A Current Affair" broadcast in June a segment titled "The Curse of Crosby," imagining a dark secret and hidden curse among the Crosbys revealed in the suicide of Dennis in May 1991, implying that it all stemmed from Bing. Lindsay had killed himself at age 51 in December 1989. Of course, the atmosphere had been poisoned by the hostile memoir of Rinker, intensified by Shepherd and Slatzer, but no one other than Rinker and Gary accused Bing of being "hollow" and cruel.

Bing was most important in music. One historian states that only recordings of Crosby and Louis Armstrong were allowed in Harlem jukeboxes in the 1930s. John Rockwell writes, "It would be hard to imagine James Taylor without Bing Crosby" (Oct. 15, 1977). He names Bing the "Norman Rockwell of music," and asserts, "Pop stars of today are not always so nice or so natural. Perhaps they dig deeper into all our emotions and hence are truer to today's realities than Mr. Crosby's gentler assurances." In this sense, many of the rock stars have slung about as much mire as most people in the 1990s can bear, and the realities of the 1990s seem to be rebounding.

Rockwell states that Bing worked out his lively techniques on radio and in his early films, but that he soon "turned into something different and more familiar to us today." This is the strain extended throughout Bing's songs and films, which became central to the 1940s but irrelevant to the radicalism since 1960 and its music and films of irresponsible youths, explicitly oversexed men and women, and violent people. Rockwell suggests, however, that Bing's central stock of songs are "prized by pre-rock pop defenders of today as the result of a golden age of sophisticated songwriting," but the songs are "often ludicrously kitschy, anticipating the nadir of Tin Pan Alley songs of the early '50s, which triggered the rock rebellion" (Oct. 29, 1982). Are many current rock songs more eloquent and meaningful than ballads of the early 1950s?

On Bing's death, Bob Hope promptly produced his two-hour NBC special, titled "On the Road with Bing." The ABC network aired a two-hour tribute in 1978, and the superb "Remembering Bing," produced by WTTW of Chicago, appeared on the Public Broadcasting System for an hour in 1987, with a long slate of friends and film clips.

Bing was a gentle, generous, intelligent, educated, productive, and talented singer, actor, sportsman, and entrepreneur, one of the most important figures, popular or professional, of the century. Writing in Parade Magazine April 27, 1986, Walter Scott answered the accusations: "Bing Crosby . . . may not have been a particularly good father to his four sons by Dixie Lee Crosby, but he certainly was no 'cowardly monster.' He believed that sparing the rod would spoil the child. He had a particularly difficult time rearing his first son, Gary. . . . He was not a sadistic child-abuser, however, and should not be held responsible for Gary's capitulation to alcoholism."

Uncontested by host Joan Lunden, Suzanne Somers said on ABC on the morning of September 24, 1992, that Gary had told her that Bing was a sadist, but Gary has been careful to explain that even the beatings he took would have been acceptable had he felt an equal amount of praise and encouragement. Life magazine in September 1990 declared Bing one of the hundred most important and influential people of the century. Bing's many accomplishments would make heroes of a dozen individuals or a tad more than another Bob Hope.

Bing was unique, developed a singing style that changed popular music, and influenced all later singers without himself being surpassed, as Ken Crossland, a British fan, expressed it in October 1991. Reviewing two CD's of Bing, Peggy Lee, and Ella Fitzgerald in 1993 in Jazz on CD and Cassette, Earl Orkin writes, "Bing Crosby was one of the greatest of all jazz singers. Although he could and often did sing just about anything, he grew up in the world of Bix Beiderbecke and Hoagy Carmichael, and jazz was always what he loved best. (Unlike Sinatra, for instance, he always phrased the music, not the words.) Short of Louis Armstrong or Billie Holiday perhaps, there is no better role-model for an aspiring jazz singer than Bing" (qtd. Bing 104: 44).

Bob Hope said, "The melody Bing Crosby sang will linger as long as there's a phonograph to be played . . . and a heart to be lifted." Harry Lillis "Bing" Crosby was a good man, generous and sensitive, an astounding person and performer, the supreme entertainer who achieved worlds more than merely singing in tune. His voice, piety, patriotism, playfulness, modesty, generosity, old-fashioned manliness, and love of jazz served him and the world to the end.

Chronology

ECONOMIC AND POPULATION COMPARISONS (1929/30-1990)

Approximate Monetary Values and Income Over the Years

$100 in year	equals this in 1990	Per Capita Income Annually
1929	$700.00	$ 692.00
1933	$950.00	$ 369.00
1940	$900.00	$ 587.00
1950	$525.00	$ 1,501.00
1960	$425.00	$ 2,219.00
1970	$330.00	$ 3,893.00
1980	$150.00	$ 9,910.00
1990	$100.00	$18,685.00

Relative Population and Sales Over the Years

Year	People relative to each million in 1930	Sales relative to 200,000 in 1990	Sales relative to one million in 1990
1930	1.00 million	100,000	0.50 million
1940	1.07 million	107,000	0.54 million
1950	1.23 million	123,000	0.62 million
1960	1.46 million	146,000	0.73 million
1970	1.65 million	165,000	0.83 million
1980	1.83 million	183,000	0.92 million
1990	2.00 million	200,000	1.00 million

(These tables are useful in comparing sales, in the sense that 500,000 sales in 1930 would compare to one million in 1990 because the population doubled.)

1903
May 3   Harry Lillis "Bing" Crosby is born at home, fourth child of Harry Lowe and Catherine (nee Harrigan) Crosby, in Tacoma, Washington. Three siblings preceded Bing: Laurence Earl "Larry" (Jan 3, 1895), Everett Nathaniel (Apr 5, 1896), and Henry Edward "Ted" (Jul

30, 1900); and three siblings were born later. Bing
always believed he was born May 2, 1904.

May 31   Is baptized at St. Patrick's Roman Catholic Church
at North G Street and Starr.

1904
Oct 3   Catherine Cordelia Crosby, a sister, is born.

1906
May 3   Mary Rose Crosby, a sister, is born.
Jul   The family is reunited in Spokane, where father
Harry is a bookkeeper for Inland Brewery.

1909
Fall   Enrolls at Webster Grade School.

1910
Bing's playmate dubs him "Bingo" after a newspaper
comic feature "The Bingville Bugle."

1913
Jul   The Crosbys build a nine-room house at 508 East
Sharp Street, Spokane.
Aug 25   George Robert "Bob" Crosby is born, the youngest
of the seven children.

1916
Jun   Overseen by Kate, Bing wins seven first- and sec-
ond-place medals in a swimming meet at Mission Park.

1917
Sep   Enters the high school of Gonzaga as a "commuter"
and makes the Junior Yard Association football team.

1918
Fall   Organizes a quartet and plays drums "borrowed"
from Gonzaga for the dance combo the Juicy Seven.

1921
Wins the Senior Oratorical Contest.
Jun   Graduates from Gonzaga High School. Plays semi-
professional baseball for a laundry, and Jimmy Cottrell
coaches him in boxing.
Sep   Enters Gonzaga College and plays varsity baseball.

1922
Buys a set of drums and has a part-time job in the
props department of Spokane's Auditorium Theatre. He
sees his idol, Al Jolson, and other performers.
Summer   Hops on trains to play professional baseball at
Los Angeles, losing interest in Northern California.
Goes to Portland to brother Ev, spends a night in jail,
and cuts a knee with an axe with a logging company;
loses his baseball position.

1923
Sep   Begins his junior year in college and declares a
pre-law major.

1924
Spring   Al Rinker hires Bing as the singing drummer for
     the Musicaladers. Introduces Al to golf at the Down-
     river Park.
Summer   The band plays at Lareida's Dance Pavilion for $25
     a week.
Sep   Becomes a senior in college.

1925
Jan   Quits college on learning he earns more money
     singing part time than an assistant lawyer.
Sep   The Musicaladers disbands, but Bing joins a quar-
     tet for two weeks at a theater with Rinker as the
     accompanist. Then Bing sings solos to Rinker's piano
     until the manager cancels the show.
Oct 15   Bing and Al leave Spokane; two days later they
     reach Seattle and play a week at the Butler Hotel.
Nov 9?   They arrive in Los Angeles, staying three weeks
     with Mildred Bailey, audition for Mike Lyman, and
     become "Crosby and Rinker, Two Boys with a Piano," at
     the Tent Cafe downtown and at the Lafayette Cafe.
Dec 7?   The Fanchon and Marco Time Agency hire them for 18
     weeks for the Syncopation Idea at the Boulevard Theatre
     and the Loew's Circuit. They each earn $75 a week.

1926
Apr   They are hired by Will Morrissey's Orange Grove
     Revue at the Majestic Theatre at $65 weekly each,
     becoming a top attraction for another two months.
          The revue goes to San Diego, then to San Francisco
     for six weeks, and closes in Santa Barbara.
Jul   The duo sings at the Metropolitan Theatre in Los
     Angeles and at the Granada and the Warfield in San
     Francisco, outdrawing Paul Whiteman, and then back at
     the Metropolitan. The billing: "Two Boys and a Piano--
     Singing Songs Their Own Way."
Sep   Paul Whiteman hires them for five years at $150
     weekly each, commencing in Chicago in December.
Oct 18   Makes his first record, "I've Got the Girl,"
     singing the chorus anonymously with Don Clarke's Bilt-
     more Hotel Orchestra.
Nov 23   The duo performs in Spokane until Nov 27; once at
     the Davenport Hotel, earning $175 to $200 each, but the
     money was stolen. Bing has put on weight.
Dec 15   The duo opens with Whiteman in Chicago and are a
     hit. Bing is late to some rehearsals and performances.
Dec 22   Whiteman produces their second record, "Wistful
     and Blue," which forges the duo's new style. They
     perform in several cities on their way East.

1927
Jan   At the Paramount Theatre in New York the duo is a
     dud and sings in the lobby to the overflow crowd.
Feb 18   They are hardly noticed in performances at the
     opening of the Paul Whiteman Club.
          They form a trio when Harry Barris joins them at
     the Whiteman Club and the new group becomes Paul White-
     man's Rhythm Boys one month later.
Mar 22   The Rhythm Boys open in Whiteman's musical <u>Lucky</u>

at the New Amsterdam Theatre, lasting about two months.
Earning $150 a week each, the trio also appears un-
billed on the new Whiteman radio program.

Aug   The trio goes on a vaudeville circuit for 45 weeks
without Whiteman. Bing earns $300 a week. On tour the
trio becomes lazy and misses connections.

1928

Jan 4   Joins Whiteman on his first Old Gold radio show
but receives no billing.

May 12   Whiteman and the Rhythm Boys begin recording on
the Columbia label.

Jun   The tour of the Rhythm Boys ends.

1929

Mar 5   Whiteman's radio program becomes a weekly affair
with the Rhythm Boys and two or three solos by Bing.

Mar 14   Sings for his first record as a solo artist.
Rejects an offer by an agent to go solo.

May 24   Records two songs in New York accompanied by Eddie
Lang (for the first time) and two other musicians.

May 26   Old Gold leases a special train with stops at 16
cities across the nation.

Jun 6   The train arrives at Los Angeles' Union Station.

Jun 28   Whiteman's film The King of Jazz is delayed and
Whiteman brings his group East with Hoagy Carmichael.

Sep 3   Whiteman begins broadcasting from New York; Bing
has solos and a duet with Mildred Bailey.

Nov 1   Filming The King of Jazz commences. Whiteman pays
Crosby $400 a week.

Nov   Drives a girl home from a studio party and has an
accident. A week later Bing is sentenced to 45 days
in jail, but he is released under escort for filming.
Loses a featured solo to John Boles, and the movie is
slightly delayed.
First meets Dixie Lee at the Cocoanut Grove.

1930

Makes a short film titled Ripstitch the Taylor for
Pathe as a test, but the studio never shows it.

Mar 21   Joins the chorus behind vocalist John Boles for
the recording of "Song of the Dawn," and records a solo
the next day. The filming ends for The King of Jazz.

May   The trio leaves Whiteman in Seattle and returns to
Los Angeles, where they spend 13 weeks on local radio.

May   William Perlberg places the trio for a smash week
at the Montmartre Cafe in Hollywood, each earning $400.
Dixie Lee is often in the audience.
Meets Dixie Lee at a house party and drives her
home. They begin dating nearly every night.

Jun   Hires agent Edward Small. Appears in Two Plus
Fours, a short for Pathe that uses the earlier test.
Unbilled, the trio sings "Just One More Chance" in
Paramount's Confessions of a Co-ed. Jim Ryan, the
casting director at Fox, tells Bing to forget movies
because of his ears.

Aug 26   The trio records "Three Little Words" with Duke
Ellington for RKO's Check and Double Check, but editing
makes the band seem to do the singing.

Sings "When the Folks High Up Do the Mean Low Down" in <u>Reaching for the Moon</u>, the first film with Bing speaking a line and singing a featured solo.

Sep   Becomes a singing sensation when the Rhythm Boys are featured at $100 each a week with Arnheim's orchestra at the Cocoanut Grove. Develops a unique "catch" or "Crosby Cry" in a transition to mastery over the microphone, and his solos steal the show.

Sep 29   Marries Dixie Lee (Wilma Winfred Wyatt). Is called "an obscure crooner" and "Murray Crosey."

1931

Jan 19   Records "I Surrender, Dear" for his first hit.
Mack Sennett stars Bing in <u>I Surrender, Dear</u>, Bing's first two-reel musical comedy.

Mar 4   Dixie announces a separation.

Mar 15   Goes to Dixie in Mexico and they reconcile.
Stops drinking for months, and never again does the bottle gain the upper hand.

Mar 30   Begins his first solo recording contract, singing on the Brunswick label.

May 4   Records "Just One More Chance," another solo hit.
Bing, Al, and Barris walk out on their contract at the Cocoanut Grove. Abe Frank blacklists them locally.

Jun   Films five more two-reelers; also films two shorts for the Christy Brothers and one for Hal Roach, and hires his brother Ev as his manager.

Aug 31   Is unable to sing at 7 p.m. for CBS in New York for an unsponsored radio show because of laryngitis.

Sep 2   After a second postponement, Bing completes his first solo radio show with Eddie Lang playing guitar. NBC soon hires Russ Columbo in "the Battle of the Baritones."

Nov 3   Becomes "The Cremo Singer" on CBS at 7:15 p.m. six nights a week to Feb 27.

Nov 8   Begins an engagement at the Paramount Theatre, which runs for a record 20 weeks (perhaps 29 weeks).

Nov 23   Records "Where the Blue of the Night."

Dec   Strains his vocal cords so that he seeks medical attention and narrowly escapes surgery that could have destroyed his voice. He rests his voice completely for two weeks, and it returns a tone or two lower.

1932

Prominent people denounce crooners, and Bing says he is not one.

Feb 20   Is the guest of honor of the Friars at a midnight dinner in New York.

Mar 26   Ends his second 10-week appearance at Paramount, which, according to many, goes 29 weeks in all.

Jun 4   Begins filming <u>The Big Broadcast</u> for Paramount-Publix for five weeks. Rents a house on Cromwell Street in Hollywood and hires brother Larry to project a new serious image.

Jul 27   Last broadcast for Chesterfield until Jan 4, 1933, as Ev demands better terms. Earning $3500 a week, he goes on a tour for Paramount.

Sep 16   At the Paramount in San Francisco the receipts for a live performance amount to $40,000, a new record.

Takes Dixie on a personal appearance tour East.

Oct 14   <u>The Big Broadcast</u> opens in New York. Reviewers rave over Bing's presence and poise in the film.

Oct   Ev works out the new radio contract for $2000 weekly, to begin next year.

Dec 2   Sings and ad-libs at the Capitol Theatre, New York, where Bob Hope and he alternate as the emcee for two weeks.

1933

Mar 26   Bing's closest friend, Eddie Lang, dies at the Park West Hospital, New York, during a tonsillectomy. Bing accompanies the body to Philadelphia on Mar 29.

Apr   Builds his first home, on Foreman Avenue in the Toluca Lake District.

Films <u>College Humor</u> (released Jun 22, 1933).

Films <u>Too Much Harmony</u> (released Sep 22, 1933).

Hires Leo Lynn as his chauffeur; he remains close to the family and serves as Bing's factotum and stand-in for movie cameramen until Bing's death.

Films <u>Going Hollywood</u> (released Dec 22, 1933), singing "Temptation" and four other songs, earning $2000 weekly, $40,000 total, and receives a three-picture contract from Paramount worth about $300,000.

Jun 22   <u>College Humor</u> opens as a hit in New York.

Jun 27   Gary Evan Crosby is born, weighing 7 3/4 pounds.

Buys his parents a house in Toluca Lake.

Oct 16   Returns to CBS, now on Mondays for Woodbury Soap, first with Lennie Hayton's orchestra, and with 1934 the Mills Brothers become regulars.

Nov   Films <u>We're Not Dressing</u> on Catalina Island for three weeks.

Dec 22   <u>Going Hollywood</u> is released, and Bing first becomes one of the top ten film stars.

1934

Invests $10,000 in the new Santa Anita race track, Arcadia, in order to obtain a choice box seat.

Mar 20   A serious kidnap threat to son Gary is revealed.

X-rays show Dixie pregnant with twins, with one in a complicating position.

May   Films <u>She Loves Me Not</u>, <u>Here Is My Heart</u>, and the short <u>Just an Echo</u>, 1934 releases. While filming <u>She Loves Me Not</u> Bing refuses to have his ears glued back any longer.

Summer   Films <u>Mississippi</u> (released Apr 1935). Weighing 190 pounds, Bing wears a girdle.

Buys an office building at 9028 Sunset Boulevard and occupies the top floor.

Jul   Forms Bing Crosby Limited, Inc.

Buys a 100-acre estate at Rancho Santa Fe.

Jul 5   Records "Love in Bloom" and three other songs to conclude his contract with Brunswick.

Jul 13   Dixie gives birth to twins: Philip Lang and Dennis Michael. The babies are premature.

Aug 8   Records Decca's first songs, "I Love You Truly," "Let Me Call You Sweetheart," and two others, under contracts that go to Dec 27, 1955.

Seriously considers retiring from radio and films.

Sep 18   Returns to radio and Woodbury Soap, now for a half
            hour on Tuesdays, to Jun 11, 1935, with a contract that
            pays him $6000 a week as a package with-total control.
            Begins filming Here Is My Heart
Dec 21   Here Is My Heart is released.

1935
Feb 21   Records four popular songs and then "Silent
            Night" for the St. Columban Missionary Society, and
            later waxes "Adeste Fideles" and two other religious
            songs for the second side for the missionaries.
            Sings "With Every Breath I Take" in Star Night at
            the Cocoanut Grove, a short for M-G-M.
            Films Two for Tonight and appears in The Big
            Broadcast of 1936.
            Builds stables and an exercise track at Rancho
            Santa Fe and buys his first racehorses. With Lindsay
            Howard he also founds Binglin Breeding Stables.
Aug 30   Two for Tonight is released in New York; Bing and
            Dixie attend the premiere.
Sep 13   The Big Broadcast of 1936 is released.
Fall   Buys seven acres in Toluca Lake on Camarillo
            Street for a home closer to the Lakeside golf course.
Nov   Films Anything Goes.
Nov 12   Records six songs, including "Adeste Fideles" and
            "Silent Night" as commercial waxings but with earnings
            assigned to charity.
Dec 5   Is paid $3000 weekly for the hour-long "Kraft
            Music Hall" on Thursdays as a trial.

1936
Jan 2   Begins the "Kraft Music Hall" under his own con-
            tract. Earns $5000 weekly.
            Begins building the Del Mar Track and Turf Club
            north of San Diego with several partners.
Feb 5   Anything Goes is released.
Spring   Films Rhythm on the Range, and later (for Colum-
            bia) Pennies from Heaven with John Scott Trotter.
Apr 8   Places his prints and name in cement at Grauman's
            Chinese Theatre.
Jul 29   Rhythm on the Range is released.
Aug 19   Bing and Dixie sing three duets for Decca, Dixie's
            last recordings.
Aug   Takes Dixie to Hawaii and discovers Harry Owens'
            "Sweet Leilani," which Bing sings in Waikiki Wedding.
Dec 9   Pennies from Heaven is released.
Dec 24   Broadcasts his first special Christmas radio show.

1937
Jan   Films Double or Nothing.
            Begins his professional-amateur golf tournament at
            Rancho Santa Fe. Films a 30-minute short on golf
            titled Swing with Bing.
Mar 24   Waikiki Wedding is released.
Jun   Named "Hollywood's Most Typical Father for 1937."
Jul 3   The Del Mar Turf Club opens and Saturday radio
            shows begin for Jul and Aug.
            Brother Ted joins Bing's organization, especially
            to publicize Del Mar, but he lasts only a year or two.

Aug 2   <u>Double or Nothing</u> is released.
Oct 16   Defeats Bob Hope in a golf tournament; Hope has to
perform for free in <u>Doctor Rhythm</u> as a penalty.
Oct 21   Accepts the honorary degree of Doctor of Philosophy in Music from Gonzaga University.

1938
Jan 5   Lindsay Harry is born, Bing's fourth son.
Stars in a 32-minute short on golf titled <u>Don't
Hook Now</u> with Bob Hope.
Apr 22   <u>Doctor Rhythm</u> is released.
Donates a $1600 organ to St. Charles Church, North
Hollywood, and dedicates it by singing a concert.
Jul 14   Bob Hope is the radio guest for the first time.
Films <u>Paris Honeymoon</u>.
Aug 12   Special race at Del Mar between Bing's Ligaroti
and Seabiscuit, with the latter winning.
Aug 14   <u>Sing, You Sinners</u> is released at Saratoga, NY,
following the Aug 12 premiere at Del Mar.
Films <u>East Side of Heaven</u> for Universal.
Dec 13   <u>Paris Honeymoon</u> is released.
Song promoters vote Bing "Number One Crooner of
the Unites States."

1939
Films <u>The Star Maker</u>.
Apr 4   <u>East Side of Heaven</u> is released.
Aug 21   <u>The Star Maker</u> is released.
Oct 8   Draws the largest attendance at the Golden Gate
International Exhibition in San Francisco.
Nov   Bing, Bob Hope, and Dorothy Lamour film <u>Road to
Singapore</u>, the first of a famous series.

1940
Feb   Founds the Crosby Research Foundation.
Films <u>If I Had My Way</u> and <u>Rhythm on the River</u>.
Mar 13   <u>Road to Singapore</u> premieres in New York City.
Apr 25   <u>If I Had My Way</u> is released.
Aug 16   <u>Rhythm on the River</u> is released.
Bing, Hope, and Lamour film <u>Road to Zanzibar</u>.
Nov 4   Speaks briefly on radio in support of Presidential
candidate Wendell Willkie.
Nov 7   Asks the country (possibly on his Nov 14 radio
show) to unite behind President Roosevelt, and never
again endorses a political candidate.

1941
Films <u>Birth of the Blues</u>.
Apr 9   <u>Road to Zanzibar</u> is released, a bigger hit than
the first <u>Road</u> film.
Aug   Sails from New York to Argentina, where Buenos
Aires dismisses schools "in honor of this great Ameri-
can singer." Buys part interest in a horse farm.
Films <u>Holiday Inn</u>, singing the perennial "White
Christmas."
Dec   The military requisitions the Del Mar property for
Army service and then Marine training.
Dec 10   <u>Birth of the Blues</u> is released.
Dec 25   Sings "White Christmas" on radio with the Music

Maids before its release in <u>Holiday Inn</u>.

1942

Volunteers for military service but is asked to entertain the servicemen. Selects programs for the Armed Forces Radio Service.

Holds his last golf tournament at Rancho Santa Fe.

Films <u>Road to Morocco</u>.

Sings the title song of the short <u>Angels of Mercy</u> (M-G-M, 1942) to honor the American Red Cross.

Films and sings "Old Glory" in <u>Star Spangled Rhythm</u> in which Gary Crosby appears. Has a cameo appearance in Bob Hope's <u>My Favorite Blonde</u> (1942).

Jan 29   Sends the radio show as a popular request to American forces besieged in the Philippines.

Feb 12   Misses his radio show this week and the next; he and Hope are on an exhibition golf tour.

Apr 29   Misses a White House party for the Hollywood Victory Caravan but catches the tour of 65 cities.

Jul   Begins playing exhibition golf matches with Bob Hope to benefit the P.G.A.'s war relief fund.

Aug 4   <u>Holiday Inn</u> is released.

Films <u>Dixie</u>.

Nov 11   <u>Road to Morocco</u> is released.

The Clambake Follies, financed by Bing's charities, entertain at military bases throughout the Southwest, often with Bing and Jimmy Van Heusen, who travel 5000 miles this year for the war effort.

Dec 30   <u>Star Spangled Rhythm</u> is released.

1943

Jan 2   The Crosby home burns down. Replaces it with a 17-room Georgian Colonial home in Holmby Hills, near the Los Angeles Country Club.

Jan 7   "Kraft Music Hall" becomes a half-hour program.

Appears in <u>Show Business at War</u> (1943) and sings the title song in the short <u>The Road to Victory</u> (1943).

Mar 4   "White Christmas" wins the Oscar as Best Song.

Jun 23   <u>Dixie</u> is released.

Jul 4   Joins Rinker and Barris on CBS as a Rhythm Boys reunion on Paul Whiteman's summer radio program.

Aug   The production of <u>Going My Way</u> slowly develops.

Nov   Begins filming <u>Road to Utopia</u> with Hope.

Dec   Fire consumes Bing's Malibu Beach house.

Jack Kapp signs Bing for a longer recording contract, running through 1955.

The <u>Downbeat</u> poll lists Frank Sinatra as overtaking Bing Crosby, Perry Como, Dick Haymes, and Bob Eberly as the most popular singer.

1944

Jan   Filming of <u>Going My Way</u> is completed.

Feb 1   Sings a duet with Sinatra for the Hollywood Victory Caravan's short wave broadcast to the military.

Feb   Buys an 8700-acre working ranch outside Elko, Nevada, and the next year replaces that with a 19,000-acre cattle ranch 50 miles to the north.

Mar   Sings "Don't Fence Me In" in the short <u>Swingtime with the Stars</u>.

May 2   <u>Going My Way</u> is released.
May   The songs "Swinging on a Star," "There'll Be a Hot
         Time in the Town of Berlin," and "Don't Fence Me In"
         are successive Hit Parade selections. Pope Pius XII
         writes Bing of his approval of the role of a "human-
         ized" priest. Fan mail increases, and Paramount signs
         Bing to a ten-year contract.
Jun   Films <u>Here Come the Waves</u>.
Aug 25   Arrives in Scotland to entertain the troops in
         Britain and broadcasts from London to the Germans.
Sep 1   Lands with his troupe at Cherbourg, entertaining
         from there to Paris, Nancy, and Metz. Once rides a
         jeep into German-held territory.
Oct 12   Returns to America and broadcasts remote from New
         York.
Oct   Dubs three songs mouthed by Eddie Bracken in <u>Out
         of This World</u> (Jun 1945) as a parody of Sinatra.
Nov 16   Frank Sinatra makes his first guest appearance on
         Bing's radio show, singing remote from New York.
         Paramount films the short <u>Hollywood Victory Cara-
         van</u> (1945); Bing sings "We've Got Another Bond to
         Buy." Has a cameo appearance in Hope's <u>The Princess
         and the Pirate</u> (released Feb 1945). Produces <u>The Great
         John L</u> and later <u>Abie's Irish Rose</u>. New York critics
         give <u>Going My Way</u> the Golden Globe Award.
Dec 28   Film exhibitors name Bing the top film star of the
         year for the first of five consecutive years.

1945
Feb   Sings a parody of "Swinging on a Star" in <u>Duffy's
         Tavern</u>.
Mar 12   Is in a special "Command Performance" on NBC and
         CBS, a spoof on Dick Tracy.
Mar 15   Escorts Dixie to receive his Oscar from Gary
         Cooper for <u>Going My Way</u>, the dinner emceed by Bob Hope.
Apr   Sings "Buy, Buy Bonds" for 20th Century-Fox's
         short <u>All Star Bond Rally</u> (1945).
May 17   Leaves his radio program after this show, return-
         ing briefly after six weeks, seeking to replace it.
Jun   The National Father's Day Committee names Bing
         "Number One Screen Father for 1945."
Jul   Filming of <u>The Bells of St. Mary's</u> is completed.
Jul 25   Sings "Don't Fence Me In" with the Andrews Sisters
         in a half hour; it becomes a big hit.
Aug   Begins filming <u>Blue Skies</u> with Fred Astaire.
Sep 5   <u>Duffy's Tavern</u> is released.
Nov   A fire consumes much of the property at Rancho
         Santa Fe.
Dec 6   <u>The Bells of St. Mary's</u> is released, and the New
         York Newspaper Guild presents Bing a "Page One Award"
         at Madison Square Garden.
         Receives many American and British film accolades,
         and soldiers and students express overwhelming approval
         of Bing as the top recording star.
         Sells $14.5 million in War Bonds in four years.
         Earns more than $1 million annually and hires Basil
         Grillo to organize Bing Crosby Productions. Grillo
         reorganizes all the enterprises.
         Is nominated for an Academy Award for Best Actor

in The Bells of St. Mary's but does not win.

1946
Buys a home at Pebble Beach. Promotes Minute Maid frozen orange juice, and invests in Bing's Things, oil leases in Louisiana and Oklahoma, banks in California and Arkansas, 6000 cattle in the United States and South America, a music publishing company, and an ice cream distributorship. Most do poorly, except Minute Maid and the oil leases.

Jan 2   Filming Road to Rio begins.
Feb 7   Road to Utopia is released.
Feb 7   Returns to the radio program under a compromise to break the contract.
Apr 15   Sells his interest in the Del Mar track and soon sells the home at Rancho Santa Fe and his stables.
May 9   His final broadcast for the "Kraft Music Hall."
The Women's Home Companion poll names Bing as the leading film star and for the next four years.
Aug   Buys about 20 percent of the Pittsburgh Pirates. He halfheartedly thinks again of retiring, and has investments in two semi-professional baseball teams.
Aug 15   Signs a contract with Philco Radio Corporation to do "The Crosby Show" as a transcribed radio program.
Films The Emperor Waltz in Canada.
Oct 16   Blue Skies is released and Bing commences the Wednesday night half-hour series for the "Philco Radio Time" on ABC.
Filming Road to Rio (fifth of the series) continues, financed by Bing, Bob Hope, and Paramount, and Bing has a cameo role in Hope's My Favorite Brunette.

1947
Broadcasts a series of 15-minute radio programs for Minute Maid, in return for 20,000 shares.
Jan   Revives his golf tournament at Pebble Beach, now a three-day affair on three courses.
Films Welcome Stranger.
Bing Crosby Electronics Division finances the Ampex Co. to design a tape recording system.
Jan 15   Al Jolson becomes a guest on Bing's radio show.
Feb 19   Road to Rio is released.
Mar   Bing and Bob Hope perform a golfing sketch for Variety Girl (released Oct. 1947).
Aug 1   Transcribes his first fall radio program (for Oct. 1) to enter the Jasper National Park Invitational Golf Tournament (which he wins), go moosehunting, and begin filming A Connecticut Yankee with Rhonda Fleming.
Aug 6   Welcome Stranger is released.
Dec   Has a heavy recording load, anticipating a strike of the Petrillo-led American Federation of Musicians.

1948
Apr 21   His sons debut on the radio show.
Jun 17   The Emperor Waltz is released.
Nov   Makes eight appearances at the Empress Hall, London, for $400,000.
Is the top film star for the fifth year in a row; Motion Picture Herald declares his feat "the all-time

boxoffice championship."

1949

	Films <u>Top o' the Morning</u> at Fox studios.
Jan 22	Signs with CBS for radio and TV appearances.
Apr 7	<u>A Connecticut Yankee in King Arthur's Court</u> is released.
Jun 1	Airs his last Wednesday broadcast for Philco.
Jun 23	Records his narrative for <u>Ichabod</u>.
Aug 9	An oil well in West Texas succeeds, yielding $3.5 million each for Bing and Hope.
Aug 31	<u>Top o' the Morning</u> is released.
Sep 21	The new radio program "Chesterfield Cigarettes Presents the Bing Crosby Show" begins on CBS.
	Films <u>Riding High</u>, directed by Frank Capra.
Dec 13	Buys 10 percent of Los Angeles Rams football team.
for	The <u>Downbeat</u> poll for 1949 places Bing in a tie for third with Mel Torme as favorite male vocalists.

1950

Jan 9	The Golf Writers Association votes Bing the year's outstanding contributor to golf, awarding him the Richardson Trophy.
	Films <u>Mr. Music</u>; thinks the title presumptuous.
Mar	Has an appendectomy in Santa Monica. Attends his bon voyage party in Hollywood, which Dixie avoids.
Apr 1	Spends the day in Front Royal, Virginia, celebrating "Bing Crosby Day." Helps endow their baseball stadium and premieres <u>Riding High</u>.
Apr 14	Arrives at Cherbourg.
May 8	Attorney John O'Melveny and brother Larry admit that Bing's marriage is "strained."
May 22	Plays in the British Amateur Open Golf Tournament, St. Andrews, Scotland, in terrible weather. He is eliminated in the first round.
Jun 20	Returns to Holmby Hills.
Jun 23	Records "Sam's Song" and "Play a Simple Melody" with Gary. The first becomes Bing's 21st gold record.
Sep 5	Bing and his four sons record <u>A Crosby Christmas</u>.
Oct 4	Bing's father dies at age 79.
Dec 20	<u>Mr. Music</u> is released.

1951

Mar 21	Has surgery for a kidney stone.
	Tries for the last time to spank Gary with a cane.
May 2	Dixie celebrates Bing's "fiftieth" birthday in southern France while Bing is fishing in Idaho.
Jun 29	<u>Here Comes the Groom</u> is released, directed by Frank Capra. The song "In the Cool, Cool, Cool of the Evening" wins an Oscar.
Summer	Gary's radio program replaces Bing's for the summer.
Jul 30	Attends the world premiere of <u>Here Comes the Groom</u> at Elko, Nevada.
Sep	Appears in <u>Angels in the Outfield</u>, a baseball film shot at the Pittsburgh Pirates ballpark.
Sep 29	Takes Dixie to the Cocoanut Grove for their 21st wedding anniversary.
Nov	Films <u>Just for You</u>.

1952

Jan   Has a cameo in Hope's <u>Son of Paleface</u>.
Apr   Signs for <u>Little Boy Lost</u> while filming <u>Road to</u>
            <u>Bali</u>. Bing and Hope have a cameo in Cecil B. DeMille's
            <u>The Greatest Show on Earth</u> and in the Martin and Lewis
            film <u>Scared Stiff</u>.
May 2   Dixie gives a surprise birthday party for Bing.
Jun 18   Dixie has exploratory surgery, with the patholo-
            gist finding terminal ovarian cancer.
Jun 21   Joins Bob Hope to host a telethon to help finance
            the American Olympic team, Bing's second TV show.
Jun 25   Concludes his Wednesday "Chesterfield" radio
            program, and Dixie goes home.
Aug   Filming <u>Road to Bali</u> is completed.
Sep 18   Arrives at Plymouth, England, by ship.
Sep 22   Flies to Paris to film <u>Little Boy Lost</u>. Later
            receives a letter stating that Dixie is dying.
Oct 4   Returns to Dixie awaiting him at the Los Angeles
            Union Station.
Oct 7   <u>Just for You</u> is released.
Oct 9   Commences his new transcribed radio program for
            General Electric, still on CBS but now on Thursdays.
Nov 1   Dixie Lee Crosby dies at 9:50 a.m.
Nov 3   Dixie is interred in the Crosby plot, Holy Cross
            Cemetery. The funeral is upset by the media. Kate
            moves in to take over at the home in Holmby Hills.
            With his autobiography at the publisher, Bing
            writes a chapter that eulogizes Dixie.

1953

Jan   Attends but does not perform at his 13th annual
            golf tournament.
Jan 29   Broadcasts from Palm Springs for the next 15
            weeks, except once from Hollywood.
Feb   Films interior scenes at Paramount to complete
            <u>Little Boy Lost</u> and meets Kathryn Grandstaff, age 19.
May 21   Begins broadcasting from Paris for seven weeks.
Jul   Bing and Lindsay return home.
Jul 23   Begins selling his 65 racehorses at Hollywood Park
            to raise nearly $1 million for taxes on Dixie's will.
Aug   Begins filming <u>White Christmas</u>.
Sep 21   <u>Little Boy Lost</u> is released.
Oct   Begins filming <u>The Country Girl</u>.
Oct 11   Has an automobile accident in Hollywood.
Dec   Films his first television special.

1954

Jan 3   "The Bing Crosby Show," a 30-minute television
            special, airs on CBS-TV.
Jan   Kathryn interviews Bing for her column.
Mar 21   Frank Sinatra is the radio guest. He returns the
            next week and sings two solos and one duet.
Apr 9   Is evicted from his Paramount bungalow and then
            attends a party at Kathryn's.
            Decca begins assembling a special five-disc col-
            lection of Bing's songs; Bing re-records many and
            comments on each song.
Apr 25   "The Bing Crosby Show" is Bing's second TV spe-
            cial.

May 2   Celebrates his birthday at Kathryn's.
May 30   Concludes his prime-time radio shows that had
   aired for 25 years, 18 as one of the most popular.
Oct 14   White Christmas is released with previews of
   Country Girl.
Oct 31   Proposes to Kathryn at Palm Springs.
Dec 3   Is interviewed by Edward R. Murrow on the "Person
   to Person" show on CBS-TV.
Dec 9   Settles the Oct 1953 automobile accident out of
   court for $100,000.
Dec 16   Country Girl is released.
          The American National Board of Review of Motion
   Pictures votes Bing the Actor of the Year.

1955
Jan   Kathryn phones from New York; Bing suggests a
   wedding for Feb 7 in Carmel.
Jan 17   Has surgery Jan 18 for a kidney stone; Jan 22 he
   has another cystoscopy and delays the wedding.
Mar 30   Escorts Kathryn to the Academy Awards dinner.
Apr   Films Anything Goes and appears in two shorts:
   Bing Presents Oreste and Hollywood Fathers.
May 13   The second wedding date is postponed.
Sep 3   Meets Kathryn's plane at Spokane.
Sep 8   Kathryn flies home, canceling the third wedding
   attempt. Bing writes that there were impediments.
Nov   Films "High Tor" in 12 days for television and
   records his songs on Dec 27.
Dec 24   Hosts a live hour radio special "Christmas Sing
   with Bing Crosby," including eight choirs at the Grand
   Central Station, New York. Kathryn is in Texas.
Dec 27   Records "When You're in Love," "John Barleycorn,"
   and other songs in Los Angeles to reach 21 years with
   Decca.
Dec 31   Offers to marry Kathryn, now on Mar 17.

1956
          Buys the Rising River Ranch in northern Califor-
   nia. Sells the video tape of Bing's electronics divi-
   sion to the Minnesota Mining and Manufacturing Co.
Jan 6   Donates $100,000 toward the Crosby Memorial Li-
   brary at Gonzaga University.
Jan   Has minor eye surgery in Palm Springs and conva-
   lesces beyond Mar 17.
Feb   Filming continues on High Society.
Feb 22   Bing and Grace Kelly record "True Love." The song
   becomes Bing's 22nd gold record.
Mar 10   "High Tor" is broadcast.
Mar 21   Paramount releases Anything Goes, Bing's last film
   for them.
Jul 15   Sings "True Love" live on "The Ed Sullivan Show"
   after returning from a brief trip to England.
Aug 9   M-G-M releases High Society, a blockbuster film.
Sep   Publicity causes Bing to postpone the wedding at
   Spokane. Kathryn soon returns to Hollywood.
Oct 6   Appears as a guest on "You're the Top," a tribute
   to and hosted by Cole Porter.
Dec   Tours the Antilles, Cuba, and the South from New
   Orleans to Aiken, South Carolina, with Phil Harris.

1957
Jan 13   Kathryn refuses to go to dinner with him.
          Films <u>Man on Fire</u>.
          Buys two radio stations and builds a new home in
          Palm Desert.
May   Golfs again in the British Amateur Open but fails
          to qualify.
Jun   Wins the French golf championship.
Jun 23   Writes the U.S. Senate that much radio music is
          "so much trash" and blames pressure by Broadcast Music,
          Inc. (BMI), the rival of ASCAP.
Jul 24   Obtains Kathryn's unlisted number by pretending he
          needs her deposition in a law suit.
Aug 22   <u>Man on Fire</u> is released.
Sep 22   Kathryn, returning from Spain, rejects Bing.
Oct 13   Hosts "The Edsel Show."
Oct 22   Writes Kathryn, offering to "marry you--any time,
          any place you wish."
Oct 24   They wed in Las Vegas and fly to Palm Desert.
Oct 28   Kathryn returns alone Holmby Hills; Bing has a
          golf game in Palm Springs.
          Buys 5.5 % interest in the Detroit Tigers baseball
          team, keeping his 20 % interest in the Pirates.
Nov 3   Goes to Spokane for the dedication Nov 4 of the
          $700,000 Bing Crosby Memorial Library at Gonzaga.
          Guests on Sinatra's Christmas television show.

1958
Jan   The Crosby tournament is televised for the first
          time, and Billy Casper wins for his first time.
May 4   Denny marries a Las Vegas showgirl.
Jun   Signs a five-year contract with ABC to star in ten
          TV shows and to produce another ten for $2 million.
Aug 8   Drives Kathryn to Queen of Angels Hospital, where
          she gives birth to Harry Lillis III two months early.
Oct   Begins another 15-minute daily radio series, "The
          Ford Radio Show." It lasts till 1962.
Nov 17   Sells his Nevada ranch for more than $1 million.
Dec   Begins playing a priest in <u>Say One for Me</u>, pro-
          duced in four months by Bing for 20th Century-Fox.

1959
Jan 16   The Crosby Pro-Am commences; Kathryn learns she is
          pregnant again.
Feb   Completes filming <u>Say One for Me</u> and produces his
          own television special.
Mar 31   Gives an interview, saying he failed his boys "by
          giving them too much work and discipline, too much
          money, and too little time and attention."
Jun 19   <u>Say One for Me</u> is released.
Sep 14   Kathryn gives birth to Mary Frances.
Oct 16   The Crosby Boys play at the Moulin Rouge in Holly-
          wood and Bing and the boys reconcile. Later the Crosby
          Boys fight among themselves in Montreal.

1960
Feb 1   Begins filming <u>High Time</u>; sings "The Second Time
          Around," which is nominated for an Oscar.
Feb 28   Bing's and Rosemary Clooney's 20-minute daily

radio show premieres on CBS at 11:40 a.m.
Mar 16   Appears in New York on Perry Como's "Kraft Music
           Hall" show on NBC.
           Takes Kathryn to New York, Florida, and Jamaica
           for golf; they meet William Paley and Lillian Hellman.
Apr 1   Takes Kathryn to the Master's Golf Tournament.
           Learns he has bursitis in both shoulders.
Jun 9   Receives from the Hollywood Chamber of Commerce a
           platinum record of "White Christmas" on a plaque that
           notes he has sold more than 200 million records.
Jun 15   Completes <u>High Time</u> and films cameos in <u>Let's Make
           Love</u> and <u>Pepe</u>, completing three films on one day.
Jul   Rides as the Grand Marshal of the Calgary Stampede
           parade.
Aug 16   <u>High Time</u> is released.
           Goes with Kathryn to London.
Sep 2   Goes to the Olympic Games in Rome; discovers the
           song "Domenica" and writes English lyrics. Bing has
           his first audience with the Pope, John XXIII.
Sep 12   Visits Sienna; then Florence, and Venice Sep 16.
Sep 28   Wins the Invitational Golf Tournament at Mitter-
           sill, Austria, and goes to Paris.

1961
Mar 31   Golfs in Palm Beach, Florida, with President
           Kennedy, Kennedy's father, and Chris Dunphy.
May 1   Decides to build a home at Las Cruces in Baja
           California and buys a house there for an orphanage.
Jul   Pays for treatment for Gary's alcoholism, and the
           son stops drinking.
Jul 17   Leaves for filming in England; sends for Kathryn
           and Harry Aug 3.
Aug 2   Bing and Bob Hope begin filming <u>Road to Hong Kong</u>
           with Joan Collins at the Shepperton Studios in England.
           Aug 27   Golfs with Joseph Kennedy in Spain.
Oct 29   Kathryn gives birth in Los Angeles to Nathaniel
           Patrick while Bing is in England.
Dec 25   Has an attack in Pebble Beach of kidney stones and
           is hospitalized; then flies to an L.A. hospital.

1962
Jan 4   Has surgery on one kidney for four stones.
Mar 22   President Kennedy arrives at Bing's Palm Desert
           home, staying till Mar 25. Kennedy chooses Bing's home
           later for a second stay of a week.
Apr 3   <u>The Road to Hong Kong</u> is released in Britain.
Jun 22   Returns from Las Cruces and soon takes Kathryn and
           children to Kauai, Hawaii, meeting John Wayne.
Jun 27   <u>The Road to Hong Kong</u> is released in America.
Jul 29   Goes alone to Biarritz, France; Kathryn, Mary,
           Harry, and Kathryn's mother fly there Aug 9. The party
           goes to Monaco and visits with Princess Grace and
           Prince Rainier.
Sep 28   The daily radio program of Bing and Clooney ends.
Oct 14   Goes to St. John's Hospital with kidney stones.
Dec 24   The TV Christmas special is the first program ABC
           broadcasts in color.

1963

Golfs at Palm Springs and in the Hawaiian Open;
does a TV special with Mary Martin.

Jan 29   Goes to St. John's Hospital for surgery for kidney
stones.

Philip commits Lindsay to Santa Monica Hospital
for psychiatric observation. Bing flees to Las Cruces.

Mar 22   Buys a 60-foot fishing boat called <u>True Love</u>.

Jul   Flies with Bud Boyd to Iceland for Atlantic salmon
fishing for ABC's "American Sportsman."

Goes to Ohio to see Kathryn in a play and sells
the Holmby Hills house for $250,000.

Fall   Kate suffers a severe stroke. Tapes the premiere
of "The Hollywood Palace."

Oct 29   Records a dozen songs and on Oct 31 in Nashville,
Tennessee, for an album of country music.

Nov 29   Performs "Don't Be a Do Badder" at Warner Bros.
studio, with Kathryn and the children watching.

Dec 19   Kathryn graduates from nursing school.

1964

Jan 4   "The Hollywood Palace" premieres and Bing enters a
semi-retirement.

Jan   Shows Kathryn the 25-room house in Hillsborough.

Jan 6   Bing's mother dies in Santa Monica, nearly age 91.

Aug 5   <u>Robin and the Seven Hoods</u> is released.

Sep 14   "The Bing Crosby Show," a half-hour situation
comedy, premieres; it lasts one season.

Oct 1   The Crosbys find and soon buy a 14-room Tudor-
style mansion on the other side of Hillsborough.

1965

Mar 10   Hosts "The Grand Award of Sports" live on ABC-TV
from the N.Y. World's Fair. Kathryn is a guest.

Harry and Bing have tonsillectomies, and soon
Kathryn has the surgery too.

Jun 26   Attends a race of his horse Meadow Court and wins
the Irish Derby at The Curragh, Dublin.

Jul   Begins filming <u>Stagecoach</u>, his last major film.

Aug 9   Returns to Hillsborough as filming is delayed.

The couple is unable to go to England to watch
Meadow Court run in the St. Leger at Doncaster, for
Bing has more kidney stones and surgery.

Sep 13   Tapes a "Hollywood Palace" show and has another
kidney stone attack. The cystoscopy fails; Bing rests
for two weeks.

Sep 29   Goes with Kathryn to France to watch Meadow Court
run; the horse comes in seventh on Oct 3. Bing goes to
Madrid.

Dec   Son Harry joins Bing on the Christmas show on "The
Hollywood Palace."

1966

May 9   Has his only recording session of 1966.

June 15   <u>Stagecoach</u> is released.

Jul 13   Brother Everett dies, age 70, in Connecticut.

Sep   The couple goes to England. Bing fishes for
salmon for "The American Sportsman" for ABC-TV.

1967
Sep   Cox Broadcasting Corp. buys Bing Crosby Productions for $2 million in stock.
Oct 31   Has his only recording session for 1967.

1968
           Alan Fisher and his wife briefly leave the Crosbys, bored by the lack of entertaining.
           Has two recording sessions in February, three in March, and two in November for 1968, singing 41 songs.

1969
Feb 17   Goes to New York to receive the Golden Tee Award from the Golf Writers of America.
Apr 25   Bing and Kathryn donate $1 million to the now-defunct Immaculate Heart College in Hollywood.
           Sells his Sunset Boulevard building.
Jun 16   Joins Kathryn, Mary Frances, and Nathaniel for the TV show "Goldilocks."

1970
Feb 7   Hosts the final show of "The Hollywood Palace."
Feb 16   Is in benefit at N.Y. Waldorf-Astoria for the Eisenhower Medical Center; televised on NBC Feb 27.
           Now owns a string of banks and TV stations.
Sep 15   Decca Records awards Bing a platinum record of "Silent Night" on a plaque that notes Bing's sales of more than 300,650,000 records.
Nov 16   Sings four Christmas songs in his only recording date of 1970.
Nov 17   Appears on a BBC TV show for Bob Hope.

1971
Jan 19   "Dr. Cook's Garden" is aired as a TV movie. Bing soon guests on the premiere of "The Pearl Bailey Show."
Mar   Joins four others to offer millions of ransom money for American Prisoners of War in Vietnam.
Jul 6   Serves as a pallbearer at the funeral of Louis Armstrong.
Sep 7   Sings six Christmas songs on this and the next day as his only recordings of 1971.

1972
Jan 12   Serves as the national chairman of the 1972 fund drive of the Arthritis Foundation.
Feb 28   Sings 12 songs, including one for Flip Wilson's TV show, to Mar 1 as his only recordings of 1972.
           Has a cameo role in Hope's <u>Cancel My Reservation</u>, released in September.
May   The couple goes on Bing's eighth African safari.
           Buys an estate at Guadalajara, Mexico, and invests in a real estate.

1973
Jun 8   Sings four songs for his only recordings of 1973.
Sep   Is in Africa with Mary Frances on his 11th safari.
Dec 9   "Bing Crosby's Sun Valley Christmas Show" attains the record audience of 49,270,000.
Dec 25   Dixie's father dies, but Bing is ill and unable to

attend the funeral.

1974
Jan 1   Kathryn drives Bing to the Burlingame Hospital,
           where doctors diagnose pneumonia and discover a rapidly
           growing tumor in his left lung.
Jan 13   Has surgery and two-fifths of his left lung is
           removed. The tumor is a rare fungus.
Jan 26   Goes home to recuperate and stops smoking. Misses
           his golf tournament for the only time.
Feb   Appears as one of the hosts for M-G-M's That's
           Entertainment.
Mar 15   The first Bing Crosby International Classic under
           the Ladies Professional Golf Association occurs at
           Guadalajara.
Oct 17   In his only recording date of 1974, Bing sings two
           songs, one with Johnny Mercer. Days earlier Bing, Ken
           Barnes, and Pete Moore establish the songs for two
           special albums.
Oct 25   Is interviewed with Phil Harris on Kathryn's
           morning TV talk show in San Francisco.
Dec 15   "Christmas with the Bing Crosbys" airs and is very
           popular, rating third of the season.

1975
Jan 16   Has many recording sessions from Jan 16 to Sep 15.
Feb 11   Rejects, like Bob Hope, the terms of the PGA,
           which wants some of the TV revenue from private tourna-
           ments.
Feb 12   Brother Larry, age 80, dies in Los Angeles.
Feb 18   Is in London to record two albums with Barnes.
           Bing sings the next day and regularly to Feb 26.
Jul   Appears as a guest of Dame Vera Lynn on her London
           TV program.
Aug 21   Joins the Mills Brothers Charity Show, a telethon
           that continues the next day.
           Finances and sings for a taped three-hour jazz
           session accompanied by piano.
           Assembles the Bing Crosby and Friends show with
           Kathryn, Rosemary Clooney, and the Joe Bushkin trio,
           which travels for the next two years.

1976
Jan 19   Has many recording sessions this date to Nov 5.
Mar 21   Co-hosts with Liza Minnelli the 90-minute "Bell
           Telephone Jubilee" on NBC.
Apr   Thompson's authorized biography of Bing goes on
           sale in the United States.
May 25   Is hospitalized in Columbus, Ohio, after choking
           on food; withdraws from a golf tournament.
Summer   The stage show appears at the Palladium (Jun 21-
           Jul 4) and several music halls in Scotland and Ireland;
           Kathryn tours Britain with Bing, acting in plays.
           Bing and Rosemary Clooney are guests at Buckingham
           Palace.
Fall   Is among the honored guests at a benefit charity
           ball in Los Angeles for the Thalians.
Dec 3   The 40th Christmas show is televised on CBS.
Dec 6   Gives a solo performance at New York's Avery

Fisher Hall as a benefit for Fordham Prep School.
Dec 7   _Bing Crosby on Broadway_ opens for a two-week run
at the Uris Theater.

1977
Jan 20   The 37th Crosby National Pro-Am Tournament begins
at Pebble Beach, with the final rounds Jan 22-23.
Mar 3   After videotaping a three-hour performance, Bing
falls into the orchestra pit of the Ambassador Audito-
rium, Pasadena, California.
Mar 20   "Bing!," a 90-minute television special, airs on
CBS at 9 ET sponsored by Kraft.
Mar 23   A myelogram reveals a ruptured spinal disc.
Apr 5   Is released from a hospital in Millbrae, CA.
May 31   "Barbara Walters Special" appears on ABC, in which
Bing talks about his children.
Jun 27   Files his last will.
Aug 15   Says he is "still a little limpy" from his acci-
dent and "I'd never retire completely."
Aug 16   Performs at Concord, California, with his family.
Aug 25   Bing and family arrive at Oslo's Fornebu Airport,
Norway, for a performance Aug 27 at Momarkedet.
Sep   Tapes his final Christmas Show in London for CBS.
Sep 12   Begins recording his last album.
Sep 22   The British tour opens at the Guild Hall, Preston,
England, with Bing's voice "still strong."
Sep 26   The concert opens at the Palladium, London.
Oct 4   Sings "Now You Has Jazz" and "Sail Away from
Norway" as his last recordings. Bing is inducted into
the Dancer's Big Band Hall of Fame, Davenport, Iowa.
Oct 8   The show ends at the Palladium; it appears at
Brighton Oct 10.
Oct 13   Goes to Spain for golf and hunting. Lord Lew
Grade announces the film production of _Road to Fountain
of Youth_ with a July starting date.
Oct 14   Friday, Bing Crosby falls unconscious from a
massive heart attack after completing the 18th hole at
La Moraleja Golf Club. He dies en route to the Red
Cross Hospital, Madrid.
Oct 16   Harry III and Fisher claim Bing's body in Spain
and return to Los Angeles that night. Several memorial
services are held around the world.
Oct 17   A private wake is held at a Los Angeles hotel.
Oct 18   Tuesday, before dawn, private funeral services are
held at St. Paul's Church in Westwood. Bing's casket
is lowered beside Dixie's at Holy Cross Cemetery.
Nov 30   "Bing Crosby's Merrie Olde Christmas" is televised
on CBS. It is Bing's 42nd Christmas special.

Discography

ARC: American Record Corp.-Brunswick   BR: Brunswick
CAP: Capital   CL: Clarion   COL: Columbia
DE: Decca   GO: Golden   OK: Okeh
REP: Reprise   UA: United Artists
VEL: Velvetone   VER: Verve   VIC: Victor, RCA
WB: Warner Bros.

The Matrix number follows the label designation.
Rejected means the record was never issued.

As Brian Rust, an authority on discographies, has stated,
matrix, or master, numbers, which are usually inscribed by
hand on the record (not the record number printed on the
label) are important for 78's, which predominated through
1956 (Brian Rust's Guide to Discography, Greenwood [1980],
113). Hence, matrix numbers are often omitted after 1956,
regularly replaced by album numbers in the album listing.
Many masters were leased to other companies for further
releases. For example, 32 Brunswick masters have been
released on 12 other labels. "Home on the Range," recorded
Sept. 27, 1933, was also released by Melotone, Perfect, Banner, Oriole, Okeh, Vocalion, Conqueror, Columbia, Romeo,
Silvertone, and Lucky. The 32 songs were recorded from Apr.
23, 1932 ("Sweet Georgia Brown"), to July 5, 1934 ("Love in
Bloom," "Give Me a Heart to Sing To," "I'm Hummin', I'm
Whistlin'," and "Straight from the Shoulder"). "Sweet
Georgia Brown" and "Love in Bloom" were reissued by Melotone, Perfect, Banner, Oriole, Okeh, Vocalion, Conqueror,
and Romeo; the other three recorded July 5, 1934, were reissued by the same labels except Okeh and Vocalion.
The entry "D" numbers represent recordings, not separate discs. Often recordings on a single day were released
on different records.

Entry and Date
Title   Composers and Lyricists
    Orchestra and Accompaniment   Company and Matrix Number

1926
D1-2. Oct 18
I've Got the Girl   W. Donaldson
    Don Clarke Biltmore Hotel Orchestra   COL W 142785
Don't Somebody Need Somebody A. Lyman, F. Rose
                              COL W 142786 Rejected

D3-4. Dec 22
Wistful and Blue   R. Etting, J. Davidson
    Paul Whiteman Orchestra   VIC BVE 37285
Pretty Lips   W. Donaldson, C. Straight
                              VIC BVE 37286 Rejected

1927
D5. Feb 10
Shanghai Dream Man   B. Davis, H. Akst
    Paul Whiteman Orchestra   VIC BVE 37764

D6. Feb 25
That Saxophone Waltz   J. Mingo, B. Sisk
    Paul Whiteman Orchestra   VIC BVE 38118

D7. Feb 28
Pretty Lips   W. Donaldson, C. Straight
    Paul Whiteman Orchestra   VIC BVE 38124

D8. Mar 3
I'm Coming, Virginia   W.M. Cook, D. Heywood
    Paul Whiteman Orchestra   VIC BVE 38135 Rejected

D9. Mar 7
Muddy Water   P. DeRose, J. Trent,
                                  H. Richman
    Paul Whiteman Orchestra   VIC BVE 38143

D10-12. Apr 29
I'm Coming, Virginia   W.M. Cook, D. Heywood
    Paul Whiteman Orchestra   VIC BVE 38135
Victor Test Medley   Unknown
    Paul Whiteman's Rhythm Boys   VIC Unknown
Side by Side   H. Woods
    Paul Whiteman Orchestra   VIC BVE 38378

D13. May 6
Missouri Waltz   J.R. Shannon, F.K. Logan
    Paul Whiteman Orchestra   VIC BVE 38392 Rejected

D14. May 9
I'm in Love Again   C. Porter
    Paul Whiteman Orchestra   VIC BVE 38394

D15. May 24
Magnolia   B.G. DeSylva, R. Henderson,
                                  L. Brown
    Paul Whiteman Orchestra   VIC BVE 38779

D16-17. Jun 20
Mississippi Mud/I Left My Sugar Standing in the Rain
                    H. Barris, J. Cavanaugh, S. Fain, I. Kahal
     Paul Whiteman's Rhythm Boys   VIC BVE 39271
Sweet Li'l/Ain't She Sweet?   H. Barris, J.Yellen, M. Ager
                                        VIC BVE 39272

D18. Jul 6
My Blue Heaven   W. Donaldson, G. Whiting
     Paul Whiteman Orchestra   VIC BVE 39627

D19. Aug 16
The Five Step   B.G. DeSylva, R. Henderson, L. Brown
     Paul Whiteman Orchestra   VIC BVE 39569

D20. Aug 17
Ooh! Maybe It's You
     Paul Whiteman Orchestra   VIC BVE 39572 Rejected

D21. Aug 19
The Calinda   H. Hupfeld
     Paul Whiteman Orchestra   VIC BVE 39575

D22. Aug 20
It Won't Be Long Now   B.G. DeSylva, R. Henderson, L. Brown
     Paul Whiteman Orchestra   VIC BVE 39577

D23. Aug 22
Ooh! Maybe It's You
     Paul Whiteman Orchestra   VIC BVE 39572

D24. Sep 21
Missouri Waltz   J.R. Shannon, F.K. Logan
     Paul Whiteman Orchestra   VIC BVE 38392

D25. Nov 11
That's Grandma   B. Crosby, H. Barris, J. Cavanaugh
     Paul Whiteman's Rhythm Boys   VIC BVE 40846

D26-27. Nov 17
Miss Annabelle Lee   S. Clare, H. Richman, L. Pollack
     Paul Whiteman's Rhythm Boys   VIC BVE 40894
     Note: Crosby may have sung for the following selection
     by a group from Paul Whiteman's Orchestra. Hoagy
     Carmichael was the scheduled vocalist, but Whiteman
     asked Crosby to be present to render possible assist-
     ance, and he may have sung for one of the alternate
     takes (2, 3, 5, 6, or 7).
Washboard Blues   H. Carmichael
     Arranged by Challis   VIC BVE 40901

D28. Nov 23
Changes   W. Donaldson
     Paul Whiteman Orchestra   VIC BVE 40937

D29. Nov 25
Mary (What Are You Waiting For?) W. Donaldson
     Paul Whiteman Orchestra   VIC BVE 40945

1928
D30. Jan 4
Ramona   R. Gilbert, M. Wayne
    Paul Whiteman Orchestra   VIC BVE 41293

D31. Jan 11
Ol' Man River   O. Hammerstein II, J. Kern
    Paul Whiteman Orchestra   VIC BVE 41607

D32. Jan 12
From Monday On   H. Barris, B. Crosby
    Paul Whiteman's Rhythm Boys   VIC BVE 41612

D33-34. Jan 20
From Monday On   H. Barris, B. Crosby
    Frank Trumbauer Orchestra   OK W 400033
Mississippi Mud   H. Barris
                                    OK W 400034

D35. Jan 27
Make Believe   O. Hammerstein II, J. Kern
    Paul Whiteman Orchestra   VIC BVE 41470

D36. Feb 7
Poor Butterfly   E. Golden, R. Hubbell
    Paul Whiteman Orchestra   VIC BVE 41680

D37. Feb 8
There Ain't No Sweet Man That's Worth the Salt of My Tears
                                    F. Fisher
    Paul Whiteman Orchestra   VIC BVE 41681

D38-39. Feb 13
Sunshine   I. Berlin
    Paul Whiteman Orchestra   VIC BVE 41688
From Monday On   H. Barris, B. Crosby
                                    VIC BVE 41689

D40. Feb 18
Mississippi Mud   H. Barris
    Paul Whiteman Orchestra   VIC BVE 41696

D41-42. Feb 28
High Water   J.K. Brennan, M. McCurdy
    Paul Whiteman Orchestra   VIC CVE 43117
From Monday On   H. Barris, B. Crosby
                                    VIC BVE 41689

D43. Mar 1
What Price Lyrics?   B. Crosby, H. Barris, M. Malneck
    Paul Whiteman's Rhythm Boys   VIC BVE 43121

D44. Mar 12
I'm Wingin' Home   B. Russell, H. Tobias
    Paul Whiteman Orchestra   VIC BVE 43140

D45. Mar 14
Metropolis   F. Grofe
    Paul Whiteman Orchestra   VIC CVE 43143

D46. Mar 15
Lovable   R. Holmes, S. Simons, R. Whiting
        Paul Whiteman Orchestra   VIC BVE 43145

D47. Mar 16
March of the Musketeers   R. Friml, C. Grey, P.G. Wodehouse
        Paul Whiteman Orchestra   VIC BVE 43148

D48. Apr 21
I'm Afraid of You   E. Davis, L. Daly, A. Gottler
        Paul Whiteman Orchestra   VIC BVE 43660

D50-52. Apr 22
My Pet   J. Yellen, M. Ager
        Paul Whiteman Orchestra   VIC BVW 43662
It Was the Dawn of Love   J.F. Coots, L. Davis
                                         VIC BVE 43663
Dancing Shadows   E. Golden
                                         VIC BVE43664

D53. Apr 23
Louisiana   A. Razaf, B. Schafer, J. Johnson
        Paul Whiteman Orchestra   VIC BVE 43667

D54-55. Apr 24
Grieving   W. Aztell
        Paul Whiteman Orchestra   VIC BVE 43668
Do I Hear You Saying?   R. Rodgers, L. Hart
                                         VIC BVE 43669

D56. Apr 25
You Took Advantage of Me   R. Rodgers, L. Hart
        Paul Whiteman Orchestra   VIC BVE 43760

D57-58. May 12
La Paloma   S. Yradier
        Paul Whiteman Orchestra   COL W 98533 Rejected
La Golondrina (The Swallow)   N. Serradell
                                         Col W 98534

D59. May 13
Evening Star   R. Turk, F. Ahlert
        Paul Whiteman Orchestra   COL W 146250 Rejected

D60. May 17
C-O-N-S-T-A-N-T-I-N-O-P-L-E
                        B.G. DeSylva, R. Henderson, L. Brown
        Paul Whiteman Orchestra   COL W 146291

D61-63. May 21
La Paloma   S. Yradier
        Paul Whiteman Orchestra   COL W 98533
Evening Star   R. Turk, F. Ahlert
                                         COL W 145250
'Tain't So, Honey, 'Tain't So W. Robinson
                                         COL W 146316 Rejected

D64-65. May 22
Get Out and Get Under the Moon   C. Tobias, L. Shay, W.Jerome

Paul Whiteman Orchestra   COL W 146319
I'd Rather Cry Over You   D. Dougherty, P. Ponce, J. Yellen
                                 COL W 146320 Rejected

D66. May 23
'Tain't So, Honey, 'Tain't So W. Robinson
    Paul Whiteman Orchestra   COL W 145316 Rejected

D67-68. May 25
Wa Da Da   H. Barris, J. Cavanaugh
    Paul Whiteman's Rhythm Boys   COL W 146336 Rejected
That's Grandma   B. Crosby, H. Barris, J. Cavanaugh
                                 COL W 146344 Rejected

D69-70. Jun 10
'Tain't So, Honey, 'Tain't So W. Robinson
    Paul Whiteman Orchestra   COL W 146316
I'd Rather Cry Over You   D. Dougherty, P. Ponce, J. Yellen
                                 COL W 146320

D71-74A. June 17
I'm on a Crest of a Wave
                    B.G. DeSylva, R. Henderson, L. Brown
    Paul Whiteman Orchestra   COL W 146541
That's My Weakness Now   B. Green, S. Stept
                                 COL W 146542
Georgie Porgie   B. Mayerl, G. Paul
                                 COL W 146543
If You Don't Love Me   J. Yellen, M. Ager
                                 COL W 146545
Lonesome in the Moonlight   A. Baer, B. Russell
                                 COL W 146546

D75-76. Jun 18
Because My Baby Don't Mean 'Maybe' Now W. Donaldson
    Paul Whiteman Orchestra   COL W 146549
Out o' Town Gal   W. Donaldson
                                 COL W 146550

D77-78. Jun 19
Wa Da Da   H. Barris, J. Cavanaugh
    Paul Whiteman's Rhythm Boys   COL W 146336
That's Grandma   B. Crosby, H. Barris, J. Cavanaugh
                                 COL W 146344

D79-80A. Sep 19   Christmas Melodies, Parts 1, 2
Silent Night, Holy Night   F. Gruber, J. Mohr
    Paul Whiteman Orchestra   COL W 98585
Noel/<u>Adeste Fideles</u>   Traditional
                                 COL W 98586

D81-82. Nov 10
My Suppressed Desire   N. Miller, C. Conn
    Paul Whiteman's Rhythm Boys   COL W 147500
Rhythm King   J. Trent, J. Hoover, J. Robinson
                                 COL W 147501

D83. Dec 11
Makin' Whoopee   W. Donaldson, G. Kahn

Paul Whiteman Orchestra   COL W 147540 Rejected

D84. Dec 12
Sweet Dreams   J. Yellen, M. Ager
      Paul Whiteman Orchestra   COL W 147535 Rejected

D85. Dec 14
Let's Do It, Let's Fall in Love C. Porter
      Paul Whiteman Orchestra   COL W 147536 Rejected

D86-87. Dec 22
Let's Do It, Let's Fall in Love C. Porter
      Paul Whiteman Orchestra   COL W 147536
Makin' Whoopee   W. Donaldson, G. Kahn
                                 COL W 147540

D88-89. Dec 28
I'll Get By   R. Turk, F. Ahlert
      The Ipana Troubadours   COL W 147545
The Rose of Mandalay   T. Koehler, F. Magine
                                 COL W 147546

1929
D90. Jan 3
Sweet Dreams   J. Yellen, M. Ager
      Paul Whiteman Orchestra   COL W 147535 Rejected

D91. Jan 11
My Angeline   L.W. Gilbert, M. Wayne
      Paul Whiteman Orchestra   COL W 147751

D92-95. Jan 25
So the Bluebirds and the Blackbirds Got Together
                                 H. Barris, B. Mohl
      Paul Whiteman's Rhythm Boys   COL W 147888 Rejected
I'm Crazy Over You   A. Sherman, A. Lewis
      Sam Lanin Famous Players   OK W 401555
Susianna   S. Williams
                                 OK W 401556
If I Had You   J. Campbell, R. Connelly, T. Shapiro
                                 OK W 401557

D96-98. Jan 26
The Spell of the Blues   A. Johnston, H. Ruby, D. Dreyer
      Dorsey Brothers Orchestra   OK W 401560
Let's Do It, Let's Fall in Love C. Porter
                                 OK W 401561
My Kinda Love   J. Trent, L. Alter
                                 OK W 401562

D99-100. Feb 28
My Angeline   L. Gilbert, M. Wayne
      Paul Whiteman Orchestra   COL W 147751 Rejected
Coquette   I. Berlin
                                 COL W 148013

D101. Mar 7
My Angeline   L. Gilbert, M. Wayne
      Paul Whiteman Orchestra   COL W 147751

D102-03. Mar 14
My Kinda Love   J. Trent, L. Alter
    Bing Crosby (solo artist)   COL W 148073
Till We Meet   T. FioRito
                                 COL W 148074

D104. Mar 15
Louise   L. Robin, R.A. Whiting
    Paul Whiteman Orchestra   COL W 148086

D105-06. Apr 5
Little Pal   B.G. DeSylva, R. Henderson, L. Brown
    Paul Whiteman Orchestra   COL W 148184 Rejected
I'm in Seventh Heaven B.G. DeSylva, R. Henderson, L. Brown
                                 COL W 148183

D107-08. Apr 10
So the Bluebirds and the Blackbirds Got Together
                                 H. Barris, B. Mohl
    Paul Whiteman's Rhythm Boys   COL W 147888
Louise   L. Robin, R.A. Whiting
                                 COL W 148428

D109. Apr 25
Little Pal   B.G. DeSylva, R. Henderson, L. Brown
    Paul Whiteman Orchestra   COL W 148184

D110. May 3
Reachin' for Someone   W. Donaldson, E. Leslie
    Paul Whiteman Orchestra   COL W 148408

D111-13. May 4
Oh! Miss Hannah   J. Deppen, T. Hollingsworth
    Paul Whiteman Orchestra   COL W 148421
Your Mother and Mine   J. Goodwin, G. Edwards
                                 COL W 148422 Rejected
Orange Blossom Time   J. Goodwin, G. Edwards
                                 COL W 148423

D114-15. May 16
Your Mother and Mine   J. Goodwin, G. Edwards
    Paul Whiteman Orchestra   COL W 148422
S'posin'   P. Denniker, A. Razaf
                                 COL W 148544

D116-17. May 24
I Kiss Your Hand, Madame   S.M. Lewis, J. Young,
    Bing Crosby   F. Rotter, R. Erwin,
                                 COL W 148619
Baby, Oh Where Can You Be?   T. Koehler, F. Magine
                                 COL W 148620

D118-19. Sep 6
At Twilight   W. Tracey, M. Pinkard
    Paul Whiteman Orchestra   COL W 148985
Waiting at the End of the Road   I. Berlin
                                 COL W 148986 Rejected

D120-21. Sep 13
Waiting at the End of the Road I. Berlin
      Paul Whiteman Orchestra   COL W 148986
When You're Counting the Stars Alone
                        B. Russell, V. Rose, J. Murray
                              COL W 149005

D122-23. Sep 27
Can't We Be Friends?   K. Swift, P. James
      Bing Crosby   COL W 149066
Gay Love   S. Clare, O. Levant
                              COL W 149067

D124-25. Oct 9
Without a Song   B. Rose, E. Eliscu, V. Youmans
      Paul Whiteman Orchestra   COL W 149125
Great Day   B. Rose, E. Eliscu, V. Youmans
                              COL W 149124

D126-27. Oct 16
I'm a Dreamer, Aren't We All?
                        B.G. DeSylva, R. Henderson, L. Brown
      Paul Whiteman Orchestra   COL W 149149
If I Had a Talking Picture of You
                        B.G. DeSylva, R. Henderson, L. Brown
                              COL W 149150

D128-31. Oct 18
A Bundle of Old Love Letters A. Freed, N.H. Brown
      Paul Whiteman Orchestra   COL W 149158
After You've Gone   H. Creamer, J.T. Layton
                              COL W 149159
Moonlight and Roses
            B. Black, E. Lemare, M. Moret, C. Daniels
                              COL W 91790
Southern Medley   Traditional
                              COL W 91791
            (Only ten records were pressed of "Moonlight and
      Roses/Southern Medley." Columbia released a Southern
      Medley album in early 1978, in which Bing solos on two
      songs: "Old Black Joe" and "Carry Me Back to Old Vir-
      ginny." He was in the four-voice chorus on "Moonlight"
      [Zwisohn 59].)

D132. Oct 31
A Bundle of Old Love Letters A. Freed, N.H. Brown
      Paul Whiteman Orchestra   COL W 149379

1930
D133. Feb 10
Happy Feet   J. Yellen, M. Ager
      Paul Whiteman Orchestra   COL W 149810

D134. Mar 21
Song of the Dawn   J. Yellen, M. Ager
      Paul Whiteman Orchestra   COL W 149822

D135. Mar 22
Livin' in the Sunlight, Lovin' in the Moonlight

```
                                  A. Lewis, A. Sherman
         Paul Whiteman Orchestra       COL W 149824

D136-38. Mar 23
A Bench in the Park               J. Yellen, M. Ager
   Paul Whiteman Orchestra             COL W 149825
I Like to Do Things for You       J. Yellen, M. Ager
                                       COL W 149826
You Brought a New Kind of Love to Me
                                  S. Fain, I. Kahal, P. Norman
                                       COL W 149827

D139-40. May 23
A Bench in the Park               J. Yellen, M. Ager
   Paul Whiteman's Rhythm Boys     COL W 149840
Everything's Agreed Upon          B. Crosby, H. Barris
                                       COL W 149841 Rejected

D141. Aug 26
Three Little Words                B. Kalmar, H. Ruby
   Duke Ellington Cotton Club Orchestra   VIC PVBE 61013

D142-43. Oct 29
Fool Me Some More                 P. DeRose, H. Gillespie
   Gus Arnheim Cocoanut Grove Orchestra   VIC PBVE 61047
        (Russ Columbo on violin, Fred MacMurray on tenor
   sax and clarinet.  Columbo remained through Jan 19,
   1931.  MacMurray remained through May 1, 1931.)
It Must Be True                   H. Barris, G. Arnheim, G. Clifford
                                       VIC PBVE 61048

D144. Nov 20
Them There Eyes              M. Pinkard, W. Tracey, D. Tauber
   Gus Arnheim Cocoanut Grove Orchestra   VIC PBVE 61057

D145. Nov 25
The Little Things in Life    I. Berlin
   Gus Arnheim Cocoanut Grove Orchestra   VIC PBVE 61058

1931
D146. Jan 19
I Surrender, Dear                 H. Barris, G. Clifford
   Gus Arnheim Cocoanut Grove Orchestra   VIC PBVE 61068

D147-50. Mar 2
Thanks to You                     G. Clarke, P. Wendling
   Gus Arnheim Cocoanut Grove Orchestra   VIC PBVE 61075
One More Time              B.G. DeSylva, R. Henderson, L. Brown
                                       VIC PBVE 61076
Wrap Your Troubles in Dreams  H. Barris, T. Koehler, B. Mohl
                                       VIC PBVE 61077
Just a Gigolo                I. Caesar, J. Brammer, L. Casucci
                                       VIC PBVE 61078

D151-52. Mar 30
Out of Nowhere                    J. Green, E. Heyman
   Bing Crosby (Studio Orchestra)  BR LA 983
If You Should Ever Need Me    A. Dubin, Joe Burke
                                       BR LA 984
```

D153-54. May 1
Ho Hum!   E. Heyman, D. Suesse
        Gus Arnheim Cocoanut Grove Orchestra .VIC PVBE 61091
I'm Gonna Get You
                G. Arnheim, J. Lemare, H. Tobias, C. Daniels
                                 VIC PBVE 61092

D155-56. May 4
Were You Sincere?   V. Rose, J. Meskill
        Victor Young Orchestra   BR LA 1036
Just One More Chance   A. Johnston, S. Coslow
                                 BR LA 1037

D157-60. Jun 12
I'm Through with Love   G. Kahn, M. Malneck, F. Livingston
        Bing Crosby and Studio Orchestra BR LA 1024
Many Happy Returns of the Day A. Dubin, Joe Burke
                                 BR LA 1042
I Found a Million Dollar Baby H. Warren, B. Rose, M. Dixon
                                 BR LA 1043
How the Time Can Fly   W. Donaldson
                                 BR LA 1044 Rejected

D161. Jun 24
At Your Command   B. Crosby, H. Barris, H. Tobias
        Bing Crosby   BR LA 1051

D162-64. Aug 19
I Apologize   A. Goodhart, E. Nelson, A. Hoffman
        Brunswick Studio Orchestra   BR E 37085
Dancing in the Dark   H. Dietz, A. Schwartz
                                 BR E 37086
Stardust   H. Carmichael, M. Parish
                                 BR E 37087

D165-66. Sept 2
Just One More Chance   A. Johnston, S. Coslow
        CBS Studio Orchestra   VIC PBS 68309
I'm Through with Love   G. Kahn, M. Malneck,
                                 VIC PBS 68311

D167. Sept 11
Sweet and Lovely
                H. Tobias, G. Arnheim, J. Lemare, C. Daniels
        Studio Orchestra   BR E 37156

D168-69. Oct 6
Now That You're Gone   G. Kahn, T. FioRito
        Victor Young Orchestra   BR E 37281
A Faded Summer Love   P. Baxter
                                 BR E 37282

D170-71. Oct 8
Too Late   S. Lewis, J. Young
        Victor Young Orchestra   BR E 37284
Goodnight, Sweetheart   R. Noble, J. Campbell, R. Connelly
                                 BR E 37285

D172-73 Oct 25
    Gems from <u>George White's Scandals</u> Parts 1 and 2
The Thrill Has Gone   L. Brown, B. Henderson
    Victor Young Orchestra   BR E 37320
Life Is Just a Bowl of Cherries L. Brown, B. Henderson
                                     BR E 37321

D174. Nov 23
Where the Blue of the Night (Meets the Gold of the Day)
                        R. Turk, B. Crosby, F. Ahlert
    Brunswick Studio Orchestra   BR E 37373

D175. Dec 3
I'm Sorry Dear   A. Weeks, H. Tobias, Lady J. Scott
    Studio Orchestra   BR E 37440

D176. Dec 16
Dinah   S. Lewis, J. Young, H. Akst
    Bing Crosby and the Mills Brothers BR E 37467

D177-78. Dec 21
Can't We Talk it Over?   N. Washington, V. Young
    Paramount Theatre Organ   BR E 37474
I Found You   R. Noble, J. Campbell, R. Connelly
                                     BR E 37525

1932
D179. Jan 21
Snuggled on Your Shoulder (Cuddled in Your Arms)
                        J. Young, C. Lombardo
    Bennie Krueger Orchestra   BR B 11163

D180. Feb 11
St. Louis Blues   W.C. Handy
    Duke Ellington Famous Orchestra ARC BX 11263

D181-82. Feb 16
Starlight (Help Me Find the One I Love) J. Young, B. Petkere
    Studio Orchestra   BR B 11291
How Long Will It Last?   J. Meyer, M. Lief
                                     BR B 11292

D183-84. Feb 23
Love, You Funny Thing   F. Ahlert, R. Turk
    Studio Orchestra   BR B 11330
My Woman   B. Crosby, I. Wallman, M. Wartell
                                     BR B 11331

D185. Feb 29
Shine   L. Brown, F. Dabney, C. Mack
    Bing Crosby and the Mills Brothers BR B 11376

D186-87. March 8
    Face the Music Medley
Soft Lights and Sweet Music I. Berlin
    Victor Young Brunswick Orchestra BR BX 11416
Shadows on the Window   V. Young, N. Washington
                                     BR B 11417

D188-89. Mar 15
Paradise   N.H. Brown, G. Clifford
    Studio Orchestra   BR B 11480
You're Still in My Heart   J. Yellen, D. Dougherty
                                      BR B 11481

D190. Apr 13
Lawd, You Made the Night Too Long S. Lewis, V. Young
    Don Redman Orchestra   BR BX 11701

D191-93. Apr 23
Sweet Georgia Brown   B. Bernie, M. Pinkard, K. Casey
    Isham Jones Orchestra   BR JC 8592
Waltzing in a Dream   B. Crosby, V. Young, N. Washington
                                  BR JC 8593
Happy-Go-Lucky You (and Broken Hearted Me)
                    J. Murray, A. Goodhart, A. Hoffman
                                  BR JC 8594

D194-95. Apr 24
Lazy Day   G. and G.C. Kahn, G. Martin, G. Posford
    Isham Jones Orchestra   BR JC 8596
Let's Try Again   C. Newman, I. Jones
                                  BR JC 8597

D196-97. May 25
Cabin in the Cotton   M. Parish, F. Perkins
    Lennie Hayton Orchestra   BR JC 8635
With Summer Coming On   F. Ahlert, R. Turk
                                      BR JC 8636

D198-99. May 26
Love Me Tonight   B. Crosby, V. Young, N. Washington
    Studio Orchestra   BR JC 8640
Some of These Days   S. Brooks
                                      BR JC 8641

D200. Sept 16
Please   L. Robin, R. Rainger
    Anson Weeks Orchestra   BR JC SF 11

D201-03. Oct 14
How Deep Is the Ocean   I. Berlin
    Studio Orchestra   BR B 12472
Here Lies Love   L. Robin, R. Rainger
                                      BR B 12473
(I Don't Stand) A Ghost of a Chance with You
                    B. Crosby, V. Young, N. Washington
                                      BR B 12474

D204-07. Oct 25
Linger a Little Longer in the Twilight
                    H. Woods, J. Campbell, R. Connelly
    Lennie Hayton Orchestra   BR B 12500
We're a Couple of Soldiers (My Baby and Me) H. Woods
                                      BR B 12501
Brother, Can You Spare a Dime? E.Y. Harburg, J. Gorney,
                                      BR B 12502
Sweet Sue, Just You   W. Harris, V. Young

        Lennie Hayton, piano   BR B 12505
           (This song was written in 1928 for Sue Carol.)

D208-09. Oct 28
Let's Put Out the Lights (and Go to Sleep) H. Hupfeld
        Studio Orchestra   BR B 12510
I'll Follow You   F. Ahlert, R. Turk
                                 BR B 12519

D210-11. Nov 4
Just an Echo in the Valley
                        H. Woods, J. Campbell, R. Connelly
        Studio Orchestra   BR B 12530
           (The above was recorded as a possible replacement
        signature song, but it was used as such only briefly.)
Someday We'll Meet Again   M. Ager, A. Hoffman, A. Goodhart
                                 BR B 12531

D212-13. Dec 9
Street of Dreams   S. Lewis, V. Young
        Studio Orchestra   BR B 12706
It's Within Your Power   M. Gordon, H. Revel
                                 BR B 12707

1933
D214-15. Jan 9
I'm Playing with Fire   I. Berlin
        Studio Orchestra   BR B 12856
Try a Little Tenderness   H. Woods, J. Campbell, R. Connelly
                                 BR B 12857

D216-18. Jan 12
You're Getting to Be a Habit with Me A. Dubin, H. Warren
    Guy Lombardo Royal Canadians BR B 12887
Young and Healthy   A. Dubin, H. Warren
                                 BR B 12888
You're Beautiful Tonight, My Dear C. Lombardo, J. Young
                                 BR B 12889

D219-20. Jan 26
I've Got the World on a String T. Koehler, H. Arlen
    Dorsey Brothers Orchestra   BR B 12991
My Honey's Lovin' Arms   H. Ruby, J. Meyer
    with the Mills Brothers   BR B 12992

D221-22. Feb 9
What Do I Care? It's Home!   R. Turk, H. Smolin
        Studio Orchestra   BR B 13043
You've Got Me Crying Again   C. Newman, I. Jones
                                 BR B 13044

D223-25. Mar 14
Someone Stole Gabriel's Horn
                        N. Washington, E. Hayes, I. Mills
        Studio Orchestra   BR B 13149
Stay on the Right Side of the Road T. Koehler, R. Bloom
                                 BR B 13150
Here Is My Heart   P. Ballard, R. Henderson
                                 BR B 13151 Unissued

D226-29. Jun 9
Learn to Croon   S. Coslow, A. Johnston
    Jimmy Grier Orchestra   BR B 779 Rejected
Moonstruck   S. Coslow, A. Johnston
                                BR B 780
My Love   V. Young, N. Washington
                                BR B 781
I've Got to Pass Your House to Get to My House L. Brown
                                BR B 782

D230-33. Jun 13
Blue Prelude   J. Bishop, G. Jenkins
    Jimmy Grier Orchestra   BR B 791
I Would If I Could But I Can't
                            B. Crosby, M. Parish, L. Grey
                                BR B 792
Learn to Croon   S. Coslow, A. Johnston
                                BR B 793
Shadow Waltz   A. Dubin, H. Warren
                                BR B 794

D234-36. Jun 16
I've Got to Sing a Torch Song A. Dubin, H. Warren
    Jimmy Grier Orchestra   BR B 803
There's a Cabin in the Pines B. Hill
                                BR B 804
Down the Old Ox Road   S. Coslow, A. Johnston
                                BR B 805

D237-40. Aug 27
Thanks   S. Coslow, A. Johnston
    Jimmy Grier Orchestra   BR LA 1
The Day You Came Along   S. Coslow, A. Johnston
                                BR LA 2
I Guess It Had to Be That Way S. Coslow, A. Johnston
                                BR LA 3
Black Moonlight   S. Coslow, A. Johnston
                                BR LA 4

D241-44. Sep 27
*Beautiful Girl   N.H. Brown, A. Freed
    Lennie Hayton Orchestra   BR LA 19
The Last Roundup   B. Hill
                                BR LA 20
*After Sundown   N.H. Brown, A. Freed
                                BR LA 21
Home on the Range   Traditional
                                BR LA 22
    (The two marked songs above were sent to Jack
Kapp, then the recording manager for Brunswick, with
false labels identifying the singer as Bill Williams,
Bing's character in Going Hollywood [1933], and a note
saying the new discovery was willing to sign a contract. Kapp ran to Los Angeles and was very annoyed at
the hoax, but he kept the disc, which an American
collector bought in 1957 [Barnes 109n].)

D245-47. Oct 22
We'll Make Hay While the Sun Shines N.H. Brown, A. Freed

```
              Lennie Hayton Orchestra          BR LA 68
Temptation                              N.H. Brown, A. Freed
                                                 BR LA 69
Our Big Love Scene                      N.H. Brown, A. Freed
                                                 BR LA 70


D248-49. Dec 11
Did You Ever See a Dream Walking?  M. Gordon, H. Revel
       Lennie Hayton Orchestra           BR LA 89
Let's Spend an Evening at Home   H. Barris, A. Freed
                                                 BR LA 90
```

1934
```
D250-53. Feb 25
Love Thy Neighbor                  M. Gordon, H. Revel
    Nat W. Finston Paramount Orchestra  BR LA 134
Once in a Blue Moon                M. Gordon, H. Revel
                                                 BR LA 135
Goodnight, Lovely Little Lady   M. Gordon, H. Revel
                                                 BR LA 136
May I?                             M. Gordon, H. Revel
                                                 BR LA 137


D254-55. Mar 10
Little Dutch Mill                  H. Barris, A. Freed
       Jimmy Grier Orchestra             BR LA 144
Shadows of Love                    A. and M. Kaufman, M. Kippel
                                                 BR LA 145


D256-57. Mar 13
She Reminds Me of You              M. Gordon, H. Revel
       Jimmy Grier Orchestra             BR LA 146
Ridin' Around in the Rain          C. Lombardo, G. Austin
                                                 BR LA 147


D258-61. Jul 5
I'm Hummin', I'm Whistlin', I'm Singin'  M. Gordon, H. Revel
       Irving Aaronson Commanders    BR LA 181
Love in Bloom                      L. Robin, R. Rainger
                                                 BR LA 182
Straight from the Shoulder      M. Gordon, H. Revel
                                                 BR LA 183
Give Me a Heart to Sing To
                        M. Judell, N. Washington, V. Young
                                                 BR LA 184


D262-65. Aug 8
I Love You Truly                   C.J. Bond
       Georgie Stoll Orchestra           DE DLA 6
Just A-Wearyin' for You            C.J. Bond
                                                 DE DLA 7
Let Me Call You Sweetheart      B. Whitson, L. Friedman
                                                 DE DLA 8
Someday, Sweetheart                J. and B. Spikes
                                                 DE DLA 9


D266-69. Oct 5
The Moon Was Yellow (and the Night Was Young)
                                   E. Leslie, F. Ahlert
```

```
        Georgie Stoll Orchestra       DE DLA 64
The Very Thought of You        R. Noble
                               DE DLA 65.
Two Cigarettes in the Dark     P.F. Webster, L. Pollack
                               DE DLA 66
The Sweetheart Waltz           C. Lombardo, M. Drake, W. Kent
                               DE DLA 67


D270-77. Nov 9
With Every Breath I Take       L. Robin, R. Rainger
        Georgie Stoll Orchestra       DE DLA 70
June in January                L. Robin, R. Rainger
                               DE DLA 71
Love Is Just Around the Corner L. Robin, L. Gensler
                               DE DLA 72
Maybe I'm Wrong Again          J. Bennett, J. Trent
                               DE DLA 73
```

Note: The following selections may be unissued takes of Crosby with Georgie Stoll and his Orchestra recorded about November 1934, all from radio broadcasts. The matrix numbers are uncertain:

```
Blame It on My Youth           O. Levant, E. Heyman
                               DE DLA 1158
Clouds                         W. Donaldson, G. Kahn
                               DE DLA 1159
Lullaby of Broadway            A. Dubin, H. Warren
                               DE DLA 1160
Ole Faithful                   M. Carr, J. Kennedy
                               DE DLA 1161
```

1935
```
D278-82. Feb 21
Soon                           R. Rodgers, L. Hart
        Georgie Stoll Orchestra       DE DLA 93
Down By the River              R. Rodgers, L. Hart
                               DE DLA 94
It's Easy to Remember          R. Rodgers, L. Hart
    with the Rhythmettes & Three Shades of Blue
                               DE DLA 95
Swanee River                   S. Foster
    with The Crinoline Choir   DE DLA 96
*Silent Night, Holy Night      F. Gruber, J. Mohr
    with the Crinoline Choir   DE DLA 97
        *Decca White Label Special Pressing
```

```
D283-85. Feb
```
Adeste Fideles/Lift Up Your Hearts/Stabat Mater
```
    Pipe Organ                 DE B 2078
        Decca White Label Special Pressing
        (Recorded, like D282, as a fund-raiser for the St.
Columban Missionary Society.  Commercial releases of
carols D282-283 were recorded later.)
```

```
D286-91. Aug 14
From the Top of Your Head      M. Gordon, H. Revel
    Dorsey Brothers Orchestra         DE 39852
I Wish I Were Aladdin          M. Gordon, H. Revel
                               DE 35853
Takes Two to Make a Bargain    M. Gordon, H. Revel
```

	DE 35854
Two for Tonight	M. Gordon, H. Revel
	DE 35855
Without a Word of Warning	M. Gordon, H. Revel
	DE 35856
I Wished on the Moon	R. Rainger, D. Parker
	DE 35857

D292-96. Nov 12
Red Sails in the Sunset   J. Kennedy, H. Williams, W. Grosz
        Victor Young Orchestra   DE DLA 253
Take Me Back to My Boots and Saddle
                            T. Powell, L. Whitcup, S. Samuels
                                        DE DLA 254
On Treasure Island   Joe Burke, E. Leslie
                                        DE DLA 255
Adeste Fideles   Traditional
                                        DE DLA 256
Silent Night, Holy Night   F. Gruber, J. Mohr
        with the Guardsmen Quartet   DE DLA 261

D297-99. Nov 13
Sailor Beware   L. Robin, R. Whiting
        Georgie Stoll Orchestra   DE DLA 259
My Heart and I   L. Robin, F. Hollander
                                        DE DLA 260
Moonburn   H. Carmichael, E. Heyman
                                        DE DLA 262

1936
D300-04. Mar 24
We'll Rest at the End of the Trail F. Rose, C. Poulton
        Victor Young Orchestra   DE DLA 306
Twilight on the Trail   S. Mitchell, L. Alter
                                        DE DLA 307
The Touch of Your Lips   R. Noble
                                        DE DLA 308
Lovely Lady   T. Koehler, J. McHugh
                                        DE DLA 309
Corrine Corrina   M. Parish, B. Chatman, J. Williams
                                        DE DLA 311

D305-09. Mar 29
Would You?   N.H. Brown, A. Freed
        Victor Young Orchestra   DE DLA 322
Robins and Roses   E. Leslie, Joe Burke
                                        DE DLA 323
I Got Plenty o' Nuttin'   G. and I. Gershwin, D. Heyward
                                        DE DLA 324
It Ain't Necessarily So   G. and I. Gershwin, D. Heyward
                                        DE DLA 325
Robins and Roses (Parody)   E. Leslie, Joe Burke
                                        DE DLA 326
        (The above parody was of Jewish music publishers,
    who dominated the industry; it became a collector's
    item [Barnes 111n].)

D310. Jul 8
Take My Heart   F. Ahlert, V. Young

Victor Young Orchestra   DE DLA 429

D311-12. Jul 14
Empty Saddles
          B. Hill, adapted from a poem by J. Kiern Brennan
     Victor Young Orchestra   DE DLA 436
     with the Guardsman Quartet
Round-Up Lullaby   C. Clark, G. Ross
     Victor Young Orchestra   DE DLA 437

D313-15. Jul 17
I Can't Escape from You   L. Robin, R. Whiting
     Jimmy Dorsey Orchestra   DE DLA 440
The House That Jack Built   L. Robin, F. Hollander
                               DE DLA 441

I'm an Old Cowhand   J. Mercer
                               DE DLA 442

D316-17. Jul 23
Song of the Islands   C. King
     Dick McIntire Harmony Hawaiians DE DLA 452
Aloha Oe (Farewell to Thee)   Queen Liliuokalani
                               DE DLA 453

D318-19. Jul 24
So Do I   J. Burke, A. Johnston
     Georgie Stoll Orchestra   DE DLA 462
Pennies from Heaven   J. Burke, A. Johnston
                               DE DLA 463

D320-21. Jul 29
Let's Call a Heart a Heart   J. Burke, A. Johnston
     Georgie Stoll Orchestra   DE DLA 478
One, Two, Button Your Shoe   J. Burke, A. Johnston
                               DE DLA 479

D322-24. Aug 4
Shoe Shine Boy   S. Cahn, S. Chaplin
     Jimmy Dorsey Orchestra   DE DLA Unissued
South Sea Island Magic   L. Tomerlin, A. Long
     Dick McIntire Harmony Hawaiians DE DLA 522
Hawaiian Paradise   H. Owens
                               DE DLA 523

D325-27A. Aug 10
For Love Alone   B. Siever
     Victor Young Orchestra   DE DLA 550
I Never Realised   C. Porter, M. Gideon
                               DE DLA 551

Beyond Compare   H. Barris, M. Greene
                               DE DLA 552
I Have So Little to Give   B. Siever, P. Thayer
                               DE DLA 553

D328-29. Aug 12
Dear Old Girl   R. Buck, T. Morse
     Ivan Ditmars on piano with the Three Cheers
                               DE DLA 554
Just One Word of Consolation F. Williams, T. Lemonier

DE DLA 555

D330-31. Aug 17
Pennies from Heaven Medley, including "So Do I"
                           J. Burke, A. Johnston
     Jimmy Dorsey Orchestra with Frances Langford and Louis
     Armstrong   DE DLA 579
Pennies from Heaven   J. Burke, A. Johnston
                                     DE DLA 580

D332-34. Aug 19
The Way You Look Tonight   J. Kern, D. Fields
     Victor Young Orchestra with Dixie Lee Crosby
                                     DE DLA 587
A Fine Romance   J. Kern, D. Fields
     with Dixie Lee Crosby   DE DLA 588
          (Bing sang the above song in a higher pitch than
     normal to accommodate Dixie's range.)
Me and the Moon   W. Hirsch, L. Handman
                                     DE DLA 589

1937
D335-36. Feb 23
Sweet Leilani   H. Owens
     Lani McIntire Hawaiians   DE DLA 722
Blue Hawaii   L. Robin, R. Rainger
                                     DE DLA 723
          ("Sweet Leilani" became Bing's first gold record.)

D337-38. Feb 28
In a Little Hula Heaven   L. Robin, R. Rainger
     Jimmy Dorsey Orchestra   DE DLA 729
Never in a Million Years   M. Gordon, H. Revel
                                     DE DLA 730

D339-41. Mar 3
What Will I Tell My Heart?
               P. Tinturin, J. Lawrence, I. Gordon
     Jimmy Dorsey Orchestra   DE DLA 737
Too Marvelous for Words   J. Mercer, R. Whiting
                                     DE DLA 738
Peckin'   H. James, B. Pollack
                                     DE DLA 739

D342-44. Mar 5
The One Rose (That's Left in My Heart) D. Lyon, L. McIntire
     Victor Young Orchestra   DE DLA 741
Sweet Is the Word for You   L. Robin, R. Rainger
                                     DE DLA 742
Moonlight and Shadows   L. Robin, F. Hollander
                                     DE DLA 743

D345-47. Mar 8
Sentimental and Melancholy   J. Mercer, R. Whiting
     Victor Young Orchestra   DE DLA 745
My Little Buckaroo   M. Jerome, J. Scholl
                                     DE DLA 746
What is Love?   V. Young, L. Robin, R. Rainger
                                     DE DLA 747

D348-51. Jul 12
It's the Natural Thing to Do J. Burke, A. Johnston
     John Scott Trotter Orchestra DE DLA 829
All You Want to Do Is Dance J. Burke, A. Johnston
                                DE DLA 830
The Moon Got in My Eyes   J. Burke, A. Johnston
                                DE DLA 831
Smarty   R. Freed, B. Lane
                                DE DLA 832

D352-55. Sep 11
Dancing Under the Stars   H. Owens
     Lani McIntire Hawaiians   DE DLA 906
Palace in Paradise   H. Owens
                                DE DLA 907
When You Dream About Hawaii H. Ruby, B. Kalmar, S. Silvers
                                DE DLA 908
Sail Along, Silv'ry Moon   H. Tobias, P. Wenrich
                                DE DLA 909

D356-59. Sep 20
Can I Forget You?   O. Hammerstein II, J. Kern
     John Scott Trotter Orchestra DE DLA 939
The Folks Who Live on the Hill O. Hammerstein II, J. Kern
                                DE DLA 940
I Still Love to Kiss You Goodnight H. Spina, W. Bullock
                                DE DLA 941
Remember Me?   H. Warren, A. Dubin
                                DE DLA 942

D360-61. Sep 25
Basin Street Blues   S. Williams
     John Scott Trotter Orchestra DE DLA 971
     with Connie Boswell
Bob White (Whatcha Gonna Swing Tonight?)
                             J. Mercer, B. Hanighen
                                DE DLA 972

D362-63. Nov 12
There's A Goldmine in the Sky N. and C. Kenny
     Eddie Dunstedter, pipe organ DE DLA 1051
When the Organ Played 'O Promise Me'
                             A. Sherman, J. Meskill, A. Silver
                                DE DLA 1052

D364-65. Nov 15
Let's Waltz for Old Times' Sake T. Koehler, S. Stept
     Eddie Dunstedter, pipe organ DE DLA 1071
In the Mission by the Sea   P. DeRose, B. Hill
                                DE DLA 1072

1938
D366-69. Jan 21
My Heart is Taking Lessons   J. Burke, J. Monaco
     John Scott Trotter Orchestra DE DLA 1148
          (Johnny Burke took the title phrase from Crosby.)
This Is My Night to Dream   J. Burke, J. Monaco
                                DE DLA 1149
On the Sentimental Side   J. Burke, J. Monaco

DE DLA 1150
The Moon of Manakoora   F. Loesser, A. Newman
DE DLA 1151

D370-71A. Jan 26
Alexander's Ragtime Band   I. Berlin
    Victor Young Orchestra   DE DLA 1152
    with Connie Boswell and Eddie Cantor
Home on the Range/True Confession Traditional
    Victor Young Orchestra   DE DLA 1153

D372-73. Apr 13
Sweet Hawaiian Chimes L. McIntire, G. McConnell, D. Sanford
    Harry Owens Royal Hawaiian Hotel Orchestra
DE DLA 1210
Little Angel   H. Owens
DE DLA 1211

D374-75. Apr 22
Let Me Whisper I Love You
          E. Heyman, D. Gasparre, P. Pattison, E. Rossell
    John Scott Trotter Orchestra DE DLA 1276
Don't Be That Way   B. Goodman, E. Sampson, M. Parish
DE DLA 1277

D376-79. April 25
Little Lady Make Believe   C. Tobias, N. Simon
    Eddie Dunstedter, pipe organ DE DLA 1287
When Mother Nature Sings Her Lullaby L. Yoell, G. Brown
DE DLA 1288
Darling Nellie Gray   B.R. Hanby
    Paul Taylor Orchestra   DE DLA 1289
Swing Low, Sweet Chariot   Traditional
DE DLA 1290

D380-83. May 23
I've Got a Pocketful of Dreams J. Burke, J. Monaco
    John Scott Trotter Orchestra DE DLA 1293
       (Johnny Burke took the title phrase from Crosby.)
Now It Can Be Told   I. Berlin
DE DLA 1294
It's the Dreamer in Me   J. Van Heusen, J. Dorsey
DE DLA 1295
Don't Let That Moon Get Away J. Burke, J. Monaco
DE DLA 1296

D384-86. Jul 1
Small Fry   H. Carmichael, F. Loesser
    Victor Young Small Fryers   DE DLA 1297
    and Johnny Mercer
Mr. Gallagher and Mr. Shean   E. Gallagher, A. Shean
DE DLA 1298
Mr. Crosby and Mr. Mercer E. Gallagher, A. Shean, J. Mercer
DE DLA 1299

D387-88. Jul 8
Summertime   G. and I. Gershwin, D. Heyward
    Matty Malneck Orchestra   DE DLA 1310
A Blues Serenade

M. Parish, F. Signorelli, J. Lytell, V. Grande
DE DLA 1311

D389-93. Jul 11
I've Got a Pocketful of Dreams J. Burke, J. Monaco
    John Scott Trotter Orchestra DE DLA 1312
Don't Let That Moon Get Away J. Burke, J. Monaco
                               DE DLA 1313
Silver on the Sage   L. Robin, R. Rainger
                               DE DLA 1314
Laugh and Call It Love   J. Burke, J. Monaco
                               DE DLA 1315
Mexicali Rose   H. Stone, J. Tenney
                               DE DLA 1316

D394-96. Oct 14
You Must Have Been a Beautiful Baby J. Mercer, H. Warren
    Bob Crosby Orchestra   DE C 91511
Old Folks   W. Robinson, D. Hill
                               DE C 91512
My Reverie   C. Debussy, L. Clinton
                               DE C 91513

D397-400. Nov 4
You're a Sweet Little Headache L. Robin, R. Rainger
    John Scott Trotter Orchestra DE DLA 1547
I Have Eyes   L. Robin, R. Rainger
                               DE DLA 1548
The Funny Old Hills   L. Robin, R. Rainger
                               DE DLA 1549
Joobalai   L. Robin, R. Rainger
                               DE DLA 1550

D401-04. Dec 2
When You're Away   V. Herbert, H. Blossom
    Victor Young Orchestra   DE DLA 1605
Ah! Sweet Mystery of Life   V. Herbert, R. Young
                               DE DLA 1606
Sweethearts   V. Herbert, R. Smith
                               DE DLA 1607
Thine Alone   V. Herbert, H. Blossom
                               DE DLA 1608

D405-06. Dec 9
Gypsy Love Song   V. Herbert, R. Smith
    Victor Young Concert Orchestra DE DLA 1624
    and Frances Langford
I'm Falling in Love with Someone V. Herbert, R. Young
                               DE DLA 1625

D407-10. Dec 12
My Melancholy Baby   E. Burnett, G. Norton
    John Scott Trotter Orchestra DE DLA 1633
I Cried for You   A. Freed, G. Arnheim, A. Lyman
                               DE DLA 1634
The Lonesome Road   N. Shilkret, G. Austin
                               DE DLA 1635
When the Bloom Is on the Sage F. Howard, N. Vincent
                               DE DLA 1636

D411-14. Dec 19
Between a Kiss and a Sigh   J. Burke, A. Johnston
      John Scott Trotter Orchestra   DE DLA 1689
Just a Kid Named Joe   J. Livingston, M. David
                                DE DLA 1690
It's a Lonely Trail   V. DeLeath, N. and C. Kenny
                                DE DLA 1691
Let's Tie the Old Forget-Me-Not J. Gorney, P.F. Webster
                                DE DLA 1692

1939
D415-18. Mar 10
East Side of Heaven   J. Burke, J. Monaco
      John Scott Trotter Orchestra   DE DLA 1718
Hang Your Heart On a Hickory Limb J. Burke, J. Monaco
                                DE DLA 1719
That Sly Old Gentleman   J. Burke, J. Monaco
                                DE DLA 1720
Sing a Song of Sunbeams   J. Burke, J. Monaco
                                DE DLA 1721

D419-21. Mar 15
Ida, Sweet as Apple Cider   E. Leonard, E. Munson
      John Scott Trotter Frying Pan   DE DLA 1722
      Five with the Foursome
Poor Old Rover   D. Porter, R. Johnson
                                DE DLA 1723
Down By the Old Mill Stream   T. Taylor
                                DE DLA 1724

D422-23. Mar 22
Deep Purple   P. DeRose, M. Parish
      Matty Malneck Orchestra   DE DLA 1733
Stardust   H. Carmichael, M. Parish
                                DE DLA 1734

D424-25. Mar 27
God Bless America   I. Berlin
      John Scott Trotter Orchestra   DE DLA 1739
The Star Spangled Banner   F.S. Key, J. Smith
                                DE DLA 1740

D426-29. Mar 31
If I Had My Way   L. Klein, J. Kendis
      John Scott Trotter Orchestra   DE DLA 1742
Little Sir Echo   L. Smith, J. Fearis, J. and A. Marsala
                                DE DLA 1743
      (The above song was recorded at the insistence of
      young Gary Crosby and became a hit.)
I Surrender, Dear   H. Barris, G. Clifford
                                DE DLA 1744
I'm Building a Sailboat of Dreams C. Friend, D. Franklin
                                DE DLA 1745

D430-32. Apr 3
Alla en el rancho grande (El Rancho Grande)
            E. Uranga, B. Costello, J. Del Moral, S. Ramos
      John Scott Trotter Frying Pan Five DE DLA 1752
It Must Be True   G. Arnheim, H. Barris, G. Clifford

DE DLA 1753
S'posin'   A. Razaf, P. Denniker
                              DE DLA 1754

D433-34. Apr 5
Whistling in the Wildwood   J. Cavanaugh, V. Rose, L. Stock
    John Scott Trotter Orchestra   DE DLA 1757
And the Angels Sing   Z. Elman, J. Mercer
                              DE DLA 1758

D435-37. Jun 9
Wrap Your Troubles in Dreams H. Barris, T. Koehler, B. Mohl
    John Scott Trotter Orchestra   DE DLA 1767
Girl of My Dreams   S. Clapp
                              DE DLA 1768
Missouri Waltz   F. Logan, J. Shannon
                              DE DLA 1769

D438-41. Jun 12
Still the Bluebird Sings   J. Burke, J. Monaco
    John Scott Trotter Orchestra   DE DLA 1770
Go Fly a Kite   J. Burke, J. Monaco
                              DE DLA 1771
A Man and His Dream   J. Burke, J. Monaco
                              DE DLA 1772
Just One More Chance   S. Coslow, A. Johnston
                              DE DLA 1773

D442-43. Jun 13
To You, Sweetheart, Aloha   H. Owens
    Dick McIntire Harmony Hawaiians   DE DLA 1774
My Isle of Golden Dreams   W. Blaufuss, G. Kahn
                              DE DLA 1775

D444-46. Jun 14
Maybe   G. and I. Gershwin
    Victor Young Orchestra   DE DLA 1776
Somebody Loves Me   G. Gershwin, B.G. DeSylva, R.
                              Henderson, L. Brown, B. MacDonald
                              DE DLA 1777
Home on the Range   Traditional
                              DE DLA 1778

D447-48. Jun 22
Start the Day Right   C. Tobias, A. Lewis, M. Spitalny
    John Scott Trotter Orchestra   DE DLA 1781
    with Connie Boswell
An Apple for the Teacher   J. Burke, J. Monaco
                              DE DLA 1782

D449-55. Jun 30
Neighbors in the Sky   H. Barris
    John Scott Trotter Orchestra   DE DLA 1793
What's New?   J. Burke, B. Haggart
                              DE DLA 1794
Cynthia   W. Donaldson
                              DE DLA 1795
Gus Edwards' Medley: Sunbonnet Sue/Jimmy Valentine/If I
    Were a Millionaire   G. Edwards, W. Cobb

                                        DE DLA 1796
In My Merry Oldsmobile   G. Edwards
    with the Andrews Sisters   DE DLA 1797

D456-57. Sep 20
Ciribiribin   H. James, J. Lawrence, A. Pestalozza
    Joe Venuti Orchestra   DE 66632
    and the Andrews Sisters
Yodelin' Jive   H. Prince, D. Raye
                                DE 66633

D458-61. Dec 15
Too Romantic   J. Burke, J. Monaco
    John Scott Trotter Orchestra DE DLA 1907
The Moon and the Willow Tree V. Schertzinger, J. Burke
                                DE DLA 1908
Sweet Potato Piper   J. Burke, J. Monaco
    with the Foursome and John Scott Trotter's Frying Pan
    Five   DE DLA 1909
Between 18th and 19th on Chestnut Street W.Osborne, D.Rogers
    with Connie Boswell   DE DLA 1910

1940
D462-65. Feb 9
Marcheta   V. Schertzinger
    John Scott Trotter Orchestra DE DLA 1918
Tumbling Tumbleweeds   B. Nolan
                                DE DLA 1919
If I Knew Then (What I Know Now) D. Jurgens, E. Howard
                                DE DLA 1920
The Girl with the Pigtails in Her Hair S. Chaplin, S. Cahn
                                DE DLA 1921

D466-68. Feb 25
Devil May Care   H. Warren, J. Burke
    John Scott Trotter Orchestra DE DLA 1951
The Singing Hills   M. David, D. Sanford, S. Mysels
                                DE DLA 1952
I'm Waiting for Ships That Never Come In A. Olman, J.Yellen
                                DE DLA 1953

D469-72. Mar 22
Beautiful Dreamer   S. Foster
    John Scott Trotter Orchestra DE DLA 1967
I Dream of Jeannie with the Light Brown Hair S.Foster
                                DE DLA 1968
Yours Is My Heart Alone
            F. Lehar, L. Herzer, B.F. Loehner, H. Smith
                                DE DLA 1969
Sierra Sue   J. Carey
                                DE DLA 1970

D473-76. Apr 12
Meet the Sun Half Way   J. Burke, J. Monaco
    John Scott Trotter Orchestra DE DLA 1981
April Played the Fiddle   J. Burke, J. Monaco
                                DE DLA 1982
I Haven't Time to Be a Millionaire J. Burke, J. Monaco
                                DE DLA 1983

The Pessimistic Character   J. Burke, J. Monaco
                                DE DLA 1984

D477-78. Apr 15
Mister Meadowlark   J. Mercer, W. Donaldson
    Victor Young Orchestra   DE DLA 1985
    and Johnny Mercer
On Behalf of the Visiting Firemen J. Mercer, W. Donaldson
                                DE DLA 1986

D479-81. Jul 1
Trade Winds   C. Friend, C. Tobias
    Dick McIntire Harmony Hawaiians DE DLA 2013
A Song of Old Hawaii   G. Beecher, J. Noble
                                DE DLA 2014

Aloha Kuu Ipo Aloha   L. McIntire, R. Ball
                                DE DLA 2015

D482-85. Jul 3
When the Moon Comes Over Madison Square J. Burke, J. Monaco
    John Scott Trotter Orchestra DE DLA 2031
That's for Me   R. Rodgers, O. Hammerstein II
                                DE DLA 2032
Only Forever   J. Burke, J. Monaco
                                DE DLA 2033
            (Johnny Burke took the title phrase from Crosby.)
Rhythm on the River   J. Burke, J. Monaco
                                DE DLA 2034

D486-89. Jul 6
Ballad for Americans--Part 1 (Narration)
                                E. Robinson, J. Latouche
    Victor Young Concert Orchestra DE DLA 2035
    and Ken Darby Singers
Ballad for Americans--Parts 2-4   DE DLA 2036/38

D490-93. Jul 10
Rhythm on the River   J. Burke, J. Monaco
    John Scott Trotter Orchestra DE DLA 2042
That's for Me   J. Burke, J. Monaco
                                DE DLA 2043
I Found a Million Dollar Baby   H. Warren, M. Dixon, B. Rose
                                DE DLA 2044
Can't Get Indiana off My Mind   H. Carmichael, R. DeLeon
                                DE DLA 2045

D494-98. Jul 20
The Waltz You Saved for Me   W. King, E. Flindt, G. Kahn
    Paradise Island Trio   DE DLA 2057
Where the Blue of the Night   B. Crosby, R. Turk, F. Ahlert
                                DE DLA 2058
When You're a Long, Long Way from Home G. Meyer, S. Lewis
                                DE DLA 2059
When I Lost You   I. Berlin
                                DE DLA 2060
Paradise Isle   S. Koki
                                DE DLA 2061

D499-500. Jul 23
Do You Ever Think of Me?   H. Kerr, J. Cooper, E. Burnett
    Victor Young Orchestra   DE DLA 2066
You Made Me Love You   J. Monaco, J. McCarthy
    with the Merry Macs   DE DLA 2067

D501-04. Jul 27
Legend of Old California   H. Warren, J. Mercer
    John Scott Trotter Orchestra DE DLA 2072
Please   L. Robin, R. Rainger
                                 DE DLA 2073
You Are the One   J.S. Trotter, C. Carroll
                                 DE DLA 2074
Prairieland Lullaby   V. Young, F. Loesser
                                 DE DLA 2075

D505-08. Dec 3
Along the Santa Fe Trail   A. Dubin, W. Grosz, E. Coolidge
    John Scott Trotter Orchestra DE DLA 2251
Lone Star Trail   C. Walker
                                 DE DLA 2252
It's Always You   J. Van Heusen, J. Burke
                                 DE DLA 2253
I'd Know You Anywhere   J. Mercer, J. McHugh
                                 DE DLA 2254

D509-12. Dec 9
De Camptown Races   S. Foster
    Victor Young Orchestra   DE DLA 2259
    and the King's Men
Did Your Mother Come from Ireland? J. Kennedy, M. Carr
                                 DE DLA 2260
My Old Kentucky Home   S. Foster
                                 DE DLA 2261
Where the River Shannon Flows J. Russell
                                 DE DLA 2262

D513-14. Dec 13
Tea for Two   V. Youmans, I. Caesar
    Bob Crosby Bob Cats   DE DLA 2271
    and Connie Boswell
Yes Indeed!   S. Oliver
                                 DE DLA 2272

D515-16. Dec 16
San Antonio Rose   B. Wills
    Bob Crosby Orchestra   DE DLA 2274
        (The above song became Bing's second gold record.)
It Makes No Difference Now   F. Tillman, J. Davis
                                 DE DLA 2275

D517-20. Dec 20
You're Dangerous   J. Van Heusen, J. Burke
    John Scott Trotter Orchestra DE DLA 2286
A Nightingale Sang in Berkley Square E.Maschwitz, M.Sherwin
                                 DE DLA 2287
You Lucky People, You   J. Van Heusen, J. Burke
                                 DE DLA 2288
Birds of a Feather   J. Van Heusen, J. Burke

DE DLA 2289

D521-22. Dec 23
Dolores   L. Alter, F. Loesser
    Bob Crosby Bob Cats   DE DLA 2290
    with the Merry Macs
Pale Moon   F. Logan, J. Glick
                                    DE DLA 2291

D523-26. Dec 30
Chapel in the Valley   L. Rene, J. Lange, L. Porter
    Victor Young Orchestra   DE DLA 2312
I Only Want a Buddy Not a Sweetheart E. Jones
                                    DE DLA 2313
When Day Is Done   B.G. DeSylva, Dr. R. Katscher
                                    DE DLA 2314
My Buddy   W. Donaldson, G. Kahn
                                    DE DLA 2315

    NOTE: ASCAP, the composer's union, had a five-month
    strike in 1941 against recording companies in an at-
    tempt to keep records off radio. Bing waxed 22 songs
    in December 1940 and 33 more in two months after the
    strike.

1941
D527-31. May 23
Who Calls?   D. Hill, J. Marks
    John Scott Trotter Orchestra DE DLA 2398
Lullaby (The Cradle Song)   J. Brahms, N. Macfarren
                                    DE DLA 2399
You and I   M. Willson
                                    DE DLA 2400
Be Honest with Me   G. Autry, F. Rose
                                    DE DLA 2401
Goodbye, Little Darlin', Goodbye G. Autry, J. Marvin
                                    DE DLA 2402

D532-33. May 26
The Waiter and the Porter and the Upstairs Maid
                                 J. Mercer
    Jack Teagarden Orchestra   DE DLA 2411
    and Mary Martin
The Birth of the Blues B.G. DeSylva, R. Henderson, L. Brown
                                    DE DLA 2412

D534-37. Jun 14
Clementine   P. Montrose
    John Scott Trotter Orchestra DE DLA 2437
    with the Music Maids and Hal
The Old Oaken Bucket   S. Woodworth, G. Kiallmark
                                    DE DLA 2438
(Lights Out) 'Til Reveille   S. Cowan, B. Worth
                                    DE DLA 2439
Sweetheart of Sigma Chi   B. Stokes, F. Vernon
                                    DE DLA 2440

D538-42. Jun 16
Sweetly She Sleeps, My Alice Fair S. Foster

```
                John Scott Trotter Orchestra   DE DLA 2442
Dream Girl of Pi K. A.            E. Shields
                                      DE DLA 2443
I Wonder What's Become of Sally  J. Yellen, M. Ager
                                      DE DLA 2444
Old Black Joe                    S. Foster
                                      DE DLA 2445
Mary's a Grand Old Name          G. Cohan
                                      DE DLA 2446


D543-48. Jul 5
Oh! How I Miss You Tonight    Joe Burke, B. Davis, M. Fisher
      John Scott Trotter Orchestra   DE DLA 2500
Don't Break the Spell            A. Dubin, D. Franklin
                                      DE DLA 2501
Dear Little Boy of Mine          J. Brennan, E. Ball
                                      DE DLA 2502
Nell and I                       S. Foster
                                      DE DLA 2503
Danny Boy                        F. Weatherly
                                      DE DLA 2504
Where the Turf Meets the Surf  B. Crosby, J.Burke, J. Monaco
                                      DE DLA 2505
      [Written about 1937, the song was recorded to
   promote Bing's Del Mar racetrack, where it continues to
   be played twice each racing day.  It has never been
   commercially released.]


D549-52. Jul 8
You Are My Sunshine              J. Davis, C. Mitchell
      Victor Young Orchestra          DE DLA 2515
Ridin' Down the Canyon           G. Autry, S. Burnette,
                                      DE DLA 2516
You're the Moment of a Lifetime  R. Charles, S. DeKarlos
                                      DE DLA 2517
No te importe saber (Let Me Love You Tonight)
                                 M. Parish, R. Touzet
                                      DE DLA 2518


D553-56. Jul 14
Ol' Man River                    O. Hammerstein II, J. Kern
      Victor Young Orchestra          DE DLA 2538
Day Dreaming                     J. Kern, G. Kahn
                                      DE DLA 2539
Darling, je vous aime beaucoup   A. Sosenko
                                      DE DLA 2540
The Anniversary Waltz            A. Dubin, D. Franklin
                                      DE DLA 2541


D557-58. Jul 30
Let's All Meet at My House       J. Van Heusen, J. Burke
      Woody Herman Orchestra          DE DLA 2597
      and Muriel Lane
Humpty-Dumpty Heart              J. Van Heusen, J. Burke
                                      DE DLA 2598


D559-60. Jul 30
The Whistler's Mother-in-Law  B. Stevens, L. Wagner
      Woody Herman Woodchoppers       DE DLA 2599
```

```
      and Muriel Lane
I Ain't Got Nobody               S. Williams, R. Graham
                                    DE DLA 2600


D561-62. Oct 24
Shepherd Serenade                F. Spielman, K. Goell
   Harry Sosnik Orchestra            DE 69863
Do You Care?                     L. Quadling, J. Elliott
                                    DE 69864
```

1942
```
D563-65. Jan 18
I Want My Mama     A. Stillman, E.Garcia, V.Paiva, J.Calazans
   Woody Herman Woodchoppers          DE DLA 2827
Deep in the Heart of Texas     J. Hershey, D. Swander
                                    DE DLA 2828
I'm Thinking Tonight of My Blue Eyes  A. Carter
                                    DE DLA 2829


D566-69. Jan 19
Sing Me a Song of the Islands  H. Owens, M. Gordon
   Dick McIntire Harmony Hawaiians  DE DLA 2830
I'm Drifting Back to Dreamland
               J. Sadler, F. Charlesworth, C. Harrison
                                    DE DLA 2831
The Singing Sands of Alamosa  B. Reisfeld, K. Gannon
                                    DE DLA 2832
Remember Hawaii                M. Willson
                                    DE DLA 2833


D570-73. Jan 24
Miss You                       H., C., and H. Tobias
   John Scott Trotter Orchestra  DE DLA 2840
Mandy Is Two                   F. McGrath, J. Mercer
                                    DE DLA 2841
Angels of Mercy                I. Berlin
                                    DE DLA 2842
Skylark                        H. Carmichael, J. Mercer
                                    DE DLA 2843


D574-77. Jan 26
Nobody's Darlin' But Mine      J. Davis
   Victor Young Orchestra          DE DLA 2844
When the White Azaleas Start Blooming  B. Miller
                                    DE DLA 2845
The Lamplighter's Serenade    H. Carmichael, P.F. Webster
                                    DE DLA 2846
Blue Shadows and White Gardenias  H. Owens, M. Gordon
                                    DE DLA 2847


D578-80. Jan 27
Blues in the Night             J. Mercer, H. Arlen
   John Scott Trotter Orchestra  DE DLA 2857
Moonlight Cocktail             L. Roberts, K. Gannon
                                    DE DLA 2858
I Don't Want to Walk Without You  F. Loesser, J. Styne
                                    DE DLA 2859
```

D581-82. Mar 13
Lili of Laguna   L. Stuart, T. FioRito, P.F. Webster
     John Scott Trotter Orchestra DE DLA 2946
     and Mary Martin
Wait Till the Sun Shines, Nellie H. Von Tilzer, A. Sterling
                                  DE DLA 2947

D593-95. Mar 16
Got the Moon in My Pocket   J. Van Heusen, J. Burke
     John Scott Trotter Orchestra DE DLA 2948
Just Plain Lonesome   J. Van Heusen, J. Burke
                                  DE DLA 2949
The Waltz of Memory   J. Burger, P. Norman
                                  DE DLA 2950

D596-98. May 25
Lazy   I. Berlin
     Bob Crosby Orchestra   DE DLA 2989
Let's Start the New Year Right I. Berlin
                                  DE DLA 2990
I've Got Plenty to Be Thankful For I. Berlin
                                  DE DLA 2991

D599-602. May 27
I'll Capture Your Heart   I. Berlin
     Bob Crosby Orchestra   DE DLA 2996
     with Fred Astaire and Margaret Lenhardt
Longing   Unissued, Test Pressing
When My Dreamboat Comes Home   C. Friend, D. Franklin
     Bob Crosby Bob Cats   DE DLA 2998
Walking the Floor Over You   E. Tubb
                                  DE DLA 2999

D603-05. May 29
White Christmas   I. Berlin
     John Scott Trotter Orchestra DE DLA 3009
        (The above song became Bing's third gold record
     and sold more than any other record in history.)
Abraham   I. Berlin
     with the Ken Darby Singers   DE DLA 3010
Song of Freedom   I. Berlin
                                  DE DLA 3011

D606-09. Jun 1
The Bombardier Song   R. Rodgers, L. Hart
     John Scott Trotter Orchestra DE DLA 3012
     with the Music Maids and Hal
Easter Parade   I. Berlin
     John Scott Trotter Orchestra DE DLA 3013
Happy Holiday   I. Berlin
     with the Music Maids and Hal DE DLA 3014
Be Careful, It's My Heart   I. Berlin
     John Scott Trotter Orchestra DE DLA 3015

D610-13. Jun 8
Adeste Fideles   Traditional
     John Scott Trotter Orchestra DE DLA 3025
     with Max Terr Mixed Chorus
Silent Night, Holy Night   F. Gruber, J. Mohr

DE DLA 3026
(The above two songs became Bing's fourth gold
      record.)
Faith of Our Fathers   Traditional
      with the Andrews Sisters   DE DLA 3027
God Rest Ye Merry, Gentlemen Traditional
                              DE DLA 3028

D614-16. Jun 10
Conchita, Marquita, Lolita, Pepita, Rosita, Juanita Lopez
                        J. Styne, H. Magidson
      Vic Schoen Orchestra   DE L 3029
The Road to Morocco   J. Van Heusen, J. Burke
                              DE L 3030
Ain't Got a Dime to My Name   J. Van Heusen, J. Burke
                              DE L 3031

D617-20. Jun 12
My Great, Great Grandfather   E. Fischer, A. Garman
      John Scott Trotter Orchestra DE L 3032
      with Chorus
A Boy in Khaki, a Girl in Lace A. Wrubel, C. Newman
                              DE L 3033
Moonlight Becomes You   J. Van Heusen, J. Burke
                              DE L 3034
            (Johnny Burke took the title phrase from Crosby.)
Constantly   J. Van Heusen, J. Burke
                              DE L 3035

D621-23. Jul 9
By the Light of the Silv'ry Moon G. Edwards, E. Madden
      Capt. Eddie Dunstedter, West Coast American Air Force
      Training Center Orchestra   DE L 3087
But Not for Me   G. and I. Gershwin
                              DE L 3088
Hello, Mom   E. Dunstedter, F. Loesser
                              DE L 3089 Rejected

D624. Jul 27
Hello, Mom   E. Dunstedter, F. Loesser
      Capt. Eddie Dunstedter West Coast A.A.F
      Training Center Orchestra   DE L 3147

NOTE: From Aug 1, 1942, to Sep 1, 1943, the American
Federation of Musicians under James C. Petrillo imposed
a recording ban on musicians, making recordings necessarily a cappella or with choral groups. Bing had only
three recording sessions during this period.

1943
D625-26A. Jul 2
Sunday, Monday or Always   J. Van Heusen, J. Burke
      Ken Darby Singers   DE L 3172
            (The above song became Bing's sixth gold record.)
If You Please   J. Van Heusen, J. Burke
                              DE L 3173
Duke the Spook   J. Van Heusen, J. Burke
                              DE Unknown

D627-28. Jul 4
Mississippi Mud   H. Barris, J. Cavanaugh
    Paul Whiteman Orchestra   VIC VI 20783
I Left My Sugar Standing in the Rain
                                   H. Barris, S. Fain, I. Kahal
                                       VIC VI 24240
         (The above two songs were recorded when the Rhythm
    Boys had a reunion on Whiteman's summer program on CBS
    for Chase and Sanborn Coffee. Part of the show was
    released in an album titled <u>Paul Whiteman's 50th Anni-
    versay Grand Award</u>, Victor, reissued by Spartan No. 33-
    901.)

D629-30. Aug 23
People Will Say We're in Love R. Rodgers, O. Hammerstein II
    The Sportsman Glee Club   DE L 3181
    and Trudy Erwin
Oh! What a Beautiful Morning R. Rodgers, O. Hammerstein II
                                   DE L 3182

D631-34. Sept 27
Pistol Packin' Mama   A. Dexter
    Vic Schoen Orchestra   DE L 3197
    and the Andrews Sisters
         (The above became Bing's seventh gold record.)
Vict'ry Polka   J. Styne, S. Cahn
                                   DE L 3198
Jingle Bells   J. Pierpont
                                   DE L 3199
         (The above became Bing's eighth gold record.)
Santa Claus Is Coming to Town H. Gillespie, J. Coots
                                   DE L 3200

D635-36. Oct 1
Poinciana (Song of the Tree) N. Simon, B. Bernier
    John Scott Trotter Orchestra DE L 3202
I'll Be Home for Christmas   W. Kent, B. Ram, K. Gannon
                                   DE L 3203
         (The above song became Bing's fifth gold record.)

D637-39. Dec 29
It Could Happen to You   J. Van Heusen, J. Burke
    John Scott Trotter Orchestra DE L 3273
September Song   K. Weil, M. Anderson
                                   DE L 3274
San Fernando Valley   G. Jenkins
                                   DE L 3275

1944
D640-42. Feb 7
Swinging on a Star   J. Van Heusen, J. Burke
    John Scott Trotter Orchestra DE L 3307
    and the Williams Brothers Quartet
         (The above song became Bing's ninth gold record.)
The Day After Forever   J. Van Heusen, J. Burke
                                   DE L 3308
Going My Way   J. Van Heusen, J. Burke
                                   DE L 3309

D643-45. Feb 11
I Love You   C. Porter
     John Scott Trotter Orchestra DE L 3314
I'll Be Seeing You   S. Fain, I. Kahal
                             DE L 3315 Rejected
Night and Day   C. Porter
                             DE L 3316

D646-49. Feb 17
Amor, amor   G. Ruiz, S. Skylar
     John Scott Trotter Orchestra DE L 3317
I'll Be Seeing You   S. Fain, I. Kahal
                             DE L 3318
One Sweet Letter from You   H. Warren, L. Brown, S. Clare
                             DE L 3319
On the Atcheson, Topeka and the Santa Fe
                             H. Warren, J. Mercer
     with Six Hits and a Miss   DE L 3320

D650-53. May 3
Long Ago (and Far Away)   J. Kern, I. Gershwin
     John Scott Trotter Orchestra DE L 3409
Like Someone in Love   J. Van Heusen, J. Burke
                             DE L 3410
Begin the Beguine   C. Porter
                             DE L 3411
Dearly Beloved   J. Kern, J. Mercer
                             DE L 3412

D654-55. Jun 30
(There'll Be a) Hot Time in the Town of Berlin
                             Sgt. J. Bushkin, Pvt. J. DeVries
     Vic Schoen Orchestra   DE L 3449
     and the Andrews Sisters
Is You Is, or Is You Ain't (Ma Baby)? B. Austin, L. Jordan
                             DE L 3450

D656-58. Jul 7
I'll Remember April   P. Johnston, D. Raye, G. DePaul
     John Scott Trotter Orchestra DE L 3455
Too-ra-loo-ra-loo-ral   J. Shannon
                             DE L 3456
         (The above song became Bing's tenth gold record.)
Moonlight on a White Picket Fence J.S. Trotter, C. Carroll
                             DE L 3457

D659-62. Jul 17
Iowa   M. Willson
     John Scott Trotter Orchestra DE L 3458
         (Recorded, along with another, D708, on Mar 3,
     1945, for the 1946 centennial celebration of Iowa, and
     was sold only in that state.)
Welcome to My Dreams   J. Van Heusen, J. Burke
                             DE L 3459
It's Anybody's Spring   J. Van Heusen, J. Burke
                             DE L 3460
Let Me Call You Sweetheart   L. Friedman, B. Whitson
                             DE L 3461

D663-65. Jul 19
Sleigh Ride in July   J. Van Heusen, J. Burke
     John Scott Trotter Orchestra DE L 3462
A Friend of Yours   J. Van Heusen, J. Burke
                                 DE L 3463
Would You?   J. Van Heusen, J. Burke
                                 DE L 3464

D666-69. Jul 24
Just a Prayer Away   C. Tobias, D. Kapp
     Victor Young Orchestra, the Ken Darby Singers,
     Ethel Smith on the organ   DE L 3471
My Mother's Waltz   D. Franklin
                                 DE L 3472
Beautiful Love
          H. Gillespie, V. Young, E. Van Alstyne, W. King
                                 DE L 3473
Dear Friend   R. Rodgers, O. Hammerstein II
                                 DE L 3474

D670-71. Jul 25
Don't Fence Me In   C. Porter
     Vic Schoen Orchestra   DE L 3475
     and the Andrews Sisters
          (The above became Bing's 11th gold record, and he
     recorded the complex arrangement after only a 30-minute
     rehearsal.)
The Three Caballeros   M. Esperon, E. Cortazar, R. Gilbert
                                 DE L 3476

D672-73. Jul 26
My Baby Said Yes   T. Walters, S. Robin
     Louis Jordan Tympany Five   DE L 3477
Your Socks Don't Match   L. Carr, L. Corday
                                 DE L 3479

D674-75. Jul 31
You've Got Me Where You Want Me H. Warren, J. Mercer
     Joseph Lilley Orchestra   DE L 3485
     and Judy Garland
Mine   G. and I. Gershwin
                                 DE L 3486

D676-77. Oct 13
Evalina   H. Arlen, E.Y. Harburg
     "Toots" Camarata Orchestra DE W 72427
The Eagle and Me   H. Arlen, E.Y. Harburg
     with Mixed Chorus   DE W 72428

D678-79. Nov 24
The Eagle and Me   H. Arlen, E.Y. Harburg
     "Toots" Camarata Orchestra DE W 72578
     with Mixed Chorus
Evalina   H. Arlen, E.Y. Harburg
     "Toots" Camarata Orchestra DE W 72579

D680-83. Dec 4
Let's Take the Long Way Home J. Mercer, H. Arlen
     John Scott Trotter Orchestra DE L 3678

Out of This World   J. Mercer, H. Arlen
                              DE L 3679
I Promise You   J. Mercer, H. Arlen
                              DE L 3680
More and More   J. Kern, E.Y. Harburg
                              DE L 3681

D684-87. Dec 8
There's a Fella Waiting in Poughkeepsie J. Mercer, H. Arlen
      Vic Schoen Orchestra   DE L 3684
      and the Andrews Sisters
Ac-Cent-Tchu-Ate the Positive J. Mercer, H. Arlen
      [Accentuate the Positive]   DE L 3685
Put It There, Pal   J. Van Heusen, J. Burke
      Vic Schoen Orchestra and Bob Hope DE L 3686
The Road to Morocco   J. Van Heusen, J. Burke
                              DE L 3687

D688-90. Dec 11
Strange Music   E. Grieg, R. Wright, G. Forrest
      John Scott Trotter Orchestra DE L 3692
June Comes Around Every Year J. Mercer, H. Arlen
                              DE L 3693
More and More   J. Kern, E.Y. Harburg
                              DE L 3694

D691-93. Dec 15
I Promise You   J. Mercer, H. Arlen
      John Scott Trotter Orchestra DE L 3705
I Love You   E. Grieg, R. Wright, G. Forrest
                              DE L 3706
These Foolish Things   H. Marvell, J. Strachey, H. Link
                              DE L 3707

1945
D694-96. Jan 21
I'd Rather Be Me   S. Coslow, F. Bernard. E. Cherkose
      John Scott Trotter Orchestra DE L 3724
Just One of Those Things   C. Porter
                              DE L 3725
All of My Life   I. Berlin
                              DE L 3726

D697-700. Jan 28
Baia   A. Barroso, R. Gilbert
      Xavier Cugat Waldorf-Astoria Orchestra
                              DE L 3731 Rejected
You Belong to My Heart   A. Lara, R. Gilbert
                              DE L 3732 Rejected
Siboney   E. Lecuona, D. Morse
                              DE L 3733 Rejected
Hasta mañana   E. DeLange, O. Farres
                              DE L 3734 Rejected

D701-04. Feb 11
Siboney   E. Lecuona, D. Morse
      Xavier Cugat Waldorf-Astoria Orchestra
                              DE L 3735
Baia   A. Barroso, R. Gilbert

Hasta mañana   DE L 3736
                                          E. DeLange, O. Farres
                                          DE L 3737
You Belong to My Heart   A. Lara, R. Gilbert
                                          DE L 3738

D705-08. Mar 3
Why Do I Like You?   J. Van Heusen, J. Burke
    John Scott Trotter Orchestra   DE L 3746
        (The above is a Special Limited Edition Pressing
    for the Building Fund of St. John's Hospital, Santa
    Monica, CA. It was never released commercially, and
    1000 one-sided plastic records were sold at $5 each.)
Temptation   N.H. Brown, A. Freed
                                    DE L 3747
Close as Pages in a Book   S. Romberg, D. Fields
                                    DE L 3748 Rejected
Early American   J. Van Heusen, J. Burke
                                    DE L 3749
        ("Early American," along with "Iowa," D659, of Jul
    17, 1944, was sold only in Iowa in 1946 for the Iowa
    centennial celebration.)

D709-10. Mar 9
Connecticut   H. Martin, R. Blane
    Joseph Lilley Orchestra   DE L 3750
    and Judy Garland
Yah-Ta-Ta, Yah-Ta-Ta (Talk, Talk, Talk)
                                    J. Van Heusen, J. Burke
                                    DE L 3751

D711-15. Apr 18
Too-ra-loo-ra-loo-ral   J. Shannon
    John Scott Trotter Orchestra   DE L 3800 Rejected
If I Loved You   R. Rodgers, O. Hammerstein II
                                    DE L 3801
Close as Pages in a Book   S. Romberg, D. Fields
                                    DE L 3802
I Love You Truly   C. Bond
                                    DE L 3803
Just A-Wearyin' for You   C. Bond
                                    DE L 3804

D716-17. Apr 25
Home Sweet Home   J. Payne, H. Bishop
    Victor Young Orchestra   DE L 3815 Rejected
Ave Maria   F. Schubert
                                    DE L 3816 Rejected

D718-19. Jun 29
Along the Navajo Trail   E. DeLange, L. Markes, D. Charles
    Vic Schoen Orchestra   DE L 3876
    and the Andrews Sisters
Good, Good, Good   A. Roberts, D. Fisher
                                    DE L 3877

D720-21. Jul 3
Wedding Day (The Wedding Polka) M. Willson
    Vic Schoen Orchestra   DE L 3887 Rejected

and the Andrews Sisters
Betsy   D. Kapp, J. Eaton, T. Shand
                                        DE L 3888

D722-23. Jul 12
It's Been a Long, Long Time   J. Styne, S. Cahn
    Les Paul Trio   DE L 3889
Whose Dream Are You?   M. Willson
                                        DE L 3890

D724-27. Jul 17
Too-ra-loo-ra-loo-ral   J. Shannon
    John Scott Trotter Orchestra DE L 3895
The Rose of Tralee   C. Glover, C. Spencer
                                        DE L 3896
Where the Blue of the Night   B. Crosby, R. Turk, F. Ahlert
                                        DE L 3897
I'll Take You Home Again, Kathleen T. Westendorf
                                        DE L 3898

D728-29. July 30
Home Sweet Home   H. Bishop, J. Payne
    Victor Young Orchestra with Choir DE L 3902
Ave Maria   F. Schubert
                                        DE L 3903

D730-31. Aug 7
I Can't Begin to Tell You   J. Monaco, M. Gordon
    Carmen Cavallaro on piano   DE L 3904
        (The above became Bing's 12th gold record.)
I Can't Believe You're in Love with Me J. McHugh, C.Gaskill
                                        DE L 3905

D732-33. Aug 9
Save Your Sorrow for Tomorrow B.G. DeSylva, A. Sherman
    Eddie Heywood Orchestra   DE L 3910
Baby, Won't You Please Come Home? C. Williams, C. Warfield
                                        DE L 3911

D734-35. Aug 17
That Little Dream Got Nowhere J. Van Heusen, J. Burke
    Eddie Heywood Orchestra   DE L 3918
Who's Sorry Now?   H. Ruby, B. Kalmar, T. Snyder
                                        DE L 3919

D736-39. Aug 21
The Happy Prince Part 1   O. Wilde, B. Herrman
    Victor Young Orchestra, Orson Welles,
    Lurene Tuttle, with Supporting Cast DE L 3929
The Happy Prince Parts 2-4   DE L 3930/32

D740-41. Aug 29
Give Me the Simple Life   R. Bloom, H. Ruby
    Jimmy Dorsey Orchestra   DE L 3937
It's the Talk of the Town
                        J. Livingston, M. Symes, A. Neiburg
                                        DE L 3938

D742-43. Sep 5
I've Found a New Baby   S. Williams, J. Palmer
    Eddie Heywood Orchestra   DE L 3949
Who's Sorry Now?   H. Ruby, B. Kalmar, T. Snyder
                                     DE L 3950

D744-45. Sep 6
Sweet Lorraine   C. Burwell, M. Parish
    Jimmy Dorsey Orchestra   DE L 3953
A Door Will Open   D. George, J. Brooks
                                     DE L 3954

D746-48. Sep 10
In the Land of Beginning Again G. Meyer, G. Clarke
    John Scott Trotter Orchestra DE L 3960
Aren't You Glad You're You   J. Van Heusen, J. Burke
                                     DE L 3961
The Bells of St. Mary's   A. Adams, D. Furber
                                     DE L 3962

D749-51. Sep 13
Day by Day   S. Cahn, A. Stordahl, P. Weston
    Mel Torme Mel Tones and Instrumental Trio DE L 3965
Prove It by the Things You Do A. Roberts, D. Fisher
                                     DE L 3966
Symphony   R. Bernstein, J. Lawrence, A. Alstone, A. Tabet
    Victor Young Orchestra   DE L 3968

D752-54. Dec 4
Mighty Lak' a Rose   E. Nevin, F. Stanton
    Ethel Smith (organ) and the Song Spinners DE W 73212
The Sweetest Story Ever Told   R.M. Stulz
                                     DE W 73213
Mighty Lak' a Rose   DE WX 73214 Test Pressing

D755-58. Dec 6
It's the Same Old Shillelagh P. White
    Bob Haggart Orchestra and the Jesters DE W 73218
McNamara's Band   S. O'Connor, J. Stamford
                                     DE W 73219
        (The above became Bing's 13th gold record.)
Dear Old Donegal   S. Graham
                                     DE W 73220
Who Threw the Overalls in Mrs. Murphy's Chowder? G. Geifer
                                     DE W 73221

D759-61. Dec 18
J'attendrai (I'll Be Yours)
        D. Oliveri, A. Sosenko, L. Poterat, N. Rastelli
    Camarata Orchestra   DE W 73249
Till the Clouds Roll By   J. Kern, P.G. Wodehouse,
                                     DE W 73250
We'll Gather Lilacs   I. Novello
                                     DE W 73251

D762-63. Dec 27
Sioux City Sue   D. Thomas, R. Freedman
    Bob Haggart Orchestra   DE W 73255
You Sang My Love Song to Somebody Else A. Roberts, D.Fisher

                              DE W 73256

D764-66. Dec 31
All Through the Day   J. Kern, O. Hammerstein II
    Camarata Orchestra   DE W 73261
Ol' Man River   J. Kern, O. Hammerstein II
                                     DE W 73262
I've Told Ev'ry Little Star   J. Kern, O. Hammerstein II
                                     DE W 73263

1946
D767-69. Jan 16
Blue (and Broken Hearted)   G. Clarke, E. Leslie, L. Handman
    Eddie Condon Orchestra   DE W 73278
After You've Gone   H. Creamer, J. Layton
                                     DE W 73279
Personality   J. Van Heusen, J. Burke
                                     DE W 73280
         (The songs recorded Jan 16 were sung between 3:34
     and 5:15, although "Personality" had not been rehearsed
     earlier and three separate pianists were used with the
     orchestra. The pianists were Gene Sullivan, Joe Sulli-
     van, and Joe Bushkin, respectively [Barnes 125n].)

D770-71. Jan 21
Pinetop's Boogie Woogie   C. Smith, N. Gimbel
    Lionel Hampton Orchestra   DE W 73287
On the Sunny Side of the Street J. McHugh, D. Fields
                                     DE W 73288

D772-74. Jan 22
Just My Luck   J. Van Heusen, J. Burke
    Jay Blackton Orchestra   DE W 73297
You May Not Love Me   J. Van Heusen, J. Burke
                                     DE W 73298
They Say It's Wonderful   I. Berlin
                                     DE W 73299

D775-76. Mar 22
Oh, But I Do   A. Schwartz, L. Robin
    John Scott Trotter Orchestra   DE L 4133 Rejected
A Gal in Calico   A. Schwartz, L. Robin
                                     DE L 4134 Rejected

D777-80. May 7
When Irish Eyes Are Smiling   E. Ball, G. Graff, C. Olcott
    John Scott Trotter Orchestra   DE L 4168
A Gal in Calico   A. Schwartz, L. Robin
                                     DE L 4169
Oh, But I Do   A. Schwartz, L. Robin
                                     DE L 4170
That Tumbledown Shack in Athlone
                              M. Carlo, R. Pascoe, A. Sanders
                                     DE L 4171

D781-82. May 11
(Get Your Kicks on) Route 66! B. Troup
    Vic Schoen Orchestra   DE L 4177
    and the Andrews Sisters

South America, Take It Away   H. Rome
                              DE L 4178
            (The above became Bing's 14th gold record.)

D783-84. May 15
Pretending   A. Sherman, S. Symes
     Les Paul Trio   DE L 4183
Gotta Get Me Somebody to Love   A. Wrubel
                                   DE L 4184

D785-86. Jul 13
Lullaby (from Jocelyn)   B. Godard
     Victor Young Orchestra   DE L 4227
     and Jascha Heifetz on violin
Where My Caravan Has Rested   H. Loehr, E. Teschemacher
                                   DE L 4228

D787-92. Jul 18
All by Myself   I. Berlin
     John Scott Trotter Orchestra DE L 4229
Blue Skies   I. Berlin
     with Choir   DE L 4230
You Keep Coming Back Like a Song I. Berlin
     with Vocal Quartet   DE L 4231
Getting Nowhere   I. Berlin
     with Vocal Quartet   DE L 4232
Everybody Step   I. Berlin
                                   DE L 4233
A Serenade to an Old-Fashioned Girl I. Berlin
                                   DE L 4234

D793-95. Jul 24
A Couple of Song and Dance Men I. Berlin
     John Scott Trotter Orchestra DE L 4246
     with Fred Astaire
I'll See You in C-U-B-A   I. Berlin
     with Trudy Erwin   DE L 4247
I've Got My Captain Working for Me Now I. Berlin
                                   DE L 4248

D796. Aug 1
The Things We Did Last Summer   J. Styne, S. Cahn
     Jimmy Dorsey Orchestra   DE L 4257

D797-98. Aug 9
When You Make Love to Me   J. Hoyl, M. Goetschius
     Victor Young Orchestra   DE L 4259
So Much in Love   J. Hoyl, M. Goetschius
                                   DE L 4260

D799-800. Aug 15
The Star Spangled Banner (Recitation) F.S. Key, J. Smith
     Victor Young Orchestra   DE L 4265
Old Ironsides (Recitation)   O.W. Holmes, V. Young
                                   DE L 4266

D801-04. Aug 22
My Heart Goes Crazy   J. Van Heusen, J. Burke
     Russ Morgan Orchestra with Male Chorus   DE L 4275

Among My Souvenirs   H. Nicholls, E. Leslie
                              DE L 4276
So Would I   J. Van Heusen, J. Burke
                              DE L 4277
Does Your Heart Beat for Me? R.Morgan, M.Parish, A.Johnson
                              DE L 4278

D805-07. Nov 14
As Long As I'm Dreaming   J. Van Heusen, J. Burke
     John Scott Trotter Orchestra   DE L 4323
Smile Right Back at the Sun   J. Van Heusen, J. Burke
                              DE L 4324
The One I Love (Belongs to Somebody Else)   I. Jones, G. Kahn
                              DE L 4325

D808-09. Nov 19
Country Style   J. Van Heusen, J. Burke
     John Scott Trotter Orchestra   DE L 4329
     with the Calico Kids
My Heart Is a Hobo   J. Van Heusen, J. Burke
                              DE L 4330

D810-11. Dec 17
That's How Much I Love You   E. Arnold, W. Fowler, J. Hall
     Bob Crosby Bob Cats   DE L 4337
Rose of Santa Rosa   A. Hoffman, A. Roberts, J. Livingston
     with the Chickadees   DE L 4338

1947
D812-13. Jan 17
I Kiss Your Hand, Madame
                    S. Lewis, J. Young, R. Erwin, F. Rotter
     Victor Young Orchestra   DE L 4345
The Kiss in Your Eyes   J. Burke, R. Heuberger
                              DE L 4346

D814-16. Feb 13
Gotta Get Me Somebody to Love A. Wrubel
     Les Paul Trio   DE L 4355
What Am I Gonna Do About You? S. Cahn, J. Styne
                              DE L 4356
Drifting and Dreaming
        H. Gillespie, E. van Alstyne, E. Schmidt, L. Curtis
                              DE L 4357

D817-19. Mar 17
Friendly Mountains   J. Burke
     Victor Young Orchestra with Mixed Chorus   DE L 4371
Emperor Waltz   J. Strauss, J. Burke
                              DE L 4372
I Still Suits Me   J. Kern, O. Hammerstein II
     with Lee Wiley   DE L 4373

D820-24. Mar 19
White Christmas   I. Berlin
     John Scott Trotter Orchestra   DE L 4374
     with Ken Darby Singers
          (The <u>Merry Christmas</u> album DL-5019 [1947], featur-
     ing D820-21 and six others, became the 15th gold "re-

cord," although earlier versions appeared about 1945 as
A-396, A-403, and A-550 albums. See D2408.)
Silent Night, Holy Night   F. Gruber, J. Mohr
                                DE L 4375
The Christmas Song   M. Torme, R. Wells
                                DE L 4376
Anything You Can Do   I. Berlin
    Vic Schoen Orchestra   DE L 4377
    with the Andrews Sisters and Dick Haymes
There's No Business Like Show Business I. Berlin
                                DE L 4378

D825-28. Mar 20
The Small One Part 1 (A Christmas Story) C.Tazewell, V.Young
    Victor Young Orchestra with Supporting Cast DE L 4379
The Small One Parts 2-4   DE L 4380/82

D829-30. Mar 25
Alexander's Ragtime Band   I. Berlin
    Morris Stoloff Orchestra with Al Jolson DE L 4386
        (The above became Bing's 16th gold record.)
The Spaniard That Blighted My Life B. Merson
                                DE L 4387

D831-32. Mar 26
Go West, Young Man!   B. Kalmar, H. Ruby
    Vic Schoen Orchestra and the Andrews Sisters DE L 4396
Tallahassee   F. Loesser
                                DE L 4397

D833-38. Mar 28
Happy Birthday (Open Version) [P. and S. Hill]/Auld Land
Syne [R. Burns]
    Victor Young Orchestra with Ken Darby Singers DE L 4398
Happy Birthday/Auld Lang Syne   DE L 4399 Unissued
The Anniversary Song   A. Jolson, S. Chaplin, I. Ivanovici
                                DE L 4400
O Fir Tree Dark   Traditional
                                DE L 4401

D839-40. May 8
Feudin' and Fightin'   A. Duben, B. Lane
    Bob Haggart Orchestra with the Jesters DE W 73909
Goodbye, My Lover, Goodbye   Traditional
                                DE W 73910

D841-43. May 12
I Do, Do, Do Like You   A. Wrubel
    John Scott Trotter Orchestra DE W 73911
    with the Skylarks
Kokomo, Indiana   M. Gordon, J. Myrow
                                DE W 73912
The Old Chaperone   R. Idriss, G. Tibbles
                                DE W 73913

D844. May 29
The Freedom Train   I. Berlin
    Vic Schoen Orchestra   DE W 73927
    with the Andrews Sisters

D845-46. Jun 4
You Do   M. Gordon, J. Myrow
    Carmen Cavallaro, piano   DE W 73938
How Soon?   C. Lucas, J. Owens
                                  DE W 73939

D847-48. Jun 5
Whiffenpoof Song
        G. Pomeroy, T. Galloway, M. Minnigerode, R. Vallee
    Fred Waring Glee Club   DE W 73940
        (The above became Bing's 17th gold record.)
Kentucky Babe   R. Buck, A. Geibel
                                  DE W 73941

D849-50A. Jun 12
Lullaby Land   A. Wilder
    John Scott Trotter Orchestra   DE L 4447
Suspense   A. Rinker
                                  DE L 4448
You Took Advantage of Me   R. Rodgers, L. Hart
                                  DE L 4449 Rejected

D851-54. Jun 13
The Man Without a Country Part 1 (Recitation; see D2404)
                        E.E. Hale, J. Holloway, V. Young
    Victor Young Orchestra and Supporting Cast   DE L 4450
The Man Without a Country Parts 2-4   DE L 4451/53

D855-56. Nov 8
Now Is the Hour   C. Scott, M. Kaihan, D. Stewart
    Instrumental Quartet with Ken Darby Choir   DE L 4541
        (The above became Bing's 18th gold record.)
Silver Threads Among the Gold H. Danks, E. Rexford
                                  DE L 4542

D857-60. Nov 12
Embraceable You   G. and I. Gershwin
    John Scott Trotter Orchestra   DE L 4551
    with the Chickadees
Pass That Peace Pipe   R. Edens, H. Martin, R. Blane
                                  DE L 4552
They Can't Take That Away from Me G. and I. Gershwin
    John Scott Trotter Orchestra   DE L 4553
Love Walked In   G. and I. Gershwin
                                  DE L 4554

D861-63. Nov 13
My Girl's an Irish Girl   J. Popplewell
    Victor Young Orchestra   DE L 4555
But Beautiful   J. Van Heusen, J. Burke
                                  DE L 4556
Experience   J. Van Heusen, J. Burke
                                  DE L 4557

D864-65. Nov 18
Ain't Doin' Bad Doin' Nothin' J. Venuti, L. Jarvis
    Joe Venuti Orchestra   DE L 4567
Ida, I Do   G. Kahn, I. Jones
                                  DE L 4568

D866-67. Nov 25
Apalachicola, F-L-A   J. Van Heusen, J. Burke
      Vic Schoen Orchestra   DE L 4576
      with the Andrews Sisters
You Don't Have to Know the Language J. Van Heusen, J. Burke
                              DE L 4577

D868-70. Nov 27
I'll See You in My Dreams   G. Kahn, I. Jones
      John Scott Trotter Orchestra DE L 4580
Swingin' Down the Lane   G. Kahn, I. Jones
                              DE L 4581
Memories   G. Kahn, E. van Alstyne
                              DE L 4582

D871. Nov 27
Galway Bay   Dr. A. Colahan
      Victor Young Orchestra   DE L 4583
          (The above became Bing's 19th gold record.)

D872-75. Dec 3
Ballerina   B. Russell, C. Sigman
      John Scott Trotter Orchestra DE L 4603
      with the Rhythmaires
Golden Earrings   V. Young, J. Livingston, R. Evans
                              DE L 4604
Pretty Baby   G. Kahn, E. van Alstyne, T. Jackson
                              DE L 4607
Rosalie   C. Porter
                              DE L 4608

> NOTE: The discography in Ulanov's 1948 biography lists
> 731 songs released as singles and 29 albums (including
> 227 songs and recitations on 122 78-r.p.m. sides). It
> also lists another seven special albums, as for Beider-
> becke and patriotic songs, in which Bing appears on 29
> sides. Through "Golden Earings," D873, Ulanov's list
> has 987 songs by Bing, many of them re-releases in some
> albums, but it does not list unissued recordings.

D876-78. Dec 11
Laroo Laroo Lilli Bolero   S. Lippman, E. Moore, S. Dee
      Victor Young Orchestra   DE L 4644
      with Ken Darby Choir
Blue Shadows on the Trail   J. Lange, E. Daniel
                              DE L 4645
The Story of Sorrento E. DeCurtis, B. Russell, S. Gallagher
                              DE L 4646

D879-80. Dec 17
A Hundred and Sixty Acres   D. Kapp
      Vic Schoen Orchestra with the Andrews Sisters DE L 4676
At the Flying 'W'   A. Wrubel
                              DE L 4677

D881. Dec 18
Once and for Always   J. Van Heusen, J. Burke
      Victor Young Orchestra with Rhonda Fleming   DE L 4720

D882-89. Dec 24
Love Me or Leave Me   W. Donaldson, G. Kahn
    John Scott Trotter Orchestra DE L 4728
Oh, You Crazy Moon   J. Van Heusen, J. Burke
                             DE L 4729 Unissued
Easy to Love   C. Porter
                             DE L 4730
I've Got You Under My Skin   C. Porter
                             DE L 4731
Imagination   J. Van Heusen, J. Burke
                             DE L 4732
I'd Love to Live in Loveland (With a Girl Like You)
                             W. Williams DE L 4733
Katrina   G. DePaul, D. Raye
    with the Rhythmaires   DE L 4734
If I Loved You   R. Rodgers, O. Hammerstein II
    John Scott Trotter Orchestra DE L 4735

D890-91. Dec 27
Once and for Always   J. Van Heusen, J. Burke
    Victor Young Orchestra   DE L 4745
    with the Ken Darby Choir
Busy Doin' Nothin'   J. Van Heusen, J. Burke
    with Sir Cedric Hardwicke   DE L 4746
    and William Bendix

D892-95. Dec 30
If You Stub Your Toe on the Moon J. Van Heusen, J. Burke
    Victor Young Orchestra   DE L 4779
Lili Marlene   N. Schultze, H. Liep, T. Connor
                             DE L 4780
Ichabod   G. DePaul, D. Raye
    Vic Schoen Orchestra with the Rhythmaires DE L 4781
The Headless Horseman   G. DePaul, D. Raye
                             DE L 4782

D896-899. Dec 31
Haunted Heart   A. Schwartz, H. Deitz
    John Scott Trotter Orchestra DE L 4795
A Fella with an Umbrella   I. Berlin
                             DE L 4796
Love Thy Neighbor   M. Gordon, H. Revel
                             DE L 4798
A Bluebird Singing in My Heart M. Emer, S. Gallop
    Victor Young Orchestra   DE L 4797

    NOTE: A year-long strike of the American Federation of
    Musicians, James C. Petrillo, virtually halted record-
    ing in 1948. Decca amassed a backlog toward the end of
    1947 for the announced strike. The issue was licensing
    material for radio broadcasts.

1948
D901-02. Nov 25
Tarra-Ta-Larra-Ta-Lar   M. Symes, J. Farrow
    Studio Orchestra with Ken Darby Choir DE L 4843
Far Away Places   A. Kramer, J. Whitney
    Studio Rhythm Accompaniment   DE L 4844
    with Ken Darby Choir

1949
D903-04. Jan 4
So in Love   C. Porter
    Vic Schoen Orchestra   DE L 4856 Unissued
Why Can't You Behave?   C. Porter
                                DE L 4857

D905. Feb 4
Sing Soft, Sing Sweet, Sing Gentle J. Durante, J. Barnett
    Roy Bargy Orchestra with Jimmy Durante ?DE L 4890

D906-07. Mar 10
Bali Ha'i   R. Rodgers, O. Hammerstein II
    John Scott Trotter Orchestra DE L 4921
Some Enchanted Evening   R. Rodgers, O. Hammerstein II
                                DE L 4922

D908-09. Mar 18
How It Lies, How It Lies, How It Lies J. Burke, P.F.Webster
    Vic Schoen Orchestra   DE L 4932
    with Evelyn Knight and the Rhythmaires
Everywhere You Go   L. Shay, J. Goodwin, M. Fisher
                                DE L 4933

D910-11. Mar 22
(Ghost) Riders in the Sky   S. Jones
    Studio Accompaniment,   DE L 4939
    Perry Botkin on Guitar with Ken Darby Singers
Careless Hands   B. Hilliard, C. Sigman
    with Ken Darby Singers   DE L 4940

D912-13. Apr 14
Be Bop Spoken Here   M. Malneck, M. DeLugg
    Vic Schoen Orchestra with Patty Andrews DE L 4973
Wedding Day   C. Hayes, C. Kalish
    with the Andrews Sisters   DE L 4974

D914-21. May 6
Holy, Holy, Holy   J. Dykes, R. Heber
    Ken Darby Choir with organ   DE L 4992
Mother Dear, O Pray for Me   Traditional
                                DE L 4993
O Lord, I Am Not Worthy   Traditional
                                DE L 4994
Rock of Ages   T. Hastings, A. Toplady
                                DE L 4995
What a Friend We Have in Jesus J. Scriven, C. Converse
                                DE L 4996
He Leadeth Me   W. Bradbury, J. Gilmore
                                DE L 4997
All Hail the Power of Jesus' Name O.Holden, Rev. E.Perronet
                                DE L 4998
O God, Our Help in Ages Past   W. Croft, I. Watts
                                DE L 4999

D922-27. May 10
A Sure Thing   J. Van Heusen, J. Burke
    Victor Young Orchestra   DE L 5000
    with Jeff Alexander Chorus

You're in Love with Someone   J. Van Heusen, J. Burke
                                DE L 5001
Sunshine Cake   J. Van Heusen, J. Burke
    with Carole Richards, Jeff Alexander Chorus DE L 5002
You're Wonderful   V. Young, J. Livingston, R. Evans
    Victor Young Orchestra   DE L 5003
The Twelve Days of Christmas   Anonymous
    Vic Schoen Orchestra and the Andrews Sisters DE L 5004
Here Comes Santa Claus   G. Autry, O. Haldeman
                                DE L 5005

D928-31. May 11
The Meadows of Heaven   J. Meyer, J. McCarthy
    Victor Young Orchestra with Ken Lane Singers DE L 5006
The Last Mile Home   W. Kent, W. Farrar
                                DE L 5007
The First Noel   Traditional
                                DE L 5008
You're All I Want for Christmas G. Moore, S. Ellis
                                DE L 5009

D932-38. May 31 (Christmas Carols Medley Parts 1-2)
Deck the Halls/Away in a Manger [M. Luther, J. Murray]/I Saw
Three Ships
    Simon Rady Orchestra with Studio Choir DE L 74948
Good King Wenceslas/We Three Kings of Orient Are/Angels We
    Have Heard on High   DE L 74949
Oh 'Tis Sweet to Think   T. Moore
    Simon Rady Orchestra with Ann Blyth DE L 74950

D939-40. Jun 6
The Four Winds and the Seven Seas D. Rodney, H. David
    Carmen Cavallaro on piano   DE W 74987
Make Believe (You Are Glad When You're Sorry)
                                J. Shilkret, B. Davis
                                DE W 74988

D941-42. Jun 17
The Iowa Indian Song   M. Willson
    Fred Waring Pennsylvanians with Glee Club DE W 75002
'Way Back Home   F. Waring, A. Lewis
                                DE W 75003

D943-46. Jun 21
Someplace on Anywhere Road   J. Van Heusen, J. Burke
    Victor Young Orchestra   DE L 5048
    with Jeff Alexander Chorus
Top o' the Morning   J. Van Heusen, J. Burke
                                DE L 5049
The Donovans   A. Needham, F. Fahy, W. Kent
                                DE L 5050
The Horse Told Me   J. Van Heusen, J. Burke
                                DE L 5051

D947. c. Jun
Spoken Introductions to Decca Selections
    from Top o' the Morning   DE TNY 1386

D948-52. Jun 23
Ichabod Part 1 (The Legend of Sleepy Hollow)
                              D. Raye, G. DePaul
        Victor Young Orchestra   DE L 5052
        with Supporting Cast and Chorus (the Rhythmaires?)
Ichabod Parts 2-4 (Ichabod, Katrina, The Headless Horseman)
                              DE L 5053/55
It's More Fun Than a Picnic   J. McHugh, H. Adamson
        with Jeff Alexander Chorus   DE L 5056

D953-54. Oct 26
Mule Train   ʼ   J. Lange, H. Heath, F. Glickman
        Perry Botkin String Band   DE L 5161
            (The two songs recorded this day were completed
        between 8 and 8:40 a.m., although Bing had not heard
        the above song and was told of it only the day earli-
        er. The whipping sound was enhanced by cracking a whip
        on newspaper scattered on the floor. Decca's "Mule
        Train" was hurried for release before Frankie Laine's
        noted version and sold 250,000 more copies.)
Dear Hearts and Gentle People   S. Fain, B. Hilliard
        with Jud Conlon's Rhythmaires DE L 5162
            (The above became Bing's 20th gold record.)

D955-56. Nov 6
Eileen   S. Fine, M. Liebman
        Victor Young Orchestra   DE L 5189
How Can You Buy Killarney?
        J. Kennedy, G. Morrison, F. Grant, T. Steels
                              DE L 5190

D957-59. Nov 16
Sorry   R. Whiting, B. Pepper
        John Scott Trotter Orchestra DE L 5205
        with the Jud Conlon Singers
Stay Well   K. Weill, M. Anderson
                              DE L 5206
The Little Gray House   K. Weill, M. Anderson
                              DE L 5207

D960-61. Nov 25
Quicksilver   I. Taylor, G. Wyle, E. Pola
        Vic Schoen Orchestra and the Andrews Sisters DE L 5215
Have I Told You Lately That I Love You? S. Wiseman
                              DE L 5216

D962-63. Dec 5
This Could Be Forever   J. Scott, H. Ruby
        Russ Morgan Orchestra with Louanne Hogan   DE L 5238
Helpless   R. Wells
                              DE L 5239

D964-65. Dec 22
My Own Bit of Land   J. Whitney, A. Kramer,
        Studio Rhythm Accompaniment   DE L 5291
        with Ken Darby Singers
When the Sun Goes Down   W. O'Keefe, I. Orton
                              DE L 5292

D966-67. Dec 23
The Yodel Blues   J. Mercer, R.E. Dolan
     Russ Morgan Orchestra with the Morganaires DE L 5293
The Big Movie Show in the Sky J. Mercer, R.E. Dolan
                             DE L 5294

1950
D968-69. Jan 3
Bibbidi-Bobbidi-Boo   J. Livingston, A. Hoffman, M. David
     Vic Schoen Orchestra with the Rhythmaires DE L 5304
Chattanoogie Shoe Shine Boy   H. Stone, J. Stapp
                             DE L 5305

D970-71. Feb 14
The Dixieland Band   B. Hanighen, J. Mercer
     Vic Schoen Orchestra   DE L 5388 Rejected
Jamboree Jones   J. Mercer
                             DE L 5389 Rejected

D972-73. Feb 15
Lock, Stock and Barrel   S. Fain, P.F. Webster
     Vic Schoen Orchestra and the Andrews Sisters DE L 5390
Ask Me No Questions   D. Saxon, R. Wells
                             DE L 5391

D974-75. Mar 24
Life Is So Peculiar   J. Van Heusen, J. Burke
     Vic Schoen Orchestra and the Andrews Sisters DE L 5451
High on the List   J. Van Heusen, J. Burke
                             DE L 5452

D976-79. Apr 8
The Dixieland Band   B. Hanighen, J. Mercer
     Bob Haggart Orchestra   DE W 76113
Jamboree Jones   J. Mercer
     with the Tattlers   DE W 76114
I Didn't Slip, I Wasn't Pushed, I Fell   E. Pola, G. Wyle
     Sy Oliver Orchestra with the Aristokats DE W 76115
*So Tall a Tree   T. Hall
                             DE W 76116
          (*The studio manager considered dismissing the
     Aristokats when the group had difficulty with its part.
     Bing, sitting aside reading a book, told the manager,
     "Give the kids a chance; I'm goin' nowhere. Take your
     time and get the chorus worked out, then call me when
     you're ready," according to Sy Oliver [Barnes 131n]).

D980-81. Apr 11
Accidents Will Happen   J. Van Heusen, J. Burke
     Jay Blackton Orchestra with Dorothy Kirsten DE W 76123
Milady   J. Van Heusen, J. Burke
                             DE L 76124

D982. Apr 12
Home Cookin'   J. Livingston, R. Evans
     Perry Botkin String Band   DE W 76144
     with Jud Conlon's Rhythmaires

D983-86. Jun 21
And You'll Be Home   J. Van Heusen, J. Burke
     Victor Young Orchestra with Ken Lane Singers DE L 5686
Once More the Blue and White J. Van Heusen, J. Burke
                              DE L 5687
Accidents Will Happen   J. Van Heusen, J. Burke
                              DE L 5688
Wouldn't It Be Funny?   J. Van Heusen, J. Burke
                              DE L 5689

D987-90. Jun 22
The Teddy Bears' Picnic   J. Bratton, J. Kennedy
     Victor Young Orchestra   DE L 5694
     with Jud Conlon's Rhythmaires
Rudolph the Red Nosed Reindeer J. Marks
     John Scott Trotter Orchestra DE L 5695
     with Jud Conlon's Rhythmaires
I Cross My Fingers   W. Kent, W. Farrar
     Axel Stordahl Orchestra with Studio Chorus DE L 5696
La vie en rose   Louiguy, E. Piaf, M. David
                              DE L 5697

D991-95. Jun 23
Play a Simple Melody   I. Berlin
     "Gary Crosby and Friend"   DE L 5698
     Matty Matlock All Stars
Sam's Song   L. Quadling, J. Elliott
                              DE L 5699
          (The above became Bing's 21st gold record.)
The Friendly Islands   H. Arlen, R. Blane
     Victor Young Orchestra   DE L 5700
     with Jeff Alexander Chorus
All My Love   P. Durand, M. Parish, H. Contet
                              DE L 5701
Early American   J. Van Heusen, J. Burke
                              DE L 5702

D996-1005. Sep 5
Harbor Lights   J. Kennedy, H. Williams
     Lyn Murray Orchestra with Chorus DE L 5815
Beyond the Reef   J. Pitman
                              DE L 5816
I Will Remember You   R. Anderson, C. Nott
                              DE L 5817
Here Ends the Rainbow   J. Burke, C. King
                              DE L 5818 Unissued
     A Crosby Christmas Part 1 DE L 5819
     John Scott Trotter Orchestra *J. Van Heusen, J. Burke
Deck the Halls (with Chorus) Traditional
That Christmas Feeling* with Gary Crosby and Chorus
I'd Like to Hitch a Ride with Santa Claus*
     with Lindsay Crosby and Chorus
     A Crosby Christmas Part 2 DE L 5820
The Snowman* with Philip and Dennis Crosby and Chorus
That Christmas Feeling* with Gary Crosby
I'd Like to Hitch a Ride with Santa Claus*
     with Lindsay, Dennis, and Philip Crosby and Chorus

D1006. Sep 6
That Christmas Feeling   J. Van Heusen, J. Burke
    John Scott Trotter Orchestra   DE L 5821
    with Jeff Alexander Chorus

D1007-09. Sep 7
Autumn Leaves   J. Kosma, J. Mercer, J. Prevert
    Axel Stordahl Orchestra   DE L 5826
I've Never Been in Love Before F. Loesser
                                    DE L 5827
This Is the Time   V. Young, N. Washington
                                    DE L 5828

D1010-12. Sep 7
Poppa Santa Claus   J. Van Heusen, J. Burke
    Vic Schoen Orchestra and the Andrews Sisters DE L 5829
Mele Kalikimaka (Merry Christmas) R. Anderson
                                    DE L 5830
If I Were a Bell   F. Loesser
    with Patty Andrews   DE L 5831

D1013. Sep 8
Silver Bells   J. Livingston, R. Evans
    John Scott Trotter Orchestra   DE L 5832
    with Carole Richards

D1014-15. Sep 8
Looks Like a Cold, Cold Winter
                    J. Fulton, A. Goering, C. James
    Sonny Burke Orchestra with Lee Gordon Singers DE L 5833
Marshmallow World   P. DeRose, S. Sigman
                                    DE L 5834

D1016-17. Sep 21
Marrying for Love   I. Berlin
    Sonny Burke Orchestra   DE L 5849
The Best Thing for You   I. Berlin
                                    DE L 5850

D1018-19. Dec 13
A Perfect Day   C. Bond
    Ken Darby Orchestra with Ken Darby Singers   DE L 5953
May the Good Lord Bless and Keep You M. Willson
                                    DE L 5954

1951
D1020-23. Jan 7
The Girl Friend   R. Rodgers, L. Hart
    Tommy Dorsey Orchestra   DE L 5986
Without a Word of Warning   M. Gordon, H. Revel
                                    DE L 5987
You Gotta Show Me   D. Brooks, N. Castle
                                    DE L 5988
Then You've Never Been Blue   T. FioRito, J. Young, S. Lewis
                                    DE L 5989

D1024-27. Feb 1
Black Ball Ferry Line   D. Thompson, J. Rarig
    Vic Schoen Orchestra   DE L 6030

The Yodeling Ghost   J. Jerome
                                      DE L 6031
With My Shillelagh Under My Arm B. O'Brien, R. Wallace
                                      DE L 6032
St. Patrick's Day Parade   J. Lange, H. Heath
   with the Mellomen   DE L 6033

D1028-29. Feb 2
Sentimental Music   B. Wayne, R. Care
   John Scott Trotter Orchestra DE L 6034
Silver Moon   S. Romberg, D. Donnelly
                                      DE L 6035

D1030-33. Feb 5
Copacabana   A. Stillman, J. DeBarro, A. Ribeiro, C. Braga
   Banda da Lua with Vocal Quartet DE L 6040
Quizas, quizas, quizas   O. Farres, J. Davis
                                      DE L 6041
Maria Bonita   B. Worth, A. Lara
                                      DE L 6042
Granada   D. Dodd, A. Lara
                                      DE L 6043

D1034-38. Feb 7
I Might Be Your Once-in-a-While V. Herbert, R. Smith
   John Scott Trotter Orchestra DE L 6049
Indian Summer   V. Herbert, A. Dubin
                                      DE L 6050
More I Can Not Wish You   F. Loesser
                                      DE L 6051
The Loneliness of Evening   R. Rodgers, O. Hammerstein II
                                      DE L 6053
Let Me Look at You   H. Arlen, D. Fields
                                      DE L 6054

D1039-41. Feb 8
Any Town Is Paris When You're Young J.S. Trotter, T. Adair
   John Scott Trotter Orchestra DE L 6052
   with the Jud Conlon Choir
Forsaking All Others   W. and R. Watkins
   Vic Schoen Orchestra with the Andrews Sisters DE L 6044
Sparrow in the Tree Top   B. Merrill
                                      DE L 6045

D1042-44. Feb 9
Here Ends the Rainbow   J. Burke, C. King
   Lyn Murray Orchestra with Betty Mullin DE L 6057
With This Ring I Thee Wed   R. and E. Asherman, A. Cornett
                                      DE L 6058
We All Have a Song in Our Hearts C. and R. Yale
   Lyn Murray Orchestra   DE L 6059

D1045. Mar 22
Moonlight Bay   P. Wenrich, E. Madden
   Matty Matlock All Stars with Gary Crosby DE L 6181

D1046. Mar 27
When You and I Were Young Maggie Blues
            J. Butterfield, G. Johnson, M. McHugh, J. Frost

Matty Matlock All Stars with Gary Crosby   DE L 6182

D1047-50. Apr 9
I Whistle a Happy Tune   R. Rodgers, O. Hammerstein II
    Victor Young Orchestra   DE L 6218
Hello Young Lovers   R. Rodgers, O. Hammerstein II
                                  DE L 6219
Getting to Know You   R. Rodgers, O. Hammerstein II
                                  DE L 6220
Something Wonderful   R. Rodgers, O. Hammerstein II
                                  DE L 6221

D1051-52. Apr 25 (From radio shows.)
Old Soldiers Never Die   J. Glazer
    John Scott Trotter Orchestra DE L 6254
    with the Rhythmaires
Gone Fishin'   N. and C. Kenny
    with Louis Armstrong   DE L 6262

D1053-55. Jun 8
I've Got to Fall in Love Again J. Van Heusen, J. Burke
    Dave Barbour Orchestra   DE L 6307
Shanghai   B. Hilliard, M. DeLugg
                                  DE L 6308
Row, Row, Row   Traditional
    John Scott Trotter Orchestra DE L 6309

D1056-59. Jun 20
In the Cool, Cool, Cool of the Evening
                              H. Carmichael, J. Mercer
    Matty Matlock All Stars   DE L 6318
    with Jane Wyman and Six Hits and a Miss
Misto Cristofo Columbo   J. Livingston, R. Evans
                                  DE L 6319
Bonne nuit   J. Livingston, R. Evans
    John Scott Trotter Orchestra DE L 6320
Your Own Little Own   J. Livingston, R. Evans
                                  DE L 6321

D1060-61. Oct 1
Christmas in Killarney   R. Redmond, J. Cavanaugh, F. Weldon
    John Scott Trotter Orchestra DE L 6462
    with the Rhythmaires
It's Beginning to Look a Lot Like Christmas M. Willson
                                  DE L 6463

D1062-63. Oct 4
When the World Was Young
                M. Philippe-Gerard, J. Mercer, A. Vannier
    John Scott Trotter Orchestra DE L 6464
Domino   D. Raye, J. Plante, L. Ferrari
                                  DE L 6465

D1064-65. Oct 19
A Weaver of Dreams   V. Young, J. Elliott
    John Scott Trotter Orchestra DE L 6494
I Still See Elisa   A. Lerner, F. Loewe
                                  DE L 6495

D1066-67. Dec 19
At Last, at Last   C. Trenet, F. Miles
     John Scott Trotter Orchestra DE L 6575
The Isle of Innisfree   D. Farrelly
                                    DE L 6576

1952
D1068-73. Feb 14
A Flight of Fancy   H. Warren, L. Robin
     Toots Camarata Orchestra   DE L 6643
Just for You   H. Warren, L. Robin
                                    DE L 6644
Sailin' Down the Chesapeake Bay G. Botsford, J. Havez
                                    DE L 6645?
Ida, Sweet as Apple Cider   E. Leonard, E. Munson
                                    DE L 6646?
Nobody's Sweetheart
                G. Kahn, E. Erdman, B. Myers, E. Schoebel
                                    DE L 6647?
It Had to Be You   G. Kahn, I. Jones
     John Scott Trotter Frying Pan Five   DE L 6650
     with Red Nichols
                (The last four above were recorded from radio
          shows: "Sailin' Down the Chesapeake Bay" Feb 13, "Ida"
          Jan 23, "Nobody's Sweetheart" Feb 6, and "It Had to Be
          You" Feb 13. Some matrix numbers are uncertain.)

D1074-76. Feb 19
Two Shillelagh O'Sullivan   P. Botkin, P. Foster
     Perry Botkin String Band with the King's Men DE L 6655
Rosaleen   T. Seymour, A. Goodhart, M. Fryberg
                                    DE L 6656
Don't Ever Be Afraid to Go Home C. Sigman, B. Hilliard
                                    DE L 6657

D1077-79. Feb 21
I'll Si-Si Yah in Bahia   H. Warren, L. Robin
     John Scott Trotter Orchestra DE L 6658
     with the Andrews Sisters
The Live Oak Tree   H. Warren, L. Robin
                                    DE L 6659
Spring Fever   H. Warren, L. Robin
                                    DE L 6660 Rejected

D1080. Mar 23
Just a Little Lovin'   E. Arnold, Z. Clements
     Grady Martin Slew Foot Five   DE W 82553

D1081. Apr 24
Till the End of the World   V. Horton
     Grady Martin Slew Foot Five   DE W 82774

D1082-83. May 8
On the 10:10 from Ten-Ten-Tennessee H. Warren, L. Robin
     Nathan Van Cleeve Orchestra with Ben Lessy DE L 6755
Zing a Little Zong   H. Warren, L. Robin
     with Jane Wyman and the Rhythmaires DE L 6756

D1084-85. May 16
The Moon Came Up with a Great Idea Last Night
                              J. Van Heusen, J. Burke
     Vic Schoen Orchestra with Peggy Lee DE L 6768
Watermelon Weather   H. Carmichael, P.F. Webster
                              DE L 6769

D1086-87. Jun 17
You Don't Know What Lonesome Is F. Carling, C. Washburne
     Perry Botkin and the Cass County Boys DE L 6813
Open Up Your Heart   F. Carling, C. Washburne
     with the King's Men   DE L 6815

D1088. Jun 20
To See You Is to Love You   J. Van Heusen, J. Burke
     Axel Stordahl Orchestra   DE L 6817

D1089-90. Jun 23
Hoot Mon   J. Van Heusen, J. Burke
     Joe Lilley Orchestra   DE L 6819
     with Bob Hope and the Mellomen
Chicago Style   J. Van Heusen, J. Burke
     with Bob Hope   DE L 6820

D1091-92. Jun 24
The Road to Bali   J. Van Heusen, J. Burke
     Sonny Burke Orchestra   DE L 6821
     with Bob Hope and the Rhythmaires
The Merry-Go-Runaround   J. Van Heusen, J. Burke
     with Bob Hope and Peggy Lee DE L 6822

D1093-94. Sep 5
South Rampart Street Parade B. Haggart, R. Bauduc, S. Allen
     Matty Matlock Orchestra   DE L 6870
     with the Andrews Sisters
Cool Water   B. Nolan
                              DE L 6871

D1095-96. Nov 12
Keep It a Secret   J. Robinson
     John Scott Trotter Orchestra DE L 6935
     with the Rhythmaires
Sleigh Bell Serenade   J. Burke, P.F. Webster
                              DE L 6936

D1097-1101. Nov 17   (Songs taken from radio broadcasts.)
Fatherly Advice   J.S. Trotter, T. Adair
     John Scott Trotter Orchestra DE L 6894 Unissued
     with Gary Crosby
Sleigh Ride   L. Anderson, M. Parish
     with the Rhythmaires   DE L 6895
I Love My Baby   H. Warren, B. Green
                              DE L 6896
Little Jack Frost, Get Lost A. Stillman, S. Ellis
     with Peggy Lee   DE L 6897
That's A-Plenty   R. Gilbert, L. Pollack
     with Connie Boswell   ?DE L 6898

D1102-03. Dec 15
Mother Darlin'   M. Willson
    Fred Waring Pennsylvanians   DE W 83728
Hush-a-Bye   J. Selen, S. Fain, A. Thomas
                                 DE W 83729
        (Bing may have recorded the lyrics to "Hush-a-Bye"
    on the golf course on a portable recorder after the
    orchestra and chorus completed their parts in the
    studio [Barnes 135n].)

1953
D1104-07. Feb 9
There's Music in You   R. Rodgers, O. Hammerstein II
    John Scott Trotter Orchestra   DE L 7041
Ohio   L. Bernstein, B. Comden, A. Green
    with the Rhythmaires   DE L 7042
The Magic Window   J. Van Heusen, J. Burke
    John Scott Trotter Orchestra   DE L 7043 Rejected
A Quiet Girl   L. Bernstein, B. Comden, A. Green
                                 DE L 7044

D1108-09. Feb 10
Tenderfoot   B. Brill (Bing Crosby), B. Bowen, P. Botkin
    The Perry Botkin Guitars   DE L 7045
Walk Me by the River   R. Stewart, P. King, M. Rothgeb
                                 DE L 7046

    NOTE: The following recordings often lack matrix
    numbers as many were songs for long-playing albums.
    See the list of albums that follows individual record-
    ings for album numbers (see page 178).

D1110-13. Mar 12
Cela m'est égal (If It's All the Same to You)
                                 J. Van Heusen, J. Burke
    John Scott Trotter Orchestra   DE L 7082
The Magic Window   J. Van Heusen, J. Burke
                                 DE L 7083
Violets and Violins
            J. Lawrence, M. Laparcerie, A. and J. Richepin
A propos de rien   J. Van Heusen, J. Burke

D1114-23. May 16
Embrasse-moi bien   P. Durand, H. Contet
    Paul Durand et son grand orchestre   DE W 84782
Au bord de l'eau   A. Grassi
La mer   C. Trenet, J. Lawrence
Tu ne peux pas te figurer   P. Misraki
La Seine   A. Roberts, A. Holt, G. Lafarge, F. Monod
Mademoiselle de Paree
                 P. Durand, H. Contet, M. Parish   DE W 84783
Mon coeur est un violon   M. Laparcerie, A. and J. Richepin
La vie en rose   M. David, Louiguy, E. Piaf
Embrasse-moi (in English)   P. Durand, R. Driscoll
Mademoiselle de Paree (in English)
                     P. Durand, E. Maschwitz, M. Parish
        (The above songs were recorded on one day in Paris
    for the album Le Bing: Song Hits of Paris.)

cysd3

D1124-31. Jun 26
Sleepy Time Gal   R. Whiting, A. Lorenze,
                                      J. Alden, R. Egan
      Buddy Cole and his Trio   DE L 7205
Somebody Loves Me   G. Gershwin, B. MacDonald,
                                      B.G. DeSylva
Do You Ever Think of Me?   E. Burnett, H. Kerr, J. Cooper
I Never Knew   T. FioRito, G. Kahn
After You've Gone   H. Creamer, J. Layton
Dinah   H. Akst, S. Lewis, J. Young
I Never Knew   G. Kahn, T. FioRito
I Can't Give You Anything but Love J. McHugh, D. Fields

D1132-33. Nov 4
What a Little Moonlight Can Do H. Woods
      John Scott Trotter Orchestra DE L 7453
      with Gary Crosby
Down By the Riverside   D. Jordan
                                    DE L 7454

D1134-35. Nov 14
Y'all Come   A. Duff
      Perry Botkin Orchestra   DE L 7461
      with the Cass County Boys
Changing Partners   J. Darion, L. Coleman
      with the Rhythmaires   DE L 7462

D1136. Dec 1
You Are Too Beautiful   R. Rodgers, L. Hart
                                    DE Unknown

D1142-43. Dec 30
If There's Anybody Here   W. Robinson, T. Shand
      Matty Matlock All Stars   DE L 7507
      with Donald O'Connor
Back in the Old Routine   W. Stone
                                    DE L 7508

D1144-51. Dec 31
Cornbelt Symphony   R. Mellin, N. Simons
      John Scott Trotter Orchestra
Call of the South   I. Berlin
      with Gary Crosby and Matty Matlock's All Stars

I Love Paris   C. Porter
      John Scott Orchestra   DE L 7513
Secret Love   S. Fain, P.F. Webster
                                    DE L 7514
Stranger in Paradise   R. Adler, J. Ross
                                    DE L 7515
Vaya con Dios   B. Pepper, L. Russell,
                                      I. James, C. Hoff
                                    DE L 7516
No Other Love   R. Rodgers, O. Hammerstein II
                                    DE L 7517
My Love, My Love   B. Haymes, N. Acquaviva
                                    DE L 7518

NOTE: Bing recorded many songs from 1954 to 1957 (a few in 1958 and 1960) with the Buddy Cole Trio, mainly for radio; 71 (72?) songs and 5 recitations were released after stereophonic augmentation in 1978 and 1979 by the Pete Moore Orchestra (Barnes 154-56). These are listed under the dates they were augmented (p. 175).

1954
D1152-53. Jan 29
Young at Heart   R. Richards, C. Leigh
     Guy Lombardo Royal Canadians DE W 85798
Oh Baby Mine, I Get So Lonely P. Ballard
                                  DE W 85799

D1154-57. Mar 31
Liebchen   J. Sherman, S. Wayne
     John Scott Trotter Orchestra DE L 7614
Tobermorey Bay   J. Hancock, J. Johnston, A. Montgomery
                                  DE L 7615
Lost in Loveliness   S. Romberg, L. Robin
                                  DE L 7616
The River   C. Concina, R. Mellin
                                  DE L 7617

D1158-60A. Apr 1
White Christmas   I. Berlin
     Joseph J. Lilley Orchestra   DE L 7622
     with Danny Kaye, Peggy Lee, Trudy Stevens
Snow   I. Berlin
     with Danny Kaye, Peggy Lee, DE L 7623
     Trudy Stevens and Chorus
The Old Man/Gee, I Wish I Was Back in the Army I. Berlin
     with Danny Kaye and Chorus   DE L 7624

NOTE: Most of the songs recorded in Apr, May, and Jun below were for Bing: A Musical Autobiography, including introductions by Bing. Most of them were songs originally recorded for Brunswick, Columbia, and Victor.

D1161-74. Apr 21
It Must Be True   H. Barris, G. Arnheim, G. Clifford
     Buddy Cole and his Trio
Wrap Your Troubles in Dreams B. Moll, T. Koehler, H. Barris
Just One More Chance   S. Coslow, A. Johnston
Sweet and Lovely   G. Arnheim, H. Tobias, J. Lemare
Where the Blue of the Night   R. Turk, F. Ahlert, B. Crosby
Paradise   G. Clifford, N.H. Brown
Just an Echo in the Valley
                        H. Woods, J. Campbell, R. Connelly
A Ghost of a Chance   V. Young, N. Washington, B. Crosby
Learn to Croon   S. Coslow, A. Johnston
Thanks   S. Coslow, A. Johnston
Muddy Water   P. DeRose, H.Richman, J. Trent
Mississippi Mud   J. Cavanaugh, H. Barris
My Kinda Love   J. Trent, L. Alter
I Surrender Dear   G. Clifford, H. Barris

D1175. Apr 28
Oh Tell Me Why   Traditional

John Scott Trotter Orchestra with Male Chorus DE L 7652

D1176. Apr 30
If You Love Me   M. Monnot, G. Parsons, E. Piaf
    John Scott Trotter Orchestra   DE L 7648

D1177-94. May 3
Down the Old Ox Road   S. Coslow, A. Johnston
    Buddy Cole and his Trio
Black Moonlight   S. Coslow, A. Johnston
The Day You Came Along   S. Coslow, A. Johnston
After Sundown   N.H. Brown, A. Freed
Temptation   N.H. Brown, A. Freed
Love Thy Neighbor   M. Gordon, H. Revel
May I?   M. Gordon, H. Revel
Love in Bloom   L. Robin, R. Rainger
June in January   L. Robin, R. Rainger
Love Is Just Around the Corner L. Robin, L. Gensler
It's Easy to Remember   R. Rodgers, L. Hart
I Wished on the Moon   R. Rainger, D. Parker
Silent Night, Holy Night   F. Gruber, J. Mohr
I'm an Old Cowhand   J. Mercer
Song of the Islands   C. King
Sweet Leilani   H. Owens
Blue Hawaii   L. Robin, R. Rainger
I Love You Truly   C. Bond

D1195-96. May 4
What Can You Do with a General? I. Berlin
    Joseph J. Lilley Orchestra   DE L 7649
Count Your Blessings Instead of Sheep I. Berlin
                             DE L 7650

D1197-98. May 21
Liza   G. and I. Gershwin, G. Kahn
    John Scott Trotter Orchestra DE L 7704 Unissued
In the Good Old Summertime G. Evans, R. Shield
                             DE L 7705

D1199-1212. Jun 16
Out of Nowhere   E. Heyman, J. Green
    Buddy Cole Trio
Stardust   H. Carmichael, M. Parish
Soon   R. Rodgers, L. Hart
The One Rose   L. McIntire, D. Lyon
There's a Goldmine in the Sky C. and N. Kenny
My Heart Is Taking Lessons J. Monaco, J. Burke
I've Got a Pocketful of Dreams J. Monaco, J. Burke
Mexicali Rose   H. Stone, J. Tenney
That Sly Old Gentleman   J. Monaco, J. Burke
Alla en el rancho grande (El Rancho Grande)
              E. Uranga, B. Costello, S. Ramos, J. Del Moral
Tumbling Tumbleweeds   B. Nolan
Only Forever   J. Monaco, J. Burke
Did Your Mother Come from Ireland? M. Carr, J. Kennedy
Lullaby   J. Brahms, N. Macfarren

D1213-14. Jun 19
I Can't Escape from You   L. Robin, R. Whiting

Buddy Cole Trio
Pennies from Heaven   J. Burke, A. Johnston

D1215-16. Jun 21
All She'd Say Was 'Umh-hum'
                    M. Emery, K. Zany, G. Kahn, J. Schenck
    Les Brown Band of Renown   DE L 7741
She's the Sunshine of Virginia H. Carroll, B. MacDonald
                                 DE L 7742

D1217-19. Sep 9
Blue Skies/Mandy/I'd Rather See a Minstrel Show I. Berlin
    Joseph J. Lilley Orchestra   DE W 86772

D1220-21. Sep 23
Who Gave You the Roses?   I. Newman
    Alfred Newman Orchestra with Jud Conlon Choir DE L 7933
We Meet Again (The Song from Desiree) A. Newman, K. Darby
                                 DE L 7934

D1222-23. Nov 4
Peace Prayer of St. Francis (Recitation) Traditional
    Padre Choristers
Blessing of St. Francis (Recitation) Tradional

D1224-27. Dec 23
The Land Around Us   I. Gershwin, H. Arlen
    Joseph J. Lilley Orchestra with Chorus DE L 8068
It's Mine, It's Yours   I. Gershwin, H. Arlen
    with Girl Trio   DE L 8069
The Search Is Through   I. Gershwin, H. Arlen
                                 DE L 8070
Dissertation on the State of Bliss (Love and Learn)
    with Patty Andrews and Male Chorus DE L 8071

D1228. Dec 31
Nobody   B. Williams, A. Rogers
    John Scott Trotter Orchestra DE L 8218

1955
D1229-30. Mar 11
Jim, Johnny and Jonas   J. Bond
    Ken Darby Orchestra with Chorus DE L 8232
Farewell   T. Blackburn, G. Bruns
                                 DE L 8233

D1231. Apr 9 (From the soundtrack of Anything Goes.)
Ya Gotta Give the People Hoke S. Cahn, J. Van Heusen
    Joseph Lilley Orchestra

D1232. May 23 (From the soundtrack of Anything Goes.)
A Second-Hand Turban and a Crystal Ball
                            S. Cahn, J. Van Heusen
    Joseph Lilley Orchestra with Donald O'Connor

D1233. June 1 (From the soundtrack of Anything Goes.)
Blow, Gabriel, Blow   C. Porter
    Joseph Lilley Orchestra
    with Donald O'Connor, Jeanmaire, Mitzi Gaynor

D1234-35. Jul 1
Angel Bells   H. Spencer, E. Hagan, H. Ruby
      Studio Orchestra with Chorus DE L 8527
Let's Harmonize   S. Burke, A. Skinner, D. Finch
      with the Mellomen   DE L 8529

D1236-40. Nov 22 (Recorded from radio broadcasts.)
Christmas Is A-Comin'   F. Luther
      Buddy Cole Orchestra with the Rhythmaires DE L 8805
The Possibility's There   J. Van Heusen, J. Burke
      with Peggy Lee
The First Snowfall   S. Burke, P.F. Webster
      with the Rhythmaires   DE L 8806
The Next Time It Happens   R. Rodgers, O. Hammerstein II
      with the Rhythmaires   DE L 8808
Is Christmas Only a Tree?   M. Rebek
      Buddy Cole Orchestra   DE L 8820

D1241-48. Nov 23 (Recorded from radio broadcasts.)
Something in Common   J. Van Heusen, J. Burke
      Buddy Cole Trio
Look to Your Heart   J. Van Heusen, S. Cahn
Suddenly There's a Valley   C. Meyer, B. Jones
Moments to Remember   R. Allen, A. Stillman
Is Christmas Only a Tree?   M. Rebek
The Longest Walk   F. Spielman, E. Pola
Ol' Man River   J. Kern, O. Hammerstein II
In a Little Spanish Town   M. Wayne, O. Lewis, J. Young

D1249-50. Dec 13
Ol' Man River   J. Kern, O. Hammerstein II
      Buddy Cole Trio   DE L 8848
In a Little Spanish Town   M. Wayne, O. Lewis, J. Young
                                     DE L 8849

D1251-59. Dec 24
Happy Holiday   I. Berlin
Joy to the World   G.F. Handel, I. Watts
White Christmas   I. Berlin
The First Noel   Traditional
Good King Wenceslas   Traditional
Away in a Manger   M. Luther, J. Murray
Deck the Halls with Boughs of Holly Traditional
O Little Town of Bethlehem   P. Brooks, L. Redner
Silent Night, Holy Night   F. Gruber, J. Mohr
      (The above are taken from the Christmas radio
      program broadcast live Dec 24, 1955, at the Grand
      Central Terminal, New York.)

D1260-66. Dec 27
      (These were for "High Tor," with all songs by
      Arthur Schwartz and Maxwell Anderson. See Albums.)
Living One Day at a Time   A. Schwartz, M. Anderson
      Joseph J. Lilley Orchestra   DE L 8896
A Little Love, a Little While
John Barleycorn
Once Upon a Long Ago
A Little While
John Barleycorn (with chorus)

When You're in Love

> NOTE: Bing's exclusive recording contract with Decca
> expired at the end of 1955, a contract signed in Jul
> 1943. From 1956 he freelanced his recordings, still
> often appearing on the Decca label.
>   Also, see recordings about this time listed in
> "Songs on Cardboard" (p. 155) and "A Treasure Trove of
> Songs" (p. 175), the latter being recordings augmented
> in late 1978 and early 1979.

1956
D1267-68. Jan 6
Little One   C. Porter
    Louis Armstrong (trumpet)
I Love You, Samantha   C. Porter

D1269. Jan 17
Well, Did You Evah!   C. Porter
    Johnny Green M.G.M. Studio Orchestra
    with Frank Sinatra   CAP 15468

D1270. Jan 18
Now You Has Jazz   C. Porter
    Louis Armstrong All Stars   CAP 15405

D1271. Jan 22
True Love   C. Porter
    Johnny Green M.G.M. Studio Orchestra
    with Grace Kelly   CAP 15409
        ("True Love" became Bing's 22nd gold record; even
    his 23rd, as it sold a million in the album and as a
    single. Songs of Jan 6-22 are collected in Capitol's
    High Society album.)

D1272-73. Feb 23
All Through the Night   C. Porter
    Joseph Lilley Orchestra with Mitzi Gaynor
You're the Top   C. Porter
        (Songs in Decca's Anything Goes album.)

D1274-81. Apr 17.
        (Songs of Apr 17-18 were for Decca's album Songs I
    Wish I Had Sung the First Time Around.)
April Showers   B.G. DeSylva, L. Silvers
    Jack Pleis Orchestra with the Rhythmaires DE L 9150
Blues in the Night   J. Mercer, H. Arlen
                                DE L 9151
Prisoner of Love   L. Robin, C. Gaskill, R. Columbo
                                DE L 9152
Memories Are Made of This   T. Gilkyson, R. Dehr, F. Miller
                                DE L 9153
My Blue Heaven   W. Donaldson, G. Whiting
                                DE L 9154
Paper Doll   J. Black
                                DE L 9155
Ain't Misbehavin'   "Fats" Waller
                                DE L 9156
When My Baby Smiles at Me

H. von Tilzer, A. Sterling, T. Lewis, B. Munro
DE L 9157

D1282-85. Apr 18
A Little Kiss Each Morning   H. Woods
    Jack Pleis Orchestra
This Love of Mine   S. Parker, H. Sanicola, F. Sinatra
Mona Lisa   J. Livingston, R. Evans
Thanks for the Memory   L. Robin, R. Rainger

D1286-87. May 22
Honeysuckle Rose   Fats Waller, A. Razaf
    Buddy Cole Trio   DE L 9261
Swanee   G. Gershwin, I. Caesar
        DE L 9262

D1288-93. Jun 11   VER BR 20155/60
    (Songs of Jun 11-12 were for Verve's album <u>Bing</u>
<u>Sings While Bregman Swings</u>; two marked with an asterisk
did not appear on the Metro reissue of the album.)
Blue Room   R. Rodgers, L. Hart
    Buddy Bregman Orchestra
Jeepers Creepers   H. Warren, J. Mercer
I've Got Five Dollars   R. Rodgers, L. Hart
*'Deed I Do   F. Rose, W. Hirsch
Nice Work If You Can Get It   G. and I. Gershwin
*The Song Is You   J. Kern

D1300-05. Jun 12   VER BR 20161/66
They All Laughed   G. and I. Gershwin
    Buddy Bregman Orchestra
Heat Wave   I. Berlin
September in the Rain   H. Warren, A. Dubin
Cheek to Cheek   I. Berlin
Have You Met Miss Jones?   R. Rodgers, L. Hart
Mountain Greenery   R. Rodgers, L. Hart

D1306-08. Oct 3
Around the World   V. Young, H. Adamson
    Buddy Cole Orchestra   DE L 9584
I Heard the Bells on   H.W. Longfellow, J. Marks
    Christmas Day   DE L 9585
Love in a Home   J. Mercer, G. DePaul
        DE L 9586

SONGS ON CARDBOARD

In 1956 Bing recorded the six following songs to
be released as cardboard Bing Crosby Phonocards for
greeting cards, mainly 6-inch 78 rpm. "Because" was so
released by his Phonocards, but the release of others
is uncertain (Zwisohn 60):

D1309-14.
Because (with Buddy Cole on organ)
The Pied Piper of Hamelin
Jack and the Beanstalk
Simple Simon
Old Mother Hubbard

Rip Van Winkle

> NOTE: Bing also recorded the following songs on card-
> board about 1956 and later as 5-in. to 7-in. discs
> (Ralph S. Harding, Bing 95 [Aug 1990]: 5-6):

D1315-20.
Music to Shave By. With Louis Armstrong, Rosemary Clooney,
     the Hi-Lo's, for the Adjustable Remington Roll-a-Matic
     Shaver and billed as the first Hi-Fi record in a na-
     tional magazine advertisement. A medley of a parody of
     "When You're Smiling," "Ain't Misbehavin'," "I'm Shav-
     ing Myself for You," and Bing singing and saying that
     the razor is "the greatest invention since the guillo-
     tine." Columbia (Auravision), 5 in., 33 1/3 rpm.
I'm the Best Dressed Man in the World. A parody of D1357
     for a Prestodine Production for Y-Iron Drip-Dry Shirts.
     33 1/3 rpm.
Swinging on a Star. A Crosby Phonocard parody advertising
     Gas Cookers (orig. song by J. Van Heusen and J. Burke).
     78 rpm.
You Took Advantage of Me. The Rhythm Boys and Paul White-
     man's Orchestra, issued as RCA Victor E3-CS-7922 for
     Halo Shampoo, apparently the same as the Victor BVE
     43760 [Victor 21398] recorded Apr 25, 1928. 78 rpm.
A Personal Message from Bing Crosby. The Longines Symphon-
     ette Society, advertising its Bing Crosby Treasury: The
     Songs I Love album of 1968. The sleeve offers holders
     of a Bank Americard credit card a free copy of [Bing
     Crosby's] All-Time Hit Parade (1966) and the chance to
     win $100. 33 1/3 rpm.
How Lovely Is Christmas (A. Wilder, A. Sundgaard). Slightly
     different from the song for Golden Records, it is a
     promotion for Goodyear Tires. 33 1/3 rpm.

> NOTE: Matrix numbers are seldom available after 1956
> for long-playing discs; albums are listed at the end of
> the Discography. The sessions often list the
> albums.

1957
D1321-22. Jan ?
Seven Nights a Week   J. Van Heusen, S. Cahn
     Nelson Riddle Orchestra   CAP
Man on Fire   S. Fain, P.F. Webster
                                    CAP

D1323-24A. Feb 19
     (The songs recorded Feb 19-20 were for the RCA
     album Bing with a Beat, which also includes "I'm Gonna
     Sit Right Down and Write Myself a Letter," "Some Sunny
     Day," and "Dream a Little Dream of Me.")
Exactly Like You   J. McHugh, D. Fields
     Bob Scobey's Frisco Jazz Band
Let a Smile Be Your Umbrella   I. Kahal, S. Fain, F. Wheeler
Tell Me   J. Callahan, M. Kortlander

D1325-30. Feb 20
Mama Loves Papa   C. Friend, A. Baer

Bob Scobey's Frisco Jazz Band
Down Among the Sheltering Palms J. Brockman, A. Olman
Last Night on the Back Porch L. Brown, C. Schraubstader
Along the Way to Waikiki   R. Whiting, G. Kahn
Whispering   J. Schonberger, R. Coburn, V. Rose
Mack the Knife   K. Weill, M. Blitzstein, B. Brecht

D1331-66. Mar 14
Alabamy Bound   B.G. DeSylva, R. Henderson, B. Green
    Buddy Cole Trio   DE L 9936
When I Take My Sugar to Tea
                   S. Fain, I. Kahal, P. Norman, P. Connor
Between the Devil and the Deep Blue Sea H. Arlen, T.Koehler
Georgia on My Mind   H. Carmichael, S. Gorrell
I'm Confessin   D. Dougherty, E. Reynolds, A. Neiburg
If I Could Be with You   H. Creamer, J. Layton
Avalon   V. Rose, A. Jolson, B.G. DeSylva
Chinatown, My Chinatown   W. Jerome, J. Schwartz
You're Driving Me Crazy   W. Donaldson
On the Alamo   I. Jones, G. Kahn
Chicago   F. Fisher
Softly as in a Morning Sunrise S. Romberg, O.Hammerstein II
        (The above 12 songs were for the Decca album New
    Tricks.)
More Than You Know   V. Youmans, B. Rose, E. Eliscu
Year In, Year Out   S. Cahn, M. Rodgers
    Arthur Norman Orchestra and Choir
My Own Individual Star   ditto
Open Sesame   ditto
Oh Rich Brother (Kassim)   ditto
They All Lived Happily Ever After ditto
I Love You Whoever You Are   ditto
        (The above six songs were for Golden's Ali Baba
    and the Forty Thieves.)
How Lovely Is Christmas   A. Sundgaard, A. Wilder
An Axe, an Apple, and a Buckskin Jacket ditto
Boy at a Window   ditto
Young Jethro Swung His Mighty Axe ditto
Johnnny Appleseed   ditto
An Incident on Roger's Creek ditto
How Lovely Is Christmas   ditto
        (The above seven songs were for Golden's A Christ-
    mas Story: An Axe, an Apple and a Buckskin Jacket.)
The Best Dressed Man in the World
                   M. Keith, A. Bergman, L. Spence
Never Be Afraid   M. Keith, A. Bergman, L. Spence
        (The above two songs were for Golden's The Emper-
    or's New Clothes.)
An Early Autumn Afternoon   A. Baer, D. Fuller
Old King Cole   Traditonal
Sing a Song of Sixpence   ditto
Mistress Mary Quite Contrary ditto
Little Boy Blue (medley)   ditto
For Want of a Nail   ditto
Starlight, Starbright   ditto
Jack B. Nimble   ditto

        (Eight songs for Golden's Jack Be Nimble; called
    Mother Goose Songs in 1977 with Crosby narrations for

Wonderland (WLP-79) and <u>Mother Goose Fantasy</u>. The fol
lowing were issued by Golden Records as children's 78
rpm six-inch yellow discs. They were released in 1957-
58 and collected in the <u>Never Be Afraid</u> album. These
are the last known 78 rpm recordings by Crosby.)

```
GO R-339 Open Sesame                S. Cahn, M. Rodgers
GO R-339 They All Lived Happily Ever After
                                    S. Cahn, M. Rodgers
GO R-371 How Lovely Is Christmas    A.Wilder, A.Sundgaard
GO R-386 Boy at a Window            A. Wilder, A. Sundgaard
GO R-386 An Axe, an Apple and a Buckskin Jacket  ditto
GO R-350 An Incident on Roger's Creek  ditto
GO R-355 Never Be Afraid    A. Bergman, M. Keith, L. Spence
GO R-395 Old King Cole               Traditional
GO R-395 Sing a Song of Sixpence     Traditional
GO R-364 Mistress Mary Quite         Traditional
    Contrary
GO R-364 Humpty Dumpty               Traditional
GO R-396 Little Boy Blue             Traditional
```

```
D1367-68. Dec 27
Trust Your Destiny to Your Star  C. Porter
    Pete King Orchestra
Gigi                            A. Lerner, F. Loewe
        (A 1958 Decca 45 rpm release, No. 37851.)
```

```
D1369-70. Dec 31
Straight Down the Middle     J. Van Heusen, S. Cahn
    Buddy Cole Orchestra
Tomorrow's My Lucky Day      J. Van Heusen, J. Burke
```

1958
```
D1371-71A. Feb 24
Paris Holiday                J. Van Heusen, S. Cahn
    Joseph Lilley Orchestra with Bob Hope
Nothing in Common            J. Van Heusen, S. Cahn
        (For the United Artists 1958 album Paris Holiday.)
```

```
D1372-75. Jul 28
        (The songs recorded Jul 28-Aug 11 were for RCA's
    album Fancy Meeting You Here, matrix Nos. J2PP-6357 and
    J2PP-6358.  Two songs marked with an asterisk are not
    on the 1969 reissue titled Rendevous by Camden.)
Brazil                       B. Russell, A. Barroso
    Billy May Orchestra with Rosemary Clooney
How About You?               A. Freed, B. Lane
Love Won't Let You Get Away  S. Cahn, J. Van Heusen
On a Slow Boat to China      F. Loesser
```

```
D1376-79. Aug 7
It Happened in Monterey      M. Wayne, B. Rose
    Billy May Orchestra with Rosemary Clooney
Hindustan                    O. Wallace, H. Weeks
Fancy Meeting You Here       S. Cahn, J. Van Heusen
*Calcutta                    J. Livingston, R. Evans
```

```
D1380-84. Aug 11
*Isle of Capri               J. Kennedy, W. Grosz
```

Billy May Orchestra with Rosemary Clooney
Say 'Si si'   E. Lecuona, A. Stillman, F. Luban
You Came a Long Way from St. Louis B. Russell, J. Brooks
I Can't Get Started   I. Gershwin, V. Duke
Love Won't Let You Get Away   S. Cahn, J. Van Heusen

D1385-86. Oct 17
Church Bells   P. Sanders
     Buddy Cole Trio
Rain   E. Ford, C. Morgan, A. Swanstrom

1959
D1387-88. Mar 6
          (Songs from Mar 6 to 25, except the last [marked],
     are in the album Say One for Me, matrix Nos. 45841/2.)
I Couldn't Care Less   S. Cahn, J. Van Heusen
     Lionel Newman Orchestra with Buddy Cole on piano
Say One for Me   ditto
     with Debbie Reynolds

D1389-92. Mar 25
I Couldn't Care Less   S. Cahn, J. Van Heusen
     Frank De Vol Orchestra
Say One for Me   ditto
The Secret of Christmas   ditto
*Just What I Wanted for Christmas ditto

D1393-97. Jul 20 (All for RCA.)
Shenandoah   Traditional, adapted by J. and A. Lomax
     Bob Thompson Orchestra
Old Settlers Song   F. Henry
Skip to My Lou   Traditional
     with Rosemary Clooney
Streets of Loredo   Traditional
All 'Pewtrified' (narration)   Traditional

D1398-1402. Jul 21 (All for RCA.)
Will You Come to the Bower?   Traditional
     Bob Thompson Orchestra   Adapted by Tom Roberts
When I Went Off to Prospect   John A. Stone
Nine Hundred Miles Traditional, adapted by J. and A. Lomax
Hang Me, Oh Hang Me   ditto
Git Along Little Dogies   ditto

D1403-06. Jul 23 (All for RCA)
Crossing the Plains*   J. Stone
     *with Rosemary Clooney   Adapted by Tom Roberts
Buffalo Gals*   Cool White
Green Grow the Lilacs   Adapted by Tom Roberts
Jennie Jenkins*   Adapted by J. and A. Lomax

D1407-09. Jul 24
Bound for the Promised Land* Adapted by J. and A. Lomax
     Bob Thompson Orchestra *with Rosemary Clooney
Red River Valley   Adapted by J. and A. Lomax
Buckskin Joe   J. Driftwood

D1410-37. Dec 16, 17 (All for RCA.)
Daisy Bell (On a Bicycle Built for Two) H. Dacre

Jack Halloran Orchestra and Chorus
The Bowery	P. Gaunt, C. Hoyt
After the Ball	C.K. Harris
When You Wore a Tulip	J. Mahoney, P. Wenrich
You Were Meant for Me	A. Freed, N.H. Brown
When I Grow Too Old to Dream	S. Romberg, O. Hammerstein II
Doodle Do Do	A. Kassel, M. Stitzel
All I Do Is Dream of You	A. Freed, N.H. Brown
Take Me Out to the Ball Game	J. Norworth, A. von Tilzer
Meet Me in St. Louis	K. Mills, A. Sterling
Peggy O'Neill	H. Pease, E. Nelson, G. Dodge
Give My Regards to Broadway	G.M. Cohan
You're a Grand Old Flag	G.M. Cohan
K-K-K-Katy	G. O'Hara
Mairzy Doats	M. Drake, A. Hoffman, J. Livingston
Old MacDonald Had a Farm	Adapted by J. Halloran
Goodbye My Lady Love	J. Howard
Linger Awhile	H. Owens, V. Rose
The Gang That Sang 'Heart of My Heart'	B. Ryan
Long, Long Ago	T. Bayly
I Was Seeing Nellie Home	J. Fletcher, F. Kyle
Aura Lee	G. Poulton, W. Fosdick
Cuddle Up a Little Closer	O. Harbach, K. Hoschna
Shoo Fly Don't Bother Me	B. Reeves, F. Campbell
Oh Dem Golden Slippers	J. Bland
On the Road to Mandalay	R. Kipling, O. Speaks
A Hot Time in the Old Town Tonight	J. Hayden, T. Metz
Toot-Toot-Tootsie	

G. Kahn, E. Erdman, D. Russo, R. King, T. FioRito
(The December recordings are in RCA's Join Bing
and Sing Along, [1960], matrix Nos. L2 PP2714-45, L2
PP2715-15, album LPM-22276.)

1960
D1438-40A. Jan 28
*The Music of Home	F. Loesser

Bob Thompson Orchestra
The New Ashmoleon Marching Society and Students
Conservatory Band   F. Loesser
*It's a Good Day   P. Lee, D. Barbour
(The above two marked songs were released as an
RCA 45 rpm single No. 47-7685 in 1960.)
Aloha Means I Love You   J. Noble, R. Lubens

D1441-43. Jun
Pennies from Heaven   J. Burke, A. Johnston
Johnnie Green and the Columbia Studio Orchestra
Let's Fall in Love   H. Arlen, T. Koehler
South of the Border   J. Kennedy, M. Carr
(Songs in Colpix's Pepe album; Bing sang "Incura-
bly Romantic" on Jun 15 for the film Let's Make Love.)

D1444-53. Jun 22
Pagan Love Song   N.H. Brown, A. Freed
Billy May Orchestra
Cuban Love Song   H. Stothart, J. McHugh, D. Fields
How High the Moon   M. Lewis, N. Hamilton
Old Devil Moon   E.Y. Harburg, B. Lane
Marta   L. Gilbert, M. Simons

The Rose in Her Hair   H. Warren, A. Dubin
C'est magnifique   C. Porter
Taking a Chance on Love   J. Latouche, V. Duke, T. Fetter
In the Still of the Night   C. Porter
I Could Have Danced All Night A. Lerner, F. Loewe

D1454-63. Jun 23
Heavenly Night   M. Keith, A. Bergman
     Billy May Orchestra
My Shawl   S. Adams, X. Cugat, C. Fernandez
Down Argentine Way   H. Warren, M. Gordon
What a Difference a Day Makes M. Grever, S. Adams
Ramona   M. Wayne, L. Gilbert
Amapola   J. LaCalle, A. Gamse
Malaguena (At the Crossroads) E. Lecouna, B. Russell
The Breeze and I (Andalucia) A. Stillman, E. Lecouna
Again   L. Newman, D. Cochran
Allez-vous-en (Go Away)   C. Porter
          (The recordings of Jun 22-23 are in MGM's El Señor
     Bing, matrix Nos. 60-MG-774, 60-MG-775.)

D1464-67. Jun 28
Sugar (That Sugar Baby o' Mine)
                    M. Pinkard, S. Mitchell, E. Alexander
     Billy May Orchestra
Way Down Yonder in New Orleans H. Creamer, J. Layton
Let's Sing Like a Dixieland Band A. Bergman
Brother Bill   L. Armstrong

D1468-75. Jun 29
Muskrat Ramble   E. Ory, R. Gilbert
     Billy May Orchestra with Louis Armstrong
Dardanella   F. Bernard, J. Black, F. Fisher
Bye Bye Blues   F. Hamm, D. Bennett, B. Lown, C. Gray
Up a Lazy River   S. Arodin, H. Carmichael
Preacher   H. Silver, B. Gonzales
Rocky Mountain Moon   J. Mercer
*Li'l Ol' Tune   J. Mercer
At the Jazz Band Ball   N. LaRocca, L. Shields, J. Mercer,
                              E. Edwards, T. Sbarbaro
          (The recordings of Jun 28-29 are in MGM's Bing and
     Satchmo, matrix Nos. 60-MGM-658/659. The song marked
     with an asterisk is not in the Capitol 1977 release
     titled Bing Crosby/Louis Armstrong. "Lazy River" was
     released in a benefit album for the United Nations.)

D1476-77. Aug 25 (Songs for MGM 45 rpm single.)
Incurably Romantic   S. Cahn, J. Van Heusen
     Pete King Orchestra
The Second Time Around   S. Cahn, J. Van Heusen

D1478-1578. Dec 20, 23, 27, and 28 (For Warner Bros.)
     101 Gang Songs: Parts 1 and 2--listed on page 177.
          (The songs were issued by Warner Bros. in 1962 in
     various versions, at least one with 101 songs, another
     with 51. See the albums list.)

1961
D1579-84. May 8
C'est si bon*   H. Betti, A. Hornez, J. Seelen
     Malcolm Lockyer Orchestra
Under Paris Skies*   H. Giraud, K. Gannon, J. Drejac
Morgen*   P. Mosser, N. Sherman
Melancholie*   A. Romans, R. Blake, P. Dudan
April in Portugal   R. Ferraro, J. Galhardo, J. Kennedy
More 'n' More Amor   A. Testa, C. Rossi, D. Manning
          (Four marked songs were first recorded in London
     Oct 15, 1960, but were rejected.)

D1585-90. May 9
Moment in Madrid   B. Thompson, R. Roberts, B.Katz, B.Thiele
     Malcolm Lockyer Orchestra
Never on Sunday   M. Hadjidakis, B. Towne
Pigalle   G. Ulmer, G. Koger, C. Newman
My Heart Still Hears the Music M. Panzeri, M. Karter
Two Shadows on the Sand   G. Becaud, M. Vidalin, M. Karter
Domenica   P. Garinei, S. Giovannini, B. Crosby, G. Kramer
          (Bing wrote the English lyrics to "Domenica" in
     Rome in 1960. All songs recorded May 8-9 appear in
     Decca's 1962 Holiday in Europe.)

D1591-93. Sep 1
Let's Not Be Sensible   S. Cahn, J. Van Heusen
     Robert Farnon Orchestra with Joan Collins
Team Work   S. Cahn, J. Van Heusen
     with Bob Hope
The Road to Hong Kong   S. Cahn, J. Van Heusen
          (In Liberty's 1962 album of Road to Hong Kong.
     Bing did not sing the last word of "Let's Not Be Sensi-
     ble" in the film; it was added by Mike Sammes.)

1962
D1594-1612. Apr 30
          (These recordings were for MGM's Great Standards,
     although Zwisohn states they were recorded by Warner
     Bros.)
Singin' in the Rain   A. Freed, N.H. Brown
Darktown Strutter's Ball   S. Brooks
Around Her Neck She Wore a Yellow Ribbon
                               J. Valentine, J. Ansell
My Little Grass Shack in Kealakekua, Hawaii
                          T. Harrison, J. Noble, B. Cogswell
Me and My Shadow   A. Jolson, D. Dreyer, B. Rose
Five Foot Two, Eyes of Blue R. Henderson, S. Lewis, J.Young
Marching Along Together   E. Pola, M. Dixon, F. Steininger
Should I?   A. Freed, N.H. Brown
Blue Moon   R. Rodgers, L. Hart
Cecilia   D. Dreyer, H. Ruby
Gimme a Little Kiss   R. Turk, J. Smith, M. Pinkard
When the Red Red Robin, Comes Bob, Bob Bobbin' Along
                               H. Woods
The Loveliest Night of the Year
                          J. Rosas, P.F. Webster, I. Aaronson
Don't Sit Under the Apple Tree L. Brown, C. Tobias, S.Stept
My Pony Boy   B. Heath, C. O'Donnell
The Man on the Flying Trapeze (The Daring Young Man)

```
                                G. Leybourne, A. Lee
Billy Boy                       Adapted by Billy Conn
A-Tisket, A-Tasket              E. Fitzgerald, A. Feldman
Forever and Ever                F. Winkler, M. Rosa
```

D1613-33. Jun 21, 26
      (Bing recorded many songs for Project, his own
    record company, which he sold about Apr 1963 to Colum-
    bia Records, but none has been released [Zwisohn 61].
    They include the following 22:)

```
All Alone                       I. Berlin
Always                          I. Berlin
The Band Played On              C. Ward, J. Palmer
(Only) A Bird in a Gilded Cage  A. Lamb, H. von Tilzer
Blueberry Hill                  L. Stock, A. Lewis, V. Rose
How Can I Leave Thee?           Anonymous
If I Didn't Care                J. Lawrence
In the Shade of the Old Apple Tree
                                H. Williams, E. van Alstyne
The Last Rose of Summer         R. Milliken, J. Moore
Look for the Silver Lining      J. Kern, B.G. DeSylva
My Bonnie Lies Over the Ocean   H. Fulmer, J. Wood
Now the Day Is Over             J. Barnaby, S. Baring-Gould
A Pretty Girl Is Like a Melody  I. Berlin
Put on Your Old Gray Bonnet     S. Murphy, P. Wenrich
Roll On, Silver Moon            J. Turner
Say It with Music               I. Berlin
Sidewalks of New York           J. Blake, C. Lawlor
Together    B.G. DeSylva, R. Henderson, L.Brown, S.Ballantine
Tom Dooley                      F. Warner, A. Lomax
What'll I Do?                   I. Berlin
Wishing (Will Make It So)       B.G. DeSylva
```

D1634-47. Oct 5
```
Winter Wonderland                   F. Bernard, D. Smith
     accompanied by Bob Thompson, Jack Halloran, Peter Matz
Have Yourself a Merry Little Christmas  H. Martin, R. Blane
What Child Is This?                 Traditional
The Holly and the Ivy               Traditional
The Little Drummer Boy       K. Davis, H. Simeone, H. Onorati
O Holy Night                        Traditional
The Littlest Angel                  M. David, S. Rady
Let It Snow! Let It Snow!           S. Cahn, J. Styne
Hark! The Herald Angels Sing     Traditional
It Came Upon the Midnight Clear  Traditional
Frosty the Snowman                  S. Nelson, J. Rollins
Pat a Pan                           Traditional
While Shepherds Watched Their Sheep  Traditional
I Wish You a Merry Christmas     Traditional
```
        (Recorded for Warner Bros. album I Wish You a
    Merry Christmas, reissued in 1977 by Capitol as Christ-
    mas Classics.)

1963
D1648-49. Jul 29
```
Fugue for Tinhorns              F. Loesser
     Morris Stoloff Orchestra
     with Frank Sinatra and Dean Martin
The Oldest Established Permanent Floating Crap Game in New
```

York   F. Loesser
        (Recorded for Reprise as a 45 rpm, No. 20217.)

D1650-53. Aug 8
Something Sort of Grandish   B. Lane, E.Y. Harburg
    Morris Stoloff Orchestra with Debbie Reynolds
Younger Than Springtime   R. Rodgers, O. Hammerstein II
Tower of Babel   R. Allen, D. Lampert, P. Farrow
    Ray Ellis Orchestra
My Favorite Story (narrated introduction to 13 stories told
    by other artists)
        (The first three above were recorded for REP, UA,
    and DE, respectively. My Favorite Story is a 20th
    Century-Fox album, matrix No. 3106, the same as the
    album number.)

D1654-57. Aug 21
The Old Plantation (Kuu Home)
                        J. Shannon, D. Nape, M. Montano
    Nelson Riddle Orchestra
Forevermore (Lei Aloha, Lei Makamae) C. King, M. Raskin
My Tane (My Man)   A. Goupil, J. Noble, R. Gump
Love and Aloha   J. Blaisdel

D1658-61. Oct 16
Frangipani Blossom   J. Livingston, R. Evans
    Nelson Riddle Orchestra
Lovely Hula Hands   R. Anderson
Keep Your Eyes on the Hands   T. Todaro, M. Johnston
The Hukilau Song   J. Owens, C. Lucas
        (Recordings of Aug 21 and Oct 16 were for Reprise,
    Return to Paradise, matrix Nos. 10293-1B, 10294-1B.)

D1662-63. Oct 21
Christmas Dinner Country Style R. Freed, G. Saxon
    Ralph Carmichael Orchestra
Do You Hear What I Hear?   N. Regney, G. Shayne
        (A Capitol 45 rpm, No. 55088.)

D1664-67. Oct 29
Still   B. Anderson
    Bill Justis Orchestra
Wabash Cannonball   A.P. Carter
A Little Bitty Tear   H. Cochran
Jealous Heart   J. Carson

D1668-75. Oct 31
Four Walls   M. Moore, G. Campbell
    Bill Justis Orchestra
Wolverton Mountain   M. Kilgore, C. King
Hello Walls   W. Nelson
*Crazy Arms   C. Seals, R. Mooney
Oh, Lonesome Me   D. Gibson
Bouquet of Roses   S. Nelson, B. Hilliard
Heartaches by the Number   H. Howard
*Sunflower   M. David
        (Recordings of Oct 29, 31 were for Capitol's Bing
    Crosby Sings the Great Country Hits, matrix Nos. ST1-
    2346-A1, ST24-2346-A1, reissued by Capitol [SM-11737]

without two songs marked by an asterisk.)

D1676-79. Dec 9 (Songs for Reprise, No. R-6106.)
Home in Hawaii (King's Serenade) C. King, P.F. Webster
    Nelson Riddle Orchestra
Beautiful Kahana   C. King, M. Montano
Adventures in Paradise   L. Newman, D. Cochran
Return to Paradise   N. Washington, D. Tiomkin

1964
D1680-84. Feb 4
This Is a Great Country   I. Berlin
    Fred Waring and his Pennsylvanians
This Land Is Your Land   W. Guthrie
A Home in the Meadow   S. Cahn, R.E. Dolan
You Never Had It So Good   S. Cahn, J. Van Heusen
    with Frank Sinatra
Let Us Break Bread Together   Adapted by Roy Ringwald
       (In the 1964 Reprise album <u>America, I Hear You
    Singing</u>.)

D1685-87. Apr 10
Style   S. Cahn, J. Van Heusen
    Nelson Riddle Orchestra
    with Frank Sinatra, Dean Martin, Sammy Davis, Jr.
Mr. Booze   S. Cahn, J. Van Heusen
Don't Be a Do Badder   S. Cahn, J. Van Heusen
    with a Boy Choir
       (In Reprise, <u>Robin and the Seven Hoods</u>, 1964.)

D1688-92. Jun 19
It's Christmas Time Again   J. Elliot, S. Burke, J. Harwood
    Fred Waring and his Pennsylvanians
Go Tell It on the Mountain   Adapted by Jack Halloran
    with Frank Sinatra
The Secret of Christmas   S. Cahn, J. Van Heusen
    Fred Waring and his Pennsylvanians
Christmas Candles   K. O'Dea
We Wish You the Merriest   L. Brown
    with Frank Sinatra
       (For Reprise, <u>Twelve Songs of Christmas</u>.)

D1693-96. Aug 15
That Travelin' Two Beat   J. Livingston, R. Evans
    Billy May Orchestra
    with Rosemary Clooney
The Poor People of Paris M. Monnot, R. Rouzard, J. Lawrence
<u>Adios senorita</u>   J. Livingston, R. Evans
Roamin' in the Gloaming   H. Lauder

D1697-1700. Oct 4
I'm Confessin'   D. Dougherty, E. Reynolds, A. Neiburg
    Buddy Cole Orchestra
Avalon   V. Rose, A. Jolson, B.G. De Sylva
Chinatown, My Chinatown   W. Jerome, J. Schwartz
Alabamy Bound   R. Henderson, B.G. DeSylva, B. Green
       (Songs for "The Bell Telephone Hour" television
    program.)

D1703-06. Dec 2
Come to the Mardi Gras
        M. Bulhoes, M. de Oliviera, E. Drake, J. Shirl
     Billy May Orchestra with Rosemary Clooney
Ciao, ciao, bambino   D. Modugno, E. Verde, M. Parish
The Daughter of Molly Malone J. Livingston, R. Evans
I Get Ideas   D. Cochran, J. Sanders, C. Vedani

D1707-10. Dec 3
Hear That Band (Hear Dem Bells) J. Livingston, R. Evans
     Billy May Orchestra with Rosemary Clooney
New Vienna Woods   J. Strauss, J. Livingston, R. Evans
Knees Up, Mother Brown   J. Livingston, R. Evans
That Travelin' Two Beat   J. Livingston, R. Evans
        (All recordings of Aug 15, Dec 2, 3 were for
     Capitol's That Travelin' Two Beat, 1965.)

1965
D1711. Sep 28
The White World of Winter   H. Carmichael, M. Parish
     Sonny Burke Orchestra
        (Reprise 45 rpm release in 1965 with "The Secret
     of Christmas, recorded Jun 19, 1964, No. S-424. Reis-
     sued for Goodyear by Columbia Special Products, The
     Great Songs of Christmas, Album Six, No. CSS-388.]

D1712-19. Nov 30
Stormy Weather   H. Arlen, T. Koehler
     Michel Piastro and Longines Symphonette Orchestra
Always   I. Berlin
Isn't This a Lovely Day to Be Caught in the Rain? I. Berlin
In the Chapel in the Moonlight B. Hill
Lonesome and Sorry   B. Davis, C. Conrad
All Alone   I. Berlin
Coquette   C. Lombardo, J. Green, G. Kahn
South of the Border   M. Carr, J. Kennedy

D1720-27. Dec 2
When My Sugar Walks Down the Street
                    G. Austin, J. McHugh, I. Mills
        Michel Piastro and Longines Symphonette Orchestra
The Breeze and I (Andalucia) E. Lecuona, A. Stillman
I'll Take Romance   B. Oakland, O. Hammerstein II
Rock-A-Bye Your Baby   J. Schwartz, S. Lewis, J.Young
Tenderly   W. Gross, J. Lawrence
Amapola   J. LaCalle, A. Gamse
Ole Buttermilk Sky   H. Carmichael, J. Brooks
My Prayer   J. Kennedy, G. Boulanger
        (The 16 songs recorded Nov 30, Dec 2 were for All-
     Time Hit Parade for Longines.)

1966
D1728-29. May 9
Far from Home   J. Morris, G. Freedman
     Johnny Keating Orchestra
How Green Was My Valley   J. Morris, G. Freedman
        (A 45 rpm for Reprise, No. S-4781, issued 1966.)

1967
D1730-31B. Oct 31
*Step to the Rear   C. Leigh, E. Bernstein
     Ernie Freeman Orchestra
*What Do We Do with the World?   H. Mancini, B. Russell
          (*A Reprise 45 rpm No. S-3080, 1967.)
Don't Let a Good Thing Get Away C. Leigh, E. Bernstein
Live a Little   C. Leigh, E. Bernstein

1968
D1732-36. Feb 9
Thoroughly Modern Millie   S. Cahn, J. Van Heusen
     "Bugs" Bower Orchestra
Talk to the Animals   L. Bricusse
Ding Dong the Witch Is Dead E.Y. Harburg, H. Arlen
High Hopes   S. Cahn, J. Van Heusen
My Friend the Doctor   L. Bricusse

D1737-43A. Feb 12
I Call You Sunshine   B. Bower, J. Wolf, J. Howard
     "Bugs" Bower Orchestra
Where the Rainbow Ends   R. Cook, R. Greenaway
What's More American   K. Millet
Up, Up and Away   J. Webb
Puff the Magic Dragon   P. Yarrow, L. Lipton
Chim Chim Charee   R. and R. Sherman
Love Is Blue   B. Blackburn, P. Cour, A. Popp
*That's All I Want from You M. Rotha
          (Except for one marked, the Feb 9 and 12 record-
          ings were for Pickwick, Thoroughly Modern Bing, 1968.
          Reissued on 8-track tape without "Where the Rainbow
          Ends" and as a CD titled A Visit to the Movies [1991]
          without "I Call You Sunshine.")

D1744-63. Mar 26-28
Marie   I. Berlin
     Michel Piastro and Longines Symphonette Orchestra
That Old Gang of Mine   M. Dixon, R.Henderson, B. Rose
One for My Baby   H. Arlen, J. Mercer
River Stay Away from My Door M. Dixon, H. Woods
What'll I Do?   I. Berlin
Ballin' the Jack   C. Smith, J. Burris
The Song Is Ended   I. Berlin
I've Heard That Song Before S. Cahn, J. Styne
Remember   I. Berlin
Puttin' on the Ritz   I. Berlin
Thank You for a Lovely Evening D. Fields, J. McHugh
Love Makes the World Go 'Round B. Merrill
Sentimental Gentleman from Georgia F. Perkins, M. Parish
There's Danger in Your Eyes, Cherie
                            H. Richman, J. Meskill, P. Wendling
Say It Isn't So   I. Berlin
Say 'Si si'   E. Lecuona, A. Stillman, F. Luban
Friendly Persuasion   P.F. Webster, D. Tiomkin
I Hear Music   F. Loesser, B. Lane
How Come You Do Me Like You Do? G. Austin, R. Bergere
Dance with a Dolly   J. Eaton, D. Kapp, T. Shand, J. Hodges
          (These twenty songs were for Bing Crosby Treasury,
     Bing's second Longines Symphonette Society album.)

D1764-67. Nov 21
Hey Jude   J. Lennon, P. McCartney
     Jimmy Bowen Orchestra
Those Were the Days   G. Raskin
Lonely Street   C. Belew, K. Sowder, W. Stevenson
It's All in the Game   C. Sigman, Gen. C. Dawes

D1768-68E. Nov 25
*Both Sides Now   J. Mitchell
     Jimmy Bowen Orchestra
The Straight Life   S. Curtis
Little Green Apples   B. Russell
Livin' on Lovin'   D. Burgess
*More and More   T. Karen, R. Robinson, A.Reuss
Just for Tonight   B. Knight
          (Nov 21, 25 recordings were for Amos, Hey Jude,
     Hey Bing, reissued twice without two songs marked.)

1969
D1769-71A. Jun 16
Take a Longer Look   R. and R. Sherman
The Human Race   ditto
Take a Longer Look   ditto
     with Kathryn Crosby
Take a Longer Look   ditto
     with Kathryn, Mary Frances and Nathaniel Crosby
               (The TV soundtrack of "Goldilocks" from Decca.)

1970
D1772-75. Nov 16
A Time to Be Jolly   L. Hale, L. Brown, S. Burke
     Les Brown Orchestra and the Jack Halloran Singers
And the Bells Rang   L. Hale, J. Herron
The First Family of Christmas S. Burke, P.F. Webster
When You Trim Your Christmas Tree
                         S. Burke, B. Carey, E. Powell

1971
D1776-82. Sep 7, 8 (Songs for Daybreak.)
Christmas Is   P. Faith, S. Maxwell
     Les Brown Orchestra and the Jack Halloran Singers
A Christmas Toast   K. Lane, I. Taylor
I Sing Noel   N. Regney, G. Shayne
The Song of Christmas   K. Lee
'Round and 'Round the Christmas Tree J. Livingston, R.Evans
Christmas Is Here to Stay   B. Angelos, A. Kohan
          (These songs completed Crosby's A Time to Be Jolly
     Christmas album; three were recorded Nov 16, 1970. Re-
     issued on 8-track tape titled Holiday Treat (1979).
An Old Fashioned Christmas (A demonstration record, never
     released, No. DL 187.)

1972
D1783-94A. Feb 28, 29, Mar 1
Have a Nice Day   S. Nestico, J. Mercer
     Count Basie Orchestra
All His Children   H. Mancini, A. and M. Bergman
Sunrise, Sunset   J. Bock, S. Harnick
Little Green Apples   B. Russell

Gentle on My Mind   J. Hartford
Snowbird   G. MacLellan
Everything Is Beautiful   R. Stevens
Gonna Build a Mountain   A. Newley, L. Bricusse
*If I Had a Hammer   L. Hays, P. Seger
Sugar, Don't You Know?   L. Bellson, J. Hayes, P. Lee
Put Your Hand in the Hand   G. MacLellan
Hangin' Loose   S. Nestico, J. Mercer
          (Recordings for Bing 'n' Basie album for Daybreak,
     which omits the song marked.)
The Bunny Club (Bing sings part of "Auld Lang Syne" for a
     sketch for the "Flip Wilson" TV Show, V185.)

D1795-96. Dec 28
Christmas Star   J. Sweeny
     with Old St. Mary's Choir
We Love Old St. Mary's   R. Moonan
          (These two songs were a limited edition record of
     1000 copies sold at $4.95 each to benefit Old St.
     Mary's Church, San Francisco [Zwisohn 60].)

1973
D1797-98. Jun 8
Tie a Yellow Ribbon Round the Old Oak Tree
                             I. Levine, L. Brown
     Billy Byer's Orchestra
It's Not Where You Start   C. Coleman, D. Fields
          ("Tie a Yellow Ribbon" and "It's Not Where You
     Start" are Bing's last songs for a single record, for
     Daybreak. Barnes lists "We Love Old St. Mary's" and
     "Christmas Star" as recorded on Jun 8, not on Dec 28,
     1972.)

1974
D1799-1800A. Oct 17
The Pleasure of Your Company J. Mercer, A. Previn
     with Johnny Mercer, arranged by Pete Moore
Good Companions   J. Mercer, A. Previn
And Points Beyond   J. Mercer, A. Previn
          (These songs were released by United Artists, Los
     Angeles, in 1976 album That's What Life Is All About,
     No. UA-LA 554-G.)

1975
D1801-06. Jan 16
Sleepy Time Down South   L. and O. Rene, C. Muse
     Paul Smith Orchestra
Carolina in the Morning   W. Donaldson, G. Kahn
Way Down Yonder in New Orleans H. Creamer, J. Layton
Stars Fell on Alabama   M. Parish, F. Perkins
Alabamy Bound   R. Henderson, B.G. DeSylva, B. Green
Where the Morning Glories Grow R. Whiting, R. Egan, G. Kahn

D1807-12. Jan 21 (for Decca.)
Georgia on My Mind   H. Carmichael, S. Gorell
     Paul Smith Orchestra
Sailin' Down the Chesapeake Bay J. Havez, G. Botsford
Swanee   G. Gershwin, I. Caesar
She's the Sunshine of Virginia B. MacDonald, H. Carroll

On the Alamo   I. Jones, G. Kahn
Crying for the Carolines   S. Lewis, J. Young, J. Warren

D1813-15. Feb 19 (For UA.)
That's What Life Is All About
                        B. Crosby, L. Reed, P. Dacre, K. Barnes
        Pete Moore Orchestra
I Love to Dance Like They Used to Dance A. and M. Bergman
The Good Old Times   K. Barnes, P. Moore

D1816-18. Feb 20 (For UA.)
The Best Things in Life Are Free
                        B.G. DeSylva, L. Brown, R. Henderson
        Pete Moore Orchestra
No Time at All   S. Schwartz
Bon vivant   J. Mercer, R.E. Dolan
        (Recordings of Feb 19-20 appeared in That's What
        Life Is All About in 1976, matrix No. UA-LA 554-G.)

D1819-23. Feb 22 (For UA.)
I Got Rhythm   G. and I. Gershwin
        Pete Moore Orchestra
Heat Wave   I. Berlin
My Heart Stood Still   R. Rodgers, L. Hart
How Are Things in Glocca Morra? E.Y. Harburg, B. Lane
Something to Remember You By H. Dietz, A. Schwartz

D1824-28. Feb 24 (For UA.)
Hello Dolly   J. Herman
        Pete Moore Orchestra
Great Day   B. Rose, E. Eliscu, V. Youmans
Looking at You   C. Porter
Cabaret   F. Ebb, J. Kander
Thou Swell   R. Rodgers, L. Hart

D1829-32. Feb 25 (For UA.)
Some Sunny Day   I. Berlin
        Pete Moore Orchestra
Breezing Along with the Breeze
                        R. Whiting, S. Simons, H. Gillespie
*Razzle Dazzle   F. Ebb, J. Kander
Have a Nice Day   H. Axton
        (More songs, except for "Razzle Dazzle," for UA
        That's What Life Is All About, along with "Send in the
        Clowns, recorded Feb 26.)

D1833-36. Feb 26
Send in the Clowns   S. Sondheim
        Pete Moore Orchestra
Yours Sincerely   R. Rodgers, L. Hart
With a Song in My Heart   R. Rodgers, L. Hart
I'll Never Fall in Love Again B. Bacharach, H. David

D1837-41. Jun 23
The Breeze and I (Andalucia) E. Leucona, A. Stillman
        Paul Smith Orchestra
Maria Bonita   A. Lara, B. Worth
Eres tu   J. Calderon, J. Livingston, R. Evans
Amapola   J. LaCalle, A. Gamse

Frenesi   A. Dominguez, R. Charles, R. Russell
        (Recordings for Bingo Viejo by Anahuac (1977),
    matrix No. 22998.)

D1842-44. Jul 15
Sing   J. Raposo
    Pete Moore Orchestra and the Johnny Evans Singers
    with Fred Astaire
How Lucky Can You Get   J. Kander, F. Ebb
In the Cool, Cool, Cool of the Evening
                        J. Mercer, H. Carmichael

D1845-48. Jul 16
Pick Yourself Up   D. Fields, J. Kern
    Pete Moore Orchestra with Fred Astaire
A Couple of Song and Dance Men I. Berlin
Mr. Keyboard Man (The Entertainer) S. Joplin
Roxie   J. Kander, F. Ebb

D1849-53. Jul 17
Top Billing   K. Barnes, P. Moore
    Pete Moore Orchestra with Fred Astaire
Top Billing (Reprise)
Spring, Spring, Spring   J. Mercer, G. DePaul
I've a Shooting Box in Scotland C.Porter, T.Lauranson-Riggs
Change Partners   I. Berlin
        (Bing Crosby solo)
            (Recordings of Jul 15-17 for A Couple of Song and
        Dance Men, 1976, matrix No. UA-LA 588-G.)

D1854. Sep 3, 5
Tom Sawyer by Mark Twain (Three-L.P. set of abridged read-
    ings for Argo.)

D1855-59. Sep 15
Green Eyes   N. Menendez, A. Utrera, E. Woods, E. Rivera
    Paul Smith Orchestra
Besame mucho   C. Velasquez, S. Skylar
Spanish Eyes   B. Kaempfert, C. Singleton, E. Snyder
Cuando caliente el Sol
                C. and M. Rigual, C. Martinoli, S. Skylar
La borracita   I. Esperon
        (More songs for Anahuac's Bingo Viejo.)

1976
D1860-63. Jan 19 (Three for UA, England.)
The Only Way to Go   T. Rice, M. Hamlisch
    Pete Moore Orchestra
Children   H. Shaper, C. Ornadel
At My Time of Life   H. Shaper, C. Ornadel
Spring Will Be a Little Late This Year F. Loesser
        (The last song above was for Seasons, Polydor, No.
    1-6128.)

D1864-1926. Jun 24, 25 (Live, for K-Tel.)
The Pleasure of Your Company J. Mercer, A. Previn
    Pete Moore Orchestra
Mary Lou   G. Waggner, J. Robinson, A. Lyman
Where the Morning Glories Grow R. Egan, R. Whiting, G. Kahn

At My Time of Life   H. Shaper, C. Ornadel
On a Slow Boat to China   F. Loesser
    with Rosemary Clooney
Send in the Clowns (solo)   S. Sondheim
Gone Fishin' (with Ted Rogers) N. and C. Kenny
Now You Has Jazz   C. Porter
    with the Joe Bushkin Quartet
Sing (with the Crosby Family) J. Raposo
You've Got a Friend (with Harry Crosby) King
My Cup Runneth Over (with Kathryn Crosby) Jones, Schmidt
Play a Simple Melody (with Harry Crosby) I. Berlin
Row, Row Your Boat (solo)   Traditional
Frere Jacques   Traditional
A Kukuberra Sits in the Old Gum Tree Traditional
Loch Lomond   Traditional
Annie Laurie   W. Douglas, Lady Scott
My Bonnie   Traditional
The Daring Young Man on the Flying Trapeze Traditional
Whiffenpoof Song
        G. Pomeroy, T. Galloway, M. Minnigerode, R. Vallee
Drinking Song   S. Romberg, S. Donnelly
Drink to Me Only   Traditional
Dark Eyes   Traditional
You Are My Sunshine   J. Davis, C. Mitchell
She'll Be Coming 'Round the Mountain Traditional
Swing Low, Sweet Chariot   Traditional
Row, Row, Row Your Boat   Traditional
    with Kathryn, Harry, Mary Frances and Nathaniel Crosby
    arranged by Ken and Mitzi Welch
The Way We Were (solo)   M. Hamlisch, A. and M. Bergman
Cuando caliente el Sol
            M. and C. Rigual, C. Martinoli, S. Skylar
    The Crosby Medley (solo except as indicated below)
I Surrender, Dear   G. Clifford, H. Barris
    Pete Moore Orchestra
Swinging on a Star   J. Van Heusen, J. Burke
Wrap Your Troubles in Dreams T. Koehler, B. Moll, H. Barris
True Love   C. Porter
    with Mary Frances Crosby
Don't Fence Me In   C. Porter
Pennies from Heaven   A. Johnston, J. Burke
Blue Hawaii   L. Robin, R. Rainger
Sweet Leilani   H. Owens
That's an Irish Lullaby   J. Shannon
Just One More Chance   S. Coslow, A. Johnston
Them There Eyes   M. Pinkard, W. Tracey, D. Tauber
Moonlight Becomes You   J. Van Heusen, J. Burke
You Are My Sunshine   J. Davis, C. Mitchell
I'll Be Seeing You   S. Fain, I. Kahal
The White Cliffs of Dover   N. Burton, W. Kent
When the Lights Go on Again
            E. Seiler, S. Marcus, B. Benjamin
Ac-Cent-Tchu-Ate the Positive H. Arlen, J. Mercer
Please   L. Robin, R. Rainger
Baby Face   B. Davis, H. Akst
South of the Border   J. Kennedy, M. Carr
Galway Bay   Dr. A. Colahan
Dinah   S. Lewis, J. Young, H. Akst
San Fernando Valley   G. Jenkins

I Found a Million Dollar Baby   H. Warren
San Antonio Rose   B. Wills
I'm an Old Cowhand   J. Mercer
In a Little Spanish Town   M. Wayne, S. Lewis, J. Young
Wait Till the Sun Shines Nellie A. Sterling, H. von Tilzer
     with Kathryn Crosby
It's Easy to Remember   R. Rodgers, L. Hart
Blue Skies   I. Berlin
It's Been a Long, Long Time   J. Styne, S. Cahn
Mississippi Mud   H. Barris, J. Cavanaugh
Ol' Man River   J. Kern, O. Hammerstein II
     with the Joe Bushkin Quartet
That's What Life Is All About
                          B. Crosby, L. Reed, K. Dacre, K. Barnes
          (The sessions of Jun 24-25 were Bing's only com-
     mercial live album, K-Tel's Bing Crosby Live at the
     London Palladium, selected from two performances.)

D1927-30. Jul 20
Nevertheless   B. Kalmar, H. Ruby
When I Leave the World Behind   I. Berlin
As Time Goes By   H. Hupfeld
The Way We Were   A. and M. Bergman, M. Hamlisch

D1931-34. Jul 21
Time on My Hands   V. Youmans, H. Adamson, M. Gordon
     Alan Cohen Orchestra
The Night Is Young and You're So Beautiful
                           D. Suesse, I. Kahal, B. Rose
Once in a While   M. Edwards, B. Green
The Rose in Her Hair   A. Dubin, H. Warren

D1935-37. Jul 22
Old Fashioned Love   C. Mack, J. Johnson
     Alan Cohen Orchestra
Feels Good, Feels Right   M. and K. Welch
There's Nothing That I Haven't Sung About
                                L. Duddy, J. Bresler

D1938-41. Aug 17
That Ol' Black Magic   H. Arlen, J. Mercer
     Alan Cohen Orchestra
At Last   H. Warren, M. Gordon
I'm Getting Sentimental Over You G. Bassman, N. Washington
What's New?   B. Haggart, J. Burke

D1942-44. Oct 19
When a Child Is Born   F. Jay, Zacar
What I Did For Love   E. Kleban, M. Hamlisch
White Christmas   I. Berlin
          (This was a 38-second version of "White Christmas"
     that Crosby hoped to include in his 30-minute medley
     for the album Bing Crosby Live at the London Palladium,
     but MCA Records, the successor to Decca, refused their
     permission, and it has never been released [Zwisohn
     60].)

D1945-50. Oct 29
The More I See You   H. Warren, M. Gordon

Deja vu   K. Barnes, P. Moore
My Resistance Is Low   H. Carmichael, M. Parish
A Little Love
     and Understanding   G. Becaud, M. Stellman
The Woman on Your Arm   R. Edelman
Come Share the Wine   D. Black, U. Jurgens

D1951-53. Nov 5
We've Only Just Begun   P. Williams, R. Nichols
     Pete Moore Orchestra
Beautiful Memories   R. Cook, H. Flowers
Seasons   G. Becaud, K. Barnes

1977
D1954. Apr 15
Don't Get Around Much Anymore D. Ellington, B. Russell
         (For a A Tribute to Duke, a Concord Jazz 1977
     album on Duke Ellington.)

D1955-58. Sep 12
September Song   K. Weill, M. Anderson
     Pete Moore Orchestra
June in January   L. Robin, R. Rainger
Autumn in New York   V. Duke
Yesterday When I Was Young   C. Aznavour, H. Kretzmer

D1959-62. Sep 13
On the Very First Day of the Year K. Barnes, P. Moore
     Pete Moore Orchestra
Sleigh Ride   L. Anderson, M. Parish
In the Good Old Summertime   G. Evans, R. Shields,
June Is Bustin' Out All Over   R. Rodgers, O. Hammerstein II

D1963-70. Sep 14
April Showers   B.G. DeSylva, L. Silvers
Summer Wind   J. Mercer, H. Bradtke, H. Meyer
Seasons   G. Becaud, K. Barnes
         (The commercial master of "Seasons" was a combina-
     tion of this vocal in London and another in Nov 1976 in
     Los Angeles and the orchestral backing recorded Aug
     1976 [Barnes 150n]. Recordings of September were for
     Seasons, Polydor, 1977, matrix No. 1-6128. It has also
     been released on 8-track tape and as a cassette.)

     NOTE: The following are poetry readings, London, Sep
     14, 1977. Music composed and arranged by Pete Moore
     and recorded Jan 23, 1979.
Around the Corner   Anon
The Singers   H.W. Longfellow
If   R. Kipling
Lucy Gray (or Solitude)   W. Wordsworth
The Slave's Dream   H.W. Longfellow

D1971-72. Oct 4
Now You Has Jazz   C. Porter
     Joe Bushkin Quartet
Sail Away from Norway   Traditional
                      arranged by Joe Bushkin, Johnny Smith

A TREASURE TROVE OF SONGS

The following is a list of songs Bing recorded mainly
from 1954 to 1957 (years in parentheses) with the Buddy Cole
Trio and not previously released. Some may also have been
recorded for Bing's own record company called Project (see
Jun 1962). Ken Barnes found 225 unissued songs and had 72
of them augmented (<u>Crosby Years</u> 152-56), although he lists
only 71. Pete Moore set the music to five poetry readings
of Sep 14, 1977, and conducted the stereophonic augmentation
of the songs in late 1978 and early 1979.

D1973-2125. Barnes found about 153 (154?) songs that are in
    addition to those augmented in the following sessions.

1978
D2126-29. Nov 30
Love's Old Sweet Song (1955)   G. Bingham, L. Molloy,
    Augmented by Pete Moore
True Love (1957)   C. Porter
Try a Little Tenderness (1955)
                        H. Woods, J. Campbell, R. Connelly
Straight Down the Middle (1957) S. Cahn, J. Van Heusen

D2130-37. Dec 2
Yes Sir That's My Baby (1956) G. Kahn, W. Donaldson
You're the Top (1956)   C. Porter
Unchained Melody (1955)   Zaret,   North
It's All Right with Me (1955)   C. Porter
Nice Work If You Can Get It (1955) G. and I. Gershwin
Just You, Just Me (1954)   Klages, Greer
You're in Kentucky--Sure as You're Born
                        L. Shay, Little, H. Gillespie
Count Your Blessings Instead of Sheep (1955) I. Berlin

D2138-41. Dec 20
Love Is the Sweetest Thing (1954) R. Noble
Manhattan (1956)   R. Rodgers, L. Hart
I Guess I'll Have to Change My Plan (1954)
                        H. Dietz, A. Schwartz
How Long Has This Been Going On? (1955) G. and I. Gershwin

D2142-44. Dec 21
What Is This Thing Called Love? (1955) C. Porter
So Rare (1957)   Sharpe
The Tender Trap (1955)   S. Cahn, J. Van Heusen

D2145-49. Dec 22
Moonglow, theme from <u>Picnic</u> (1956)
        W. Hudson, E. DeLange, S. Allen, I. Mills, G. Duning
You're Sensational (1956)   C. Porter
They Didn't Believe Me (1956) J. Kern, H. Reynolds
All Through the Night (1955) C. Porter

1979
D2150-53. Jan 16
Yours (1956)   G. Roig
I Wish You Love (1956)   Beach, C. Trenet
I See Your Face Before Me (1955) H. Dietz, A. Schwartz

I've Got a Crush on You   (1956)   G. and I. Gershwin

D2154-61. Jan 17
Where or When (1960)   R. Rodgers, L. Hart
Papa Loves Mambo (1955)   Hoffman, Manning, Reichman
I Can't Get Started (1956)   I. Gershwin, V. Duke
I've Grown Accustomed to Her Face (1956)
                              A. Lerner, F. Loewe
At the Jazz Band Ball (1956)
                    N. LaRocca, E. Shields, J. Mercer
Way Down Yonder in New Orleans (1956) H. Creamer, J. Layton
The Banjo's Back in Town (1955) Shuman, Shuman, Brown
When the Red, Red Robin Comes Bob-Bob-Bobbin' Along (1956)
                              H. Woods

D2162-69. Jan 29
When My Baby Smiles at Me (1956) Munro
Mandy (1954)   I. Berlin
Keepin' Out of Mischief Now (1954) A. Razaf, Fats Waller
We're in the Money (1954)   A. Dubin, H. Warren
What Is There to Say? (1955) E.Y. Harburg, V. Duke
Don't Take Your Love from Me (1954) Nemo
We'll Be Together Again (1956) F. Laine, Fischer
Come Rain or Come Shine (1956) J. Mercer, H. Arlen

D2170-73. Jan 30
Crazy Rhythm (1956)   I. Caesar, G. Kahn, Meyer
You Turned the Tables on Me (1956) J. Mitchell, L. Alter
She's Funny That Way (1955)   N. Moret, R. Whiting
Please Don't Talk About Me When I'm Gone (1957) S. Stept

D2174-81. Feb 13
Ain't Misbehavin' (1954)   S. Brooks, A. Razaf, Fats Waller
Margie (1956)   B. Davis, C. Conrad, J. Robinson
Waitin' for the Evenin' Mail (1956) Baskette
Isle of Capri (1956)   W. Grosz, J. Kennedy
Old Cape Cod (1957)   C. Rothrock, A. Jeffrey, M. Yakus
It's Not for Me to Say (1957) A. Stillman, T. Allen
You'll Never Know (1957)   M. Gordon, H. Warren
Misty (1960)   S. Burke, E. Garner

D2182-85. Feb 14
Little Man, You've Had a Busy Day (1956)
                              Sigler, Hoffman, M. Wayne
Chances Are (1957)   A. Stillman, T. Allen
My Funny Valentine (1956)   R. Rodgers, L. Hart
My Ideal (1955)   L. Robin, Chase, R. Whiting

D2186-92. Feb 26
The Lady Is a Tramp (1955)   R. Rodgers, L. Hart
Sunday (1955)   Miller, Conn, Stein
'Deed I Do (1955)   B. Rose, W. Hirsch
This Can't Be Love (1954)   R. Rodgers, L. Hart
Don't Blame Me (1956)   D. Fields, J. McHugh
Meet Me Tonight in Dreamland (1957) B. Whitson, L. Friedman
Let's Put Out the Lights and Go to Sleep (1958) H. Hupfeld

D2193-97. Feb 27
My Baby Just Cares for Me (1956) G. Kahn, W. Donaldson

Just Around the Corner (1956)   Singer, H. von Tilzer
Anything Goes (1956)   C. Porter
New Sun in the Sky (1955)   H. Dietz, A. Schwartz
Heartaches by the Number (1960) J. Howard

SONGS FOR WARNER BROS. 101 Gang Songs D1478-1578.

The album includes these 94 songs recorded Dec 1960:   Abdul
Abulbul Amir (F. Crumit); Ach Du Lieber Augustine (Anon.);
America the Beautiful (K. Bates); Anchors Aweigh (C. Zimmer-
man, A. Miles, D. Savino, G. Lottman); Annie Laurie (W.
Douglas, Lady John Scott); Asleep in the Deep (H. Petrie, A.
Lamb); Battle Hymn of the Republic (J. Howe, W. Steffe); The
Bear Went Over the Mountain (Anon.); Believe Me If All Those
Endearing Young Charms (T. More); Big Rock Candy Mountain
(M. McClintock); Bill Bailey, Won't You Please Come Home?
(H. Cannon); Blow the Man Down (Anon.); Blue Bells of Scot-
land (A. Grant, D. Jordan); Careless Love (Anon.); Carry Me
Back to Old Virginny (J. Bland); Casey Jones (T. Seibert, E.
Newton); Cindy (Anon.); Come Back to Erin (Claribel); Come
Where My Love Lies Dreaming (S. Foster); Coming Through the
Rye (R. Burns); Dear Evelina (Anon.); Down in the Valley
(Anon.); Drink to Me Only with Thine Eyes (B. Jonson); Du Du
Liegst Mir In Herzen (Anon.); Ezekiel Saw the Wheel (Anon.);
Finiculi, Finicula (L. Denza, E. Oxenford); Flow Gently
Sweet Afton (R. Burns, J. Spilman); For He's a Jolly Good
Fellow (Anon.); Forty-five Minutes from Broadway (G. Cohan);
The Fountain in the Park (While Strolling Through the Park)
(E. Haley, R. Keiser); The Girl I Left Behind (Anon.);
Goodnight Ladies (Anon.); Goodnight to You All (J. and M.
Watson); The Gospel Train's A-Coming (Anon.); Grandfather's
Clock (H. Work); Gumtree Canoe (Tom Bigbee River) (A. Winne-
more, S. Steele); Hand Me Down My Walking Cane (J. Bland);
Harrigan (G. Cohan); Heaven, Heaven (Anon.); Hello, Ma Baby
(J. Howard, I. Emerson); I Don't Want to Play in Your Yard
(H. Petrie, P. Wingate); I've Been Working on the Railroad
(Anon.); In the Evening By the Moonlight (J. Bland); In the
Gloaming (A. Harrison); Joshua Fit de Battle of Jericho
(Anon.); Juanita (C. Norton); Keemo Kimo (Anon.); Killarney
(E. Falconer, M. Balfe); Li'l Liza Jane (A. de Lachau);
Listen to the Mockingbird (Septimus Winner, D. Milburn);
Litttle Annie Rooney (M. Nolan); Little David, Play on Your
Harp (Anon.); Loch Lomond (Anon.); Love's Old Sweet Song (J.
Molloy); The Man Who Broke the Bank at Monte Carlo (F.
Gilbert); Maryland, My Maryland (J. Randall); The Minstrel
Boy (T. Moore); My Gal Sal (P. Dresser); My Sweetheart's the
Man in the Moon (J. Thornton); My Wild Irish Rose (C. Ol-
cott); Nobody Knows the Trouble I've Seen (Anon.); On Top of
Old Smokey (Anon.); Oh Susanna (S. Foster); Oh Where Has My
Little Dog Gone (Septimus Winner); Nut Brown Maiden (Anon.);
O Mary Don't You Weep (Anon.); O Sole Mio (E. di Capua, G.
Capurro, E. Lockton); Oh Dear, What Can the Matter Be?
(Anon.); Oh How Lovely Is the Evening (Anon.); Our Boys Will
Shine Tonight (Anon.); Polly Wolly Doodle (Anon.); Pop Goes
the Weasel (Anon.); Roll Jordan Roll (Anon.); Santa Lucia
(T. Cottrau, T. Oliphant), Schnitzelbank (Anon.); She'll Be
Coming 'Round the Mountain (Anon.); Shine On Harvest Moon
(J. Norworth, N. Bayes); So Long, Mary (G. Cohan); Sweet
Adeline (H. Armstrong, R. Gerard); Sweet Genevieve (G.

Cooper, H. Tucker); Sweet Rosie O'Grady (M. Jerome); That's
Where My Money Goes (W. Daniels, R. Lilly); There Is a
Tavern in the Town (W. Hills); This Old Man (Anon.); Three
Blind Mice (Anon.); Today Is Monday (Anon.); Tramp, Tramp,
Tramp (G. Root); Wait for the Wagon (G. Knauff); Walk To-
gether, Children (Anon.); When Johnny Comes Marching Home
Again (L. Lambert); When the Saints Go Marching In (Anon.);
Where Did You Get That Hat? (J. Sullivan); While Strolling
Through the Park (E. Haley, R. Keiser).

COMPOSERS' AND LYRICISTS' PSEUDONYMS

Bill Brill (Bing Crosby), Claribel (Charlotte Arlington
Barnard), Vernon Duke (Vladimir Dukelsky), Ralph Freedman
(Max Freedman), Ziggy Elman (Harry Finkelman), Ralph Erwin
(Erwin Ralph Vogl), Ed Haley (Robert A. Kaiser), Joe Hoover
(J. Russell Robinson), Jim Hoyl (Jascha Heifetz), Caesar
James (Caesar Petrillo), Mickey Leader (Dave Kapp), Jules
Lemare (Charles N. Daniels), Edward Lockton (Edward Teschem-
acher), Louiguy (Luis Guglielmi), Cecil Mack (Richard C.
MacPherson), Eric Martin (Eric Maschwitz), Eddie Maxwell
(Eddie Cherkose), Pierre Norman (Pierre Norman Connor),
Billy O'Brien (Coomber Scott), Charles E. Pratt (H.J. Fulm-
er), Old Put (John A. Stone), Malia Rosa (May Singhi Breen),
Joe Saunders (George Leybourne), Lady John Scott (Alicia Ann
Spottiswoode), Cool White (John Hodges), Hugh Williams (Will
Grosz), W.R. Williams (Will Rossiter), Septimus Winner
(Alice Hawthorne), Lawrence Wright (Horatio Nicholls)

ALBUMS
ST: film soundtrack TV: television R: radio
(Discography entry numbers appear at every tenth
album. The order is alphabetical. See below for albums
released only as 78 rpm discs, not 33 1/3 LP.)

D2198.
Accentuate the Positive (DE DL-4258 BH 9) ST
Ali Baba and the Forty Thieves
     (GO 20, Wonderland WLP-314) Recorded Mar 1957.
D2200.
All-Time Hit Parade, [Bing Crosby's] (Longines 224)
     Recorded Nov, Dec 1965 (17 songs).
All the Way (Blue and Gold 1)
America, I Hear You Singing, with Frank Sinatra, Fred Waring
     (REP R/FS-2020 [1964])
     Recorded Feb 4, 1964 (5 songs).
The Andrews Sisters Live (Amalgamated 210) R
The Andrews Sisters on Radio (Radiola 1033) R
Anything Goes (Caliban 6043) ST (1936 Version)
Anything Goes (DE DL-4264 BH 15 [1962], DL-8318 [1956])
     Recorded Feb 1956. ST (1956 version)
Around the World with Bing (DE DL-8687)
At My Time of Life (UA England 29956)
     Recorded Feb 1975, Jan 1976.
Auld Lang Syne (10" DE DL-5028)
D2210.
Beautiful Memories (UA England)
     Recorded Feb 1975, Jan, Oct 1976.

Beloved Hymns (10" DE DL-5351)
The Best of Bing (DE DXB-184/DXS-7184, MCA 4045)
The Big Broadcast (Soundtrack 101) ST
The Big Broadcast of 1935
     (Kasha King 1935, Amalgamated 196) ST
Bing (DE DX-151)
Bing--A Musical Autobiography, Vol. 1-5 (DE DX151,
     ED-1700 [45rpm], DL-9054, 9064, 9067, 9077, 9078)
     New songs and narration recorded Apr-Jun 1954.
Bing and Al, Vol. 1-6, with Al Jolson
     (Totem 1003, 1007,1013, 1015, 1016, 1017) R
Bing and Bob Hope (Spokane 22) R
Bing and Connee (10" DE DL-5390) with Connee Boswell
D2220.
Bing and Connie Boswell--On the Air (Spokane 18) R
Bing and Dinah Shore (Spokane 32) R
Bing and Hoppy (Critter 8901, Amalgamated 147) R
     with William Boyd
Bing and Louis (Metro M/S-591) with Louis Armstrong. A
     reissue of Bing and Satchmo.
Bing and Mary--Rhythm on the Radio (Star-Tone 225) R
     with Mary Martin
Bing and Satchmo (MGM E/SE-3882P, MGM GAS-137)
     with Louis Armstrong. Recorded Jun 1960.
Bing and the Dixieland Bands
     (10" DE DL-5323, DL-8493)
Bing and the Music Maids (Spokane 21)
Bing and Trudy Erwin (Spokane 23)
Bing at His Extra Special (Avenue International 1018)
D2230.
Bing, Bob and Judy (Totem 1009) R
     with Bob Hope, Judy Garland
Bing Crosby (Going Hollywood) [no label number]
Bing Crosby (Metro M/S-523) A reissue of Bing Sings While
     Bregman Swings omitting two songs (see Jun 11, 1956).
Bing Crosby and Al Jolson Duets (Amalgamated 0003)
Bing Crosby and Bob Hope (Radiola 1044) with Dorothy Lamour
Bing Crosby and Dorothy Lamour--Live (Amalgamated 237) R
Bing Crosby and Friends (Broadcast 0001) R
Bing Crosby and Friends (Magic 3) R
Bing Crosby and Friends, Vol. 2 (Magic 10) R
Bing Crosby and Friends (4-Murray Hill 894637) R
D2240.
Bing Crosby/Louis Armstrong (CAP SM-11735) A reissue of
     Bing and Satchmo, omitting "Lil Ol' Tune."
Bing Crosby and Louis Armstrong--Havin' Fun
     (Sounds Rare 5009) R
Bing Crosby and Louis Armstrong--More Fun
     (Sounds Rare 5010) R
Bing Crosby and Perry Como (Broadway Intermission 123)
Bing Crosby and Red Nichols--Together Again
     (Broadway Intermission 142)
Bing Crosby and the Andrews Sisters (MCA Coral 804)
Bing Crosby and the Andrews Sisters, Vol. 1-3
     (Coral 80, 91, 112)
Bing Crosby and the Music Maids--On the Air
     (Spokane 22) R
Bing Crosby and the Rhythm Boys (Arcadia 5001)
Bing Crosby at the Music Hall (Joyce 1117)

D2250.
Bing Crosby, Boris Karloff, Victor Moore
    (Almagamated 1004) R
Bing Crosby Classics, Vol. 1-3 (CAP SM 11738-40)
A Bing Crosby Collection, Vol. 1-3
    (COL C-35093, C-35094, C-35748)
Bing Crosby, Duke Ellington and Nat "King" Cole Live
    (Amalgamated 252) R
Bing Crosby, Groucho Marx and Maurice Chevalier--Live
    (Amalgamated 221) R
Bing Crosby--His Greatest Hits (Musidisc 30CV1356)
Bing Crosby in Hollywood (COL C2L-43)
Bing Crosby in the Thirties, Vol. 1-3 (JSP 1076, 1084, 1104)
Bing Crosby Live (Amalgamated 153, 162) R
Bing Crosby Live at the London Palladium (K-Tel 951)
    Recorded Jun 24-25, 1976, Bing's only commercially
    released live recording of a concert; 2 discs.
D2260.
Bing Crosby, Lucille Ball and Spike Jones--Live
    (Amalgamated 239) R
Bing Crosby on the Air (Sandy Hook 2002) R
Bing Crosby on the Air (Spokane 1) R
Bing Crosby on the Air (Totem 1008) R
    with the Boswell Sisters
The Bing Crosby Radio Shows (Golden Age 5023) R
Bing Crosby Reads <u>Tom Sawyer</u> (Argo 561-63)
The Bing Crosby Show
        (Facit 192, Memorabilia 705, Radiola 1044) R
Bing Crosby Sings (VOC VL 3603)
Bing Crosby Sings for Children (VOC VL 73769)
Bing Crosby Sings the Great Country Hits
    (CAP T/ST-23461, CAP SM-11737 less two songs)
    Recorded Oct 1963, Nashville, Tenn.
D2270.
Bing Crosby Sings the Great Songs (MCA 2721)
Bing Crosby Sings the Great Standards (VER 4129)
Bing Crosby Sings the Hits (10" DE DL-5220)
The Bing Crosby Story, Vol. 1 (COL Special Products 201)
The Bing Crosby Story, Vol. 1: The Early Jazz Years
    (Epic E2E-201)
Bing Crosby--The Best (Music for Pleasure 5814)
Bing Crosby: The Chronological Years, Vol. 13 (Jonzo 13)
    British, songs of 1932. See D2314.
Bing Crosby Treasury (Longines 344)
    Recorded Mar 1968 (20 songs).
Bing Crosby with Glenn Miller--Rare Radio
    (Broadway Intermission 114) R
Bing Crosby with Special Guests (Amalgamated 1007) R
D2280.
Bing Crosby's Greatest Hits (MCA 3031)
Bing Goes Latin (MGM 2354-028)
Bing in Paris (DE DL-8780)
Bing in the Hall (Spokane 17) R
Bing in the Thirties, Vol. 1-8
    (Spokane 12, 14, 24, 25, 26, 27, 28, 29)
Bing is Back (Totem 1002)
Bing 'n' Basie (Daybreak 2014) with Count Basie
    Recorded Feb, Mar 1972.
Bing 1932-34 (COL Special Products 14369)

Bing 1975-1976 (DE England)   Recorded Aug 17, 1976.
Bing on the Happy Side (WB)   Recorded Apr 30, 1962.
D2290.
Bing Sings (Reader's Digest 127)
Bing Sings Broadway (MCA 173)
Bing Sings Crosby (Broadway Intermission 139)
Bing Sings While Bregman Swings (VER 2020)
        with Buddy Bregman. Recorded Jun 1956; Bing's first
        album after leaving Decca.
Bing with a Beat (RCA LPM-1473)
        with Bob Scobey's Frisco Jazz Band
        Recorded Feb 1957, plus three more (see Feb 1957).
Bingo Viejo (Anahuac International ANC-3901 [1977])
        Recorded Jun, Sep 1975.
Bing's Beaus (Amalgamated 151, 805) R
        with Tallulah Bankhead, Marlene Dietrich
Bing's Music (Magic 1) R
Bing's Music Hall Highlights Vol. 1-2 (Spokane 16, 19) R
Bing's Party (Artistic 001)
D2300.
Birth of the Blues (Spokane 9) R
Bix 'n' Bing (ASV 5005) with Bix Beiderbecke, Paul Whiteman
Blue Hawaii (DE DFL-8269)
Blue of the Night (10" DE DL-4259) with Fred Astaire
Blue Skies (DE A-481 [78rpm], DL-4259 <u>BH 10</u>) ST
Bob Hope Collection (Deja Vu DVLP 2124) Bing on 8 songs.
Both Sides of Bing Crosby (Curtain Calls 10012) R
But Beautiful (DE DL-4260 <u>BH 11</u>) ST
The Chesterfield Show, Vol. 1-2 (Joyce 1133, 6050)
Christmas Classics (CAP SM-11732 [1977]). A Reissue of <u>I</u>
    <u>Wish You a Merry Christmas</u>.
D2310.
Christmas Greetings, with the Andrews Sisters
        (DE 715 [78 rpm]; 10" DL-5020)
Christmas Sing with Bing--Around the World (DE-8419) R
        Recorded Dec 24, 1955. See R116.
A Christmas Story: An Axe, an Apple and a Buckskin Jacket
        Recorded Mar 1957 (GO)
Christmas with Bing Crosby, Nat "King" Cole and Dean Martin
        (CAP SL-6925)
The Chronological Bing Crosby, Vol. 1-12 (Jonzo 1-12)
The Classic Years (BBC 648)
Cole Porter Songs (10" DE DL-5064)
Collection of Early Recordings, Vol. 1-2
        (10" BR BL-5800, 5801)
Collector's Classics, Vol. 1-8 (10" DE DL-6088-6015)
Command Performance, U.S.A. (Tulip 108)
D2320.
The Complete Bing Crosby (Silver Eagle)
Cool of the Evening (DE DL-4262 <u>BH 13</u>) ST
Country Crosby (Axis AX-701369) Australia
Country Style (10" DE DL-5321)
A Couple of Song and Dance Men, with Fred Astaire
        (UA-LA588-G [1976], UA-EA588-H 8-track)
        Recorded in London, Jul 1975.
Cowboy Songs, Vol. 1-2 (DE A-69, A-514 (Vol. 1) [78 rpm],
        DL-5107, 5129)
The Crooner (COL C4X-44229)
Crosby Classics, Vol. 1-2 (COL M-555 [78rpm], 10" CL-6027,

CL-6105)
Crosby, Columbo and Sinatra (10" RCA   LPT-5)
    with Russ Columbo, Frank Sinatra
Crosbyana, Vol. 1-2 (DE A-221 [78rpm], Broadway Intermission
    111, 116) R
D2330.
Dark Moon (Magic 7) R
Day Dreaming (Coral 113)
Der Bingle (10" COL CL-2502)
Der Bingle, Vol. 1-5 (Spokane 5, 10, 20, 30, 32) R
Dick Powell, Bing Crosby (Amalgamated 162)
The Dinah Shore-Bing Crosby Shows (Sunbeam 309) R
Distinctively Bing (Sunbeam 502) with Guy Lombardo
Don't Fence Me In (DE A-417, A-550 [78 rpm], 10" DL-5063)
Down Memory Lane, Vol. 1-2 (Ace of Hearts 40, 88)
Drifting and Dreaming (DE A-578 [78 rpm], 10" DL-5119,
    DL 8268)
D2340.
The Early Bing Crosby (Ajazz 526)
Early Film Soundtracks (Biograph BLP-M-1) ST
Early Gold (COL Special Products P4-13153)
The Early Thirties, Vol. 1-2 (Ace of Hearts 40, 88)
East Side of Heaven (DE DL-4253 <u>BH 4</u>) ST
Easy to Remember (DE DL-4250 <u>BH 1</u>, Saville 190) ST
El Bingo (DE A-547 [78 rpm], 10" DL-5011)
El Señor Bing (MGM E/SE-3890) Recorded Jun 1960.
The Emperor's New Clothes (GO 79) Recorded Mar 1957.
Fancy Meeting You Here, with Rosemary Clooney
    (RCA LPM/SLP-1854, RCA International 89315)
    Recorded Jul-Aug 1958.
D2350.
Favorite Hawaiian Songs, Vol. 1-2 (DE A-460/61 [78 rpm], 20
    sides, 1946; 10" DL-5122, 5299. Earlier version DE A-
    140 [78 rpm].)
Feels Good, Feels Right ([British 1976] London PS-679)
    Recorded Jul-Aug 1976.
Fifty-one Good Time Songs (WB M/S-1435) See <u>Join Bing . . .</u>
Forever (RCA International 89535)
From Bing's Collection, 2 vols.
    (Broadway Intermission 135, 136)
From the Forties (Joyce 6052)
George Gershwin Songs (DE A-96 [78rpm], 10" DL-5081)
Going My Way/The Bells of St. Mary's (DE A-405 [78 rpm],
    10" DE DL-5052) ST
Golden Memories (COL Special Products P614370)
Goldilocks (DE DL-3511, Evans Black Carpets DL-3511)
    1969 TV Recorded Jun 16, 1969.
D2360.
Go West Young Man (10" DE DL-5302)
Great Country Hits (CAP T/ST-2346, CAP SM-11737)
Great Standards (MGM E/SE-4219P) Recorded Apr 1962.
The Greatest Christmas Show (Music for Pleasure 210)
The Greatest Hits of Bing Crosby (M.F./MCA 7007)
Happy Holidays (Spokane 6) R
The Happy Prince/The Small One (DE DA-420; 10" DL-6000)
Havin' Fun (Sounds Rare 5009) with Louis Armstrong
Hawaiian Collection (Good Music MSM-35082) 24 songs.
Here Lies Love (ASV 5043) British, songs of 1930-34

D2370
Here Is My Heart (Caliban 6042) ST
Hey Bing! (MCA 915)
Hey Jude-Hey Bing! (Amos 7001, London (U.K.), Springboard SP
    -4003 less two songs; see D1764-67) Recorded Nov 1968.
High Society (CAP W/SW-750) ST
    Recorded Jan 1956.
High Tor (DE DL-8272) TV
    Recorded Dec 27, 1955.
Holiday in Europe (DE DL-4281/74281 [1962])
    Recorded Oct 1960, May 1961.
Holiday Inn with Fred Astaire (DE A-396 [78 rpm],
    10" DL-5092, DE DL-4256 BH 7, MCA 25205,
    Soundtrack 112) ST
Holiday Inn/The Bells of St. Mary's
    (Sandy Hook 2049, Spokane 15) ST
Holiday Treat (20th Century-Fox S-551 [1979]) A reissue of
    A Time to Be Jolly.
Home on the Range (DE DL-8210)
D2380.
How Lovely Is Christmas: An Axe, an Apple and a Buckskin
    Jacket (Narration) (GO 121, Wonderland WLP-121)
    Mitch Miller Orchestra and Chorus Recorded Mar 1957.
How the West Was Won (RCA Victor)
    with Rosemary Clooney and others
    Recorded Jul 20, 21, 23, 24, 1959.
I Love You Truly (Coral 79)
I Wish You a Merry Christmas (WB M/S-1484) Reissued by
    CAP as Christmas Classics, 1977.
    Recorded Oct 5, 1962.
I'll Sing You a Song of the Islands (Coral 90)
In a Little Spanish Town (DE DL-8846)
Jack Be Nimble (GO 23) Recorded Mar 1957.
The Jazzin' Bing Crosby (Top Classic Historia 622)
Jerome Kern Songs (10" DE DL-5001) Cf. D2703.
Joe Bushkin Celebrates 100 Years of Recorded Sound
    (UA England) Includes "Now You Has Jazz" and "Sail
    Away from Norway," Bing's last two recordings.
D2390.
Join Bing and Sing Along (RCA LPM-22276)
    Recorded Dec 16-17, 1959.
Join Bing and Sing Along: 51 Good Time Songs (WB M/S-1435)
    Another 1962 release, selected from 101 Gang Songs.
Join Bing in a Gang Song Sing Along (WB M/S-1422)
    A 1962 reissue of 101 Gang Songs (WB 1401)
Judy and Bing Together (Legend 1973) R
    with Judy Garland
Just Breezin' Along--A Tenth Anniversary Memento (EMI 1274)
Just for Fun, Vol. 1-2 (Broadway Intermission 134, 138)
Just for You (10" DE DL-5417) ST
The Kay Thompson Reviews (Amalgamated 179) R
King of Jazz (Caliban 6025) ST
Kraft Music Hall, Vol. 1-7 (Spokane 2, 3, 4, 7, 11, 13, 17)
    (Vol. 3-5 also on Spokane 24, 25, 26) R
D2400.
Le Bing (10" DE DL-5499)
A Legendary Performer (RCA CPL1-2086)
Live with Bing Crosby (Amalgamated 214) R
Lullaby Time (DE DL-8110) with Fred Waring

Mail Call, Vol. 1-2 (Tandem 1903, 1904) R
     Bing's performances on <u>Mail Call</u> during the Second
     World War for Armed Forces Radio.
A Man Without a Country/What So Proudly We Hail. Dramatiza-
     tion with Frank Lovejoy/Chorus (DE DL-89020)
Many Happy Returns (VOC 1)
The Marx Brothers (4-Murray Hill 931680) R
Merry Christmas (DE A-396, A-403, A-550 [78rpm], 10"
     DL-5019, DL-8128/78128, MCA 167). A-403 (1945) has ten
     sides [five discs, Nos. DE-18429, DE-18510-11, DE-
     18570, DE-23281]: White Christmas**; Let's Start the
     New Year Right**. Adeste Fideles**; Silent Night, Holy
     Night**. Faith of Our Fathers**; God Rest Ye Merry,
     Gentlemen**. I'll Be Home for Christmas***; Danny Boy*.
     Jingle Bells***; Santa Claus Is Coming to Town***. A-
     550 (1945) has eight sides [four discs, Nos. DE-
     23777/79, DE-23281], omitting Let's Start the New Year
     Right and Danny Boy. DL-5019 (1947) re-recorded White
     Christmas+ and Silent Night+. DL-8128 (1951) has 12
     songs, adding Silver Bells++, It's Beginning to Look a
     Lot Like Christmas+++, Christmas in Killarney+++, and
     Mele Kalikimaka++. <u>Recording dates</u>: * Jul '41; ** May-
     Jun '42; *** Sep-Oct '43; + Mar '47; ++ Sep '50; +++
     Oct '51. Album A-396 is virtually unknown and is
     probably a version of A-403. The 1947 album became
     Bing's 15th certified gold record in 1970 (proving
     sales were slow in those days).
More Fun! (Sounds Rare 5010) with Louis Armstrong
D2410.
Mother Goose Songs (Wonderland WLP-79)
     Narration and songs recorded Mar 1957.
Mr. Crosby and Mr. Mercer (with Johnny Mercer)
     (MCA Coral 8025, Music for Pleasure 50554)
Mr. Music (10" DE DL-5284) ST
Music! (Grappenhauser 1001)
Music Hall Highlights, Vol. 1-2 (Spokane 16, 19) R
My Golden Favorites (DE DL-4086)
Never Be Afraid (GO 22) Recorded Mar 1957.
New Tricks (DE DL-8575, Memoir 202)
     with Buddy Cole and his Trio. Recorded Mar 1957.
1945 Command Performance U.S.A. (Tulip 108) R
     Bing's performances on "Command Performance" for the
     Armed Forces Radio during the Second World War.
Old Masters (DE DX-152)
D2420.
On the Air (Sandy Hook 2002, Spokane 1, Totem 1008) R
On the Happy Side (WB-1482)
101 Gang Songs [two records] (WB-1401 [1962])
     Recorded Dec 1960. Reissued as <u>Join Bing in a Gang
     Song Sing Along</u> and selected for <u>Join Bing and Sing
     Along: 51 Good Time Songs</u>, all in 1962.
Only Forever (DE DL-4255 <u>BH 6</u>)
Original Radio Broadcasts (Mark 56762) R
Paris Holiday (UA 40001) ST
     with Bob Hope on two songs (Bing not in film)
     Recorded Feb 24, 1958.
Pennies from Heaven (DE DL-4251 <u>BH 2</u>) ST
Pepe (Colpix 507) ST Recorded Jun 1960.
Philco Radio Time (Totem 1002, Radiola 1044) R

Philco Radio Time, Vol. 2 (Totem 1003) R
D2430.
Pocketful of Dreams (DE DL-4252 <u>BH 3</u>)
Pop Music of the '40s: 2 vols. (EMI T-BILL.260816/260963)
    Bing sings nine songs on Vol. 1 and eight on Vol. 2.
Pop Music of the '50s: Vol. 2 (EMI T-BILL.791807) Bing
    sings two songs, none on Vol. 1.
<u>Poupees de Paris [Les Poupees]</u> (RCA LOC/LSO-1090) Orig. Cast
Radio Cavalcade of 1936 (Amalgamated 252) R
Rare Early Recordings, 1929-33 (Biograph 13)
Rare 1930-31 Brunswick Records (MCA 1502)
The Rare Ones (Broadway Intermission 128)
Rare Style (Ace of Hearts 164)
Remembering (Happy Days 123)
D2440.
Rendezvous (Camden CAS-2330) with Rosemary Clooney. A 1969
    reissue of <u>Fancy Meeting You Here</u>, omitting two songs.
Return to Paradise Island (Reprise 6106)
    Recorded Aug, Oct, Dec 1963.
Rhythm on the Range (Coral 81)
Rip Van Winkle (10" DE DL-6001)
The Road Begins (DE DL-4254 <u>BH 5</u>) ST
The Road to Bali (10" DE DL-5444) ST
The Road to Hong Kong (Liberty LOM-16002/LOM-17002) ST
    Recorded Sep 1961.
Robin and the Seven Hoods (REP R/FS-2021) ST
    "Don't Be a Do Badder" recorded Apr 10, 1964.
St. Patrick's Day (DE A-495; 10" DL-5037)
St. Valentine's Day (10" DE DL-5039)
D2450.
The San Francisco Experience (S.F.E. 101)
Say One for Me (COL CL-1337/CS-8147) ST
    Recorded Oct 17, 1958, Mar 1959.
Seasons (Polydor PD-1-6128, 8T-1-6128 8-track,
    CT-1-6128 cassette) Recorded Sep 1977 ("Spring Will Be
    a Little Late This Year" Jan 19, 1976). Bing's last
    album.
Selections from <u>The Country Girl</u> and <u>Little Boy Lost</u>
    (10" DE DL-5556)
She Loves Me Not (Caliban 6042) ST
She Loves Me Not (Totem 1004) ST
Shh! Bing (Crosbyana LLM-02)
Shillelaghs and Shamrocks (DE DL-8207)
Show Hit Tunes (10" DE DL-5298)
Sing, You Sinners (Spokane 8) ST
D2460.
Singularly Bing (Broadway Intermission 137)
The Small One/The Happy Prince (DE DL-4283/74283)
Soft Lights and Sweet Music (Pelican 104)
Some Fine Old Chestnuts (DE DL-5508 10", DL-8374 12") R
    Songs taken from Bing's radio programs.
Song Hits from Hit Musicals (10" DE DL-5000)
Songs Everybody Knows (DE DL-4415/74415)
Songs I Wish I Had Sung the First Time Around
    Recorded Apr 1956. (DE DL-8352)
Southern Medley (COL album of 1978 which first released
    songs recorded Oct 18, 1929, with Whiteman.)
A Southern Memoir (Decca, England) Recorded Jan 1975.
A Souvenir Program, with Paul Whiteman and the Rhythm Boys

(VIC P-100 [78 rpm])
D2470.
The Special Magic of Bing (MGM 2353-084)
    with Louis Armstrong
Star Spangled Rhythm (Curtain Calls 100/20, Sandy Hook 2045)
    ST
Stardust (DE A-181 [78 rpm], 10" DL-5216)
State Fair (Box Office Productions 19761, CIF 2009,
    CIF 3007, Sound/Stage 2310) ST
Stephen Foster Songs (DE A-440, A-482 [78rpm], 10" DL-5010X)
Sunshine Cake (DE DL-4261 BH 12) ST
Swinging on a Star (DE DL-4257 BH 8) ST
That Christmas Feeling (DE DL-8781)
That Travelin' Two-Beat (CAP T/ST-2300 [1965])
    with Rosemary Clooney; recorded Aug, Dec 1964.
That's What Life Is All About (UA LA-554-G [1976])
    Recorded Oct 1974, Feb, Mar 1975.
D2480.
Themes and Songs from The Quiet Man (10" DE DL-5411)
This Is Bing Crosby (RCA DPS-2066)
Thoroughly Modern Bing (Pickwick International [PIP] 6802
    [1968], PIP P8-3583 8-track less one song, Laserlight
    15-411 CD titled A Visit to the Movies less one song
    [see Feb 1968]). Recorded Feb 1968.
Three Billion Millionaires (UA UXI-4UXS-4) ST
    Bing recorded "Tower of Babel" Aug 1963; album a
    benefit for the United Nations.
A Time to Be Jolly (Daybreak 2006, P8DR-2006 8-track,
    P4DR-2006 cassette) Reissued as Holiday Treat in 1979.
    Recorded Nov 1970, Sep 1971.
Too Much Harmony/Going Hollywood (Caliban 6039) ST
Top Hat, White Tie and Golf Shoes (Facit 124)
    with Fred Astaire, Ginger Rogers
Top o' the Morning/The Emperor Waltz (10" DE DL-5272)
Traditional Carols (WLSM 1170) with the Bonaventura Choir
A Tribute to Duke (Concord Jazz S-50 [1977])
    Includes Bing's "Don't Get Around Much Anymore," his
    last American recording, Apr 15, 1977, San Francisco.
D2490.
Twelve Songs of Christmas (REP R/FS-2022 [1965])
    with Frank Sinatra, Fred Waring
    Recorded Jun 19, 1964 (5 songs).
20th Anniversary in Show Business (Joyce 1128)
Twilight on the Trail (DE DL-8365)
Variety Girl (Caliban 6007) ST
The Very Best of Bing Crosby (MGM E/SE-4203)
The Very Best of Bing Crosby (World Record Club SHB-291-96)
The Very First Radio Broadcast
    (Amalgamated 128, Frogbien 6309) R
Victor Herbert Melodies (DE A-505 [78 rpm], 10" DL-5355)
    Orig. album title: Bing Crosby--Victor Herbert.
A Visit to the Movies (Laserlight 14-411, a 1991 CD reissue
    of Thoroughly Modern Bing, omitting one song. See Feb
    1968.
The Voice of Bing in the Thirties (BR BL-54005)
D2500.
The War Years (Broadway Intermission 129)
A Warm and Wonderful Christmas Eve with Bing and Frank
    (Ho-Ho-Ho 1088) TV (1957 Sinatra show)

Way Back Home (10" DE DL-5310)
When Irish Eyes Are Smiling (10" DE DL-5403, DL-8262)
Where the Blue of the Night Meets the Gold of the Day
    (Music for Pleasure 50249)
White Christmas (DE DL-8083) ST
White Christmas (MCA 1777) with Danny Kaye, Peggy Lee
Wrap Your Troubles in Dreams (RCA LPV-584)
The Young Bing Crosby (X LVA-1000, RCA LPM-2071)
Yours Is My Heart Alone (10" DE DL-5326)
Zing a Little Zong (DE DL-4263 BH 14) ST

COMPACT DISCS

        Generally, anthologies are listed that have two or
more songs by Bing Crosby. Virtually all are available
in cassette format, most with the same basic number.
To keep current with the world-wide Crosby releases,
the collector should subscribe to Bing from the International Crosby Circle, discography by Derek Parkes,
and to BingTalks from BingThings Society, discography
by Charles Baillie. See B52, B77, B304, and B306.

D2511.   One cassette that is not on CD is Young Bing, 3
    vols. with songs from 1927 to 1941 (Evergreen Melodies
    EVR12/14, United Kingdom) Total of 42 tracks.

D2512.
Alexander's Ragtime Band (Patricia-All Star Series CD 23107)
    16 songs. Denmark
The All-Time Best of Bing Crosby (Curb D2-77340) 10 songs,
    including a duet with Louis Armstrong and one with the
    Andrews Sisters.
The American Songbook Series: Irving Berlin (Smithsonian
    Collection RD 048-1/SONY Special Products A-22403) Two
    songs by Bing of 13 tracks.
The Andrews Sisters Show (Dec 31, 1944) (Radiola CDMR-1033)
    Includes two duets with Bing. See R66.
The Andrews Sisters--Sing, Sing, Sing (Axis CDAX-701596)
    Two duets with Bing. Australia
Around the World (Entertainers CD-0211) Three duets with
    Bing and Rosemary Clooney. Italy.
The Beiderbecke Affair (Double Play GRF-079) Includes two
    songs with Bing. U.K.
Best Collection (TF T-1859) 16 songs. Japan
D2520-29A.
The Best of Bing Crosby (Entertainers CD-0248) 23 songs.
    See The Crooners, in which this 1987 disc was collected
    with others. U.K.
The Best of Bing Crosby (MCA DMCL-1607) U.K.
The Best of the Classic Years in Digital Stereo (BBC CD-667)
    Two songs by Bing. U.K.
Best 22 Songs (MCA 35XD-501) Japan
Billboard 1935-1954 Greatest Christmas Hits (Rhino R2-70637)
    Two songs by Bing out of 10.
Bing and Louis Live (Spectrum U-4016) U.K.
Bing Crosby (Ariola Express 295040-201 [Germany], RCA BPCD-
    5092 [Australia]). 16 songs; 14 with Gus Arnheim Orches-
    tra, one with Whiteman, one with Ellington.

Bing Crosby (Bella Musica BMCD-89921) A mono CD with 18
    songs.
Bing Crosby (Echo Jazz EJCD-12) 16 songs. U.K.   Sometimes
    referred to as Big Band Days.
Bing Crosby (Intertape 500-027) U.K.
Bing Crosby (Stagedoor SDC-8087) U.K.
D2530-39A.
Bing Crosby and Friends (Magic Dawe 3) Includes 15 radio
    duets with Ethel Merman, Judy Garland, the Andrews
    Sisters, Bob Crosby, Patti Page, Al Jolson, and others.
    U.K.
Bing Crosby and Jimmy Durante--Start Off Each Day with a
    Song (JSP JSPCE-701) U.K.
Bing Crosby and Judy Garland (JSP JSPCD-702) U.K.
Bing Crosby and Liberace Christmas (MCA MCAD-2052) Six songs
    by Bing.
Bing Crosby and Some Jazz Friends (DE GRD-603, MCA GRP-
    16032) Early songs, many duets.
Bing Crosby and Val Doonican (J&B JB-452CD) 10 songs by Bing
    (four are Buddy Cole/Pete Moore versions) and 10 by
    Doonican.   Australia
Bing Crosby Christmas Collection (Dejavu DVCD-2078) 12
    songs, including "Baby, It's Cold Outside" duet with
    James Stewart.
Bing Crosby [Classics] (Collection OR-0084) 18 songs. U.K.
A Bing Crosby Collection, Vol. 1 (Pickwick) 14 songs from
    Columbia, "Collector's Choice." The selections run
    from "Anyone Can See with Half an Eye I'm Crazy Over
    You" to "We're a Couple of Soldiers," originally re-
    leased by Brunswick and Okeh.
The Bing Crosby Collection (Lasertech 944D)
Bing Crosby--Dream a Little Dream of Me (Ariola Express
    295040) U.K.
D2540.
Bing Crosby--Eleven Historic Recordings (Conquistador CONQ-
    004) 11 songs; same selections as Everything I Have Is
    Yours CD (D2600).
The Bing Crosby EP Collection (See for Miles, No. unavail-
    able) The latest release of Crosby songs, the CD
    includes 26 tracks of 45 rpm recordings selected by Ken
    Crossland, then Editor of Bing magazine. MCA allowed
    the release of 19 of its masters. 1992. U.K.
Bing Crosby: 1926-1932 (Timeless Jazz Nostalgia CBC 1-004)
    24 songs.
Bing Crosby: 1927-1934 (ABC-836172-2 [Australia], BBC CD-648
    [U.K.]) From an LP The Golden Years in Digital Stereo,
    or Classic Years in U.K.
Bing Crosby--Please (Evasound EMD-002) Australia
Bing Crosby Sings Again (MCA MCAD-5764 JVC-499)
Bing Crosby Sings Christmas Songs (MCA MCAD-5765 JVC-500)
Bing Crosby Sings More Great Songs (Pickwick PWK-088) U.K.
Bing Crosby Sings the Great Songs (Pickwick PWK-065) U.K.
The Bing Crosby Story, Vol. 1, 2CD's (CBS Special Products
    A2-201) 16 songs on each disc.
D2550.
The Bing Crosby Story (Dejavu DVRECD-16) U.K.
Bing Crosby--That's Jazz (Flapper Past CD-9739) U.K.
Bing Crosby the Crooner: The CBS Years 1928-1934. 3 CD's
    (CBS 465596) Identical to the following entry. U.K.

Bing Crosby the Crooner: The Columbia Years 1928-1934. 3
    Cd's (COL C3K-44229 [44304-44306]) Identical to the
    above entry.
Bing Crosby--The Most Welcome Groaner (Parade PAR 2021) U.K.
Bing Crosby--White Christmas (MCA DMCAT-111) Three songs in
    an 8-minute CD. U.K.
Bing Crosby with Gary Crosby and the Andrews Sisters (Star-
    lite CDS-51058)
The Bing Crosby Years. 6 CD's (Readers Digest RDCD-121-6)
    112 tracks, about 45 songs by Bing. U.K.
Bing Crosby's Christmas Classics (See Christmas Classics)
Bing Crosby's Greatest Hits (MCA MCAD-1620)
D2560.
Bing: Feels Good, Feels Right (London 820 586-2) U.K.
Bing 'n' Basie (EmArcy 824 705-2, Pickwick PKD-3022 [Austra-
    lia])
Bing Sings: All About Love (Silver Eagle SED-10633, Disc 1
    of 3) See The Complete Crosby.
Bing Swings (Magic Dawe 48) 19 songs with many accompanists
    and duets, including Armstrong and Venuti, from the
    Philco and Chesterfield radio shows. U.K.
Bing Swings: Straight Down the Middle (Silver Eagle SED-
    10633 Disc 2 of 3) See The Complete Crosby.
Bing with a Beat (RCA BVCJ-2029) Japan
Bix Beiderbecke (The Collection OR-0072) Six songs by Bing.
    U.K.
Bix Beiderbecke--Bix Lives (Bluebird CD-6845-2) Eight songs
    by Bing.
The Bix Beiderbecke Collection (Dejavu DVCD-2049) Two songs
    by Bing. U.K.
Bix Beiderbecke--Jazz Me Blues (Pro-Arte CDD-490) Three
    songs by Bing.
D2570.
The Bix Beiderbecke Story (Dejavu DVRFCD-14) Three songs by
    Bing. U.K.
Bix 'n' Bing (ASV Living Era CD AJA-5005-R) U.K.
Blue Skies (MCA MCAD-25989)
Blue Skies Soundtrack (Sandy Hook SH-2095)
Bob Hope and Friends--Thanks for the Memory (DE MCAD 10611)
    Bing sings on eight of 13 tracks, with two takes of
    "Put It There Pal" and "Road to Morocco."
The Bob Hope Collection (Dejavu DVLP-2124) Nine songs with
    Bing. U.K.
Bob Hope's Christmas Party (Vintage Jazz Classics VJC-1031-
    2) Includes three songs by Bing, one with Hope.
Boogie Woogie Bugle Boy (Pro-Arte CDD-506) Two songs by
    Bing.
Brother Can You Spare a Dime (Pro-Arte CDD-486) Two songs by
    Bing out of 20.
Celebrating V Disc 50th Anniversay (V Disc Vol. 1 CD-1)
    Includes a medley of three songs by Bing from the Kraft
    Music Hall radio show.
D2580.
Christmas--All-Time Greatest Records (Curb D2-77351) Three
    songs by Bing, out of 12.
Christmas Classics (CAP CDP-7-91009-2) A reissue of WB's LP
    of I Wish You a Merry Christmas; 10 songs (omits "Pat a
    Pan").
Christmas Love Songs (Arcade 94820-2) Includes "Santa Claus

Is Coming to Town" and "Silent Night."   U.K.

Christmas with Bing (Pickwick PWKS-561) U.K.

Christmas with Bing and Frank (Pilz CD 44-5446-2) 12 tracks, including three instrumentals, from a 1957 Sinatra TV show.

Christmas with Bing Crosby (Telstar TCD-2468)   20 songs with a duet with David Bowie on two songs.   U.K.

Christmas with the Andrews Sisters (Pickwick PWK-082) Five duets with Bing. U.K.

Classic Crosby 1931-1938 (BBC CD-766, U.K.; ABC 838985, Australia) 18 songs.

Classic Performances [16 Classic Performances] (Regal 1572742) 16 standards.   Australia

The Collection (Castle Comm. CCSCD-275)   24 songs with Buddy Cole augmented by Pete Moore's Orchestra. U.K.

D2590.

Command Performance--Victory Extra (Radiola CDMR 1100) Two songs and show hosted by Bing for the armed forces on Aug 15, 1945, with a large cast.

The Complete Bing Crosby. 3 Cd's (Silver Eagle SED-10633, 3 discs)   Issued in U.K. as 10th Anniversary Collection, Warwick 1005, 3 discs. See D2562, D2564, D2603, D2659.

The Complete Bix Beiderbecke. 9 CD's (IRD BIX1 to BIX9) Several songs with Bing, especially Discs 5 (6), 7 (9), and 8 (6). Italy

The Crooners, Vol. 2 (Entertainers CD-0248) The Best of Bing Crosby (23 songs). Vols. 1, 3 (CD-0213, CD-0224) are on Sinatra and Dean Martin. U.K.

Crooners Originals, Vol. 1 (Always the Best ALW-060) Four songs by Bing. EEC

Crosby Classics (Regal uncertain) Many sing-along tracks from WB 101 Gang Songs. Australia

Crosby Classics II (Regal 1572042) 72 sing-along tracks, including 17 medleys, from WB 101 Gang Songs. Australia

Crosby Family Christmas (Pilz CD 44-5445-2) 10 tracks, five with Gary and other sons, perhaps from radio shows.

The Dorsey Brothers (Pro-Arte CDD-508)   Two songs by Bing.

The Dorsey Brothers--Harlem Lullaby (HEP CD 1006)   Three songs by Bing. U.K.

D2600.

Everything I Have Is Yours (Double Play GRF-016) 29 songs. EEC   See D2540.

Fancy Meeting You Here (RCA R25J-1003) 13 duets with Rosemary Clooney. Japan

'40s Hits--Great Records of the Decade (Curb D2-77353) Two songs by Bing of 13 tracks.

From Broadway to Hollywood (Silver Eagle SED-10633 Disc 3 of 3) See The Complete Bing Crosby.

From the Time You Say Goodbye (Scana 7706/7) Two songs by Bing. U.K.

From This Moment On--The Songs of Cole Porter. 4 CD's (Smithsonian Collection RD 047/SONY Music Special Products A4-22481) Two songs by Bing on Disc 2.

The Genius of Bix Beiderbecke (Flapper Past CD-9765)   Three songs with Bing. U.K.

A Golden Hour with Bing Crosby (Knight KSHCD-170) U.K.

Golden Memories of the '40s. 4 CD's. (Reader's Digest RC7-094) One song by Bing on Disc 2; two on Disc 3; three on Disc 4.

The Great Entertainers, Vol. 2 (MFP CD-MFP-6057) Two songs
    by Bing, from radio in 1938 and 1952. U.K.
D2610.
Great Songs! Great Bands! In a Sentimental Mood Part 1.
    (Reader's Digest RDCD314) Fourth disc of 6-disc set The
    Dance Band Days. Two songs of 18 tracks.
The Great Victor Duets (RCA 9967-2-R) Two duets with Rose-
    mary Clooney, out of 20 songs.
Guy Lombardo: 16 Most Requested Songs (COL CK-44407) Three
    songs by Bing.
Guys and Dolls (REP Musical Repertory Theater 9-45014-2)
    Two songs with Bing. Sinatra, Dean Martin, Jo Staf-
    ford, the McGuire Sisters, Dinah Shore, Debbie Reyn-
    olds, Clark Dennis, and Sammy Davis, Jr. also appear on
    the 14 tracks.
Here Lies Love (ASV AJA-5043) 18 songs. U.K.
High Society (CAP TOCP-6587) Japan; (World Star WSC-99056)
    Australia
Hits of '39 (ASV CD AJA 5086) Three songs by Bing. U.K.
Holiday Inn (MCA MCAD-25205)
The Hollywood Musicals (Dejavu DVRECD-26) Two songs by Bing.
    U.K.
Hollywood Stars (Accord 129011) Three songs by Bing. U.K.
D2620.
Homecoming 1945. 2 CD's (Good Music GMCD-8037) Bing on one
    song on the first CD and on three on the second.
I Wish You a Merry Christmas (Axis CDAX-260300) Reissue of
    WB LP, 11 songs. Australia [See Christmas Classics.]
Irving Berlin--100th Anniversary Collection (MCA MCAD-39324)
    Three songs by Bing.
It's Christmas Time (Lasterlight 15152) 10 songs by Bing of
    19 tracks, 1991 (only 4 of 17 in the 1989 release)
It's Christmas Time Again (Pickwick PWK-083) Three songs by
    Bing. U.K.
It's Easy to Remember (Rainbow RCD-307) 21 songs. Australia
Jascha Heifetz--The Decca Masters, Vol. 2 (MCA MCAD-42212)
    Two songs by Bing.
The Jazzin' Bing Crosby, 1927-1940. 2 CD's (Affinity CD AFS
    1021-2) 48 songs by Bing; includes a 24-page booklet.
    EEC
Jerome Kern--A Fine Romance (Parade PAR-2019) Two songs by
    Bing. U.K.
Jimmy Durante and Bing Crosby (JSP JSPCD-701) U.K.
D2630.
Judy Garland--Changing My Tune: The Best of the Decca Years,
    Vol. 2 (DE MCAD 10504) Three songs by Bing of 14.
Juke Box Saturday Night--24 Hits from the Fabulous '40s (SPA
    CD YDG-74619) Four songs by Bing. U.K.
Just Breezin' Along (EMI CDP 7-48272-2) U.K.
The Legendary Big Band Vocalists (CBS Special Products
    A21135) Two songs by Bing with the Dorsey Brothers, of
    10 tracks.
Louis Armstrong's Greatest Hits (Curb D2-77339) Six duets
    with Bing.
Mail Call with Judy Garland and Bing Crosby (Laserlight
    15413) Six solos and duets with Garland, Bob Hope,
    Sinatra of 12 tracks, from World War II Armed Forces
    Radio. Side Two is a "Command Performance."
Memories of You. 4 CD's (Reader's Digest RF-062) Bing sings

four songs.
Merry Christmas (Entertainers CD-0200) Five songs by Bing.
U.K.
Merry Christmas (Lotus CD-50013) Three songs by Bing. U.K.
Merry Christmas (MCA 33XD-511) 14 songs by Bing. Japan
D2640.
Merry Christmas (MCA MCAD-31143, Rainbow RXMCD-5024 [Austra-
lia]) 12 songs by Bing.
Merry Christmas--All Time Christmas Hits (PMF-90527-2)
Includes "White Christmas" and "Rudolph the Red Nosed
Reindeer." Holland
The Mills Brothers, Chronological, 2 vols. (JSP JSPCD-301,
302) Four songs with Bing on vol. 1; two on the other.
U.K.
The Mills Brothers 1931-1934 (Giants of Jazz CD53086) Four
songs with Bing of 27 tracks. Italy
The Mills Brothers--Tiger Rag (Conifer TQ-152) Two songs
with Bing. U.K.
The Movie Hits (Flapper Past CD9784) 22 songs from Bing's
early films.
My Greatest Songs--Bing Crosby (MCA MCD 18348) 14 songs.
Australia
New Tricks (DE 25P2-2833) 14 songs, including "More Than You
Know" and "Rain" as the last two. Japan
On the Sentimental Side (ASV AJA-5072) 20 songs. U.K.
The Original Dick Tracy (Pro-Arte CDD-505) The transcription
of a "Command Performance" hour special aired Feb 15,
1945, in which Bing plays Dick Tracy, Dinah Shore plays
Tess Truehart, Bob Hope plays Flat Top, and many other
guests participate. Bing sings on four songs.
D2650.
The Other Side of "The Singing Detective" (BBC CD-708) Two
songs by Bing. U.K.
Out of Nowhere (London 820-553-2) U.K.
Paper Moon--Paul Whiteman (Pro-Arte CDD-437) Nine songs with
Crosby.
Paul Whiteman and His Orchestra: The Victor Masters (RCA
9678-2-R) Eight songs with Bing.
Peggy Lee with Bing Crosby (Parrot PARCD-001) Duets with
Peggy Lee and Fred Astaire. U.K.
Pennies from Heaven (Pro-Arte CDD-432)
Pocketful of Dreams (Pro-Arte CDD-457) 18 songs.
Pops! The Happy Sound of Louis Armstrong (Jazz and Jazz
CDJJ-626) Two songs by Bing of 14 tracks, including
"Music to Shave By" ("When You're Smiling" parody),
D1315. Italy
Portrait of a Song Stylist (Harmony HARCD-120) 14 songs with
Buddy Cole and augmented by Pete Moore's Orchestra.
U.K.
The Quintessential Bing Crosby. 2 CD's (BNR CD 211) 50 songs
selected from The Complete Bing Crosby, D2591. 1992.
D2660.
The Radio Years, Vol. 1 (GNP Crescendo GNPD-9044) 12 solos
and duets with Judy Garland, Connee Boswell, George
Burns.
The Radio Years, Vol. 2 (GNP Crescendo GNPD-9046) 12 solos
and duets.
The Radio Years--1931-1943 (GNP Crescendo GNPD-9051)
The Radio Years--1944-1953 (GNP Crescendo GNPD-9052)

Remembering 1927-1934 (Conifer CDHD-123) U.K.
Sentimental Journey: The Love Songs of World War II, 2 vols.
    (BBC CD-2007) Three songs by Bing. U.K.
Sincerely Bix Beiderbecke 2 vols. (Sunbeam) Bing sings 11
    songs and other alternate takes on Vol. 1; 27 songs and
    other alternate takes on Vol. 2 (52 of 287 tracks
    total).
Sing a Song of Sunbeams (Saville CDSVL219) 18 songs. U.K.
The Singing Detective (BBC CD-608) Two songs by Bing. U.K.
Sixteen Original World Hits--Golden Gate Collection (MCA 256
    137-2, Rainbow Music for Pleasure MFPCD-023) All by
    Crosby. Australia
D2670.
Sixty Christmas Classics. 2 CD's (Sessions [no number]) Two
    songs by Bing on Disc 1 and one on Disc 2.
The Song Is . . . Cole Porter (ASV AJA-5044) Two songs by
    Bing out of 16. U.K.
The Song Is . . . Jerome Kern (ASV AJA-5036) Two songs by
    Bing out of 16. U.K.
The Song Is . . . Richard Rodgers and Lorenz Hart (ASV AJA-
    5041) Two songs by Bing out of 16. U.K.
Songs I Wish I Had Sung (DE 25P2-2832) 12 songs. Japan
Stage Door Canteen. 2 CD's (Heartland HD-1051/2) Five songs
    by Bing on Disc 1 (CBS Special Product A20162). Songs
    of the 1940s.
Star Spangled Rhythm (Sandy Hook SH-2045) Bing's song from
    the soundtrack of the 1942 film.
The Stars in Song (Axis CDAX-701592) Bing sings duets with
    several others. Australia
Swing Time--<u>Die Highlights der Swin-Ara</u>. 2 CD's (Polystar
    515509-2) Two songs by Bing on Disc 1 and one on Disc
    2. Germany
Swinging on a Star (MCA MCAD-31367) 12 songs; <u>BH 8</u> of Dec-
    ca's series of 1962, the third CD from the series.
D2680.
That Travelin' Two Beat (Axis CDAX-701597) Includes the <u>Bing
    and Louis</u> album from MGM. Australia
These Were Our Songs: The Early '50s. 6 CD's (Reader's
    Digest RDCD 161/166) Two songs on Disc 3; two songs on
    Disc 4 (of 112 tracks in the set). U.K.
Through the Years: Vol. 5 (Limited Edition Club JGB-1012) 13
    songs and one by Connee Boswell from 1936 to 1950. U.K.
Timeless Historical Presents Bing Crosby 1926-1932 (Timeless
    CBC 1-004). U.K.
The Time-Life Treasury of Christmas 2 vols. (Time-Life TL-
    107/108) Vol. 1 has Bing's "White Christmas" and "Do
    You Hear What I Hear?"; Vol. 2 has Bing's "Jingle
    Bells," "I'll Be Home for Christmas," and "Rudolph the
    Red Nosed Reindeer."
Tommy Dorsey--The Carnegie Hall V-Disc Session--April 1944
    (Hep CD-40) Two Crosby songs from NBC's "All Time Hit
    Parade" aired Jun 18, 1944.
A Tribute to Duke (Concord Jazz CDD-4050) One song by Bing.
    EEC
Twenty Beautiful Christmas Songs (Jingle Bells JB-004)
    Includes five Crosby songs.
Twenty Golden Greats (MCA DMCTV 3) 20 songs. U.K.
Twenty Golden Memories (Companion 6187152) Denmark

D2690.
A Visit to the Movies (Laserlight 15-411 [1991]) A reissue
    of Thoroughly Modern Bing, omitting one song. See Feb
    1968. See D1737-43.
We Must Never Say Goodbye. 3CD's (Parade PAK-904) A pack
    that includes Bing Crosby--The Most Welcome Groaner and
    other CD's without Crosby. See D2554.
We Wish You a Merry Christmas (Pickwick PWK-084) Two songs
    by Bing. U.K.
When I Fall in Love: 24 Love Songs (SPA CD-YDG-74621) Two
    songs by Bing. U.K.
Where the Blue of the Night (London 820-552-2) U.K.
White Christmas (Laserlight 15-444) 17 songs, perhaps from
    the Kraft Music Hall radio programs. U.K.
White Christmas (MCA DMCL-1777) 10 songs, nine with Bing;
    film soundtrack. U.K.
White Christmas (MCA 255-199-2) 5" CD with four songs.
White Christmas (World Star WSC-99055 [Australia], Lotus CD-
    5001 [Italy]) 14 songs, including two Irish ones.
You're the Top--The Songs of Cole Porter (Conifer CDHD 181)
    Two songs by Bing of 20 tracks. U.K.

NOTE: Scores of radio programs that included Bing
Crosby as a guest are available on cassette tapes. See
Michael R. Pitts, Radio Soundtracks: A Reference Guide (2nd
ed., Metuchen, N.J.: Scarecrow, 1986) pp. 4-183.
    Decca produced in 1962 a series of 15 albums of sound-
tracks from many of Crosby's films from Here Is My Heart to
Anything Goes, albums numbered from DL-4250 to DL-4264.
They called the series Bing's Hollywood, indicated in the
above lists as BH and the number in the series. Zwisohn
states that the series "is probably the largest number of
albums ever issued by one popular artist at one time" (p.
63). The jackets carry an early, if not the first, publication of a famous outline of Bing's head from the front, the
drawing with a soft hat, large feather, and long pipe.

    SOME ALBUMS IN 78 R.P.M.

    NOTE: The albums listed here are 78 r.p.m. multi-disc
    sets not listed in the Albums section above (all long
    playing discs and many 78 r.p.m. issues). Many may
    have been released under other titles and for selec-
    tions for other LP albums and CD's.

D2700.
Ballad for Americans: 4 parts. DE A-134. See D2715.
Bells of St. Mary's. DE A-410. Four songs, two discs.
Bing Crosby: 2 vols. BR B-1012/15. Brunswick reissues.
Bing Crosby--Jerome Kern. DE A-485. Eight sides; incl. two
    songs with Dixie Lee. 1946. Cf. D2388.
Bix Beiderbecke Memorial Album, with Paul Whiteman's Orches-
    tra. Bing sings on 10 of 12 sides. VIC P-4.
Christmas Music. DE A-159. Bing sings two of the songs.
Hawaii Calls. DE A-193. Bing sings two of the songs.
Music of Hawaii. DE A-10. Bing sings two of the songs.
Patriotic Songs for Children. DE A-50. Bing sings two of
    the songs, the same two in What So Proudly We Hail.

Paul Whiteman: 50th Anniversary Grand Award. 2 vols; two
    songs at the Rhythm Boys' reunion in 1943. VIC; reis-
    sued by Spartan 33-901.
D2710.
Road to Utopia. DE A-423. Six songs, three discs. ST
St. Valentine's Day--Bing Crosby. DE A-621. Eight songs,
    four discs.
A Souvenir Program. Paul Whiteman's Orchestra. VIC P-100.
    Bing sings on nine of the ten sides, issued 1941.
Under Western Skies. DE A-250. Ten songs, five discs.
Welcome Stranger. DE A-531. ST
What So Proudly We Hail. DE DA-453. Two songs in addition
    to four sides of Ballad for Americans. Three discs.
    See D2700 and D2708.

GOLD RECORDS

Title	Date Recorded	Year It Went Gold

[The numbers after most entries indicate the weeks as a
best selling record and the highest number in the charts.]

1. Sweet Leilani   Feb 23, 1937
2. San Antonio Rose   Dec 16, 1940   1946
        7th in the charts.
3. White Christmas   May 29, 1942   1946
                          and Mar 19, 1947
    Sold 30 million in U.S. by 1968; by 1980 it sold 68
    million discs in U.S. and 32 million abroad, and 5.5
    million sheet music in North America alone.
        72 weeks, No. 1 for 11 weeks, and seasonally.
4. Silent Night/Adeste Fideles   Jun 8, 1942
    Sold more than 7 million discs by 1984 with royalties
    donated to charity.
        4th in the charts.
5. I'll Be Home for Christmas Oct 1, 1943
        3rd in the charts.
6. Sunday, Monday or Always Jul 2, 1943
        18 weeks, No. 1 for 7 weeks.
7. Pistol Packin' Mama Sep 27, 1943
    A duet with the Andrews Sisters.
        9 weeks, No. 2.
8. Jingle Bells   Sep 27, 1943
    Another duet with the Andrews Sisters. Has sold more
    than 6 million.
9. Swinging on a Star   Feb 7, 1944
        20 weeks, No. 1 for 9 weeks.
10. Too-ra-loo-ra-loo-ral   Jul 7, '44, Jun 17, '45
        9 weeks, No. 4.
11. Don't Fence Me In   Jul 25, 1944
    A third duet with the Andrews Sisters; their fifth gold
    record.
        18 weeks, No. 1 for 8 weeks.
12. I Can't Begin to Tell You   Aug 7, 1945
        17 weeks, No. 1 for 1 week.
13. McNamara's Band   Dec 6, 1945
14. South America, Take It Away May 11, 1946
    The fourth duet with the Andrews Sisters to sell a
    million copies.

17 weeks, No. 2.
15. Merry Christmas (album issued 1947 on 78s, 10" LP 1954,
    12" 1963 with additional songs) R.I.A.A. Gold Disc 1970.
    The best selling album in the industry. See D2408.
16. Alexander's Ragtime Band Mar 25, 1947
    The only duet Bing recorded with Al Jolson.
17. Whiffenpoof Song   Jun 5, 1947   1950
    No. 7.
18. Now Is the Hour   Nov 8, 1947
    23 weeks, No. 2.
19. Galway Bay   Nov 27, 1947
    17 weeks, No. 3.
20. Dear Hearts and Gentle People Oct 26, 1949
    Patty Andrews and Gordon Jenkins and his Orchestra also
    sold gold records of the song.
    16 weeks, No. 2.
21. Sam's Song   Jun 23, 1950
    A duet with son Gary Crosby.
    19 weeks, No. 3.
22. True Love (Capitol album High Society) Jan 22, 1956
23. True Love, Capitol single Jan 22, 1956
    Nos. 22 and 23 are separate issues of the same duet
    with Grace Kelly.
24. Seasons, Bing's last album, went gold in England in
    1977.
        Sources: Joseph Murrells, Million Selling Records
    (N.Y.: Arco, 1984); Ken Barnes, The Crosby Years (N.Y.:
    St. Martin's, 1980), p. 30.

OSCAR-NOMINATED AND OSCAR-WINNING SONGS

Title/Year   Film   Composers

(Asterisks [*] indicate the five that won the Academy
Award for Best Song that year.)

Love in Bloom, 1934
            She Loves Me Not, Leo Robin, Ralph Rainger
Pennies from Heaven, 1936
            Pennies from Heaven
                        Johnny Burke, Arthur Johnston
*Sweet Leilani, 1937
            Waikiki Wedding, Harry Owens
Only Forever, 1940
            Rhythm on the River
                        Johnny Burke, James V. Monaco
*White Christmas, 1942
            Holiday Inn, Irving Berlin
*Swinging on a Star, 1944
            Going My Way, Johnny Burke, Jimmy Van Heusen
Ac-Cent-Tchu-Ate the Positive, 1945
            Here Come the Waves
                        Johnny Mercer, Jimmy Van Heusen
Aren't You Glad You're You, 1945
            The Bells of St. Mary's
                        Johnny Burke, Jimmy Van Heusen
*It Might as Well Be Spring, 1945
            State Fair

Richard Rodgers, Oscar Hammerstein II
(Jeanne Crain featured the above song in the film,
but Bing contributed some share in singing, boobooing,
and whistling several bars in a cameo appearance. On
his radio show Bing featured the song as the Oscar
winners were being selected. Bing never recorded this
song commercially.)
You Keep Coming Back Like a Song, 1946
Blue Skies, Irving Berlin
*In the Cool, Cool, Cool of the Evening, 1951
Here Comes the Groom
Johnny Mercer, Hoagy Carmichael
Zing a Little Zong, 1952
Just for You, Leo Robin, Harry Warren
Count Your Blessings Instead of Sheep, 1954
White Christmas, Irving Berlin
True Love, 1956
High Society, Cole Porter
The Second Time Around, 1960
High Time, Sammy Cahn, James Van Heusen,

BING AND ELVIS

Bing Crosby recorded more than 2200 songs (many as
duplicates) through 52 years and more than 1600 individual
songs; Elvis Presley, who also began by imitating Crosby's
vocalizing, recorded more than 500 through 24 years. Laurence J. Zwisohn (p. 57) notes that 31 of Bing's were recorded by Elvis, including "Blue Hawaii," "Spanish Eyes,"
"True Love," "White Christmas," "Winter Wonderland," and
several other Christmas songs. Both singers have sold about
500 million records.

BING AS SONGWRITER

Of course, Bing was also a songwriter, composing or
revising the lyrics, especially verses, to about 23 songs,
although he recorded commercially only 15 of them. Zwisohn
summarizes this aspect of Crosby (pp. 43-45) and his contribution to such songs as "That's Grandma," "From Monday On,"
and "At Your Command" with Harry Barris from 1927 to 1931,
the verse to "Where the Blue of the Night" (1931), "My
Woman," "I Don't Stand a Ghost of a Chance with You" and
"Love Me Tonight" with Victor Young and Ned Washington in
1932, "Where the Turf Meets the Surf" with Johnny Burke and
James Monaco in 1938 for the Del Mar Race Track, "Tenderfoot" in 1953 under the pseudonym of Bill Brill, and "Anthem
of the Clams" in 1960 for his fishing excursions with Jimmy
Van Heusen and Phil Harris.
Bing Crosby also composed the English lyrics to "Domenica" in 1960, the last eight bars of "That's What Life Is
All About," and the English lyrics to his final recording of
"Sail Away from Norway." He wrote others that have been
lost, although "You're Just a Beautiful Melody of Love"
(1932) was a selection four times on his radio program but
never a commercial recording. He wrote "I Was So Alone,
Suddenly You Were There" (1932), inspired by Greta Garbo's

dialogue in <u>Grand Hotel</u>, a 1932 film. Bing never recorded
this one either. His choice of Bill Brill as a pseudonym on
"Tenderfoot" is a wry allusion to the Brill Building of New
York, which houses many music publishers.

Bob Hope laughs at a Bing Crosby joke on a radio show in the 1940s.

Sans toupee, Bing Crosby singing at the Stage Door Canteen, London, in 1944. (Photo by the late Sir Lancelot Vining)

Bing Crosby in May 1945 at the Club de Golf Islamere, Laval, Quebec. (Photo courtesy of Jean-Paul Frereault)

Bing Crosby at a racetrack about 1946.

Bing Crosby standing between assistant director Martin Ritt (left) and Van Heflin on location while filming *Stagecoach*. (Photo courtesy of Father Robert Murphy)

Bing golfing out of a sandtrap at Southport, England, on September 24, 1972. (Photo courtesy of Jim Cassidy)

Bing Crosby singing at his 1977 concert in Preston, England. (Photo courtesy of Jim Cassidy)

A collection of Bing Crosby recordings and the 100th issue of *Bing*, of the International Crosby Circle. (Albums courtesy of Stanley; photo by Tuunanen)

Filmography

The first section includes the title of the film, any unusual role (guest, image, voice), the studio, running time, and the date of first release or preview. The letters mean the following:
        d: director; asst: assistant director; ep: executive producer; p: producer; ap: associate producer; w: writer; ad: adaptation; s: story; m: music; l: lyrics; md: musical direction or supervision; o: orchestration; v: vocal supervision; va: vocal arrangements; a: musical arrangements; ma: musical adviser; ch: choreography; cos: costume design; art: art direction; sd: scenic designs; mu: make-up; e: editing; c: camera; fx: special effects, process photography; anim: animators; ta: technical adviser; bw: black and white; col: color.
        The second section lists the cast; the third summarizes the plot and lists any songs; the fourth has relevant notes; and the fifth section excerpts some major initial reviews.
        This Filmography lists all known films in one chronological order. A "Guest" role means a brief cameo appearance, not a supporting role. Most films that include only a Crosby song, recording, or imitation are presented only briefly.

F1.   Ripstitch the Tailor (1930, Pathe) Screen test Short.
        Never released, as Bing seemed a poor prospect for the studio. It was an enterprise arranged by producer Ray McCarey, but his superiors at Pathe did not like it, perhaps for the same reasons that the Fox studio gave Bing later. Jim Ryan, the casting director at Fox, said Bing's "ears are too wingy," that he looked like a taxi cab with both doors open, and that the camera would have to be confined to a three-quarter view. Most footage, if not all, was probably used in Two Plus Fours (see F3 below).

F2.   The King of Jazz (1930, Universal) Supporting role 105 min. col d: John Murray Anderson asst: Robert Ross p: Carl Laemmle w: Harry Ruskin, Charles MacArthur m: Milton Ager, Mable Wayne l: Jack Yellen, Billy Rose o: Ferde Grofe art, sd, cos: Herman Rosse ch: Russell E.

Markert   anim: Walter Lantz, Bill Nolan   c: Hal Mohr, Jerry
Ash, Ray Rennahan   sound: C. Roy Hunter   e: Robert Carlisle.
May 2; May 5, Roxy Theatre, New York
          Paul Whiteman and his Orchestra, John Boles, Laura
La Plante, Jeanette Loff, Glenn Tryon, William Kent, "Slim"
Summerville, the Rhythm Boys (with Bing Crosby), Kathryn
Crawford, Beth Laemmle, Stanley Smith, Charles Irwin (an-
nouncer), George Chiles, Jack White, Frank Leslie, Walter
Brennan, Churchill Ross, Johnson Arledge, Al Norman, Jacques
Cartier (clarinet, voodoo dancer), Paul Howard, Nell O'Day
and Adagio Dancers, Tommy Atkins Sextette, Marion Statler,
Don Rose and his Rag Doll Dancers, the Russell Markert
Girls, Merna Kennedy, Stanley Smith, Otis Harlan, Sisters
G., Jeanie Lang, Grace Hayes, Wilbur Hall, John Fulton,
Nancy Torres, Charlie Murray, George Sidney, Carla Laemmle,
Cathryn Bessette, Yola D'Avril, 'Snowdrop,' Al Norman
(legmania dancer), Paul Howard (dancer), the Hollywood
Beauties, the Brox sisters, Roy Bargy (piano)
          A musical revue of pages from the career of Whiteman
and his Orchestra, featuring George Gershwin's "The Rhapsody
in Blue" with Gershwin on piano (debuted by Whiteman in
1924), Joe Venuti's swing violin, other specialty songs and
dances, and innovative scenic designs, like gigantic pianos,
drums, and bugles. Songs: Among 91 musical numbers, Bing
sings "Music Hath Charms" solo over the titles; "My Lord
Deliver Daniel" solo and, with the Rhythm Boys, "Music Hath
Charms" in a cartoon on Whiteman's early success in jazz;
"Mississippi Mud," "So the Bluebirds and the Blackbirds Got
Together" with a solo, and "How I'd Like to Own a Fish
Store" as part of the Rhythm Boys and chorus; "A Bench in
the Park" with the trio, the Brox Sisters, Jeanette Loff and
others; and "Happy Feet" with the trio.
          NOTE: The film won an Academy Award for scenic designs
by Herman Rosse, especially for the "Melting Pot" finale.
Not all of Bing's parts are significant: For "How I'd Like
to Own a Fish Store" he does not sing but takes part in the
scene, and for "A Bench in the Park" he and the rest of the
trio merely scat behind the Brox Sisters. Bing was supposed
to sing "Dawn" as a featured solo but lost the opportunity
by being jailed on a charge of drunken driving. He was
released from jail daily, accompanied by a guard, who turned
him over to Jimmy Gillespie at the studio. He once escaped
Gillespie and spent a night with a bottle of bootleg whiskey
in the dressing room of Jeanette Loff. John Boles, a Hollywood tenor and actor, was given Bing's featured solo. It is
a dramatic rendering in a cowboy setting. Bing feared his
career might have been ruined, and the credits do not list
him beyond the trio, although Barris does call Bing by name
after "Mississippi Mud." The early five-minute cartoon, the
world's first in Technicolor, was mainly the work of Lantz
before he created Woody Woodpecker or Andy Panda. The
Markert Girls became the famous Rockettes. The process was
two-color Technicolor, while Becky Sharp (1935) with Miriam
Hopkins has the first full-Technicolor (three-color) process
designed by Robert Edmond Jones and Rennahan. The production ran from Jan to Mar 20, 1930, and was cut to 98 min.
for the New York premiere of May 5. Violinist Mario Perry
was killed and Joe Venuti suffered a broken arm in an automobile accident on Jul 31, 1929, during the first attempt at

filming. In 1930 Paramount and songwriter Sam Coslow wanted
Bing as a singing waiter at $200 a week for the film Honey,
but Whiteman refused to release Bing from a scheduled tour.
     "This Technicolor potpourri of songs, dancing and fun
is a marvel of camera wizardry, joyous color schemes, charming costumes and seductive lighting effects.... John Boles,
a far better John Boles than was seen in 'Captain of the
Guard,' sings something about a romance on the Rio Grande.
The Brox Sisters also render a melody in a skit called
'Bench in the Park.' . . . " No mention of the Rhythm Boys,
not even in cast list. Mordaunt Hall, N.Y. Times, May 3.
     "I have heard that they were not so enthusiastic about
the film in America, but here, where we have had none of
this sort, it was soothing both to eye and ear. . . . Arnold
Korff, one of the finest of the older German actors, was the
master of ceremonies in the German version. He accomplished
that difficult task with ease and charm. . . ." C. Hooper
Trask [from Berlin], N.Y. Times, Nov 23.
     ". . . John Boles sings ['Dawn' by Ager and Yellen and
'Monterey' by Mabel Wayne], and well, with each extensively
produced. They will help, but can't make the picture."
Sime., Variety, May 7.

F3.   Two Plus Fours (1930, RKO-Pathe) 17 min bw   d:
Raymond McCarey p: E.B. Derr s: McCarey, Charles Callahan
md: Josiah Zuro e: John Link. Aug 10
     Nat Carr, Thelma Hill, Ed Deering, Harry Barris,
Alton Rinker, Bing Crosby, Spec O'Donnell (the last five
playing the College Boys)
     Carr plays Tailor Ginsburg, Hill the girl, and the
College Boys sing "The Stein Song (University of Maine)."
The Rhythm Boys, with Crosby, also sing a scat version of
the song and then a parody chorus.
     NOTE: Filmed about June 1930. Reynolds states that it
is a longer (two-reel) version of Ripstitch the Tailor, in
which the tailor is first called Ripstitch, later Ginsburg
(p. 22). He also suggests that portions of the film may
have been edited into The Sound of Laughter of 1963.

F4.   Check and Double Check (1930, Radio) Voice only
70 min. bw d: Melville Brown p: William LeBaron w: J.
Walter Ruben ad: J. Walter Ruby m,l: Bert Kalmar, Harry
Ruby o: "Duke Ellington's all-colored orchestra" c: Wil-
liam Marshall sound: George E. Ellis. N.Y. preview Oct 3
     Freeman F. Gosden (Amos), Charles V. Correll
(Andy), Sue Carol, Irene Rich, Ralf Harolde, Charles S.
Morton, Edward Martindel, Rita LaRoy, Russell Powell, Roscoe
Ates, Duke Ellington and his Cotton Club Orchestra with
Ethel Waters
     Amos 'n' Andy, connived by Kingfish (Powell), use their
Fresh Air Taxi to drive a black band to the Blair mansion in
Hartsdale. Then the Mystic Knights of the Sea lodge, led by
Kingfish, sends Amos 'n' Andy to a haunted house in Harlem
one rainy night at midnight to retrieve a paper left there a
year earlier, while Ralph Crawford (Harolde) and a thug
arrive to steal the deed to defeat Richard Williams
(Morton), who hopes to keep the family house and marry Jean
Blair (Carol). Amos 'n' Andy find their paper, on which is
written "Check and Double Check," and seek to leave another

written on the deed they find. The villains demand the deed
and receive the other sheet. Later, Andy thinks his paper
reads "Dead," but Amos realizes its worth. They dash to
their taxi and Pennsylvania Station before Williams departs
for Georgia and turn the document over to him at the last
moment. Songs include Bing and others on "Three Little
Words"; Ellington's Orchestra also perform "Ring Dem Bells"
and "Old Man Blues."
    NOTE: Amos 'n' Andy's first film was very popular and
included the voices of the Rhythm Boys singing "Three Little
Words" at a dance but edited to look like the song was sung
by Duke Ellington's band. The stars were whites, Gosden and
Correll, in blackface. The film premiered by opening
R.K.O.'s New York theater, the plush and air-conditioned
Mayfair, Broadway and 47th St. Reynolds states in error
that the trio was filmed in the background, making them
unrecognizable (p. 23). The Rhythm Boys had no billing.
Sue Carol was a close friend of Dixie Lee, whom Bing married
in 1931, and the Rhythm Boys recorded "Three Little Words"
with Duke Ellington on Aug 26.
    "While the villain is plotting and the hero bemoaning
his ill-luck, this cinema work is amateurish, but the moment
Amos 'n' Andy come to its rescue, the merriment starts
again." Mordaunt Hall, N.Y. Times, Nov 1.
    "'Check and Double Check' as a story is a little too
wan to stand up to criticism. . . . It is, however, comic
to gaze upon Amos 'n' Andy." N.Y. Times, Nov 9: 30.
    "With Amos and Andy good for another Radio talker,
unlike Rudy Vallee another of Radio's freak attractions, who
was washed up with his first." Sime. Variety, Oct 8, 1930.

    EXTRA: a specious test film of Bing Crosby and Russ
Columbo at the Cocoanut Grove may have been produced in 1930
or 1931, but Reynolds summarizes the alleged provenance of
supposed ten copies and concludes that "the claims must be
suspected of being spurious," and Crosby had no recollection
of such a film (p. 24).

F5.   Reaching for the Moon (1930, United Artists)
Supporting role   90 min.   bw   d: Edmund Goulding   p: Joseph
M. Schenck   w: Goulding, Elsie Janis   s, m, l: Irving Berlin
sd: William Cameron Menzies   c: Ray Nanee   sound: Oscar
Logerstrom.   NY Criterion Theatre Dec 29
        Douglas Fairbanks, Sr., Bebe Daniels, Edward
Everett Horton, Jack Mulhall, Claude Allister, June MacCloy.
        Larry Day (the elder Fairbanks in modern dress) learns
the joys of romance over Wall Street on meeting Vivian
Benton (Daniels) on a transatlantic voyage, where he learns
to woo her despite the presence of her fiance and the stock
market crash. A young and thin Bing Crosby as a member of
the crew has a chorus of the song "When the Folks High Up Do
the Mean Low Down" (a title corrupted by reviewers) with
Daniels.
    NOTE: Bing was featured, though unbilled, as the
singing sailor of "When the Folks High Up Do the Mean Low
Down." He also had a brief line: "Hi, gang." He sang with
his sprightly jazz rhythms of those days. He never recorded
the song and his career seemed settled on a low plateau. He
was hired in an emergency when Daniel's singing of "Reaching

for the Moon" was deemed unsuitable; Crosby did his scene at
night after singing at the Cocoanut Grove. Irving Berlin
had written several songs for the film, but only one remained in the final edit, the studio thinking the public had
become weary of songfests.

"None of the Berlin songs is left other than a chorus
of hot number apparently named 'Lower Than Lowdown.' Tune
suddenly breaks into the running in the ship's bar when Bing
Crosby, of the Whiteman Rhythm Boys, gives it a strong start
for just a chorus which, in turn, is ably picked up by Miss
Daniels, also for merely a chorus, and then an exterior shot
to the deck where June MacCloy sends the lyric and melody
for a gallop of half a chorus." Sid., _Variety_, Jan 7, 1931.

"There is only one song, which is called 'High Up and
Low Down." Mordaunt Hall, N.Y. _Times_, Dec 30.

F6.   _Confessions of a Co-ed_ (1931, Paramount-Publix)
alternate: _Her Dilemma_ Supporting role   74 min. bw   d:
David Burton, Dudley Murphy   w: anonymous   c: Lee Garmes.
Jun 19

Phillips Holmes, Sylvia Sidney, Norman Foster,
Claudia Dell, Florence Britton, Martha Sleeper, Dorothy
Libaire, Bing Crosby, Al Rinker, Harry Barris

Hal Evans (Foster) plots to eliminate roommate Dan
Carter (Holmes) with the aid of Patricia Harper (Sidney) to
win Peggy Wilson (Dell), who has designs on Dan. Patricia
becomes pregnant by Dan as Dan and Peggy are expelled over a
fatal auto accident, and Patricia marries Hal. Three years
later Dan learns the male child is his, with poetic justice
on Hal and Patricia, as the natural parents arrange to
marry. Bing plays "band vocalist Crosby." _Songs_ include
"Out of Nowhere" and, with the Rhythm Boys, "Ya Got Love."
Others sing "Betty Co-Ed," "Tabu," "Home Sweet Home,"
"Jingle Bells," "Ho Hum," "When I Take My Sugar to Tea," "My
Ideal," and "Consolation."

NOTE: Crosby had his last small part in this film.
"Just One More Chance" was sung by Bing but edited from the
film, but Bing recorded this fateful song on May 4, which
Bing's brother Ev sent to CBS radio. The film production
occurred in April, for which the Rhythm Boys left Chicago.
Bing earned $500. The writers refused to have a billing,
the film being credited as "based on the diary of an anonymous college girl."

"It is no wonder that the author of 'Confessions of a
Co-Ed,' the current talking picture at the Paramount, should
prefer to remain anonymous, for it is a most trivial and
implausible story, although the scenes are nicely photographed and attractively staged. . . . The [live] stage
contribution is 'College Rhythm,' with Ethel Merman and Rudy
Vallee." Mordaunt Hall, N.Y. _Times_, Jun 20.

" . . . the story and direction are hardly worthy of
the talent of the players." N.Y. _Times_, Jun 28: 3.

"The high school faction may deem it worthy, inasmuch
as they have yet to enter college, but those both over and
under the prep school level will not be impressed or convinced." Sid., _Variety_, Jun 23.

F7.   _I Surrender, Dear_ (1931, Fox) 22 min. d, p: Mack
Sennett   s,w: John A. Waldron, Earle Rodney, Harry McCoy.

Sep 13
        Bing Crosby, Marion Sayers, Luis Alberni, Arthur
Stone, Julia Griffith, George Gray, Alice Adair
        Bing (as himself) and his band are heard on the radio
by a girl (Sayers) aboard a train as she is reprimanded by
her mother (Griffith) for resisting marrying a phony marquis
(Alberni). Bing and his friend Jerry (Stone), expecting to
meet Bing's sister at a railroad depot, mistake Sayers for
her and Bing kisses her. The marquis pulls a sword from his
cane and chases Bing, who escapes. Ensuing chases through
hotel rooms, especially annoying an Irish husband, develop
surprises, and the girl hides in the room of George Dobbs
(Gray), another friend of Bing's, a man with a jealous wife
(Adair). From the closet of George's room, the girl emerges
when Bing sings "At Your Command," proving his identity.
The girl elopes with Bing pursued by her mother and the
marquis, who find a marriage certificate hanging below a "Do
Not Disturb" sign outside the couple's hotel room. Songs
include "I Surrender, Dear," "Out of Nowhere," "At Your
Command," and "A Little Bit of Heaven."
        NOTE: This is the first of six shorts with Bing pro-
duced by Mack Sennett and released over the next two years
by Fox Films and Paramount Pictures. The Sennett shorts,
each running about 20 minutes, were filmed between April and
August 1931. Bing earned $600 for the first and filmed it
while singing at the Cocoanut Grove. He recorded "I Surren-
der Dear" on Jan 19, 1931, with Gus Arnheim's Orchestra;
"Out of Nowhere" on Mar 30; and "At Your Command" Jun 24.
Bing wrote "At Your Command" with Harry Barris and Harry
Tobias, and "I Surrender Dear" with Gordon Clifford and
Harry Barris. Educational Pictures owned the first four
Sennett shorts but went bankrupt in 1939, when they became
owned by Astor Pictures and went to Raymond Rohauer in 1964.
I Surrender Dear was an Educational-Mack Sennett Featurette
No. S2094.

F8.   One More Chance (1931, Fox) 20 min. d, p: Mack
Sennett s,w: John A. Waldron, Earle Rodney, Harry McCoy,
Lew Foster. Nov 15
        Bing Crosby, Patsy O'Leary, Arthur Stone, Matty
Kemp
        Bing Bangs (Bing), married to Ethel (O'Leary), is a
salesman of Magic washing machines in Hoboken, NJ. Ethel's
Uncle Joe (Stone) wishes she would marry richer Percy Howard
(Kemp). To escape a muscular irate customer, Bing accepts a
promotion and a transfer to the California branch. Encoun-
tering such problems as a gun battle with gangsters near
Chicago, a tornado that drives them off course, and a detour
that brings them back to Hoboken (adventures depicted in an
animated map), they set off cross-country again, and Bing
encounters a buxom and amorous Indian maiden, is hit in the
rear by arrows, wrecks his convertible, and causes an old
bus to sink in a mudhole. Ethel vows to divorce Bing and
leaves him on the road, but later she enters a restaurant in
Hollywood with Percy and Uncle Joe, where Bing, now called
Sunny Monday, is the new radio vocalist pleading for "just
one more chance." His show is being broadcast, sponsored by
the Magic Washing Machine Company. She leaves her uncle and
new beau for her old husband. Songs include "Magic C.O.D.,"

a parody of "I Surrender, Dear"; "Wrap Your Troubles in Dreams"; "I'd Climb the Highest Mountain"; and "Just One More Chance."
NOTE: The film is commonly called <u>Just One More Chance</u>. It was the second short Bing made for Sennett and possibly began the practice of singing to recorded music, a pipe organ, ukeleles, and choirs, as Bing, now paid $750, and the rest of the Rhythm Boys had been blacklisted by Abe Frank of the Cocoanut Grove for walking out in May 1931 on their low-paid engagement. "I Surrender Dear." was recorded Jan 19, "Wrap Your Troubles" on Mar 2, and "Just One More Chance" on May 4. The short was an Educational-Mack Sennett Featurette No. S2687.

EXTRA: probably specious, <u>At Your Command</u> (1931, Educational) Short   bw.
Probably a confusion with <u>I Surrender Dear</u> (1931 Short) in which Bing sings "At Your Command" (F7).

F9.   <u>Dream House</u> (1932, Fox) 19 min. d: Del Lord p: Mack Sennett s,w: John A. Waldron, Earle Rodney, Harry McCoy, Lew Foster. Jan 17
Bing Crosby, Ann Christy, Katherine Ward, Eddie Phillips, William Davidson, Vernon Dent
Bing Fawcett (Bing) is a plumber engaged to Betty Brooks (Christy), for whom he is building a cottage with his own hands when her mother (Ward) takes her to Hollywood and films. Bing catches Betty at the train and gives her an engagement ring, saying the house will be done in three months. Weeks later the mother mails him the ring. Bing runs to Hollywood but is thrown out of the Monarch Studio, where Betty is a star. He looks through a knot hole in the fence, when his face is painted black, and is hired as a Negro singer for Betty's <u>Hot Kisses</u>. Dressed as a eunuch, Bing kicks the light plug out, throws a tomato into the face of the leading man, Reginald Duncan (Phillips), hits him again, and confuses the director (Dent). Then Bing and Betty realize that her ambitious mother was keeping their letters from them. Bing escapes the axe-wielding mother by entering a room with a lion. Bing bolts out, runs upstairs, and he and the lion crawl into an upright piano, which tumbles downstairs. Bing and Betty drive away, pursued by the lion and the mother in the back seat of a taxi. The mother clubs the lion into submission and throws him onto the road, but the lovers escape to return to their cottage. <u>Songs</u> include "When I Take My Sugar to Tea," "It Must Be True," "Merrily We Roll Along," and "Dream House."
NOTE: Bing recorded "It Must Be True" Oct 29, 1930. The film was an Educational-Mack Sennett Featurette No. S2688. A briefer version that included all the songs was released as <u>Crooner's Holiday</u> by Astor Pictures in 1935.

F10.   <u>Billboard Girl</u> (1932, Fox) 21 min. d: Leslie Pearce p: Mack Sennett s,w: John A. Waldron, Earle Rodney, Marry McCoy, Lew Foster. Mar 20
Bing Crosby, Margie "Babe" Kane, Dick Stewart, Jimmy Eagles, Lincoln Stedman, George Pearce
Bing (as Bing) and Jerry (Stewart) sell magazine subscriptions house to house to earn college tuition as Bing

has fallen in love with Mary Malone (Kane) pictured on a
billboard. He had been writing her at Benson College, where
she was a student, but her brother (Eagles) intercepts the
letters and replies with a gushing invitation. Driving a
car powered by an airplane engine and propeller, they go off
to Bensonhurst. When Bing arrives, he kisses Mary and is
felled by Whitney (Stedman), her boyfriend. The brother
impersonates Mary in the dark in the garden, but the real
Mary hears Bing singing and replaces her brother and jilts
stuffy Whitney. At the end her father (Pearce) and brother
hear Bing singing in her bedroom and notice a marriage
license posted on the door. Songs include "We're on Our Way
to Bensonhurst" with Stewart, a parody of "Pop Goes the
Weasel"; "Were You Sincere?"; and "For You."
     NOTE: Bing recorded "Were You Sincere?" May 4, 1931.
The film was An Educational-Mack Sennett Featurette No. 2709
and was the fourth short Bing filmed for Sennett. Astor
Pictures released a briefer version titled Bring on Bing in
1935 (F34) in which only the songs "For You" and "Were You
Sincere?" were retained.

F11.   Hollywood on Parade Z2-No. 2 (1932, Paramount) 10
min.   bw   p: Louis Lewyn.
     Stuart Erwin, Bing Crosby, Gary Cooper, George
Burns and Gracie Allen, Olson and Johnson
     Bing introduces George Burns and they banter about
Gracie Allen, whom Bing wants to meet and who expects him to
be Morton Downey. Perplexed, Bing claims to be Rudy Vallee
and sings "Auf wiedersehen, My Dear" to her on learning she
is married to George Burns. Bing wears a double-breasted
suit, unlike the version in Blue of the Night (F14), where
he wears a tuxedo, although the song could be an outtake
from the other short.
     NOTE: The short was in a series produced from 1932 to
1934 at Paramount by Lewyn especially to introduce radio
personalities, who may not have been paid for their appearances. A videotape of some of the series exists as Hollywood on Parade, 59 min. (films of 1932-34) from Discount
Video Tapes, and may include Bing Crosby (see F17-19).

F12.   The Big Broadcast (1932, Paramount) 79 min. bw
d:Frank Tuttle   w: George Marion Jr.   s: Wild Waves, play by
William Ford Manley   m, l: Ralph Rainger and Leo Robin   c:
George Folsey.   Oct 14
     Stuart Erwin, Bing Crosby, Leila Hyams, Sharon
Lynne, George Burns and Gracie Allen, George Barbier, Major
Sharp and Minor, Ralph Robertson, Spec O'Donnell, Kate
Smith, the Boswell Sisters, Cab Calloway and orchestra,
Mills Brothers, Arthur Tracy (the Street Singer), Vincent
Lopez and orchestra, Donald Novis, Eddie Lang, and actual
radio announcers: Don Ball (for Mills Brothers), James
Wallington (Lopez, Novis, Calloway), Norman Brokenshire
(Boswells), William Brenton (Smith)
     Bing Crosby (Crosby), as the Grip-Tight Troubadour, is
an irresponsible crooner on the failing radio station WADX,
owned by Burns, when the important sponsor, Mr. Clapsaddle
(Barbier), owner of Grip-Tight Girdles, demands Bing be
fired. Driving the taxi himself, Bing arrives late, is
mauled by forty adoring female fans, and sings one line of

"I Surrender Dear" as the program ends. Anita Rogers
(Hyams), Burns's secretary, loves Bing and is unable to take
dictation on learning that Bing is to marry. Gracie Allen,
the receptionist, is called in to try dictation, and a trio
of singing telephone operators announces that Bing is probably in a speakeasy. Later spurned by Mona Lowe (Lynne) for
a rich broker, Bing brings Leslie McWhinney (Erwin) home.
Bing thinks the Texas oilman destitute for having lost
$100,000 to a jilting widow. By candlelight in a three-
piece suit, Bing attempts suicide by gas with Leslie.
Anita, with news that Bing would be rehired, arrives with a
black attendant, who lights a match, causing an explosion
that ends the mortal attempt without harming the apartment.
On awaking the next morning with Bing in his bedroom, Leslie
asks, "Are we married?" Anita had been an old flame of
Leslie's and explains that she loves Bing because of "the
funny little catch in his voice when he sings." Leslie,
still worth $900,000, buys the station, arranges for an
international broadcast, and, believing Bing is dead drunk
in Mona's apartment as the program begins, tries to obtain a
recording of "Please" by Bing on Famous Records. Bing fumes
at Mona's jealous rage over Anita. With the last disc
warped by a cigar lighter in the lobby at the studio, Leslie
attempts to imitate Bing. At the last moment Bing arrives
to finish "Please." Mona with a black eye arrives at the
end of the broadcast, and Leslie gets Anita as Mona pledges
herself to Bing. Songs include "I Surrender Dear," "Dinah,"
"Please" accompanied twice by Eddie Lang, "Here Lies Love"
with Arthur Tracy ("The Street Singer"), "I've Got Five
Dollars," and "Where the Blue of the Night." Others are
"Rose of the Wildwood" and "Here Lies Love" (Tracy and his
accordion), "Hold That Tiger" (Mills Brothers), "I'm the
Drummer" (Lopez Orchestra), "Trees" (Novis), "Crazy People"
(Boswell Sisters [Connie is the one on the left at the
piano]), "When the Moon Comes Over the Mountain" and "And
You Were Mine" (Smith), "Minnie the Moocher" and "Kicking
the Gong Around (Where Is Minnie?)" (Cab Calloway Orchestra).
     NOTE: This was Bing's first starring role in a major
film. The script was based on the Broadway play Wild Waves,
about a crooner with an inferiority complex. Bing won his
role over Morton Downey and Rudy Vallee, rewrote it to suit
his personality, and refused to star alone. He is called
Crosby in the film but his character is called Hornsby in
the credits. Bing's version of "Dinah" is an excellent
example of his ability with jazz and scatting to the rhythm
of a black shoeshine boy. Two versions of "Please" may be
the only times guitarist Eddie Lang, Bing's best friend,
appears on film with him, and off camera he accompanies Bing
on "Dinah." Calloway's gestures in his song of Smoky Joe in
search of Minnie make clear that "kicking the gong around"
means sniffing cocaine. The song is a version of "Minnie
the Moocher." Paramount paid Bing $200,000, according to
some sources, for three films when the studio executives
voted for Bing over Rudy Vallee on a close poll, 33 to 32.
Burns and Allen were popular New York entertainers, and
Gracie Allen dyed her blonde hair black for this film.
Bing's ears were held back by spirit gum. As Bing contem-
plates suicide, he sings a duet of "Here Lies Love" with

Arthur Tracy, who filmed his part in New York City. Kate
Smith, the Boswell Sisters, Donald Novis, and the Lopez and
Calloway orchestras also filmed their parts in New York.
Bing sings passages from "Where the Blue of the Night" three
times. In the morning after the suicide attempt Bing sings
"When the blue of the night," getting the first word wrong,
as he did earlier on introducing himself to Leslie in a
lounge, and transposes other lyrics to "And the blue of her
eyes crowns the gold of her hair." All the specialty artists appeared under their own names. Production occurred
from Jun to Sep 1932. The "Big Broadcast" in the film was
scheduled for Monday, Jul 7 (a date that occurred only in
1930 and 1940). On a later tour in which Paramount paid
Bing $35,000 a week, he recorded "Please" in San Francisco
Sep 16 and "Here Lies Love" and two others in New York Oct
14. He had recorded "Where the Blue of the Night" on Nov
23, 1931, and "Dinah" with the Mills Brothers Dec 16, 1931.
The film was popular and became the first of a series of
four Big Broadcast's; Bing appears again in the second (of
1936) and Bob Hope appears in the last (of 1938). Paramount
had later annual variety shows under other titles.
     "It is a pity that [Donald Novis] has not the opportu-
nity to repeat [singing Joyce Kilmer's 'Trees'] as often as
Mr. Crosby warbles about 'When the blue of the night meets
the gold of the day.'. . . George Barbier is the moneyed
individual named Clapsaddle, who pays for the hour and has
the distinction of discharging Bing. . . . Leslie is im-
pelled to imitate Bing himself, which he does extraordinari-
ly well. The popular Bing, the hero of hundreds of thousands of women, finally reports to the studio, pulls Leslie
away from the microphone and continues the song." Mordaunt
Hall, N.Y. Times, Oct 15.
     "The film is a credit to Crosby as a screen juve possi-
bility, although he has a decidedly dizzy and uncertain role
which makes him misbehave as no human being does. . . .
Just why Bing Hornsby, the crooner (Crosby) should be so
carelessly late has no foundation in fact, for the biggest
of ether [radio] names know better." Abel., Variety, Oct
18.

F13.   Crosby, Columbo and Vallee (1932, Warner Bros.)
Short Cartoon.
     Depicts the foremost singers of the time.

F14.   Blue of the Night (1933, Paramount) 20 min. d:
Leslie Pearce p: Mack Sennett. Jan 6
     Bing Crosby, Margie "Babe" Kane, Franklin Pang-
born, Toby Wing, Bud Jamison
     Bing (as Bing Crosby) makes a farewell appearance at a
nightclub, singing "My Silent Love" and "Auf Wiedersehen"
wearing a tuxedo, and boards a train to another engagement.
On board he meets Margie (Kane), who tells him she is engaged to Bing Crosby after people mistake them as newlyweds.
He sings to her from his berth as she listens in hers,
thinking it is on the radio. At their destination, he tells
reporters of her engagement, which upsets rival Gilbert
Sinclair (Pangborn) as Bing plays a reporter named Jack
Smith. Sinclair later loses his bet of his Cadillac car
against Crosby's five dollars that Crosby is not the real

Bing. Bing proves his identity by singing "Where the Blue
of the Night" with a police officer and Margie's friends
present and holding the keys to the Cadillac. <u>Songs</u> include
"My Silent Love," "<u>Auf Wiedersehen</u>, My Dear," "Ev'ry Time My
Heart Beats," "There's a Hot Time in the Old Town Tonight,"
and "Where the Blue of the Night Meets the Gold of the Day."
     NOTE: This is the first film in which Bing sang "Where
the Blue of the Night," which he first recorded Nov 23,
1931. The concluding sequence in which Bing leaves the
nightclub is reminiscent of his leaving the Cocoanut Grove
about May 1931. The film, produced about July 1931, was An
Educational-Mack Sennett Featurette No. S3628, and was
probably filmed after <u>Sing, Bing, Sing</u> to number six Sennett
shorts. The film was produced when Russ Columbo was already
singing the title song, and it was months later that it
became Bing's signature song on radio from New York. Bing
probably had sung the song frequently on radio before leaving the Cocoanut Grove, or it would not have been associated
with him when he only dreamed of a New York show.

F15.   <u>Sing, Bing, Sing</u> (1933, Paramount) 19 min. d:
Babe Stafford p: Mack Sennett. Mar 24
     Bing Crosby, Florine McKinney, Irving Bacon,
Franklin Pangborn, Arthur Stone, Marvin Loback
     Bing (as Bing), a radio vocalist, broadcasts an elope-
ment cue to Helen (McKinney) overheard by her father
(Bacon), who hates crooners and obstructs their plot with
the aid of two detectives. In a later attempt, they drive
away, helped by her father's pet gorilla, which defeats the
father, Helen's official fiance (Pangborn), and the clumsy
detectives, whom Bing calls "defectives." Bing and Helen
escape in one automobile, chased by her father, the detectives, and the gorilla in a second, followed by her fiance
in nightshirt pedaling a bicycle. The pursuers splash into
a river as Bing and the girl fly away in a chartered airplane. <u>Songs</u> include "In My Hideaway," "Between the Devil
and the Deep Blue Sea," "Lovable," and "Snuggled on Your
Shoulder."
     NOTE: Raymond Rohauer, who owns all the Sennett films,
lists Fox and Paramount as the releasing agencies, although
such is not listed in the credits. Bing recorded "Snuggled
on Your Shoulder" Jan 21, 1932. The film, produced in 1931,
was an Educational-Mack Sennett Featurette No. S3627 and may
have been filmed before <u>Blue of the Night</u>.

F16.   <u>College Humor</u> (1933, Paramount) 68 min. bw d:
Wesley Ruggles w: Claude Binyon, Frank Butler s: Dean
Fales m, l: Sam Coslow, Arthur Johnston c: Leo Tover. Jun
22
     Bing Crosby, Jack Oakie, Richard Arlen, Mary
Carlisle, Mary Kornman, Joseph Sauers (later Joe Sawyer),
George Burns, Gracie Allen, Lona Andre, James Burke
     Frederick Danvers (Crosby) is a singing professor of
drama at Mid-West University. "Mondy" Mondrake (Arlen) and
Tex Roust (Sauers) are the football stars, and Mondrake
rooms with the freshman player Barney Shirrel (Oakie) and
falls for Barney's sister Barbara Shirrel (Carlisle).
Barbara, however, prefers the Professor. Burns and Allen
appear as caterers at a fraternity dance. Jealous Mondrake

is expelled for drunkenness and trying to punch the Professor, and Barney becomes the new grid star in the defeat of
Eastern College. Danvers objects to the dismissal and
resigns, taking Barbara with him as he becomes famous on
radio as the Crooning Cavalier. Songs include "(Down) The
Old Ox Road," "Moonstruck," "Learn to Croon," "Play Ball,"
and a medley of "Just an Echo in the Valley," "Learn to
Croon," "Please," "I Surrender Dear," and "Just One More
Chance."
    NOTE: In one scene, Bing, dressed in a double-breasted
suit, parodies himself in singing "Learn to Croon" to a
chorus of adoring co-eds in his class. The durability of
the film stems from its lighthearted treatment of the
script. The film was supposed to be filmed in January, but
it was delayed to April because Paramount refused to pay
$3000 a week so that Bing's radio program could be broadcast
from Hollywood. Mary Carlisle, a step-daughter of industrialist Henry J. Kaiser, appeared in two more films with Bing
of 1937 and 1938. Richard Arlen became close to Bing for
years.
    "Mr. Crosby turns out to have a sense of humor and his
subterranean blue notes are easy to listen to." Andre
Sennwald, N.Y. Times, Jun 23.
    "'Learn to Croon' is most catchy of the Coslow-Johnson
[sic] score, but the picture . . . could have used a more
outstanding lead tune. Crosby does the singing. Between
Crosby for romance and Oakie for laughs, the picture has
strong pair of male leads. . . . Crosby makes his best
showing to date with a chance to handle both light comedy
and romance." Bige., Variety, Jun 27.

F17.   Hollywood on Parade Z3-No. 1 (1933, Paramount) 12
min. bw p: Louis Lewyn.
    Eddie Borden, Mr. and Mrs. Richard Arlen, Theda
Bara, Mary Pickford, Bing Crosby, Jackie Cooper, Tom Mix,
and others
    Borden plays a mailman to the celebrities; rides with
Pickford to the studio, listening to Bing sing "(Down) The
Old Ox Road" on radio.
    NOTE: See listing of a videotape at Hollywood on
Parade Z2-No. 2 (1932), above (F11; see also F18-19).

F18.   Hollywood on Parade Z3-No. 4 (1933, Paramount) 11
min. bw p: Louis Lewyn.
    Douglas MacLean, Bing Crosby, Jack Oakie, Skeets
Gallagher, Roscoe Ates, Ann Dvorak, John Miljan, Constance
Bennett, Mr. and Mrs. James Gleason, Carole Lombard, Groucho
and Harpo Marx, John Boles, Will Rogers, Governor James E.
Rolph, Charles Laughton, and others
    Bing, Oakie, and Gallagher sing "Boo-boo-boo" to estab-
lish the rhythm for girls on exercise machines to counter
the lack of rhythm of stuttering Ates. Then Oakie imitates
Crosby in "Learn to Croon." Bing sings "Buckin' the Wind"
while driving to a celebrity miniature auto race started by
Lombard, with Harpo flagged the winner by Laughton.

F19.   Hollywood on Parade Z3-No. 7 (1933, Paramount) 12
min. bw p: Louis Lewyn.
    Mack Gordon, "Shipwreck" Kelly (the champion flag-

pole sitter), Joe E. Brown, Carole Lombard, Johnny Weissmuller, Leila Hyams, golfer Jimmy Thompson, John Barrymore,
Bing Crosby, Harry Langdon, and many others
     Bing appears in a skit with Barrymore and Langdon on
the golf course as Thompson instructs his wife, Viola Dana.

     EXTRA: Bing was asked by Paramount to play the role of
Mock Turtle in Alice in Wonderland (1933) and sing "Beautiful, Beautiful Soup," but he refused. Russ Columbo was
considered but Cary Grant did the role.

F20.   Too Much Harmony (1933, Paramount) 76 min. bw d:
Edward Sutherland p: William LeBaron w: Joseph L. Mankie-
wicz, Harry Ruskin m, l: Arthur Johnston, Sam Coslow. Sep
22
     Bing Crosby, Jack Oakie, Richard "Skeets" Galla-
gher, Judith Allen, Harry Green, Lilyan Tashman, Ned Sparks,
Kitty Kelly, Grace Bradley, Mrs. Evelyn Offield Oakie
     Eddie Bronson (Crosby) is a famous singer who befriends
entertainer Ruth Brown (Allen) and takes her to New York,
where she outsmarts nasty Lucille Watson (Tashman) with the
aid of song and dance men Benny Day and Johnny Dixon (Oakie
and Gallagher). Lucille learns that Eddie might jilt her
for Ruth and threatens to cause a scandal. Benny and Johnny
appeal to Lucille's greediness to let Eddie go, making him
available to Ruth. Mrs. Day (Mrs. Evelyn Oakie, Jack's
mother) is Benny's mother. Songs include "The Day You Came
Along," "Black Moonlight," "Thanks" with Allen, "Boo-boo-
boo," and "Buckin' the Wind" with Allen.
     NOTE: The production occurred about Jun and Jul. The
film was Bing's last of his first three-film contract.
Judith Allen could not sing and the dubbing for her was
inept.
     "Even persons who delight in Mr. Crosby's peculiar
ballads may be somewhat disappointed in his attempts to
register admiration and affection, for, although he is one
of the most popular singers in his line, his acting is often
apt to make one uneasy." Mordaunt Hall, N.Y. Times, Sep 23.
     "Between Bing Crosby and Jack Oakie the literary defi-
ciencies are modified. . . At least one of the several
songs should make the best seller grade in the competent
hands of Crosby. His singing ability he always had, but
Crosby now has also found himself in the trouping department. It makes him a cinch." Bige., Variety, Sep 26.

F21.   Going Hollywood (1933, Cosmopolitan, M-G-M) 75
min. bw d: Raoul Walsh w: Donald Ogden Stewart s:
Frances Marion m,l: Nacio Herb Brown, Arthur Freed md:
Lennie Hayton c: George Folsey. Dec 22
     Marion Davies, Bing Crosby, Fifi D'Orsay, Stuart
Erwin, Ned Sparks, Patsy Kelly, Bobby Watson, Sterling
Holloway, Lennie Hayton and his Orchestra, the Radio Rogues
     Bill Williams (Crosby) is the crooner of a troupe that
includes Lili Yvonne (D'Orsay) and travels from New York to
Hollywood. Sylvia Bruce (Davies), a teacher who loves
crooning and Bill, follows them. Having become Lili's maid,
Sylvia makes a movie in which Sylvia wins Lili's part be-
cause the latter is too temperamental. Ernest B. Baker
(Erwin) is the film's "angel," and cynical Conroy (Sparks)

is the director. Bill and Lili run away to Tijuana and
tequila, but Bill relents and returns to the film and Syl-
via's heart. Songs include "Our Big Love-Scene," "We'll
Make Hay While the Sun Shines" with Davies and chorus,
"Temptation," "After Sundown," "Beautiful Girl," "Just an
Echo in the Valley," and "Going Hollywood" with chorus.
Others include "Cinderella's Fella" by D'Orsay and Davies
and four songs by the Radio Rogues (trio): "Remember Me?"
"When the Moon Comes Over the Mountain," "You Call It Madness But I Call It Love," and "My Time Is Your Time."
    NOTE: Bing was paid $5000 a week on loan to M-G-M and
did not mind that the director and Davies proceeded very
slowly. Davies was the mistress of William Randolph Hearst,
who financed the film and later demanded more production.
The production took about ten weeks, from Aug to Dec.
Barely one scene a day was completed, and not until Davies
had been entertained daily by her private orchestra and
catered dinners. "Temptation," sung to a glass of tequila,
was Bing's first staged dramatic song. The film did little
to rejuvenate Davies' career. Holloway also appears in Star
Spangled Rhythm and as Bing's milkman-friend in Dr. Rhythm;
he became famous as the voice of Winnie the Pooh and other
cartoon characters.
    "Bing Crosby has a manner and a voice, both pleasant,
and the songs . . . have a tinkle and the list. From the
competent routine sentiments of 'Our Big Love-Scene' and the
pleasing little pastoral lyric 'We'll Make Love When It
Rains,' they range down to that brooding song ['Temptation']
which Mr. Crosby, loaded with whisky and sorrow, sings
across a Mexican bar while the glamourous Miss Davies is far
away." Andre D. Sonnewald, N.Y. Times, Dec 23.
    "Marion Davies is starred and Bing Crosby featured, but
Crosby will draw the bulk of what this one gets. . . . From
start to finish Crosby is constantly singing. It must be
good singing because it doesn't get tiresome, despite that
it's laid on so heavy. . . . At least three songs in the
generally excellent score, as played by Lennie Hayton's
orchestra, sound promising. With Crosby there to sing 'em
the songs get a break, too." Bige., Variety, Dec 26.

F22.   Please (1933, Paramount) 22 min. bw d,p: Arvid
E. Gillstrom s: Dean Ward, Vernon Dent. Dec 15
          Bing Crosby, Mary Kornman, Vernon Dent, Dick
Elliott, Dickie Kilby
    Bing helps Mary with her car, annoying Dent, and takes
singing lessons from Mary. Bing and Dent compete in a
recital, but Bing's dog howls through Dent's song. Bing
placates Mary by singing "Please," and they drive away past
Dent's service station. Songs include "Please," "You're
Getting to Be a Habit with Me," and "I Don't Stand a Ghost
of a Chance." Bing may also have sung "Rocked in the Cradle
of the Deep," "How Dry I Am," and "My Darling" (Reynolds
50).
    NOTE: No copy of the film survives, but it was filmed
at Metropolitan Studios, Hollywood, in 1933 as Bing's seventh short musical, not counting studio promotional films.

    EXTRA: Bing became one of the top ten film actors in
1934.

F23.   <u>Just an Echo</u> (1934, Paramount) 20 min. bw d,p:
Arvid Gillstrom. Jan 19
        Bing Crosby, Vernon Dent, Mary Kornman, Carl
Harbaugh, Alice Ardell
        Bing plays a ranger in Yosemite Valley, who takes a
cigarette away from a girl, who starts her car, spooking the
horse to run away. After a long walk home, Bing again takes
her cigarette away, but his captain blames him for smoking.
He takes the blame and hides his romantic feelings until the
girl, the captain's daughter, feigns suicide and is saved by
Bing. <u>Songs</u> include "Just an Echo in the Valley," "Going,
Going, Gone," "Play, Fiddle, Play," "Two Tickets to
Georgia," and "You're Beautiful Tonight, My Dear."
        NOTE: The production occurred in late 1933 as Bing's
eighth short film (not counting studio promotional shorts).
Bing recorded "Just an Echo" Nov 4, 1932, and "You're Beau-
tiful Tonight" Jan 12, 1933.

F24.   <u>Who Killed Cock Robin?</u> (1930s) Short Cartoon
        Portrays several stars, including Bing Crosby and Mae
West.

F25.   <u>Toyland Broadcast</u> (1934, M-G-M) Short Cartoon d:
Hugh Harman, Rudy Ising.
        Toys in a shop come to life, with the jack-in-the-box
as Bing Crosby and Humpty Dumpty as Paul Whiteman directing
the Sambo Jazz Band composed of clocks.

F26.   <u>We're Not Dressing</u> (1934, Paramount) 80 min. bw
d: Norman Taurog ap: Benjamin Glazer w: Horace Jackson,
Francis Martin, George Marion, Jr. s: Sir James M. Barrie's
play <u>The Admirable Crichton</u> m, l: Harry Revel, Mack Gordon
c: Charles Lang. Apr 23
        Bing Crosby, Carole Lombard, George Burns, Gracie
Allen, Ethel Merman, Leon Errol, Jay Henry, Raymond Milland,
John Irwin, Charles Morris, Ben Hendricks, Droopy the bear
        Stephen Jones (Crosby) is a singing deckhand on rich
Doris Worthington's (Lombard's) yacht and exercises Doris's
pet bear. She finds Jones attractive but taunts him rather
than reveal it. He saves her life after a shipwreck in a
fog and on a strange island, but only later does she learn
this and allow herself to reveal her love. Burns and Allen
are explorers on the island; the others are passengers on
the yacht. Prince Alexander Stofani (Henry) and Prince
Michael Stofani (Milland) are scoundrel suitors for Doris's
hand, and her tipsy but hard-headed Uncle Hubert (Errol)
feels that Jones is reliable. Only Jones has the ability to
survive, and he makes his companions do their share of the
work. Doris finds the explorers, borrows clothes and tools,
and learns that a ship will come in a month, which she keeps
to herself. The rambunctious and overly affectionate bear
would relax only when Crosby sings "Good Night, Lovely
Little Lady."   Rescued at the end, Jones reveals he is an
architect working his way to a job in New York, and Doris
changes from one ship to another to sail with him. <u>Songs</u>
include "Love Thy Neighbor," "Goodnight, Lovely Little
Lady," "May I?" "She Reminds Me of You," "Ridin' Around in
the Rain," a medley of six songs ("I Positively Refuse to
Sing," "Stormy Weather," "On the Road to Mandalay," "The

Last Roundup," "Who's Afraid of the Big, Bad Wolf?" and "Annie Doesn't Live Here Anymore"), and "Once in a Blue Moon." Merman sings "It's the New Spanish Custom."
    NOTE: A jungle song, "It's the Animal in Me," by Ethel Merman was cut from the film, later appearing in The Big Broadcast of 1936 by the same director. When Bing slapped Lombard's face in once scene, she went berserk and thrashed the crooner soundly. When the bear once grabbed a female extra, she was rescued by the trainer, but he died ten days later from wounds he suffered (Reynolds 60). The shipwreck scene was filmed over seven weeks about Nov 1933 on Catalina Island; the rest was shot early in 1934. Feb 1934 the New York World Telegram published a poll naming Crosby as the most popular male singer. Others of the many versions of Barrie's play appeared as the earlier DeMille's Male and Female with Gloria Swanson and Thomas Meighan, and two later British films. One is the 1957 The Admirable Crichton (retitled Paradise Lagoon), directed by Lewis Gilbert, starring Kenneth More, Diane Cilento, Cecil Parker, Sally Ann Howe, and Martita Hunt. Another is the 1975 Italian film Swept Away, directed by Lina Wertmuller.
    "With all due respect to Mr. Crosby's earnest rendition of the song 'Love Thy Neighbor,' the fun afforded by the dependable Miss Allen and the unstable Mr. Errol wins the honors." Mordaunt Hall, N.Y. Times, Apr 26.
    "Where it's light and familiar on the story it's heavy on sturdy croonology by Bing Crosby, who makes the footage a vocal delight. . . . Carole Lombard is negligible and not favorably impressive opposite Crosby. . . . It's Burns and Allen who really rate the second honors to Crosby, the unofficial star. Crosby himself is most of the picture. He screens his best and sings better." Abel., Variety, May 1.

F27.   She Loves Me Not (1934, Paramount) 83 min. bw d: Elliott Nugent p, w: Benjamin Glazer s: Howard Lindsay's play, Edward Hope's novel m, l: Mack Gordon, Harry Revel, Ralph Rainger, Leo Robin c: Charles Lang. Sep 7
    Bing Crosby, Miriam Hopkins, Kitty Carlisle, Edward Nugent, Henry Stephenson, Warren Hymer, Lynne Over-man, Judith Allen, George Barbier, Henry Kolker
    Paul Lawton (Crosby) and Buzz Jones (Nugent) are Princeton students who find a cabaret girl, Curly Flagg (Hopkins), and hide her in their room from gangsters because she had witnessed a murder in Philadelphia. Mugg Schnitzel (Hymer) is a goofy gangster sent to "rub her out," but he mistakes Frances Arbuthnot (Allen) for Curly, who is dis-guised as a man. Paul loves Frances, who accuses him of the mix-up and cancels their engagement. Midge Mercer (Car-lisle), the daughter of Dean Mercer (Stephenson), and every-one, including a movie producer (Barbier) and a publicity man (Overman) who intend to put Curly in a movie after suitable publicity, become involved in the madcap mayhem, like students knocking a thug and the dean unconscious. Paul resigns from Yale but is reinstated by popular demand, and he and Frances drive away as Flagg obtains a movie role. Songs include "I'm Hummin,' I'm Whistlin', I'm Singin'" Robin's and Rainger's "Love in Bloom" with Carlisle, and "Straight from the Shoulder" with Carlisle. A chorus sings several college songs.

NOTE: "Love in Bloom" was nominated for an Academy
Award, losing to "The Continental." While filming this
picture, the spirit gum holding Bing's ears back failed.
Bing insisted on completing the film with his ears out: he
said, "In the first part I looked like a whippet in full
flight. In the second part I looked like Dumbo." He never
glued his ears back again, but continued to wear his toupee
whenever he could not convince a director to allow him to
wear a hat. Bing wore his "thatch" only for the camera.
The film was the third of Bing's second contract. Gary
Cooper rejected the male lead because he felt Miss Hopkins
had the better role. Bing nearly stole the film, and Hopkins left Paramount permanently. The film opened while
Lindsay's play was in its 47th week on Broadway, and Bing's
song "Love in Bloom" was number one on the Hit Parade.
    "[The songs] are rendered quite effectively by Mr.
Crosby and Miss Carlisle." Mordaunt Hall, N.Y. Times, Sep
8.
    "Crosby is most of it [plenty for the gate]. He looks
better than ever (somehow his stature has been built up
although the faintest suggestion of embonpoint doesn't quite
jell with a Princeton undergrad), but he acts intelligently
and sings those tunes. . . . the distinguished Crosby vocalizing (Miss Carlisle is the vis-à-vis in most of it) more
than offsets these portions [of dullness]. The bit with the
pair doing crosspatter in song to hoodwink the dean is one
of these outstanding bright moments." Abel., Variety, Sep
11.

F28.   Here Is My Heart (1934, Paramount) 75 min. bw d:
Frank Tuttle p: Louis D. Lighton w: Edwin Justus Mayer,
Harlan Thompson s: Alfred Savoir's comedy The Grand Duchess
and the Waiter m, l: Ralph Rainger, Leo Robin, Lewis
Gensler c: Karl Struss. Dec 21
    Bing Crosby, Kitty Carlisle, Roland Young, Alison
Skipworth, Reginald Owen, William Frawley, Cecilia Parker,
Marian Mansfield, Charles E. Arnt, Akim Tamiroff, Arthur
Housman
    J. Paul Jones (Crosby), descended from the famous
admiral, is a successful American crooner who performs many
eccentric activities on becoming a millionaire. Claire
(Mansfield) is a guest on Jones's yacht. He returns to
Monte Carlo on learning the mate to his John Paul Jones
pistol is there, as he wants to donate the pair to the Naval
Academy. In his plot to woo penniless Princess Alexandra
(Carlisle) and obtain the pistol she owns, he secretly buys
the hotel and, as a singing waiter, persuades her to sell
the gun to pay bills, some illegal, and hires her royal
relatives. These include Prince Nicholas (Young), Countess
Rostova (Skipworth), and Prince Vladimir (Owen). Later Paul
convinces the princess of his sincerity, and she returns his
love. Songs include "June in January" with a reprise with
Carlisle, "Love Is Just Around the Corner" with Parker and
later solo, and "With Every Breath I Take."
    NOTE: The film hardly resembles the source play and
has never been shown on television. Reynolds states that
the production was the fifth and last film of Bing's first
contract with Paramount (p. 65). Gary Cooper rejected the
male lead because he felt that sophisticated comedy was not

his forte, and recommended Bing for the part. The film was
a remake of a silent film titled <u>The Grand Duchess and the
Waiter</u>.

". . . the new Bing Crosby film at the Paramount is a
witty, lyrical and debonair farce, and a first-rate addition
to the holiday bounties. . . . Mr. Crosby, who has already
shown that his talents include a gift for light comedy,
emerges this time as a celebrated songbird. . . ." The
stage program featured Fred Waring and his Pennsylvanians
and Rosemary and Priscilla Lane. Andre Sennwald, N.Y.
<u>Times</u>, Dec 22.

"Crosby gets a music cue every few feet, and always
answers, but never tires. He can make a songalog into a
feature picture because he gives the vocalizing something
more than just a voice. To change the pace the director has
him singing while doing everything but hanging from a chan-
delier. One well planned departure has Crosby in a duet
with himself with a phonograph for a teammate." Bige.,
<u>Variety</u>, Dec 25.

F29.   <u>Let It Be Me</u> (1935, Warner Bros.) Caricature
<u>Merrie Melodies</u> cartoon 8 min. col ep: Leon Schlesinger.
Mr. Bingo is a crooning rooster wearing spats, bow tie,
straw hat, boutonniere, and carrying a cane. He sings "Let
It Be Me," entrancing wives and young hens on the radio and
at the Poultry Broadcasting Company. One rooster discovers
a picture of Mr. Bingo hidden by his wife. Driving a big
roadster with a horn that goes "boo-boo-boo-boo," Bingo
picks up Emily, a "little maid," taking her away from her
bumpkin boyfriend. He romances her at a club until he
fancies a French singer and has Emily kicked out. Months
later the bumpkin hears Mr. Bingo on the radio and throws it
to the floor, where it moans "boo-boo-boo-aaa." He goes to
the PBC building, beats Bingo up behind closed doors, and
discovers Emily selling violets on the street in the snow.
Later, with a brood of chicks, they hear one of them singing
"boo-boo-boo" at their piano and throw a book at him.
NOTE: The cartoon is the inverse of a Sennett short in
that Bing becomes the dastardly seducer. Bing never recorded a song with the lyrics, "When someone steals your heart
away, let it be me," a song that perhaps imitates others.

F30.   <u>Mississippi</u> (1935, Paramount) 75 min. bw d: A.
Edward Sutherland p: Arthur Hornblow, Jr. w: Claude Bin-
yon, Herbert Fields, Frances Martin, Jack Cunningham s:
Booth Tarkington m: Richard Rodgers l: Lorenz Hart c:
Charles Lang. Apr 18
Bing Crosby, W.C. Fields, Joan Bennett, Queenie
Smith, Gail Patrick, Claude Gillingwater, John Miljan, Ed
Pawley, Fred Kohler, Sr., King Baggott, Mahlon Hamilton,
Jack Mulhall, Matthew Bets, the Cabin Kids
Tom Grayson (Crosby), a gentle Philadelphian engaged to
marry Elvira Rumford (Patrick) of Kentucky circa 1860, is
ostracized by Gen. Rumford (Gillingwater) when he refuses a
duel with rival Major Patterson (Miljan). After Lucy
(Bennett), Elvira's younger sister, expresses her love and
admiration of his principles, he joins a troupe on a riverboat and saves braggart Commodore Jackson (Fields) by raising a folding chair as an angry poker player throws a Bowie

knife. The Commodore had five aces, and two of the other
three players, as crooked as the Commodore, had four each.
Tom becomes billed as the Notorious Colonel Steele, the
Singing Killer, a billing reinforced when he fights mean
Captain Blackie (Kohler, Sr.) and causes him to shoot himself. The Commodore lies that Tom also killed Harry Rumford, the general's son, and Lucy scorns him on learning his
new identity. Tom ultimately runs to the Rumfords, intimi-
dates the men of the house, including Joe Patterson (Pawle-
y), Lucy's betrothed, and wins the heart of Lucy. Songs
include "Soon" (twice), "It's Easy to Remember" with a
female chorus, "Swanee River" with the Cabin Kids, and "Down
By the River." The Cabin Kids, five "pickaninnies from
radio and vaudeville," also sing "Little David, Play on Your
Harp" and, with Queenie Smith and chorus, "Roll Mississippi."
        NOTE: Bing not only wore his toupee and a mustache, he
had to add a girdle for the tight wardrobe, for he had added
a few pounds to his stocky frame. Jack Oakie called him
"the robot of romance." Fields labored in vain to steal his
scenes, and later complained that Bing had not played fair
in singing so well. Crosby had the film re-edited to damper
Fields' expansive comedy. Ann Sheridan has an unbilled spot
at a riverboat poker game. It was filmed about Feb-Mar 1935
and loosely relates to Tarkington's Magnolia; Tarkington
also published Monsieur Beaucaire (1900), source of a 1946
Bob Hope film. Gail Patrick used her native dialect of
Birmingham, AL, and later became the creator of the famed
"Perry Mason" TV series.
        "Mr. Crosby, who is a personable light comedian as well
as a husky-voiced master of the croon, makes an excellent
partner for Mr. Fields." Andre Sennwald, N.Y. Times, Apr
18.
        "None of it is convincing, for even a moment. The
Crosby part was written with Lanny Ross in mind and even
when he's singing it's no go. They've pasted a bit of a
mustache on Crosby's lip, which doesn't help, either."
Kauf., Variety, Apr 24.

F31.   Two for Tonight (1935, Paramount) 61 min. bw d:
Frank Tuttle p: Douglas MacLean w: George Marion, Jr.,
Jane Storm, Harry Ruskin s: Play by Max Lief, J. O. Lief
m, l: Mack Gordon, Harry Revel. Aug 30
        Bing Crosby, Joan Bennett, Mary Boland, Lynne
Overman, Thelma Todd, Ernest Cossart, James Blakeley, Doug-
las Fowley, Maurice Cass, Charles E. Arnt, Jack Mulhall,
Arthur Housman
        Gilbert Gordon (Crosby) and his two half-brothers,
Buster Da Costa and Pooch Donahue (Blakeley and Fowley), are
ne'er-do-well writers of musical comedies, and their mother,
Mrs. J.S.K. Smythe (Boland), is ambitious. Bobbie Lockwood
(Bennett) is the aviatrix-secretary of a stage producer in
search of a play for Lily Bianca (Todd), a temperamental
actress who prefers scenes in a bathing suit. Bobbie crash-
es her plane into a tree Gilbert is hiding in as he vainly
tries to interest a deaf music publisher, Alexander Myers
(Arnt), in his song. The Broadway producer, Harry Kling
(Overman), thinks Gilbert's explanation is a scenario and
orders the final version in a week. Lily entertains Gil-

bert, who is arrested for a brawl, and the musical is endan-
gered until Homps, the producer's inarticulate Hungarian
butler (Cossart), receives a large inheritance, which ena-
bles him to finance it. Gilbert then convinces Bobbie of
his love for her. <u>Songs</u> include "Two for Tonight," "I Wish
I Were Aladdin," "Without a Word of Warning," "Takes Two to
Make a Bargain," and "From the Top of Your Head to the Tip
of Your Toes."
     NOTE: Filmed about Jun-Jul 1935. Regarded as perhaps
the silliest story of Crosby's films, it's the songs and
Bing's smoother voice that carried the day. Bennett was not
a singer and did not sing. Cossart was the younger brother
of composer Gustave Holst.
     "If . . . the new Bing Crosby film at the Paramount had
a second act as richly comic as its first there is little
doubt but that it would be hailed this morning as one of the
merriest comedies of the season. Unfortunately for us all,
the battery of writers neglected to bring up their reserves.
. . . The boo-boo-booing Mr. Crosby figures here as one of
the three song-writing sons. . . . " Frank S. Nugent, N.Y.
<u>Times</u>, Aug 31.
     "The songs, the competent cast, the fetching title and
mostly Crosby will have to offset the other deficiencies.
. . ." Abel., <u>Variety</u>, Sep 4.

F32.   <u>Star Night at the Cocoanut Grove</u> (1935, M-G-M)
two-reel short col d,p: Louis Lewyn. Apr 12
     Leo Carillo as the M.C., Bing Crosby, Gary Cooper,
Jack Oakie, the Fanchon and Marco Girls, Ted FioRito and his
Orchestra, Eduardo Durant's Rhumba Band, and others
     NOTE: This short is one of a series called <u>Colortone
Musicals</u>. Mary Pickford introduces Bing at the Cocoanut
Grove, chats briefly, then, as M-G-M reported to Reynolds,
Bing sings "With Every Breath I Take," a song he recorded
Nov 9, 1934. The studio numbered the short LP 5303. Some
date it as 1933 and the song as "I Saw the Stars."

     EXTRA: Bing was asked to sing opera in the Paramount
<u>Vienna Nightingale</u> (1935) after singing a "legitimate" solo
to acclaim on his radio station. Paramount bought Herman
Bahr's operetta <u>The Yellow Nightingale</u> for him, but he felt
his voice was not appropriate and refused.

F33.   <u>Crooner's Holiday</u> (1935) Short Abbreviated version of <u>Dream House</u> (1932, Astor) (F9).
     An edited version that includes all the songs of the
original short.

F34.   <u>Bring on Bing</u> (1935) Short Abbreviated version of
<u>Billboard Girl</u> (1932, Astor) (F10).
     Only two songs, "For You" and "Were You Sincere?" are
retained.

F35.   <u>The Big Broadcast of 1936</u> (1935, Paramount) Guest
97 min. bw d: Norman Taurog p: Benjamin Glazer w: Walter
DeLeon, Francis Martin, Ralph Spence m, l: Ralph Rainger,
Richard Whiting, Leo Robin, Dorothy Parker, Mack Gordon,
Harry Revel, Ray Noble ch: LeRoy Prinz c: Leo Tover. Sep
13

Jack Oakie, George Burns, Gracie Allen, Lyda Roberti, Wendy Barrie, Henry Wadsworth, C. Henry Gordon, Benny Baker, Samuel S. Hinds, Akim Tamiroff, specialties by Bing Crosby, Ethel Merman, Amos 'n' Andy, Ray Noble's band, Ina Ray Hutton's band, Mary Boland-Charles Ruggles, Bill Robinson, Willy, West and McGinty, Vienna Boys Choir, and others.

Burns sells the Radio Eye, a television invention, to Spud (Oakie), owner of the failing radio station WHY and the talking half of the romantic lead Lochinvar. Spud and Smiley (Wadsworth) (the crooning half of Lochinvar) become threatened on a private island by Gordonio (Gordon), the jealous caretaker for the unwitting Countess Ysobel de Nargila (Roberti), who loves the Lochinvar parts of Spud and Smiley. Sue (Barrie) is the countess's skeptical secretary who falls for Smiley. The special numbers are caught by the Radio Eye; Crosby's song is seen aboard the yacht heading for the fateful island. Spud and Smiley are saved by Burns with a charging speedboat full of Marines, directed by the Radio Eye. Songs include Bing's two choruses of "I Wished on the Moon" in a country setting for four minutes with a chorus. Merman's jungle song, "It's Just the Animal in Me," had been cut from We're Not Dressing. Roberti sings "Trying to Be True to Two," and another song is "Why Dream."

NOTE: This was the only Big Broadcast film to show a loss, although Taurog filmed acts whenever they passed through Los Angeles over 13 months and added Merman's song from the cutting room floor of a 1934 Crosby film.

"Bing Crosby, in a mercifully brief appearance, sings a likable ballad. . . ." Andre Sennwald, N.Y. Times, Sep 16.

"Bing Crosby gets an exterior log cabin set for his song . . . with choral accompaniment. It's just Crosby and just singing, and that couldn't be bad." Bige., Variety, Sep 18.

F36.   Hollywood Steps Out (1930s) Short Cartoon.
Caricatures of Clark Gable, Humphrey Bogart, Bing Crosby, and the Three Stooges.

F37.   Anything Goes (1936, Paramount) alternate: Tops Is the Limit 92 min. bw d: Lewis Milestone p: Benjamin Glazer s: Howard Lindsay, Russel Crouse, Cole Porter from a play by Guy Bolton, P.G. Wodehouse m, l: Porter, Leo Robin, Richard Whiting, Frederick Hollander, Hoagy Carmichael, Edward Heyman art: Hans Dreier, Ernest Fegte sd: A.E. Freudeman cos: Travis Banton c: Karl Struss e: Eda Warren sound: Jack Goodrich, Don Johnson fx: Farciot Edouart. Feb 5

Bing Crosby, Ethel Merman, Charles Ruggles, Ida Lupino, Grace Bradley, Arthur Treacher, Robert McWade, Richard Carle, Margaret Dumont, Jerry Tucker, Matt Moore, Pat Collins, Edward Gargan, Harry Wilson, Matt McHugh, Bud Fine, Billy Dooley, Rolfe Sedan, Jack Mulhall, Jack Norton, the Avalon Boys (led by Chill Wills)

Billy Crocker (Crosby) is a stockbroker attending a bon voyage party for Reno Sweeney (Merman) and her female troupe, when he sees Hope Harcourt (Lupino) crying and whom he believes is being kidnapped by two detectives (Gargan and McHugh) for Sir Evelyn Oakleigh (Treacher) onto an ocean

liner. Billy attends the sailing and decides to stay
aboard, although his boss, Mr. Whitney (McWade), is sailing
and has put him in charge of the firm. Billy first hides as
Mr. Hill (the pseudonym of Snake Eyes Johnson, Public Enemy
Number One), an accomplice of "Moonface" Martin (Ruggles),
who is Public Enemy Number Thirteen. Moonface's companion
is Bonnie Le Tour (Bradley), actually Snake Eyes' wife.
Billy demands to know where Hope is from the detectives when
they leave the ship for the pilot boat, and they knock him
unconscious. Assisted by Reno, Moonface, and Bonnie, Billy
hides in a lifeboat, as a member of the crew, and finally as
a Russian, until a large dog knocks his beard off, a beard
fashioned from the fur of a small dog, as Moonface wins a
"crap shooting" contest by shooting clay pigeons with his
machine gun. Hope finally tells Billy she is being returned
home and later scorns him when he and Moonface are put in
the brig. After an elaborate dockside show, Moonface steals
a Paramount News van at Southampton docks and Billy jumps
in. He grabs Hope on the way and they are reconciled when
Bonnie reveals the real Snake Eyes has been captured and the
police declare "Moonface" no longer wanted. Moonface ends
up with Bonnie and Oakleigh gets Reno. <u>Songs</u> include
"You're the Top" with Merman, "My Heart and I" with a reprise in a Russian accent, "Sailor Beware," "There'll Always
Be a Lady Fair" with the Avalon Boys, and the Heyman-Carmi-
chael "Moonburn"; Merman sings "Anything Goes," "I Get a
Kick Out of You" with the line on cocaine and a reprise,
reprises "You're the Top," and sings "Shanghai-dee-ho." The
Avalon quartet also sings "A Sailor's Life" and "There'll
Always Be a Lady Fair" with Wills singing and playing a jug.
Finally Bing joins Merman again on "You're the Top" and
"Shanghai-dee-ho."
    NOTE: Bing is billed as the sole "star." Included are
three Porter songs; omitted are four of the popular songs by
Porter for the 1934-35 Broadway hit, and added are four
others (three by Robin and Hollander and one by Heyman and
Carmichael). Bing's harmonizing of "There'll Always Be a
Lady Fair" with the Avalon Boys, a trio with Chill Wills, is
one song Bing did not record commercially. <u>Variety</u> calls
the Avalon Boys the Pug-Uglies, a quartet by themselves but
a trio with Bing. Porter named the lead male role after his
San Francisco financier of his early years, and Merman
reprised her original stage role. Dixie Lee Crosby was the
original choice to play Merman's role of Reno Sweeney, but
she declined and never made another film. Victor Moore was
originally sought to play Moonface. Paramount remade the
film in 1956, also starring Crosby in an extensively revised
story. The 1934 musical of Bolton and Wodehouse was rewritten in three weeks by Howard Lindsay and Russel Crouse after
the fire on the <u>Morro Castle</u> Sep 8, 1934, off Asbury Park,
NJ, which killed 134 passengers, making a maritime disaster
musical unthinkable (and, ironically, months after the 1956
film was released, another disaster killed 51 people when
the <u>Andrea Doria</u>, colliding with the <u>Stockholm</u>, sank off
Long Island. Porter's 1934 musical ran to 420 performances.
    ". . . Bing Crosby is an acceptable substitute for the
show's William Gaxton in almost every subdivision except
that in which he joins Miss Merman in 'You're the Top.' It
doesn't seem possible, but Mr. Crosby croons it." Frank S.

Nugent, N.Y. <u>Times</u>, Feb 6.
  "Crosby is fine singing 'Sailor Beware' alone and
working in with three ship's crew members (The Pug-Uglies)
who sing as a trio, and he's also there as usual when it
comes to getting his quota of laughs. And there's also a
few sotto voce cracks in his vocal swingin' for the special
benefit of the boys at the Famous Door." Bige., <u>Variety</u>,
Feb 12.

F38.   <u>Rhythm on the Range</u> (1936, Paramount) 85 min. bw
d: Norman Taurog p: Benjamin Glazer w: Walter DeLeon,
Francis Martin, John C. Moffitt, Sidney Salkow s: Mervin J.
Hauser m, l: Billy Hill, Sam Coslow, Leo Robin, Richard
Whiting, Frederick Hollander, Johnny Mercer md: Boris
Morros art: Hans Dreier, Robert Usher sd: A.E. Freudeman
mu: Bud Westmore e: Ellsworth Hoagland c: Karl Struss.
Jul 29
        Bing Crosby, Frances Farmer, Bob Burns, Martha
Raye, Samuel S. Hinds, Warren Hymer, Lucille Webster Glea-
son, George E. Stone, James Burke, Clem Bevans, Charles
Williams, Leonid Kinskey, Bud Flanagan (later Dennis O'-
Keefe), Charles E. Arnt, Irving Bacon, Louis Prima, Bessie
Patterson, Sons of the Pioneers (with Roy Rogers)
        Jeff Larabee (Crosby), a cowhand of Penelope Ryland
(Gleason), rides in a rodeo in Madison Square Garden, and
returns West with a prize bull called Cuddles, finding
Penelope's rich niece, Doris Halloway (Farmer), hidden in
the boxcar, wearing a gown, and pretending to be a cook.
Jeff manages a dude ranch in Southern California with the
aid of Buck Burns (Burns), who returns home ahead of Jeff.
Thwarting kidnappers hoping to return her home to her fi-
ance, Doris falls for Jeff and Jeff gradually obliges. Emma
Mazda (Raye) is the high-society woman at the ranch whom
slow-witted Buck intends to marry. At a celebration, Jeff
announces he and Doris will also wed. <u>Songs</u> include "Empty
Saddles," "I Can't Escape from You," "Round-Up Lullaby,"
"Rhythm on the Range," "Drink It Down," "The House That Jack
Built for Jill" with Farmer, and "I'm an Old Cowhand" with
Raye and the cast. Raye also sings "Mr. Paganini" and "If
You Can't Sing It You'll Have to Swing It."
  NOTE: Bing is billed as the sole "star"; the others
are featured and Raye, age 27, and Bob Burns are introduced.
Bing is overshadowed in this Western by Burns and Raye. The
production occurred about Apr-May 1936. Dressed in a cowboy
suit with "Jeff" monogrammed over the left pocket, Bing's
costume for the film, he appeared at Grauman's Chinese
Theatre on Apr 8, 1937, to place his hand prints and boot-
prints in concrete. It is Bing's only musical Western, and
it was remade as <u>Pardners</u> (Paramount, 1956) with Dean Martin
and Jerry Lewis, with Martin in Crosby's role and again
directed by Taurog, script by Sidney Sheldon, filmed in Nov
1955. The Martin-Lewis team was splitting as their movie
was released. The only other Western Bing is in is the 1966
remake of <u>Stagecoach</u>.
  "Assisting [Raye] in the genial task of stealing the
picture from the laryngeal Mr. Crosby and the decorative
Frances Farmer is Bob Burns, radio's monologist and bazooka
player from Van Buren, Ark." Frank S. Nugent, N.Y. <u>Times</u>,
Jul 30.

"Bing Crosby shoots par, on singing and light comedy but, because of story handicap, he might have had some tough going minus the aid of a pair of new faces [Raye and Bob Burns], clicking on their first picture attempt." Bige., Variety, Aug 5.

F39.   Stowaway (1936, 20th Century-Fox) Impersonation 86 min. bw d: William A. Seiter p: Buddy G. DeSylva, Earl Carroll, Harold Wilson w: William Conselman, Arthur Sheekman s: Sam Engel M, l: Mack Gordon, Harry Revel, Irving Caesar md: Louis Silvers e: Lloyd Nosler c: Arthur Miller.
    Shirley Temple, Robert Young, Alice Faye, Eugene Pallette, Helen Westley, Arthur Treacher, J. Edward Bromberg, Astrid Allwyn, Allan Lane, Robert Greig
    Ching-Ching (Temple), daughter of slain missionaries, is stranded in Shanghai, where she meets playboy Tommy Randall (Young) and enters an amateur contest in which a Chinaman imitates Bing Crosby singing "Please." She stows away on Randall's yacht and later in divorce court under Judge Booth (Bromberg), she brings Randall and wife, Susan Parker (Faye), together. Songs include the impersonation of Crosby's "Please," "One Never Knows, Does One?" by Faye and "Good Night, My Love" and "You gotta S-M-I-L-E to Be H-A-Double P-Y" by Temple.
    "A clever little baggage when she is kept in her place, Shirley has been permitted to dominate 'Stowaway' without monopolizing it." Frank S. Nugent, N.Y. Times, Dec 19.
    "In addition to her customary singing, dancing and exceptional line reading for a child her age, Miss Temple this time goes in for talking Chinese, quoting Oriental proverbs, giving imitations of Jolson, Cantor and Fred Astaire and other departures. She even handles a tearful dramatic exit expertly." Bige., Variety, Dec 23.

F40.   Bingo Crosbyana (1936, Warner Bros.) Caricature cartoon 8 min. col p: Leon Schlesinger d: I. Freleng m: Norman Spencer anim: Cal Dalton, Sandy Walker.
    Bingo Crosbyana is an ant, a guitar-playing crooner from Havana, who sings a song of his native land, entrancing the female ants in a human's kitchen, except an old female who dumps a cup of water on him. A female trio of ants sings "Bingo Crosbyana," with lyrics that he is "a sheik who murders the weaker gender." After singing a parody with the words "Where the Blue of the Night Meets the Gold of Mañana" and dancing with the prettiest ant, he impresses the females with high-speed stunt flying until a spider appears. Bingo literally turns yellow, jumps into an empty cup and follows the females into a roll of waxed paper. When the other male ants attack the spider and drive him onto a sheet of fly paper, Bingo emerges and says, "Well, we certainly got him this time." The other males get rid of Bingo by bouncing him into a cup full of coffee.
    NOTE: The impersonator does better in singing like Bing rather than talking like him. This is another cartoon that makes fun of Bing and crooning. Later cartoons are regularly respectful.

    EXTRA: Paramount proposed a musical-comedy-murder

mystery <u>Fly by Night</u> (1936) for Bing, written by Eric Hatch,
but it did not work out. A film of the title appeared in
1942 as a film about uncovering a Nazi spy ring.

F41.   <u>Pennies from Heaven</u> (1936, Columbia) 81 min. bw
d: Norman Z. McLeod p: Emanuel Cohen (Major Pictures) w:
Jo Swerling s: Katherine Leslie Moore's <u>The Peacock Feather</u>
m,l: Arthur Johnston, John Burke md: George Stoll va: John
Scott Trotter c: Robert Pittack sound: Glen Rominger. Dec
9
        Bing Crosby, Madge Evans, Edith Fellows, Donald
Meek, John Gallaudet, Louis Armstrong and his Band, Tom
Dugan, Nan Bryant, Charles Wilson
        Larry (Crosby), imprisoned on a trumped-up smuggling
charge, leaves prison promising to deliver a letter to the
New Jersey family of a man an inmate had murdered. Hoping
to go to Venice, he sings for pennies and performs stunts in
an automobile at a fairgrounds. Later he takes Daisy
(Fellows), a 13-year-old daughter of the murdered man, and
her grandfather, Gramp (Meek), to a farm house owned by the
executed killer, where Larry sings a lullaby in a storm and
founds a profitable roadhouse called Haunted House Cafe with
the aid of several businessmen. Henry (Armstrong) is a
musician friend. Miss Howard (Bryant) tries to run an
orphanage, and Carmichael (Stack) is the welfare commissioner. Susan (Evans) is the harassing county welfare agent who
later loses her job, joins the group, and falls for Larry.
<u>Songs</u> include "Let's Call a Heart a Heart," "Old MacDonald,"
"Pennies from Heaven," "Now I've Got Some Dreaming to Do,"
"One, Two, Button Your Shoe," "What This Country Needs," and
"So Do I." Louis Armstrong plays "Skeleton in Your Closet."
        NOTE: Bing is billed as the sole "star," and Louis
Armstrong made his film debut. Crosby financed half the
production for half the large profits, as an outside feature
permitted by his contract with Paramount. It was filmed
about Jul-Sep 1936 by Major Pictures at Paramount Studios,
although Columbia released it. The title song was nominated
for an Academy Award, losing to "The Way You Look Tonight."
This was Crosby's first association with John Scott Trotter,
whom Johnny Burke suggested as the arranger of Bing's songs.
A 1981 film of the same title, starring Steve Martin and
Bernadette Peters, is not a remake.
        "A wholesome, lightly sentimental and genial comedy, it
is all the more ingratiating by contrast to its predecessor
[Mae West's prolonged session at the Paramount]. . . . In
sum, [it] is one of Mr. Crosby's best." Frank S. Nugent,
N.Y. <u>Times</u>, Dec 10.
        "Film won't advance Crosby although Crosby may overcome
its faults to some extent." Land., <u>Variety</u>, Dec 16.

F42.   <u>Waikiki Wedding</u> (1937, Paramount) 89 min. bw d:
Frank Tuttle p: Arthur Hornblow w: Frank Butler, Don
Hartman, Walter DeLeon, Francis Martin s: Butler, Hartman
m, l: Leo Robin, Ralph Rainger, Harry Owens ch: LeRoy Prinz
cos: Edith Head sd: A.E. Freudeman exterior d: Robert C.
Bruce c: Karl Struss sound: Gene Merritt, Louis Mesenkop
e: Paul Weatherwax. Mar 24
        Bing Crosby, Bob Burns, Martha Raye, Shirley Ross,
George Barbier, Leif Erikson, Grady Sutton, Granville Bates,

Anthony Quinn, Maurice Lieu, Mitchell Lewis, Racquel Eche-
verria, Lotus Liu, Prince Lei Lani

Tony Marvin (Crosby), publicity man for the Imperial
Pineapple Company, connives to have the Pineapple Girl,
Georgia Smith (Ross) of Birch Falls, to board a yacht with
her friend Myrtle Finch (Raye) and his friend Shad Buggle
(Burns) as crew and chaperones to learn that Hawaii is not
boring but romantic. Georgia is pursued by her uncle, J.P.
Todhunter (Barbier), his son Everett (Sutton), and a dentist
from home, Dr. Victor P. Quimby (Erikson), who is engaged to
Georgia. Georgia and Myrtle are fooled into believing they
have a sacred black pearl that would quell a volcano, learn-
ing otherwise only later. The Hawaiian priest (Prince Lei
Lani) assists in the romantic fiction of the saving pearl.
Shad arranges to have Dr. Quimby arrested and then himself,
and Tony hires an old woman to pose as his mother, who
boards Georgia's liner to convince her to marry Tony.
Aboard the waiting ship Tony convinces her that he loves
her. <u>Songs</u> include "Blue Hawaii" with Ross, "Sweet Is the
Word for 'You'" with Ross, "<u>Nani Ona Pua</u>" with a chorus, and
"Sweet Leilani." Ross also sings "In a Little Hula Heaven";
Raye sings "<u>Okolehao</u>"; and a chorus offers "<u>Aloha Oe</u>."
NOTE: Bing led the "featured" cast, none billed as a
"star," and from 1940 on Bing shared "star" billing. "Sweet
Leilani," a song by Harry Owens that Bing discovered in
Honolulu and insisted on singing in the film, won the Oscar
for Best Song of 1937 and became Bing's first million seller. Bing had to convince Owens to let him sing it, to the
annoyance of songwriters Robin and Rainger. The studio
decorations by Freudeman and Bruce are exceptionally convincing in recreating Hawaii.
"Regretting that he has but one voice to give, Bing
Crosby is surrendering it cheerfully at the Paramount to the
uses of the Hawaiian Board of Trade, the pineapple industry
and sundry tourist agencies. . . . Mr. Crosby is still the
pleasantest of our crooners and Miss Ross was all right,
too. . . ." Frank S. Nugent, N.Y. <u>Times</u>, Mar 25.
"The prime possible b.o. deterrent with this pic is
that it comes so soon after the release of Crosby's 'Pennies
from Heaven' for Columbia, but this damper should not be
drastic. . . . [Crosby] also makes the best of his songs, a
couple of them spotted in night sailboat scenes that are
very well photographed and directed." Scho., <u>Variety</u>, Mar
31.

F43.   <u>Screen Snapshots</u> No. 5 (1937, Columbia) Short.

F44.   <u>It Happened in Hollywood</u> (1937, Columbia) U.K.
title <u>Once a Hero</u> Impersonation 67 min. bw d: Harry
Lachman w: Ethel Hill, Harvey Fergusson, Sam Fuller s:
Myles Connolly c: Joseph Walker. Oct 1
Richard Dix, Fay Wray, Victor Kilian, Franklin
Pangborn, Charlie Arnt, Granville Bates, William B. David-
son, Arthur Loft, Edgar Dearing, James Dolan, Billy Burrud
Tim Bart (Dix) was a cowboy star of silent films now
rejected for sound, although his leading lady, Gloria Gay
(Wray), succeeds. Bart stays in Hollywood and goes broke
because his self-image won't let him accept popular gangster
roles. Slim (Kilian) is his friend, Sam Bennet (Bates) is a

producer, and Mr. Forsythe (Pangborn) a dialogue director.
A faded star, Tim later rejoins Gloria after helping an
idolizing crippled boy (Burrud). Tim shoots three bank
robbers, and his fame induces the studio to put him back in
the saddle. At the end many doubles of film stars appear,
including one of Bing Crosby singing "Let's Fall in Love."
     "A friendly fable of the rise and fall (and rise again)
of a movie cowboy hero, the new back-studio piece contains
sardonic references to the coming of the talkies, has an
approving word for fan mail and adds a pious commentary on
the transiency of fame." Frank S. Nugent, N.Y. Times, Oct
2.
     "Not only has the story of a pic star washed up when
films found voice, been done before, but it has been done so
much better." Bert., Variety, Oct 6.

     EXTRA: A poll by Motion Picture Herald placed Bing as
the fourth most popular film star of 1937, trailing Shirley
Temple, Clark Gable, and Robert Taylor.

F45.   Double or Nothing (1937, Paramount) 90 min. bw
d: Theodore Reed p: Benjamin Glazer w: Charles Lederer,
Erwin Gelsey, John C. Moffitt, Duke Atterbury s: M. Coates
Webster m, l Arthur Johnston, Johnny Burke, Sam Coslow, Al
Siegel, Ralph Freed, Burton Lane md: Boris Morros v: Al
Siegel a: Max Terr, Victor Young ma: Arthur Franklin c:
Karl Struss e: Edward Dmytryk. Los Angeles Paramount Aug
2; N.Y Sep 1
     Bing Crosby, Martha Raye, Andy Devine, Mary Car-
lisle, William Frawley, Benny Baker, Samuel S. Hinds, William Henry, Fay Holden, Bert Hanlon, Gilbert Emery, Walter
Kingsford, John Gallaudet, Harry Barris, specialties by Ames
and Arno, Alphonse Berg, Frances Faye, Ed Rickard, Calgary
Brothers
     Lefty Boylan (Crosby), a destitute crooner, competes
with Liza Lou Lane (Raye), Half-Pint (Devine), and Peterson
(Frawley) to win a million-dollar inheritance by honestly
doubling $5000 in 30 days. The challenge was the bequest of
a deceased millionaire to prove the honesty and intelligence
of people; only four of 25 wallets were returned. If they
failed the intelligence part, the estate would go to Jonathan (Hinds), brother of the deceased, who seeks to sabotage
their plans. Lefty's competitors fail and become partners
with him to open a nightclub, selling half interest at the
last moment for $10,000. The orchestra leader is Harry
Barris, leading a "sing band" of 20 voices. Lefty ends up
with Vicki Clark (Carlisle), the daughter of the millionaire. Songs include "Smarty," "After You" with Raye, Faye,
Barris, and chorus, "It's the Natural Thing to Do," "The
Moon Got into My Eyes," and "All You Want to Do Is Dance."
Other songs are "It's On, It's Off" by Raye as a strip tease
and "Listen, My Children."
     NOTE: Bing was the sole "star" of the film.
     "Although Bing delivers five songs in his customary
agreeable voice and makes a pleasant enough suitor for the
fair Mary Carlisle, it is really the explosive Miss Raye,
[Ames and Arno and the Calgary Brothers] . . . who provide
the brighter moments. Miss Raye . . . [satirizes] the
'strip tease' artistes in much the same fashion as . . .

Imogene Coca, although with considerably less finesse."
Thomas M. Pryor, N.Y. Times, Sep 2.
    "This is not the first time that Crosby has carried a
heavy load on his broad shoulders. Point is, can he keep on
doing it indefinitely? He is strictly a personality, just
passing fair as an actor, but his croon is unique and the
wide radio exploitation he has had keeps him a valuable
asset for theatres. . . . Value of the Crosby warble is
dimmed because he sings in nearly every episode in which he
appears. Some of it is so casual that his major effort near
the end of the picture falls rather flat." Flin., Variety,
Aug 18.

F46.   Don't Hook Now (1938, Paramount) 32 min. bw d,
p: Herbert Polesie, Everett Crosby, Inc., for the Profes-
sional Golfers Association.
        Bing Crosby, Bob Hope, Ben Hogan, Sam Snead, Byron
Nelson, Jimmy Demaret, Ralph Guldahl, Jimmy Hines
    It was filmed at Bing's second Pro-Am Tournament at
Rancho Santa Fe. Bing sings Burke's and Van Heusen's
"Tomorrow's My Lucky Day" before teeing off. He recorded
the song nearly twenty years later, on Dec 31, 1957.
    NOTE: Some sources indicate it was released by United
Artists. Reynolds states that it was filmed at Crosby's
Pro-Am Tournament in Jan 1942 and ran 18 min. (p. 120). One
item of internal evidence suggesting a 1942 date is that Van
Heusen replaced James V. Monaco as Burke's composer in 1940,
but they could have collaborated earlier. Burke and Monaco
collaborated on the 1940 short Swing with Bing (F53). The
annual "Clambake" resumed in 1947 at Pebble Beach.

F47.   Doctor Rhythm (1938, Paramount) 80 min. bw d:
Frank Tuttle asst: Russell Matthews p: Emanuel Cohen
(Major Pictures) ap: Herbert Polesie w: Jo Swerling,
Richard Connell, Dion Titheradge s: O. Henry's "The Badge
of Policeman O'Roon" m, l: Johnny Burke, James V. Monaco
md: George Stoll o: John Scott Trotter ch: Jack Crosby c:
Charles Lang. Los Angeles Paramount Apr 22
        Bing Crosby, Mary Carlisle, Beatrice Lillie, Andy
Devine, Rufe Davis, Laura Hope Crews, Fred Keating, John
Hamilton, Sterling Holloway, Henry Wadsworth, Franklin
Pangborn, Harold Minjir, William Austin, Gino Corrado, Harry
Stubbs, Frank Elliott, Louis Armstrong, Bob Hope
    Dr. Bill Remsen (Crosby), a physician, has a 15th high
school reunion (Brooklyn P.S. 43) of the relay team in the
Central Park Zoo at midnight with three chums: Patrolman
Lawrence O'Roon (Devine), zookeeper Al (Davis), and Luke
(Holloway), an ice cream vendor. O'Roon becomes incapaci-
tated by a bite from a seal after he released caged monkeys
and nearly a lion the day after the drunken fete, leading to
Bill's taking on the patrolman's task of protecting socialite Judy Marlowe (Carlisle) from a fortune-hunting gambler
named Chris LeRoy (Keating). Mrs. Lorelei Dodge-Blodgett
(Lillie), Judy's aunt, is sponsoring and planning the annual
policeman's benefit. Messrs. Stanchfield, Martingale, and
Coldwater (Pangborn, Minjir, Austin) are the confused clerks
as Mrs. Dodge-Blodgett orders napkins. The lady becomes so
distraught that Mrs. Twombling (Crews) takes her to see Dr.
Remsen, who scarcely hides his impersonation. After Judy

fails several times to elope, O'Roon arrests the gambler and
is promoted to sergeant. In Judy's final attempt to elope,
Bill corners her in an amusement park and takes her to the
benefit show, where they fall for each other. Songs include
"Doctor Rhythm," "Public School 43" with Holloway, Devine,
and Davis, "On the Sentimental Side," "This Is My Night to
Dream," "Only a Gypsy Knows" with Lillie and chorus, "The
Trumpeter's Lament," and "My Heart Is Taking Lessons."
Lillie sings "There's Rhythm in This Heart of Mine."
   NOTE: Bing, Carlisle, and Lillie were the "co-stars."
Hundreds of monkeys escaped the studio during the production
and haunted the landscape for months. Lillie performs her
"Double Dozen Double-Damask Dinner Napkins" routine, made
famous in the Andre Charlot Revues. Bob Hope appears briefly at no charge, his penalty for losing a well-publicized
golf match to Bing Oct 16, 1937, during the filming.
   "[Beatrice Lillie is] one up on Mr. Crosby, whose
crooning is almost too liquid this time. [His songs] were
not so much sung as wrung out. Too bad, too, for they're
good numbers." Frank S. Nugent, N.Y. Times, May 19.
   "[The film] will keep Crosby at his present high box-
office rating." Flin., Variety, Apr 27.

F48.   Sing, You Sinners (1938, Paramount) 88 min. bw
d, p: Wesley Ruggles w: Claude Binyon l: John Burke m:
James V. Monaco "Small Fry," special song by Frank Loesser,
Hoagy Carmichael c: Karl Struss e: Paul Weatherwax.
Saratoga Springs, NY, Aug 14
        Bing Crosby, Fred MacMurray, Ellen Drew, Donald
O'Connor, Elizabeth Patterson, John Gallaudet, Tom Dugan,
Irving Bacon, Harry Barris
        Joe Beebe (Crosby) is a swap-happy ne'er-do-well who
loses his gas-station job because of swapping fuel for
things. He goes away, swapping race tickets for winners,
those for a swap shop, and that for a horse, Uncle Gus, in
Los Angeles, where he intends to care for his family, brothers David (MacMurray) and Mike (O'Connor, age 13) and his
mother (Patterson). Joe invites his family, although he has
a house rented for only two months. David believes he can
now afford to marry Martha (Drew), but he discovers that Joe
is broke and argues with Martha. The boys sing in a club to
finance the horse, sing "Small Fry" in blackface, fight
mobsters with their fists, and with Mike as the jockey, win
the big race, when David weds Martha. Secure at the end,
Joe and his brothers continue singing at the club. Songs
include "Don't Let That Moon Get Away" (Bing's only solo),
"I've Got a Pocketful of Dreams" with MacMurray and O'Connor, "Shall We Gather at the River" with most of the cast,
"Laugh and Call It Love" with MacMurray and O'Connor, and
"Small Fry" with MacMurray and O'Connor.
   NOTE: Bing and MacMurray were the "co-stars." Donald
O'Connor, singing "Small Fry" with Crosby, returned at age
31 to co-star with Bing in the 1956 remake of Anything Goes.
O'Connor won the earlier role over Guy Mitchell. The Na-
tional Board of Review named the film the fifth best of the
year. Much of the film was made at Bing's Del Mar Turf
Club, which opened in 1937, and the film was first shown
there, probably Aug 12, before the premiere at Saratoga
Springs. Aug 12 was the date of a famous race at Del Mar

between Bing's Ligaroti and Seabiscuit. Bernard Huff and
Forest O. Bobitt made a brief controversy at South Bend, IN,
with a suit alleging plagiarism in "Pocketful of Dreams"
from a song of theirs called "Just an Old Romance."   Burke
and Monaco also wrote "Where Is Central Park?" for the film,
but it was not used.

   "The happily accidental conjunction of Bing Crosby and
horse racing (which is Bing's other love, besides crooning,
as you may have read somewhere) has turned out to be the
funniest comedy on Broadway. . . . in the movies Crosby's
horse wins--an unprecedented thing which may be explained by
the fact that Bing undoubtedly must have had a hand in the
script. . . . [The jockey wins] in spite of crooks and the
most rousing fist-fight on the local screen in the last
decade. . . ." B.R. Crisler, N.Y. _Times_, Aug 18.

   "A new and interesting Bing Crosby emerges in 'Sing You
Sinners,' a likable ne'er-do-well who believes that the
secret of success lies in taking gambles. He is less the
crooner, and, for added relief of tiring Crosby fans, if
any, less of a delight for fluttering maidenly hearts.
Instead, he's something of a pain in the neck to a forgiving
mother and two brothers. Crosby and a small but good cast
combine with an excellent story and good direction for
surefire box office. . . . Crosby plays his part strongly,
but with restraint. He doesn't hog anything from MacMurray
nor moppet O'Connor." Char., _Variety_, Aug 17.

F49.   _Paris Honeymoon_ (1938, Paramount) 83 min. bw
d:Frank Tuttle asst: Stanley Goldsmith p: Harlan Thompson
w: Frank Butler, Don Hartman s: Angela Sherwood md: Boris
Morros m,l: Ralph Rainger, Leo Robin md: Boris Morros ma:
Arthur FRanklin art: Hans Dreier, Roland Anderson sd: A.E.
Freudeman ch: LeRoy Prinz cos: Edith Head c: Karl Struss
sound: Earl Hayman, Walter Oberst e: Archie Marshek. Preview, L.A. Paramount Dec 13

   Bing Crosby, Franciska Gaal, Akim Tamiroff, Shirley Ross, Edward Everett Horton, Ben Blue, Gregory Gaye,
Rafaela Ottiano, Alex Melesh, Victor Kilian, Michael Visar-
off, Luana Walters

   "Lucky" Lawton (Crosby), a wealthy Texan, takes his
fiancee, Barbara Wayne, Countess de Remi (Ross), to Paris to
hasten her divorce from Count de Remi (Gaye). Lucky jour-
neys to mythical Graustarkia in the Balkans to inspect the
honeymoon castle, and becomes involved with a clever village
girl, Manya (Gaal). As the Rose Queen, she is allowed to
stay at the castle for a week, and Lucky vainly tries to
scare her away. Later, at the last minute, he drops Barbara
at the altar in Paris and runs back to Manya, just in time
to save her from marrying the scoundrel Peter Karloca
(Tamiroff), mayor-innkeeper of Pushtalnick. Ernest Figg
(Horton) is Lucky's valet, and Sitska (Blue) is the village
dunce. _Songs_ include "Funny Old Hills" and reprised with
Gaal and Horton, "Sweet Little Headache," "I Ain't Got
Nobody," "The Maiden by the Brook," "I Have Eyes" with Ross,
and "Joobalai" with Gaal and chorus. The peasant-chorus
sings "Work While You May."

   NOTE: Bing was the sole "star." This was one of only
two American films to include Franciska Gaal, the other
being _The Buccaneer_ (1938) with Frederic March. The film

was completed in a few weeks
    "The Old World charm of Bing Crosby in a ten-gallon hat
is the principal Parisian motif in [the film] which marks a
return to the ancient Crosby formula of the days before
'Sing You Sinners.' . . . One thing about Bing, you never
catch him acting. He is always himself." B.R. Crisler,
N.Y. _Times_, Jan 26, 1939.
    "Bing Crosby, back with a bundle of tuneful melodies,
nonchalantly meanders through a light romance of the Prince
Charming-peasant Cinderella type, displaying a more convincing personality than heretofore.... There's a greater ease
and assurance displayed by Crosby in his handling of the
lead spot than previously. He times his lines better, and
gives a corking performance throughout." _Variety_, Dec 21.

F50.   _East Side of Heaven_ (1939, Universal) 85 min. bw
d: David Butler p: Independent ap: Herbert Polesie w:
William Conselman s: Butler, Polesie m, l: James V. Mona-
co, Johnny Burke art: Jack Otterson sd: Russell A. Gausman
cos: Vera West c: George Robinson sound: Bernard B. Frown.
Preview, Alexander, Glendale, Calif., Apr 4; World Premiere,
Lincoln Theatre, Miami Beach Apr 7
    Bing Crosby, Joan Blondell, Mischa Auer, Irene
Hervey, C. Aubrey Smith, Jerome Cowan, "Sandy" [Lee Hen-
ville, age 11 months], J. Farrell MacDonald, Mary Carr,
Robert Kent, Douglas Wood, Arthur Hoyt, Russell Hicks,
Jackie Gerlich, Edward Earle, Dorothy Christy, Jane Jones,
the Music Maids, Matty Malneck and his Orchestra.
    Denny Martin (Crosby), a New York singing messenger and
cab driver, brings home an abandoned baby ("Sandy") to his
roommate, Nicky (Auer). The back of Nicky's dressing robe
reads, "Moscow Golden Gloves 1919." Denny's fiancee, Mary
Wilson (Blondell), helps them avoid the baby's misunder-
standing grandfather, Cyrus Barrett, Sr., (Smith), who
claims guardianship. Then the mother, Mona Barrett
(Hervey), returns from her hunt for her husband, Cyrus Jr.
(Kent), and clears things up to the satisfaction of her
father-in-law. _Songs_ include "Rings on My Fingers," "Ida,"
"East Side of Heaven," "Sing a Song of Sunbeams," "That Sly
Old Gentleman," and "Hang Your Heart on a Hickory Limb" with
the Music Maids.
    NOTE: Crosby, co-starring with Blondell, financed half
the production for half the profits, as an outside feature
allowed by his contract with Paramount. He had a similar
deal with Columbia for _Pennies from Heaven_ (1936). The
Music Maids, Bing's radio chorus, made their only film
appearance with Bing, singing "Hang Your Heart on a Hickory
Limb." The baby won the role in a nationwide contest, and
only after the filming did Bing and others learn it was a
girl. As a telephone singer early in the film, Bing calls
"Mr. and Mrs. James Monaco," reaching them during a bitter
quarrel. Bing had a Moscow boxing title embroidered on
Auer's robe without Auer's knowledge.
    "If there is anything in motion pictures more subtly
calculated to paralyze the critical faculty than Bing Crosby, it is the formula which Universal has happily hit upon
in 'East Side of Heaven,' at the Music Hall: Bing Crosby
and a baby. . . . Even for persons who hate crooning, the
spectacle of Mr. Crosby dutifully chanting holiday greetings

over the telephone for Postal Union Telegraph . . . should
afford a certain sadistic pleasure. . . . And those rare,
dyspeptical types who hate both crooners and babies will
derive an evil joy from the scenes in which Bing . . . walks
the floor in his pajamas, crooning to the helpless infant."
B.R. Crisler, N.Y. Times, May 5.
      "Despite his financial interests, Crosby gives support
plenty of work and opportunity for some fat lines and situations. . . . Picture is smartly paced, hitting a nice tempo
at the start and rolling merrily to the finish." Variety,
Apr 12.

F51.   The Star Maker (1939, Paramount) 85 min. bw   d:
Roy Del Ruth p: Charles R. Rogers w: Frank Butler, Don
Hartman, Arthur Caesar   s: Caesar, William A. Pierce based
on career of Gus Edwards m, l: Johnny Burke, James V.
Monaco   md: Alfred Newman art: Hans Drier, Robert Usher
sd: A.E. Freudeman cos: Edith Head c: Karl Struss   sound:
Charles Hisserich, Richard Olsen. Preview Aug 21
      Bing Crosby, Louise Campbell, Linda Ware, Ned
Sparks, Laura Hope Crews, Janet Waldo, Walter Damrosch as
himself, Thurston Hall, Clara Blandick, Oscar O'Shea, John
Gallaudet, Darryl Hickman, and Richard Denning, Frank Fayl-
en, Los Angeles Philharmonic Orchestra conducted by Damrosch
      Larry Earl (Crosby) is a songwriter cum vaudeville
producer-director, who successfully promotes child actors
and singers like Jane Gray (Ware, age 14) and deals with
stage mothers like former opera singer Carlotta Salvini
(Crews) with the aid of his ingenious wife (Campbell) and
publicity man named "Speed" King (Sparks), who hates children. "Speed" suggests a national audition tour by train
and becomes quarantined with the youngsters in a measles
epidemic. Jane Gray becomes a hit, but Welfare prohibits
children under 12 from performing after 10 p.m. Jane joins
Damrosch, but Larry is poor again until he thinks of putting
the children on radio. Dr. Damrosch conducts the Philharmonic Orchestra in the finale. Songs include "If I Were a
Millionaire" with children, "Go Fly a Kite" with children,
"I Wonder Who's Kissing Her Now," "An Apple for the Teacher"
with Ware and children, "A Man and His Dream," "Still the
Bluebird Sings" with children, and the traditional "School
Days" with Ware and children, "In My Merry Oldsmobile" with
children, and "(Look Out for) Jimmy Valentine."
      NOTE: Crosby was the sole "star," the rest of the cast
being "featured" players. Edwards' proteges included George
Jessel, Eddie Cantor, Ray Bolger, Sally Rand, the Lane
Sisters, Eleanor Powell, Groucho Marx, Mervyn LeRoy, and
Walter Winchell, and he wrote such songs as "By the Light of
the Silv'ry Moon," which Crosby sings in Birth of the Blues
(F61). Filming occurred about May-Jul 1939. The film was
updated under the same title for TV in 1981 with Rock Hudson
and Suzanne Pleshette, as an opportunistic television producer offered several discoveries.
      "Mr. Crosby sings in his usual lullaby manner and
hasn't many good lines to play with. . . . But it is all,
if Mr. Edwards will pardon us, too much like a Gus Edwards
revue and far too much of that." Frank S. Nugent, N.Y.
Times, Aug 31.
      "Audiences will quickly and cheerfully respond to the

gayety [sic] which pervades the film. . . . 'School Days' is recreated in an elaborate production number, including an interpolation when Crosby, speaking directly from the screen to the film audience, invites and obtains a spirited if somewhat vocally uncertain choral participation." Flin., Variety, Aug 22.

F52.   Songmakers of the Nation Unknown

F53.   Swing with Bing (1940?, Universal) 30 min. d,p: Herbert Polesie w: Grant Garret m: John Scott Trotter and his Divot Diggers. Sep 4, 1940
        Bing Crosby, Roger Keene as narrator, Arthur W. Bryan, Byron Nelson, Jimmy Thompson, Bud Ward, Walter Hagen, Ed Oliver, Jimmy Demaret, Tony Penna, Ty Cobb, Henry McLemore, Richard Arlen, and others
        An independent sports short subject, produced by Everett Crosby and the Professional Golfers Association. It was probably filmed Jan 1940, the fourth appearance of Crosby's Pro-Am Tournament at Rancho Santa Fe. The Crosby was canceled in 1936 because of rain. Some sources say it was filmed in 1937 and runs 12 or 19 min. and is titled Swinging with Bing. The Song is "The Little White Pill on the Little Green Hill," sung by Bing and written by Johnny Burke and James V. Monaco. The song was never commercially recorded by Bing.

F54.   Road to Singapore (1940, Paramount) 84 min. bw d: Victor Schertzinger p: Harlan Thompson w: Don Hartman, Frank Butler s: Harry Hervey m, l: James V. Monaco, Johnny Burke, Schertzinger md: Victor Young c: William C. Mellor ch: LeRoy Prinz art: Hans Dreier, Robert O'Dell e: Paul Weatherwax c: William Mellor sound: Earl Hayman, John Cope. Preview, Los Angeles Paramount Feb 20
        Bing Crosby, Dorothy Lamour, Bob Hope, Charles Coburn, Judith Barrett, Anthony Quinn, Jerry Colonna, Johnny Arthur, Pierre Watkin, Gaylord Pendleton, Miles Mander, Pedro Regan, Greta Grandstedt, John Kelly, Ed Gargan, Kitty Kelly, Richard Keene, Jack Pepper, Robert Emmett O'Connor
        Josh Mallon (Crosby), the playful son of a shipping tycoon, Joshua Mallon, IV, (Coburn), performs the "pat-a-cake" routine on a Mallon ship with Ace Lannigan (Hope) to help Ace avoid having to wed a girl named Cherry. Engaged to Gloria Wycott (Barrett), Josh brawls with Gloria's brother Gordon (Pendleton) with Ace's aid. Josh calls Gordon one of the "zeros of the high-society 400." He leaves his fiancee to sail with Ace to Kaigoon, in the South Seas. They grub for money and cause another brawl to rescue Mima (Lamour) from Caesar (Quinn), who attempts to get her back under his bullwhip. Then Caesar reveals that the boys have no passports, and authorities issue a warrant dated March 25, 1940. Achilles Bombanassa (Colonna) has his white jacket eaten away by Ace's overly acidic Spotto cleaner and reveals Josh's location to his father. Ace concocts Scrammo, an exterminator, which allows the boys and Mima to darken their skin and dress as natives for a feast, where Josh unwittingly participates in a native wedding dance. Josh is saved by Ace and Mima. Josh's intended and his father appear, Josh hears Mima say she prefers Ace, and he

sails for home, but at a port enroute he learns that Ace and
Mima are there demonstrating Spotto. Mima had ceased pre-
tending to spurn Josh for his best interest. The film ends
with Josh and Ace performing another "pat-a-cake" routine to
save Ace from being arrested for destroying a millionaire's
suit with Spotto. Songs include "Captain Custard" with
Hope, "The Moon and the Willow Tree," "An Apple for the
Teacher" with Hope and Lamour, "Sweet Potato Piper," "Carry
Me Back to Old Virginny" by Colonna, "Too Romantic" with
Lamour and reprised solo, and "Kaigoon" by a chorus.
     NOTE: Paramount took a story they had, tried to inter-
est Fred MacMurray and Jack Oakie in it, and offered it to
Crosby, Burns, and Allen, although the latter two had to
withdraw, replaced by Lamour and Hope. It gave Hope international fame, increased Crosby's stature, and began a
famous team and series. Hope and Crosby hired Barney Dean
as their personal gag man. The running "pat-a-cake" routine
in which Crosby and Hope slug their spellbound opponents was
introduced early and performed five times, twice on Quinn.
The soap-bubble effect for Spotto led to an off-screen
"bubble" fight among the three stars, which concluded when
Lamour dumped a pailful over Bing and Hope at the Commissary. It was hours before filming could resume. Colonna,
Hope's radio sidekick, plays himself in Road to Rio and Star
Spangled Rhythm and has a cameo in The Road to Hong Kong.
Filming occurred about Nov 1939-Jan 1940, and encouraged
greater ad-libbing in the sequels. The film began the most
successful series of its time, the seventh and last film
appearing in 1962.
     "[The film] is cobbled with good intentions, is blessed
intermittently with smooth-running strips of amiable non-
sense, but is altogether too uneven for regular use. We
would not go so far as to call the road closed, merely to
say one proceeds at his own risk, with heavy going after
Lamour." Frank S. Nugent, N.Y. Times, Mar 14.
     "Initial teaming of Bing Crosby and Bob Hope . . .
provides foundation for continuous round of good substantial
comedy that will click up and down the line. Paramount
should carry the team through a series of pictures. . . ."
Variety, Feb 28.

F55.   Picture People No. 1 (1940, RKO) Short.

F56.   What's Up, Doc? (1940?, Warner Bros.) Caricature
Short cartoon.
     Elmer Fudd rejects the likes of Bing Crosby, Edward G.
Robinson, Jack Benny, and Al Jolson as hasbeens and makes a
star out of Bugs Bunny.

F57.   If I Had My Way (1940, Universal) 93 min bw d,p:
David Butler asst: Richard H. Riedel w: William Conselman,
James V. Kern s: Butler, Conselman, Kern m,l: James V.
Monaco, Johnny Burke o: Frank Skinner cos: Vera West sd:
Russell A. Gausman. Alexander, Glendale, CA, Apr 25
     Bing Crosby, Gloria Jean (age 12), Charles Win-
ninger, El Brendel, Allyn Joslyn, Claire Dodd, Moroni Olsen,
Nana Bryant, Donald Woods, Kathryn Adams, Brandon Hurst,
Eddie Leonard, Grace LaRue, Blanche Ring, Trixie Friganza,
Julian Eltinge, Six Hits and a Miss

Buzz Blackwell (Crosby), a crooning steelworker, and
Axel Swenson (Brendel) care for Patricia Johnson (Jean) when
her father, Fred (Woods), dies in a construction accident.
They take her to New York, where her rich uncle rejects her,
but her great-uncle named Joe Johnson (Winninger), an old
vaudevillian, takes her in.   When Axel buys a worthless
restaurant, Buzz oversees its reclamation by manipulating
worthless stock and with the aid of Joe's vaudeville
friends, including (as themselves) Eddie Leonard singing
"Ida" in blackface and Blanche Ring and Grace LaRue singing
"Rings on My Fingers."   Songs include "Meet the Sun Half
Way" with Jean, "I Haven't Time to Be a Millionaire" with
Brendel and Jean, "Pessimistic Character," "April Played the
Fiddle" with Six Hits and a Miss, and "If I Had My Way."
Others are "Ida" by Leonard in blackface and "Rings on My
Fingers" by LaRue and Ring.
    NOTE: Crosby partly financed the film. Gloria Jean
was the "co-star," not just featured, and from this film on
Bing constantly shared "star" billing.
    "Add [to Crosby and Jean] the fact that the melodious
couple are accompanied by El Brendel, the comical squigeegum
Swede who almost swallows himself, and encounter in New York
Gloria's rollicking, frolicking great-uncle, Charlie Win-
ninger, and you have a roster of the picture's assets. . . .
The sum total is but a moderately amusing musical, more
often flat than sharp. . . ." Bosley Crowther, N.Y. Times,
May 6.
    "Bing Crosby will likely want to forget this cinematic
adventure just as quickly as possible. . . . Even the
valiant nonchalance of Crosby, the personality of Gloria
Jean and Brendel's comedy fail to provide much lift to a
creaky story chassis." Walt., Variety, May 1.

F58.   Rhythm on the River (1940, Paramount) 92 min. bw
d: Victor Schertzinger p: William LeBaron w: Dwight Taylor
s: Billy Wilder, Jacques Thery o: John Scott Trotter m, l:
Johnny Burke, James V. Monaco, Schertzinger md: Victor
Young ma: Arthur Franklin art: Hans Dreier, Ernest Fegte
cos: Edith Head c: Ted Tetzlaff sound: Earl Hayman, Richard Olsen e: Hugh Bennett. Preview, Del Mar racetrack Aug
16; Aug 28
    Bing Crosby, Mary Martin, Basil Rathbone, Oscar
Levant, Oscar Shaw, Charlie Grapewin, Lillian Cornell,
William Frawley, Jean Cagney, Helen Bertram, John Scott
Trotter, Ken Carpenter, Charles Lane, Harry Barris on saxophone, Wingy Manone and his Band
    Bob Summers (Crosby), an unambitious man who wants to
own a 25-foot catboat, ghostwrites melodies in New York for
Oliver Courtney (Rathbone), who also hires Cherry Lane
(Martin) to ghostwrite the lyrics. Cherry is annoyed by the
playing of Barris and Manone's band at her rooming house,
and Courtney sends her to Nobody's Inn in Tarrytown, unaware
its Bob's uncle's retreat. Bob and Cherry meet there,
inspect the grounded riverboat Arabella, discover their
connection, and strike out on their own. After testing the
band in a pawn shop with the jumping "Rhythm on the River,"
Bob drumming, he decides to use them to back their auditions. Their songs, however, are considered Courtney rip-
offs by publisher Mr. Westlake (Frawley) and others. Court-

ney then appropriates their "Only Forever," which becomes a hit, and is forced, after Bob calls him "Hambone" and demands a correction, to announce them as collaborators on his new musical. Starbuck (Levant) is Courtney's deadpan assistant, once seen reading A Smattering of Ignorance, a book by Levant. Trotter is an orchestra leader and Carpenter the announcer. Songs include "Only Forever" with Martin, "Rhythm on the River," "When the Moon Comes Over Madison Square," "That's for Me" with Martin, and "What Would Shakespeare Have Said?" with Cornell.

NOTE: Mary Martin is the "co-star," not just featured. The song "Only Forever" was nominated for an Academy Award but lost to Disney's "When You Wish Upon a Star." Trotter and Levant made their screen debuts; Barris and Manone have featured roles. At a press preview at the Del Mar Turf Club attended by Pat O'Brien, Crosby and Martin sang; Bing included Johnny Burke's "Where the Turf Meets the Surf," and Martin, Burke, Schertzinger, Carpenter, Cornell, and Trotter sang couplets, broadcast on NBC. The film was originally called "Ghost Music" and occurred about May-Jul 1940.

"One producer may come along with a supercolossal whopper . . . and folks will find . . . a dull and pretentious fizzle. And then along will come . . . an after-you sort of entry . . . and, behold, it turns out to be one of the most likeable musical pictures of the season. . . . What's there to it? Well, there's Bing, whose frank and guileless indifference, whose apparent dexterity with ad libs is, in this case, beautiful to behold. . . . It's a funny business, all right." Bosley Crowther, N.Y. Times, Aug 29.

"Some may tab this as the best picture Crosby has appeared in for several years. It's certainly one of his toppers. . . . Crosby tackles his acting assignment with the nonchalance that has proven effective in past releases and on the air." Walt., Variety, Aug 21.

F59.   Road to Zanzibar (1941, Paramount) 89 min. bw d: Victor Schertzinger p: Paul Jones w: Frank Butler, Don Hartman s: Hartman, Sy Bartlett's "Find Colonel Fawcett" md: Victor Young ch: LeRoy Prinz m, l: Johnny Burke, Jimmy Van Heusen art: Hans Dreier, Robert Usher c: Ted Tetzlaff sound: Earl Hayman, Don Johnson cos: Edith Head e: Alma Macrorie. Studio Projection Room Mar 10; Apr 9

Bing Crosby, Dorothy Lamour, Bob Hope, Una Merkel, Joan Marsh, Eric Blore, Iris Adrian, Ethel Greer, Douglass Dumbrille, Luis Alberni, Georges Renavent, Lionel Royce, Leo Gorcey as Boy, Ken Carpenter, Richard Keene

Chuck Reardon (Crosby) and Fearless Frazier (Hope) are inept carnival performers who sell a phony diamond mind to a European cut-throat named Le Bec (Royce) and have to flee. They become stranded in Africa, yearning for Birch Falls back home, pick up hucksters Donna Latour (Lamour) and Julia Quimby (Merkel), and safari after a rich white hunter whom the boys think is Donna's long-lost brother. Chuck and Fearless, abandoned by the girls, become caught by cannibals, for whom Fearless has to wrestle a gorilla to prove he is a god. After his loss, they "pat-a-cake" an escape to find the girls at a seaport, where they reconcile and stage another show. Songs include "It's Always You" reprised with

Hope and Lamour, "You Lucky People, You," and "African
Etude" with a native chorus.   Lamour sings "You're Dangerous," Hope sings "Home Sweet Home," Adrian sings "Feathers
Can-Can," and background music includes "Birds of a
Feather."
       NOTE: Bing, Lamour, and Hope are the "co-stars."   The
gorilla that defeats Hope was played by Charlie Gemora, who
specialized in playing large apes.   This second Road film
was even more successful, but music sales slumped because of
a strike Jan 1, 1941, by the American Society of Composers,
Authors and Publishers (ASCAP), which led the National
Association of Broadcasters to form rival Broadcast Music
Incorporated (BMI), which boycotted ASCAP material for
months.   Bing could not record songs until May 23, after
which he recorded 34 songs in barely two months.
       "Pity the poor motion picture which ever again sets
forth on a perilous (?) safari, now that Bing Crosby and Bob
Hope have traversed the course! . . . Yessir, the heart of
darkest Africa has been pierced by a couple of wags. . . .
the travelers of the 'Road to Zanzibar' make little use of
[the script]. . . . Needless to say, Mr. Crosby and Mr.
Hope are most, if not all, of the show--with a slight edge
in favor of the latter, in case any one wants to know."
Bosley Crowther, N.Y. Times, Apr 10.
       "Comedy episodes generally lack the sparkle and tempo
of 'Singapore,' and musical numbers are also below par for a
Crosby picture." Walt., [Hollywood, Mar 7] Variety, Mar 12.

F60.   Where the Turf Meets the Surf at Del Mar (1941)
Voice only Short.
         Franky Jenks
     Bing's song "Where the Turf Meets the Surf" by Johnny
Burke and James V. Monaco, recorded Jul 5, 1941, by Decca,
is heard over the titles and again as the races commence.
The song has not been released commercially.

F61.   Birth of the Blues (1941, Paramount) 80 min. d:
Victor Schertzinger P: B.G. DeSylva for Monta Bell w:
Harry Tugend, Walter DeLeon s: Tugend a: Robert Emmett
Dolan ma: Arthur Franklin m,l: Johnny Mercer and 14 pop
excerpts by such composers as Robert Emmett Dolan, W.C.
Handy, Lew Brown, and Gus Edwards art: Ernest Fegte, Hans
Dreier c: William Mellor, Farciot Edouart sound: Earl
Hayman, John Cope cos: Edith Head e: Paul Weatherwax.
Preview, N.Y. tradeshow Aug 28; New Orleans and Memphis Dec
1
       Bing Crosby, Mary Martin, Brian Donlevy, Carolyn
Lee, Eddie "Rochester" Anderson, Jack Teagarden, J. Carrol
Naish, Warren Hymer, Horace MacMahon, Ruby Elzy, Barbara
Pepper, Dan Beck, Harry Barris, Perry Botkin, Harry Rosen-
thal, Donald Kerr, Minor Watson, Roscoe Ates, Ronnie Cosbey,
and Jack Teagarden's Orchestra, John Gallaudet, the Hall-
Johnson Negro Choir
     Jeff Lambert (Cosbey), 12 years old and schooled in
classical clarinet, is rebuked by his father for his devotion to jazz.   The boy plays with blacks in a dive on Bourbon Street until he grows up and forms his own group.   Jeff
(Crosby), now grown and in need of a hot trumpet player,
discovers Memphis (Donlevy) in jail, who is great with the

horn. With singer Betty Lou Cobb (Martin), Jeff leads his
group of Basin Street musicians to success. Trying to leave
the posh Bourbon Street club owned by a gangster named
Blackie (Naish), they brawl with mobsters and Louey (Anderson) is seriously hurt and nursed by his wife, Ruby (Elzy).
The band plays briefly at a better club, but Blackie's men
(Hymer, MacMahon) kidnap them until Blackie is killed by one
of his own. The group succeeds in Chicago with a finale
with Ted Lewis, the Dorseys, Duke Ellington, Louis Armstrong, George Gershwin, and Paul Whiteman. Songs include
Mercer's "The Waiter and the Porter and the Upstairs Maid"
with Martin and Teagarden, and many standards: "Birth of the
Blues," "Memphis Blues," "St. James Infirmary," "Melancholy
Baby," "St. Louis Blues" by Elzy, "Wait Till the Sun Shines,
Nellie" with Martin, and "By the Light of the Silv'ry Moon."
    NOTE: It is a loose recreation of Nick LaRocca's
Original Dixieland Jazz Band, noted as the first white group
to play black music. Drummer Suds (Barris), guitarist Leo
(Botkin), and "Piano Player" (Rosenthal) are band members.
One of the musical highlights is the duet with Bing and Mary
Martin singing and whistling "Wait Till the Sun Shines,
Nellie"; others are "Memphis Blues" by Teagarden's Orchestra, and Ruby Elzy singing "St. Louis Blues." Buddy DeSylva, producer, was the co-lyricist of the title song. Scenes
involving Martin were filmed hastily, as she was pregnant.
The Negro band that opens the film was patterned after the
Razzy Dazzy Spasm Band that played along Basin Street. The
film premiered Dec 1 in both New Orleans and Memphis, both
claiming to originate the blues, but Schertzinger died a few
days before. Gary Crosby tested for the role of young Jeff
but did not obtain the part.
    ". . . here is a film straight down the groove--a blend
of jump-and-jive music that should make the 'hep cats' howl
with some sweet bits of romantic chaunting that should
tickle the 'ickies,' too. . . . And for dipping deep on the
low chords, you can't ask for anything more than Mr. Crosby's 'Melancholy Baby' and those mournful 'St. Louis Blues,'
sung by one Ruby Elzy, with the Teagarden band moaning
behind." Bosley Crowther, N.Y. Times, Dec 11.
    "'Birth of the Blues' is Bing Crosby's best filmusical
to date. . . . Cofeatured in the band that ultimately
proves his point are Jack Teagarden . . . plus Harry Barris
(of the original Rhythm Boys: Al Rinker, now a CBS producer,
was the third in the actual combo). . . . Carolyn Lee [is]
a cute kidlet who, for once, may make good the show biz hope
for 'another Shirley Temple.' . . . The detail is as faith-
ful as Lindy's, excepting of course those 1941 arrangements
in early 1900 background." Abel., Variety, Sep 3.

F62.   Angels of Mercy (1941, Metrotone News) Newsreel
Short with other versions by Paramount, M-G-M, and 20th
Century-Fox. Dec 5
    A short dramatizing the efforts of Red Cross workers,
featuring Crosby singing Irving Berlin's "Angels of Mercy."
The separate versions varied in content but all used Crosby's title song. It was released in early 1942 by some
studios, and Crosby recorded the song Jan 24, 1942.

F63.   My Favorite Blonde (1942, Paramount) Guest   78

min. bw d: Sidney Lanfield asst: Arthur Black p: Paul
Jones w: Don Hartman, Frank Butler s: Melvin Frank, Norman
Panama c: William Mellor e: William O'Shea. N.Y. tradeshow Mar 16
        Bob Hope, Madeleine Carroll, Gale Sondergaard,
George Zucco, Victor Varconi, Lionel Royce, Bing Crosby
        Larry Haines (Hope), a vaudevillian (earning $30 weekly
while his penguin earns $500), is enlisted by Karen Bentley
(Carroll), a British agent with a secret message bound for
Los Angeles, to hurry West to forestall the Nazi spies who
seek to sabotage a flight of Lockheed bombers. In California Bing Crosby directs Larry and Karen to a picnic of Irish
teamsters, after which Hope wonders if it was Bing. The
song is "When Irish Eyes Are Smiling," by Hope, Carroll, and
a busload of Irish teamsters.
        NOTE: In his first cameo appearance in a Bob Hope
film, Bing is leaning against a post when Hope asks, "Hey,
pardon me, bud. What is this line for?" "Oh," says the
crooner, "the secretary there, he tells you what bus to get
in." "What for? The picnic?" Bing replies, "Yeah, at the
Humbolt Park. You going out?" "Ah, I think I will. Be all
right." Then Bing asks, "Ya got a match?" "Yeah." Taking
the match Bing says, "Thanks." Hope says, "It's okay," and
walks several steps before muttering, "It couldn't be." In
Star Spangled Rhythm (1942) Bob Hope explains to Betty
Hutton, "Did you see that nice shot I gave Crosby in My
Favorite Blonde? You know, I like to throw all the work his
way that I can, because those kids eat like horses." Blonde
was one of Hope's favorites.
        ". . . there is also one truly inspired sight gag in
which a famous star appears anonymously. . . . . in these
times we can't have too much Hope." Bosley Crowther, N.Y.
Times, Apr 2.
        The producer and director "permitted themselves still
another conceit when Bing Crosby is seen idling at a picnic
bus station. Crosby directs the lammister Hope and Miss
Carroll toward the picnic grounds. As Hope gives Crosby one
of those takes, he muses, 'No, it can't be.' That's all,
and it's one of the best laughs in a progressively funny
film." Abel., Variety, Mar 18.

F64.   Holiday Inn (1942, Paramount) 100 min. bw d, p:
Mark Sandrich w: Claude Binyon ad: Elmer Rice s, m, l:
Irving Berlin a: Robert Emmett Dolan ma: Arthur Franklin
va: Joseph Lilley dance ensembles: Danny Dare art: Hans
Dreier, Roland Anderson c: David Able sound: Earl Hayman,
John Cope cos: Edith Head mu: Wally Westmore e: Ellsworth
Hoagland. N.Y. tradeshow Jun 12; Premiere, Benefit for Navy
Relief Society, N.Y. Paramount Aug 4
        Bing Crosby, Fred Astaire, Marjorie Reynolds,
Virginia Dale, Walter Abel, Louise Beavers, Irving Bacon,
James Ball, John Gallaudet, Shelby Bacon, Joan Arnold,
Special Accompaniments by Bob Crosby's Band [the Bob Cats],
and unbilled: Marek Windham, Jacques Vanaire, Judith Gibson,
Harry Barris, Ronnie Rondell, Keith Richards, Reed Porter,
Lynda Grey, Kitty Kelly, Edward Arnold, Jr., Bud Jamison
        Jim Hardy (Crosby), planning to retire to Connecticut
with dancer Lila Dixon (Dale), is jilted by her in favor of
their partner, Ted Hanover (Astaire). Escaping Broadway and

his agent, Danny Reid (Abel), Jim goes alone to Midville, CT, and once returns to New York, where he announces his new musical inn ("Open Holidays Only") and meets ambitious Linda Mason (Reynolds), who pretends she knows Ted. Danny gives Linda Jim's card, and she goes to audition. Danny falls for her, but an inebriated Ted appears on New Year's Eve, for Lila has jilted him too (for a phony millionaire). Ted dances with Linda and wants her to become his partner, but he falls dead drunk and later tries to identify her. Jim hides her in blackface for Lincoln's Birthday and proposes for St. Valentine's Day, but she is uncovered and pursued by Ted. When Jim receives a cable from Lila that she learned her fiance was broke and left him, Jim plots to reunite her with Ted, but Linda is angry at being kept from the Fourth of July show and possibly missing a Hollywood film. After Ted dances solo the Firecracker Number and Bing sings "Song of Freedom," Hollywood decides to film the inn's story. Linda accepts Ted's offer to dance with him, and Jim agrees to write the music, but in Connecticut. A confused cartoon turkey chases Thanksgiving Day from the November 20 to 27, but Jim finds heart, runs West, and finds Linda singing "White Christmas" on the set. Jim joins in and takes Linda away from Ted, who is reunited with Lila for a finale in Midville. <u>Songs</u> are "I'll Capture Your Heart Singing" with Astaire and Dale, reprised with Astaire and Reynolds, "Lazy," "You're Easy to Dance With" by Astaire and reprised with Astaire, "White Christmas" with Reynolds, "Happy Holiday" with Reynolds, "Let's Start the New Year Right" and reprised with cast, "Abraham" with Reynolds, Beavers, Arnold, and Bacon, "Be Careful, It's My Heart," "Washington's Birthday Minuet" (with Crosby in a powdered wig at the harpsichord jazzing up Astaire's number) with lyrics "(I Gotta Say I Love You 'Cause) I Can't Tell a Lie" by Astaire, "Easter Parade," "Say It with Firecrackers" by chorus, "Song of Freedom" (with Bing as "an American troubadour"), "I've Got Plenty to Be Thankful For."
     NOTE: The song "White Christmas" was premiered and won the Academy Award as best song of the year, first sung as a duet with Reynolds, while Bing whistled and used his pipe to ring bells on the Christmas tree behind the upright piano, and repeated later in the Hollywood-reproduced inn, sung by a chorus, Reynolds, and, after she finds his pipe, Bing joins in. Astaire performed the Firecracker number for 38 takes, losing 14 of his 142 pounds. Some sources exaggerate the takes at about 100. Mary Martin could not accept the female lead because of her pregnancy, and Rita Hayworth was considered before it went to Reynolds, who appeared in her first feature role. Martha Mears dubbed Reynold's singing. Bob Crosby and his Bob Cats provide the band behind many of the numbers. Berlin provided all new songs except the reprises of his "Lazy" and "Easter Parade." Bing sings "Song of Freedom" with a passage from "Any Bonds Today." The popularity of "White Christmas," selling more records than any other song, inspired Bing's 1954 film <u>White Christmas</u>. Bing premiered the song on his radio program Dec 25, 1941, more than seven months ahead of the film's premiere. The stage show at the premiere featured Skinnay Ennis and his Orchestra, the Ink Spots, the Knight Sisters, Willie Shore, Clayton Case, and Al Hendrickson.

"If there are no tunes in 'Holiday Inn' that quite match those of [his concurrent stage show at the Paramount for the Navy Relief Society], Mr. Berlin still has created several of the most effortless melodies of the season--the sort that folks begin humming in the middle of a conversation for days afterward. . . . That it comes off, of course, is largely due to the casual performances of Bing Crosby, who can sell a blackface song like 'Abraham' or turn an ordinary line into sly humor without seeming to try. . . ." Theodore Strauss, N.Y. Times, Aug 5.

"[There is a] cinematic montage of U.S. planes, battleships, armaments, MacArthur, F.D R. and finally Old Glory. That kinda puts a topper to the George M. Cohan technique--in spades. But it fits the occasion and, in the 1942 idiom, it's topical and socko. . . . The production is ultra, and the musical interpretations, with Bob Crosby's Bobcats [sic] backing up brother Bing, make the song idioms ultra-modern." Walt., Variety, Jun 17.

F65.   Curtain Razor (1942, Warner Bros.) Caricature Cartoon   Short.
        Bing Crosby, Al Jolson, and Frank Sinatra are depicted.

F66.   Road to Morocco (1942, Paramount) 83 min. bw d: David Butler asst: Hal Waller p: Paul Jones w: Butler, Don Hartman m,l: James Van Heusen, Johnny Burke md: Victor Young c: William Mellor, Farciot Edouart, Gordon Jennings sound: Loren Ryder cos: Edith Head e: Irene Morra c: William Mellor N.Y. tradeshow Oct 1; Nov 11
        Bing Crosby, Bob Hope, Dorothy Lamour, Anthony Quinn, Doña Drake, Vladimir Sokoloff, Mikhail Rasumny, George Givot, Andrew Tombes, Leon Belasco, Jamiel Hasson, Monte Blue, Dan Seymour, Ralph Penney, George Lloyd, Sammy Stein, Pete Katchenaro, Brandon Hurst, Richard Loo, Leo Mostovoy, Yvonne de Carlo
        Jeffrey Peters (Crosby) and Orville "Turkey" Jackson (Hope) wash ashore in North Africa after Turkey causes an explosion on ship by smoking in the powder room (gunpowder), hitch a camel (which spits at Turkey) for Karameesh, where a pasha (Seymour) buys Turkey from Jeff, and Princess Shalmar (Lamour) buys him from the trader. Jeff finds a letter from Turkey stating that he is being tortured and that Jeff should flee. Aunt Lucy (Hope in drag) pricks Jeff's conscience in a vision and sends him to rescue her nephew, whom he finds enjoying the princess. Jeff gets her to fall for him instead, but she insists on marrying Turkey first, for her horoscope had revealed that her first husband would die in a week. Aided by a corrected interpretation of the stars by Hyder Khan (Sokoloff), she agrees to Jeff's pleas and Turkey falls for a palace maid named Mihirmah (Drake). Then the two couples head for a ship as cruel Mullay Kasim (Quinn), a desert sheik, arrives, finds Jeff hiding under a blanket, and captures the princess for himself, tying the boys and leaving them to die in the desert. (Crosby and Hope try their pat-a-cake routine on Quinn, but he expects it and smashes their heads together. Crosby remarks, "Yes sir, Junior, that thing sure got around.") Miraculously freed, they tread to Kasim's camp, are jailed, and Turkey

wastes three wishes of a magic ring. They escape, perform
several tricks that incite a fight between rival tribes, and
leave with the princess. The camel says, "This is the
screwiest picture I was ever in." Turkey causes an explosion on an ocean liner by smoking in the powder room, but
the four paddle a raft to New York. Songs include "Road to
Morocco" with Hope, "Ain't Got a Dime to My Name [Ho Ho
Hum]," "Constantly" by Lamour, and "Moonlight Becomes You,"
which is reprised by Bing, Hope, and Lamour in each others'
voices.
        NOTE: The screenplay and the sound recording of Ryder
won Academy Award nominations. Bing and Hope each financed
a third of the production, and Lamour's billing went below
Hope's with this third film of the series. At one point
Hope jokes about a new five-year contract with Paramount.
The camel spit at Hope, prompting Bing to congratulate the
beast and pat him on his neck, a surprise left in the film.
The charging horses in the street in the back lot of 20th
Century-Fox almost trampled Bing and Hope when the director
failed to give them the cue to jump out of the way. Leonard
Maltin, in TV Movies and Video Guide, rates the film among
the best of the Road films (three stars of a possible four),
better than its two predecessors (two and a half stars
each). Lamour was annoyed that she was not allowed to
partake of the financing. Bing recorded "Moonlight Becomes
You" and "Constantly" Jun 12, 1942.
        "Let us be thankful that Paramount is still blessed
with Bing Crosby and Bob Hope, and that it has set its
cameras to tailing these two irrepressible wags on another
fantastic excursion. . . . It is, in short, a lampoon of
all pictures having to do with exotic romance, played by a
couple of wise guys who can make a gag do everything but lay
eggs." Bosley Crowther, N.Y. Times, Nov 12.
        "Crosby, of course, is still more or less straighting
for Hope's incessantly streaming gags. The two have never
teamed better, nor have they, seemingly, romped with such
abandon. Miss Lamour is decorative, as usual, and perhaps
even more so garbed in the Hollywood interpretation of
Arabian flimsy." Kahn., Variety, Oct 7.

F67.   Star Spangled Rhythm (1942, Paramount) 99 min. d:
George Marshall ap: Joe Sistrom (unbilled) w: Harry Tugend
(sketches by George Kaufman, Arthur Ross, Mel Frank, Norman
Panama) m, l:Johnny Mercer, Harold Arlen score: Robert
Emmett Dolan va: Joseph J. Lilley ch: Danny Dare, George
Ballanchine cos: Edith Head c: Leo Tover e: Arthur
Schmidt. N.Y. tradeshow Dec 29; Dec 30
        Bing Crosby, Bob Hope, Fred MacMurray, Franchot
Tone, Ray Milland, Victor Moore, Dorothy Lamour, Paulette
Goddard, Vera Zorina, Mary Martin, Dick Powell, Betty Hut-
ton, Eddie Bracken, Veronica Lake, Alan Ladd, Rochester
(Eddie Anderson); featuring William Bendix, Jerry Colonna,
Macdonald Carey, Walter Abel, Susan Hayward, Marjorie Reyn-
olds, Betty Rhodes, Doña Drake, Lynne Overman, Gary Crosby,
Johnnie Johnston, Gil Lamb, Cass Daley, Ernest Truex, Kath-
erine Dunham, Arthur Treacher, Walter Catlett, Sterling
Holloway, Walter Dare Wahl & Co., Golden Gate Quartet;
including Cecil B. DeMille, Preston Sturges, Ralph Murphy,
Albert Dekker, Edward Fielding, Anne Revere, Edgar Dearing,

William Haads, Maynard Holmes, James Millican, Eddie Johnson
(in all, 36 studio stars and executives)
     Sailor Jimmy Webster (Bracken) is misled by his girl-
friend Polly (Hutton), a studio telephone operator, and his
father, William "Bronco Billy" Webster (Moore), now a studio
guard, into believing his father heads the studio. Jimmy
brings his buddies from a destroyer at San Pedro to ogle the
starlets, and Polly and the father cause trouble for B.G.
DeSoto (Abel) by usurping his position by arranging a benefit show and annoying DeMille. Bing arrives with Gary, who
states he came because Lamour was working, and Bing accepts
Polly's plea to join in the show. Polly kisses Gary, who
says, "I still think you've got the wrong Crosby." Hope
helps DeSoto uncover the fraud but joins the cast when Bing,
Goddard, Lamour, Lake, Ladd, Treacher, and others leave for
the show at the Navy base, where Jimmy expects to marry
Polly. The father, unaware that Polly has assembled a show,
attempts to confess to the audience when Bing parts the
curtain and ushers out 20 stars behind the dejected man.
Mr. DeSoto fails to stop the show that Hope emcees, and it
ends when Bing sings the finale, presenting people from New
Hampshire to the Georgia who praise the nation, but then the
sailors are ordered back to the ship. Unable to marry
Polly, Jimmy gives her the ring as a pledge. Bing <u>sings</u>
"Old Glory" with a chorus in the finale. <u>Others' Songs</u>
include "Time to Hit the Road to Dreamland" by Mary Martin,
Dick Powell, and the Golden Gate Quartet; "A Sweater, a
Sarong and a Peek-a-Boo Bang" by Goddard, Lamour, and Lake
(imitated by Treacher, Catlett, and Holloway; Lake's voice
was dubbed by Martha Mayer); "That Old Black Magic" by
Johnston to Zorina's dancing; "Working the Swing Shift" by
Drake, Reynolds, and Rhodes; "I'm Doing It for Defense" by
Hutton in a jeep full of sailors; and "Sharp as a Tack" by
"Rochester" Anderson in a zoot suit with dancer Dunham.
     NOTE: Bing's final scene has a replica of the monumen-
tal sculpture at Mount Rushmore as a backing; the four
Presidential heads (Washington, Jefferson, Teddy Roosevelt,
and Lincoln) were completed by Gutzon Borgium after more
than 10 years and dedicated by President Coolidge in 1927.
The film was the most successful "back lot" film in the
tradition of the annual Paramount parade of stars, last
appearing as <u>The Big Broadcast of 1938</u>, which included Hope,
and his <u>They Got Me Covered</u> was released at the same time as
<u>Star Spangled</u>. Daley sings her acrobatic routine as an
audition, joined by rubber-legged Lamb on the harmonica;
Tone, Milland, MacMurray, and Overman depict effeminate card
players in a twist on the vaudeville sketch "If Women Played
Poker Like Men"; Hope, Bendix, and Colonna do a sketch about
an unfaithful wife; Wahl and Company perform their sticky-
fingered acrobatic act while trying to help Polly climb over
the studio wall. Audiences at the premiere gave the Golden
Gate Quartet an ovation. Zorina, a prima ballerina, dances
to choreography by her husband, George Ballanchine. Fielding (unbilled) plays Y. Frank Freemont, a take-off on producer Y. Frank Freeman, and the B.G. DeSoto character mim-
icks B.G. DeSylva (a songwriter and now the Paramount head
of production). Mercer and Arlen also wrote "He Loved Me
Till the All-Clear Came," which was cut. Bob Dorian of the
American Movie Classics TV cable recalls that the New York

premiere included the stage show with Benny Goodman's orchestra, Frank Sinatra, and Peggy Lee. Some critics denounced the Rochester zoot-suit routine as demeaning to
blacks, an uncommon complaint of the time. The performance
features an exaggerated suit, which Rochester replaces at
the end for a more appealing Army uniform. This was Hutton's second film; she was a regular on Hope's radio shows.
Gary Crosby made his first screen appearance and had prominent billing, even in the trailer. Bauer quotes one critic
as writing that Crosby's patriotism "was the most graceful
flag-waving of the year" (p. 42).

     "That quaint old Paramount custom of producing an
annual all-star variety show, which was allowed to lapse
into the past tense after 'The Big Broadcast of 1938,' has
been hopefully revived with new vigor. . . . Half of the
contract players on the studio's lot are jam-packed into
it. . . . And the whole thing is topped off by Bing Crosby
in a patriotic tableau called 'Old Glory.'" Bosley Crowther, N.Y. Times, Dec 31.

     "'Old Glory' is used for a patriotic finale which seems
out of place and tacked on as an after-thought. . . . [The
director and writer tossed] in the foibles of a number of
studio execs. These provide a flock of laughs that the
general public, unfortunately, will never get. Par studio
head, for instance, is named 'B.G. DeSoto' (B.G. DeSylva),
with Walter Abel playing the part. His boss is 'Mr. Freemont' (Y. Frank Freeman), with Edward Fielding in the brief
role and pouring himself a Coca-Cola (Freeman is a Southern-
er and addicted to cokes)." Variety, Dec 30.

F68.   What's Cookin', Doc? (1943, Warner Bros.) Impersonation Short Part cartoon-part live col d: Robert
Clampett.
     Bugs Bunny seeks an Oscar at an Academy Awards ceremony
at the Cocoanut Grove by imitating Bing Crosby, Bette Davis,
Edward G. Robinson, and others. James Cagney wins the
Oscar, and actually won it in 1943 for the 1942 film Yankee
Doodle Dandee. Bugs is hit with a similar statuette. He
accepts it and says he will sleep with it, until he realizes
it is an animated male rabbit.

F69.   Dixie (1943, Paramount) 89 min. col d: A. Edward
Sutherland p: Paul Jones w: Karl Tunberg, Darrell Ware
ad: Claude Binyon s: William Rankin m, l: Johnny Burke,
James Van Heusen, Dan Emmett md: Robert Emmett Dolan va:
Joseph J. Lilley art: Hans Dreier, William Flannery ch:
Seymour Felix cos: Raoul Pene duBois c: William C. Mellor
sound: Earl Hayman, John Cope e: William Shea. Jun 23
     Bing Crosby, Dorothy Lamour, Marjorie Reynolds,
Billy DeWolfe, Lynne Overman, Eddie Foy, Jr., Raymond Wal-
burn, Grant Mitchell, Clara Blandick, Tom Herbert, Olin
Howard, Robert Warwick, Fortunio Bonanova, Brandon Hurst,
Josephine Wittell, Paul McVay, Harry Barris
     Dan Emmett (Crosby) is a struggling Kentucky composer
engaged to Jean Mason (Reynolds) and his pipe burns down his
fiancee's house. Dan boards a riverboat and meets Mr. Bones
(DeWolfe), who cheats at cards and takes Dan's money. Dan
pursues Bones to a restaurant in antebellum New Orleans,
where the cardsharp pacifies Dan with a meal. They take a

room from old showman Mr. Cook (Walburn), whose daughter
Millie (Lamour) hounds them for the rent and later agrees to
marry Dan. Dan returns to tell Jean, whom he now finds
paralyzed, and marries her out of pity. They try New York,
where Dan refuses to sell his slow version of "Dixie," and
they travel to New Orleans, where Dan forms the first minstrel troupe with Mr. Bones, Cook, Pelham (Foy), and Witlock
(Overman). At the theater, Jean leaves Dan a goodbye letter, which Millie burns, causing a conflagration that results in a rousing rendition of "Dixie" as Dan attempts to
calm the audience. Millie and Dan are finally together.
Songs include "Sunday, Monday or Always" and reprised with a
chorus, "Swing Low, Sweet Chariot" with chorus, "She's from
Missouri" and reprised with chorus, "A Horse That Knows the
Way Back Home," "If You Please," Emmett's traditional
"Dixie," "Kinda Peculiar Brown," and both "Old Dan Tucker"
(by Emmett) and "The Last Rose of Summer" with DeWolfe, Foy,
and Overman. Also, Foy and Overman sing "Laughing Tony" and
the chorus sings "Minstrel Show," "Buffalo Gals," and
"Turkey in the Straw."
   NOTE: This film is Bing's first Technicolor film (since
King of Jazz [1930]), and he and Lamour are billed as co-
stars. Filmed in late 1942, Hope mentions it as Bing's
previous film in Road to Utopia (1946). The story is very
loosely the career of Daniel Decatur Emmett. DeWolfe debuted at Paramount and then joined the Army. Lamour and Reynolds do no singing in the film. Lynne Overman died shortly
after the filming. Harry Barris appears as a drummer.
Burke and Van Heusen also wrote "Miss Jemima Walks By,"
which is not in the film.
   "[Dan Emmett, the original 'Virginia Minstrels' man is]
the role which the old booper, Bing Crosby, plays. . . . And
when Bashful Bing is warbling such sparkless but adequate
songs . . . it is easy to sit back and listen. . . . Mr. De
Wolfe, with some coaching, might do in an amateur show, but
he is definitely a minus quantity in a spot generally filled
by Bob Hope." Bosley Crowther, N.Y. Times, June 24.
   "[De Wolfe is] a cinch for a comeback. . . . the crooner is never from Dixie when it comes to lyric interpretations. The weaker the film vehicles, the greater is the
impact of the Crosby technique. . . . Crosby now is as
standard among the male singing toppers as the Four Free-
doms, and today he shapes up more and more as the Will
Rogers-type of solid American actor-citizen. He enjoys a
stature, especially because of his radio programs, enjoyed
by no other singing star in show business." Abel., Variety,
Jun 30.

F70.   Erroneous attribution of a guest appearance by
Bing Crosby: Higher and Higher (1943, RKO) Mentions 90 min.
bw d, p: Tim Whelan ad: Jay Dratler, Ralph Spence, William
Bowers, Howard Harris s: Gladys Hurlbut, Joshua Logan m,
l: Rodgers and Hart, Jimmy McHugh, Harold Adamson m stag-
ing: Ernst Matra e: Gene Milford c: Robert De Grasse.
N.Y. preview Dec 1
      Michele Morgan, Jack Haley, Frank Sinatra, Leon
Errol, Marcy McGuire, Victor Borge, Mary Wickes, Elisabeth
Risdon, Barbara Hale, Mel Torme, Paul Hartman, Dooley Wilson
      Drake (Errol) is a bankrupt man who, inspired by his

valet named Mike (Haley), schemes with his servants to raise money. Frank (Sinatra) is a neighbor. Millie (Morgan), secretly in love with Mike, is the maid selected to marry Sir Bictor Fitzroy Victor (Borge), a phony lord, but Mike finds a secret door at the Drake mansion and a horde of expensive wines and a harpsichord. He stops the wedding at the last minute and saves Millie for himself, after the cellar had been turned into a successful nightclub. Songs include Sinatra singing "I Couldn't Sleep a Wink Last Night," "I Saw You First," "The Music Stopped," and "This Is a Lovely Way to Spend an Evening" with Morgan, and the cast singing "Minuet in Boogie" and "When It Comes to Love You're on Your Own."

NOTE: Bing Crosby is mentioned in a few scenes, giving rise to the apocryphal account of him and Sinatra riding bicycles past each other and sticking their tongues out. Several sources repeat the error. Errol runs downstairs after Sinatra sings "I Couldn't Sleep a Wink Last Night" and asks, "Who was that singing down there, Bing Crosby?" Wickes replies, "Bing-bang Sinatra." Later, as McGuire falls off the bicycle Sinatra is pedaling after he mentioned a previous love, she says, "What other love affair, you double-crosser? From now on I'll listen to Crosby." The film was Sinatra's first major film role. He previously had a song in Columbia's 1942 Reveille with Beverly. Toward the end of Step Lively (1944) with George Murphy, Adolphe Menjou, and Gloria DeHaven, Sinatra tests his voice by singing "Where the Blue of the Night" like Bing, to which Murphy says, "He's losing his voice."

" . . . Frankie appears at such times as he is graciously permitted to warble and ooze out what passes for charm." Bosley Crowther, N.Y. Times, Aug 1.

"There may be some folks who can't figure out the reasons for Sinatra's meteoric rise, or might be wondering whether he's here to stay or not, but in his first starring role on the screen he at least gets in no one's way. Though a bit stiff on occasion and not as photogenic as may be desired, he generally handles himself ably in song as well as a few brief dialog scenes." Char., Variety, Dec 15.

F71.   Show Business at War (1943, 20th Century-Fox) Short.

F72.   Going My Way (1944, Paramount) 126 min. bw d, p: Leo McCarey ep: B.G. DeSylva w: Frank Butler, Frank Cavett s: McCarey m, l: Johnny Burke, James Van Heusen md: Robert Emmett Dolan, Troy Sanders va: Joseph J. Lilley art: Hans Dreier, William Flannery sd: Steve Seymour c: Lionel Lindon fx: Gordon Jennings sound: Gene Merritt, John Cope cos: Edith Head mu: Wally Westmore e: Leroy Stone. Los Angeles tradeshow Feb 25; May 2

Bing Crosby, Risë Stevens, Barry Fitzgerald, James Brown, Gene Lockhart, Jean Heather, Frank McHugh, Eily Malyon, Stanley Clements, Fortunio Bonanova, Anita Bolster, William Frawley, and the Robert Mitchell Boys' Choir

Father Charles Francis Patrick "Chuck" O'Malley (Crosby) is sent to revive Father Fitzgibbon's (Fitzgerald's) Eastside St. Dominic's Church, which he does by turning neighborhood toughs into a choir, admired by Jenny Linden

(Stevens) (an old friend and opera star). Fitzgibbon gradually bends to the younger curate's ways, first by donating
$10 to Carol James (Heather), a runaway who had a singing
lesson from O'Malley. O'Malley pours Fitzgibbon a "drop of
the craiture," as though drink were of the devil. Ted
Haines, Sr., (Lockhart) owns the mortgage of the church,
which he hopes to tear down for a parking lot. Father Tim
O'Dowd (McHugh), of a neighboring parish and friend of
O'Malley, arranges with music publishers an audition of a
song by O'Malley. Linden tries to sell the song "Going My
Way" to Max Dolan (Frawley) of Dolan, Lilley, Burke and Van
Heusen, but they buy "Swinging on a Star," "donating" the
money to the church. O'Malley, O'Dowd, and later, Fitzgibbon play golf. Gossipy Mrs. Quimp (Bolster) tells Fitzgibbon that Tim Haines, Jr., (Brown) has been seeing Carol at
her apartment, and O'Malley visits them. Later, Ted Sr.
finds his son at Carol's, but now in an Air Force uniform
and married, and he agrees to a new mortgage. The church
burns down, but O'Malley arranges a temporary edifice to be
replaced after the war with funds earned by a tour of Linden
and the choir. Before departing into the night to be replaced by O'Dowd, Father Chuck leaves Father Fitzgibbon in
the arms of his aged mother. Songs include "Hail, Alma
Mater" with McHugh, "Day After Forever" with Heather and
then a Heather solo, "Three Blind Mice" with Mitchell Boys'
Choir, "(Too-ra-loo-ra-loo-ral) That's an Irish Lullaby" and
reprised with the Choir, "Going My Way" and reprised by
Stevens and Choir, "Swinging on a Star" with the Choir and
Stevens, a recitative and "Habanera" (an aria from Carmen,
Act I) by Stevens, "Ave Maria" with Stevens and Choir,
"Adeste Fideles," and "Silent Night" with the Choir.
     NOTE: Six Academy Awards went to the film, Crosby
(over Alexander Knox, Cary Grant, and Charles Boyer), Fitzgerald as best supporting actor, McCarey for both direction
and original story, Butler and Cavett for the screen play,
and "Swingin' on a Star" as best original song. McCarey,
unable to sell his story to RKO, was loaned by RKO to Paramount for the film; McCarey risked his savings of $51,000
and made $2 million, and Paramount had to agree to let Bing
make a film for RKO, the 1945 Bells of St. Mary's and a
guest shot in The Princess and the Pirate (1944). The music
publishers in the film are an obvious play on four of the
composers. Filming occurred from Aug 1943 to Feb 1944. The
golfing scenes were filmed at the Riviera Country Club, near
Bing's home, leading an NBC press agent to comment, "Bing
Crosby has reached the millennium. He's being paid to play
golf." Clements (playing tough Tony Scarponi) went on to
roles in the Bowery Boys' film series. The British premiere
occurred Jul 27, raising £4000 (about $10,000) for the Stage
Door Canteen Services Fund, and Glenn Miller and his Orchestra played during the 30-minute stage show. In a month Bing
would himself be in England and visit the Canteen.
     On Crosby's arrival at the Academy Awards, held at
Hollywood's Grauman's Chinese Theatre, Mar 15, 1945, with
Bob Hope as the master of ceremonies and Gary Cooper the
presenter, a reporter wrote: "And then a man smoking a pipe,
wearing an overcoat and his hat slouched jauntily to one
side, arrived with a pretty blonde, and the crowd went wild.
It was Crosby and his wife." N.Y. Times, Mar 16, 1945: 17.

(Bob Hope and Margaret O'Brien received special Oscars for
1944.) Bing became the first male voted the top performer
by Motion Picture Herald; the National Board of Review named
Bing and Fitzgerald best actors and the film the second-best
film in English for the year. Photoplay, Film Daily, and
Golden Globe Awards cited the film as the best of the year,
and Photoplay named Bing as Best Actor. Readers of Britain's Picturegoer Magazine voted Bing the best actor. The
New York Film Critics awarded the film, its director, and
Fitzgerald (11 votes of 16 to Crosby's two) as the year's
best, and Crowther called the film one of the ten best of
the year, not quite as good as Preston Sturges's and Paramount's Hail the Conquering Hero (N.Y. Times, Dec 31, 2: 1).
    "Having hit about as high in his profession as any
average man would hope to hit--and that is to say the top
notes in the musical comedy league--Bing Crosby has switched
his batting technique (or had it switched for him) in his
latest film . . . and . . . Old Bing is giving the best show
of his career." Bosley Crowther, N.Y. Times, May 3.
    "Bing Crosby gets a tailor-made role in 'Going My Way,'
and with major assistance from Barry Fitzgerald and Risë
Stevens, clicks solidly to provide topnotch entertainment
for wide audience appeal." Walt., Variety, Mar 8.

    EXTRA: By this time Crosby had become the top film
attraction and remained at the top for a record five consecutive years.

F73.   The Shining Future (1944, Canada, Warner Bros.) 20
min. d: LeRoy Prinz ep: Jack L. Warner p: Gordon Hollins-
head, Arnold Albert w: James Bloodworth s: Emmanuel Man-
heim md: Leo F. Forbstein.
    Olive Blakeney, Jack Carson, Bing Crosby, Deanna
Durbin, Benny Goodman and his Orchestra, Cary Grant, Harry
James, James Lydon, Irene Manning, Herbert Marshall, Dennis
Morgan, Harold Peary, Charles Ruggles, Frank Sinatra
    Bing sings Loesser's "The Road to Victory" and Sinatra
sings DeVries' and Joe Bushkin's "Hot Time in the Town of
Berlin." The short was produced for Canada's Sixth War
Loan, and a shorter version was later edited for the U.S.
Treasury Department War Activities Committee (Release No.
98) as The Road to Victory (F75), which some misconstrue as
Road to Glory.

F74.   Swooner Crooner (1944, Warner Bros.) Caricature
Cartoon 7 min. col d: Frank Tashlin.
    Porky Pig, running the Flockheed Eggcraft Factory,
"100% War Work," loses his producing hens to swooning when
Frankie, a thin rooster, sings "Would I Be Wrong?" Wearing
a wide green bow tie that stands out behind the microphone
stand, Frankie also sings "As Time Goes By," causing Porky
to audition singers to keep up production. He hears caricatures of Jolson and Cab Calloway, until Bing taps him on the
shoulder and says, "Now looka here, Porky my old man, let
the Old Groaner take a whirl at those slick chicks." Wearing a battered soft hat, a loud Hawaiian shirt, and smoking
a pipe, this young rooster sings "When My Dreamboat Comes
Home." Frankie counters with "At the End of the Day"; Bing
returns with "Down Where the Trade Winds Play"; Frankie

sings "You Are Always in My Heart," but Bing commands the scene with "You Must Have Been a Beautiful Baby." With production at an amazing level, Porky asks how they did it, and both Bing and Frankie sing a bit of a wordless duet.
     NOTE: Bing's imitator is much better than Sinatra's. "Flockheed Eggcraft," of course, is a parody of Lockheed Aircraft. Bing recorded "You Must Have Been a Beautiful Baby" Oct 1938, "Trade Winds" Jul 1940, and "When My Dream-boat Comes Home" May 1942.

F75.   The Road to Victory (1944, Warner Bros.) 12 min. bw d: LeRoy Prinz p: Jack L. Warner.
         Bing Crosby, Cary Grant, Frank Sinatra, Charles Ruggles, Dennis Morgan, Irene Manning, Jack Carson, Jimmy Lydon, Olive Blakeney
         An edited version of The Shining Future (F73) for the War Activities Commission to help promote the Fifth War Loan Drive. It is set in an American home in 1951 with a flash-back to 1944, and Crosby sings the title song.

     EXTRA: Bing tested for the lead in The Story of Will Rogers in 1944 for producer Mark Hellinger and director Michael Curtiz. His scene was with Tom Tully and Dane Clark, but the 1952 film starred Will Rogers, Jr., Jane Wyman and Eddie Cantor. Will Rogers sang a good imitation of Bing in one of his films.

F75A.   Swingtime with the Stars (1944) Short Unknown
         Bing sings "Don't Fence Me In."

F76.   Pathe Gazette (1944, British, Pathe) Newsreel.
     Bing appears at the opening of the Stage Door Canteen in Piccadilly, London, Sep 20, 1944, greeted by Jack Buchan-an and sings "Amor, amor."

F77.   British Movietone (1944, British, Movietone) Newsreel.
     British Foreign Secretary Anthony Eden is shown opening the Stage Door Canteen in London Sep 20, 1944, and Bing, introduced by Dorothy Dickson, sings "San Fernando Valley."

F78.   Troops Entertainment Show (1940s) Newsreel.
     Includes a shot of Bing and Bob Hope singing "Mairzy Doats," probably filmed at March Field in 1942 or 1943.

F79.   March of Time (1940s, 20th Century-Fox) Short Documentary.
     Bing Crosby appears briefly, along with Carole Lombard, Louis Armstrong, Frank Sinatra, Jack Benny, Bob Hope, Irving Berlin, James Cagney, W.C. Fields, Alfred Hitchcock, Clark Gable, the Mills Brothers, Orson Welles, and Mickey Rooney.

     EXTRA: Bing Crosby Productions produced The Great John L. (1944), titled A Man Called Sullivan in the United King-dom. Bing's partners included James Edward Grant. It was directed by Frank Tuttle, written by James Edward Grant, scored by Victor Young, and starred Linda Darnell, Barbara Britton, Greg McClure, Lee Sullivan, Wallace Ford, Otto Kruger, Robert Barrat, and Rory Calhoun. Songs include "A

Friend of Yours," "A Perfect Gentleman," "When You Were
Sweet Sixteen," "We Have Always Been Comrades," "Take Me Out
to the Ball Game," and "When You and I Were Young, Maggie."
Burke and Van Heusen wrote the first two, Thornton wrote the
third. Released through United Artists, it was only a
moderate success.

F80.   <u>The Princess and the Pirate</u> (1944, RKO) Guest
release, Samuel Goldwyn Production 92 min. col d: David
Butler ap: Don Hartman w: Hartman, Melville Shavelson,
Everett Freeman ad: Allen Boetz, Curtis Kenyon s: Sy
Bartlett score: David Rose m, l: Jimmy McHugh, Harold
Adamson c: Victor Milner e: Daniel Mandell. N.Y. tradeshow, Oct 10
        Bob Hope, Virginia Mayo, Walter Brennan, Walter
Slezak, Victor McLaglen, Marc Lawrence, Hugo Haas
        Sylvester Crosby (Hope) is a trick entertainer who is
captured on the high seas and goes to the West Indies with
cut-throats. The pirate leader (McLaglen) wants the captured princess (Mayo), who is pursuing a commoner. Hope
dresses in drag to escape walking the plank and sparks the
interest of ugly pirate Featherhead (Brennan). Bing Crosby
gets the girl at the end, revealed as the beloved commoner.
As a sailor Bing says, "Stick around, son. Something older
may show up for you." Hope steps out of character to complain, "This is a fine thing! I knock my brains out for
nine reels and then some bit player from Paramount comes on
to grab all the goods. This is the last picture I ever do
for you, Mr. Goldwyn." Bing adds, "Pardon me," as he continues kissing Mayo. Hope complains, "Don't make a meal out
of it." Bing has the last word: "Go sell your rack
shellac," an allusion to Pepsodent toothpaste, Hope's radio
sponsor. <u>Song</u>: Mayo's "Kiss Me in the Moonlight."
        ". . . there come moments . . . when it seems that all
the authors have run out . . . . And the question seems to
hang in the balance whether [Hope] is going to take a powder
too. . . . The film has a cutely novel finish, in which 'a
bit player from Paramount' steps in and snags the girl from
Mr. Hope's arms. But they asked us not to tell you what it
is." Bosley Crowther, N.Y. <u>Times</u>, Feb 10.
        The film is "a very funny topper," and the turn at the
end is "a switch on a bit Hope and Crosby did in one of the
former's Paramount starrers." Abel., <u>Variety</u>, Oct 11.

F81.   <u>Here Come the Waves</u> (1944, Paramount) 99 min. bw
d, p: Mark Sandrich w: Allan Scott, Ken Englund, Zion Myers
l: Johnny Mercer m: Harold Arlen md: Robert E. Dolan v:
Joseph J. Lilley ma: Troy Sanders ch: Danny Dare art:
Hans Dreier, Roland Anderson sd: Ray Moyer cos: Edith Head
c: Charles Lang, Farciot Edouart sound: Hugo Grenzbach,
John Cope fx: Gordon Jennings, Paul Lerpae e: Ellsworth
Hoagland. N.Y. tradeshow Dec 15; Dec 27
        Bing Crosby, Betty Hutton, Sonny Tufts, Ann Doran,
Gwen Crawford, Noel Neill, Catherine Craig, Marjorie Hen-
shaw, Harry Barris, Oscar O'Shea, Mae Clark, Minor Watson,
Vera Marshe, Mona Freeman, Yvonne De Carlo, Roberta Jonay
        Johnny Cabot (Crosby) is a colorblind crooner who was
rejected for military service, and blonde Susie and redhead
Rosemary Allison (both Hutton) are singing twins at the

Cabaña Club. Dim-witted Susie adores Johnny, whom the twins
have not met, and mature Rosie (12 minutes older), spurning
Johnny for not enlisting, wants to join the WAVES (Women
Accepted for Volunteer Emergency Service). Susie takes
Rosie to hear Johnny at a stage show, where he croons as
bobbysoxers swoon, and Johnny puts on dark glasses and a
beard to go out with Petty Officer First Class Wendell Smith
(Tufts). At the club the bandleader, Barris, introduces the
twins, and Wendy introduces them to Johnny. Susie, eating a
Johnny Cabot sundae, reveals that Rosie said Johnny "looks
like an amorous bullfrog and sounded like one," and he falls
for Rosie, the twin Wendy also prefers. When the Navy
lowers its standards, Johnny enlists, and Susie follows
Rosie into the WAVES; Ruth (Doran) and Tex (Crawford) are
others. With "Moonlight Becomes You" playing in the background, Johnny becomes a Seaman Second Class under Wendy on
the destroyer U.S.S. Douglas in San Diego, commanded by Lt.
Commander Slade. Johnny's father had been killed aboard the
ship in World War I. Susie writes Johnny, but, with Johnny
singing parts of "Blow, Boys, Blow," Wendy places him on
guard duty and meets the twins alone. Susie causes a female
riot over Johnny when she finds him patrolling. The next
night at a restaurant where Wendy and Rosie relax, Johnny
causes the arrest of Wendy by throwing ice down the back of
a woman, enraging her escort. Johnny says, "Maybe he just
doesn't like your New England accent, those clipped speeches
of yours." Johnny takes Rosie for a walk in which she falls
for him, making Susie jealous. Susie forges the crooner's
signature on a memo suggesting a recruiting show, which
Commodore Mcpherson (O'Shea) and the Pentagon adopt and
promote Johnny temporarily to Chief Petty Office, over
Wendy. He tells Rosie that Johnny is avoiding combat, and
she now thinks the crooner a coward. Johnny puts the twins
and Wendy in the show, and one filmed rehearsal occurs on
the hangar deck of the carrier Traverse, when Johnny in
blackface and beard as a mailman sings a duet of "Accentuate
the Positive" with Wendy, in blackface as a doorman. Johnny
hopes to show the memo to Rosie to prove he did not write
it, but Susie picks his pocket and loses the paper overboard. Rosie decides to stay in the show to aid her twin.
At the Naval Training School for WAVES in the Bronx Johnny
films his and Wendy's parts to be able to return to the
ship, and at a party Wendy has Susie wear a red wig and
drink heavily, carouse, and say she is using Johnny for her
career as Johnny overhears, thinking her Rosie. Susie plays
the lead in "'If Waves Acted Like Sailors,' Set Sketches by
Milt Gross,'" in which Johnny and Wendy act like women asked
out on dates. At the big production, Johnny goes AWOL to
return to the ship, but Susie and Wendy find him and expose
his disguise on the street to his fans. Johnny retreats to
the show, when Susie confesses her forgery to Rosie. Rosie
tells the commander, Capt. Johnson, that Johnny wants combat, and the commander orders him and Wendy to fly back and
meet the ship in Los Angeles. Rosemary falls again for
Johnny and Susie falls for Wendy. In the last filmed scenes
in the show Johnny and Wendy board a destroyer and wave from
the departing warship. Songs include "Join the Navy" by
WAVES chorus, reprised by Hutton (as twins), "That Ol' Black
Magic," "Moonlight Becomes You," "Blow, Boys, Blow," "Let's

Take the Long Way Home," "Accentuate the Positive" with
Tufts, "If Waves Acted Like Sailors" by Hutton and chorus,
"There's a Fella Waitin' in Poughkeepsie (Strictly on My Own
Tonight)" by Hutton and chorus, "I Promise You" with Hutton,
and "Here Come the Waves" by a WAVES chorus.

NOTE: "Accentuate the Positive" was nominated for an
Academy Award for 1944, and the film was the most expensive
Paramount musical of the war. The role of Wendy was obviously written for Bob Hope. "Mama Thinks I'm a Star" was
written but not used. At the peak of his popularity, Bing
sings "That Ol' Black Magic," Frank Sinatra's hit of 1944,
wearing a white double-breasted suit and black bow tie while
leaning behind the microphone, with both hands on the post,
like Sinatra at the Paramount in 1944. Mona Freeman plays
the first girl to faint; De Carlo plays another girl. This
was the last film directed by Sandrich, who directed Holiday
Inn (1942) and five musicals with Fred Astaire and Ginger
Rogers. Barris appears unbilled (only the first seven
members of the cast had credits). The "If Waves Acted Like
Sailors" sketch is a twist on the standard vaudeville routine "If Women Played Poker Like Men," a sketch also re-
versed for Star Spangled Rhythm (1942). The WAVES were the
Women's Reserve of the U.S. Navy through the war. Note an
early use of some of Crosby's nicknames in the reviews.
Neill, noted as Lois Lane in Superman on TV in the 1950s,
plays the second female in the sketches. Tufts, rejected by
the military for a football injury, came from a prominent
Boston family, but by 1954, because of alcoholism, his name
became a standard joke on TV. He also appears in Duffy's
Tavern (1945). Hutton, who appears in Star Spangled Rhythm,
became bankrupt in the 1960s and worked as a waitress in
Rhode Island. Marshe is the unbilled double for Hutton.

"In this one our old friend, the Bingle, doffs mufti
for nautical attire and plays a swoon-throwing crooner who
becomes a member of Uncle Sam's fleet. . . . Mr. Crosby
sings most of the [songs] . . . and does very nicely by
them, as he does by his droll and genial role. . . . the
best part of the humor is that which has Bing crooning in
travesty of a famous 'swooner' who shall be nameless (just
this once)." Bosley Crowther, N.Y. Times, Dec 28.

"Der Bingle [and the others] are an undeniable marquee
and b.o. parlay. . . . 'Old Black Magic' is reprised in a
delicious rib on Frank Sinatra. Crosby is cast as the new
pash crooner, and his mike-clutching stance, accented by the
whinnying dames, leaves no secret as to whom Der Bingle
refers. It's a dandy take-off on The Voice, but it's not
harsh; in fact, it's a sympathetic salve for all out-of-
service crooners. . . . [The writers] do as good a job for
The Groaner as does Carroll Carroll on the radio." Abel.,
Variety, Dec 20.

F82.   All Star Bond Rally (1945, 20th Century-Fox) 11
min. bw d: Michael Audley for the War Activities Committee
and the U.S. Treasury Dept.

Bing Crosby, Frank Sinatra, Bob Hope, Harpo Marx,
Linda Darnell, Betty Grable, Jeanne Crain, Harry James and
his Orchestra, Fibber McGee and Molly

Crosby sings "Buy, Buy Bonds" and appeals for purchases
of bonds for the Seventh War Bond Drive. The short was

offered free to theaters to aid in promoting the drive.
Sinatra follows Bing to sing "Saturday Night Is the Loneli-
est Night of the Week" as Bing peeks enviously from the
wings.

F83.   Hollywood Victory Caravan (1945, Paramount) 21
min. bw d: William Russell w: Mel Shavelson. Produced
for the War Actitivies Committee and the U.S. Treasury Dept.
        Bing Crosby, Alan Ladd, Humphrey Bogart, Bob Hope,
William Demarest, Betty Hutton, Olga San Juan, Barbara
Stanwyck, Doña Drake, Franklin Pangborn, Robert Benchley,
Carmen Cavallaro, Diana Lynn
        Crosby sings "We've Got Another Bond to Buy" to promote
the sale of War Bonds.
        NOTE: There was another tour of this name in Apr and
May 1942.

F84.   Out of This World (1945, Paramount) Voice only 96
min. bw d: Hal Walker p: Sam Coslow ad: Walter DeLeon,
Arthur Phillips s: Elizabeth Meehan, Coslow m, l: Johnny
Mercer, Harold Arlen, Felix Bernard, Bernie Wayne, Coslow
ch: Sammy Lee c: Stuart Thompson e: Stuart Gilmore. Pre-
view, N.Y. Paramount Jun 4
        Eddie Bracken, Veronica Lake, Diana Lynn, Cass
Daley, Parkyakarkus, Donald McBride, Florence Bates, Don
Wilson, Mabel Paige, Charles Smith, Irving Bacon, Bing
Crosby's Kids (Gary, Philip, Dennis, Lin), Glamourette
Quartet, Piano Maestros: Carmen Cavallaro, Ted Fiorito,
Henry King, Ray Noble, Joe Reichman
        Herbie Fenton (Bracken) is a singing messenger cum
bobbysoxers' crooner, voice by Crosby in a lampoon on Sinatra, who becomes a sensation on a radio program. Herbie is
sold 125 percent to backers by bandleader Betty Miller
(Lynn), with Fanny (Daley) as the drummer. One of his new
managers is Dorothy Dodge (Lake), who hires "swooners" for
his shows. The Crosby Kids are seated in the front row of a
radio show and, on hearing the voice, one asks, "Where have
I heard that voice before?" Another says, "I was just
thinking that." A third says, alluding to Sinatra, "Aw
shucks, I'd rather hear that bow-tie guy sing anyway." The
fourth adds, "You'd better not let mother hear you say
that." Herbie is taken to New York where the females labor
to keep him from a benefit show and the over-invested backers, but he makes good in a finale with five pianists. At
the end Herbie says, "Thanks, Bing." Songs include "Out of
This World," "June Comes Around Every Year," "A Sailor with
an Eight-Hour Pass" by Daley, "All I Do Is Beat That Goldarn
Drum" by Daley, "I'd Rather Be Me," "Ghost of Mr. Chopin" by
Daley, and "It Takes a Little Bit More" by Daley.
        NOTE: The film was produced while Bing was in Europe
entertaining the soldiers, and he recorded his three songs
in Dec 1944 and Jan 1945 after his return. He rejected any
pay for singing, but his four sons were paid $6500 each.
One screen credit reads, "Eddie Bracken's songs are sung by
a great friend of his and yours."
        "Imagine a shy young singer with Eddie Bracken's looks
and the soothing voice of Bing Crosby and you have a picture
of the hero of this film. . . . That trick of movie presti-
digitation is the novel twist of the show and is good for a

laugh whenever Eddie opens his mouth and Bing's warbling
comes out. To be sure, Mr. Crosby never shows up, but his
four fair-haired youngsters are on hand in one scene to
represent the family and toss a few quips about dad. . . .
Mr. Crosby sings three fairish songs amusingly. . . ."
Bosley Crowther, N.Y. Times, Jun 7.

"A unique stunt is having Bracken play a croon-swooner,
which he isn't, with Bing Crosby's voice dubbed in to fit
Bracken's singing lip movements. Crosby isn't seen at any
point but his four young boys, Gary, Philip, Dennis and Lin,
appear in a bit shortly after the opening and are responsible for a couple cute cracks when they hear their father's
voice coming from Bracken." Char. Variety, Jun 6

F85.   State Fair (1945, 20th Century-Fox) alternate: It
Happened One Summer Voice only 100 min. bw d: Walter
Lang p: William Perlberg w: Oscar Hammerstein II ad:
Sonya Levien, Paul Green s: novel by Philip Stong m,l:
Richard Rodgers, Hammerstein md: Alfred Newman, Charles
Henderson a: Edward Powell art: Lyle Wheeler, Lewis Creber
sd: Thomas Little, Al Orenbach cos: Rene Robert mu: Ben
Nye c: Leon Shamroy, Natalie Kalmus, Richard Mueller fx:
Fred Sersen sound: Bernard Fredricks, Roger Beman e: J.
Watson Webb. N.Y. tradeshow Aug 16

Jeanne Crain, Dana Andrews, Dick Haymes, Vivian
Blaine, Charles Winninger, Fay Bainter, Donald Meek, Frank
McHugh, Percy Kilbride, Henry Morgan, Jane Nigh, William
Marshall, Phil Brown, Paul Harvey, Harlan Briggs

Margy Frake (Crain) is the daughter of Brunswick, Iowa,
super farmers Abel (Winninger) and Melissa (Bainter), one
with a prize Hampshire boar (a hog named Blue Boy), the
other with prize mincemeat and pickles for the Iowa State
Fair. Dave Miller (Kilbride) sells hay and feed. Abel
secretly fortifies his wife's mincemeat with brandy, and she
adds more. Margy daydreams on the porch swing of "Ronald
Colman, Charles Boyer, and Bing" and is cool to her beau,
Harry Ware (Brown). While the Frakes camp at the fair, one
barker (Morgan) is outsmarted by Wayne Frake (Haymes),
Margy's brother, supported by redhead Emily Edwards
(Blaine), pretending to be the daughter of the police chief.
She's actually the band singer, and Marty (Marshall) is the
male singer. A well-traveled reporter named Pat Gilbert
(Andrews), now with the Des Moines Register, covers the
fair, meets Margy on the rollercoaster, and wins her love.
McGee (McHugh) is an unscrupulous song plugger, using Wayne
to influence Emily, and Marty accuses Wayne of taking payo-
la. Emily knows better and falls for Wayne. The leading
judge (Briggs) announces Melissa's first prize for sour
pickles and special plaque for extraordinary mincemeat.
McGee tells Wayne that Emily is married. While Margy runs
off to marry Pat, Wayne is reconciled to his local girl,
Eleanor (Nigh). Songs include "State Fair" by Kilbride,
Winninger, and Bainter; "It Might as Well Be Spring" by
Crain, reprised by Crain and Bing; "That's for Me" by
Blaine; "It's a Grand Night for Singing" by Marshall,
Haymes, Crain, Blaine, and chorus; "Maybe You're Not the
One" by Haymes and Blaine; and "All I Know, I Owe Iow-ay" by
Marshall, Blaine, Winninger, Briggs, and chorus.

NOTE: A remake of Henry King's 1933 film for Fox with

Will Rogers, Janet Gaynor, Lew Ayres, Sally Eilers, and
Norman Foster. Will Rogers does an effective imitation of
Bing Crosby in one of his films, possibly the 1933 production (he died in 1935). In the 1945 version, in an early
daydream sequence, Crain hears Ronald Colman and Charles
Boyer, and then Bing singing a line from "It Might as Well
Be Spring," complete with a few bars of "boo-boo-booing" and
whistling. This song won an Oscar, but Bing never recorded
it except for the soundtrack, although he featured it on his
radio program Feb 7 and sang it himself Feb 28 and Mar 21,
1946, as the Oscar was selected. It soon becomes inimi-
cally his voice in the film. Crain's singing was dubbed by
Louanne Hogan. The film was previewed four days before the
preview of Duffy's Tavern. The film was remade again by Fox
for 1962, a film rated a "Bomb" by Leonard Maltin, directed
by Jose Ferrer, with Pat Boone, Bobby Darin, Ann-Margret,
Alice Faye, Tom Ewell, and Wally Cox. Sonya Levien was one
of the writers of all three screenplays.

F86.   Duffy's Tavern (1945, Paramount) 97 min. bw d:
Hal Walker p: Danny Dare w: Melvin Frank, Norman Panama
based on characters by Ed Gardner sketches: George White,
Eddie Davis, Matt Brooks, Abram S. Burrows, Barney Dean,
Frank, Panama m, l: Johnny Burke, James Van Heusen, Bernie
Wayne, Ben Raleigh md: Robert Emmett Dolan ch: Billy
Daniels c: Lionel Lindon e: Arthur Schmidt. N.Y. preview
Aug 20; Sep 5
        Extensive Paramount cast, starring Ed Gardner,
Bing Crosby, Betty Hutton, Paulette Goddard, Alan Ladd,
Dorothy Lamour, Eddie Bracken, Brian Donlevy, Sonny Tufts,
Veronica Lake, Barry Fitzgerald, Cass Daley, Victor Moore,
Marjorie Reynolds, Charles Cantor, Eddie Green, Ann Thomas;
with Arturo de Cordova, Diana Lynn, Robert Benchley, William
Demarest, Howard DaSilva, Billy DeWolfe, Walter Abel, Johnny
Coy, Miriam Franklin, Charles Quigley, Olga San Juan, Robert
Watson, and Gary, Philip, Dennis, and Lin Crosby
        Characters from a famous radio program of the time
overhire ex-servicemen as waiters (about 14) and have to
have a block party-benefit show to pay bills and to reopen a
recording studio. Archie (Gardner) the barkeep, Eddie
(Green) the waiter, Moocher Finnegan (Cantor), and Miss
Duffy (Thomas) help Michael O'Malley (Moore) finance reopen-
ing the recording company for jobs for the veterans. Crosby
is in a spoof of his own life story, as told by Benchley,
and in ball cap and sweatshirt, plays the piano and sings a
parody of "Swinging on a Star" with Jean Heather, Helen
Walker, Gail Russell, and others. Fitzgerald and Lamour
play Bing's parents. Other songs include "The Hard Way"
(Hutton), "You Can't Blame a Gal for Tryin'" (Daley), and
"Swinging on a Star (Parody)" (Crosby).
        NOTE: The film's opening was timed for Duffy's Tav-
ern's and Bing's new radio season. One small irony is that
Robert Benchley hailed from Worcester, MA, the old home town
of Crosby's paternal forebears.
        "Bing Crosby and a chorus of assistants, including a
likely assortment of studio 'names,' do a very amusing
parody of 'Swinging on a Star,' which finishes a Robert
Benchley recount of the high points of Bing's Career."
Bosley Crowther, N.Y. Times, Sep 6.

"Robert Benchley tells the four Bing Crosby children a fantastic Horatio Alger story of the boyhood of their father, with Bing, Barry Fitzgerald and Dorothy Lamour [as his parents] enacting the idyll, the scene seguing into a take-off of the 'Swinging on a Star' sequence from 'Going My Way,' with Der Bingle using a dozen Par stars as his 'kid choir.'" Bron., <u>Variety</u>, Aug 22.

F87.   <u>The Bells of St. Mary's</u> (1945, RKO release, Rainbow Productions) 126 min. bw d, p: Leo McCarey w: Dudley Nichols s: McCarey m, l: Douglas Furber-A. Emmett Adams, John Burke-James Van Heusen, Grant Clarke-George W. Meyer score: Robert Emmett Dolan art: William Flannery sd: Darrell Silver cos: Edith Head c: George Barnes, Vernon L. Walker sound: Stephen Dunn e: Harry Marker. L.A. tradeshow Nov 20; Radio City Music Hall ca. Dec 6
Bing Crosby, Ingrid Bergman, Henry Travers, William Gargan, Ruth Donnelly, Joan Carroll, Martha Sleeper, Rhys Williams, Dickie Tyler, Una O'Connor, Jimmy Crane
Father Chuck O'Malley (Crosby) is sent to revive another declining New York church, especially its parochial school run by Mother Superior Sister Benedict (Bergman). She clashes with the priest's permissiveness, teaches Eddie (Tyler) how to box the ears off a bully, produces a Christmas pageant by first-grade children, and deals with industrialist Mr. Bogardus (Travers). Mrs. Breen (O'Connor) is Eddie's mother. Bogardus and Sister Benedict misunderstand each other as agreeing to transfer their property to the other. Bogardus wants the school land for a parking lot. Urged by Father Chuck, however, Bogardus finally donates his factory to the school, as it would be good for his heart trouble. Father Chuck, surprised to find a student named Luther (Crane) at the Catholic school, also leads the separated parents (Gargan and Sleeper) of a schoolgirl named Patsy (Carroll) to a reconciliation. At the end he has to send Sister Benedict away to cure her tuberculosis, but only after he disobeys Dr. McKay (Williams) and confesses to her the reason for her removal. <u>Songs</u> include "Aren't You Glad You're You" with children, "<u>Adeste Fideles</u>" with children, "In the Land of Beginning Again," "O Sanctissima" with children, and "The Bells of St. Mary's" with children. Bergman sings "It's Spring" (Swedish song "<u>Vavindar Frisca Leka Och Hviska</u>").
NOTE: The song "Aren't You Glad You're You," by Burke and Van Heusen was nominated for an Oscar as best original song of the year. Crosby, Bergman, and McCarey won Oscars while shooting, Crosby and McCarey (two) for <u>Going My Way</u>, Bergman for <u>Gaslight</u>. Ruth Donnelly plays Sister Michael, and Bing's friend and Paramount's prop man, Jimmy Cottrell, taught Bergman how to box for the film. The song "The Bells of St. Mary's" was written by Adams and Furber, "In the Land of Beginning Again" by Clarke and Meyer. McCarey, a producer-director for RKO, was loaned to Paramount for <u>Going My Way</u> in return for Crosby for this film, although Frank Sinatra was considered for the lead. Ironically, Flannery's church set was later used in the Val Lewton-Boris Karloff horror film <u>Bedlam</u> (1946).
"Father O'Malley is generally consistent (and played by Bing Crosby, what else could he be?) but Sister Benedict has

not the veracity of her counterpart character which was
played by Barry Fitzgerald. . . . And the whole story-line
developed toward the wheedling of a building for the school,
with Henry Travers as the landlord who is wheedled, is
unconvincing and vaguely immoral. . . . As Father Chuck,
Mr. Crosby is--well, you know--the same easy, confident
Bing, tossing off slangy jokes and soft-soap; with the
sincerity of a practiced hand. . . . Maybe his truck with
Tin Pan Alley after writing that hit song ['Where the Blue
of the Night,' re-recorded July 17, 1945] is to blame. It
is noticeable that he hovers in the background a little more
than he did in 'Going My Way.'" Bosley Crowther, N.Y.
Times, Dec 7.
        "It's all done with the natural ease that is Crosby's
trademark. . . . Picture is packed with many simple scenes
that tug at the heart and loosen the tears as directed by
McCarey and played by the outstanding cast." Brog., Variety, Nov 28.

F88.   Road to Utopia (1946, Paramount) 90 min. bw   d:
Hal Walker   p: Paul Jones   w: Norman Panama, Melvin Frank
m, l: Johnny Burke, James Van Heusen   md: Robert Emmett
Dolan   score: Leigh Harline   va: Joseph J. Lilley   art: Hans
Dreier, Roland Anderson   sd: George Sawley   ch: Danny Dare
cos: Edith Head   animation: Jerry Fairbanks   c: Lionel Lin-
den, Farciot Edouart   sound: Hugo Genzbach   e: Stuart Gil-
more. N.Y. preview Nov 14, 1945; Jan 25, 1946; N.Y. Para-
mount Feb 7, 1946
        Bing Crosby, Bob Hope, Dorothy Lamour, Hillary
Brooke, Douglas Dumbrille, Jack LaRue, Robert Barrat, Nestor
Paiva, Will Wright, Jimmy Dundee, Robert Benchley, Billy
Benedict, Arthur Loft, Paul Newlan, Stanley Andrews, Alan
Bridge, Romaine Callendar, Jack Rutherford, Al Hill, Edward
Emerson, Ronnie Rondell, Allen Pomeroy, Jack Stoney, George
McKay, Larry Daniels, Charles Gemora, Claire James, Maxine
Fife, Ferdinand Munier, Edgar Dearing, Charles C. Wilson,
Jim Thorpe, Harry Semels
        Duke Johnson (Crosby), accompanied by two beautiful
women (James and Fife), finds rich old Chester Hooton (Hope)
and his wife, Sal (Lamour), and reminisces to 35 years
earlier: Duke and Chester, vaudevillians on the run from
San Francisco in 1900. Duke attempts to convince Chester to
try "Utopia" (Alaska) and succeeds only by lifting his
wallet. They sail to the Klondike, lose their money when
Chester thinks the porthole is a safe, lose a talent contest
to a monkey--Chester says, "Next time I'll bring Sinatra"--
and stoke the ship's boiler, with Duke merely observing as a
man in formal dress on his way to Stage 10 walks in and asks
for a light. Robert Benchley appears in a corner of the
screen several times, wisecracking about the cinematography
of it all--like, "This is how not to make a picture"--and
Crosby and Hope often address the audience directly. Pursuing the thieves of her father's map to a gold mine and the
murderers of her father's partner, Mr. Latimer (Wright), Sal
embarks on an earlier ship, meets Ace Larsen (Dumbrille),
owner of the Golden Rail, and becomes his singer. Duke and
Chester find the map in the stateroom of the two villains,
Sperry and McGuirk (Barrat and Paiva), and take their iden-
tities and beards. In Skagway Sal tries to help Ace get the

map. Thinking the killers are Duke and Chester (who have shed their beards), Sal gets half the map from Duke, and Ace dogsleds to Dawson City, needing two days to stake his claim, when he realizes he has only half. Accompanied by "a large shaggy dog" named Buck, Duke and Chester dogsled for the mine and meet Kate (Brooke), Ace's girlfriend, who hopes to get the rest of the map for Ace and takes them to a cabin. After Sal arrives, Duke catches 14 fish, Chester none, when another rises to tell Chester he is No. 15. Duke confesses his identity to Sal, who also comes clean, but she helps Kate take the map from Chester that night to save the boys from Ace, and the girls leave. After the boys sleep with a bear, whose partner later complains that he is given no lines, the real Sperry and McGuirk arrive, the boys realize they do not have any of the map, and they tie up the villains, who soon get free. The boys fall while climbing a cliff and temporarily defeat the villains when Chester causes an avalanche by hiccupping. At Larsen's Last Chance Saloon in Dawson, Duke asks for "two fingers of rotgut" and Chester for lemonade, but "in a dirty glass." The boys get the map, rescue Sal, and blow up the saloon with the two villains in it. They escape with Sal on dogsled into the wastes from Ace, Kate, Le Bec (LaRue), and the gang. Duke seems lost when the ice parts, stranding him. He offers to hold the gang off and throws Chester and Sal the map. Back in the present of 1935, Duke explains that he fought off the gang and learns of Chester's "adopted" son, who looks like a 35-year-old Bing Crosby. Songs include "Sunday, Monday or Always," "Goodtime Charlie" with Hope, "It's Anybody's Spring," "Personality" by Lamour, "Welcome to My Dreams" twice, "Put It There, Pal" with Hope, and "Would You?" by Lamour.

NOTE: This is the fourth and perhaps the best of the famous Road series, the first in three years. Hope took second star billing again; Lamour had that honor for the first two. Butler and Hartman had written the first three, but not this one. Bing and Hope played so much golf that the studio prevailed on them to stand for wardrobe fittings on the course. Robert Benchley died in 1945 shortly after the filming. Filming began in Nov 1943 (according to Faith, p. 182) and is advertised in Louella Parson's Dec 1944 article. It was released in 1946, but the print dates it as 1945. Hope names Dixie as Bing's previous film, released Jun 1943; Bing names Let's Face It as Hope's, released Aug 1943. Bing recorded "Sunday, Monday or Always" Jul 1943, "It's Anybody's Spring" Jul 1944, "Personality" Jan 1946, "Welcome to My Dreams" Jul 1944, "Put It There, Pal" Dec 1944, and "Would You?" Jul 1944. Crosby injured his back when he and Hope fell while climbing a cliff and Hope landed on top of him. One Wednesday they slept in a scene as a loose bear snuggled beside Hope, who complained of the weight on his arm, which required first aid. The next day the bear went berserk and tore its trainer's arm off. These and other incidents appear in Hal Walker's book Three Months on the Road and in Hope's This Is on Me. The delay in the release was probably to avoid infringing on the popular image of Bing as a priest reprised in the release of Dec 1945, and Bing's back injury may also have contributed to the delay. From May 17, 1945, to Feb 7, 1946, Bing avoided his Kraft radio show but for one appearance, trying to break his contract that bound him into 1950.

"Their style of slugging each other with verbal discourtesies is quite as familiar as ice cream--at least to the patrons of films. And their can-you-top-this vein of jesting runs straight through our national attitude. The only difference, in this case, is that their style seems more refined, their timing a little more expert, their insults a little more acute. Bing and Bob have apparently been needling each other for so long that they naturally stitch along a pattern which shapes the personalities of both. . . . Out of this lurid situation the Messrs. Crosby and Hope--with the help of the boys at Paramount--have ripped a titanic burlesque of brawny adventure pictures and of movies in general, indeed. . . . But where this sort of clowning might be juvenile and monotonous in other hands it has rich comic quality in the smooth paws of the gentlemen involved." Bosley Crowther, N.Y. _Times_, Feb 28.

"The highly successful Crosby-Hope-Lamour 'Road' series under the Paramount banner comes to attention once again in 'Road to Utopia,' a zany laugh-getter which digresses somewhat from the pattern by gently kidding the picture business and throwing in unique little touches, all with a view to tickling the risibilities. . . . Though this one is rich in laughs and fast, the songs turned out for it are not of heavy caliber" Char., _Variety_, Dec 5, 1945.

F89.   Screen Snapshots No. 9 (1946, Columbia) Short.

EXTRA: Bing was asked in 1946 to star in "Comin' Through the Rye," a story by Clements Ripley on the life of Robert Burns, the Scottish poet, a film perhaps never produced. He was also considered for another Road film titled "Road to Brooklyn," which was not produced.

F90.   Blue Skies (1946, Paramount) 104 min. col d: Stuart Heisler p: Sol C. Siegal w: Arthur Sheekman ad: Allan Scott s, m, l: Irving Berlin md: Robert Emmett Dolan va: Joseph J. Lilley, Troy Sanders ch: Hermes Pan art: Hans Dreier, Hal Pereira sd: Sam Comer, Maurice Goodman cos: Edith Head, Mme. Karinska mu: Wally Westmore c: Charles Lang, William Snyder, Natalie Kalmus fx: Gordon Jennings, Paul K. Lerpae, Farciot Edouart sound: Hugo Grenzbach, John Cope e: LeRoy Stone. N.Y. tradeshow Sep 25; Oct 16

Bing Crosby, Fred Astaire, Joan Caulfield, Billy DeWolfe, Olga San Juan, Mikhail Rasumny, Frank Faylen, Victoria Horne, Karolyn Grimes, Jack Norton, Roy Gordon, Joan Woodbury, John Kelly, Mary Jane Hodge, John Gallaudet

Johnny Adams (Crosby), a former vaudevillian who is not the marrying kind, dreams, croons, and likes to open and sell nightclubs around the country. Jed Potter (Astaire) is a disc jockey who reminisces: He courts and dances with Mary O'Hara (Caulfield) until he introduces her to Johnny, whom she marries. Jed spins records and reminisces about Johnny's and Mary's daughter, Mary Elizabeth (Grimes), their failed marriage, and Jed's further courtship until Johnny returns more mature. Jed is jilted again, takes to the bottle, and is crippled by falling off a bridge while danc-

ing drunk with former partner Nita Nova (San Juan). Mary
then disappears in Europe for years, to return after the
beginning of World War II as Johnny sings "You Keep Coming
Back Like a Song" on Jed's program, where the lovers are
reunited. Tony (DeWolfe) is Johnny's waiter-captain, a
former vaudevillian, and paired with Nita. Songs include "A
Pretty Girl Is Like a Melody" by a chorus and reprised by
Astaire, "I've Got My Captain Working for Me Now" with
DeWolfe, "You'd Be Surprised" by Juan, "All By Myself" with
Caulfield, "A Serenade to an Old-Fashioned Girl" by Caul-
field and male quartet, "Puttin' on the Ritz" by Astaire,
"(I'll See You in) C-U-B-A" with Juan, "A Couple of
Song-and-Dance Men" with Astaire, "You Keep Coming Back Like
a Song" with quartet and reprised with chorus, "Always" by
chorus and reprised solo, "Blue Skies" and reprised by
Caulfield, {a Crosby medley: "The Little Things in Life,"
"When You Said I'm Yours," (or "Not for All the Rice in
China"), "A Russian Lullaby,"} "Steppin' Around" (or "Everybody Step"), "How Deep Is the Ocean" with chorus, "(Running
Around in Circles) Getting Nowhere" to Grimes, "Heat Wave"
by Juan, and another Crosby medley: "Any Bonds Today," "This
Is the Army, Mr. Jones," "White Christmas" (set in Okinawa).
    NOTE: "You Keep Coming Back Like a Song" was nominated
for an Academy Award for best original song, losing to "On
the Atcheson, Topeka and the Santa Fe." The premiere occurred in several cities, the same night Bing's new Philco
Radio Show premiered on ABC, and Paramount's New York stage
show featured Stan Kenton's Orchestra, the King Cole Trio,
and others. Four songs were new: "(Running Around) Getting
Nowhere," "A Couple," "You Keep Coming Back," and "A Serenade." Bing also recorded "Say It Isn't So," "What'll I
Do?" "All Alone," "Remember," "I'm Putting All My Eggs in
One Basket," "Cheek to Cheek," and "God Bless America" for
the soundtrack, but they were not used. He was also billed
above Astaire. Mark Sandrich, who produced and directed
Holiday Inn, died suddenly while planning Blue Skies, and
Astaire, announcing prematurely that this would be his last
musical, replaced Paul Draper at the last moment, and Ginger
Rogers was considered for Caulfield's role. The budget was
a large $3 million. Astaire continued to dance in films and
on television through most of the '50s. There were already
rumors that Dixie Crosby was ill. The 1983 Blue Skies
Again, about baseball, is not a sequel.
    "...with the redoubtable Bing, [Astaire] doubles in
song while that nipper doubles in dance in a comedy gem,
written especially for the occasion, entitled 'Two Song-and-
Dance Men.'... Naturally, Mr. Crosby, as the rolling-stone
character, has his share of the spotlight and holds it with
aggressive modesty." B. Crowther, N.Y. Times, Oct 17.
    "The songs are pleasantly familiar to the World War I
generation and, for the youngsters, they are refreshing and
solid, especially as Berlin has modernized them. . . . the
dialog is inclusive of such tongue-in-cheek cracks as 'I
like kids even better than horses' (Crosby), along with
other topical innuendos on Bing's bangtails [racing] pen-
chant. . . . If [Astaire] ever seriously thought of retiring, 'Skies' should postpone any such ideas. . . . Crosby
is Crosby although a slightly heftier Bing. He's the same
troubadour, chirping the ditties as only Crosby does even

though his waistline is somewhat more generous than behooves a juve." Abel. Variety, Sep 25.

EXTRA: Bing Crosby Productions produced Abie's Irish Rose, released Dec 27, 1946, as its second film. It was directed by Edward Sutherland, written by Anne Nichols, scored by John Scott Trotter, photographed by William Mellor, and starred Joanne Dru, Richard Norris, Michael Chekhov, Eric Blore, and Art Baker. The producers hired a rabbi, a priest, and a minister as advisers, but its sensitive religious content caused controversy, showing an Irish girl marrying a Jewish boy and the clash of their families. Although the stage play written by Anne Nichols had been a huge success on Broadway from 1922 to 1927, the movie just seemed old fashioned and bombed. The company did not produce a third feature film.

F91.   My Favorite Brunette (1947, Paramount) Guest 87 min. bw d: Elliott Nugent asst: Mel Epstein p: Daniel Dare w: Edmund Beloin, Jack Rose m, l: Ray Evans, Jay Livingston score: Robert Emmett Dolan c: Lionel Lindon e: Ellsworth Hoagland fx: Gordon Jennings. N.Y. tradeshow Feb 9
    Bob Hope, Dorothy Lamour, Peter Lorre, Lon Chaney, John Hoyt, Charles Dingle, Reginald Denny, Frank Puglia, Ann Doran, Jack LaRue, William Robertson, Alan Ladd
    Ronnie Jackson (Hope), a condemned murderer, tells reporters: he is a baby photographer with a keyhole camera who gets his chance to be a private detective in lieu of Alan Ladd (in a cameo) and tries to help Carlotta Montay (Lamour) to save her scientist father from the clutches of international criminals but becomes convicted of murder. He is saved from the gas chamber at the last moment by Carlotta's discovery of a photograph that incriminates the real murderers--to the disappointment of the anxious executioner, who exclaims, "Off?" and storms away (he is Bing Crosby in uniform). Hope says, "Boy, he'll take any kind of a part." Song: Lamour sings "Beside You."
    NOTE: Hope paid Bing $25,000 for the guest appearance, money Bing had Hope send to Gonzaga University.
    "[It] is a commendably funny film. . . . Granted that it repeats the concept of Mr. Hope as a self-inflated mouse and that it rings in [Bing] Crosby for a sight gag such as has become a standard fixture in Hopeful films." Bosley Crowther, N.Y. Times, Mar 20.
    "Curtain rings down on a solid rib." Wit., Variety, Feb 19.

F92.   Welcome Stranger (1947, Paramount) 106 min. bw d: Elliott Nugent p: Sol C. Siegel w: Arthur Sheekman ad: Sheekman, N. Richard Nash s: Frank Butler m, l: Johnny Burke, James Van Heusen score: Robert Emmett Dolan art: Hans Dreier, Franz Bachelin sd: Sam Comer, John McNeil cos: Edith Head c: Lionel Linden sound: Stanley Cooley, Joel Moss e: Everett Douglas. L.A. tradeshow Apr 28; Aug 6
    Bing Crosby, Joan Caulfield, Barry Fitzgerald, Wanda Hendrix, Frank Faylen, Elizabeth Patterson, Robert Shayne, Larry Young, Percy Kilbride, Charles Dingle, Don Beddoe, Thurston Hall, Lillian Bronson

Jim Pearson (Crosby) is a young singing physician who covers for the overdue vacation of Dr. Joseph McRory (Fitzgerald) in Fallbridge, a small village in Maine, leading to clashes between modern and traditional doctors. The elder calls the younger a "blatherskite." Trudy Mason (Caulfield) is the school teacher and volunteer at the clinic whom Dr. Pearson pursues (too obviously for New England sensibilities) at the going-away barn dance in honor of Doc McRory, while Emily Walters (Hendrix) is a teenager with a crush on the young physician. Nat Dorkas (Kilbride) is one of the colorful villagers. Doc Pearson intends to leave a disapproving town, but, urged by Mrs. Gilley (Patterson), McRory's approving maid, to talk it over with McRory, the younger wins the approval of his elder during a fishing trip. Doc Pearson becomes a hero when he saves Doc McRory's life in an emergency appendectomy assisted by Trudy and then helps him save his dream of becoming the first superintendent of a new hospital by exposing an incorrect diagnosis by his out-of-town competitor, Dr. Ronnie Jenks (Young), who diagnosed the dizziness of youths smoking cigars as equine encephalitis. Songs include "Smile Right Back at the Sun," "My Heart Is a Hobo," "Country Style" at a square dance, "Smack in the Middle of Maine," and "As Long as I'm Dreaming."

"[The film] misses by a considerable margin the high mark in entertainment established by ['Going My Way']. . . . Credit for [the light bantering spirit of the film], no doubt, can be shared by [the writer and director], but we are inclined to give the lion's share to the Messrs. Crosby and Fitzgerald. Both tower over the script through sheer personality, and especially is this true in Mr. Crosby's case, for Mr. Sheekman has not invested the character of Jim Pearson with much substance." Thomas M. Pryor, N.Y. Times, Aug 7.

"Crosby and Fitzgerald take obvious pleasure in their friendly antagonist roles as young and old doctors. . . . Tag of many of smart cracks will be lost in audience roars." Brog., [Hollywood, Apr 29] Variety, Apr 30.

F93.   Road to Hollywood (1947, Astor) 55 min. bw d: Bud Pollard p: Robert M. Savini ad: John E. Gordon, Charles P. Boyle c: Frank Good, George Unholz, Don Malkames e: Pollard. ca. May 7
Bing Crosby, Luis Alberni, Ann Christy
Compilation of four Educational-Mack Sennett shorts purporting to show how Bing began in Hollywood, narrated by Pollard, president of the Eastern Chapter of the Screen Director's Guild. Songs: "I Surrender Dear," "At Your Command," "Out of Nowhere," "Wrap Your Troubles in Dreams," "I'd Climb the Highest Mountain," "Just One More Chance," "Mine, All Mine," and "When I Take My Sugar to Tea."
NOTE: The Sennett shorts were bought by "Bob" Savini, the president of Astor Pictures, and later by Raymond Rohauer.

"Savini and Pollard did a creditable job on editing the briefies, managing to integrate a faint story line with them. . . . this picture proves, at least, how terrific [Crosby] was when he first hit the Coast." Stal., Variety, May 21.

NOTE: Paramount considered casting Bing in 1947 in
"Adventures of a Ballad Hunter" on the life of folk-singer
John Avery Lomax (1867-1948), who collected American songs,
but the film was not produced. And Alex Korda, head of
London Films, announced in 1947 an untitled film written by
Damon Runyon and starring Bing Crosby, but it fell through.

F94.   Variety Girl (1947, Paramount) 93 min. col d:
George Marshall p: Daniel Dare w: Edmund Hartmann, Frank
Tashlin, Robert Welch, Monte Brice score, md: Joseph Lilley
a: Van Cleave m, l: Johnny Burke-James Van Heusen, Allan
Roberts-Doris Fisher, Frank Loesser, others ch: Billy
Daniels, Bernard Pearce c: Lionel Lindon, Stuart Thompson
fx: Gordon Jennings, Farciot Edouart e: LeRoy Stone. N.Y.
tradeshow Jul 11; Oct 15
          Mary Hatcher, Olga San Juan, DeForest Kelley,
William Demarest, Frank Faylen, Frank Ferguson, Glen Tryon,
Ann Doran, Edgar Dearing, and others, with Bing Crosby, Bob
Hope, Gary Cooper, Ray Milland, Alan Ladd, Barbara Stanwyck,
Paulette Goddard, Dorothy Lamour, Veronica Lake, Sonny
Tufts, Joan Caulfield, William Holden, Lizabeth Scott, Burt
Lancaster, Gail Russell, Diana Lynn, Sterling Hayden, Robert
Preston, John Lund, William Bendix, Barry Fitzgerald, Cass
Daley, Howard DaSilva, Billy DeWolfe, Macdonald Carey, Mona
Freeman, and others; director-producers: Cecil B. DeMille,
Mitchell Leisen, Frank Butler, George Marshall; specialties
by Pearl Bailey, Jim and Mildred Mulcay, Spike Jones and the
City Slickers, Wanda Hendrix, Mikhail Rasumny, George
Reeves, and others, and a Puppetoon by George Pal
          Catherine Brown (Hatcher) goes from vaudeville to a
Paramount screen test, learning much inside information on
the trials and techniques of filmmaking and Hollywood,
including the Brown Derby, aspiring starlets, and parties.
J.R. O'Connell (Ferguson) discovers Catherine at a theater
owned by Bill Farris (Tryon), and later Catherine and O'Con-
nell found the Variety Clubs movement as a philanthropy for
children. Crosby and Hope appear as themselves in a golf
sketch and as side-show vaudevillians in checkered suits at
a Variety Club benefit emceed by Hope. Songs include
"Tallahassee" by Ladd, Lamour, and others; "Harmony" by
Crosby, Hope, and others; and "Tired" by Pearl Bailey.
Other songs are "He Can Waltz," "Your heart," "I Must Have
Been Madly in Love," "I Want My Money Back," "Impossible
Things," and "The French."
          NOTE: This was another in the series of Paramount all-
star extravaganzas since The Big Broadcast of 1932. Betty
Hutton, the only Paramount star not included, was expecting
a baby. Based on Catherine "Variety" Sheridan's rise from a
waif, discovered in 1928 at John H. Harris's Sheridan Theater, Pittsburgh, and the founding, with Robert O'Donnell, of
the philanthropic Variety Clubs movement--O'Donnell becomes
J.R. O'Connell in the film, and Harris becomes Bill Farris.
The checkered suits Bing and Hope wear are the same they
wear in Road to Utopia. Bing recorded "Tallahassee" on Mar
26, 1947, but never recorded "Harmony."
          "The picture . . . follows the pattern established some
years ago by the Paramount studio for its 'Big Broadcast'
productions, but the new effort gets across with much more
zip and bang." Thomas M. Pryor, N.Y. Times, Oct 16.

"[The film] emerges a socko entertainment. . . . [Hope] and Crosby click with their 'Harmony' routine, a socko number for all its paraphrasing of the 'Friendship' routine out of 'Du Barry Was a Lady' which Bert Lahr and Ethel Merman made famous.' _Variety_, Jul 16.

F95.   _Road to Rio_ (1947, Paramount) 100 min. bw d: Norman Z. McLeod asst: Oscar Rudolph p: Daniel Dare w, s: Edmund Beloin, Jack Rose m, l: Johnny Burke, James Van Heusen md: Robert Emmett Dolan va: Joseph J. Lilley ch: Bernard Pearce, Billy Daniels art: Hans Dreier, Earl Hedrick sd: Sam Comer, Ray Moyer fx: Gordon Jennings, Paul Lerpae, Farciot Edouart cos: Edith Head mu: Wally Westmore c: Ernest Laszlo sound: Harold Lewis, Walter Oberst e: Ellsworth Hoagland. L.A. tradeshow Nov 10, 1946; Feb 18
        Bing Crosby, Bob Hope, Dorothy Lamour, Gale Sondergaard, Frank Faylen, Joseph Vitale, George Meeker, Frank Puglia, Nestor Paiva, Robert Barrat, Stanley Andrews, Harry Woods, the Stone-Barton Puppeteers, the Carioca Boys, the Weire Brothers, the Andrews Sisters, Jerry Colonna
    A cartoon over the music to the samba "Brazil" (or "Brasilia") blended with "But Beautiful" presents the titles. Scat Sweeney (Crosby) and Hot Lips Barton (Hope), musicians down on their luck, flee irate husbands. Scat is the wide-ranging Romeo, saying he's Sinatra in Oklahoma and Gene Autry in Texas before they join a carnival in Louisiana, which is accidentally torched after Scat "volunteers" Hot Lips as an aerialist. They escape by stowing away to Rio de Janeiro on the S.S. _Queen of Brazil_. In a cold locker they find meat labeled, "Crosby Stables, Grade AA?" Scat romances Lucia Maria de Andrade (Lamour), and he and Hot Lips seek to aide the distressed damsel, who is being forced into marrying Sherman Malloy (Meeker) against her will by her hypnotizing aunt, Catherine Vail (Sondergaard), and swindlers Trigger and Tony (Faylen and Vitale). Under a spell, Lucia reports Scat and Hot Lips. They ply the pat-a-cake routine to escape and hide in the ship's barber shop, but an irate customer causes their capture. Lucia arranges their release to join the ship's orchestra. When the captain returns Scat's pipe, he says, "Well, my old heater. Now I can smoke up and learn the truth." Lucia finds a cable Sherman sends Mrs. Vail, advising an immediate marriage as Rodrigues (Puglia) has learned about certain papers. In Rio Scat and Hot Lips pick up a dopey trio of Latins (Wiere Brothers) whom they teach a little hep talk to work in the nightclub of Mr. Cardoso (Paiva). They are hypnotized into a ineffectual duel with each other, and Rodrigues pays for a small airplane to carry them to the coffee plantation to retrieve the papers from Mrs. Vail's safe (eight people are in the two-seat plane). Rodrigues stays behind to get help, but they get the papers and have to entertain in disguise at Lucia's wedding party, doing an impromptu version of the samba "Brasilia." Trigger and Tony recognize them, but they give the mysterious papers to the prefect, saving the dazed girl and incriminating the wicked aunt without needing the attempt at rescue by a troop of gauchos led by Colonna and Rodrigues, who never arrive. Lucia selects Hot Lips for her mate, a mystifying choice clarified in their honeymoon suite at Niagara Falls when,

peeking through the keyhole, Scat sees him hypnotizing her. Songs include "Apalachicola, F-L-A" with Hope (including "Swanee River," "Carry Me Back to Old Virginy"), "But Beautiful," "You Don't Have to Know the Language" with the Andrews Sisters, "Experience" by Lamour, a parody of the samba "Brazil" with Hope, and "For What?" by the Andrews Sisters.

NOTE: This fifth film of the Road series may be less zany than Road to Utopia, but it is rated as one of the best. The scene in which Bing and Hope disguise themselves as natives, Hope as a Carmen Miranda and Bing as a pirate, and sing gibberish lyrics and dance the samba to "Brazil" is the recreation of an act the pair performed in 1937 at Del Mar and which Hope has said most brought them to the attention of Paramount producers.

". . . there are patches in this crazy quilt that are as good and, perhaps, even better than anything the boys have done before. . . . Hope reluctantly doing a high-wire bicycle act and wrecking a carnival in the process, or being unceremoniously hung up as a side of ham in a ship's refrigerator, or blowing musical bubbles out of a trumpet in a Rio de Janeiro night club may sound silly in cold print, but it's the kind of stuff that gets laughs on the screen. And, naturally, Crosby, the smoothest straight man in the business today, is in there all the time getting situations started and feeding jokes to his pal when he doesn't actually steal the play by adding a snapper to a snapper." Thomas M. Pryor, N.Y. Times, Feb 19.

"Star trio is up to all demands and gives extra punch because of obvious enjoyment of playing roles." Brog., [Hollywood, Nov 11] Variety, Nov 12.

F96.   The Baby Sitter (1947, Paramount) Cartoon Short. Bing Crosby, Bob Hope, W.C. Fields, and Jerry Colonna appear caricatured as infants performing for babies at the Stork Club.

F97.   It Happened in Brooklyn (1947, M-G-M) Mention only 105 min. bw   d: Richard Whorf.
Frank Sinatra, Jimmy Durante, Kathryn Grayson, Peter Lawford, Gloria Grahame
In one scene Durante asks Sinatra what makes Bing the singer of the age. Sinatra suggests, "His voice?" Durante replies, "It helped, but what really did it was his heart." The basic plot is about Brooklynites trying to break into show business. Songs include Sinatra singing "Time After Time" and Sinatra and Durante duet on "The Song's Gotta Have Heart."

F98.   Rough But Hopeful (1948) Short Details unknown.

EXTRA: Frank Capra wanted Bing to star with Jean Arthur in Friendly Persuasion in 1948, having sold his company, Liberty Films, and the story to Paramount. The tale was written by Jessamyn West about Quakers during the Civil War, her first novel, published in 1945, but Capra's budget of $1.5 million set by Barney Blaban, president of Paramount, was unacceptable to the director. William Wyler made the film in 1956, starring Gary Cooper and Dorothy McGuire.

Capra made two other films with Bing, in 1950 and 1951.

F99.   The Emperor Waltz (1948, Paramount) 105 min. col
d: Billy Wilder   p: Charles Brackett   w: Brackett, Wilder
score: Victor Young   m, l: James Van Heusen, Johnny Burke,
Johann Strauss   va: Joseph J. Lilley   art: Hans Dreier,
Franz Bachelin   cos: Edith Head   mu: Wally Westmore   c:
George Barnes, Natalie Kalmus   e: Doane Harrison. Hollywood
tradeshow Apr 30; Radio City Music Hall Jun 17
     Bing Crosby, Joan Fontaine, Roland Culver, Lucille
Watson, Richard Haydn, Harold Vermilyea, Sig Ruman, Julie
Dean, Bert Prival, Alma Macrorie, Roberta Jonay, Gerald
Mohr, John Goldsworthy, Doris Dowling, James Vincent, Harry
Allen, Eleanor Tennant, Vesey O'Davorn, Norbert Schiller,
Frank Elliott, Paul de Corday, Jack Gargan, Cyril Delevante,
Frank Mayo, Franco Corsaro, dogs Buttons and Scheherazade
     Virgil Smith (Crosby), an American traveling phonograph
salesman from Newark with a fox terrier named Buttons,
enters the court of Emperor Franz Joseph (Haydn) in 1901 to
introduce record players. Virgil courts a young widow,
Countess Johanna Augustus Franziska Von Stultzenberg (Fontaine), to the dismay of her father, Baron Holenia (Culver).
Virgil follows them to their hunting lodge in the Tyrol and
lamely explains, "I used to travel for a Venetian blind
company." The pooch, simulating the pose of the famous "His
Master's Voice" trademark of RCA Victor, suffers the snarls
of Johanna's poodle. The poodle becomes so nervous that a
veterinarian psychologist orders that it make friends with
Buttons, leading Johanna to bring her dog to the Golden
Fiddle Inn, where Smith is staying, and the dogs discover
they like each other. The Emperor's veterinarian, Dr.
Zwieback (Ruman), ministers to the canines. Virgil plays
his phonograph from a copse when the Emperor goes stag-
hunting, and the marching music scares away the royal prey.
Johanna helps Virgil escape the guards, and later the couple
follows her dog to Buttons on an island, where they spend
two weeks. Virgil calls her "Honey Countess." She permits
him to ask the Emperor for permission to marry, but he and
her father oppose it. Virgil pretends he was only using
Johanna, but at a ball he learns that Dr. Zwieback is about
to destroy puppies sired by Buttons. Virgil storms into the
Emperor's presence, and Johanna learns the truth. The
Emperor agrees to the marriage, and the penniless Baron
Holenia decides to marry homely Princess Bitotska (Watson).
Songs include "The Whistler and His Dog" whistled, "I Kiss
Your Hand, Madame" (from Rotter-Erwin), "Friendly Mountains"
(from Austrian yodel songs or Swiss airs), "Santa Lucia"
(Cottrau), "The Kiss in Your Eyes" (Burke-Heuberger), and
Strauss's "The Emperor Waltz," lyrics by Burke.
     NOTE: Greta Garbo was considered for the film, but she
had firmly retired seven years earlier. Filmed during the
summer of 1946 on location in Jasper's National Park, British Columbia, Canada, it was not released until after Road
to Rio. Wilder is better known for frank and penetrating
films like Five Graves to Cairo, Double Indemnity, The Lost
Weekend, Sunset Boulevard, and Ace in the Hole. For this
film, he had the side of a mountain painted, built an island
floating on gas-filled drums, painted highways, imported
4,000 white daisies, which he then decided to paint blue,

and added trees, spending $90,000 for a two-minute scene in
which the dogs meet on the island. The tennis court at
Bing's Holmby Hills home was used for one scene, and for the
ball, Wilder had to fit camp chairs under the gowns of about
250 woman so they could maintain a curtsy before the Emperor
for 70 seconds. When Buttons would not jump into a bag,
Bing yelled, "Get your damn arse right in here," and it
obeyed. For the next take Bing just looked stern, inducing
the dog to jump in on cue. The part of Baron Holenia
(Culver) is also known as Count Von Stolzenberg-Stolzenberg.
Bing said that this was the one film in which he played
"loud" (strong or aggressively in a few scenes); in other
films he played "soft." The song "The Kiss in Your Eyes"
was adapted from "Im chambre separee ("In Separate Rooms"),
a waltz by Richard J. Heuberger (1850-1914) for his operetta
Der Opernball (or The Opera Ball). Bing also sang the
Burke-Van Heusen "Get Yourself a Phonograph," which was cut
from the film.
     "[The film] is a picture which can be characterized in
a few words, but which is much more entertaining if you see
it from beginning to end. Not that there's anything stag-
gering in the way of music or plot in this spoof. . . . But,
even so, Brackett and Wilder have made up with casualness
and charm--and with a great deal of clever sight-humor--for
the meagerness of the idea. And Bing has provided the
substance which the farcical bubble may lack. . . . Our boy
is his usual delightful and completely unceremonious self,
baffled by Hapsburg pomposity and candid in his confidence
in love. . . . Bing has the air of a fellow to whom the
artificial is a bore." Bosley Crowther, N.Y. Times, Jun
18.
     "Picture has a free-and-easy air that perfectly matches
the Crosby style of natural comedy. Costar Joan Fontaine,
better known for heavy, serious roles, demonstrates adapt-
ability that fits neatly into the lighter demands and she
definitely scores with charm and talent as the Crosby foil.
One complaint likely to be made by audiences is that Crosby
doesn't sing enough." Brog., [Hollywood, Apr 30] Variety,
May 5.

F100.   A Connecticut Yankee in King Arthur's Court (1949,
Paramount) 106 min. col d: Tay Garnett asst: Oscar Ru-
dolph p: Robert Fellows w: Edmund Beloin, on Mark Twain's
1889 novel m, l: James Van Heusen, Johnny Burke score:
Victor Young, Troy Sanders va: Joseph J. Lilley special a:
Van Cleave art: Hans Dreier, Roland Anderson sd: Sam
Comer, Bertram Granger cos: Mary Kay Dodson, Gile Steele
mu: Wally Westmore c: Ray Rennahan, Farciot Edouart, Nata-
lie Kalmus, Monroe W. Burbank sound: Harold Lewis, John
Cope fx: Gordon Jennings, Jan Domela, Irmin Roberts e:
Archie Marshek. Hollywood tradeshow Feb 18; Radio City
Music Hall Apr 7
     Bing Crosby, Rhonda Fleming, Sir Cedric Hardwicke,
William Bendix, Murvyn Vye, Virginia Field, Henry Wilcoxon,
Richard Webb, Joseph Vitale, Alan Napier, Julia Faye, Mary
Field, Ann Carter
     Hank Martin (Crosby), a Hartford, CT, blacksmith cum
automobile mechanic, visits Pendragon Castle in England in
1912, finding familiar armor and a portrait of his "fair

maiden." He shows Lord Pendragon (Hardwicke), ill in bed,
the amulet that matches the one in the painting and tells
his tale: He is knocked unconscious when Tex, his horse,
bolts in a storm and Hank's head hits a low tree limb. He
awakens in Camelot of A.D. 528. Captured by Sir Clarence
Sagramore l'Desirous (Bendix), a Knight of the Round Table
in squeaky armor, Hank is condemned as a monster to burn at
the stake. Later "Saggy" says, "If there were aught I could
do to save thee." Hank replies, "Well, ain't there aught?"
He first avoids execution by using a watch lens as a magni-
fying glass to fire the execution order and Merlin's (Vye's)
gown, and a wooden match to intimidate his superstitious
prosecutors. Hank gains notoriety as a wizard, is knighted
"Sir Boss," and is given a blacksmith shop with "Saggy" as
his squire. At a ball King Arthur (Hardwicke), suffering
the same sniffles as Lord Pendragon, shouts to the trumpet-
ing herald, "Stop the music!" [an allusion to a TV show].
Hank teaches musicians to play with a beat, saying, "Putteth
in the brass and taketh out the lead." Wooing Alisande La
Carteloise (Fleming), Arthur's niece who is betrothed to Sir
Lancelot (Wilcoxon), Sir Boss has to joust his mighty romantic competitor, shunning armor to defeat him cowboy style on
Tex with a lariat. He calls his Lady "Sandy," devises a
safety pin for her, useful on diapers, and constructs a
revolver, which "Saggy" plays with. Hank finds injustice in
the kingdom, and, when the king joins him and "Saggy" to
inspect the kingdom as peasants, they and Sandy are captured
by Sir Logris (Vitale) and sold as slaves to their captor.
Merlin and Morgan La Fay (Field) connive to control the
Kingdom and Lady Alisande, whom Merlin and Sir Logris
(Vitale) kidnap. After an escape in which only "Saggy" gets
away (to bring Hank's pistol to him), Hank saves himself and
the king from the executioner's axe by pretending to cause
an eclipse of the sun with such invocations as "Walla Walla,
Washington." He found the eclipse listed in his Handbook of
Mechanics and Almanac. Freed, he goes to the castle of Sir
Logris to rescue Sandy; Logris observes him coming with an
anachronistic spyglass. Hank is again struck unconscious
after shooting Sir Logris with his pistol. He concludes his
tale to Lord Pendragon, after which he meets the lord's
niece (also Fleming), who resembles Sandy, and they embrace.
Songs include "If You Stub Your Toe on the Moon," "When Is
Sometime?" by Fleming, "Busy Doing Nothin'" with Bendix and
Hardwicke, and "Once and for Always" with the musicians,
solo, and with Fleming.
    NOTE: Filmed in fall of 1948, Bing gave Fleming her
first film kiss after she sang a duet with him on "Once and
for Always," imitating his "boo-boo-booing." Fleming was
25, twenty years Bing's junior, and she was linked romanti-
cally to him in 1953. Bing also sang "Twixt Myself and Me,"
which was cut from the film. The script by Beloin is closer
to Mark Twain's original than are any of the other film
adaptations, including a forgotten one with Tennessee Ernie
Ford as a Tennessean at King Arthur's Court. Fox filmed the
novel in 1921 with Harry C. Myers and Pauline Stark, and in
1931 as a talkie with Will Rogers, Maureen O'Sullivan, Myrna
Loy, Frank Albertson, and William Farnum, directed by David
Butler. Crosby's use of a lariat instead of a lance in
jousting was first done by Rogers. Unable to use the music

Rodgers and Hart wrote for the 1927 stage musical written by
Herbert Field, which was bought by M-G-M, Paramount used
songs by Burke and Van Heusen. The unlikely trio of Crosby,
Bendix, and Hardwicke made a hit record of "Busy Doing
Nothin'." The eclipse is film of an actual solar event. A
major theme of the film, as in Twain's novel, is the power
of technology.

        ". . . we can thank Bing Crosby, primarily and above
all, because it is Bing in the role of the Yankee who gives
this film its particular charm. . . . But it is still
Bing's delightful personality, his mild surprises and sweet
serenities, and his casual way of handling dialogue that
makes this burlesque a success. No one in current operation
could qualify, we are sure, to play the Connecticut Yankee
the way the old Groaner does." Bosley Crowther, N.Y. _Times_,
Apr 8.
        "It's closer to the Twain story than the 1921 silent
film starring Harry Myers and the 1931 Will Rogers version.
. . . Picture wears the easy casualness that's a Crosby
trademark, goes about its entertaining at a leisurely pace,
and generally comes off satisfactorily. . . . Crosby does a
lot better by the picture than its costumes do by him. His
face and figure are comically displayed in tights, jerkin
and wig without the heroic qualities that more modern tai-
loring endows, but such is his personality that he overcomes
the handicaps. It's his picture and he sparks it." Brog.,
[Hollywood, Feb 10] _Variety_, Feb 23.

        EXTRA: The popularity of television affected films, and
Crosby's next few features were not very successful, finan-
cially or artistically.
        Producer Charles Feldman wanted Bing to star in "The
Silver Whistle" in 1949, the role created on Broadway by
Jose Ferrer of a vagabond poet who stole from the rich and
gave to the poor. The film may never have been produced.

F101.   _Top o' the Morning_ (1949, Paramount) 99 min. bw
d: David Miller   p: Robert L. Welch   w: Edmund Beloin,
Richard Breen   m, l: Johnny Burke, James Van Heusen   md:
Robert Emmett Dolan   va: Joseph J. Lilley   ch: Eddie Prinz
art: Hans Dreier, Henry Bumstead   sd: Sam Comer, Emile Kuri
cos: Mary Kay Dodson   c: Lionel Lindon   sound: Philip Wis-
dom, Gene Garvin   ta: Arthur Shields   e: Arthur Schmidt.
N.Y. tradeshow July 14; Aug 31
        Bing Crosby, Ann Blyth, Barry Fitzgerald, Hume
Cronyn, Eileen Crowe, John McIntire, Tudor Owen, Jimmy Hunt,
Morgan Farley, John Eldredge, John "Skins" Miller, John
Costello, Dick Ryan, Mary Field
        Joe Mulqueen (Crosby), an investigator for an American
insurance company, goes to Ireland to capture the omadhaun
who stole the Blarney Stone. Sergeant Briany McNaughton
(Fitzgerald) and his addled assistant, Hughie Devine (Cronyn), of the Civil Guard ignore the disdain of his superior
officers of Cork, especially Inspector Fallon (McIntire),
jail Joe, disguised as a vacationing painter. Joe sings his
way into the hearts of the villagers, suspects ale-drinking
McNaughton, meets and romances his daughter, Conn (Blyth),
battles Irish superstitions and dark prophecies proclaimed
by Biddy O'Devlin (Crowe), and uses them as a ruse with the

aid of Pearse O'Neill (Hunt) to catch the crook in a wild
scramble down a hillside. Joe restores the stone to the
Blarney Castle wall. <u>Songs</u> include "You're in Love with
Someone," "Top o' the Morning," "Oh, 'Tis Sweet to Think,"
"Beautiful Kitty," "The Donovans," and Irish airs like "When
Irish Eyes Are Smiling."

" . . . the picture's effect is both agreeable and
jauntily good-humored." <u>Newsweek</u>, Sep 12.

" . . . Mr. Crosby wends a happy and comfortable course
through the whole incredible proceedings, taking complacent-
ly in stride the fitful abuse of Mr. Fitzgerald and the
romantic rue of Ann Blyth. . . . And his natural way with a
wise-crack brightens many a darkening spot." Bosley Crowther, N.Y. <u>Times</u>, Sep 1.

"Groaner, despite his having to play to a gal (Ann
Blyth) who is so obviously younger, is socko. His easy way
with a quip, combined with his fine crooning of some old
Irish tunes and a couple of new ones, is solid showmanship."
Stal., <u>Variety</u>, Jul 20.

F102.   <u>Jolson Sings Again</u> (1949, Columbia) Voice only 96
min. col d: Henry Levin.
    Larry Parks, Barbara Hale, William Demarest,
Ludwig Donath
    A loose version of the life of Jolson, a continuation
of <u>The Jolson Story</u> (1946), including Parks playing Jolson
but now also Parks meeting Jolson. Bing is heard in one
scene singing "Learn to Croon."

F103.   <u>The Adventures of Ichabod and Mr. Toad</u> (1949, Walt
Disney Production, RKO release) Voice (Narration and Songs)
68 min. Animation col d: Jack Kinney, Clyde Geronimi,
James Algar p: Ben Sharpsteen w: Erdman Penner and others,
based on Washington Irving's "The Legend of Sleepy Hollow"
(1820) and Kenneth Grahame's <u>The Wind in the Willows</u> (1908)
anim: Franklin Thomas, Oliver Johnston, Jr., Wolfgang Rei-
therman, Milt Kahl, John Lounsbery, Ward Kimball, and others
songs: Don Raye, Gene De Paul md: Oliver Wallace va: Ken
Darby o: Joseph Dubin sound: C.O. Slyfield, Robert O. Cook
e: John O. Young, Al Teeter. N.Y. tradeshow Aug 19; Oct 1
    Bing Crosby narrates and sings in <u>The Adventures</u>
<u>of Ichabod</u>, accompanied by the Studio Chorus; Basil Rathbone
(narrator), Eric Blore, and Pat O'Malley are the voices of
the first segment.
    A two-part cartoon, the first segment is the British
tale of aristocratic Mr. Toad, bored by Toad Hall and his
animal companions, likes fast automobiles and airplanes, and
barely defends himself against the charge of driving a
stolen car, sold to him by thieving weasels. Following a
transition spoken by Crosby, the second segment, with all
voices by Crosby, has Ichabod Crane, an aspiring but clumsy
and superstitious schoolmaster who seeks the money and
affections of Katrina Van Tassel, finally outwitted and
scared witless by Brom Bones, the "burly, roistering blade"
who leads the Sleepy Hollow Boys at Ye Olde Schnooker and
Schnapps Shoppe, and by the terrifying Headless Horseman.
<u>Songs</u> are "Ichabod (Who's That Coming Down the Street?),"
Singing Practice, "Katrina," a vocalized jig without lyrics,
and "The Headless Horseman."

NOTE: The video of <u>The Legend of Sleepy Hollow</u> and two
short cartoons released in 1982 lists only Crosby of the
performers, leaves the musical accompaniment and songs
anonymous, and omits Crosby's transition of introducing "Old
Icky" by observing that the "colonies" also produced some
notable characters. Crosby voices the full range of his
playful inflections. Bing recorded his songs Dec 24 (with
the Rhythmaires) and 30, 1947.
        "In the second episode Bing Crosby introduces the
Sleepy Hollow legend as if it were a new brand of breakfast
cereal. And factually true to Irving though it remains, the
resulting narrative is just about as tasteless as the Crosby
prelude. . . . [The] 'headless horseman' [is] likely to
scare children." <u>Newsweek</u>, Nov 10.
        "The amiable Mr. Crosby's narration and the couple of
songs he casually tosses in with the assistance of the
Rhythmaires, is smooth and professional. . . . The credits
outweigh the debits and Mr. Disney has included enough
elements of entertainment to make his newest film package a
solid entertainment." A.H. Weiler, N.Y. <u>Times</u>, Oct 10.
        "[The film] ranks among the best full-length cartoons
turned out by the Walt Disney studios. . . . In both cases,
it pars Disney's standard for excellence." Herm., <u>Variety</u>,
Aug 24.

F104.   <u>Down Memory Lane</u> (1949, Eagle-Lion) Anthology
70 min. bw d: Phil Karlson p: Aubrey Schenck. Preview,
N.Y. RKO Colonial Sep 6
        Bing Crosby, W.C. Fields, Donald Novis, Gloria
Swanson, Mabel Normand, Ben Turpin, Phyllis Haver, Franklin
Pangborn, Charlie Murray, James Finlayson, Mack Swain,
Irving Bacon, Frank Nelson, Yvonne Pettie, Steve Allen, Mack
Sennett, Keystone Cops
        Film is a collection of Sennett comedy shorts from the
silent days to the early talkies, with Steve Allen serving
as the thread, as a disc jockey in a television studio
searching frantically for sight material between the commercials. Sennett himself appears at the studio at the end.
        "[The film] provides personalities extending from the
Keystone Cops to the then young Bing Crosby. . . . Bulk of
this feature is made up of shorts starring Crosby in his
salad days. These shorts have faded more quickly than the
one in which the Keystone Cops roared to the rescue in their
1915 flivvers. While the early films have a genuine antique
flavor, the Crosby shorts of the early 1930s are just plain
old-fashioned. They're good for some mild laughs only.
Crosby's vocalizing on a flock of oldies, however, is pleasant to take." Herm., <u>Variety</u>, Sep 14.

F105.   <u>It's in the Groove</u> (1949) Short Unknown.

F106.   <u>Honor Caddie</u> (1949) 20 min. Unknown.
        Bing Crosby, Bob Hope, Ben Hogan, Chick Evans
        NOTE: One photograph from the film with Bing, Evans,
Hogan, and four caddies appears in the Mar-Apr 1992 issue of
<u>Golf Journal</u>, reprinted in <u>Bing</u> 101 (Aug 1992): 36. Bing
sings "Tomorrow's My lucky Day," although some list the song
as "Don't Hook Now" (never commercially released), and <u>Bing</u>
magazine speculates that the film may have reappeared as

<u>Faith, Hope and Hogan</u> (1953), F121, with Bob Hope.   "Tomor-
row's" was recorded for Columbia in Dec 1957.

F107.   <u>The Road to Peace</u> (1949, 20th Century-Fox) 18 min.
bw d: Larry Webb p: Col. J.R. Cunningham.   College of St.
Rose, Albany, Dec 8
          Bing Crosby, Ann Blyth, Father Patrick C. Peyton,
Rod O'Connor as narrator
          Film emphasizes world-wide daily prayer and Family
Rosary as the reliable road to peace;   Bing and Blyth sing
"When Irish Eyes Are Smiling" and narrate portions.   Filmed
at the College of St. Rose, Albany, it is on 16 mm; the
Hollywood studio donated its equipment and planned a 35 mm
version.
          "Crosby's voice, on miniature film track, naturally
does not sound as smooth as on standard gauge in a theatre,
and several of the medium-range shots are not over-flatter-
ing, but few viewers probably will notice it."   Jaco.,
<u>Variety</u>, Dec 14.

          EXTRA: Paramount announced in 1949 that William Boyd,
famous as Hopalong Cassidy, would make a dozen films in six
years and that the first would probably be a Western with
Bing Crosby.   Producer Paul Jones announced that one script
had been written, but Bing did not appear in any of them.
          Paramount announced in 1950 that the next <u>Road</u> film
with Bing, Hope, and Lamour would be <u>Road to Paris</u>, but it
never materialized.

F108.   <u>Riding High</u> (1950, Paramount) 112 min. bw d, p:
Frank Capra asst: Arthur Black w: Robert Riskin, Melville
Shavelson, Jack Rose s: Mark Hellinger new songs: Johnny
Burke, Jimmy Van Heusen md: Victor Young (assoc. Troy
Sanders) va: Joseph J. Lilley art: Hans Dreier, Walter
Tyler sd: Emile Kuri cos: Edith Head mu: Wally Westmore
c: George Barnes, Ernest Laszlo, Farciot Edouart sound:
Hugo Grenzbach, John Cope e: William Hornbeck.   N.Y. pre-
view Dec 15, 1949; Front Royal, Va., Apr 1, 1950; N.Y. Apr
10
          Bing Crosby, Colleen Gray, Charles Bickford,
Frances Gifford, with William Demarest, Raymond Walburn,
James Gleason, Ward Bond, Clarence Muse, Percy Kilbride,
Harry Davenport, Margaret Hamilton, Paul Harvey, Douglas
Dumbrille, Gene Lockhart, Marjorie Hoshelle, Rand Brooks,
Willard Waterman, Marjorie Lord, Irving Bacon, Joe Frisco,
Charles Lane, Frankie Darro, Dub Taylor, Oliver Hardy
          Dan Brooks (Crosby) runs away from Higginsville and his
position as head of the Paper Box Company owned by rich J.L.
Higgins (Bickford), to gamble on a racehorse, Broadway Bill.
The horse ran a practice mile at 1:42.   J.L.'s sons-in-law,
Henry Early and Arthur Winslow (Brooks and Waterman), also
run divisions and are aghast, and Dan's fiancee, J..L.'s
third daughter, Margaret (Gifford), refuses to go with him.
As help Dan has Alice Higgins (Gray), J.L.'s fourth daughter, Happy McGuire (Demarest), and Whitey (Muse), the sta-
bleboy, who also encounter a succession of track characters
(from Oliver Hardy and Joe Frisco to Max Baer and Ish Kabibble).   After Dan enters the horse in the Imperial Derby
against favored Gallant Lady, Professor Pettigrew (Walburn)

and Happy McGuire (Demarest) attempt to bilk Dan as Dan seeks money from the Professor for financing. They leave a restaurant without paying, complaining of the noise they began by singing. The horse becomes ill, pining for Skeeter, his pet white rooster, and recovers when it is brought by Alice, whom Dan calls "Princess." The Professor convinces Pop Jones (Kilbride), the stable owner, not to worry about expenses for the horse's stall and feed. The horse becomes feverish in the leaking barn, Margaret refuses to cancel the wedding, and J.L. bets on Broadway Bill. The Professor and Happy take $25 from Oliver Hardy for a tip on Doughboy, and Hardy spreads the false tip, which returns and induces the Professor to bet on him. Doughboy loses and Hardy faints. Alice pawns valuables and gives the money to Whitey for Dan, telling him to say he won it at cards. Millionaire J.P. Chase (Lockhart) bets $2 on Broadway Bill, leading to rumors he had bet $200,000, which temporarily lowers the odds. Dan is jailed for striking a deputy that whipped Broadway Bill while evicting him, but crooked gamblers Eddie Howard and Lee (Dumbrille and Bond) pay the bail and plot to make the horse lose, ridden by Ted Williams (Darro), their own jockey. The jockey tries to lose, but Broadway Bill wins, inspired by Skeeter. Being ill, the horse immediately dies. Broadway Bill is buried in the infield, with a eulogy by the Racing Secretary (Gleason). J.L., having watched the race on TV with his butler Johnson (Davenport), arrives without Margaret and later sells his companies. Bing arrives at the mansion shouting, "Release the princess from the dark tower." J.L. joins Dan and Alice, who have two new horses on their way to Santa Anita. Songs include "Sure Thing," "Someplace on Anywhere Road" with Muse, "Whiffenpoof Song" with Walburn and chorus, "Sunshine Cake" with Muse and Gray and reprised with Gray, "The Horse Told Me" with others, and Stephen Foster's "Camptown Races" with chorus.

     NOTE: Capra directed the same script as Broadway Bill (1934, Columbia), with Warner Baxter and Myrna Loy, reused much footage for the remake, and retained many original actors, like Walburn, Muse, Dumbrille, Bond, Darro, and Harvey. Some actors reappear in 16-year-old footage, as in the gambling room where Bond is much younger (age 21 rather than 37). Capra had been frustrated by Baxter's fear of horses and vowed to remake the film. Demarest took the late Lynne Overman's role. The 1934 film was released in the United Kingdom as Strictly Confidential. For the remake Capra insisted on Bing, knowing he liked horses, and his budget was limited to $1.5 million as Harry Cohn of Columbia allowed Paramount to use its original negative in return for Capra's and his Liberty Film's story of Woman of Distinction (1950) for the film that starred Rosalind Russell and Ray Milland. Capra, working with a three-film contract, wanted Joan Leslie for the female lead, but Bing insisted on Colleen Gray. New racetrack scenes were shot in ten days south of San Francisco, where the horse's funeral was filmed in less than a day as bad weather threatened. The song "Sunshine Cake" was not pre-recorded, and the direct recording, including Bing on spoons and Muse with a guitar and a box, worked so well without background music that other songs were also recorded direct. Freeman "Bones" Davis taught

Bing to play the spoons. Joe Venuti on violin, Ish Kabibble
(Merwyn Bogue) on cornet, and Candy Candido on bass play for
"The Horse Told Me." The world premiere was held at Front
Royal, VA, on Apr 1, as Bing dedicated their Bing Crosby
Stadium, raising $15,000. Apr 1 was Bing Crosby Day there
for five years. A 1943 film with Dorothy Lamour and Dick
Powell titled Riding High is unrelated to Bing's film.
Capra also directed Bing in Here Comes the Groom and hoped
to produced a film on the life of Jimmy Durante with Bing
and others, a film that never materialized.
     "'Riding High' beats [the original] by a nose--or
rather, by Mr. Crosby's casual and gay personality, which
leaps to the front at the barrier and paces the picture all
the way. . . . And the striking thing is that the screen
play . . . has not been perceptibly changed to fit Mr.
Crosby's personality or his natural disposition to star.
way with a horse--as well as with music and people--gives
that quality of richness to this film that makes it not only
amusing but deeply ingratiating, too," Bosley Crowther,
N.Y. Times, Apr 11.
     "Racetrack pix have been traditionally tough to sell
because they seem to lack femme appeal. That's certainly
not the story with this entry, however, for while a large
part of the action takes place around a gee-gee oval, the
combo of Hellinger and Capra has imbued the yarn with such
humor, good-natured pathos and real heart that the track
angle is strictly incidental to the bigger human angles
involved." Herb., Variety, Jan 11.

F109.   The Old Grey Hare (ca. 1950, Warner Bros.) Mention
Cartoon 7 min. col d: Robert Clampett anim: Robert
McKimson voices: Mel Blanc md: Carl W. Stalling.
     In this "Merry Melodies" cartoon Elmer Fudd chases Bugs
Bunny through 1950 and into the year 2000, waking up Rip Van
Winkle style, and finds a newspaper, the Daily Rocket, with
the banner headline, "Bing Crosby's Horse Hasn't Come In
Yet!" over a photograph of Bing peering through a spyglass
down the racetrack. The subhead reads: "Bing's bangtail
bungles on home stretch." Wrinkled Fudd finds a Buck Rogers
Lightning Quick Rabbit Killer and vainly pursues Bugs, who
has glasses, a cane, and a white goatee.

F110.   Mr. Music (1950, Paramount) 110 min. bw d:
Richard Haydn asst: Harry Caplan p: Robert L. Welch w:
Arthur Sheekman s: Samson Raphaelson's play Accent on Youth
m, l: Johnny Burke, James Van Heusen a: Van Cleave o:
Joseph J. Lilley, Troy Sanders ch: Gower Champion fx:
Farciot Edouart c: George Barnes e: Doane Harrison, Ever-
ett Douglas. Preview, N.Y. Paramount, Aug 23; Dec 20
          Bing Crosby, Nancy Olson, Charles Coburn, Ruth
Hussey, Robert Stack, Tom Ewell, Ida Moore, Charles Kemper,
Donald Woods, Marge and Gower Champion, Claud Curdle [really
Director Richard Haydn], Groucho Marx, Dorothy Kirsten,
Peggy Lee, the Merry Macs
     Paul Merrick (Crosby), a lazy songwriter who prefers
playing golf, arrives at his alma mater, Lawford College, to
see a revival of one of his musicals. A crowd at the rail-
road station celebrates athlete Jefferson Blake (Stack), not
Paul. Paul is accompanied by his producer, Alex Conway

(Coburn), and is supervised by a bossy alumni representative, Katherine Holbrook (Olson), who forces Paul to sing for the students and write a line about Jeff in the show. Paul's factotum-caddy is Haggerty (Ewell), whom Paul calls Cupcake. Paul pawns his awards and asks Alex for $15,000. Paul agrees to write another musical, after three years of golf, and Alex hires Kathy to assure Paul's industriousness. Alex's last four plays were bombs. Kathy's Aunt Amy (Moore) is the chaperone at Paul's penthouse. Jeff asks Paul to get tickets to a play and decides to take Kathy, who realizes her feelings for Paul. Jeff does chinups and jumps chairs at the penthouse, which Paul fails to duplicate. When the songs for <u>Mr. Music</u> are written, Paul gives a party at which Peggy Lee and Marge and Gower Champion perform. Lovelorn Jeff blames Paul for his poor performance in the high jump, for Kathy ignores him, and states that it would be Paul's fault if America does not win in the Olympics. Paul agrees to marry Lorna Marvis (Hussey), who has jilted a backer named Tippy Carpenter (Woods), who offered her a $49,000 diamond. Lorna accepts Paul's $96 ring, and Carpenter refuses to back the play. Jerome Thisby (Curdle/Haydn) offers $300. To find reasonable backers Paul and Kathy stage the musical at Lawford. Groucho Marx explains his presence as "investigating the student body," and, walking off with three girls, he says, "I hope I don't lose my faculties." The Merry Macs, Marx, and Kirsten perform, but the millionaires refuse to back Alex. Finally, Thisby gets the numbers right and provides the $300,000. Lorna tells Paul she has accepted Carpenter's ring and Jeff leaves Kathy to Paul's arms. Paul claims to be an athlete, does chinups, and obscures Kathy's view to keep her from seeing Jeff doing one-arm chinups. <u>Songs</u> include "Once More the Blue and White" by chorus, "Milady," "And You'll Be Home" with chorus and reprised by chorus, "High on the List," "Wouldn't It Be Funny?" "Accidents Will Happen" and reprised with Kirsten, "Was I There?" "Life Is So Peculiar" with Lee, by the Merry Macs, and by Bing and Marx, and "Mr. Music" by the chorus.
    NOTE: Bing thought the title presumptuous, noting that "I know relatively little about music," and he partly blamed that on the film's weak showing. Bing is seen singing one of his songs to a tape recorder designed by the Ampex Company he financed. Kirsten was an opera star and sings a duet with Bing in an "Opera vs. Vaudeville" scene. Bing hit such a good drive for the golfing scene that he followed it to complete a round while the cast and crew had to wait. The film is a remake of <u>Accent on Youth</u> (1935), directed by Wesley Ruggles and starring Sylvia Sidney, Herbert Marshall, and Philip Reed, and was again remade as <u>But Not for Me</u> (1959), directed by Walter Lang and starring Clark Gable, Carroll Baker, and Lilli Palmer. Bing recorded all the songs but two ("Wasn't I There?" and "Mr. Music") in Mar, Apr, and Jun 1950. Stack, age 30, was attempting to emerge from the stereotype of a college tennis player, which he suffered from since his film debut in 1939 and overcame only in 1954 as the copilot to John Wayne in <u>The High and the Mighty</u>, directed by William A. Wellman.
    "To brighten the Christmas season, our old friend, Bing Crosby, is in town in a role (and an entertainment) that fits him--and he it--like a glove. . . . Der Bingle (which

rhymes with Kris Kringle, we trust you will incidentally
note) plays an easy-going song-writer. . . . There's no
point in being coy about it: Bing has not been too fortu-
nate in the general characteristics of his roles in the past
three or four films. But in this light, romantic entertainment . . . he acts the sort of droll, informal fellow that
he himself happens to be. . . . It is notable that little
condescension to the so-called juvenile taste is evident
here." Bosley Crowther, N.Y. Times, Dec 21.

"The crooner-star does a good job in a role wherein he
fits in easily, and might well have been a truly convincing
characterization if not snarled by the cliche elements. By
and large, however, Crosby makes the part breathe." Abel.,
Variety, Aug 30.

F111.   Here Comes the Groom (1951, Paramount) 113 min.
bw d, p: Frank Capra w: Virginia Van Upp, Liam O'Brien,
Myles Connolly s: Robert Riskin, O'Brien m, l: Jay Living-
ston, Ray Evans, Johnny Mercer, Hoagy Carmichael md: Joseph
J. Lilley cos: Edith Head c: George Barnes, e: Ellsworth
Hoagland. Hollywood tradeshow Jun 29; Sep 20
Bing Crosby, Jane Wyman, Alexis Smith, Franchot
Tone, James Barton, Robert Keith, Jacques Gencel, Beverly
Washburn, Connie Gilchrist, Walter Catlett, Alan Reed, James
Burke, Irving Bacon, Ted Thorpe, Art Baker, Anna Maria
Alberghetti, Laura Elliot, Dorothy Lamour, Frank Fontaine,
Louis Armstrong, Phil Harris, Cass Daley
Pete Garvey (Crosby), a carefree newspaperman who aids
war orphans, returns to Boston from a long assignment in
Paris with two war orphans (Gencel and Washburn) whom he can
adopt if he marries within five days, but his ex-fiancee,
Emmadel Jones (Wyman), tired of waiting, is about to marry
wealthy Wilbur Stanley (Tone). On the returning airplane,
Pete sings with Armstong, Lamour, Harris, and the cameo
company returning from a U.S.O. tour. Degnan (Keith) is
Pete's helpful editor. Emmadel's seafaring father (Barton)
supports Pete, though her mother (Gilchrist) would rather
she married rich. Allowed by Wilbur to try to re-win Emmadel, Pete pitches the orphans, songs, and Winifred Stanley
(Smith), who loves her kissing-cousin Wilbur, at his problem, and finally a phony FBI officer (Burke) to break up the
garden wedding at the last second. Pete wins Emmadel and
Winifred catches her kissing cousin. Songs include "Bonne
nuit," "In the Cool, Cool, Cool of the Evening" with Wyman,
"Your Own Little House," "Misto Cristofo Columbo" with guest
stars, and "Caro nome" from Rigoletto by Alberghetti.
NOTE: "In the Cool, Cool, Cool of the Evening," sung
by Crosby and Wyman, won the Academy Award as the best
original song of 1951. It was an elaborately staged song
that begins in the lavish offices of the rich Bostonite,
trails down the elevator, and out onto the sidewalk. Capra,
noted for penetrating human-interest films, also directed
Bing in Riding High. The world premiere was held at Elko,
Nevada.
"Again the calculated coincidence of Frank Capra and
Bing Crosby . . . has resulted in a light, breezy item,
nicely marked with the genial Capra touch and adorned with
the cheerful disposition and the casual vocalizing of Bing.
it has to have children in it--and children mean sentiment.

use describing him--except to note that he looks a little
thinner and a little wearier under the weight of the years.
Pretty soon Mr. Crosby will have to stop playing carefree
scamps and he'll have to side-step such frisky numbers as
'In the Cool, Cool, Cool of the Evening,' which he plugs
here. He'll have to stick to the less exhausting efforts.
out of him. . . . And it's better than television, as someone says." Bosley Crowther, N.Y. _Times_, Sep 21.
      "Crosby is at his casual best, nonchalantly tossing his
quips for the most effect. Miss Wyman is a wow as the
girlfriend who makes him really work to win her." Brog.,
[Hollywood, Jul 6] _Variety_, Jul 11.

F112.   <u>Two Tickets to Broadway</u> (1951, RKO) Image only
106 min. col   d: James V. Kern   p: Howard Hughes   w: Sid
Silvers, Hal Kanter   s: Sammy Cahn   m, l: Jule Styne, Leo
Robin, Sammy Cahn, Bob Crosby, Al Hoffman, Leo Corday, Leon
Carr, Rodgers and Hart   score: Walter Scharf   ch: Busby
Berkeley   c: Edward Cronjager, Harry J. Wild, Jerry Wald,
Norman Krasna   e: Harry Marker. N.Y tradeshow Oct 8; Nov 21
      Tony Martin, Janet Leigh, Gloria DeHaven, Eddie
Bracken, Ann Miller, Smith and Dale, Barbara Lawrence, Joe
Smith, Charles Dale, Taylor Holmes, Buddy Baer, Bob Crosby
      Lew Conway (Bracken) connives to get Dan Carter (Mar-
tin), Nancy Peterson (Leigh), Hannah Holbrook (DeHaven), and
Joyce Campbell (Miller) on Bob Crosby's television variety
show. Bob Crosby acts under Bing's cloud, for Nancy Peterson from Pelican Falls, Vermont, falsely accuses Bob of
being afraid of competition, unlike Bing, and the question
of whether singer Carter is any good is settled when Bob's
manager states that Bing likes him. When Conway succeeds in
booking Carter and the act, he has to persuade Nancy at the
last minute to get off a Greyhound bus bound for Worcester
and Boston. Carter wins Nancy's heart at the end of the
show. <u>Songs</u> include an elaborate number in which Bob Crosby
sings on his TV show "Let's Make Comparisons" by Sammy Cahn
and Bob Crosby about the public's comparison between him and
big brother Bing, who "appears" as a garishly dressed pipe-
smoking mannequin that later strolls alive off stage. The
song states the Bob Crosby dresses more tastefully, has not
Bing's big ears, is not "f-a-t-s-o" like Bing, that Bob has
gone from Pop Crosby's youngest son, to Bing Crosby's brother, to Gary Crosby's uncle, and concludes that the "song is
all in fun" and that he "would rather be the brother of Bing
than anyone." Martin sings "The Closer You Are" with
Leigh, "<u>Pagliacci</u>," "There's No Tomorrow," "Are You a Beautiful Dream?" and "Big Chief Hole-in-the-Ground." Others
sing "Baby, You'll Never Be Sorry," "The Worry Bird" by
Crosby, "Pelican Falls," "It Began in Yucatán," and the
Rodgers-Hart "Manhattan."
      " . . . the newcomer is merely conventional in plot,
brisk in pace, heavily freighted with song and light in
comedy." N.Y. _Times_, Nov 22.
      "[The film], said to be one of the oldest off RKO's
unreleased shelf, comes to the screen as a breezy Technicol-
or musical replete with shapely girls and catchy tunes."
Gilb., _Variety_, Oct 10.

F113.   <u>You Can Change the World</u> (1951) 20 min. bw d:

Leo McCarey   p: William Perlberg.
     A short made for the Christopher Association with
Loretta Young, Ann Blyth, Irene Dunne, Jack Benny, Bing
Crosby, Bob Hope, Eddie "Rochester" Anderson, William Hold-
en, Paul Douglas. Bing sings "Early American" by Johnny
Burke and Jimmy Van Heusen, recorded Mar 3, 1945, and Jun
23, 1950.

F114.   A Millionaire for Christy (1951, 20th Century-Fox)
Voice only 90 min. bw d: George Marshall p: Bert E.
Friedlob-Thor w: Ken Englund s: Robert Harari m: Victor
Young e: Daniel Mandell. Hollywood tradeshow Jul 25
     Fred MacMurray, Eleanor Parker, Richard Carlson,
Una Merkel, Kay Buckley, Douglas Dumbrille, Raymond Green-
leaf, Nestor Paiva, Chris-Pin Martin, Walter Baldwin
     Christy Sloane (Parker) is a legal secretary sent from
San Francisco to Los Angeles to inform Peter Ulysses Lock-
wood (MacMurray), a radio philosopher engaged to marry June
Chandler (Buckley), of a $2 million inheritance. Patsy
(Merkel) has advised Christy, "Stop being legal, and be
lovely," to interest Lockwood. Lockwood's best friend,
psychiatrist Dr. Roland Cook (Carlson), loves June and walks
out of the wedding. Lockwood chases him with Christy.
Christy manages to marry Lockwood after they are rescued by
Mexicans after a tidal wave and after he is duped into
giving his money to charity. Dr. Cook gets June. An unseen
Crosby sings "I Don't Stand a Ghost of a Chance with You" to
Victor Young's music in a hotel scene.
     "[The film] is, despite the transparency of its plot
and the broad histrionics of the players, who seem to be
having a good time, too, an infectious trifle, which is as
harmless and palatable as a bon bon." A.W., N.Y. Times, Oct
5.
     "Miss Parker and MacMurray are an excellent team and
pull all stops in selling their goofy characters. . . .
Victor Young's music score deserves mention." Brog., Variety, Aug 1.

F115.   Angels in the Outfield (1951, M-G-M) Guest 99
min. bw d, p: Clarence Brown w: Dorothy Kingsley, George
Wells s: Richard Conlin m: Daniele Amfitheatrof art:
Cedric Gibbons, Edward Cartagno c: Paul C. Vogel e: Robert
J. Kern. Hollywood tradeshow Aug 22
     Paul Douglas, Janet Leigh, Keenan Wynn, Lewis
Stone, Spring Byington, Bruce Bennett, Donna Corcoran,
Marvin Kaplan, Jeff Richards, John Gallaudet, King Donovan,
Bing Crosby, Joe DiMaggio, Ty Cobb, Harry Ruby
     Guffy McGovern (Douglas), the tyrannical and profane
manager of a losing Pirates baseball team, benefits after
the angelic spokesman of Heavenly Choir Nine announces one
evening at second base of a miracle in the third inning of a
crucial game and of winning the pennant if McGovern reformed
and became humane. Orphan Bridget White (Corcoran) had
prayed to the Angel Gabriel to intercede. The miracle
occurs and McGovern accepts. Fred Bayles (Wynn) is a boisterous baseball announcer out to get McGovern. Sisters
Edwitha (Byington) and Veronica (Corby) are Pirates fans.
Jennifer Paige (Leigh), a reporter of household hints for a
Pittsburgh paper, interviews Bridget, who can see angels

assisting the Pirates. McGovern, hit by a foul ball, admits
angels are helping them and has to defend his sanity to the
Commissioner of Baseball, Arnold P. Hapgood (Stone); the
team wins the league pennant and everyone learns true
values. Joe DiMaggio, Ty Cobb, Harry Ruby, and Bing Crosby
make surprise appearances.
    NOTE: The games were filmed at Forbes Field of the
Pittsburgh Pirates, a team partly owned by Bing Crosby; the
film was released during the 1951 World Series, when the New
York Yankees defeated the New York Giants four games to two.
    " . . . this combination of whimsy, sports, religious
faith and romance is a heart-warming and edifying amalgam
which can pass the test of what is traditionally termed
entertainment." A.W., N.Y. _Times_, Oct 18.
    "It has so many points to recommend it, reviewers will
be at a loss where to start. First and foremost for the
fans' standpoint, probably, is the film bow of little Donna
Corcoran. Moppet has been heralded as 'another Shirley
Temple,' and she lives up to the billing." Mike., _Variety_,
Aug 29.

F116.   The Fifth Freedom (1951, Chesterfield Cigarettes)
ca. 10 min. col p: Louis de Rochemont.
    Arthur Godfrey, Perry Como, Bob Hope, Bing Crosby
    A propaganda film stressing the freedom of choice,
filmed during the Korean War. Bing appears in a loud jacket
and straw hat to _sing_ "You're a Grand Old Flag." The film
was discovered about 1983 by Bob DeFlores in an abandoned
theater in Iowa.

F117.   The Greatest Show on Earth (1952, Paramount) Guest
153 min. col d, p: Cecil B. DeMille ap: Henry Wilcoxon
w: Frederic M. Frank, Barre Lyndon, Theodore St. John s:
Frank, St. John, Frank Cavett ch: John Murray Anderson m,
l: Victor Young, Ned Washington, John Ringling North, E. Ray
Goetz, Henry Sullivan, Anderson score: Young c: George
Barnes e: Anne Bauchens. N.Y. tradeshow Dec 13, 1951; ca.
Jan 10, 1952
    Betty Hutton, Cornel Wilde, Charlton Heston,
Dorothy Lamour, Gloria Grahame, James Stewart, Henry Wilcox-
on, Lyle Bettger, Emmett Kelly, John Ringling North, Frank
Wilcoxon, Henry Ringling, cast of the Ringling Brothers-
Barnum & Bailey Circus, with Bing Crosby, Bob Hope, and
others as members of the audience during a circus perform-
ance
    Holly (Hutton) is a trapeze artist competing with
Sebastian (Wilde) and yearns for Brad (Heston), the circus
manager. Sebastian pursues Holly and takes a literal fall.
Heartless Angel (Grahame), the girl on an elephant, wants
Brad, making the pachyderm trainer, Klaus (Bettger), jealous, even as he places an elephant's foot over her nose in
an act. A detective (H. Wilcoxon) noses around, tracking
down a physician who is wanted for murder. Crosby and Hope
eat peanuts in the bleachers during Lamour's number of
"Lovely Luawana Lady," a hula number, while the chorus girls
swing from ropes. Brad fires nasty Klaus, who retaliates
with a robbery that leads to a spectacular train wreck in
which the villain dies. Buttons (Stewart), a clown and the
wanted physician who remains disguised, heals Brad and

Sebastian. Brad is injured in the wreck but makes sure the
show goes on, even with an injured cast. Holly gets Brad
and Angel decides on Sebastian. About 85 authentic acts
appear.
    NOTE: The film won Oscars for best picture and best
story. Other stars appear in the bleachers, including Mona
Freeman.
    "Everything in this lusty triumph of circus showmanship
and movie skill betokens the way with the spectacular of the
veteran Mr. DeMille." Bosley Crowther, N.Y. Times, Jan 11.
    "There's a sock laugh when two intent, peanut-eating
bleacherites prove to be Bing Crosby and Bob Hope." Herb.,
Variety, Jan 2, 1952.

F118.   Son of Paleface (1952, Paramount) Guest 95 min.
col d: Frank Tashlin asst: Bill Watson p: Robert L. Welch
w: Tashlin, Welch, Joseph Quillan m, l: Jay Livingston, Ray
Evans, Jack Brooks, Jack Hope, Lyle Moraine md: Lyn Murray
art: Hal Pereira, Roland Anderson sd: Sam Comer, Ray Moyer
ch: Josephine Earl cos: Edith Head mu: Wally Westmore c:
Larry J. Wild, Gordon Jennings, Paul Lerpae, Farciot Edouart, Richard Mueller sound: Gene Merritt, Walter Oberst e:
Eda Warren. Hollywood preview, Jul 8; Oct 1
    Bob Hope, Jane Russell, Roy Rogers and Trigger,
Bill Williams, Lloyd Corrigan, Paul E. Burns, Douglas Dumbrille, Harry Von Zell, Iron Eyes Cody, Wee Willie Davis,
Charles Cooley, Charles Morton, Don Dunning, Bing Crosby
    Junior Potter (Hope) is a cowardly Harvard braggart who
goes West and tries to avoid his father's debts. He becomes
embroiled with Roy Barton (Rogers) and Doc Lovejoy (Corrigan), government agents who suspect Mike (Russell), a saloon
owner, of leading a gang of gold robbers, including Kirk
(Williams). Ebenezer Hawkins (Burns) is Junior's partner,
helping him con Sheriff McIntyre (Dumbrille) and banker Pre.
Stoner (Von Zell). Once Junior has to share a bed with
Trigger. Mike woos Roy and Junior pursues Mike and wins,
for Roy prefers his horse. Songs include "Buttons and Bows"
(reprised from Bob Hope's The Paleface [1948]) by Hope,
"What a Dirty Shame" by female chorus, "Wing-Ding Tonight"
by Russell, "California Rose," "Four-Legged Friend" by
Rogers, and "Am I in Love?" by Hope and Russell.
    NOTE: "Buttons and Bows," sung by Bob Hope, had won an
Academy Award as best song of 1948. The film lampoons
Western film cliches. Bing Crosby appears briefly in an
opening cameo (literally an oval corner of the screen) to
comment on "Junior's" ineptness. Cecil B. DeMille and
Robert Welch also make guest appearances.
    ". . . What is delivered in this colored package is a
wild farce that comes so close to the style of those old
'Road to --' pictures of Mr. Hope, Bing Crosby and Dorothy
Lamour that you might almost shut your eyes (if you can
manage) and think you are enjoying one of the same." Bosley
Crowther, N.Y. Times, Oct 2.
    "There a jibe at video when Hope remarks: 'Let's see
'em top this on television.'" Brog. Variety, Jul 16.
F119.   Just for You (1952, Paramount) 95 min. col d:
Elliott Nugent p: Pat Duggan w: Robert Carson s: Stephen
Vincent Benet's "Famous" m, l: Harry Warren, Leo Robin md:
Emil Newman va: Joseph J. Lilley art: Hal Pereira, Roland

Anderson sd: Sam Comer, Ray Moyer cos: Edith Head, Yvonne
Wood mu: Wally Westmore c: George Barnes, Farciot Edouart,
Natalie Kalmus, Monroe W. Burbank fx: Gordon Jennings, Paul
Lerpae e: Ellsworth Hoagland. N.Y. preview Jul 10; Oct 8
        Bing Crosby, Jane Wyman, Ethel Barrymore, Robert
Arthur, Natalie Wood, Cora Witherspoon, Ben Lessy, Regis
Toomey, Art Smith, Leon Tyler, Willis Bouchey, Herbert
Vigran, Joel Marston, the Mexican Ballet
     Jordan Blake (Crosby), a widowered Broadway producer
obsessed with his career, sings "Call me Tonight," a song by
his son, Jerry (Arthur), but berates it and him when he says
he is going to pay to publish it. Jerry's friend is David
MacKenzie (Tyler). Jordan bails his daughter, Barbara
(Wood), out of jail and fires her drunken governess, Miss
Angevine (Witherspoon). He compensates for previous neglect
by taking a vacation with his children to the Adirondacks,
where he charms Allida de Bronkhart (Barrymore), unaware
she's the headmistress of St. Hilary's, the finishing school
Barbara hopes to attend. Jerry, age 18, thinks Carolina
Hill (Wyman), Jordan's musical star and girlfriend, returns
his affection while she is trying to explain that she and
his father hope to marry. Jordan, thinking to entertain by
singing "Trees" at a school tea party, meets Georgie Polans-
ski (Lessy), an old musician friend, and they give out with
vaudevillian hokum. Barbara is accepted by the school, and,
back in New York, Carolina tells the press that she and
Jordan would marry. Jerry, who has written "Just for You"
for Carolina, distrusts his father's praise of the song,
keeps it to himself, and joins the Air Force. Jordan goes
on a U.S.O. tour to find Jerry, locating him in Alaska,
where he has matured and, before the show starts, delivers
Carolina to his father. Songs include "I'll Si-Si Ya in
Bahia" with chorus, "He's Just Crazy for Me" by Wyman, "Call
Me Tonight" by Arthur and Tyler, reprised by Bing, "Checkin'
My Heart" by Wyman and chorus, "Zing a Little Zong" with
Wyman, "Flight of Fancy" (music only), "The Live Oak Tree"
with a female chorus, "The Maiden of Guadalupe" by Wyman
with chorus, "On the Ten-Ten from Ten-Ten-Tennessee" with
Lessy, "Just for You," and "Spring Fever" (music only).
     NOTE: "Zing a Little Zong" was nominated for an Acade-
my Award but lost to "Do Not Forsake Me." Filming began Nov
1951 at Paramount and much of the film was made near Stock-
ton, California, 60 miles east of San Francisco. Judy
Garland was supposed to be the co-star, but she backed out
to perform on stage, at which time Bing's close friend, Jane
Wyman, accepted the role. Bing phoned Harry Warren one day
at 6 a.m. about writing the music, and both settled on Leo
Robin for the lyrics because Johnny Mercer was unavailable.
Robin and Warren also wrote "Spring Fever" and "Flight of
Fancy" for the film, but they were used only as background
music, although Bing recorded them in Feb 1952 along with
two others with the Andrews Sisters. Two other songs were
recorded by Decca May 8. Bing was at Paramount in early
1952 when Charlie Chaplin rented the studio for three days
to film scenes for Limelight (1952, American premiere in
1972). Jerry Epstein, Chaplin's assistant, thought Bing
annoyed in the Commissary. Variety listed the film as the
17th most profitable of the year and earned $2.9 million in
North America. Ethel Barrymore was a Crosby fan, and for

her elaborate 70th birthday celebration and 50th year in show business transcribed for radio (R93) Aug 15, 1949, President Harry Truman opened the show, Winston Churchill spoke, and Bing sang "Happy Birthday."

"Solemnly, anxiously, benignly, the greying Bingle appears as a widower dad who is torn between sparking Jane Wyman and squaring himself with his [son]. . . . Whether the line of procedure arranged by the writer . . . would be approved by the real Crosby Pere is open to question, however--and we seriously doubt that it would. For the real Bing, they say, is realistic--and this little story is not. . . . the ideas are worked out in pretty tedious talk, which we rather image Mr. Crosby, as a practicing papa, would eschew." Bosley Crowther, N.Y. <u>Times</u>, Oct 9.

"[The film] should prove a stout factor in bringing back that 'lost' audience.' . . . [It] will not only satisfy the 'under 35' trade but will recapture some of the older public who have temporarily lost the film-going habit. . . . With fine material to work with, Crosby socks across one of his best portrayals." Gilb., <u>Variety</u>, Aug 6.

EXTRA: Bing wanted the lead in <u>Come Back Little Sheba</u> (1952), but Burt Lancaster got the role. Paramount proposed <u>Guys and Dolls</u> in 1952 for Bing and Bob Hope, but Samuel Goldwyn produced it in 1955 starring Marlon Brando and Frank Sinatra. Bob Hope appears with Mickey Rooney and Marilyn Maxwell in <u>Off Limits</u> (1953), a boxing film for Paramount, in which Bing is briefly shown singing on television in a bar. The title in the U.K. is <u>Military Policemen</u>.

F120.   <u>Road to Bali</u> (1953, Paramount) 91 min. col d: Hal Walker asst: John Coonan p: Harry Tugend w: Frank Butler, Hal Kanter, William Morrow s: Butler, Tugend m, l: Johnny Burke, James Van Heusen md: Joseph J. Lilley special o: Van Cleave ch: Charles O'Curran art: Hal Pereira, Joseph McMillan Johnson sd: Sam Comer, Ross Dowd cos: Edith Head mu: Wally Westmore fx: Gordon Jennings, Paul Lerpae, Franciot Edouart c: George Barnes sound: Gene Merritt, John Cope e: Archie Marshek. Hollywood preview Nov 14, 1952; Jan 29, 1953

Bing Crosby, Bob Hope, Dorothy Lamour, Murvyn Vye, Peter Coe, Ralph Moody, Leon Askin, cameos by Bob Crosby and Jane Russell, and scenes with Humphrey Bogart, Dean Martin, Jerry Lewis

George Cochran (Crosby) and Harold Gridley (Hope), rascally vaudevillians, flee Melbourne, Australia, and two irate fathers, don beards shorn from sheep, and become divers for a prince, Ken Arok (Vye), of Vatu. Each has offered the other as the diver and himself as the pumpman, unaware that four divers have already been killed by Boga Ten, a giant squid. They compete for the affection of Princess Lalah McTavish (Lamour), and Harold takes a basket and flute that conjure up a dancing girl. George practices and produces a heavy woman. When Harold says, "That Lalah! She intoxicates me," George takes a sniff and replies, "Could be; she's half scotch." When Lalah wonders where the pirates are back in the States, George explains: "The Pirates are probably hiding in the cellar somewhere." When Harold finds a bottle with a note for redeeming it for three cents at a market, George says, "Every movie has to have a message." They are hunting for sunken jewels lost when McTavish, Lalah's father, went down with his ship at a reef. George connives Harold into the diving suit, and he finds the treasure and fights Boga Ten. Harold escapes, but Boga Ten sweeps Ken Arok overboard. They sail for Bali to sell the jewels, when Hope steps out of character to say, "He's gonna sing, folks. Now's the time to go out and get the popcorn." George sings "To See You" and proposes, angering Harold, who calls George "a collapsible Como." Lalah recalls being lonely at age seven and having a monkey with Harold's face; then Harold tells Lalah that he does George's singing. They become shipwrecked, swim to an island, and Bob Crosby appears and fires a rifle. George explains, "That's my brother Bob. I promised him a shot in the picture." Then they see Humphrey Bogart pulling The African Queen through the swamp and leaving his 1951 Oscar behind. George tells Lalah, "I'm just an average American boy with an excess of charm," and Lalah has a dream of Dean Martin and Jerry Lewis. A female gorilla steals Harold, and, arguing whether the word is breast or beast in the aphorism, George sings "To See You" to soothe her. Harold pleads with George to keep singing, "And if you get tired, call Gary." Cannibals shoot the men with arrows tipped with "the laughing twitch" fluid and capture them and Lalah. She refuses to bow to Bhoma Da (Moody), the high priest of Newatah, and learns that her father was the benefactor of the natives. They let her marry both George and Harold, whose pat-a-cake routine fails again. Ken Arok arrives and persuades King Ramayana (Askin) to kill Lalah, braving the wrath of the volcano. The wedding is for the two boys, who drink the twitching potion and wake up with each other. Then the volcano erupts, allowing them to save Lalah and escape with the jewels. On the beach, Harold finds a basket, Lalah picks George, Harold draws Jane Russell out of the basket, and both women walk away with George, leaving Harold trying to stop the end of the picture. Songs include "Road to Bali" by a chorus, "Chicago Style" with Hope, "Whiffenpoof Song (Poor Little Lambs)" with Hope and "sheep," "Moonflowers" by Lamour twice, "Hoot Mon" with Hope, "To See You," "The Merry-Go-Runaround" with Hope and Lamour, and "Chant Erotica" by a chorus.

NOTE: This was the sixth Road film, rated among the best of them by Leonard Maltin, and the first in color. Bing, Hope, and Paramount each spent about $350,000 and split the considerable profits. It was filmed from about May to Aug 1952, months after Bogart won his Oscar in March. Lamour, no longer contracted to Paramount, was allowed to co-star. A long water ballet scene with Lamour was cut from the film, and most of the animal shots were from the Paramount vault. Paramount had to send to Scotland for several bolts of McTavish tartan for Bing's and Hope's kilts, and Lamour wore seven sarongs, the longest and shortest of her career, although it had been eight years since she wore one in a film. Bing celebrated a birthday, for which Lamour gave him a one-candle cake; and Hope celebrated a birthday, for which Bing showed him a gag edition of Variety with the headline, "Crosby Breaks In New Boy: Entertainment King Auditions New Stooge Replacement," over a large picture of

Bing and Jerry Lewis. The quotation argued over is by
William Congreve, to wit: "Music has charms to soothe a
savage breast" (1697). Lamour was upset when Bing and Hope
recorded "The Merry Go Runaround" with Peggy Lee on Jun 24,
1952.
    "Not since their 'Road to Rio,' some five years ago, in
fact, had this free-wheeling team of comedians been seen
together in a film. And now that they're back in 'Road to
Bali' . . . the outrage of their collective absence is just
beginning to sink in. For, all of a sudden, it is apparent
that this veteran and camera-scarred team is the neatest,
smoothest combo of comics now working the fun side of the
screen. Apart, they may be very funny or clever or quaint
or what you will, according to where you are sitting and
what sort of picture they're in. But together, and in a
'Road' picture, with the consequent freedom of style and
reckless impulse that goes with it, they are pretty nigh
nonpareil. At least, that's the word of this reviewer who
spent a small part of yesterday falling out of a seat at the
Astor while desperately clutching his sides." Bosley
Crowther, N.Y. _Times_, Jan 30.
    "Bing Crosby, Bob Hope and Dorothy Lamour are back
again in another of Paramount's highway sagas, this time in
Technicolor, with nonsensical amusement its only destination. That end is reached eventually, but the road isn't a
smooth highway and the entertainment occasionally falters."
Brog., _Variety_, Nov 19.

F121.   _Faith, Hope and Hogan_ (1953, Christopher Association) Short p: Father Keller.
    The priest filmed Bing Crosby, Bob Hope, and Ben Hogan
at a golf match in Palm Springs, CA, and televised it on his
Sunday religious program.
    NOTE: Bob Hope writes in his book _This Is on Me_ that
the film involved "an hour and a half of dialogue between
golf shots. . . . I imagine that Bing was labeled Faith on
account of his role in _Going My Way_." Cf. F106, _Honor
Caddies_ (1949).

F122.   _Scared Stiff_ (1953, Paramount) Guest 106 min. bw
d: George Marshall p: Hal Wallis w: Herbert Baker, Walter
DeLeon, Ed Simmons, Norman Lear s: play by Paul Dickey,
Charles W. Goddard m, l: Mack David, Jerry Livingston md:
Joseph J. Lilley art: Hal Pereira, Franz Bachelin cos:
Edith Head mu: Wally Westmore c: Ernst Laszlo fx: Gordon
Jennings, Paul Laerpe sound: Hugo Grenzbach, Walter Oberst
e: Warren Low Hollywood preview ca. Apr 12; Jul 2
    Dean Martin, Jerry Lewis, Lizabeth Scott, Carmen
Miranda, George Dolenz, Dorothy Malone, William Ching, with
Frank Fontaine, and Crosby and Bob Hope as surprise guests
    Larry Todd (Martin) and Myron Mertz (Lewis), having be-
friended a gun moll (Malone), flee a jealous New York gangster and go with heiress Mary Carroll (Scott) to help her
claim her zombie-haunted island near Cuba against the plots
of Tony Warren (Ching), who knows there is gold under the
castle. Larry and Myron discover that a clue means that
notes on an old organ reveal a treasure-laden hidden cellar.
Then Cortega (Dolenz) is killed and Tony is exposed. At the
end Tony peers through an opened stone to see skeletons with

shaking heads of Bing and Bob Hope. Songs include "I Don't Care If the Sun Don't Shine" by Martin, "What Have You Done for Me Lately" by Martin and Lewis, "San Domingo" by Miranda with Martin and Lewis, "When Someone Wonderful Thinks You're Wonderful" by Martin, "You Hit the Spot" by Martin, "The Enchilada Man" by Martin and Lewis, and "Mama yo quiero [I Want My Mama]" by Miranda, reprised by Lewis.

NOTE: The film is a remake of the 1940 Bob Hope film Ghost Breakers with the same director. Two silent versions appeared in 1915 with H.B. Warner and in 1932 with Wallace Reid. Bing recorded "Mama yo quiero" on Jan 18, 1942.

"It is true that the play by Paul Dickey and Charles W. Goddard . . . did an unqualified service for Bob Hope's 'The Ghost Breakers' [1940] some thirteen years ago. . . . But somehow the farcical humor . . . throwing unholy terror into the person of Mr. Hope does not emerge in the responses of Mr. Martin and Mr. Lewis to the same things." Bosley Crowther, N.Y. Times, Jul 3.

"Dean Martin & Jerry Lewis are back in a free-wheeling round of slapstick hilarity--the kind they do so well. . . ." Brog., Variety, [Hollywood, Apr 14] Apr 15.

EXTRA: Another Road film with Bing, Bob Hope, and Marilyn Monroe was announced, to be called "Road to the Moon," but it did not materialize.

F123.   Little Boy Lost (1953, Paramount) 95 min. bw d, w: George Seaton asst: Francisco Day p: William Perlberg ap: Arthur Jacobson s: novel by Marghanita Laski m, l: Johnny Burke, James Van Heusen score: Victor Young art: Hal Pereira, Henry Bumstead sd: Sam Comer, Ross Dowd cos: Gladys de Segonzal, Edith Head mu: Wally Westmore c: George Barnes, Farciot Edouart, Loyal Griggs fx: Gordon Jennings sound: Harry Mills, Gene Garvin e: Alma Macrorie. Hollywood preview Jul 2; Sep 21

Bing Crosby, Claude Dauphin, Christian Fourcade, Gabrielle Dorziat, Nicole Maurey, Colette Dereal, Georgette Anys, Henri Letondal, Michael Moore, Peter Baldwin, Gladys de Segonzal, Yola d'Avril, Bruce Payne, Jean Del Val, Adele St. Maur, Ninon Straty, Paul Magranville, Christiane Fourcade, Jacques Gallo, Karin Bengay, Tina Blagoi, Arthur Dulac

Bill Wainwright (Crosby) is an American radio reporter married to a Parisian singer named Lisa Garret (Maurey), and they have a son, John (Fourcade, age 8). At a fair Bill wins a toy dog, which they name Binkie, and the outbreak of war separates them. His wife, a member of the Resistance, gives her son to friends before the Nazis kill her. Bill searches through France from 1944 to 1947 and returns to America. Pierre Verdier (Dauphin) summons Bill in Oct 1948 with news, and Bill learns from a laundress, Madame Quilleboeuf (Anys), that she had passed a child called "Boo-boo" to an orphanage. There, counseled by the Mother Superior (Dorziat), he finds a weakling now named Jean, whom he walks with doubts to the railway station. Persuaded to bring the boy to Paris, Bill sings to him and shows him old sights. The laundress has the boy pretend to recognize his mother's perfume, but Bill sees through it and returns the boy. Bill takes a blonde named Nellie (Dereal) to a fair and wins a toy dog like Binkie, which he sends to Jean. Pierre admon-

ishes Bill to forget his morbid dreams of Lisa and makes him
hear the account of her death. At the station, a train
whistle reminds Bill of Lisa's nightmare of a lonely boy
needing help, which sends him to the orphanage. Bill
watches as Jean recognizes Binkie, and Bill takes the boy's
hand to lead him out. Songs are "Mon coeur est un violon"
by Maurey, "The Dark Town Strutter's Ball" with Maurey (with
passages in French), "A propos de rien [Apropos of Nothing]"
by Maurey, reprised by Bing, "Oh Susanna" by boy chorus, reprised by Fourcade, "Cela m'est égal" ["It's All the Same to
Me"], usually called "If It's All the Same to You," "Sur le
pont d'Avignon" by Dauphin and Fourcade, "Frère Jacques"
with Dauphin and Fourcade, and "The Magic Window."
     NOTE: The film was shot mainly in Paris in 1952 and
premiered Sep 21, 1953, at the Rivoli Theatre in New York as
a benefit for the Overseas Press Club. Bing reshot a scene
in Paris in May 1953. The film was among the year's top 20
in earnings, and Film Daily named it the ninth best of the
year. At Fourcade's insistence, his mother, Christiane
Fourcade, played a maid and his father a barker at the
circus. Paramount bought the film rights from actor John
Mills. The author was at first aghast that Bing would play
the British intellectual as a singing American but was
pleased with the performance. Maurey had her American film
debut and returned seven years later to co-star with Bing in
High Time. While filming the final railroad depot scene,
Bing received a letter from his wife's doctor, informing him
her cancer was terminal; Seaton was struck by Bing's excellent performance of despondency. While filming studio
scenes later he met Kathryn Grandstaff (renamed Grant).
     "A considerable departure for Bing Crosby from the sort
of picture and the type of role that he has been accustomed
to playing. . . . Except for two or three song numbers that
are worked in consistently, there are few other points of
contact with the bright and chipper Bingle of old. And yet
it must be said for Mr. Crosby that he manages to convey a
strong sense of real emotional torment in a tragically
wracked character and that he serves as a credible buffer in
a candidly heart-socking film. . . . [Christian Fourcade]
has the eyes, the expression and the voice that would tear
the heart out of a heathen idol and a sure sense of the
drama he plays. . . . And Mr. Seaton's command is equally
evident in the performance Mr. Crosby gives. . . ." Bosley
Crowther, N.Y. Times, Sep 22.
     "[It is a film] with an obvious pitch at family audi-
ences. . . . [It] doesn't come off with the tremendous
heart impact of the original, or of the television version
seen only a season or two back, although it does have suffi-
cient moving moments to be satisfactory family filmfare."
Brog., [Hollywood, Jul 7] Variety, Jul 8.

F124.   Popeye's 20th Anniversary (1954, Paramount) Caricature Short col.
     Popeye's testimonial dinner is hosted by Bob Hope.
Olive Oyl, Bing Crosby, Dean Martin, Jerry Lewis, and others
appear in the audience.

F125.   White Christmas (1954, Paramount) 120 min. col
d: Michael Curtiz asst: John Coonan p: Robert Emmett Dolan

w: Norman Krasna, Norman Panama, Melvin Frank m, l: Irving
Berlin md, va: Joseph J. Lilley a: Van Cleave, Troy Sand-
ers ch: Robert Alton art: Hal Pereira, Roland Anderson
sd: Sam Comer, Grace Gregory fx: John P. Fulton cos: Edith
Head mu: Wally Westmore c: Loyal Griggs, Farciot Edouart,
Richard Mueller sound: Hugo Grenzbach, John Cope e: Frank
Bracht. Hollywood preview, Aug 23; Radio City Music Hall,
Oct 14
          Bing Crosby, Danny Kaye, Rosemary Clooney, Vera-
Ellen, Dean Jagger, Mary Wickes, John Brascia, Anne Whit-
field, Richard Shannon, Grady Sutton, Sig Ruman, Robert
Crosson, Johnny Grant, Barrie Chase, Herb Vigran, Dick
Keene, Gavin Gordon, Marcel De La Brosse, James Parnell
     During a Christmas Eve show at the front in France in
1944, in honor of retiring beloved Maj. Gen. Tom Waverly
(Jagger), singer Capt. Bob Wallace (Crosby) is saved by
Private Phil Davis (Kaye), who slightly injures his arm and
plays that into teaming up with Bob after the war. They
become a successful song and dance team on radio and begin
producing their own shows. Bob is the dedicated producer,
to the dismay of fun-loving Phil, who tries to arrange dates
for his serious-minded partner, who considers the girls
worth "a dime a dozen." Through Judy's (Vera-Ellen's)
conniving, they meet the singing Haynes sisters, Betty
(Clooney) and Judy, in Miami. With Bob stuck on Betty, he
and Phil help the sisters escape a cheating landlord (Ruman)
and the sheriff (Parnell) by exiting through the dressing
room window. Phil tricks Bob into taking a train with the
sisters to the girls' booking in Pine Tree, VT, for December. Without snow, the Columbia Inn run by the 151st Division's old commander, retired Gen. Waverly, is empty. Bob
orders his whole cast from New York to the inn for a Christmas Eve opening with the sisters, and Betty thinks that Bob
is decent in arranging for performers. Bob phones Ed Harrison (Grant), host of a variety TV show, and Emma (Wickes),
the eavesdropping housekeeper, overhears half the call that
suggests he intends to take advantage of the general's
plight for publicity. Now Betty thinks Bob a heel. Phil
and Judy pretend to be engaged to assist the Bob-Betty
romance, but Betty runs away to New York, where Bob attends
her performance. Bob tells her that the general is despair-
ing as well as insolvent, then he goes on Harrison's
show--while the general is kept distracted--to appeal to the
veterans of the division to buy tickets to the inn for
Christmas Eve to honor the "old man" and see a hit show.
The benefit pulls him out of debt and the doldrums and
results in romance for Bob and Phil with the sisters, for
Betty returns, having learned Bob was her shining knight.
Then it snows. <u>Songs</u> include "White Christmas" and reprised
at end; "The Old Man" with Kaye and chorus; "Heat Wave" with
Kaye; "Let Me Sing and I'm Happy" with Kaye; "Blue Skies"
with Kaye; "Sisters" by Clooney and Vera-Ellen; "The Best
Things Happen When You're Dancing" by Kaye and reprised by
Kaye with Page Cavanaugh Trio; "Snow" with Kaye, Clooney,
and Vera-Ellen; the Minstrel Number with "Mandy" with Kaye
and Clooney; "Count Your Blessings" with Clooney and re-
prised by Bing; "Choreography" by Kaye; "Abraham" danced by
Vera-Ellen; "Love, You Didn't Do Right By Me" by Clooney;
"What Can You Do with a General?"; "Gee, I Wish I Was Back

in the Army" with Kaye, Clooney, and Vera-Ellen; and the
Santa Claus Number with "White Christmas" with Bing, Kaye,
Clooney, Vera-Ellen, and chorus.
     NOTE: The song "Count Your Blessings" was nominated
for an Academy Award but lost to "Three Coins in the Fountain." The film first displayed Paramount's excellent wide-
screen process called VistaVision with Technicolor. Berlin's story was originally broached about 1948 as a stage
musical called "Stars on My Shoulders" for Walter Huston,
who died in 1950. Berlin sold the idea to Paramount, which
decided to relate it to Holiday Inn. Berlin was happy to be
writing again, without a film score in more than ten years.
The studio added the title song and Bing. Fred Astaire was
unavailable, and Donald O'Connor became ill, so the role of
Phil Davis went to Kaye. Vera-Ellen was a Rockette in 1941
before going to Hollywood, debuted with Kaye in Wonder Man
(1945), and her singing was dubbed by Gloria Wood. "What
Can You Do with a General?" was written by Berlin in 1948.
He was so nervous about filming the song "White Christmas"
that Bing interrupted the scene to tell him to relax, that
it was already a big hit and he was familiar with it.
Kathryn Grandstaff (Grant/Crosby) interviewed Bing in September 1953 on the set for her Texas column, days after
being escorted around the set by Bing and sitting with him
while Danny Kaye filmed a dance scene. Bing refused to
dress as a woman for a duet of "Sisters" with Kaye, and did
so only when they let him merely roll up his pants. The
film became Bing's greatest hit, and he, Berlin, and Kaye
split 70 percent of the profits. By 1969 it had earned a
total of $12 million as the 50th biggest hit film in histo-
ry. Only nine films before 1954 had larger gross earnings.
Berlin wrote "Sittin' in the Sun (Countin' My Money)" for
Crosby, but with delays he sold it separately, and also "A
Singer, a Dancer" in 1952 for Bing and Astaire, revised as
"A Crooner, a Comic" for Bing and Kaye, but it was not used.
George Chakiris, the singer and actor, appeared as a dancer
in his film debut.
     "It was twelve years ago that Bing Crosby was in a
place and a film called 'Holiday Inn.' . . . The occasion
was happily historic, for a reason we scarcely need recall:
'White Christmas' and Mr. Crosby became like 'God Bless
America' and Kate Smith. . . . Three numbers are given over
to the admiration of generals and Army life, which seems not
alone an extravagance but a reckless audacity. Even the
sweetness of Dean Jagger as the old general does not justify
the expense. Someone's nostalgia for the war years and the
U.S.O. tours has taken the show awry." Bosley Crowther,
N.Y. Times, Oct 15.
     "[Crosby and Kaye click] so well the teaming should
call for a repeat. . . . Crosby wraps up his portion of the
show with deceptive ease, selling the songs with the Crosby
sock, shuffling a mean hoof in the dances and generally
acquitting himself like a champion." Brog., [Hollywood, Aug
27] Variety, Sep 1.

F126.   The Country Girl (1954, Paramount) 104 min. bw
d, w: George Seaton p: William Perlberg s: a play of the
same title by Clifford Odets score: Victor Young m: Harold
Arlen l: Ira Gershwin ch: Robert Alton art: Hal Pereira,

Roland Anderson sd: Sam Comer, Grace Gregory cos: Edith
Head c: John F. Warren sound: Gene Merritt, John Cope e:
Ellsworth Hoagland. N.Y. preview Nov 10; N.Y. Criterion Dec
15.
      Bing Crosby, Grace Kelly, William Holden, Anthony
Ross, Gene Reynolds, Jacqueline Fontaine, Eddie Ryder,
Robert Kent, John W. Reynolds, Ida Moore, Frank Scannell,
Ruth Rickaby, Jonathan Provost, Hal K. Dawson, Howard Joslin
      Frank Elgin (Crosby), a musical-comedy star fallen into
self-pity and singing commercials, has become an alcoholic
with no confidence over the death of his son, killed by an
automobile when Frank is distracted by a photographer. With
his loyal wife, Georgie (Kelly), unaware, he passes a tough
audition for a new musical called The Land Around Us to open
in a few weeks out of town in Boston, and is supported by
her, who is accused by young director Bernie Dodd (Holden),
an old fan of Frank's, of hampering his comeback. She tells
Bernie she knows nothing of show business people: "I'm just
a girl from the country." To keep Bernie from separating
them during rehearsals, Frank says she is a possessive drunk
who might commit suicide if left alone. Frank, a lying
drunk who needs to be loved, leans on his wife, whom Bernie
thinks domineering and jealous. Phil Cook (Ross) is the
doubting producer, and Larry (Reynolds) the young stage
manager. Losing his nerve from hostile Boston critics,
increased attention, and especially from a "Wanted for
Murder" poster in the play that recalls the fatal photogra-
phy, Frank "catches a cold," and Bernie orders the wife back
to New York to save Frank's part. Frank goes on a binge,
awakens in the drunk tank, and Georgie bends her pride to
reveal the truth to Bernie, who sees Frank's scarred wrist.
She wishes she could leave Frank in Bernie's care, but after
they kiss, they nurse Frank, who admits to Bernie that the
death has been only "a respectable excuse for failure." He
succeeds in New York, and with Bernie asking Georgie to
leave the revitalized star who now dominates the producer,
she confesses to Frank at a cast party that she did partly
want him dependent on her, but she gently kisses Bernie
goodbye and runs after Frank. Songs include "It's Mine,
It's Yours" [or, "The Pitchman"], "The Search Is Through
(You've Got What It Takes)," "The Land Around Us," and
"Dissertation on the State of Bliss" [or, "Love and Learn"].
      NOTE: The "world premiere" occurred in New York on Dec
16, and a benefit for the U.S. Olympic Fund was staged the
previous day with one showing. The Academy Awards, announced March 30, 1955, went to Grace Kelly as Best Actress
and George Seaton for Best Screen Play for this film (N.Y.
Times, Mar 31, 1955: 23). Bing and Seaton had been nominated. On the Waterfront and its star, Marlon Brando, won as
Best Picture and Best Actor, that film earning eight Oscars
in all. The N.Y. Times named Crosby's film one of the
year's ten best (Dec 26, 2: 7), and the N.Y. Film Critics
named Kelly Best Actress, primarily for The Country Girl but
also for Dial M for Murder and Rear Window (N Y. Times Dec
29: 18). Seaton received the Outstanding Directorial
Achievement Award from the Director's Guild of America; Bing
was named the Actor of the Year by the American National
Board of Review of Motion Pictures and received Look magazine's award as Best Actor. Film Daily's poll selected the

film as the fourth best of the year, and the National Board
of Review named Kelly Best Actress. Odets' original play
opened on Broadway in 1950, starring Paul Kelly and singer
Uta Hagen, although Kelly did not play a singer, and the
play was retitled <u>Winter Journey</u> for London. Jennifer Jones
was the first choice as Georgie, but she was pregnant, and
some say Bing asked Greta Garbo. With this film, Crosby,
glamorous Kelly, and boy-next-door Holden all enlarged their
images. To film the drunken scene at the jail, Bing stayed
up all night with Gary, and Bing's mother, watching the
filming, thought her son actually drunk and walked away in a
huff. Associated with recent Crosby films, Danny Kaye and
VistaVision also won Academy Awards for the year, Kaye for
<u>Assignment Children</u>, a Paramount short for the United Na-
tions Children's Fund. The 27th Academy of Motion Picture
Arts and Sciences ceremony was televised for 90 minutes,
March 30, 1955, by NBC from two auditoriums, Hollywood's
Pantages Theatre and New York's Century Theatre. Bing,
dressed in a tuxedo and top hat, brought Kathryn Grant to
the affair at Pantages and to a following party. Bing
recorded the four songs on Dec 23, 1954.
     " . . . with all the intense, perceptive acting of
Grace Kelly and William Holden in the other roles, it is
truly Mr. Crosby's appearance and performance as the has-
been thespian who fights and is helped back to stardom that
hits the audience right between the eyes. . . . It is
he--the degraded husband--who is the focus of attention
here. And the force and credibility of the drama depends
upon how he is played. That is why it is Mr. Crosby who
merits particular praise, for he not only has essayed the
character but also performs it with unsuspected power. . . .
He plays the broken actor frankly and honestly, goes down to
the depths of degradation without a bat of his bleary eyes
and then brings the poor guy back to triumph . . . with a
maximum of painful resolution and sheer credibility. There
is no doubt that Mr. Crosby deserves all the kudos he will
get." Bosley Crowther, N.Y. <u>Times</u>, Dec 16. See also
Crowther's follow-up comments, Dec 26: 54 and II: 1, and
Bing's article "Bing Scans His Elgin." Later Crowther made
the tenuous charge that Crosby was prejudiced against blacks
in his films and TV shows.
     "Crosby pulls a masterly switch, for it is the charac-
ter of the story that he projects: it is not the crooner in
another shallow disguise. He immerses himself into the part
with full effect, inspiring audience revulsion with his
deceit and sottiness and yet engendering just enough sympathy to make his final triumph over the bottle a welcome
development." Gene., <u>Variety</u>, Dec 1.

F127.   <u>Bing Presents Oreste</u> (1955, Paramount) 11 min.
col.
     Bing introduces Oreste Kirkop, an opera singer, who was
filming <u>The Vagabond King</u> for Paramount, directed by Michael
Curtiz and starring Kathryn Grayson, Oreste, and Rita More-
no. The opera singer appears in clips from the coming
attraction, making the short a trailer for that 1956 film
about the life of poet-robber Francois Villon. Bing's part
was evidently Paramount's attempt to spark interest in a
weak film, and Kirkop was soon forgotten. The trailer may

have been released in 1956.

F128.   Hollywood Fathers (1955, Columbia) Short.

F129.   Anything Goes (1956, Paramount) 106 min.   col   d:
Robert Lewis   asst: John Coonan   p: Robert Emmett Dolan   w:
Sidney Sheldon   s: a play by Guy Bolton, P.G. Wodehouse,
revised by Howard Lindsay, Russel Crouse, [Cole Porter] for
1934 Broadway musical   m, l: Cole Porter, Sammy Cahn, James
Van Heusen   md: Joseph J. Lilley   special a: Van Cleave   ch:
Nick Castle; Jeanmaire ballet and "I Get a Kick Out of You"
dance staged by Roland Petit; "Anything Goes" dance staged
by Ernie Platt   cos: Edith Head; ballet cos: Tom Keogh   fx:
John P. Fulton   c: John F. Warren, Richard Mueller, Farciot
Edouart   sound: Gene Merritt, Gene Garvin   e: Frank Bracht.
Hollywood preview, Jan 13; Mar 21
          Bing Crosby, Donald O'Connor, [Zizi] Jeanmaire,
Mitzi Gaynor, Phil Harris, Kurt Kasznar, Richard Erdman,
Walter Sande, Archer MacDonald, Argentina Brunetti, Alma
Macrorie, Dorothy Neumann, James Griffith, Marcel Dalio
          Bill Benson (Crosby), a veteran singer, is teamed with
young television star Ted Adams (O'Connor) by producer
Victor Lawrence (Kasznar), but the pair first vacations in
Europe and hopes to find their leading lady. On the ship
Bill meets Steve Blair (Harris), a self-exiled gambler
trying to avoid a tax rap and who sends the singer to see
his daughter dancing in London. Bill promises the role in
the new musical to her, Patsy Blair (Gaynor), who accepts
when her father says he has been cleared in America. In
Paris Ted promises the lead to Gaby Duval (Jeanmaire), and
the men argue over whom to sign while keeping them apart.
Ted smuggles Gaby aboard ship in Le Havre, and Bill and Ted
become impressed with each other's find as Gaby falls for
Bill, Patsy for Ted, and they reciprocate. Steve is caught
by Treasury Agent Alex Todd (Sande), who agrees to delay the
arrest until the ship docks. Gaby dances a dream ballet of
conquering Broadway before learning that Bill was supposed
to withdraw her contract. Gaby overhears Steve explain to
Patsy that he is going to jail, but his gamble for her was
worth it. Gaby surrenders her contract to save Patsy, who
now spurns Ted. Ted sings for the children, and Bill,
devising a solution, has the captain invite both women to a
concert. Bill and Ted explain to their loves that a new
script, based on their recent experiences, will include both
women. The show, You're the Top, is a smash, still running
two years later when Patsy's father is released from jail.
Songs include [each Porter composition marked by an aster-
isk] "Ya Gotta Give the People Hoke" with O'Connor, "Anything Goes*" by Gaynor and chorus, "I Get a Kick Out of
You*" by Jeanmaire and chorus, "You're the Top*" with Jeanmaire, O'Connor, and Gaynor, "It's De-Lovely*" by O'Connor
and Gaynor, "All Through the Night*" (in English and
French), "Dream Ballet*" danced by Jeanmaire, "You Can
Bounce Right Back" by O'Connor, "A Second-Hand Turban and a
Crystal Ball" with O'Connor, and "Blow, Gabriel, Blow*" with
O'Connor, Gaynor, Jeanmaire, and chorus.
          NOTE: The film, Crosby's last for Paramount, is an
extensive revision of the 1934 musical and Bing's 1936 film.
O'Connor, age 31, was teamed at age 13 with Crosby in Sing,

<u>You Sinners</u> (1938). The remake was notorious for brief and
sexy costumes of the dancers, especially "an incredibly
tight, closer-than-skin, black outfit" (<u>Variety</u>) worn by
Jeanmaire for a number staged by Roland Petit for "I Get a
Kick Out of You," costume by Edith Head. Jeanmaire thought
the costumes rather tame. Petit was Jeanmaire's husband and
also staged the Dream Ballet, occurring after Bing sings
"All Through the Night" to her. The shipboard scenes of the
1934 musical were hastily rewritten after the fire on the
<u>Morro Castle</u> Sep 8, 1934, off Asbury Park, NJ, making a
maritime disaster musical unthinkable (and months after the
1956 film was released, another disaster occurred on Jul 25,
1956, in which 51 people died when Italy's <u>Andrea Doria</u>,
colliding with the Swedish <u>Stockholm</u>, sank off Long Island).
Leo Robin and Frederick Hollander wrote "Am I Awake" and
"Hopelessly in Love" for the film, but they were not used.
Seven Porter songs and scores were used, supplemented by
three by Cahn and Van Heusen. Only three Porter songs were
in the 1936 film.
     " . . . the chief trouble with 'Anything Goes' is too
much concern for its lavish production and too little for
such simple ingredients as humor and originality." <u>News-</u>
<u>week</u>, Mar 26.
     "Bing Crosby, who obviously can't help being profes-
sional, croons . . . with individual charm. But while he
can toss off an urbane wisecrack with characteristic ease,
one gets the impression that he is slightly apathetic about
it. Perhaps it's natural. He's been through it all
before." A.H. Weiler, N.Y. <u>Times</u>, Mar 22.
     "Script provides Crosby with plenty of those sotto
voce, throw-away cracks he and his fans dote on, as well as
an overall comedic setup against which to bounce the musical
numbers." Brog., [Hollywood, Jan 23] <u>Variety</u>, Jan 25.

F130.   <u>High Society</u> (1956, Metro-Goldwyn-Mayer) 107 min.
col d, ch: Charles Walters asst: Arvid Griffen p: Sol C.
Siegel w: John Patrick s: unbilled, Philip Barry's play
<u>The Philadelphia Story</u> m, l: Cole Porter md: Johnny Green,
Saul Chaplin o: Nelson Riddle, Conrad Salinger, M-G-M
Studio Orchestra: Johnny Green art: Cedric Gibbons, Hans
Peters sd: Richard Pefferle, Edwin Willis cos: Helen Rose
mu: William Tuttle hair: Sydney Guilaroff fx: A. Arnold
Gillespie c: Paul C. Vogel, Charles K. Hagedon sound: Dr.
Wesley C. Miller e: Ralph E. Winters. N.Y. tradeshow, Jul
11; Radio City Music Hall, Aug 9
     Bing Crosby, Grace Kelly, Frank Sinatra, Celeste
Holm, John Lund, Louis Calhern, Sidney Blackmer, Louis
Armstrong and his Band (Trummy Young, Ed Hall, Billy Kyle,
Arvell Shaw, Barrett Deems), Margalo Gillmore, Lydia Reed,
Gordon Richards, Richard Garrick, Richard Keene, Ruth Lee,
Helen Spring, Paul Keast, Reginald Simpson, Hugh Boswell
     Louis Armstrong begins as the narrator, introducing
C.K. Dexter-Haven (Crosby), a Newport "juke-box hero" and
socialite divorced from the perfectionist Tracy Lord
(Kelly). Dexter, sponsoring the Jazz Festival and housing
Armstrong and his band, attends his former in-laws next
door, especially free-thinking Uncle Willie (Calhern), and
annoys Tracy's stuffy fiance, George Kittredge (Lund).
Meddling and precocious young Caroline Lord (Reed) prefers

Dexter. Seth Lord (Blackmer) is the straying father while
the mother (Gillmore) tries to maintain propriety. Black-
mailed by the editor (Keast) of Spy magazine, lest they
print a story of Seth and a chorus girl, Mrs. Lord permits
them to cover the wedding. Feature reporter Mike Connor
(Sinatra) and photographer Liz Imbrie (Holm) arrive, to whom
Tracy, in a parody of refinement, introduces Willie as
"Papa." Seth, scorned by Tracy, returns and has to pretend
he is Uncle Willie, and Tracy upbraids Mike for his unfair
opinions of the wealthy. Dexter's wedding present is a
model of his yacht, True Love, on which he and Tracy had
their honeymoon, and Tracy realizes she still loves Dexter.
With Armstrong and his band, Dexter attends the pre-wedding
party at Uncle Willie's mansion, sings a duet with Mike in
the library, and Seth reveals he is the real father. Mike
drives Tracy home, where she jumps drunkenly into the pool,
and he rescues her, carrying her past Dexter and George to
her bedroom. The reporters quit the magazine. After Tracy
and George learn that Mike had harmlessly put her to bed,
she rebounds from George's hesitancy to remarry Dexter.
Mike proposes to Liz, and the Lords are reconciled. Songs
include "High Society Calypso" by Armstrong and Band,
"Little One" with Band, reprised by Reed, "Who Wants to Be a
Millionaire" by Sinatra and Holm, "True Love" with Kelly,
reprised by Kelly, "You're Sensational" by Sinatra and
Kelly, "I Love You, Samantha" with Band, "Now You Has Jazz"
with Armstrong and Band, "Well, Did You Evah!" with Sinatra,
and "Mind If I Make Love to You?" by Sinatra. Other Porter
melodies used as background are "Easy to Love," "I've Got
You Under My Skin," and "I've Got My Eyes on You."
     NOTE: The song "True Love" was nominated for an Acade-
my Award but lost to "Que sera sera." The star billing is
alphabetical, but it is not so noted in the credits. The
album of the soundtrack sold a million copies, as did a
single disc of "True Love," accounting for the 22nd and 23rd
gold records for Bing, and the only ones for Kelly, who
earned $30,000 in royalties for her contribution. Bing
earned $200,000 and five percent of the profits through Bing
Crosby Productions, for the fourth highest money-maker of
the year. Bing also sang "Let's Vocalize," which was cut
from the film, and Porter also wrote unused "A Step
Montage," "Caroline," "So What?" and "Hey, Sexy." The film
is a musical version of a 1939 play and the M-G-M 1940 film
directed by George Cukor, both starring Katharine Hepburn.
Cary Grant, James Stewart, and Ruth Hussey starred in older
film, in roles played in the Newport story by Crosby, Sinatra, and Holm, respectively. The 1956 film is the first in
which Bing and Sinatra appear together, and it is Grace
Kelly's last film before becoming Princess Grace of Monaco.
It has Porter's first film score in more than ten years, and
he wrote "Well, Did You Evah!" for the 1939 Broadway musical
Du Barry Was a Lady, sung by Betty Grable and Charles Walters, the director of High Society. Porter revised the
lyrics for the film. Six days after the new musical premiered, Sinatra's film Johnny Concho opened at the New York
Paramount with a week-long personal appearance by Sinatra
and the joint band of Tommy and Jimmy Dorsey to "a capacity
audience of loud enthusiasts, clearly reminiscent of those
who gathered at the Paramount in the Forties when Mr. Sina-

tra appeared frequently as a soloist with Tommy Dorsey's band . . . " (Bosley Crowther, <u>Variety</u>, Aug 16: 30). One of the music directors, Chaplin, had also written the lyrics to "Anniversary Song," a hit Crosby record of 1947.

"Lightheaded nostalgia." <u>Newsweek</u>, Aug 6.

"In the musical line, Mr. Sinatra and Bing Crosby also sing some fetching songs that more or less contribute to a knowledge of what is going on. . . . However, there do come tedious stretches in this socially mixed-up affair, and they are due in the main to slow direction and the mildness of Miss Kelly in the pivotal role. . . . And we must say that Mr. Crosby seems a curious misfit figure in the role of the young lady's cast-off husband who gets her back at the very end. He wanders around the place like a mellow uncle, having fun with Mr. Armstrong and his boys and viewing the feminine flutter with an amiable masculine disdain. He strokes his pipe with more affection than he strokes Miss Kelly's porcelain arms." Bosley Crowther, N.Y. <u>Times</u>, Aug 10.

"Although Sinatra has the top pop tune opportunities, the Groaner makes his specialties stand up and out on show-manship and delivery, and Miss Kelly impresses as the femme lead with pleasantly comedienne overtones." Abel., <u>Variety</u>, Jul 18.

F131.   <u>High Tor</u> (1956, CBS-Ford Star Jubilee) 90 min. bw Mar 10, CBS-TV d James Neilson p, w, m, l: Arthur Schwartz s: Maxwell Anderson (1937) md, o: Joseph J. Lilley and "Skip" Martin.

Bing Crosby, Julie Andrews, Nancy Olson, Everett Sloane, Hans Conreid, Lloyd Corrigan, John Picaroll

Van Van Dorn (Crosby) labors in vain to keep his Hudson River land from rapacious development and modernization, inspired by ghosts of the 16th-century Dutch forbears on the mountain High Tor, especially by the ghosts of Capt. DeWitt (Sloane), and his wife, Lisa (Andrews). <u>Songs</u>: "Living One Day at a Time," "When You're in Love" and reprised by Sloane and Andrews and again by Sloane, "Sad Is the Life of the Sailor's Wife" by Andrews, "A Little Love, a Little While," "John Barleycorn," and "Once Upon a Long Ago" by Andrews, reprised by Bing.

NOTE: This television movie was produced in 12 days, with Bing recording seven numbers on Dec 27, 1955. The reviews were cool toward the weak production values, except for the music. It may never have been rebroadcast and has never been released to theaters. Based on Anderson's 1937 Broadway drama, it and was Arthur Schwartz's second venture into television, which he thought freer than the stage. He had produced several popular Broadway musicals. It was filmed after Bing and Kathryn Grant had again postponed their wedding. Schwartz produced <u>Surprise from Santa</u>, a 90-minute TV special in 1948, and was stunned by criticism that the first serious TV special, with a cast of four boys and four dancing girls, had "too many people." With <u>High Tor</u> he returned to offer the first full-length musical filmed specially for TV.

"[The show] was only a starter in [Schwartz's] full-scale return to TV sets. . . . Schwartz's change of mind about TV's possibilities has been even more fervent than his earlier abandonment of the medium." <u>Newsweek</u>, Mar 19.

F132.   <u>The Heart of Show Business</u> (1957, Columbia) Narrator Documentary 40 min.   d: Ralph Staub.
          Narrators: Bing Crosby, Cecil B. DeMille, Burt
Lancaster, Edward G. Robinson, James Stewart. With Bob
Hope, Harry Belafonte, Victor Borge, Maurice Chevalier, Lena
Horne, Art Linkletter, Sophie Tucker, Jimmy Durante, Edgar
Bergen and Charlie McCarthy, Cantinflas
          The film traces the history of the Variety Clubs International.

F133.   <u>Man on Fire</u> (1957, Metro-Goldwyn-Mayer) 95 min.
bw d: Ranald MacDougall p: Sol C. Siegel w: MacDougall
s: Malvin Wald, Jack Jacobs m, l: Sammy Fain, Paul Francis
Webster score: David Raskin c: Joseph Ruttenberg e: Ralph
E. Winters. N.Y. preview May 20; Aug 22
          Bing Crosby, Inger Stevens, Mary Fickett, E.G.
Marshall, Malcolm Brodrick, Richard Eastham, Anne Seymour,
Dan Riss, the Ames Brothers singing the title song over the
final credits
          Earl Carleton (Crosby) is a successful businessman
desperately trying for love and hurt feelings to keep total
custody of his son, Ted (Brodrick), in a divorce from reasonable Gwen (Fickett), who has married another man, stuffy
but wise Bryan Seward (Eastham), a marriage also resented by
the son. Nina Wylie (Stevens), a lawyer, tries to comfort
and pacify Earl through his vicious and bitter moods and
drunken parties; her boss is Sam Dunstock (Marshall), Earl's
reasonable lawyer. Although the mother had technically
signed away her rights to the boy to marry, stern Judge
Randolph (Seymour), presiding over a heated custody hearing,
awards primary custody to Gwen. Then Earl, blindly angry,
tries to kidnap his son, takes him to the airport, but
finally becomes understanding after a confrontation. <u>Song</u>:
"Man on Fire" and reprise by the Ames Brothers.
          NOTE: This is Crosby's first non-singing feature film.
It introduced Fickett, direct from Broadway, and Stevens.
The Ames Brothers were to sing the title song at the opening
and ending, but when Bing recorded the song the producers
added his version to the opening. Bing recorded the song in
Jan 1957, issued by Capitol.
          "Even though buttressed by the evident undivided devotion of the son, such an attitude by a father cannot help
but look selfish and unjust. And so it took quite a bit of
courage for Mr. Crosby to expose himself in this role. The
fact that he did so is a credit to his belief in the idea of
the film. . . . Without restraint, he actually makes a
method of annoyance out of his customary glibness and
charm. . . . [Siegel] has shown you can still bring out a
good film in a conventional screen size and black and
white." Bosley Crowther, N.Y. <u>Times</u>, Aug 23.
          "Bing Crosby, who made an impact as the alcoholic actor
in 'The Country Girl,' again demonstrates his ability as a
straight dramatic performer. . . . Despite the dramatic
impact of the picture, it is not all sombre. McDougall
 . . . has provided some light dialog that fits Crosby's
familiar style. The tension is relieved on a number of
occasions by scenes designed to provide a chuckle or a

laugh." Holl., _Variety_, Jun 5.

EXTRA: Bing wanted the lead in 1957 of Meredith Willson's _The Music Man_, but the film appeared in 1962 starring
irrepressible Robert Preston in his most memorable role.
Bing and Jackie Gleason were suggested in 1957 as stars of a
film on the lives of songwriters Al Dubin and Harry Warren,
but the project seems to have died.

F134.   _The Joker Is Wild_ (1957, Paramount) alternate: _All_
the Way Voice only 123 min. bw d: Charles Vidor p:
Samuel J. Briskin w: Oscar Saul s: Art Cohn, based on the
life of Joe E. Lewis m, l: Sammy Cahn, Jimmy Van Heusen,
Harry Harris score: Walter Scharf o: Nelson Riddle art:
Hal Pereira, Roland Anderson cos: Edith Head c: Daniel L.
Fapp e: Everett Douglas. Las Vegas, El Portal Theatre Aug
23; N.Y. Aug 26
     Frank Sinatra, Mitzi Gaynor, Jeanne Crain, Eddie
Albert, Beverly Garland, Jackie Coogan, Sophie Tucker
     Joe E. Lewis (Sinatra) is a singer who has his throat
slashed in Chicago in 1927 by speakeasy mobsters, but he
makes a comeback in 1937 as a comic in a Variety Clubs
International benefit headed by Sophie Tucker. In one scene
set in 1937 in New York, a silhouette of Crosby is seen at a
backstage party singing "June in January." Joe's loyal
pianist, Austin Mack (Albert), Austin's wife, Cassie (Garland), and hanger-on Swifty Morgan (Coogan) follow him
through boozing days and nights as he loses his love, Lettie
Page (Crain), and marries and separates from his wife and
movie actress, Martha Stewart (Gaynor), leading him to try
to set his life aright. _Songs_ include, besides Crosby's
"June in January," Sinatra's Oscar-winning new song "All the
Way" (which is the title of the reissued film), "At
Sundown," "I Cried for You," "If I Could Be with You," a
parody "[My Bookie Came] From Out of Nowhere," and a parody
of Crosby's "Swinging on a Star." Crosby's voice on "June
in January" was probably from the May 1954 Decca recording.
     "But perhaps the brightest thing about the picture is
the excellent dialogue--peppery, amusing and sensitive in
turn. Add, certainly, the consistently fine acting of Mr.
Sinatra, on view virtually every minute, armed to the hilt
with period songs." H.H.T., N.Y. _Times_, Aug 27.
     "[Sinatra's] believeable and forceful--alternately
sympathetic and pathetic, funny and sad." Gene., _Variety_,
Aug 28.

F135.   _Showdown at Ulcer Gulch_ (1958, Saturday Evening
Post) Short p: Shamus-Culhane.
     Bing Crosby, Bob Hope, Ernie Kovacs, Edie Adams,
Groucho Marx, Chico Marx, Orson Bean, Salome Jens
     Billed as "An Adult Eastern," it promoted _The Saturday_
Evening Post and was shown on television and in some thea-
ters.

EXTRA: Bing was named in 1959 as the star of _Bachelor's_
Baby, a Cinemascope film from 20th Century-Fox directed by
Dick Powell, but this did not work out. Bing was much more
serious about playing one of Jimmy Durante's partners, Eddie
Jackson, in "The Jimmy Durante Story," proposed by Frank

Sinatra for Columbia, who would play Durante, while Dean
Martin would play another partner, Lou Clayton. Crosby,
Sinatra, Frank Capra, Martin, and Columbia planned to share
equally in the production with a $5 million advance by the
studio, but a Writer's Guild strike stalled the script,
which Capra then wrote himself. It was unsatisfactory to
his partners, so that in Jan 1960 he withdrew. An actor's
strike ensued in Mar-Apr 1960, killing the project.

F136.   <u>Alias Jesse James</u> (1959, United Artists) Guest 92
min. col d: Norman McLeod p: Jack Hope, Hope Enterprises
w: William Bowers, Daniel D. Beauchamp s: Robert St. Aubrey, Bert Lawrence m: Joseph J. Lilley c: Lionel Lindon
e: Marvin Coil, Jack Bachom. Hollywood preview, Picwood
Theatre Mar 9; May 16
        Bob Hope, Rhonda Fleming, Wendell Corey, Jim
Davis, Gloria Talbot, Will Wright, Mary Young, with surprise
guests Bing Crosby, Gary Cooper, Gene Autry, Roy Rogers,
James Arness, Hugh O'Brien, Ward Bond, Gail Davis, Jay
Silverheels, James Garner
        Milford Farnsworth (Hope) is a cowardly life insurance
salesman in the 1880s who inadvertently sells a $100,000
policy in New York to cold-eyed Jesse James (Corey) and has
to try to protect his life. Milford is sent West, where he
meets a young piano player named Harry Truman. James hopes
to kill Milford, have him identified as the outlaw, and keep
the money and the beneficiary, his reluctant girlfriend,
Cora Lee Collins (Fleming), who loves Milford. She is known
as the Duchess. Milford poses as a parson, and his lucky
maneuvers at a barbecue in a fight against the James gang,
with help from a horde of lawmen, including Crosby, save the
day. Dressed as a cowboy, Bing fires a revolver from an
open window, hitting one of the James gang, and says, "This
fella needs all the help he can get." <u>Song</u>: "Ain't A-Han-
kerin'" by Hope and Fleming.
        ". . . it is only half-way through these sporadic
goings-on that the gags and quips fly with any regularity
and effect. . . . But all things considered, an observer
cannot help but agree with his pal, a famed singer who
appears, as one of the unbilled gunmen who aid him in the
climactic fight, when he says: 'This boy needs all the help
he can get.'" Bosley Crowther, N.Y. <u>Times</u>, May 18.
        "[The film has] the kind of gags and situations that
Hope can play off his left hand. Unfortunately, not enough
script has been given him for even one finger of the left
hand, and the result is an extremely mild comedy." Powe.,
[Hollywood, Mar 13] <u>Variety</u>, Mar 18.

F137.   <u>Say One for Me</u> (1959, 20th Century-Fox) 119 min.
col d, p: Frank Tashlin asst: Joseph E. Rickards w:
Robert O'Brien m, l: Sammy Cahn, James Van Heusen md:
Lionel Newman o: Earle Hagen, Herbert Spencer, Pete King
v: Charles Henderson art: Lyle R. Wheeler, Leland Fuller
sd: Walter M. Scott, Eli Benneche ch: Alex Romero cos:
Charles LeMaire, Adele Palmer mu: Ben Nye hair: Helen
Turpin c: Leo Tover, Leonard Doss sound: E. Clayton Ward,
Harry M. Leonard e: Hugh S. Fowler. Preview N.Y. Paramount
Jun 2; Jun 19
        Bing Crosby, Debbie Reynolds, Robert Wagner, Ray

Walston, Les Tremayne, Connie Gilchrist, Frank McHugh, Joe
Besser, Alena Murray, Stella Stevens, Nina Shipman, Sebastian Cabot, Judy Harriet, Dick Whittinghill, Robert Montgomery, Jr., Murray Alper, Richard Collier, David Leonard

Father Conroy (Crosby), an off-Broadway priest, conducts 2 a.m. Masses for show people--he has his own "late,
late, LATE show" and "the padre runs an after-hours joint."
He promises an ailing vaudevillian to protect his daughter,
Holly LaMaise (Reynolds), who leaves school for show business and auditions for and then lives with hustler-comic-
producer Tony Vincent (Wagner). Holly begins to work with
Tony, who vainly tries to seduce her. Tony thinks the
priest a "square" ("Know what I mean?") and accuses him, in
front of Monsignor Stradford (Cabot), of stealing his material for a vaudevillian. The priest's penance is to furnish
Tony a few good jokes, which he tests in the 2 a.m. Mass.
Phil Stanley (Walston) is Tony's drunken pianist, who has
written "The Secret of Christmas"; Mary Manning (Gilchrist)
is the witty housekeeper; June January (Harriet) is a hopeful songstress; and the priest baptizes the illegitimate
baby of a showgirl, saying, "There are only illegitimate
parents." Tony hopes to take Holly to Miami, but his booking is canceled. Keeping the cancellation secret, he allows
the priest to bribe him into abandoning Holly in return for
a spot on the nationally televised benefit for the Actors
Medical Fund. Holly is furious, tries to seduce Tony, but
now he loves her and abstains. For the grand church show,
the priest, Holly, and Tony, wearing a jacket much too
small, perform, the first two succeeding, the last bombing
until saved by Father Conroy. Tony decides to make an
honest woman of Holly, and, married, they go to Miami. The
final title reads, "The Beginning." Songs include "Say One
for Me" with Reynolds, reprised solo; "You Can't Love 'Em
All" by Wagner and Reynolds; "The Girl Most Likely to Succeed" by Reynolds and Wagner; "I Couldn't Care Less,"
"Chico's Choo-Choo" by Reynolds and Wagner; "The Secret of
Christmas" by Walston, reprised by Bing, Walston, and Reynolds; and "The Night That Rock 'n' Roll Died (Almost)" by
Harriet.
NOTE: Bing financed this film himself, and it took
four months to complete, from about Nov 1958 to Feb 1959,
when he sold his ranch for over $1 million. This is the
third film in which Bing plays a priest, this one inspired
by the monsignor of St. Malachy's, West 48th St., which
holds 2 a.m. Masses for Broadway. As he began filming, Bing
tripped over his cassock and fell. He said, "I forgot you
had to hitch these things up." Walston's piano playing was
dubbed by Buddy Cole. Bing recorded "Say One For Me," "I
Couldn't Care Less," and "The Secret of Christmas" on Mar 6
and again on Mar 25, 1959; he recorded the third song again
Jun 19, 1964.
"It is a pleasant show-world entertainment. . . . As
for Bing--well, he's just about as usual, a little less
lively, perhaps, a little older looking, but still casual
and sincere. He'll never make Monsignor. He'll always be a
parish priest, whenever he turns his collar backward, because you always sense a sport shirt underneath." Bosley
Crowther, N.Y. Times, Jun 20.
". . . something went wrong in the development; the

entertainment values are short of impressive. . . . Crosby
turns in a curiously inhibited performance. He plays the
role tight, not at all like the free-wheeling, leisurely-
paced Crosby of yore, but the voice is still there." Gene.,
Variety, Jun 10.

F138.   This Game of Golf (1959) Short Unknown.

F139.   Your Caddy, Sir (1959) Short Unknown.

EXTRA: Bing liked the lead of William Gibson's Two for
the Seesaw after seeing the play in 1959, but the film
appeared in 1962 starring Robert Mitchum and Shirley Ma-
cLaine, directed by Robert Wise.
Bing was offered the role in 1960 of any of the three
brothers Grimm (Wilhelm, Karl, or Jakob) for an M-G-M film,
but Bing did not accept. M-G-M also proposed to co-produce
"The Great Western Story" with Crosby Productions, inspired
partly by Bing's album How the West Was Won (RCA Victor
1959) and a series in Life magazine. The Western was produced by M-G-M and Cinerama as How the West Was Won (1962),
directed by John Ford and others and starring John Wayne,
James Stewart, Henry Fonda, George Peppard, Debbie Reynolds,
and others, while Bing Crosby Enterprises owned the score.
The film won Oscars for Screenplay (James R. Webb) and
editing (Harold F. Kress). Bing, Gary Cooper, and Clark
Gable were considered for the lead in F. Scott Fitzgerald's
Tender Is the Night (20th Century-Fox 1962), but they were
thought too old and Jason Robards got the role.

F140.   Let's Make Love (1960, 20th Century-Fox) Guest
118 min. col d: George Cukor p: Jerry Wald w: Norman
Krasna, Hal Kanter m, l: Sammy Cahn, James Van Heusen m
numbers staged: Jack Cole md: Lionel Newman c: Daniel L.
Fapp e: David Bretherton. Preview, N. Y. Paramount, Aug
18; Sep 8
Marilyn Monroe, Yves Montand, Tony Randall,
Frankie Vaughan, Wilfrid Hyde-White, David Burns, Michael
David, Mara Lynn, Dennis King, Jr., Joe Besser, Madge Kennedy, Ray Foster, Mike Mason; guests Bing Crosby, Gene Kelly,
Milton Berle
Amanda (Monroe) is an off-Broadway singer and night
school student who becomes pursued by the billionaire-play-
boy Jean-Mare Clement (Montand) when he learns that he's to
be satirized in a New York avant-garde musical revue produced by Oliver Burton (Burns) and starring Tony Danton
(Vaughan). An incognito Jean-Mare is hired to play Jean-
Mare, causing nerves for his public relations man (Randall)
and his chief assistant (Hyde-White). Like his ancestors,
the playboy pursues busty women, and takes comedy, dancing,
and singing lessons--the last from Crosby--to win Amanda's
heart. Bing advises Jean-Mare, "Take a dip down there;
that's where the money is." When the student "boo-boo-
boos," Bing says, "Don't do that around here, you'll get
arrested," and recommends dancing lessons as he phones Gene
Kelly. Amanda likes droll humor, dancing, and Vaughan's
singing, but the billionaire wins her heart before she
learns he is rich. The song Bing sings is "Incurably Romantic," with Montand, reprised by Monroe and Montand and again

by Monroe and Vaughan. Other songs are "Let's Make Love" by
Monroe, Vaughan, Montand; "My Heart Belongs to Daddy" by
Monroe; "Give Me the Simple Life" by Vaughan; "Crazy Eyes"
by Vaughan; and "Specialization" by Monroe.
     NOTE: Montand and British singer Vaughan made their
American film debuts. After Berle gives up on polishing
Montand's comic timing, he phones Bing, who arrives to teach
crooning and low tones. When Bing gives up, he phones
Kelly. Jack Benny, Sinatra, and Astaire were supposed to do
the guest shots filled by Berle, Bing, and Kelly but filming
delays caused by an actors' strike in Mar and Apr 1960 kept
them away. Kelly flew from Paris for his one-day assignment, and Marilyn's singing is supplemented by Gloria Wood.
Marilyn was having a well known romance with Montand. Bing
completed his guest appearance on Jun 15, 1960, the same day
he completed a second guest appearance and also completed
filming High Time. Let's Make Love is a version of On the
Avenue (1937) starring Dick Powell, Madeleine Carroll, and
Alice Faye, directed by Roy Del Ruth, with songs by Irving
Berlin, including "I've Got My Love to Keep Me Warm."
     "Who (aside from his mother) would ever have expected
to see Milton Berle steal a show, without much effort, from
Marilyn Monroe and Yves Montand? . . . Bing Crosby and Gene
Kelly are brought in to give the pupil further lessons. The
only humor in their appearance is the idea. The futility of
their efforts is more ironic." Bosley Crowther, N.Y. Times,
Sep 9.
     "[The film is] a cheerful lightweight comedy-with-
music, very familiar in form but still delightful in execution. . . . Another highlight is a comedy sequence in which
Montand brings on Milton Berle, Bing Crosby and Gene Kelly
(playing themselves) to coach him in the musical comedy
arts." Anby., Variety, Aug 24.

F141.   High Time (1960, 20th Century-Fox) 102 min. col
d: Blake Edwards   p: Charles Brackett, Bing Crosby Produc-
tions   w: Tom and Frank Waldman   s: Garson Kanin   m, l:
Sammy Cahn, James Van Heusen   score: Henry Mancini   art:
Herman A. Blumenthal, Duncan Cramer   ch: Miriam Nelson   mu:
Ben Nye   c: Ellsworth Fredericks   (DeLuxe Color)   e: Robert
Simpson.   N.Y. Warner Theater Sep 16
     Bing Crosby, Fabian, Tuesday Weld, Nicole Maurey,
Richard Beymer, Patrick Adiarte, Yvonne Craig, Jimmy Boyd,
Gavin MacLeod, Kenneth MacKenna, Nina Shipman, Paul Schreib-
er, Angus Duncan, Dick Crockett, Frank Scannell
     Harvey Howard (Crosby), a 51-year-old widower who
became a millionaire with a chain of 1,433 hamburger res-
taurants, decides "it's high time someone in the family get
a college education," rooms with Gil "Sparrow" Cuneo (Fabian), Bob Bannerman (Beymer), and an Indian exchange student,
T.J. Padmanabhan (Adiarte), tries to help Gil romance Joy
Elder (Weld), who has a crush on Harvey. The freshman of
the Class of 1960 agonize over their teams, the right fra-
ternities and sororities, hazing, picnics, studying math and
biology, including defining ecology, and the Freshman bon-
fire before the big game. For the fire, Harvey takes a
chair from under a porch, which then collapses. The tenant
is widowed Professor Helene Gauthier (Maurey), the French
teacher, who is mollified when Harvey pays for the damage.

To join Xi Delta Pi Harvey has to dress in an antebellum
gown and pass for a woman at the ball. To keep the professor from going to New York after his sophomore year, Harvey
hires her as his tutor for the summer. Harvey Jr. (Duncan)
and daughter Laura Howard (Shipman) feel humiliated at their
father's exuberance and second childhood, and during his
junior year he takes his friends to a Harvey Howard Smoke-
house, finding the hamburgers overdone. The manager, Thayer
(MacLeod), gets haughty until Harvey reveals himself and
shows the staff how to cook. Harvey wins the professor for
a $100 bid in the charity Faculty Auction, winning a home-
cooked Sunday dinner. Pinehurst U feels scandalized at the
close fraternization between a professor and a student.
Helene is virtually ostracized, but Harvey demands justice,
backed by the students. President Tribble (MacKenna) delays
a decision on her resignation and later does not accept it.
She goes to France the next summer and misses Harvey. She
suggests marriage during a hayride, but Harvey says, "I
could no more get married again than I could fly." With Joy
now in love with Gil, all students graduate. As the vale-
dictorian for the commencement ceremony, Harvey repudiates
negativism and the feeling that people could no more do
things than they could fly, when he is raised by wires to
fly above the audience as a proposal to the professor for
his "second time around." Songs include "The Second Time
Around"; "You Tell Me Your Dream" with Maurey and chorus;
"It Came Upon the Midnight Clear" with Fabian, Maurey, and
others; and "Foggy, Foggy Dew" by Fabian. Instrumentals are
"High Time," "The Old College Try Cha-Cha," "Tiger," and
"Frish Frosh." Other songs considered for the film are
"Nobody's Perfect" by Fabian "Camptown Races," "The Limerick
Song," and "Be My Girl," most if not all recorded but omit-
ted at least from some editions of the film.
   NOTE: The song "The Second Time Around" was nominated
for an Academy Award but lost to "Never on Sunday." Bing
recorded "The Second Time Around" on Aug 25, 1960, and it
sold very well. Nicole Maurey previously co-starred with
Bing in Little Boy Lost (1953) and accepted the role in
Paris only ten days before filming began, the script unseen.
Bing phoned her, and she trusted his judgment. This film is
the only time Bing would wear a dress. The script was
originally written for Spencer Tracy and provisionally
called "Daddy-O." The campus scenes were filmed at Wake
Forest University, Winston-Salem, NC, the city that became
home to the Crosby annual golf tournament at the Bermuda Run
Country Club in 1986. Filming began Feb 1, 1960, and the
five-week actors' strike of Mar and Apr delayed the comple-
tion until Jun. One record is that on Jun 15 Crosby completed filming and also completed guest roles for Let's Make
Love and Pepe.
   "Thus Mr. Crosby, still pretending to be youthful, goes
to college again, but a few necessaries are lacking. One of
them is a script. The other is youth. . . . [Crosby] tries
hard to be casual and boyish, to prove modestly that he's in
the groove, to match the animal spirits of the swarming
youngsters . . . [but] there is a terrible gauntness and
look of exhaustion about Mr. Crosby when the camera gets
close and peers at this face. We don't blame his children
(in the film) for objecting to his going to college. He

should have stayed at home with his feet to the fire."
Bosley Crowther, N.Y. Times, Sep 17.
    "High Time is pretty light-weight fare for a star of
Bing Crosby's proportions, and all the draw of the Groaner,
who only trills twice, will be required to sell it. . . .
Crosby handles his role in his usual fashion, perfectly
timing his laughs. . . ." Whit., Variety, Sep 21.

F142.   Pepe (1960, Columbia) Guest 195 min. col d, p:
George Sidney w: Dorothy Kingsley, Claude Binyon ad:
Leonard Spigelgass, Sonya Levien s: play by L. Bush-Fekete
md: Joe Green m editor: Maury Winetrobe cos: Edith Head
c: Joe MacDonald e: Viola Lawrence, Al Clark. N.Y. preview
Dec 19; Dec 21.
        Cantinflas, Dan Dailey, Shirley Jones, Carlos
Montalban, Vicki Trickett, Matt Mattox, Hank Henry, Suzanne
Lloyd, Joe Hyams, with guest stars Maurice Chevalier, Bing
Crosby, Richard Conte, Bobby Darin, Sammy Davis, Jr., Jimmy
Durante, Judy Garland (voice), Ernie Kovacs, Andre Previn,
Debbie Reynolds, Edward G. Robinson, Frank Sinatra, William
Demarest, Bunny Waters, Charles Coburn, and dozens more
        Pepe (Cantinflas) is a Mexican groom of a stallion
bought by declining director Ted Holt (Dailey) and parlays
small change into a fortune in Las Vegas. He goes to Holly-
wood and finances a movie for Ted, who roughs up Hollywood
hopeful Susie Murphy (Jones), whom Pepe vainly yearns for.
Among the dozens of cameo appearances, Chevalier sings
"September Song," Crosby autographs a tortilla, and Garland
sings off screen.
        NOTE: Bing's part was done the same day he had his
guest appearance in Let's Make Love and completed High Time.
        "The rare and wonderful talents of Mexican comedian
Cantinflas, who was nicely introduced to the general public
as the valet in 'Around the World in 80 Days,' are pitifully
spent and dissipated amid a great mass of Hollywooden dross
in the oversized, over-peopled [film]." Bosley Crowther,
N.Y. Times, Dec 22.
        "[The producer-director and writers] obviously have
taken a cue or more from the late Mike Todd's 'Around the
World in 80 Days.' . . . Sidney has provided an obviously
expensive and impressive production--but too much." Gene.,
Variety, Dec 21.

F143.   Kitty Caddy (1961, Columbia) Cartoon Short col.
    Bing Crosby and Bob Hope are depicted as golfers.

    EXTRA: Otto Preminger wanted Bing in 1961 for Advise
and Consent (1962), but Bing had committed himself to film
The Road to Hong Kong in England. Later in 1961 he considered another political film tentatively called "The Art of
Llewellyn Jones," but he did not sign on.

F144.   The Road to Hong Kong (1962, United Artists; British) 91 min. bw d: Norman Panama asst: Bluey Hill p:
Melnor Films, Ltd. (Melvin Frank) w: Panama, Frank m, l:
Sammy Cahn, Jimmy Van Heusen md: Robert Farnon, Bill
McFuffie Quartet background m and conducted: Robert Farnon
art: Sydney Cain, Bill Hutchinson sd: Maurice Fowler
production design: Roger Furse ch: Sheila Meyers, Jack

Baker mu: Dave Aylott fx: Wally Veevers, Ted Samuels
animation: Biographic Cartoon Films, Ltd. c: Jack Hildyard
sound: A.G. Ambler, Red Law, Chris Greenham titles: Maurice
Binder e: John Smith. London Mar 29; Jun 27
         Bing Crosby, Bob Hope, Joan Collins, Dorothy
Lamour, Robert Morley, Walter Gotell, Roger Delgardo, Felix
Aylmer, Alan Gifford, Robert Ayres, Robin Hughes, Peter Mad-
den, Jacqueline Jones, Mei Ling, Katya Douglas, Sue Chang,
Yvonne Shima, Peter Sellers, Dave King, Julian Sherrier,
Bill Nagy, Guy Standeven, John McCarthy, with special guests
Frank Sinatra, Dean Martin, David Niven, Jerry Colonna
    Harry Turner (Crosby) and Chester Babcock (Hope) are
vaudevillians at London's Palladium with a backdrop with
"Bing Crosby" writ large and "Bob Hope" small, and another
with "Bob Hope" writ large and "Bing Crosby" in tiny Chinese
characters. Then they become con men selling space-suit
kits to natives in Ceylon and Calcutta. Chester, who has
hidden their money, is knocked unconscious while demonstrating the suit and suffers amnesia. A Hindu psychiatrist
(Sellers) does not help and sends them for a memory potion
at a lamasery in Tibet. At the airport Diane (Collins), a
secret agent for the nefarious Third Echelon, thinks Chester
her contact and slips a stolen Russian formula for rocket
fuel into his pocket. In Tibet, Lamas memorize great literature, although David Niven works on <u>Lady Chatterly's Lover</u>,
and the Grand Lama (Aylmer) cures Chester. Harry and Chester abscond with herbs that produce a photographic memory,
escaping through their pat-a-cake routine. Chester finds
the formula, memorizes it, and burns the paper before Diane
accosts them with a revolver. Chester boasts to Harry, "I'm
as chicken as you are--chickener." For $25,000 Harry plots
to send Chester to her headquarters in Hong Kong, telling
Chester they are going to audition their mind-reading act
and split $2500. On the next plane, Jhinnah (Delgardo), the
agent of the Grand Lama, replaces the herbs with tea.
Performing before the Leader (Morley), who plots to rule the
world, Chester can't remember the formula. The Leader
replaces monkeys with the men in a space capsule where they
receive the food for the monkeys as, back to back, they
rocket around the moon. Back on earth, Chester is hypno-
tized by Diane's moon-shaped earrings and remembers part of
the formula, and Diane is ordered to seduce him to obtain
the rest. Then Diane decides to run away with them in a
submarine and through Hong Kong, where "Special Effects"
provides the clothes of coolies. They meet Colonna, and a
goldfish swallows a key Chester drops into the bowl. Chester takes all the goldfish, and he and Harry hide in a
nightclub where Lamour is singing. She puts them in her act
to save them ("from the critics"), when Chester, losing the
fish, sees a stage moon and recites the rest of the formula.
Harry and Chester return to the headquarters to save the
world from a second rocket with a warhead, and Diane brings
American Secret Service agents, who settle the issue.
Trapped in the capsule, Diane, Harry, and Chester are sent
aloft by the dying Leader. Diane redirects the ship to the
planet Plutonius, where they share everything, including the
girl. Then they find her kissing Dean Martin and Frank
Sinatra, who landed in spacesuits from "Special Effects."
Harry and Chester eliminate them the same way. Then Chester

asks that Harry be sent home, but Chester is launched as
Harry keeps kissing Diane. <u>Songs</u> include "Team Work" with
Hope, reprised with Hope and Collins; "Road to Hong Kong"
with Hope; "Let's Not Be Sensible" with Collins; "Personality" and "Warmer Than a Whisper" by Lamour; and "(It's) The
Only Way to Travel" with Hope. Music includes Farnon's
tunes "Reluctant Astronaut," "Lamasery Chant," "Moon Over
Hong Kong," and "The Chase."
     NOTE: This is the seventh and final <u>Road</u> film, after a
ten-year hiatus of the formula that stretched 22 years. It
was one of the top-grossing films of the year, was the only
one filmed outside the United States (at Shepperton Studios,
Middlesex, near London), and the only one without Lamour as
the female star. It was filmed from Aug 2 to Nov 3, with
the songs recorded in September. After Brigitte Bardot,
Gina Lollobrigida, and Sophia Loren were considered, the
female lead went to Collins. Lamour accepted a small role
after it was expanded and her songs were given less distrac-
tion. The script was based on "The Bamboo Kid," bought by
Bob Hope from Danny Kaye in 1959. Many special sets, like a
Tibetan monastery, an underwater headquarters, a rocketship,
submarine, a Hong Kong nightclub, and planet terrain, were
constructed, and three versions of the film were released,
altering some dialogue for American, British, and international audiences. Sellers performs a burlesque of the
Indian physician he played in <u>The Millionairess</u> (British,
1960) with Sophia Loren, directed by Anthony Asquith.
Hope's name in the film is the real name of composer James
Van Heusen [Edward Chester Babcock], used as a private joke,
especially when Hope disparages it as Crosby tries to re-
store his memory. Bing and Hope each had a third financial
interest in the film, and just by May 1962 records indicated
a return of $2 million each. It was rated in Britain by
<u>Films and Filming</u> as the fifth most successful film of the
year. Fred Reynolds (p. 4) states the film, seeming old
fashioned, is not as good as the other <u>Road</u> films, and that
one British critic faults Panama's and Frank's jokes, designed to make Bing and Hope feel at ease, with appealing
primarily to viewers their own age (p. 264). Lamour demanded a bigger part than first offered to appear and stated in
a 1992 interview on the American Movie Channel that she had
no quarrel with Collins: She "never [had] a feud . . . and
when I do it'll be with the star." This is the only <u>Road</u>
film that includes the definite article in the title.
     "Age may have withered somewhat the glossy hides of
Bing Crosby and Bob Hope, and custom may have done a little
something to stale their brand of vaudeville. But the old
boys still come through nicely in another turn in the old
'Road' act. . . . This sequence, with the boys in the space
suits tailored to fit the somewhat more bulky gorillas and
being fed by a rotary machine that pokes bananas at them, is
the liveliest and funniest in the film. It may not serve to
popularize space travel, but it sure makes hilarious monkeys
of Bing and Bob." Bosley Crowther, N.Y. <u>Times</u>, Jun 28.
     "Perhaps the old formula creaks occasionally, but not
enough to cause any disappointment while the zany situations
and razor-edge wisecracks keep the whole affair bubbling
happily. . . . The result is an amiable comedy which should
please nostalgic customers and entice those who haven't seen

any of the previous 'Road' pix." Rich., [London, Apr 3],
Variety, Apr 4.

EXTRA: Dore Shary asked Bing in 1962 to play the lead
in "The Devil's Advocate," to be directed by Henry King and
co-starring Frederic March and Sophia Loren, but evidently
the project died. Producer David Susskind wanted Bing in
1962 to star in his All the Way Home (1963), but Robert
Preston got that role, co-starring with Jean Simmons, directed by Alex Segal. A further Road film was suggested, to
be called either "Road to Calcutta" or "Road to Bombay." In
1964 the title became "Road to India," but it was not produced. Bing also attempted in 1962 to buy the film rights
to Paul Ford's stage musical Never Too Late, which was
filmed in 1965 with Paul Douglas and Connie Stevens, directed by Bud Yorkin.

F145.   Search for Venus (1962) Impersonation.
A nudist exploitation film in which the starlet Carole
Wilson leads a visit to several nudist camps. The sound-
track includes several voice impersonations, including those
of Bing, Cary Grant, Groucho Marx, James Stewart, James
Mason, and Winston Churchill.

F146.   The Sound of Laughter (1962, Union Films) Antholo-
gy 75 min. bw d: John O'Shaughnessy p: Barry B. Yellen,
Irvin S. Dorfman w: Fred Saidy (continuity, narration).
Dec 17
Danny Kaye, Bing Crosby, Bob Hope, Buster Keaton, Harry
Langdon, Shirley Temple, the Ritz Brothers, Andy Clyde,
Edgar Kennedy, Imogene Coca, Bert Lahr, Milton Berle, Billy
Gilbert, Will Mahoney, and others. Narrated by Ed Wynn.
Clips from short films of the early 'thirties,
with rare early shots of Crosby, Hope, and others.
"There's a frightful scene of a skinny Bing Crosby
caught in a cage with a lion [Dream House (1932)]--and
another of Bob Hope, made-up sweetly, singing a love song to
a girl in a grocery store [Going Spanish (1934)]. A young
Milton Berle acts like a scarecrow in a poisonous bit with
some dancing girls and Danny Kaye, still fresh from the
borscht circuit, does a frantically labored skit in formal
dress. . . . [Wynn] is only funny because he is so bad."
Bosley Crowther, N.Y. Times, Dec 18.

EXTRA: An untitled film project was considered in 1963
for both Bing and Lucille Ball. Bing also attempted to
obtain the film rights in 1963 to the The Rain Maker (a 1956
film) for a musical version. The musical was produced
without Bing's participation as 110 in the Shade. He also
sought to buy the rights to Meredith Willson's Broadway
musical Here's Love but failed.

F147.   Robin and the Seven Hoods (1964, Warner Bros.-7
Arts) 123 min. col d: Gordon Douglas p: Frank Sinatra
and P-C Productions ep: Howard Koch c, ap: William H.
Daniels w: David R. Schwartz m, l: Sammy Cahn, James Van
Heusen score: Nelson Riddle o: Gilbert C. Grau art: LeRoy
Deane   sd: Raphael Bretton ch: Jack Baker mu: Gordon Bau
hair: Jean Burt Reilly dialogue supervision: Thomas Conroy

sound: Everett Hughes, Vinton Vernon e: Sam O'Steen.
Hollywood preview, Academy Awards Theatre Jun 19; Aug 5 (Jul
23 in the U.K.)

Frank Sinatra, Dean Martin, Sammy Davis, Jr., Bing
Crosby, Peter Falk, Barbara Rush, Victor Buono, Hank Henry,
Jack LaRue, Robert Foulk, Phil Crosby, Barry Kelley, Hans
Conreid, Sig Ruman, Allen Jenkins, Robert Carricart, Phil
Arnold, Sonny King, Richard Simmonds, Harry Swoger, Harry
Wilson, Richard Bakalyan, Bernard Fein, Carol Hill, Joseph
Ruskin, Maurice Manson, Milton Rudin, Diane Sayer, Bill
Zuckert, Chris Hughes, Edward G. Robinson

Alan A. Dale (Crosby) is the stuffy secretary of an
orphanage. In 1928, Guy Gisborne (Falk) has Big Jim (Robinson) shot, betrayed by Sheriff Octavius Glick (Foulk) during
a lavish birthday party, and elects himself the new Number
One. Robbo (Sinatra), with Will Scarlet (Davis) as others
of his gang, warns Guy to avoid the North Side, Robbo's
turf. Vermin and Tomatoes (Jenkins and LaRue) are in Guy's
gang. Robbo meets poolsharp Little John (Martin) from
Indiana, who joins Robbo and inspires an attack on Guy's
club. Meanwhile, Guy destroys Robbo's club. Socialite
Marian Stevens (Rush), daughter of Big Jim and using her
mother's maiden name, offers Robbo $50,000 to avenge her
father. She pays him after the sheriff's murder, but Guy
had killed him and has him placed in the concrete cornerstone of the new police station. Potts (Buono), always
drinking cocoa, is the new sheriff, and Will, ordered by
Robbo to "dump" the money, donates it to Dale's Blessed
Shelter Orphans Home in Robbo's name, which brings him civic
adulation. Naive Dale offers himself as Robbo's publicity
and charity director. Six Seconds (Henry) hears Dale's
vocabulary and says, "I sink there's sumthin' wrong wid his
troat." He is hired at $100 a week, saying, "Oh boy, I'm a
Hood, a Hood." One Hood (Bakalyan) practices knitting.
Robbo inspires Dale to dress with style and opens a gambling
casino, built by Mr. Ricks (Conreid) in two months, that
converts into a Skid Row mission when the police arrive with
Guy. The officers hear a 17-year-old girl (Sayer) and
others testify against "booze." Guy frames Robbo, who is
tried for murdering Glick, and while he is in jail, Marian
and John become counterfeiters, using Robbo's soup kitchen
as their front. The prosecutor (Simmonds) leads Guy and
Potts in their testimony as Dale defends Robbo to the orphans. Robbo is acquitted, upbraids John, and slaps Marian.
Marian asks Guy to kill Robbo, but Guy ends up in the cornerstone of a pretzel factory dedicated by Hammacher
(Ruman). John leaves Marian, who organizes the Women's
League for Better Government and leads women to destroy
Robbo's locations. Defeated, Robbo, John, and Will end up
in Santa Claus suits, ringing bells for Christmas for a
mission and freezing in the snowfall. Marian alights from a
limousine, followed by Dale in formal dress. He drops a
donation from a bulging wallet into each bucket and, taking
Marian's arm, struts into the new Women's League building,
where Potts lies in the cornerstone. Songs include "All for
One and One for All" by Falk and his group; "Give Praise,
Give Praise" by a group of mourners; "I Like to Lead When I
Dance" by a male chorus at Robbo's; "Any Man Who Loves His
Mother" by Martin; "Bang, Bang" by Davis; "Style" with

Sinatra and Martin; "Charlotte Couldn't Charleston" by
female chorus; "Mr. Booze" with Sinatra, Martin, Davis, and
group; "Don't Be a Do-Badder" with children, reprised by
Sinatra, Martin, and Davis; and "My Kind of Town" by Sinatra
and chorus.

NOTE: The film took months to complete, from about Sep
1963 to Feb 1964, and most of it was filmed at night at
Sinatra's insistence. Sinatra also sang "I Like to Lead
When I Dance," intended for an early song to Rush, but it
was omitted from the film. Bing was supposed to film "The
Devil's Advocate," but when it did not materialize he took
the role of Allen A. Dale. He brought his wife and younger
children to the studio on Nov 29, 1963, when he sang "Don't
Be a Do-Badder," and Nathaniel vomited on him. Philip
Crosby appeared as a member of Robbo's gang and had one
line, saying, "Sit down, Pops," when he offered Bing a
chair. President Kennedy was assassinated (Nov 22, 1963)
during the production, and Bing and Hyde-Whyte became
friends at the studio, often talking about horses. Davis
was so struck by Bing's singing of "Mr. Booze" that he
missed his cue for one take. Upbraided by Sinatra, Sammy
said, "To hell with you, Frank. I'm listening to Bing."
Robinson reprised a role like the one he had in Little
Caesar (1930), which established the gangster genre and
helped spark a public reaction against films that were
excessively violent, indecent, and glorifying crime. Jenkins and LaRue were also staples in old gangster films.

". . . as though there weren't enough aping in it, Mr.
Crosby sings a moralizing song, 'Don't Be a Do-Badder' in a
roomful of charity-home boys. Well, at least, one can say
this for it: The usual Sinatra arrogance is subdued."
Bosley Crowther, N.Y. Times, Aug 6.

"Performance-wise, Falk comes out best. His comic
gangster is a pure gem and he should get plenty of offers
after this. Sinatra, of course, is smooth and Crosby in a
'different' type of role rates a big hand. Martin seems
lost in the shuffle. Davis is slick and Miss Rush, going
heavy, is beautiful to look at." Whit., [Hollywood, Jun 18]
Variety, Jun 24.

EXTRA: Bing, Dean Martin, Frank Sinatra, Sammy Davis,
Jr., Louis Armstrong, and others were reported by M-G-M in
1965 as ready to star in "Say It with Music," an Irving
Berlin musical to be directed by Vincente Minnelli, but in
1969 the project was canceled.

Bing had agreed to film Rocket to the Moon in 1966 in
Ireland, playing Phineas T. Barnum of the Jules Verne's
novel, but Bing became ill and Burl Ives took the role. The
film is not to be confused with the 1954 film starring Sonny
Tufts and retitled Cat Women of the Moon. Bing was also
proposed for Bloomer Girl in 1966, The Absence of a Cello,
Mad Dogs and Englishmen, and The Family Band with Walt
Disney.

F148.   Cinerama's Russian Adventure (1966, United Road-
show Presentations release) Narration 145 min. col d:
Leonid Kristy, Roman Karmen, and others p: Harold J. Dennis, J. Jay Frankel, Soviet Kinopanorama production super-
visor: Thomas Conroy m: Aleksandr Lokshin and others c:

Nikolai Generalov and others music e: William E. Wild.
Chicago, McVickers Cinerama Theatre Mar 29; London Apr 7;
New York, Warner Cinerama Theater Apr 13

Bing Crosby appears in a small screen, sings
briefly, playing a balalaika (three strings, triangular
body), and then narrates this Cinerama tour of Russian culture and geography produced by Russians and released under
the auspices of the Cultural Exchange Program. The original
narrator was Homer McCoy, replaced by Crosby in this re-
edited release.

NOTE: This is a completely Russian production of six
directors and seven cameramen. The Cinerama format includes
a 180-degree screen. Russians spent eight years on the
film. The original narrator was Homer McCoy, replaced by
Bing about Jan 1966. Another version was edited down to 122
min. The intent of the exchange was to let each country see
and better understand the other.

"As narrator for this package, they have that old
gadabout and Russophile, Bing Crosby, whose jolly tone and
lingo tend to embrace all the Russians as chums. His narration provides meager information, however, aside form the
fact that the Soviet Union spans 10 time zones. That is the
most striking fact about Russia you are likely to get from
this film." Bosley Crowther, N.Y. _Times_, Apr 14.

"Bing Crosby, who handles the narration and appears
briefly in the beginning to introduce the picture, turns in
a first-rate job, easily projecting the affable aura around
the entire production." Ron., _Variety_, Apr 6.

F149.   _Stagecoach_ (1966, 20th Century-Fox) 114 min. col
d: Gordon Douglas asst: Joseph E. Richards, Ray Kellogg p:
Martin Rackin ap: Alvin G. Manuel w: Joseph Landon s:
former screenplay by Dudley Nichols of a story by Ernest
Haycox score: Jerry Goldsmith o: Arthur Morton m, l: Lee
Pockriss, Paul Vance art: Jack Martin Smith, Herman Blumenthal sd: Walter M. Scott, Stuart A. Reiss mu: Ben Nye
hair for Ann-Margret: Sydney Guilaroff c: William H. Cloth-
ier fx: L.B. Abbott, Emil Kosa, Jr. sound: Bernard Fredericks, Elmer Raguse e: Hugh S. Fowler unit production
manager: Harry Caplan, Arthur Steloff portraits: Norman
Rockwell. Preview, Hollywood, 20th-Fox Studio May 11

(alphabetical order) Ann-Margret, Red Buttons,
Michael Connors, Alex Cord, Bing Crosby, Bob Cummings, Van
Heflin, Slim Pickens, Stefanie Powers, Keenan Wynn; with
Brad Weston, Joseph Hoover, John Gabriel, Oliver McGowen,
David Humphreys Miller, Bruce Mars, Brett Pearson, Muriel
Davidson, Ned Wynn, Norman Rockwell, Edwin Mills, Hal Lynch

Doc Josiah Boone (Crosby) is a drunken physician in
Dryfork who witnesses a saloon brawl started by two troopers
over a loose dancehall girl named Dallas (Ann-Margret).
Both soldiers die. Cavalry Capt. Mallory (Gabriel) demands
that the bartender (Lynch) purify the town by expelling Doc
and Dallas while he assembles his troop and pursues the
Sioux who have just scalped several soldiers. Doc and
Dallas ride the Concord stagecoach to Cheyenne. Also in the
coach are Hatfield (Connors), a Southern gambler-gunman;
Henry Gatewood (Cummings), a gutless bank clerk absconding
with $10,000 from his father-in-law's bank; Mr. Peacock
(Buttons), a whiskey drummer attended closely by Doc; and

Southern Mrs. Lucy Mallory (Powers), pregnant and riding to the fort to join her husband, the captain. On the trail the coach, driven by Buck (Pickens) with Marshal Curly Wilcox (Heflin) riding shotgun, picks up the Ringo Kid (Cord), who has escaped from prison, having been framed by land-hungry Luke Plummer (Keenan Wynn), who had killed Ringo's father and brother. Curly expected Ringo the head for Cheyenne and arrests him for the $500 reward and seeks to save him from the Plummers. At the stage at Horseshoe Bend, the Cavalry escort departs, but the passengers vote to proceed. Doc reluctantly sobers up to deliver the baby, assisted by Dallas, whom Mrs. Mallory had despised. Dallas helps Ringo escape, but he returns when he spots Indians. The coach departs fast, and they fight the Indians along the trail. Peacock is wounded and Hatfield dies, but the stage gets through. Sadistic Luke and his two sons, Matt and Ike (Weston and Ned Wynn), have taken over the El Dorado Saloon, and Curly handcuffs Ringo. Curly learns of Gatewood's theft; Gatewood offers the Plummers money if allowed to escape. Curly follows and demands Gatewood, but one son blasts him in the leg and they throw him out of the saloon. Doc aims a gun at the station manager and orders Ringo's release. Luke kills Gatewood, and Ringo challenges Luke to come out. The Plummers open fire, and Ringo dives in through a window and shoots all three, setting the saloon ablaze. Curly frees Ringo, who walks away with Dallas. Song "Stagecoach to Cheyenne" is sung by Wayne Newton at the end over Rockwell's portraits of the principals.
     NOTE: The film is based on the 1939 John Ford Western for United Artists, produced by Walter Wanger, that was based on a 1937 Collier's short story "Stage to Lordsburg" and Guy de Maupassant's "Boule de suif" (1880). The remake is largely rewritten and was filmed on location near Boulder, Colorado. The following lists some of the cast with that of the original cast in parentheses: Crosby (Thomas Mitchell), Cord (John Wayne), Pickens (Andy Devine), Heflin (George Bancroft), Ann-Margret (Claire Trevor), Cummings (Berton Churchill), Connors (John Carradine), Buttons (Donald Meek), Powers (Louise Platt), Wynn (Tom Tyler), Weston (Vester Pegg) and Hoover, playing Lt. Blanchard, (Tim Holt). Cord did his own riding for the remake, while Yakima Canutt performed the horse stunts for Wayne. The original was set in Arizona (filmed in Utah), the remake set in post-Civil War Colorado. For the remake, Norman Rockwell's portraits of the stars are featured at the end, and the artist, who also designed the film's logo, appears in the early saloon scene. Bing made a blooper that had to be reshot: he was supposed to say that he and Dallas were victims of social prejudice, but he said, "You see, my dear, we are both victims of a social disease." Crosby braved his role, taking his own risks, ignoring the Oscar-winning style of Thomas Mitchell in the original. Bing was widely expected to win an Oscar, but he was not even nominated for Best Supporting Actor. Oscars went to the 1939 film for Best Supporting Actor (Mitchell) and Best Score, and the New York critics named Ford the Best Director. Other versions include Apache Uprising (1966), directed by R.G. Springsteen and starring Rory Calhoun and Corinne Calver, and a television movie titled Stagecoach (1986), directed by Ted Post

and starring Willie Nelson, Kris Kristofferson, Johnny Cash,
Waylon Jennings, John Schneider, Elizabeth Ashley, Tony
Franciosa, Anthony Newley, Mary Crosby, and June Carter.
Leonard Maltin rates the TV film as "average," but notes
that the actors disdained "the simple-minded script." Mary
Crosby is Bing's daughter, playing the roles done by Platt
and Powers in the earlier versions.

John Ford was disturbed when he learned his masterpiece
was being remade, for which Douglas had a $5 million budget.
Filming began in Hollywood Jul 6, 1965, and went to Colorado
on Jul 10. On Aug 3 they were back in the studio, on Aug 19
they moved to the studio's ranch in Malibu Canyon, back to
the studio on Aug 30 for some night scenes, and filming
ended Sep 10. Bing joined the cast on the first day and
completed his work Sep 2. In Colorado Bing suffered from
bursitis and had an attack of kidney stones as soon as he
finished, but the next week his factotum, Leo Lynn, delivered a special key chain to each member of the cast. The
mementos were made of silver, with a stagecoach sculpted on
one side and on the other a message engraved in goldleaf in
Bing's hand: "Thanks, Bing / Stagecoach, 1965." Muriel
Davidson, who played a woman in the film, and her sister
Janet Rale, listed as a publicity coordinator, were actually
charged with writing a journal of the filming for The Saturday Evening Post (B113) and only Bing had been informed.
Twenty-four Sioux from South Dakota were hired as extras,
but only ten remained at the end. One was fired for fighting, another for threatening a stuntman, two for stealing
beer, one was injured by powder burns, another by a horse.
Chief Yellow Horse and others rode to nearby Nederland and
sold passes for $1 each to visit the set and enjoy free
food. By the time 14 had been discharged, however, most of
their scenes had been completed.

"In a decided departure from the norm, Bing Crosby, as
the unshaven, sodden surgeon, is casual, natural, glib and
mildly funny. . . . Superb sound and fury make [the film]
an enjoyable trip most of the way." A.H. Weiler, N.Y.
Times, Jun 16.

"Crosby projects eloquently the jaded worldliness of a
down-and-outer who still has not lost all self-respect.
Much humor evolves from his running gag with Red Buttons,
the preacher-dressed and mannered liquor salesman played
earlier by the late Donald Meek." Murf., [Hollywood, May
12] Variety, May 25.

EXTRA: Bing was proposed in 1967 for The Great St. Bernard, another untitled film to reunite Bing with Fred Astaire, and for the Frank Sinatra film The Detective (1968)
with Lee Remick.

F150.   The Private Navy of Sgt. O'Farrell (1968, United
Artists) Guest (stock footage) 92 min. col d: Frank
Tashlin p: John Beck w: Tashlin.
Bob Hope, Phyllis Diller, Jeffrey Hunter, Gina
Lollobrigida, Mylene Demongeot, John Myhers, Mako
Sgt. O'Farrell (Hope) tries to obtain nurses for an
island to improve the morale of his men, but he receives
only Phyllis Diller. Bing Crosby is seen in a clip singing
"Pennies from Heaven." Leonard Maltin states that this film

may be Hope's worst.

F151.   <u>Bing Crosby's Washington State</u> (1968, Cenecrest)
Documentary 28 min. d: Dave Gardner p: Washington State
s: Robert Brown, Ruth Davis c: Brown, Davis, Gardner.
    Bing narrates this travelogue of the State of Washing-
ton to promote tourism. Besides ships, mountains, and
cultural institutions, the film shows Spokane (where he grew
up), Tacoma (his birthplace), and Olympia (the capital where
Bing's great grandfather's home is a museum). At the end
Bing states that his childhood in Washington put a song in
his heart. It was filmed about Sep 1967.

    EXTRA: Bing was encouraged in 1968 to join Bob Hope for
a film called "Road to Christmas." Paramount offered Bing
the lead in <u>Paint Your Wagon</u> (1969), but he evidently
thought the role of a grubby prospector involved in a <u>menage
a trois</u> unsuitable. Lee Marvin took the role. Bing also
refused in 1968 to join the film cast of the play <u>Spofford</u>.

F152.   <u>Richard Hamilton</u> (1969, The Arts Council of Great
Britain; U.K.) Guest (stock footage) Short.
    The film shows paintings by Richard Hamilton, and for
one titled <u>I'm Dreaming of a White Christmas</u>, Bing is shown
in a color negative singing "White Christmas."

F153.   <u>Golf's Golden Years</u> (1970) Narrator Short Unknown.
    Bing Crosby is the narrator.

F154.   <u>Dr. Cook's Garden</u> (1971, Paramount Pictures Tele-
vision and ABC-TV) 90 min. col d: Ted Post p: Bob Markell
ap: George Goodman w: Art Wallace s: Ira Levin m: Robert
Drasnin art: William C. Molyneaux c: Urs Ferrer e: Jack
McSweeney. Jan 19, ABC-TV "Tuesday Night Movies" (See V171)
    Bing Crosby, Frank Converse, Blythe Danner, Abby
Lewis, Barnard Hughes, Bethel Leslie, Staats Cotsworth,
Jordan Reed, Helen Stenborg, Carol Morley, Fred Burrel,
Thomas Barbour
    Dr. Leonard Cook (Crosby), a mild town doctor in Ver-
mont and the idol of Jimmy Tennyson (Converse), is uncovered
when Jimmy becomes a doctor, returns home, and learns that
Cook is obsessed with perfection to the point of euthanasia
on the bad and ill people in town. Jane Rausch (Danner),
Elias Hart (Hughes), Ted Rausch (Cotsworth), and the minister (Barbour) are some of the villagers. Cook wants the
town as free of "weeds" as his garden. On a picnic Cook
feeds Jimmy a poisoned ham sandwich, but Jimmy tricks Cook
into administering an antidote. After Cook explains that he
murders out of pity for the ill, Jimmy confesses that he had
tricked Cook, who becomes enraged and tries to kill Jimmy
with a garden hoe. The exertion causes Cook to suffer a
heart attack, and Jimmy refuses to give him the life-saving
nitroglycerin tablets. Cook pleads for help, and Jimmy
replies that he believes he is helping the elderly doctor,
who says, "You see how it begins."
    NOTE: This is the only film in which Crosby plays a
villain, albeit a generally mild-mannered psychopath. The
film has never been released to theaters, and has been

revived on television only once or twice. The script is
based on Ira Levin's 1967 Broadway play in which Burl Ives
starred and Keir Dullea co-starred, a play that had a brief
run. The TV film was shown in the United Kingdom in 1972
and 1974.

F155.   Cancel My Reservation (1972, Warner Bros.) Guest
MPAA rating: G 99 min.   col   d: Paul Bogart   p: NAHO (NBC-
Bob Hope), Gordon Oliver   exec. p: Bob Hope   w: Arthur Marx,
Robert Fisher   s: Louis L'Amour's The Broken Gun   m: Dominic
Frontiere   art: Roland M. Brooks   sd: Anthony Mondell.
Preview Warner Bros., Burbank Sep 12
          Bob Hope, Eva Marie Saint, Ralph Bellamy, Forrest
Tucker, Anne Archer, Keenan Wynn, Henry Darrow, Doodles
Weaver, Chief Dan George, Betty Ann Carr, Herb Vigren,
Gordon Oliver, Paul Bogart, Buster Shaver, Marsha Umberhauer
          Dan Bartlett (Hope) is a late-night TV host whose wife,
Sheila (Saint), makes his program popular; Dan is so annoyed
he travels to Arizona for rest as Bing Crosby is scheduled
to substitute on the show. Dan becomes embroiled in an
Indian girl's mysterious murder, solved through the efforts
of another Indian girl (Carr) and mystic Old Bear (George).
While in jail, Dan suffers an anxiety daydream of being
lynched by a mob, a dream in which his wife (Sheila/Saint),
Bing Crosby, Johnny Carson, John Wayne, and Flip Wilson
appear. When Dan asks Bing, "Aren't you going to help me?"
Bing, in a blue crush hat and black sweater, laughs and
replies, "Help you? Who do you think bought the rope?"
          NOTE: Most of the film was made in Arizona.
          " . . . a tame murder comedy. . . . Hope's one-liner
voiceovers frame, sustain and prop up the fumbling plot, in
which the funniest scene is a lynching nightmare. . . .
Hope's regular tv appearances have at least the topicality
of current events . . . and the eventual tv licensing will
make everything all right in the accounting department."
Murf. Variety, Sep 20.

F156.   Paper Moon (1973, Paramount) Voice only 102 min.
bw   d: Peter Bogdanovich   w: Alvin Sargent   s: Joe David
Brown's play Addie Pray.
          Ryan O'Neal, Tatum O'Neal, Madeline Kahn, John
Hillerman, P.J. Johnson, Burton Gilliam, Randy Quaid
          A con man (R. O'Neal) teams with a bright child (T.
O'Neal, Ryan's daughter) in the 1930s to make easy money.
In one scene Bing is heard on the radio singing "Just One
More Chance." Tatum won an Oscar as best supporting ac-
tress.

          EXTRA: Bing and Bob Hope bid $1 million in 1973 but
were outbid for the Neil Simon play The Sunshine Boys
(1975), about two former Vaudeville partners who hate each
other. Walter Matthau and George Burns starred in the film.

F157.   That's Entertainment (1974, Metro-Goldwyn-Mayer
United Artists release) Co-host MPAA rating: G 132 min.
col   d, p, w: Jack Haley, Jr.   ep: Daniel Melnick   c: Gene
Polito, Ernest Laszlo, Russel Metty, Ennio Guarnieri, Allan
Green   optics: Robert Hoag, Jim Liles   e: Bud Friedgen,
David E. Blewitt   ms: Jesse Kaye, Henry Mancini. Preview,

M-G-M Studio, Culver City Apr 12
        (Alphabetical order) Fred Astaire, Bing Crosby,
Gene Kelly, Peter Lawford, Liza Minnelli, Donald O'Connor,
Debbie Reynolds, Mickey Rooney, Frank Sinatra, James Stewart, Elizabeth Taylor
        The stars host a nostalgic collection of clips from
nearly 100 M-G-M musicals, including Esther Williams, Clark
Gable singing and dancing, Jimmy Durante, and Eleanor Powell
dancing with Astaire. Near the end of the film Bing comments on <u>Going Hollywood</u> (1933) and <u>High Society</u> (1956), his
own M-G-M musicals, and others, and is shown singing "Going
Hollywood" and "Well, Did You Evah!," the latter with Sinatra. Sinatra opens and closes the film.
        NOTE: The musicals appeared from 1929 to 1958, although
the mastery of M-G-M in musicals began only about 1940, when
Arthur Freed, the former songwriter, became a major producer. The studio earlier trailed the musicals by Warner Bros.
and RKO. The film includes clips from about 100 films. The
version released in the United Kingdom ran for 137 min. and
included a third Crosby song: "True Love."
        "[The film] is a consciousness-raising delight, and
immediate high, a revue that doesn't only evoke the past
but, in addition, lays the past out there to compete with
the present on its own terms. . . . It asks a question:
what the hell ever happened to the American movie musical?
. . . you'll see how the American musical film grew out of
its innocence to peak in wit and sophistication in the
fifties, only to slide back into the pious, lugubrious,
pseudo-innocence of recent years." Vincent Canby, N.Y.
<u>Times</u>, Jul 7.
        "[The film is] an outstanding, stunning, sentimental,
exciting, colorful, enjoyable, spirit-lifting, tuneful,
youthful, invigorating, zesty, respectful, heart-warming,
awesome, cheerful, dazzling, and richly satisfying feature
documentary. . . . Is it possible that the unabashed arti-
fice of older films communicates more strongly with the
subconscious than the synthetic 'reality' of modern films?"
Murf., <u>Variety</u>, Apr 17.

        EXTRA: Bing and Bob Hope were asked in 1975 to play
widowed grandfathers with Dorothy Lamour in a film called
"Road to Tomorrow," but it fell through.

F158.   <u>Brother, Can You Spare a Dime?</u> (1975, Sandford
Lieberson-David Putnam Production) Voice only Documentary
106 min.
        America in the Great Depression of the 1930s is depict-
ed in newsreel footage and film clips. Bing appears in two
cartoon caricatures and singing the title song and "Where
the Blue of the Night." Bing recorded "Brother Can You
Spare a Dime" Oct 25, 1932. The film is often replayed on
the American Movie Classics cable.

F159.   <u>That's Entertainment, Part 2</u> (1976, Metro-Goldwyn-
Mayer United Artists release) Guest MPAA rating: G   133
min. col d: Gene Kelly ass't: William R. Poole p: Saul
Chaplin, Daniel Melnick w: Leonard Gershe c: George Folsey
e: Bud Friedgen, David Blewitt, David Bretherton, Peter C.
Johnson ms: Nelson Riddle special l: Howard Deitz, Chaplin

optics: Jim Liles   new anim: Hanna-Barbera.   Preview, Culver
City Apr 13
          Fred Astaire and Gene Kelly co-host this sequel,
which now includes comedy and drama as well as musicals.
     About 30 minutes into the film Bing Crosby appears
singing "Temptation" from <u>Going Hollywood</u> and "Now You Has
Jazz" with Louis Armstrong from <u>High Society</u>.   Shortly after
Bing's first song, Ethel Waters, one of Bing's idols, appears singing "Takin' a Chance on Love" from the all-black
film <u>Cabin in the Sky</u> (1943).
     NOTE: The film includes clips from about 72 feature
films and other short subjects, with about 100 performers.
     "Certainly 'That's Entertainment, Part 2' is as much
fun as the first film, and perhaps even more interesting as
Hollywood history. . . Frank Sinatra, seen in a montage of
sequences covering his M-G-M career, including the early,
unintentionally hilarious "Old Man River" sequence from
'Till the Clouds Roll By,' not only got better and better as
a singer as the years rolled by but his appearance changed
considerably, also for the better." Vincent Canby, N.Y.
<u>Times</u>, May 31.
     "The very handsome and polished sequel . . . transforms
excerpts from perhaps $100,000,000 worth of classic Metro
library footage into a billion dollars worth of fun, excite-
ment, amusement, escapism, fantasy, nostalgia and happi-
ness." Murf., <u>Variety</u>, May 5.

F160.   <u>The Man Who Fell to Earth</u> (1976, British Lion;
U.K.) Voice only 140 min. col d: Nicolas Roeg s: novel
by Walter Tevis.
          David Bowie, Rip Torn, Candy Clark, Buck Henry,
Bernie Casey, Jackson D. Kane
     Bowie plays an extraterrestrial posing as a corporate
giant who is actually seeking water for his planet. Bing is
heard singing "True Love." The film was remade for American
television in 1987; the original film was cut to 118 min.
for the United States.

F161.   <u>Tracks</u> (1976) Voice only 90 min. col d: Henry
Jaglom.
          Dennis Hopper, Taryn Power, Dean Stockwell, Topo
Swope, Michael Emil, Zack Norman
     Hopper plays a Vietnam veteran escorting the body of a
fallen comrade by train across the country and loses his
mind.   The soundtrack includes Bing singing "These Foolish
Things" and "There'll Be a Hot Time in the Town of Berlin."
Two characters played by Emil and Norman are reprised in
<u>Sitting Ducks</u> (1980).

     EXTRA: Bing agreed in 1977 to join Bob Hope and Dorothy
Lamour in a film called "Road to the Fountain of Youth,"
produced by Lew Grade and being written by Mel Shavelson
when Bing died in October.

F162.   <u>Funny Business: Comedy from the Movies' Greatest
Era</u> (1978, Universal) Anthology 2 hrs. ep: Leonard B.
Stern d, p, w: Richard Schickel narrator: Walter Matthau.
          W.C. Fields, the Marx Brothers, Laurel and Hardy,
Bing Crosby and Bob Hope, Mae West, Abbott and Costello,

"and an all star cast"
     Scenes from the 1930s and 1940's narrated by Walter
Matthau. Bing appears with Bob Hope in several scenes from
Road films.   Dorothy Lamour sings "Moonlight Becomes You,"
Bing and Hope sing "On the Road to Morocco," Bing quiets an
histrionic Hope on the raft at the end of Morocco, Bing and
Hope appear stoking the boiler in Utopia, sing "Put it
There" in Utopia, greet a younger Crosby at the end of
Utopia, and perform their "pat-a-cake" routine in Singapore.
Other stars presented are Edward Everett Horton, Veronica
Lake, Joel McCrea, Charles Coburn, John Barrymore, Edgar
Bergen and Charlie McCarthy, Olson and Johnson, George Burns
and Garcie Allen, Jack Benny, and Fred Allen.

F163.   Grace Kelly (1983) Impersonation Television Movie
100 min. col d: Anthony Page w: Cynthia Mandelberg.
          Cheryl Ladd, Lloyd Bridges, Diane Ladd, Alejandro
Rey, Ian McShane, William Schallert, Marta DuBois, Salome
Gens, Edith Fellows
     Grace Kelly (C. Ladd) rises from starlet to the Prin-
cess of Monaco, married to Prince Rainier (McShane) and
pleasing her father, Jack Kelly (Bridges). Bing Crosby,
Gary Cooper, William Holden, Clark Gable, Alfred Hitchcock,
and Edith Head (Fellows) appear in impersonations. Scenes
from The Country Girl (1954) are reenacted. Kelly died in
late 1982, reportedly having approved this script.

F164.   Christmas Comes to Tattertown (1988, Wang Film
Production Co., Ltd.) Voice only Animation 60 min. A
Bakshi Animation Production-Cukoo's Nest Studio col.
     The cartoon depicts a pessimistic attempt to capture
the spirit of Christmas in Tattertown. At the end, as the
attempt has failed, Bing Crosby's rendition of "White
Christmas" is played as a contrast. The song is credited as
"Courtesy of MCA Records."

F165-79. Bing Crosby recordings have also been played in
the following feature films since 1978. (Most of those of
the 1980s are listed in Bing 96 (Dec 1990): 22.)

Year	Film	Song(s)
1978	The Brinks Job	Accentuate the Positive
1978	F.I.S.T.	Santa Claus Is Coming to Town
1982	Pennies from Heaven	Did You Ever See a Dream Walking?
1982	Some Kind of Hero	Silver Bells
1982	Frances	Love Is So Terrific
1983	A Christmas Story	Jingle Bells
		It's Beginning to Look a Lot Like Christmas
		Santa Claus Is Coming to Town
1984	Racing with the Moon	Moonlight Becomes You
1985	A Nightmare on Elm Street: Part 2: Freddy's Revenge	Did You Ever See a Dream Walking?
1986	Tough Guys	Don't Get Around Much Anymore

1987	Radio Days	Pistol Packin' Mama
1987	Someone to Love	Long Ago and Far Away
1989	National Lampoon's Christmas Vacation	Mele Kalikimaka (The Hawaiian Christmas Song)
1989	When Harry Met Sally	Have Yourself a Merry Little Christmas
1991	November Days	Song of Freedom

[Irving Berlin's "Song of Freedom" is interspersed throughout this TV documentary on the fall of the Berlin Wall, produced by Marcel Ophuls for the BBC.]

| 1993 | Grumpy Old Men | Winter Wonderland |

NOTE: Most of Bing's films are available on home videos. See Home Videos, pages 363-65.

A SAMPLER OF BOB HOPE'S LINES ON BING

Bob Hope probably referred to or alluded to Bing in a score of films and in scores of radio and television programs. The following mentions a few more feature films, in addition to those delineated above. See the end of the Videography for a sample comment on television.

F180.   In They Got Me Covered (1943, Paramount), a film in which Hope becomes embroiled with spies and is helped by Dorothy Lamour, he is taken to a hotel bedroom in Niagara, where he opens a musical cigarette box and hears Bing singing the line, "When the Blue of the Night" [instead of "Where the Blue"] and ending with several "boo-boo-boos." Hope says, "That guy's haunting me." Bing frequently sang the wrong word to begin his famous signature song. Hope wrote his first book, published 1941, titled like this film, a paperback that features a foreword by Bing. The book's success inspired the film's title. In his book he calls Bing "the little fat man who sings" and lampoons his horses (p. 61).

F181.   In Monsieur Beaucaire (1946, Paramount), directed by George Marshall, Hope plays the barber to King Louis (Reginald Owen) of France and impersonates a French duke in Spain about to marry a Spanish princess. A Spanish lord (Joseph Schildkraut), seeking trouble with France, imprisons the real French duke (Patric Knowles), ostensibly as an impostor. When M. Beaucaire (Hope) asks the Spanish nobleman what would happen to a man impersonating a duke, he explains that they would stand him against a wall and, "bing, bing," shoot him dead. Beaucaire says, "Bing? What an awful thought." In the end the real duke marries the Spanish princess (Marjorie Reynolds) and Beaucaire escapes to America with the French king's maid, Mimi (Joan Caulfield). Their child is the image of Bob Hope (not Bing Crosby, as some sources assert. The child that looks like Bing at 35 appears at the end of Road to Utopia, also released in 1946.) The story was by Booth Tarkington, who wrote the novel Bing's Mississippi (1935) was based on, but Hope's film takes broad liberties.

F182.   In My Favorite Spy (1951, Paramount), directed by

Norman Z. McLeod, Hope plays Peanuts "Boffo" White, who
resembles Eric Augustine, a spy killed by American agents,
and again gets involved in international intrigue. He is
aided by Hedy Lamarr, Augustine's lover. At the home in
Tangier of the chief villain, Hope picks up a skull, studies
it, and says, "Looks like a fella I know who sings." Another film of the same title appeared in 1942 with Kay Kyser
and Jane Wyman.

F183.   In Here Come the Girls (1953, Paramount), directed
by Claude Binyon, starring Bob Hope, Tony Martin, Arlene
Dahl, Rosemary Clooney, Millard Mitchell, William Demarest,
Fred Clark, and Robert Strauss, Hope plays an incompetent
chorus boy named Stanley Snodgrass in New York in 1900.
Stanley is picked unawares by the musical producer Fraser
(Clark) and detective Logan (Demarest) to seem to be the
lover and costar of Irene Bailey (Dahl) to protect Allan
Trent (Martin). The Slasher, a man named Bennett (Strauss),
seeks to kill Irene's lover and stalks Stanley, who believes
he has become the star. Before Stanley's first starring
performance, he meets a boy outside his dressing room and
tells him, "Just watch me from the wings and someday you too
may be a star. What is your name, sonny boy?" The boy
says, "Crosby." "What's your first name?" Stanley asks.
"Bang," the boy answers. "That's pretty close," replies
Stanley. After the terrible performance, Bang kicks Stanley
in the shin, but when the producer realizes he still needs
Stanley until the murderer is caught, Stanley turns and
kicks the boy's shin. When Stanley realizes he is a mere
goat, he receives a run-of-the-play contract and performs
reluctantly until the Slasher is caught. Stanley marries
chorus girl Daisy (Clooney), but two years later he remains
unable to get onstage to perform.

BING'S ACADEMY NOMINATIONS AND AWARDS FOR ACTING

      Role   Film and Year
Father Chuck O'Malley   Going My Way, 1944
      Bing won the Oscar as Best Actor

Frank Elgin   The Country Girl, 1954
      Bing was nominated for Best Actor, but Marlon Brando
won the Oscar.

      NOTE: See the end of the Discography for songs that won
Nominations and Oscars as Best Songs.

BING'S HIGHLY POPULAR FILMS

    * Films that won Academy Nominations (not for songs)
    ** Films that won Oscars (not for songs)
    *** Films with Academy Award Nominated songs
    **** Films with Academy Award Oscar-Winning songs

Title	Studio and Year
1. The King of Jazz	Universal, 1930 **
2. She Loves Me Not	Paramount, 1934 ***
3. Rhythm on the Range	Paramount, 1936
4. Pennies from Heaven	Columbia, 1936 ***
5. Waikiki Wedding	Paramount, 1937 ****
6. Road to Singapore	Paramount, 1940
7. Rhythm on the River	Paramount, 1940 ***
8. Road to Zanzibar	Paramount, 1941
9. Holiday Inn	Paramount, 1942 ****
10. Road to Morocco	Paramount, 1942 *
11. Star Spangled Rhythm	Paramount, 1943
12. Dixie	Paramount, 1943
13. Going My Way	Paramount, 1944 **/****
14. Here Come the Waves	Paramount, 1945 ***
15. Duffy's Tavern	Paramount, 1945
16. Bells of St. Mary's	RKO, 1945 ***
17. Road to Utopia	Paramount, 1946
18. Blue Skies	Paramount, 1946 ***
19. Welcome Stranger	Paramount, 1947
20. Road to Rio	Paramount, 1947
21. The Emperor Waltz	Paramount, 1948
22. A Connecticut Yankee in King Arthur's Court	Paramount, 1949
23. Here Comes the Groom	Paramount, 1951 ****
24. Just for You	Paramount, 1952 ***
25. The Greatest Show on Earth	Paramount, 1952 **
26. Road to Bali	Paramount, 1953
27. Little Boy Lost	Paramount, 1953
28. White Christmas	Paramount, 1954 ***
29. The Country Girl	Paramount, 1954 **
30. High Society	M-G-M, 1956 ***
31. Say One for Me	20th Century-Fox, 1959
32. High Time	20th Century-Fox, 1960 ***
33. The Road to Hong Kong	United Artists, 1962
34. Robin and the Seven Hoods	Warner Bros., 1964

Radiography

Entry numbers generally refer to shows of the fall and spring seasons and to special appearances.

The ratings are listed in Harrison B. Summers, ed., <u>A Thirty-Year History of Programs Carried on National Radio Networks in the United States, 1926-1956</u> (New York: Arno, N.Y. Times, 1958). The ratings represent the percentage of American homes tuned in during a week in January. The Cooperative Analysis of Broadcasting ratings are given from 1929 to 1935; C.E. Hooper, Inc., ratings from 1936 to 1949; and the A.C. Nielsen ratings after 1949.

Dates	Stations or Networks	Programs and Sponsors

1928
R1.   Jan 4   WNBC, NY   Old Gold Cigarettes Presents The King of Jazz, Paul Whiteman   Wed.
Also on Jun 19 on WEAF, Sep 18 on WNBC, Nov 15 on KMBC (Kansas City, Ivanhoe Auditorium)--mainly on Tuesdays. Crosby sang as many solos as he did numbers with the Rhythm Boys.

1929
R2.   Feb 5   WABC, NY   Old Gold/Paul Whiteman   Tue.

R3.   Mar 5-May 21   WABC, NY   Old Gold/Paul Whiteman   Tue.

R4.   May 25   WJAS, Syria Mosque (Chicago)   Old Gold/Paul Whiteman   Sat.

R5.   May 28-Aug 27   Old Gold/Paul Whiteman
On the Road: especially Chicago, St. Louis, San Francisco, Los Angeles from Jun 18 to Aug 27. Mainly Tuesdays; from Jul 2 Crosby sang many solos.

R6.   Sep 3-17   WABC, NY   Old Gold/Paul Whiteman   Tue.

R7. Sep 24-Dec 31 KMTR, L.A. Old Gold/Paul Whiteman   Tue.
Crosby may not have appeared on all programs.

1930

R8.   Jan 7-Mar 25 KMTR, L.A. Old Gold/Paul Whiteman Tue.
       Crosby may not have appeared on all programs.
       The unrated hour program, Whiteman's first full
season on radio, ended when he began his Northwest
tour, which Crosby and the Rhythm Boys left in Seattle.
Crosby appeared on no more Old Gold Hours.

R9.   Mar 30-Dec Los Angeles   The Cocoanut Grove Presents
       Gus Arnheim
       It is uncertain exactly when the Rhythm Boys
joined Arnheim and his radio broadcasts, which usually
aired thrice weekly, usually on Tuesdays, Wednesdays,
and Saturdays. Arnheim's shows began at an earlier
date without the Rhythm Boys.

1931

R10.   Jan-May 31 Los Angeles   The Cocoanut Grove (cont.)
       The Rhythm Boys left the show about the end of May
1931, when they walked out on the Cocoanut Grove and
disbanded the trio. They were subsequently blacklisted
in California while Bing continued to film shorts for
Mack Sennett.
       Rudy Vallee's 2nd season (60 min., 8 p.m., Thur.)
was rated at 36.5; sponsor: Fleischmann.

R11.   Sep 2-Oct 31 CBS, WABC, NY Presenting Bing Crosby
       15 min., six days a week, 6:45 p.m., Mon. to Sat.
from Sep 14. Sustaining (unsponsored).
       The signature song was "Love Came Into My Heart"
for a few weeks before it became "Where the Blue of the
Night."

R12.   Nov 3-Dec 31 CBS, WABC, NY Bing Crosby--The Cremo
       Singer 15 min., six days a week, Mon. to Sat.;
broadcast live nationally. Cremo was a popular cigar
brand. Every broadcast began with "Where the Blue of
the Night" as the theme song. No rating.

1932

R13.   Jan 1-Feb 27 CBS, WABC, NY Bing Crosby/Cremo Singer
       Six days a week, Mon. to Sat.
       Crosby may not have appeared on the final program.
       1931-32: 6.9 share; Vallee, 24.7; Whiteman, 19.1;
Columbo, no rating. Russ Columbo's program aired three
nights a week on the Blue Network at 10 p.m.

       Chesterfield Cigarettes Presents Music That
              Satisfies CBS, New York
              Feb 29, 1932-Apr 15, 1933 from 9-9:15 p.m.;
five days a week to twice a week. Five-month break
after Jul 1932.
       Music: Lennie Hayton's Orchestra with Eddie Lang,
Artie Shaw, Tommy Dorsey, Joe Venuti, and Arnold Brill-
hart.
       Announcer: Norman Brokenshire (Paul Douglas as
Standby).
       Theme songs: "Just an Echo in the Valley" for a
week or two in 1933, and then "Where the Blue of the

Night" returned.

R14.   Feb 29-Jul 27 CBS, WABC, NY Chesterfield Presents
        Gradually reduced from five weekly shows to four
(with Mar 14), to three (with Apr 25), to two days a
week (with Jun 6), ending on Mon. and Wed. Probably
broadcast from Los Angeles from about Jun 1, as Bing
began filming The Big Broadcast.

1933
R15.   Jan 4-Apr 15 CBS, WABC, NY   Chesterfield Presents
        Twice weekly, Wednesdays and Saturdays at 9 p.m.
Unrated, like Russ Columbo's show, now twice a week at
6:15. Shows of Mar 15, Apr 1 featured the song "Farewell to Arms" to promote the new Paramount release of
the same title (novel by Hemingway) with Gary Cooper.
Eddie Lang died the day after the Mar 25 show.
        1932-33: no rating; Vallee, 33.9; Downey, 5.6.

        The Woodbury Soap Show CBS, New York
            Oct 16, 1933-Jun 11, 1935, at 8:30 p.m. Mon.;
        Tue. at 9 p.m. with Sep 1934.
        Theme song: "Where the Blue of the Night."
        Writers: Burt McMurtrie, then Carroll Carroll.

R16.   Oct 16-Dec 15 CBS, WABC, NY   The Woodbury Soap Show
        With the Lennie Hayton Orchestra.

1934
R17.   Jan 1-May 28 CBS, WABC, NY   Woodbury Soap (cont.)
        The Mills Brothers became regulars Jan 1 to Mar
26. The Gus Arnheim Orchestra replaced Hayton Jan 15.
The Carol Lofner Orchestra played the first three shows
in March, replaced Mar 26 by the Jimmy Grier Orchestra.
        1933-34: 25.1 audience share; Amos 'n' Andy, 30.3;
Burns and Allen, 30.2; Jack Benny, 25.3; Paul Whiteman
with Al Jolson, 29.9.

R18.   Sep 18-Dec 25 CBS, WABC, NY   The Woodbury Soap Show
        With the Georgie Stoll Orchestra (to Jun 1935) and
the Boswell Sisters (to Dec 18, 1934). Guests Dec 25:
Irene Taylor, Charlie Bourne.

1935
R19.   Jan 1-Jun 11 CBS, WABC, NY   Woodbury Soap (cont.)
        The Mills Brothers became regulars Jan 8 to Mar
12; the Georgie Stoll Orchestra remained.
        1934-35: 15.5 share. Amos 'n' Andy 22.6; Benny,
36.4; Rudy Vallee, 38.5; Kate Smith, 15.0; Bob Hope,
unrated as he began his radio career on the Blue Network for the 1934-35 season on Fridays at 8:30 p.m.

        [Jul 6, Sat, Dixie Lee Crosby and Richard Barthel-
mess were the guests on CBS, Shell Chateau, 60 min.]

        Kraft Music Hall   NBC, Los Angeles
            Dec 5, 1935-May 9, 1946
            Hour Thur. shows at 9 p.m. through 1942; then
        half hour shows at 9 p.m. with 1943.

Orchestra: Jimmy Dorsey to 1937, followed by John Scott Trotter. Announcer: Don Wilson, then Roger Krupp, then Ken Carpenter.

Theme Song: "Where the Blue of the Night"

Writers: Carroll Carroll, David Gregory, Leo Sherin, Ed Helwick, and Matty Mannheim.

Directors: Cal Kuhl, Ezra MacIntosh, Ed Gardner, and Bob Brewster.

Carroll Carroll is credited with developing the casual Crosby banter (Variety, Oct 19, 1977).

R20.   Dec 5-26   NBC, Los Angeles Kraft Music Hall
These first four programs included remotes with the Paul Whiteman Orchestra in New York as Crosby was being tested to replace Whiteman. No Christmas special show Dec 19, nor Dec 26.

1936
R21.   Jan 2-Aug 20 NBC, L.A.   Kraft Music Hall (cont.)
Guests: Joe Venuti, Jan. 9; John Barrymore, Jan 16.

1935-36: 14.8 audience share; Jolson, 20.9; Bob Hope, 7.0 (on CBS Sat., half hour, 7 p.m. for Atlantic Oil); Eddie Cantor, 16.1; Vallee, 28.2. KMH dominated the Thursday night broadcasts.

R22.   CBS   Ford V-8 Review   30 min.
A brief series starring Bing Crosby

R23.   Oct 15-Dec 31 NBC, L.A.   Kraft Music Hall
Guest: Jack Oakie, Dec 17. Crosby's first Christmas Special aired Dec 24; Bing sang "Adeste Fideles," "Trust Me," "Diane," "Did You Mean It?," "Pennies from Heaven," and "Silent Night."

1937
R24.   Jan 7-Jul 1 NBC, L.A.   Kraft Music Hall (cont.)
Guests: Gail Patrick, Zasu Pitts, Rudolph Gonz, and Bob Burns, May 27; Charlie Ruggles, McClellan Barkley, and Natalie Bodagna, Jun 3; William Frawley, Jun 10.

John Scott Trotter replaced Jimmy Dorsey by July, and Roger Krupp replaced Don Wilson as the announcer.

1936-37: 22.4 audience share; Jolson, 19.1; Burns and Allen, 24.0; Cantor, 29.1; Jack Benny, 28.6; Kate Smith, 12.2; Vallee, 15.7; Amos 'n' Andy, 18.3; Bob Hope not listed.

R25.   Oct 7-Dec 30 NBC, L.A.   Kraft Music Hall
Guests: Robert Young and Marian Marsh, Oct 28; Ralph Bellamy, Dec 16; Basil Rathbone and Madge Evans, Dec 23; guests now became a regular attraction.

R26.   Nov 8   CBS   Lux Radio Theatre: She Loves Me Not
60 min. Melville Ruick, announcer; Louis Silvers, music. Mon.

Host: Cecil B. DeMille. Guests: Bing Crosby, Joan Blondell

Bing reprises his role in his 1934 film.

1938

R27.   Jan 6-Jul 21 NBC, L.A.   Kraft Music Hall (cont.)
        Guests included: Miriam Hopkins, David Niven, and
Morris Rosenthal, Mar 10; George Brent, Mar 24; Walter
Huston and Beaulah Bondi, May 5; Humphrey Bogart, May
19; Joel McCrea and Mary Astor, Jun 2; Bob Hope, Jul 14
(probably Hope's first appearance); Donald O'Connor,
Jul 21.
        By this time Ken Carpenter had replaced Roger
Krupp as the announcer.
        1937-38: 23.1 share; Jolson 23.5; Burns and
Allen, 27.5; Charlie McCarthy with Don Ameche, 39.4;
Cantor, 23.1; Jack Benny for Jello, 34.0; Kate Smith
for Calumet, 9.1; Amos 'n' Andy, 17.4; Bob Hope not
listed.

R28.   Jul 3   NBC, Del Mar   Opening at Del Mar 30 min.
        Sponsor: Kraft Foods. The opening show before the
first races at the Del Mar Turf Club. Sat.
        Host: Bing Crosby. Guests: Pat O'Brien, George
Jessel, Dixie Lee Crosby, Hoagy Carmichael, and many
others.
        The program was aired for years as a half-hour
show Sat. mornings during the Del Mar racing season.
The frequent emcee was George Jessel. Bing Crosby and
Ken Carpenter often interviewed guests and then Bing
would sing a few songs accompanied by Perry Botkin on
guitar at the Jockey Club.

R29.   Jul 20   NBC   The Raleigh-Kool Show 30 min.
        Starring Tommy Dorsey and his Orchestra. Wed.
        Guests: Jack Benny, Bing Crosby, Dick Powell, Ken
Murray, Shirley Ross

R30.   Oct 20-Dec 29 NBC, L.A.   Kraft Music Hall
        Guests included: Ogden Nash and Henry Fonda, Oct
27; Johnny Mercer, Marie Wilson, and Robert Young, Nov
17; Leslie Howard, Dec 15; Jack Carson, Dec 29.

1939

R31.   Jan 5-Jun 15 NBC, L.A.   Kraft Music Hall (cont.)
        Guests included: Freddie Bartholomew, May 25; Bert
Lahr, Lucille Ball, and Linda Ware, Jun 8.
        1938-39: 24.5 share; Bob Hope, 16.2 (for Pepso-
dent, Tue from 10 to 10:30 on NBC); Jolson, 16.8;
Charlie McCarthy, 35.1; Benny, 31.4; Burns and Allen,
18.6; Kate Smith, 16.7; Amos 'n' Andy, 14.4.

R32.   Feb 5   CBS   The Gulf Screen Guild Show: Revue
        60 min. John Conte, announcer; Oscar Bradley,
music; Wesley Ruggles, guest director; Edward Freeman,
Frank Butler, writers. Sun.
        Host: George Murphy. Guests: Bing Crosby, Hugh
Herbert, Jane Withers, the Yacht Club Boys
        Bing sings "This Can't Be Love" from the Broadway
show The Boys from Syracuse.
        The program was a benefit for the Motion Picture
Relief Fund.

R33. Jul 20   NBC, L.A.   Kraft Music Hall   Thur.
      Crosby did a one-hour show with Pat Friday and
resumed his vacation.

R34. Sep 28-Dec 29 NBC, L.A.   Kraft Music Hall
      Guests included: Wendy Barrie, Oct 5; Jack Oakie,
Oct 19; Chester Morris and Lucille Ball, Nov 9; Jackie
Cooper and Maria Ouspenskaya, Dec 7.

R35. Dec 10   CBS The Gulf Screen Guild Theatre: Mr. Jinx
      Goes to Sea 30 min. John Conte, announcer; Oscar
Bradley, music. Sun.
      Host: Roger Pryor. Guests: Bing Crosby, Andy
Devine, Jean Parker, Chick Chandler, Raymond Walburn.
      The show was a romantic comedy. The program was a
benefit.

1940
R36. Jan 4-Aug 8 NBC, L.A.   Kraft Music Hall (cont.)
      Guests included: Marlene Dietrich, Feb 15; Brian
Donlevy, Feb 29; Annabella and Jose Iturbi, May 2;
Johnny Mercer, Nigel Bruce, John Garfield, and Geral-
dine Fitzgerald, Jul 4; Oscar Levant, Jul 18; Pat
O'Brien, Aug 1; Charles Laughton and Jose Iturbi, Aug
8.
      1939-40: 23.3 share; Hope, 25.0; Charlie McCarthy,
34.6; Benny, 34.1; Burns and Allen, 15.8; Kate Smith
with Abbott and Costello, 19.6; Amos 'n' Andy, 11.6.

R37. Jan 15   CBS   Lux Radio Theatre: Sing You Sinners
      60 min. Melville Ruick, announcer; Louis Silvers,
music. Mon.
      Host: Cecil B. DeMille. Guests: Bing Crosby,
Ralph Bellamy, Jacqueline Wells, Elizabeth Patterson
(reprised Apr 7, 1945, with some different co-stars).
      Bing recreated his role in his hit 1938 film of
the same title.

R38. Aug 16   NBC   Preview of <u>Rhythm on the River</u> at
      Del Mar Turf Club, CA. Fri.
      Bing Crosby, Pat O'Brien, Mary Martin, Johnny
Burke, Victor Schertzinger, Ken Carpenter, John Scott
Trotter, and Lillian Cornell. Bing sings Burke's song
"Where the Turf Meets the Surf."

R39. Nov 14-Dec 26 NBC, L.A.   Kraft Music Hall
      Guests included: Wingy Manone, Nov 14; Ogden Nash,
Nov 21; Charles Boyer, Connie Boswell, and Tommy Dorsey, Nov 28; Ken Darby Singers, Dec 26.

1941
R40. Jan 2-Jul 31 NBC, L.A.   Kraft Music Hall (cont.)
      Guests included: Ogden Nash, Jan 30; Paul Robeson
and Lew Ayres, Feb 6; Eddie Bracken and Bob Burns, Mar
6; Jack Teagarden, Apr 17; Priscilla Lane, May 15; Duke
Ellington, May 29; Ethel Waters, Jun 12; Rita Hayworth
and Wingy Manone, Jul 10.
      1940-41: 18.6 share; Hope, 28.2; Charlie McCarthy,
32.2; Burns and Allen, 14.9; Cantor, 14.7; Benny, 36.2;

Kate Smith, 18.1. Bing Crosby was opposite Major Bowes
Amateur Hour with a 19.8 share.
Crosby missed the programs of Feb 13, Mar 27, and
Jun 26.

R41. Feb 23   CBS   The Gulf Screen Guild Theatre: Altar
        Bound   30 min. John Conte, announcer; Oscar
Bradley, music. Sun.
        Host: Roger Pryor. Guests: Bing Crosby, Bob Hope,
Betty Grable
        Bing and Hope play bums down on their luck, res-
cued by Betty Grable. Bing sings "<u>Frenesi</u>." The
program was a benefit for the Motion Picture Relief
Fund.

R42. Oct 30-Dec 25 NBC, L.A.   Kraft Music Hall
        Guests included: Victor Borge, Dec 4; Veronica
Lake, Jerry Lester, Paul Robeson, Victor Borge, Bob
Crosby's Bob Cats, and Bob Coote, Dec 11 (the first
program after the Japanese sneak attack on Pearl Har-
bor). On Dec 25 Crosby and the Music Maids sang "White
Christmas" for the first time.

1942
R43. Jan 1-Jun 25 NBC, L.A.   Kraft Music Hall (cont.)
        Guests included: Mary Martin and Wingy Manone, Jan
1; Mary Martin, Jan 8 and regularly to Oct 15; Ronald
Reagan and Spike Jones, Apr 16; Joan Leslie and Susan
Hayward, Apr 30; Fred Astaire, Jun 25. Crosby missed
the shows of Feb 12 and 19 and May 7 and 14.
        1941-42: 21.1 share; Hope, 31.7; Gene Autry's
third season had a 10.6.

R44. Mar 8   CBS   The Gulf Screen Guild Theatre: Too Many
        Husbands   30 min. John Hiestand, announcer; Oscar
Bradley, music. Sun.
        Host: Roger Pryor. Guests: Bing Crosby, Bob Hope,
Hedy Lamarr
        Bing and Hope vie for Lamarr in a romantic comedy.
A benefit for the Motion Picture Relief Fund.

R45. Oct 1-Dec 31 NBC, L.A.   Kraft Music Hall
        Guests included: Desi Arnaz and Milton Berle, Oct
8; Cass Daley, Oct 15; Victor Borge and Judy Canova,
Oct 22; Bob Hope, Oct 29; Janet Blair, Nov 26, Dec 24,
31; Dorothy Lamour, Dec 3; Cliff "Ukulele Ike" Edwards,
Dec 10.

1943
R46. Jan 7-Apr 15 NBC, L.A.   Kraft Music Hall (cont.)
        The program was reduced to a half hour. Guests
included: Cass Daley, Feb 18, Mar 18; Eddie Bracken,
Mar 11; Lucille Ball, Apr 1; Rags Ragland, Apr 8.
        1942-43: 23.1 share; Hope, 40.9; Charlie McCarthy,
34.8; Cantor, 21.4; Benny, 33.9; Red Skelton's second
season, 40.7.

R47. Jan 11   CBS   The Lady Esther Screen Guild Players:
        Holiday Inn   30 min. Truman Bradley, announcer;

Wilbur Hatch, music; Lady Esther Cosmetics, sponsor.
Mon.
        Bing Crosby, Dinah Shore (selections from film
Holiday Inn)
        The program was a benefit for Motion Picture
Relief Fund.

R48. Apr 5   CBS   Lux Radio Theatre: Road to Morocco
        60 min. John Milton Kennedy, announcer; Louis
Silvers, music. Mon.
        Host: Cecil B. DeMille. Guests: Bing Crosby, Bob
Hope
        Crosby and Hope, without Dorothy Lamour, recreate
their roles in the 1942 film of the same title. This
is the only time they appeared together on this series.

R49. Jun 17-Dec 30 NBC, L.A.   Kraft Music Hall
        Crosby also appeared on Whiteman's July 4 CBS
radio program for a reunion with the Rhythm Boys (see
R50 below). Guests on KMH included: Phil Silvers, Sep
9, Dec 16; George Murphy, Sep 23; Lucille Ball, Oct 7,
Dec 9.
        Bob Crosby hosted the show from Oct 28 to Nov 25,
with Bing absent.

R50. Jul 4   CBS, L.A.   Paul Whiteman Presents
        Sun. A reunion of the Rhythm Boys. Dinah Shore
and Bill Goodwin were regulars. Bing sang and recorded
two songs (D627-28) for a Whiteman album (Shore's voice
was replaced by demand of her recording company).

R51. Sep 13   CBS   The Lady Esther Screen Guild Theatre:
        Birth of the Blues 30 min. Truman Bradley,
announcer; Wilbur Hatch, music; Lady Esther Cosmetics,
sponsor. Mon. A benefit.
        Bing Crosby, Ginny Simms, Johnny Mercer
        Scenes and songs from the 1941 film.

R52. Dec 20   CBS   Lux Radio Theatre: Dixie
        60 min. John Milton Kennedy, announcer; Louis
Silvers, music. Mon.
        Host: Cecil B. DeMille. Guests: Bing Crosby,
Dorothy Lamour, Barry Sullivan
        Bing reprises his role in the 1943 film.

1944
R53. Jan 6-Jul 27 NBC, L.A.   Kraft Music Hall (cont.)
        Guests included: Dale Evans, Jan 20; Gloria DeHa-
ven Jan 27; Marilyn Maxwell, Feb 3 and regularly to Jul
27; Donald O'Connor, Feb 3; Lucille Ball, Mar 2; Bob
Hope, Apr 13, Jun 15; Sonny Tufts, Apr 27, Jul 20, 27;
Gene Kelly, May 4; Cecil B. DeMille, Jun 8; Roy Rogers,
Jun 29; Tommy and Jimmy Dorsey, Jul 6. Bing left to
entertain the troops in England and France.
        1943-44: 22.2 share; Hope, 31.6; Your Hit Parade,
19.1 (sponsored by Lucky Strike cigarettes) and Lucky
Strike All Time Hit Parade (first season), 11.6; Cantor, 17.7; Kate Smith, 16.8; Whiteman, 4.6; Skelton,
31.4; Charlie McCarthy, 29.2; Burns and Allen, 18.1;

Frank Sinatra, 12.4 (his first season, CBS, 9-9:30 p.m.,
Wed.); Perry Como, unrated (his first season).
Bob Crosby hosted the program from March 16 to 23.

R54.   Feb 1   AFRS   Command Performance 30 min. Tue.
Bing and Frank Sinatra broadcast a special program
for the Hollywood Victory Committee, sent by short wave
to the Armed Forces (Carpozi 70-71). The program might
be R57, Command Performance No. 123, which includes Bob
Hope, Frank Sinatra, and others.

R55.   Apr   Tommy Dorsey: The Carnegie Hall V-Disc Session
Bing joined the show to sing "Small Fry" and
"Pennies from Heaven." The songs were aired again Jun
18, 1944, on NBC's "All Time Hit Parade."

Syndicated by AFRS Command Performance 30 min.
Aired 1942-1945. Bing Crosby was on several
shows, including the following:
R56.   No. 118: Ken Carpenter, Bing Crosby, Gypsy Rose Lee,
Bob Hope, Betty Hutton
R57.   No. 123: Jerry Colonna, Bing Crosby, Connie Haines,
Bob Hope, Lena Horne, Shirley Ross, Frank Sinatra
R58.   No. 125: Bing Crosby, Judy Garland, Bob Hope, Frank
Sinatra
R59.   No. 129: Bing Crosby, the Andrews Sisters, Judy Gar-
land
R60.   No. 154: The Andrews Sisters, Lauren Bacall, Bing
Crosby, Bob Hope, Stan Kenton, Anita O'Day
R61.   No. 165 included the "Crosby Kids," Frank Sinatra, and
others

Syndicated by AFRS Mail Call 30 min.
R62.   No. 91: The Groaner, the Canary and the Nose: Bing
Crosby, Jimmy Durante, Judy Garland, Arthur Treacher
R63.   No. 120: The Andrews Sisters, Bing Crosby, Garry
Moore, Risë Stevens, Peggy Ryan
R64.   No. 128: Bing Crosby, Cass Daley, Lauritz Melchior

R65.   Oct 12-Dec 28 NBC, L.A.   Kraft Music Hall
Oct 12 Bing broadcast remote from New York on his
return from entertaining the troops in Europe, while
his guests (Spike Jones, George Murphy, and Bob Hope)
aired from Los Angeles. Other guests included: Frank
Sinatra, Nov 16 (remote from New York); Risë Stevens,
Nov 23; Jerry Colonna, Dec 14; Kraft Choral Society,
Eugenie Baird, Dec 21 Christmas Show; Beatrice Kay and
the Les Paul Trio, Dec 28.

R66.   Dec 31   ABC   The Andrews Sisters Eight-to-the-
Bar Ranch 30 min. Sun. Starring Patty, Maxene,
Laverne Andrews, George "Gabby" Hayes, and the Riders
of the Purple Sage. Guest: Bing Crosby. See D2515.

1945
R67.   Jan 4-May 17 NBC, L.A.   Kraft Music Hall (cont.)
Guests included: Johnny Mercer, Jan 4; Duke Ell-
ington, Jan 18; the Andrews Sisters, Jan 25; Marian
Anderson, Feb 22; Joe Venuti, Mar 8; Artie Shaw, Mar

15; Frankie Carle, Mar 22; Florence Alba and the "King"
Cole Trio, Apr 5; Florence Alba and Carmen Cavallaro,
Apr 26; "King" Cole Trio, May 3; Cass Daley, May 10.
    Crosby took the next six weeks off, trying to
break his contract, and then went on "vacation" for
seven months. There may have been no Christmas Special
for 1945 except for the Armed Forces (see R75).
    1944-45: 25.8 share; Hope, 34.1; Vallee, 13.7;
Kate Smith, 8.5; Sinatra, 11.3; Dick Haymes, 11.2;
Dinah Shore, 17.6; Major Bowes Amateur Hour, 7.2 (still
opposite Crosby).

R68. Jan 8   CBS   The Lady Esther Screen Guild Play-
        ers: Going My Way 30 min. Truman Bradley, announc-
    er; Lady Esther Cosmetics, sponsor. Mon. A benefit.
        Bing Crosby, Barry Fitzgerald, George Murphy
        A version of the film Going My Way that emphasizes
    the servicemen overseas, with Bing as Father O'Malley.

R69. Feb 15   CBS, NBC Command Performance Special: Dick
        Tracy in B-Flat; or, For Goodness Sake, Isn't He
    Ever Going to Marry Tess Truehart? 60 min. Thur.
        Armed Forces Radio Service hour special: Bing
    Crosby as Dick Tracy, Dinah Shore as Tess Truehart, Bob
    Hope as Flat Top, the Andrews Sisters as the Summer
    Sisters, Judy Garland as Snowflake, Frank Sinatra as
    Shaky, Jimmy Durante as the Mole, Jerry Colonna, Frank
    Morgan, Cass Daley, and others.
        Bing sings three songs and a reprise of "Whose
    Dream Are You," with additional dialogue, and duets
    with Dinah Shore, Bob Hope, Sinatra. See V245B.

R70. Mar 7   ABC   Five Will Get You Ten 30 min. Wed.
        Bing Crosby, Pedro de Cordova, William Gargan,
    Ruth Hussey, J. Carrol Naish, Pat O'Brien, Loretta
    Young

R71. Apr 15   NBC   NBC Tribute to Franklin Delano
        Roosevelt Sun.
        Amos 'n' Andy, James Cagney, Eddie Cantor, Bing
    Crosby, Fibber McGee and Molly, Bob Hope, Kay Kyser,
    Meredith Willson and his Orchestra, and others.

R72. May 7   CBS   Lux Radio Theatre: Sing, You
        Sinners 60 min. John Milton Kennedy, announcer;
    Louis Silvers, music. Mon.
        Host: Cecil B. DeMille. Guests: Bing Crosby, Joan
    Caulfield, James Dunn, Elizabeth Patterson (reprise
    from Jan 15, 1940).

R73. Jun 28   NBC, L.A.   Kraft Music Hall
        Guests: Carmen Cavallaro and Florence Alba.

R74. Jul 2   NBC   The Bell Telephone Hour
        30 min. Mon. Starring Donald Vorhees and the
    Bell Telephone Orchestra. Guest: Bing Crosby

R75. Aug 8   AFRS   Christmas Jubilee Show
        Count Basie and his Orchestra, joined for one

song, "Gotta Be This or That," by Bing.

R76. Aug 15   AFRS   Command Performance Victory Extra
          Host: Bing Crosby.   There was a large cast.

1946
R77. Feb 7-May 9 NBC, L.A.   Kraft Music Hall
          Guests included: Eddie Duchin, Feb 7 to May 9; Les
Paul, Feb 14; Jerry Colonna, Feb 28; the Slim Galliard
Trio, Mar 21; Georgia Gibbs, Mar 28, Apr 4; Marilyn
Maxwell and the Les Paul Trio, Apr 11; Peggy Lee, Joe
Frisco, and Bob Hope, May 2; Spike Jones, May 9.
          1945-46: 17.5 share; Hope, 29.8; Cantor, 19.5;
Kate Smith, 11.0; Vallee, 12.2; Sinatra, 10.5; White-
man, unrated (sustaining program); Abbott and Costello,
19.4; Burns and Allen, 19.1; Fibber McGee and Molly,
30.8; Benny, 24.1; Skelton, 25.7; Amos 'n' Andy, 17.2.
          Crosby was absent Apr 25, and May 9 was his last
performance for the program.   He was on about 390 KMH
broadcasts since Dec 5, 1935.

R78. Aug 26   CBS   The Lady Esther Screen Guild Play-
          ers: The Bells of St. Mary's   30 min.   Truman Brad-
ley, announcer; Wilbur Hatch, music.   Mon.   A benefit.
          Bing Crosby, Ingrid Bergman, Joan Carroll
          Bing as Father O'Malley in a version of The Bells
of St. Mary's, which had been released the previous
December.   The show was reprised Oct 6, 1947 (R82).

          Philco Radio Time ABC, Hollywood, Calif.
               Oct 16, 1946-Jun 1, 1949, Wednesdays
          Crosby went to the old NBC Blue Network, which
became ABC in 1942, because he could transcribe his
programs.   They were recorded before a live audience
with two commercial breaks.   Crosby kept John Scott
Trotter's Orchestra and Ken Carpenter as his announcer.
Ironically, he once again worked under innovative Paul
Whiteman, who had become the musical director for the
network.   Despite the more leisurely hours, working
under Whiteman was a strain, which contributed to
Crosby's jumping to CBS in 1949.   The recording tape
used from the second season was developed with the 3M
Company and recorded on Ampex machines developed by the
Crosby Research Company and Ampex, which Bing financed
to use technology gained by John Mullin from Germany
after the Second World War.
          Theme Song: "Where the Blue of the Night" at open
and close.
          Directors: Bill Morrow and Murdo MacKenzie.

R79. Oct 16-Dec 25 ABC, Hollywood   Philco Radio Time
          Guests included Bob Hope, Lina Romay, Skitch
Henderson, and the Charioteers, Oct 16; Spike Jones,
Oct 23; The Les Paul Trio, Oct 30, Nov 27; Ezio Pinza,
Nov 13; Burl Ives, Nov 20; Peggy Lee, Dec 11, 18; no
special guest Dec 25 (a program rebroadcast Dec 24,
1947).

1947

R80.   Jan 1-Jun 18 ABC, Hollywood   Philco Time (cont.)
       Guests included: Peggy Lee, Jan 1 and regularly to
Apr 23; Al Jolson, Jan 15, Mar 5, Apr 2, May 7; Bob
Hope, Jan 29, Jun 18; Beatrice Lillie, Feb 5; Leo
McCarey and Judy Garland, Feb 19; the Andrews Sisters,
Feb 26; Irving Berlin, May 7; Maurice Chevalier, May
21; Ethel Merman, Jun 11.
       Crosby broadcasted on ABC from Chicago Apr 30 and
May 14, and from New York May 21 to Jun 18.
       1946-47: 16.1 share; Shore, 9.4; Kate Smith, 12.0;
Vallee 11.6; Como, 12.5; Sinatra, 10.2; Hope, 30.2;
Benny, 27.0.

R81.   Mar 16   NBC   The Jack Benny Program 30 min. Sun.
       Guests: Bing Crosby, Dick Haymes, and Andy Russell

R82.   Oct 6   CBS   Screen Guild Players: The Bells of
       St. Mary's 30 min. Michael Roy, announcer;
Wilbur Hatch, music; Camel Cigarettes, sponsor. Wed.
       Bing Crosby, Ingrid Bergman, Joan Carroll (selec-
tions from film The Bells of St. Mary's)
       The program was a benefit for the Motion Picture
Relief Fund. The show was a reprise of Aug 26, 1946
(R78).

R83.   Oct 1-Dec 31 ABC, Hollywood   Philco Radio Time
       Guests included: The Rhythmaires (regulars to Jun
1949--soon billed as Jud Conlon's Rhythmaires), Peggy
Lee, and Gary Cooper, Oct 1; Jimmy Durante, Oct 8;
Dinah Shore, Oct 15; Ozzie and Harriet Nelson, Nov 5;
Kay Thompson and the Williams Brothers, Nov 12; Barry
Fitzgerald, Nov 19; Frankie Laine, Nov 26; Al Jolson,
Dec 3.
       The Dec 24 Christmas program was a rebroadcast of
the one aired Dec 25, 1946 (R79).

1948

R84.   Jan 7-Jun 2 ABC, Hollywood   Philco Time (cont.)
       Guests included: George Burns, Jan 14; Burns and
Allen, Jan 21; Dick Haymes and Jimmy Durante, Feb 4;
Oscar Levant, Feb 11; Jack Benny, Mar 3; James Stewart,
Mar 10; Fred Astaire, Apr 7; the Crosby Brothers, Apr
21 (this is probably the first appearance of Bing's
sons on the show); Beatrice Lillie, May 26.
       From May 12 to Jun 2 (four weeks) the program
originated on ABC in New York.
       1947-48: 16.8 share; Como, 10.5; Sinatra, not
rated; Hope, 24.7; Benny, 26.0.

R85.   Apr 18   NBC   NBC Special: A Question of Pianos
       30 min. Sun. Bing Crosby, Jimmy Durante, Bob
Hope, Pat O'Brien

R86.   May 23   NBC   The Fred Allen Show 30 min. Sun.
       Bing Crosby was the guest.

R87.   Fall   CBS   The Bing Crosby-Minute Maid Show
       A transcribed daily 15-minute show aired at 9:45

a.m. EST. Philco had agreed to the venture so long as Bing included plugs for Philco products. The program lasted for several years.

R88. Sep 29-Dec 29 ABC, Hollywood   Philco Time
    Guests included: the Crosby Brothers, Sep 29; Judy Garland, Oct 6; Marilyn Maxwell, Oct 13, 20; Edgar Bergen, Nov 3; Red Nichols, Joe Venuti, and Oscar Levant, Nov 10; Kay Starr, Nov 17; Bob and Cathy Crosby, Dec 1; Morton Downey, Dec 8; Bob Hope, Dec 15; Bob Mitchell Boys' Choir, Dec 22 Christmas Show; the Mills Brothers, Dec 29.
    Oct 13 the show aired from ABC, Vancouver, B. C.; Oct 20, ABC, Spokane; Oct 27, ABC, San Francisco.

R89. Oct 14   NBC   The Screen Guild Players: Welcome Stranger   30 min. Vern Smith, announcer; Camel Cigarettes, sponsor. Thur.
    Bing Crosby, Ingrid Bergman, Joan Carroll, Barry Fitzgerald
    Selections from the film of the same title; a benefit for the Motion Picture Relief Fund.

R90. Dec 5   CBS   The Adventures of Ozzie and Harriet   30 min. Sun. Guest: Bing Crosby

1949
R91. Jan 5-Jun 1 ABC, Hollywood   Philco Time (cont.)
    Guest included: Harry James and Betty Grable, Jan 5; 'Lassus White and Hattie McDaniel, Jan 19; Abe Burrows, Jan 26; Jimmy Durante, Feb 2; Dinah Shore and Burl Ives, Mar 2; Phil Harris, Mar 9; Joe Venuti, Jack Teagarden, and Louis Armstrong, Mar 16; Ethel Merman, Mar 23; Dennis Day, Mar 30; Kay Starr and James Stewart, Apr 6; Rudy Vallee, Apr 20; Rhonda Fleming and Johnny Mercer, May 18.
    Feb 2 and 9 and Mar 2 to 30 the program was broadcast from ABC, San Francisco.
    The Jun 1 program was Crosby's 108th of the series and his last.
    1948-49: 15.7 share; Como, 8.8; Hope, 23.8; Benny, 26.4; Lamour, 10.4.

R92. May 16   The Savings Bond Show 60 min. Mon.
    Eddie "Rochester" Anderson, Edward Arnold, Lionel Barrymore, Jack Benny, Bing Crosby, Irene Dunne, Bob Hope, Al Jolson, Jules Munshin, Edward G. Robinson, Roy Rogers, Frank Sinatra, Red Skelton, Jo Stafford, Fred Waring, Esther Williams

R93. Aug 15? Ethel Barrymore's 70th Birthday and 50th Year in Show Business. Bing sings "Happy Birthday," President Harry Truman opened the program, and Winston Churchill and others participated. Bing recorded his song Aug 15; the date of broadcast is uncertain.

R94. Sep 26   CBS   Lux Radio Theatre: The Emperor Waltz   60 min. John Milton Kennedy, announcer; Rudy Schrager, music. Mon.

Host: William Kneighley. Guests: Bing Crosby, Ann Blyth
Bing reprises his role in his 1948 film.

R95. Oct 19   NBC   The Dean Martin-Jerry Lewis Show
      30 min. Fri.   Guest: Bing Crosby

Chesterfield Cigarettes Presents The Bing Crosby
   Show CBS, Hollywood, Calif.
   Sep 21, 1949-Jun 25, 1952, Wed at 9:30 p.m.
   This program retained the orchestra, announcer,
and producer-directors of The Philco Radio Time. The
transcriptions were also performed before live audiences, a practice now common to all the radio networks.
"Where the Blue of the Night" remained as the opening
and closing signature song.

R96. Sep 21-Dec 28 CBS, Hollywood Chesterfield Cigarettes
      Presents the Bing Crosby Show
      Guests included: Peggy Lee, regularly from Sep 21
to Nov 30 and less regularly thereafter; Abe Burrows,
Sep 21; Judy Garland, Oct 5; Bob Hope, Nov 2; the Mills
Brothers and Ella Fitzgerald, Nov 9; Bob and Cathy
Crosby, Nov 16; Al Jolson and Gracie Allen, Nov 30;
Jimmy Stewart and Carole Richards, Dec 14; Ethel Barry-
more, Dec 21 Christmas Show; Al Jolson, Dec 28.

1950
R97. Jan 4-May 24 CBS, Hollywood   Chesterfield (cont.)
      Guests included: Al Jolson, Jan 4, Feb 15; Gary
Crosby and Barbara Whiting, Jan 18; Peggy Lee, Jack
Teagarden, Louis Armstrong, and Joe Venuti, Jan 25; Bob
Hope, Feb 1; the Andrews Sisters and the Fire House
Five Plus Two, Feb 22, Mar 29; Bob Crosby and Bob Hope,
Mar 1; Gary Crosby, Mar 8; Philip and Dennis Crosby,
Mar 15; Arthur Godfrey and Perry Como, Apr 5; Mildred
Bailey, Apr 12; Lindsay Crosby and Carole Richards, Apr
19; Beatrice Lillie, Apr 26; Al Jolson and Ella Fitz-
gerald, May 3; Bob Hope, Perry Como, Arthur Godfrey,
and the Crosby Brothers, May 24.
      1949-50: 18.0 share (Nielsen); Sinatra, 6.9; Hope
13.9.

R98. Apr 1   ABC Premiere of <u>Riding High</u> from Front
      Royal, Virginia. Sat.
      Local WFTR disc jockeys named Rayburn and Finen
hosted the county's square dance, where Bing sang after
the premiere of the film, which was held at Front Royal
in connection with Bing's support of endowing the
city's baseball field, which was named the Bing Crosby
Stadium, and Warren County's Bing Crosby Day.

R99. Oct 11-Dec 27 CBS, Hollywood   Chesterfield
      Guests included: Judy Garland and Bob Hope, Oct
11, 18; Ella Fitzgerald and the Fire House Five Plus
Two, Nov 29; Judy Garland, Dec 6 (A Tribute to Al
Jolson); Dixie Lee Crosby and Crosby Brothers, Dec 20
Christmas Show; Dinah Shore, Louis Armstrong, and Jack
Teagarden, Dec 27.

The program had been scheduled to return Oct 4,
but Bing's father died that afternoon and his sponsor
agreed to Bing's request, as did Bob Crosby's sponsor,
that it be postponed a week. The show with Dixie Lee
on Dec 20 was her only appearance on the show, de-
scribed by Gary Crosby (pp. 136-38).

R99A. Nov 20   Martin Block Interviews Bing Crosby
          Taped Nov 19 on telephone, for anniversary of
Paramount Theater, New York, thought to be the 20th
anniversary of Bing's Nov 8, 1931, appearance.

R100. Dec 24 ABC   The Louella Parsons Show 15 min. Sun.
          With Bing Crosby, William Boyd.

1951
R101. Jan 3-Jun 20 CBS, Hollywood   Chesterfield (cont.)
          Guests included: Fred Astaire, Jan 3; Bob Hope and
Bob Crosby, Jan 10; Armstrong, Teagarden, and Venuti
Jan 17; Bob Hope, Jan 31; Judy Garland, Feb 7, Mar 7,
14, 21, 28; the Andrews Sisters and the Nat "King" Cole
Trio, Feb 28; Les Paul and Mary Ford, Mar 21; Dinah
Shore, Apr 4; Armstrong, Maxwell, Lindsay Crosby, Apr
11; Gary Crosby, Apr 18; Armstrong and Rose Marie, Apr
25; Teresa Brewer and Fred Astaire, May 9; Brewer,
Armstrong, Teagarden, May 23; Helen O'Connell, May 30;
Brewer, Jun 13; Brewer, Tommy Dorsey, Venuti, Jun 20.
          1950-51: 10.0 share; Autry, 12.4; Hope (for Camel
cigarettes) 12.7; Benny, 19.9.

R102. Jan 7   Liberty Broadcasting System   Salute to Bing
          Crosby 60 min. Sun.
          The Andrews Sisters, Frank Capra, Jerry Lewis,
Russ Morgan, Vic Schoen, Jane Wyman

R103. Jan 9   CBS   Salute to Bing Crosby 30 min. Tue.
          Amos 'n' Andy, Louis Armstrong, Judy Garland, Bob
Hope. Commemorating Bing's 20th anniversary on radio.

R104. Jan 18   ABC   The Screen Guild Players: Birth of
          the Blues 60 min. Thur.   Orville Anderson,
announcer; Basil "Buzz" Adlam, music; Buick, sponsor.
          Bing Crosby, Dinah Shore, Phil Harris
          Selections from the film of the same title; a
benefit for the Motion Picture Relief Fund.

R105. Sep 24   CBS   Lux Radio Theatre: Movietime,
          U.S.A. 60 min. John Milton Kennedy, announcer;
Rudy Schrager, music. Mon.
          Host: William Kneighley. Guests in alphabetical
order: Mari Aldon, Ann Blyth, Leslie Caron, Claudette
Colbert, Gary Cooper, Wendell Corey, Bing Crosby, Dan
Dailey, John Derek, Joanne Dru, Gene Kelly, Vera Ral-
ston, Donna Reed, Robert Ryan, Forrest Tucker, John
Wayne, Jane Wyman
          Guests performed scenes from recent and scheduled
film releases. Crosby and Wyman did a selection from
Here Comes the Groom (released Jun 29, 1951) and sang
"In the Cool, Cool, Cool of the Evening."

R106. Oct 3-Dec 26 CBS, Hollywood   Chesterfield
      Guests included: Hoagy Carmichael and Jane Wyman,
Oct 3; Bob Hope, Oct 17; Dinah Shore, Oct 31; Dean
Martin and Jerry Lewis, Nov 7; James Stewart and Anna
Maria Alberghetti, Nov 14; Alexis Smith, Nov 21, Dec
12; Ella Fitzgerald and Louis Armstrong, Nov 28; Trudy
Erwin and Lindsay Crosby, Dec 19 Christmas Show; Doro-
thy Lamour and Bob Hope, Dec 26.

1952
R107. Jan 2-Jun 25 CBS, Hollywood   Chesterfield (cont.)
      Guests included: Bob Hope, Jan 16, Apr 9; Patti
Page, Jan 30; Fred Astaire, Feb 6; the Mills Brothers,
Feb 20; Bob and Cathy Crosby, Mar 5; Gary Crosby, Apr
2; Donald O'Connor, Apr 30; Teresa Brewer and David
Niven, May 14; Judy Garland, May 21, 28, Jun 4; Rose-
mary Clooney and Joe Venuti, Jun 11; Peggy Lee, Jun 18,
25.
      Jun 25 was the last show Crosby recorded for
Chesterfield; he had appeared on 113 programs. The
show had no rating for 1951-52.

R108. Jan 25   CBS   Screen Guild Players: The Birth of
      the Blues 30 min. Fri.
      Bing Crosby, Dinah Shore, Phil Harris, Red Nichols
(selections from film <u>Birth of the Blues</u>). Also called
the Screen Guild Theatre, it was a benefit program that
did not pay performers.

R109. Feb 17   ABC   Walter Winchell News Sun.
      Bing Crosby was the guest host for Winchell.

R110.   Guest Star Time   15 min.
      Bing Crosby was a guest in 1952 on one show.

      General Electric-The Bing Crosby Show
      CBS, Hollywood Oct 9, 1952-May 30, 1954
      The G.E. series aired Thur at 9:30 p.m. and was
Crosby's final regular weekly radio program. The
Trotter Orchestra, Ken Carpenter, and producers-direc-
tors Bill Morrow and Murdo MacKenzie remained. The
competition with television was taking its toll.

R111. Oct 9-Dec 25 CBS, Hollywood   General Electric
      Guests included: Jane Wyman, Oct 9; Judy Garland
as guest hostess, Oct 30; James Stewart, Oct 23, guest
host Nov 6 with guests Rosemary Clooney, Gordon MacRae,
and Venuti; Dinah Shore, Nov 13, 20; Clooney, Dec 4,
11; Ella Fitzgerald, Dec 18; Gary Crosby, Dec 25
Christmas Show.
      Guest hosts presided Oct 30 and Nov 6, the time of
Dixie Lee Crosby's final illness; she died Saturday,
Nov 1.

1953
R112. Jan 1-Jul 2 CBS, Various locations   G.E. (cont.)
      Guests included: Ella Fitzgerald, Jan 1; Clooney,
Hope, and Venuti, Jan 15, Fort Ord; Clooney and Venuti,
Jan 22; Kay Starr and Venuti, Jan 29, Feb 5, Palm

Springs; Jack Benny, Feb 12; Dinah Shore and Venuti, Mar
19; Clooney and Venuti, Mar 26, Apr 2, 9, 23; Lindsay
Crosby and Venuti, May 21 to Jul 2 (seven weeks),
Paris.

Although based in Hollywood, the program originated Jan 15 from Fort Ord; after the next week from
Hollywood, Crosby broadcast Jan 29 to Apr 23 (13 weeks)
from Palm Springs, regularly from the Plaza Theater;
after one week, Crosby returned to Palm Springs for May
7; after a later week from Hollywood, he took his
program to Paris from May 21 to July 2.

1952-53: 6.5 share; Hope, 5.4; Benny, 12.8.

R113. Sep 27-Dec 27   CBS, Hollywood   General Electric
Guests included: Gary Crosby, Sep 27, Oct 4, Nov
1, 8; Rosemary Clooney, Oct 11, 18, Nov 22, Dec 6; Ella
Fitzgerald, Dec 13, 27; Gloria Wood, Dec 20 Christmas
Show.

The theme song was omitted from Sep 27 to May 30,
1954, the end of the series. The song was replaced by
economic discussions of Crosby and Ken Carpenter.

1954
R114. Jan 3-May 30   CBS, Hollywood General Electric (cont.)
Guests included: Gary Crosby, Jan 10, 24; Ella
Fitzgerald, Feb 14; the Four Aces, Feb 21, 28; Frank
Sinatra, Mar 21, 28; Gary and Lindsay Crosby, Apr 4,
11, May 9, 30; Rosemary Clooney, Apr 18, May 2, 23.

Crosby ended his major weekly radio shows on May
30 as he went into television, but he began transcrib-
ing 15-minute programs with the Buddy Cole Trio, broadcast weekdays on radio to 1962. Gary Crosby took the
Sunday slot for his own radio show, summer 1954.

1953-54: 6.0 share; Hope, not rated; Benny, 8.2.

NOTE: The Bing Crosby Show became a 15-minute
weekday program in Nov 1954 on CBS for General Electric
to 1960 and for Ford into 1962. The theme song became
"Moonlight Becomes You" until 1960.

R115. Nov 22   CBS   The Bing Crosby Show
15 min., five days a week at 9:15 p.m., at 7:30 by
Dec 1955. Sponsor: General Electric
Music: Buddy Cole on piano and organ.
Announcer: Ken Carpenter.
This program went into 1960, replaced by another
daily show.

1954-55: 3.1 share; Sinatra, Clooney unrated.

1955
R116. Dec 24   CBS   A Christmas Sing with Bing Crosby
Live special Christmas program at Grand Central
Station, New York, with two large choirs. Bing may
have participated remote from Los Angeles.

The program was also carried by the Canadian
Broadcasting Corporation, Armed Forces Radio Services
overseas, and the Voice of America, covering the entire
English-speaking world. It is available as an album
(D2311). A total of eight choirs were on the air,

though probably only two with Bing. Bing did Christmas
radio shows for a few more years, through 1961 as part
of his daily series. His first regular TV Christmas
show was Dec 1961.

1956
       1955-56: 2.2 share; McCarthy/Bergen, 3.9; Gene
Autry, 3.2. Thirteen major programs were unsponsored.

1960
R117. Feb 28   CBS   The Ford Road Show with Bing Crosby
           and Rosemary Clooney
           Music: Buddy Cole on piano and organ.
           Announcer: Ken Carpenter.
           A 20-minute program that aired five mornings a
week and lasted to 1962. (Bill Osborn states the
program lasted 20 min. [Crooner 51 (Feb 1991): 2.]) It
was recorded in Hollywood and other convenient locations with Bing singing two songs, Clooney two songs,
and both on a duet. The theme songs were, first, "Side
by Side," for 73 shows, and then "Don't Worry About
Tomorrow." Bing and Clooney delivered most of the
commercials. There were 675 programs over 135 weeks.
Reynolds states that Bing hosted the show twice a week,
and Rosemary Clooney hosted the others, although they
regularly sang on each other's show (p. 248).

1962
R118. Sep 28   CBS   The Ford Road Show with Bing Crosby
           and Rosemary Clooney
           The final program of Bing Crosby's regular radio
       shows.

       Some Other Guest Appearances on Radio

R119. The Bob Burns Show   CBS, Campbell Soup
R120. The Bob Hope Show   NBC, Pepsodent
R121. The Cavalcade of America   NBC, DuPont
R122. Duffy's Tavern   CBS, Schick
R123. The Dinah Shore Show   CBS and NBC, Birdseye
                                  Foods
R124. The Eddie Cantor Show   NBC, Sal Hepatica, Pabst
                                  Blue Ribbon
R125. Family Theater   Mutual
R126. G.I. Journal (Bing appeared on at least nine shows)
R127. The Hedda Hopper Show   CBS, Sunkist and Armour
R128. Hollywood vista a las Americas (in Spanish)
R129. Millions for Defense   CBS, Treasury Department
R130. The Radio Hall of Fame   NBC-Blue, Philco
R131. The Rudy Vallee Show   NBC, Sealtest
R132. Shell Chateau   NBC, Shell Oil Company
R133. Showtime: Dixie; with Bing Crosby, Dorothy Lamour
R134. The Spike Jones Show   CBS, Coca-Cola

       Bing Crosby made nearly 4000 radio appearances, includ-
ing about 1011 for his own major series (Sep 1931-May 1954),
2000 for his daily series (Nov 1954-Sep 1962), and 300 or
more for his Minute Maid series (1948 and later).

Videography

When known, the following television productions include the following credits: d: director; ep: executive producer; p: producer; ap: associate producer; w: writer; md: music director; ma: music arranger; cd: choral director; ch: choreographer; c: camera; e: editor; a: announcer

Date	Program	Episode	Network	Length

1948
V1.   Dec 19   Philco Television Playhouse: A Christmas Carol NBC   60 min.   Fred Coe, creator.
        Crosby's television debut, apparently singing "Silent Night."

        NOTE: Television programs originating in New York were aired on the West Coast up to ten days later in kinescopes. This practice lasted until about 1954.

1949

        Paul Whiteman, Crosby's discoverer of 1926, opened Paul Whiteman's TV Teen Club on ABC Saturday night, Apr 2, 1949, a show that ran to Mar 28, 1954, and discovered singer Bobby Rydell in 1951 and Dick Clark, his announcer in 1952. Whiteman wore loud shirts and jackets, used bizarre nicknames for his young cast, and spoke in contemporary slang, perhaps imitating Crosby.

V1A. Mar 4   An Evening with Richard Rodgers NBC   Unknown
           Guests: Bing Crosby, Mary Martin, Celeste Holm, Vivienne Segal, Alfred Drake

1950

        Bob Crosby was on Bob Hope's show Sep 14.   NBC

1951
V2.   Feb 27   The Red Cross Fund Program CBS   Guest
           Host: Ed Sullivan. Guests: Bing Crosby, Bob Hope, Judy Garland, and others
           Commonly regarded as Crosby's television debut.
        He sang a few songs.

1952
V3.   Jun 21   Telethon for the U.S. Olympic Team   CBS and
NBC   14.5 hours, overnight.
        Hosts: Bob Hope, Bing Crosby, and Dorothy Lamour.
Guests: Ezio Pinza, Phil Harris, Dean Martin and Jerry
Lewis, Buddy Cole, Red Nichols
        The telethon was the idea of Vincent Flaherty of
the Los Angeles _Examiner_ and was patterned after Milton
Berle's annual telethons for the Cancer Fund. Hope and
Crosby attempted to raise $500,000 to send the Olympic
Team to the Summer Games in Helsinki, Finland, and
achieved pledges of more than $1 million. Bing wore
his toupee, complained mockingly whenever the audience
seemed bored, chatted with guests, read hundreds of
names of contributors, traded insults with Hope, and
crooned several songs, like "Home on the Range." Bing
was, according to _Time_, "glibly polysyllabic" and
"seems assured of a lively and profitable TV career
whenever he wants it. Said Bing, 'Well, I guess I'm
off on the road to vaudeville--again'" (Jun 30, 1952:
45).

        Bing Crosby Productions produced "Rebound," a
dramatic anthology airing on ABC and later on Dumont,
from Feb 8, 1952, to Jan 16, 1953. Stars included Lee
Marvin and Rita Johnson. The show featured mystery and
suspense with surprise endings.

1953
V4.   Jan 4   The Bob Hope Show/Colgate Comedy Hour   NBC
60 min. Variety show.
        Host: Bob Hope. Guest: Bing Crosby, Jack Buchanan
and others

V5.   Feb 25   I Married Joan NBC 30 min. Comedy series
episode
        Joan Davis, Jim Backus. Guest: Bing Crosby

1954
V6.   Jan 3   The Bing Crosby Special CBS 30 min. Musi-
cal special Sponsor: General Electric
        d: Fred De Cordova; p, w: Bill Morrow; md: John
Scott Trotter; a: Ken Carpenter
        Host: Bing Crosby. Guests: Jack Benny, Sheree
North
        This was Bing's first TV special. He sang "Y'all
Come," "It Had to Be You," "Changing Partners," and "I
Love Paris."

V7.   Jan 17   The Colgate Comedy Hour NBC 60 min. Variety show
        Bing Crosby presents the winner of the Crosby
National Pro-Am Golf Tournament, Pebble Beach, CA.

V8.   Mar 21   The Jack Benny Program CBS 30 min. Variety
·show (Benny states it is last show of the season.)
        Host: Jack Benny. Guest: Bing Crosby, George
Burns, Bob Hope

V9.   Apr 25   The Bing Crosby Show CBS 30 min. Musical
special Sponsor: General Electric
       d: Leslie Goodwins; p, w: Bill Morrow; ap: Sid
Brod; md: John Scott Trotter; a: Ken Carpenter
       Host: Bing Crosby. Guests: Joanne Gilbert, Buddy
Cole, the Weire Brothers

       See V246 for comments on Bing by Bob Hope on Jack
Benny's show about this time.

       NOTE: Networks began broadcasting two or three shows a
week in color.

V10.   Oct 17   Toast of the Town CBS 60 min. Variety show
       Host: Ed Sullivan. Guests: Bing Crosby, Irving
Berlin, Liberace, and others.

V11.   Dec 3   Person to Person CBS 30 min. Talk show
       Edward R. Murrow interviews Bing Crosby and
praises his work in <u>Country Girl</u>.

V12.   Dec   This Is Your Life: Laurel and Hardy NBC 30
       min.
       a: Bob Warren
       Host: Ralph Edwards. Guests: Stanley Laurel,
Oliver Hardy, Leo McCarey, Jr., and others. Exact date
unknown.
       Contrary to some reports, Bing Crosby does not
appear on this program from the El Capitan Theater, but
his two films directed by McCarey are mentioned.

1955
V13.   Mar 30   Academy Awards Show NBC
Host: Bob Hope. Bing Crosby briefly chats with Hope.

V13A.   Look Magazine Awards Unknown
       Red Skelton presents the magazine's Best Actor
Award to Bing for <u>The Country Girl</u>.

V14.   May 24   The Bob Hope Show NBC 60 min. Variety
       special
       p: Jack Hope; md: Les Brown
       Host: Bob Hope. Guests: Jane Russell, Bing Cros-
by, Don Hartman

1956
V15.   Jan 10   Shower of Stars CBS 60 min. Monthly revue
       o: David Rose
       Host: Jack Barry. Guests: Bing Crosby, Jack
Benny, Jayne Mansfield, Liberace

V16.   Mar 10   Ford Star Jubilee: High Tor CBS 90 min.
       Musical special (TV movie)
       See F131 of the Filmography for details.

V16A. Jun 17   Bob Hope Sunday Spectacular NBC Unknown
       Host: Bob Hope. Guests: Bing Crosby and others

V17.   Jul 15   Ed Sullivan Show CBS 60 min. Variety show

Host: Ed Sullivan. Guests: Bing Crosby, Frank Sinatra,
Grace Kelly, Louis Armstrong
    Bing sings "True Love" and bits of "Mississippi
Mud" and "A-Tisket, A-Tasket."

V18. Oct 6   You're the Top CBS 90 min. Variety special
Celebrating Cole Porter. Ford Star Jubilee.
    Host: Cole Porter. Guests: Sally Forrest, George
Chakiris, Dolores Gray, Peter Lind Hayes, Mary Healy,
Dorothy Dandridge, Bing Crosby, Shirley Jones, Gordon
MacRae, George Sanders, Louis Armstrong.
    Bing's part and two songs were filmed at Pebble
Beach. See V260.

V18A. Nov   Special Voting Day Telecast Unknown
    Bing Crosby, Jimmy Durante, Bob Hope, Peter Law-
ford, Groucho Marx, and others emphasize the privilege
of voting. Bing sings "The Gypsy in My Soul."

V18B. Nov 17   Ed Sullivan Show CBS 60 min. Variety
    Host: Ed Sullivan. Guests: Bing Crosby and others
Bing sings two versions of "True Love."

V18C. Dec 10   Picture Parade BBC (England)
    Bing is interviewed about High Society.

V18D. Dec   The Joyful Hour Unknown
    Bing sings "Is Christmas Only a Tree?"

1957
V19. Jan 22   Phil Silvers Show: Sgt. Bilko Presents Bing
Crosby CBS 30 min.
    Host: Phil Silvers. Guests: Bing Crosby, Everett
Crosby.
    Bing becomes an entertainer at "Fort Baxter" in
Kansas. He does not sing but recites "The Wreck of the
Hesperus" to expose a Crosby impersonator.
    This is the only time Bing's brother Everett
appeared in a program with him.

V19A. Mar 27   Academy Awards Show Unknown
    Bing sings "True Love."

    NOTE: The three major television networks began
showing most programs on videotape on Apr 28, 1957
(Rushin, "Hi Fi" 32). Before this date most programs
were televised live and recorded in kinescope.

V20. Jun 16   The Ed Sullivan Show CBS 60 min. Variety
show
    Host: Ed Sullivan. Guests: Bing Crosby, Inger
Stevens, and others.
    Bing sings "True Love" and previews, with Miss
Stevens, scenes from the film Man on Fire.
    Some sources date the show as in May.

    Bing signed a five-year contract in June for radio
and television with the ABC network. These TV shows
began in 1959, but he often appeared on other networks.

In 1964 he became a frequent host of ABC's "Hollywood Palace."

Gary Crosby and his brothers were on The Bob Hope Show Oct 16.   NBC

V21. Oct. 13 The Edsel Show   CBS   60 min. Variety special
      p: Bill Morrow
      Host: Bing Crosby. Guests: Frank Sinatra, Rosemary Clooney, Louis Armstrong, Bob Hope, Lindsay Crosby, the Four Preps
      Bing sings about 35 songs, solo and duets with others, including "September Song" and "There's a Long, Long Trail" with Sinatra and "Road to Morocco" in a cameo appearance by Bob Hope. See V259, V292.
      Some sources date the show as Oct 7.

V22. Dec 8   A Warm and Wonderful Christmas Eve with Bing and Frank ABC 60 min. Musical special
      Hosts: Bing Crosby and Frank Sinatra
      This is Bing's first TV Christmas special, although none aired on TV in 1958-60, when they were only on radio.

1958
V23. Jan 12   Bing and His Friends CBS 60 min. Golfing special
      d: Seymour Berns, Bob Quinlan; p: Cecil Barker; w: Joe Quillan; md: Buddy Cole
      Host: Bing Crosby. Guests: Howard Keel, Kathryn Grant, Fred MacMurray, Guy Madison, Dean Martin, Dennis O'Keefe, Randolph Scott
      This was the first televised Crosby-National Pro-Am Golf Tournament, which had resumed at Pebble Beach in 1947. It remained through 1985, after which AT&T took it over and the Crosby moved to Winston-Salem, NC. Bing Crosby missed only once through 1977. This (1958) was the 22nd Crosby Clambake, although it began in 1937. The annual tournament was televised until the Crosby moved to North Carolina.

V24. Mar 2   The Bob Hope Show NBC 60 min. Variety special
      d: Jim Jordan, Jr.; p: Jack Hope; md: Les Brown
      Host: Bob Hope. Guests: Robert Wagner, Natalie Wood, Bing Crosby, Anita Ekberg

V25. Sep 30   The Eddie Fisher Show NBC 60 min. Musical special
      o: Buddy Bregman
      Host: Eddie Fisher. Guests: Dean Martin, Jerry Lewis, Bing Crosby
      Bing has a cameo appearance with Martin to interrupt Lewis.

V26. Oct 1   The Bing Crosby Show ABC 60 min. Musical special Sponsor: Oldsmobile
      md: Buddy Cole
      Host: Bing Crosby. Guests: Dean Martin, Patti

Page, Mahalia Jackson

V27. Nov 22   The Dean Martin Show NBC 60 min. Variety
special Sponsor: Timex
      d, p: Jack Donohue; md: David Rose; w: Herbert
Baker
      Host: Dean Martin. Guests: Bing Crosby, Phil
Harris, and the Treniers

V28.   USO Christmas Show Variety special; taped
for overseas armed forces
      Guests: President Eisenhower, Bing Crosby, Bob
Hope, Louis Armstrong, Jack Benny, Dinah Shore, Jane
Russell, Milton Berle

1959
V29. Mar 2   The Bing Crosby Special ABC 60 min. Musi-
cal special Sponsor: Oldsmobile
      d, p: Bill Colleran; w: Bill Morrow; md: Nelson
Riddle; cd: Jimmy Joyce; songs Sammy Cahn, Jimmy Van
Heusen
      Host: Bing Crosby. Guests: James Garner, Philip
Crosby, Dennis Crosby, Jo Stafford, Tom Hanson, Thelma
Tadlock, Dean Martin

V30. Mar 19   The Dean Martin Show NBC 60 min. Musical
special
      Host: Dean Martin. Bing is a brief guest.

V31. Sep 29   The Bing Crosby Show ABC 60 min. Musical
special Sponsor: Oldsmobile
      d: Bill Colleran; p: Sammy Cahn, Bill Colleran;
w: Bill Morrow; md: Axel Stordahl
      Host: Bing Crosby. Guests: Frank Sinatra, Peggy
Lee, Louis Armstrong, George Shearing, Joe Bushkin,
Paul Smith, Jayne Turner

      The Crosby Brothers were on The Bob Hope Show Oct
8 on NBC

V32. Oct 19   The Frank Sinatra Timex Show ABC 60 min.
Musical special See V292.
      d, p: Bill Colleran; ep: Sammy Cahn, Jimmy Van
Heusen; md: Nelson Riddle; w: John Bradford
      Host: Frank Sinatra. Guests: Bing Crosby, Dean
Martin, Mitzi Gaynor, Jimmy Durante

1960
V33. Feb 29   The Bing Crosby Show ABC 60 min. Musical
special Sponsor: Oldsmobile Taped Jan 11
      d, p: William O. Harbach; w: Sheldon Keller, Saul
Ilson, Herb Sargent, James Elson; md: Vic Schoen;
ch: Tom Hanson; a: Frank Gallop
      Host: Bing Crosby. Guests: Perry Como, Philip
Crosby, Dennis Crosby, Lindsay Crosby, Elaine Dunn,
Sandy Stewart
      Bing, singing "Joshua Fit the Battle of Jericho,"
filled in for Gary, who had just left the act of the
Crosby Brothers. When the Brothers appeared on the Ed

Sullivan Show, Gary was missing then too.

V34.   Mar 16   Perry Como's Kraft Music Hall   NBC   60 min.
Taped Mar 6
          md: Mitchell Ayres
          Host: Perry Como. Guest: Bing Crosby, Genvieve,
Peter Gennaro
          Bing is the principal guest, singing about 20
songs solo and with Como. See p. 347 for note on KMH.

V35.   Mar 24   A Salute to Paul Whiteman   CBS   60 min.
Sponsor: Revlon
          Host: Mike Wallace Guests: Jack Teagarden, Peggy
Lee, Buster Keaton, Bing Crosby, Peter Nero, others
          Bing sings part of "Mississippi Mud" and "Happy
Birthday" on Whiteman's 70th "Birthday Party" and 50th
year in show business.

V36.   Oct 5   The Bing Crosby Show   ABC   60 min. Musical
special Sponsor: Oldsmobile Taped in Aug
          d, p: William O. Harbach; w: Herb Sargent, Sheldon
Keller, Saul Ilson, James Elson; md: Nelson Riddle
          Host: Bing Crosby. Guests: Rosemary Clooney,
Johnny Mercer, Carol Lawrence, Dennis Crosby, Philip
Crosby, Lindsay Crosby

V37.   Oct 18   Tonight (England) BBC Talk show
          Bing Crosby on the Sunningdale Golf Course, Eng-
land, interviewed by Derek Hart on Oct 15.

1961
V38.   Mar 20   The Bing Crosby Show   ABC   60 min. Variety
special Sponsor: Oldsmobile Taped in Feb See B216.
          md: Nelson Riddle
          Host: Bing Crosby. Guests: Maurice Chevalier,
Aldo Monaco, Carol Lawrence

          Bing produced "Ben Casey," aired on ABC Oct 2,
1961, to Mar 21, 1966. Bing Crosby also discovered
Vince Edwards, the virile star of the medical series.

V39.   Aug 3   Tonight (England) BBC
          Bing is the guest, taped Aug 2.

V40.   Aug 5   The Rosemary Clooney Show (England) ATV
Live
          Bing Crosby is a "surprise" guest and sings a duet
of "Fancy Meeting You Here" with Clooney.

V41.   Aug 26   A Big Night Out with Peggy Lee Unknown
          Bing Crosby is a guest with Sammy Cahn and Jimmy
Van Heusen (taped Jul 30).

V42.   Sep 10   Sunday Night at the London Palladium ABC
(England)
          Bing Crosby appears and sweeps the stage during
Bob Hope's act.

V43.   Sep 24   The Dupont Show--Happy with the Blues Un-

known
>   md: Paul Weston
>   With Bing Crosby, Peggy Lee, Vic Damone, La Vern
Baker, Joanie Sommers, Harold Arlen
>   Bing narrates the songwriting career of Arlen.

V44.   Nov 5   The Time, the Place and the Camera   Unknown
>   An appearance by Bing Crosby, details unknown.

V45.   Dec 11   The Bing Crosby Show ABC 60 min. Christmas
special Taped Nov 12 at Wembley Studios, London
>   md: Peter Knight
>   Host: Bing Crosby. Guests: Marion Ryan, Dave
King, Terry-Thomas, Shirley Bassey, the Happy Wander-
ers, Bob Hope
>   This marks the beginning of Bing's annual TV
Christmas shows, although he sings only one Christmas
song, "White Christmas," which is the finale.

1962
V46.   Feb 27   The Bob Hope Show NBC 60 min. Variety
special
>   d: Jack Shea; p: Jack Hope; md: David Rose
>   Host: Bob Hope. Guests: Steve Allen, Joan Col-
lins, Joanie Sommers, Jack Parr, Bing Crosby
>   Bing plays a child star with Parr and Allen.

V47.   Apr 3   Picture Parade (England) BBC
>   Bing Crosby and Bob Hope interviewed by Robert
Robinson, taped Oct 19, 1961. Bing duets "Team Work"
with Hope.

V48.   May 14   The Bing Crosby Springtime Special ABC 60
min. Musical special, taped in Apr
>   md: David Rose
>   Host: Bing Crosby. Guests: Edie Adams, Bob Hope,
Gary Crosby, Pete Fountain, Dick Smothers, Tom Smothers

V49.   c.Jun   DuPont Show of the Week: Biography of a Movie
NBC 60 min. Special documentary
>   A chronicle of all aspects of filming The Road to
Hong Kong, which was released on Jun 27.

V50.   Jun 24   The Ed Sullivan Show CBS 60 min. Variety
special
>   Bing Crosby and Bob Hope are guests on the 14th
anniversary of the program.

>   Going My Way, Crosby's 1944 masterpiece film,
inspired a TV series of the same name that aired from
Oct 3, 1962, to Sep 11, 1963, starring Gene Kelly, Leo
G. Carroll, Dick York, and Nydia Westman.

V51.   Oct 24   The Bob Hope Show NBC 60 min. Variety
special
>   d: Jack Shea; p: Jack Hope; ma: Skinnay Ennis;
md: Les Brown and his Band of Renown; ch: Tom Hansen
>   Host: Bob Hope. Guests: Juliet Prowse, Bing
Crosby, Lucille Ball

V52.   Dec 24   The Bing Crosby Christmas Show ABC   60 min.
Christmas musical special   Sponsor: Clairol
          d: Joe Lilley; p: Nick Vanoff; w: Bill Morrow, Max
Wilk; md: Andre Previn; ch: Dee Dee Wood, Marc Breaux
          Host: Bing Crosby. Guests: Mary Martin, Andre
Previn
          This is ABC's first color special. Bing sings
"Little Drummer Boy"; also "White Christmas" with Mary
Martin, a duet delayed since 1942; taped Nov. in L.A.

1963
V53.   Feb 17   The Dinah Shore Show NBC   30 min.   Talk
show. Taped in Dec.
          d: Dean Whitmore; md: Harry Zimmermann; ch: Nick
Castle
          Host: Dinah Shore. Guests: Bing Crosby, Al Hirt,
Bud and Travis

          Bing had taped commercials for Minute Maid orange
juice, and now did one for Shell Oil. He frequently
appeared in ads for Minute Maid until he died.

V53A.   The American Sportsman ABC 30 min. Sports
show Host: Curt Gowdy. Guests: Bing Crosby, Bud Boyd,
fishing for salmon in Iceland; filmed in July. Cf.
V163, Feb 21, 1970.

V53B. May 29   The Bob Hope Birthday Special
          Bing was a guest; details unknown. See note for
V142B, May 29, 1968.

V54.   Nov 7   The Bing Crosby Show CBS 60 min. Variety
show. Taped Sep 29.
          d, p: Nick Vanoff; w: Bill Morrow, Max Wilk;
md: Andre Previn; ch: Dee Dee Wood, Marc Breaux
          Host: Bing Crosby. Guests: Buddy Ebsen, Caterina
Valente, Andre Previn, the Young Americans

V55.   Tell Us More NBC 30 min. Documentary
          Host: Conrad Nagel. Presented two biographical
sketches per show, one program on Bing Crosby and Bob
Hope.
          The series aired from Sep 9, 1963, to Mar 16,
1964.

V56.   Dec   The Grammy Awards   Unknown
          Bing Crosby receives a special award for his
outstanding contribution to the recording industry.

V57.   Dec 13   A Bob Hope Comedy Special   NBC   60 min.
Variety special
          md: Les Brown and his Band of Renown
          Hosts: Bing Crosby, Jack Benny. Guests: Juliet
Prowse, Danny Thomas
          Bing and Benny fill in for Hope, who was ill.

V58.   Dec 24   The Promise   Father Peyton's Family Theater
Group Unknown
          Bing Crosby narrates the story of the birth of

Christ.

1964
V59.   Jan 4   The Hollywood Palace ABC Hour variety show
that aired Saturdays or Mondays until Feb 7, 1970.
Crosby hosted the opening show and hosted other shows
every four weeks or so, especially around Christmas,
for at least 32 appearances of the 190 shows. The
programs were staged at the Palace, the former El
Capitan, a refurbished Los Angeles theater.
ep Nick Vanoff; md Les Brown (1964), Mitchell Ayres
(1964-1969), Nick Perito (1970)
    The premiere hosted by Crosby included Mickey
Rooney, Bobby Van, Nancy Wilson, Bob Newhart, Gary
Crosby, and the Young Americans.

    Philip Crosby was on The Bob Hope Show Jan 17,
NBC.

V60.   Feb 15   The Bing Crosby Show CBS 60 min. Musical
special Sponsor: Lever Brothers. Taped Oct 27, 1963,
and Feb 3.
    d, p: Nick Vanoff; w: Howard Leeds, Sid Dorfman,
Bob Rodgers, Bill Morrow; md: John Scott Trotter
    Host: Bing Crosby. Guests: Bob Hope, Rosemary
Clooney, Kathryn Crosby, Frank Sinatra, Dean Martin,
Peter Gennaro

V60A.   ca. Jun 20   Los Expertos Contestan Syndicated
    Bing appears on a Spanish-speaking panel show to
be viewed throughout South America. His Spanish was
poor.

V61.   Sep 13   Hollywood Palace ABC 60 min. Variety
special
    Host: Bing Crosby. Guests: Mickey Rooney, Jimmy
Dean, Connie Stevens, Kathy Nolan, Tony Franciosa,
Richard Basehart, David Hedison, David Janssen, Lawrence Welk
    The program previews many shows on the new ABC
season. It is Bing's second Palace show.

V62.   Sep 14   Bing Crosby Show ABC 30 min. Comedy series
    Aired Mondays at 9:30 p.m. for one season until
Jun 14, 1965. 28 episodes. bw See V294.
    p: Steven Gethers; md: John Scott Trotter; theme
song by Jimmy Van Heusen, Sammy Cahn
    Bing Crosby, Beverly Garland, Carol Faylen,
Diane Sherry, Frank McHugh
    Bing Collins (Crosby) is a former singer who
settles down in Los Angeles with his family to work as
an electrical engineer, but his wife, Ellie (Garland),
dreams of becoming a success in show business, and
their two daughters range from the normal, boy-crazy
15-year-old Joyce (Faylen) to the intellectual 10-year-
old Janice (Sherry). Willie Walters (McHugh) is the
live-in handyman. Bing sings a song or two in each
episode, between mediating disputes and dispensing sage
advice.

NOTE: Bing sings "There's More to Life Than Just
Livin'" over the opening titles and "It All Adds Up"
over the closing titles. Staying at the Sheraton-West
or a rented bungalow during the week, he would tape
five shows (with canned laughter) in three weeks at
Desilu Studios and take two weeks off. Gary Crosby,
Kathryn Crosby, and Phil Harris were among the guests.
(See <u>Bing</u> 98 [Aug 1991]: 6-7). Two episodes are available on videotape from Discount Video Tapes, Inc.

EPISODES (Dates and Titles)
	9/14	A Fine Romance
V63.	9/21	Guess Who Is Exactly Like Who

Guest: Gary Crosby

V64.	9/28	A Bit of Fresh Danish
V65.	10/5	The Green Couch
V66.	10/12	Hoop Shots Are Hard to Get

Guest: Jimmy Boyd

V67.	10/19	Flashback--Ah, Happy Days!
V68.	10/26	The Education of Bing Collins

Guest: Macdonald Carey

| V69. | 11/9 | The Dominant Male |

Guest: Gary Crosby

V70.	11/16	The Importance of Bea 'n' Willie
V71.	11/23	The Liberated Woman
V72.	11/30	Danger! Genius at Work

Guest: Thomas Gomez

V73.	12/7	The Yardwin Report
V74.	12/14	Unknown

Guest: David Wayne

| V75. | 12/21 | Christmas Show |

Bing sings "Christmas Candles," "We Wish You the
Merriest Christmas" with cast, "<u>La Piñata</u>" with cast,
"Do You Hear What I Hear," and "White Christmas."

V76.	1/11/65	Unknown
V77.	1/18	Bugged by the Love Bugs

Bing also hosted "The Hollywood Palace" this date.

V78.	1/25	Are Parents People?
V79.	2/1	That's the Way the Suki Yakies
V80.	2/8	The Gifted Child
V81.	2/15	The Image

Guests: Kathryn Crosby, George Gobel

| V82. | 2/22 | The Keefers Come Calling |

Guests: Frankie Avalon, Vikki Carr

| V83. | 3/1 | Operation Man Save |

Guests: Joan Fontaine, Dennis Day

| V84. | 3/8 | One for the Birds |

Guest: Phil Harris

V85.	3/22	The Test
V86.	3/29	Moonlight Becomes You

Guest: Mel Torme

V87.	4/5	Unknown
V88.	4/12	Unknown
V89.	4/19	Real Estate Venture

Guest: Ruth Roman
The 28th and final episode, although repeats
appeared to Jun 14.

| V90. | Oct 4 | The Bell Telephone Hour   NBC   60 min. Varie- |

ty special
        Guests: Bing, Burl Ives, Grant Johannessen (pianist). Bing Crosby sings four songs: "I'm Confessin'," "Avalon," "Chinatown, My Chinatown," and "Alabamy Bound." <u>Bing</u> 104: 27 dates the program as Oct 6.

1965

V91. Jan 16   Hollywood Palace ABC 60 min. Variety special
        Host: Bing Crosby. Guests: Beverly Garland, George Burns, the King Family, Ed Wynn, Frank McHugh

V92. Mar 10   The Grand Award of Sports ABC
        Hosts: Bing Crosby and Kathryn Crosby.
        Broadcast live from the New York World's Fair.

V93.   The American Sportsman ABC 30 min. Sports show
        Host: Curt Gowdy. Guests: Bing Crosby, Phil Harris, Texas Gov. John Connally, on safari in Africa; filmed about May 1965.

       Jun 14   Bing Crosby Show ABC 30 min. series
        Final broadcast of the series that began Sep 14, 1964; probably repeating episodes since Apr 19.

V94. Jun 27   The Eamonn Andrews Show (England) ITV Talk show   Thames production.
        Host: Eamonn Andrews. Guests: Bing Crosby, Spike Milligan, Cilla Black, Patrick Campbell, Harry H. Corbett

V95. Jun 30   Wimbledon Lawn Tennis Championship (England) BBC
        Bing appears in a brief interview.

V96. Jul 6   Late Night Line-up (England) BBC
        Bing is interviewed.

V97. Sep 18   Hollywood Palace ABC 60 min. Variety special
        Host: Bing Crosby. Guests: Caterina Valente, the Nitwits, Jack Burns, Tim Conway

V98. Sep 25   Hollywood Palace ABC 60 min. Variety special
        Host: Bing Crosby. Guests: Louis Armstrong, Phil Harris, the Young Americans

V98A. Nov 11   CBS News Special--Sinatra CBS Unknown
        Bing is interviewed.

V99. Nov 20   Hollywood Palace ABC 60 min. Variety special
        Host: Bing Crosby. Guests: Bob Hope, Diahann Carroll, the Kessler Twins (Alice and Ellen), John Bubbles

V99A.   Art Linkletter   Unknown

Linkletter interviews Bing on the set of Stagecoach.

V100. Dec 15   A Bob Hope Comedy Special NBC 60 min.
Variety special
        d: Jack Shea; p: George Hope; w: Mort Lachman,
Lester White, Bill Larkin, John Rapp; md: Les Brown
        Host: Bob Hope. Guests: Bing Crosby, Janet Leigh,
Nancy Wilson, Mickey Rooney, Jack Benny
        Bing sings "Do You Hear What I Hear?"

V101. Dec 25   Hollywood Palace ABC 60 min. Christmas
variety special This was Bing's seventh Palace show;
his 30th annual Christmas special.
        Host: Bing Crosby. Guests: Dorothy Collins, Fred
Waring and his Pennsylvanians, Bob Crane, Harry Crosby
III

V102. Unk.   A Tribute to Irving Berlin Unknown
        Appearance by Bing Crosby. Cf. V142-42A.

V103. Bing Crosby's narration and songs for The Legend of
Sleepy Hollow appeared on Walt Disney's television
series that has aired since Oct 1954 with only a few
interruptions. See F103 for details of the 1949 cartoon titled The Adventures of Ichabod and Mr. Toad.

1966
V104. Jan 1   Hollywood Palace ABC 60 min. Variety
special
        Host: Bing Crosby. Guests: Danny Thomas, Bob
Newhart, Sonny and Cher, Donna Butterworth

V105. Jan 6   Telescope (Canada) CBC
        A profile of Bing Crosby; interview by Fletcher
Markle.

V105A. Feb 2   The American Sportsman ABC 30 min. Sports
show
        Host: Curt Gowdy. Guest: Bing Crosby

V106. Feb 19   Hollywood Palace ABC 60 min. Variety
special
        Host: Bing Crosby. Guests: Gary Crosby, Rosemary
Clooney, Edgar Bergen

V107. Mar 26   Hollywood Palace ABC 60 min. Variety
special
        Host: Bing Crosby. Guests: David Frost, Nanette
Fabray, Jackie Mason, Tammy Grimes

V108. Mar 27   The Easter Seal Show CBC (Canada) Benefit
        md: Lucio Agostini Taped Mar 7.
        With Bing Crosby, Kathryn Crosby, Juliette, Robbie
Lane and the Disciples, Art Hallman Singers

V109. April 4   The Danny Thomas Show: The Road to Lebanon
NBC 60 min. Comedy special Sponsor: Consolidated
Cigars See V285.

Host: Danny Thomas. Guests: Bing Crosby as
"Bing," Bob Hope, Sheldon Leonard, Claudine Auger,
Hugh Downs
A spoof on the Crosby-Hope Road films.

V110. May 1   The Magic of Broadcasting CBS 60 min.
Hosts: Arthur Godfrey, Lucille Ball, Bing Crosby

V111. May 21   Hollywood Palace ABC 60 min. Variety
special
Host: Bing Crosby. Guests: Johnny Mercer, Shelley
Berman, the King Family, Leslie Uggams

V112. Jun 6   Channel 9 Kaleidoscope Unknown
James Daly interviews Bing.

V113. Jun 7   Derby Grandstand (England) BBC
Bing is interviewed.

V114. Jun 9   Across the Seven Seas (England) Talk show on
private air travel to Baja California. Bing is a
guest.

V115. Jun 17   Wayne and Shuster Take an Affectionate Look
at . . . CBS 60 min. Interview show
d, p: Bob Jarvis; ep: Gil Rodin; w: Johnny Wayne,
Frank Shuster
Hosts: Johnny Wayne, Frank Shuster. Bob Hope and
Bing Crosby were the subjects of one of the first
installments of this documentary that aired from Jun 17
to Jul 29, 1966, with hosts, comedians from Canada.
Later subjects were Jack Benny, W. C. Fields, the Marx
Brothers, and George Burns.

V116. Sep 17   Hollywood Palace ABC 60 min. Variety
special
Host: Bing Crosby. Guests: George Burns, Sid
Caesar, Jane Marsh, Mamas and the Papas

V116A.   The American Sportsman ABC 30 min. Sports
show
Host: Curt Gowdy. Guest: Bing Crosby, fishing for
salmon, River Derwent, Cockermouth, England, in Sept.

V117. Oct 30   The Andy Williams Show Musical special
Host: Andy Williams. Guests: Bing Crosby, Tennessee Ernie Ford, Kate Smith, the Young Americans

V118. Nov 16   A Bob Hope Comedy Special Starring Bing and
Me NBC 60 min. Comedy special: The Bob Hope Chrysler
Theater: Fantastic Stomach
md: Les Brown
Host: Bob Hope Guests: Bing Crosby, Jackie Glea-
son

V119. Nov 26   Hollywood Palace ABC 60 min. Variety
special
Host: Bing Crosby. Guests: Dorothy Lamour, Sid
Caesar, Vikki Carr

V120. Dec 24   Hollywood Palace   ABC   60 min.   Christmas
variety special   This was Bing's 14th Palace show.
    Host: Bing Crosby. Guests: Kate Smith, Cyd Cha-
risse, the Crosby Family, Bob Newhart
    Bing's annual Christmas specials began 30 years
earlier; this was his 31st.

V121. Dec 31   Hollywood Palace   ABC   60 min.   Variety
special
    Host: Bing Crosby. Guests: The Mills Brothers,
Skitch Henderson, Charles Aznavour, Dorothy Collins

1967
V122. Jan 14   Hollywood Palace   ABC   60 min.   Variety
special
    Host: Bing Crosby. Guests: Jimmy Durante, Bob
Hope, Edie Adams, Senator E. Dirksen, rebroadcast of
Bing singing "Paper Doll" (Dec 31, 1966) with the Mills
Brothers

V122A. Jan 29   The American Sportsman   Unknown

V123. Feb 18   Hollywood Palace   ABC   60 min.   Variety
special
    Host: Bing Crosby. Guests: Ella Fitzgerald, the
Nitwits, Alice Faye, Phil Harris

V124. Mar 14   A Little Bit of Irish (Ireland)   Redifussion
60 min.   Taped Sep 1966. See V175 as U.S. repeat.
    Bing introduces Irish entertainers, including Milo
O'Shea, and sings Irish songs.

V125. Apr 1   Hollywood Palace   ABC   60 min.   Variety
special
    Host: Bing Crosby. Guests: Louis Armstrong, the
Washboard Three, Red Buttons, Nanette Fabray

V126. Apr 13   The Dean Martin Show   NBC   60 min.   Musical
special
    o: Les Brown
    Host: Dean Martin. Guests: Bing Crosby, Polly
Bergen, Don Cherry, Rowan and Martin

V127. May 13   Hollywood Palace   ABC   60 min.   Variety
special
    Host: Bing Crosby. Guests: Frances Langford,
Barbara McNair, Louis Nye, the King Family, Don Ameche

V128. Jun 4   The Eamonn Andrews Show (England)   ITV   Talk
show
    Bing has a walk-on at the end of Bob Hope's ap-
pearance.

V129. Jul 17   Conversations 1967-1968   Unknown   Taped Sep
1966
    Bing talks about his family and career.

V130. Sep 5   Hollywood Palace   ABC   60 min.   Variety
special   Taped Sep 1966.

Host: Bing Crosby. Guests: Jimmy Durante, Milton Berle, Ravi Shankar, Joey Heatherton, Diahann Carroll

The Kraft Music Hall. TV heir to the radio program that ran from 1933 to 1949 and led by Crosby from Dec 1935 to May 1946, returned to TV on NBC Sep 13, 1967, and ran until May 12, 1971, Wed, introducing many popular entertainers, and Bing Crosby appeared at least once. The series first appeared on NBC-TV 1958-62 with Milton Berle, Perry Como, and Dave King alternating as hosts (see V35).

V131. Oct 9   Danny Thomas Hour: The Demon Under the Bed
    NBC 60 min. Dramatic series.
        Episode starring Bing Crosby, Joan Collins, George Maharis, Mary Frances Crosby
        Bing plays an aging actor facing the possibility of losing his voice in an excellent performance.

V131A. Oct 25 The Joey Bishop Show ABC 90 min. Talk show
        o: Johnny Mann; a: Regis Philbin
        Bing appears with Kathryn Crosby and Dorothy Lamour

V132. Oct 31   Hollywood Palace ABC 60 min. Variety special
        Host: Bing Crosby. Guests: Victor Borge, Roger Miller, Gail Martin, Paul Lynde, the U.N. International Children's Choir

V133. Nov 21   One Night Stands ABC Documentary
        Bing narrates careers of Woody Herman, Johnny Rivers, the Fifth Dimension, and others.

V134. Nov 25   The Jackie Gleason Show CBS 60 min. Variety special
        o: Sammy Spear; a: Johnny Olsen
        Guests: Bing Crosby, Alan King, Liberace

V135. Nov 29   Today NBC Morning talk show
        Bing is interviewed by Hugh Downs in a tribute to Bob Hope.

V136. Dec 19   Hollywood Palace ABC 60 min. Christmas variety special This was Bing's 22nd Palace show.
        Host: Bing Crosby. Guests: The King Family, Louis Nye, Adam West, the Crosby Family

1968
V137. Jan 13   Hollywood Palace ABC 60 min. Variety special
        Host: Bing Crosby. Guests: Peggy Lee, Jimmy Durante, Phil Harris, Milton Berle, Gonzaga University Choir

Phil Crosby was on The Bob Hope Show Jan 18, NBC.

V138. Jan 28   The American Sportsman ABC 30 min.
        Bing Crosby and Phil Harris hunt sand grouse in

Tanzania. They sing, as they often did on their appearances on the show, a parody of "Mr. Gallagher and Mr.
Shean."

V139. Feb 12   The Bob Hope Show: The Night of the Century
NBC   60 min.   "A Salute to the U.S.O." taped Feb 11 at
the New Madison Square Garden, New York.
        md: Les Brown
        Host: Bob Hope. Guests: Bing Crosby, Rocky Mar-
ciano, Pearl Bailey, Barbara Eden
        Bing sings and acts as the referee between a Hope
and Marciano boxing match.

V140. Apr 20   Hollywood Palace   ABC   60 min.   Variety
special   Taped Mar 1.
        Host: Bing Crosby. Guests: Sid Caesar, the King
Sisters, Florence Henderson, Joe Bushkin

V141. Apr 25   The Dean Martin Show   NBC   60 min.   Variety
special
        o: Les Brown
        Guests: Bing Crosby, Lena Horne, Dom DeLuise
        Bing 104: 29 dates this program as Oct 19, 1967.

V142. May 5   The Ed Sullivan Show   CBS   60 min.   Variety
show   Taped Feb 11.
        Bing Crosby is a guest in "A Tribute to Irving
Berlin" for the songwriter's 80th birthday. Cf. V102.

V142A. May 16   Nightline   Unknown
        A tribute to Irving Berlin with Bing, Guy Lombar-
do, Rudy Vallee, Ginger Rogers, Fred Astaire, Ethel
Merman. Cf. V102 and V142.

V142B. May 29   Bing 104: 29 lists another tribute to Bob
Hope on May 29, 1968, probably for his birthday, with
Bing as a guest and details unknown; cf. V53B.

V143. Sep 28   Hollywood Palace   ABC   60 min.   Variety
special
        Host: Bing Crosby. Guests: Bobby Goldsboro, Sid
Caesar, Jeannie C. Riley, Abby Lincoln

V144. Oct 23   The Bing Crosby Show   NBC   60 min.   Musical
special
        d: Marc Breaux; p: Ray Charles; w: Bill Morrow,
Hal Fimberg; md: Mitchell Ayres
        Host: Bing Crosby. Guests: Bob Hope, Stella
Stevens, Jose Feliciano, Diana Ross and the Supremes,
Dorothy Lamour

V145. Nov 2   The Prince of Peace   Religious program
        Narrator: Bing Crosby. Guest: Frankie Avalon
        Bing narrates the life of Christ; Bing [104 (Aug
1993): 29) states the program aired Jan 2, 1968.

V145A. Dec   The Ed Sullivan Show   CBS   60 min.   Variety
show
        Bing sings "White Christmas" after a brief inter-

view. The scene appears in "Happy Holidays from Ed
Sullivan," a two-hour special on CBS Dec 20, 1992.
       Bing includes the song in the Sullivan tribute to
Berlin in V142.

V146. Dec 21   Hollywood Palace ABC 60 min. Christmas
variety special This was Bing's 26th Palace show.
       Host: Bing Crosby. Guests: The Crosby Family,
John Beyner, the Lennon Sisters, Glen Campbell

       By this time Crosby had sold Bing Crosby Produc-
tions and its name to Cox, Atlanta, which continued to
produce many of the same series.

1969
V147. Jan 4   Hollywood Palace ABC 60 min. Variety
special
       Host: Bing Crosby. Guests: Tiny Tim, Judy Carne,
Bobbie Gentry

V148. Jan   Hall of Fame Awards Unknown
       Host: Bing Crosby

V149. Feb 15   Feelin' Groovy at Marine World ABC
       Host: Bing Crosby. Guests: Kathryn Crosby, Anissa
(Buffy) Jones, the Singing Rascals
       A tour of Marineland, Redwood City, California.

V150. Feb 14   Here Come the Stars Syndicated 60 min. A
roast
       p: William Hanna, Joseph Barbera
       Host: George Jessel. Jessel, Dorothy Lamour, Phil
Harris, Rich Little, Pat Buttram, and Dorothy Kirsten
roast Bing. See V274.

V151. Feb 17   The Bob Hope Special NBC 60 min. Variety
special
       md: Les Brown
       Host: Bob Hope. Guests: Bing Crosby, George
Burns, Martha Raye, Diana Ross and the Supremes, Lisa
Miller

V152. Mar 1   Hollywood Palace ABC 60 min. Variety
special
       Host: Bing Crosby. Guests: Victor Borge, Frank
Sinatra, Jr., Gary Crosby, the Temptations
       Program taped Feb 18, 1969.

V152A. Mar 9   The American Sportsman ABC 30 min.
       Host: Curt Gowdy. Guests: Bing Crosby, Gaylord
Perry, Phil Harris
       Bing and Harris hunt quail near Pinehurst, NC,
with Perry, a pitcher with the San Francisco Giants.

V153. Apr 5   Hollywood Palace ABC 60 min. Variety
special
       Host: Bing Crosby. Guests: Philip Crosby, Shelley
Berman, the Four Tops, Sally Ann Howes
       Taped Mar 19, 1969. Bing sang a medley of "Sam's

Song," "When You and I Were Young Maggie," and "Play a Simple Melody" with Philip, songs he had recorded with Gary. It was Bing's 29th Palace show.

V154. Oct 4   The Jackie Gleason Show: The Honeymooners in Hollywood CBS 60 min. Taped Sep 15, 19. Cf. V274.
o: Sammy Spear; a: Johnny Olsen
Host: Jackie Gleason. Guests: Bing Crosby, Maureen O'Hara, Bert Parks

V155. Oct 11   Hollywood Palace ABC 60 min. Variety special
Host: Bing Crosby. Guests: Engelbert Humperdinck, Bobbie Gentry, Dick Shawn, Gwen Verdon

V156. Nov 3   The Carol Burnett Show CBS 60 min. Variety special Taped Oct 14, 17.
md: Harry Zimmermann
Guests: Bing Crosby, Ella Fitzgerald, Rowan and Martin

V157. Nov 6   Rowan and Martin's Laugh-in NBC 60 min. Variety show
o: Ian Bernard; a: Gary Owens
Bing makes two appearances.

V158. Nov 6   The Dean Martin Show NBC 60 min. Variety show Taped Sep 28.
md: Les Brown and his Band of Renown
Guests: Bing Crosby, Eva Gabor, Jack Gilford, Dom DeLuise

V159. Dec 17   Bing Crosby and Carol Burnett: Together Again for the First Time NBC 60 min. Christmas variety special Taped Nov 22, 28.
d: Grey Lockwood p: Nick Vanoff, William O. Harbach   w: Sheldon Keller, Kenny Solms, Gail Patent md: John Scott Trotter
Hosts: Bing Crosby, Carol Burnett. Guests: Juliet Prowse, Roy Clark

V159A. The Bob Hope Show Unknown Listed in *Bing* 104: 31.

1970
V160. Jan 3   The Hollywood Palace ABC 60 min. Variety special
Host: Bing Crosby. Guest: Mary Costa, Sergio Franchi
Bing sings "This Is the Life" and old favorites: "Please," "Learn to Croon," "Down the Old Ox Road," "The Waiter, the Porter and the Upstairs Maid," "Pennies from Heaven," and "Swinging on a Star." With Costa he sings "Pollution."

V161. Feb 7   The Hollywood Palace Finale ABC 60 min.
This final program of the series that began Jan 4, 1970, was hosted by Bing Crosby, with guests Ella Fitzgerald, Fred Astaire, Ethel Merman, Nat King Cole, and Judy Garland. It was a retrospective that included

performances by Jimmy Durante, Sammy Davis, Jr., Martha
Raye, Herb Alpert, Ray Bolger, Gene Kelly, Bette Davis,
Buster Keaton, Gloria Swanson, Imogene Coca, Groucho
Marx, and George Burns. Bing also sings "Until You've
Played the Palace." Bing hosted 32 shows of the series
and received $12,500 per show, which took three days to
produce. See V266.
     NOTE: The finale is available for $29.95 from
Discount Video Tapes, Inc.; Video Yesteryear; and Video
Dimensions.

V162. Feb 16   The Bob Hope Chrysler Special   NBC   60 min.
     Variety special, including excerpts from the benefit
     for the Eisenhower Medical Center staged Jan 27 at the
     Grand Ballroom of the Waldorf-Astoria, New York
          p: Bob Hope, Mort Lachman; md: Les Brown
          Host: Bob Hope. Guests: Bing Crosby, Ray Bolger,
     Johnny Cash, Raquel Welch
          President Eisenhower died Mar 1969 and Bob and
     Dolores Hope pledged to raise $7 million as one-third
     of the cost to complete the Center at Palm Springs,
     California. The benefit alone raised $2 million from
     1500 guests. Bing and Hope wore top hats and tails.

V163. Feb 21   The American Sportsman   ABC   30 min.   Sports
     show
          Host: Curt Gowdy. Guests: Bing Crosby, Bud Boyd,
     and Ted Williams, fishing for salmon in Iceland. Bing
     sings "The Land of the Midnight Sun." Cf. V53A, July
     1963. Bing 104 dates the program as Feb 8.

V164. Feb 26-27   The Movie Game   Syndicated   30 min.
          a: Johnny Gilbert
          Hosts: Sonny Fox, Larry Blyden. Guests: Bing
     Crosby, Margaret O'Brien, Army Archerd

V165. Mar 31   Goldilocks   NBC   30 min.   Partially animated
     musical
          d: Marc Breaux p: David H. DePatie, Fritz Fre-
     leng, Robert M. and Robert B. Sherman w: A.J. Caroth-
     ers production supervisor: Jim Foss c: Roy W. Sea-
     wright, John Burton, Jr. ma: Doug Goodwin sound: Brad
     Trask e: Lee Gunther, Anthony Milch animation: Lee
     Mishkin, Warren Batchelder, Manny Gould, Jim Hitz, Ed
     Love, Robert Taylor, Lloyd Vaughn backgrounds: Richard
     Thomas, Mary O'Loughlin, Tom O'Loughlin fx: Van Der
     Veer Effects
          Mary Frances Crosby, with Bing Crosby, Kathryn
     Crosby, and Nathaniel Crosby. Paul Winchell was the
     narrator
          NOTE: The music was recorded Jun 16, 1969. Bing
     and Kathryn also dubbed the voices of Papa and Mama
     Bear. Mary Frances was 10.

V166. Apr 1   Bing Crosby--Cooling It   NBC   60 min.   Varie-
     ty special
          d: Art Fisher; ep: Bob Finkel; p: Buz Kohan, Bill
     Angelos; w: Buz Kohan, Bill Angelos, Tony Webster;
     md: Nick Perito

Host: Bing Crosby. Guests: Dean Martin, Bernadette Peters, Flip Wilson
    The program focuses on a lighthearted look at
leisure.

V166A. Apr 12   The American Sportsman   ABC   30 min.
        Host: Curt Gowdy. Guest: Bing Crosby
        Bing explains a sportsman's idea of conservation.

V166B. Jul 16   Happy Days   Unknown   Talk show
        With Bing Crosby, Louis Nye, Lionel Hampton, Jack
Benny, Mary Livingstone

V167. Nov 25   This Is Your Life (England)   BBC
        Host: Eamonn Andrews. Guest: Bob Hope.
        Bing Crosby appears briefly.

V168. Nov 29   The John Wayne TV Special--Swing Out, Sweet
Land   NBC   90 min. Variety show   Sponsor: Budweiser
        Host: John Wayne   Guests: Bing Crosby, Ann-Mar-
gret, and others
        Bing appears as Mark Twain and also sings.
        Repeated Apr 8, 1971, and Jan 15, 1976.

V169. Dec 16   Bing Crosby's Christmas Show: The Bell System
Family Theater   NBC   60 min. Musical special
        d: Marty Pasetta; ep: Bill Angelos; p: Buz Kohan;
w: Buz Kohan, Bill Angelos, Rod Warren; md: Nick Perito
        Hosts: Bing Crosby, Kathryn Crosby, Mary Crosby,
Nathaniel Crosby, Harry Crosby. Guests: Melba Moore,
Jack Wild, Joe Besser, the Doodletown Pipers
        This is Bing's 35th annual Christmas show.

1971
V170. Jan 7   The Flip Wilson Show   NBC   60 min. Variety
show   See D1794.
        o: George Wyle
        Bing Crosby is the featured guest, receives a
platinum disc for selling over 300 million records,
sings, and plays in a "Bunny Club" skit with Wilson.

V171. Jan 19   Dr. Cook's Garden   ABC   90 min. A television
movie, drama filmed Sep 1970
        See the Filmography (F154) for details.

V172. Jan 23   The Pearl Bailey Show   ABC   60 min. Variety
show
        d: Dean Whitmore; p: Bob Finkel; md: Louis Bell-
son; w: Bill Angelos, Buz Kohan, Pearl Bailey; a: Roger
Carroll
        Host: Pearl Bailey. Guests: Bing Crosby, Louis
Armstrong, Andy Williams
        This was the premiere of the series, which aired
from Jan 23 to May 8, 1971.

V173. Feb 10   Frost Over America   Syndicated   Talk show
        Host: David Frost. Guests: Bing Crosby, Louis
Armstrong

V174. Feb 15   The Bob Hope Show   NBC   60 min.   Variety
      special
            p: Bob Hope, Mort Lachman; md: Les Brown
            Host: Bob Hope. Guests: Bing Crosby, Petula
      Clark, Jo Anne Worley, Teresa Graves

V175. Mar 16   St. Patrick's Day Special   NBC   60 min.
      Variety special   Rerun of V124.
            Host: Bing Crosby. Guests: Kathryn Crosby, Alma
      Carroll, John McNally, Milo O'Shea, and others

V176. Mar 18   Ver-r-r-ry Interesting: The Arte Johnson Show
      NBC   60 min.   Comedy special
            Host: Arte Johnson. Guests: Bing Crosby, Peter
      Marshall, Elke Sommer, Billy DeWolfe, Joe Flynn, Nancy
      Kulp

V177. Mar 29   The American Sportsman   ABC   30 min.
            Bing explains the rehabilitation of wildlife.

V178. Apr 8   Sing Out Sweet Land   NBC   90 min.   Variety
      special on America's development   Rerun of V168.

            "Columbo," airing about every third week on NBC
      from Sep 15, 1971, to Sep 4, 1977, made a star of
      Peter Falk. The pilot TV movie was aired in 1967. The
      producers hoped to star Bing Crosby, probably for the
      pilot TV movie in 1967 and for the resulting series,
      but Bing thought it too demanding and likely to in-
      fringe on his golf. The series aired cyclically with
      two other detective shows: "McMillan and Wife," and
      "McCloud."

V179. Oct 7   The Dean Martin Show   NBC   60 min.   Variety
      special
            o: Les Brown
            Host: Dean Martin. Guests: Bing Crosby, Claire
      and McMahon, Rip Taylor, Richard Castellano, Ken Lane,
      Kay Medford, the Ding-a-lings

V180. Nov 29   Monsanto Presents Mancini   Syndicated   60
      min.
            d, p, w: Art Fisher; md: Henry Mancini
            Host: Henry Mancini. Guests: Bing Crosby, Hoagy
      Carmichael

V181. Dec 10   Rowan and Martin's Laugh-in Christmas Show
      NBC   60 min.   Variety special
            Guests: Carroll O'Connor, Bing Crosby, Janet Leigh

V182. Dec 14   Bing Crosby and the Sounds of Christmas   NBC
      60 min.   Variety special
            d: Ray Klaussen; ep: Bob Finkel; p, w: Buz Kohan,
      Bill Angelos; md: Ray Charles
            Host: Bing Crosby. Guests: Kathryn Crosby, Mary
      Crosby, Nathaniel Crosby, Harry Crosby, Robert Goulet,
      Mary Costa, the Mitchell Boys' Choir, the Alan Copeland
      Singers

1972
V183. Feb 26   Bing Crosby and His Friends   NBC   60 min.
Variety special
            d: Marty Pasetta; p: Bob Finkel; w: Harry Crane,
Marty Farrell, Norman Barasch, Carroll Moore, Bob
Ellison; md: Nick Perito; ch: Robert Sidney
        Host: Bing Crosby.   Guests: Bob Hope, Carol Bur-
nett, Pearl Bailey, Ray Charles

V184. Mar 15   The Carol Burnett Show   CBS   60 min.   Variety
show
        Host: Carol Burnett.   Regulars: Harvey Korman,
Vicki Lawrence, Lyle Waggoner.   Guest: Bing Crosby.

V185. Mar 16   The Flip Wilson Show   NBC   60 min.   Variety
show
            o: George Wyle
        Guests: Bing Crosby, Tim Conway, Melba Moore

V186. Mar 22   This Is Your Life (England)   BBC   Talk show
        Host: Eamonn Andrews.   Subject: Dr. Michael Wood.
Bing appears in a filmed segment from East Africa.

V187. Mar 26   The American Sportsman   ABC   30 min.
        Bing Crosby narrates a feature on guide dogs for
the School for the Blind, San Rafael, CA.

V188. Dec 10   Christmas with the Bing Crosbys   NBC   60 min.
Musical special
        Hosts: Bing Crosby, Nathaniel Crosby, Kathryn
Crosby, Mary Crosby, Harry Crosby.   Guests: Sally
Struthers, David Hartman, Edward Villella,

V189. Dec 23   The Parkinson Show (England)   BBC   Talk show
        Bing was the sole guest of Michael Parkinson.

1973
V190. Jan 7   Bing Crosby--Cooling It   CBS   60 min.   Variety special   Rerun of V166.

V191. Dec 9   Bing Crosby's Sun Valley Christmas Show: A
White Christmas at Sun Valley   NBC   60 min.   Variety
special   Taped Feb.
            d: Art Fisher; p: Bob Finkel, Buz Kohan, Bill
Angelos; w: Buz Kohan, Bill Angelos, Tom Patchett, Jary
Tarses; md: Nick Perito
        Host: Bing Crosby.   Guests: Connie Stevens, John
Byner, Michael Landon, Kathryn Crosby, Mary Crosby,
Nathaniel Crosby, Harry Crosby, John Misha Petkevich

1974
V192. Oct 9   Bing Crosby and His Friends   CBS   60 min.
Variety special   Taped Aug
            d: Marty Pasetta; p: Bob Finkel; w: Harry Crane,
George Bloom, Mitzi Welch, Ken Welch; m: Peter Matz;
ch: Buddy Schwab
        Host: Bing Crosby.   Guests: Bob Hope, Sandy Dun-
can, Pearl Bailey

V193. Oct 25   The Kathryn Crosby Show San Francisco
      Weekday morning talk show
            The host interviews Bing Crosby and Phil Harris.

V194. Dec 15   Christmas with the Bing Crosbys NBC 60 min.
      Musical special
            md: Peter Matz
            Hosts: Bing Crosby and his family (Kathryn, Mary,
      Harry, Nathaniel). Guests: Karen Valentine, Mac Davis

1975
V195. Feb 22   Grandstand (England) BBC-1 60 min. Satur-
      day sports show
            Frank Bough interviews Bing intermittently.

V196. Feb 27   Pebble Mill at One (England) BBC-1
            Donny McCloud interviews Bing.

V197. Jul 24   Top of the Pops (England) BBC-1 Musical
      show
            Bing sings "That's What Life Is All About," taped
      Jul 23.

V198. Jul 25   Today (England) ITV Talk show
            Llew Gardner interviews Bing.

V199. Aug 5   ITN (England)
            Bing is interviewed at Sunningdale.

V200. Aug 8   Interview (Holland) AVRD Talk show
            Bing is interviewed and sings, taped Aug 7.

V201. Aug 30   Parkinson (England) BBC-1 Talk show
            Michael Parkinson interviews Bing, who sings
      several songs, taped Jul 18. An edited version ap-
      peared Oct 15, 1977, on BBC-1.

V202. Sep 9   The Mike Douglas Show 90 min. Syndicated
      talk show
            a: Jay Stewart
            Douglas interviews Bing Crosby, Kathryn Crosby,
      David Brenner, Joe Williams, Jack Nicklaus, Mike Prem-
      inger, Frank Gifford

V203. Sep 14   Stars on Sunday (England) ITV Religious
      talk show Four appearances from one taping session.
            Bing sings "That's What Life Is All About," taped
      in Jul. Bing also appeared on Oct 12, reading from St.
      Mark 10: 1-16; Nov 16, reading from St. Matthew 7: 1-
      12; and Dec 14, singing "The Bells of St. Mary's."

V204. Sep 24   The Vera Lynn Show (England) BBC
      Taped Jul 27
            Bing sings "Sing" with Lynn and "That's What Life
      Is All About" solo.

V205. Oct 24   Bob Hope Special: A Quarter Century of Bob
      Hope on Television NBC 2 hours Variety special with
      highlights of Hope's 25 years on television, all on NBC

d: Dick McDonough; ep: Bob Hope; p: Paul W. Keyes;
w: Keyes, Charles Lee, Gig Henry; m: Les Brown
Host: Bob Hope. Guests: John Wayne, Frank Sinatra, Bing Crosby

V206. Nov 12   Dinah   Syndicated talk show
Host: Dinah Shore. Guests: Bing Crosby, Phil Harris, Pat Boone
Dinah mentions seeing Bing shaking backstage and shows clips of a Sennett short.

V207. Nov 28   The Mike Douglas Show Syndicated Talk show
Douglas interviews Crosby and his wife Kathryn at their Hillsborough, CA, home. At the end Bing strolls around his garden singing a medley and practicing his golf swing.

V208. Dec 3   Merry Christmas, Fred, from the Crosbys NBC
60 min. Musical special, taped Nov 20, 22.
Host: Bing Crosby and his family (Kathryn, Harry, Mary Frances, and Nathaniel). Guests: Fred Astaire, the Young Americans, Joe Bushkin, Bob Hope
An hour show featuring Crosby and Astaire singing "A Couple of Song-and-Dance Men," a number shown with clips from the livelier version of the 1946 film Blue Skies. Some of the songs were also recorded as an album, Bing Crosby and Fred Astaire: A Couple of Song-and-Dance Men, on Jul 16-17, 1975, for United Artists.

V209. Dec 25   Parkinson (England) BBC Talk show
Bob Hope is the principal guest; Bing makes an appearance, taped in America with Michael Parkinson.

V210. Dec 26   Disney Time (England) BBC Variety show
Bing presents excerpts of Disney films, including Ichabod.

1976
V211. Jan 15   Sing Out Sweet Land NBC 90 min. Variety special on America's development Repeated from Nov 29, 1970 (V168); see also V178.

V212. Jan 26   The Merv Griffin Show CBS Talk show
Griffin interviews Bing, who sings "That's What Life Is All About."

V213. Jan 27   International Celebrity Golf (England)
Bing Crosby and Tom Weiskopf play against Peter Oosterhuis and Val Doonican, taped in Aug 1975.

V214. Mar 5   Tonight: With Johnny Carson NBC 90 min.
Late-night variety show Repeated as V229.
Host: Johnny Carson. Guests: Bing Crosby, Ray Bolger, Marvin Hamlisch
Bing sings "Where the Morning Glories Grow," "I Love to Dance Like They Used to Dance," and (with Bolger) "The Only Way to Go."

V215. Mar 26   Bell Telephone Jubilee: 100th Anniversary of

the Telephone NBC 90 min. Variety special
     Hosts: Bing Crosby, Liza Minnelli. Guests: Eydie
Gorme, Roy Clark, Steve Lawrence, Joel Grey, Ben Ver-
een, and excerpts from previous programs.

V216. Apr 5   The Rich Little Show NBC 60 min. Variety
     show
          Host: Rich Little. Guest: Bing Crosby
     Bing sings several duets in which Little imitates
Astaire, Armstrong, Gene Kelly, Sinatra, Bing, and Dean
Martin.

V217. Apr 21   The Bob Hope Special from Montreal NBC 90
     min. Variety special Taped Apr 12; a benefit for the
     Summer Olympics, held at Montreal.
          Host: Bob Hope. Guests: Bing Crosby, Shirley
Jones, Lynn Anderson, Freddie Prinze

V218. May 4   Tonight (England) BBC-1
     Bing is interviewed.

V219. Jun 14   Entertainment Hall of Fame Award show
     Bing Crosby is honored by Sammy Cahn, Tony Ben-
nett, and Bob Hope.

V220. Jun 16   Royal Ascot (England) BBC-1 Horse race
     Bing is interviewed.

V221. Jul 2   Tribute to Johnny Mercer (England) BBC
     Bing makes a brief introduction to the tribute.

V222. Nov 27   The Lawrence Welk Show Syndicated 60 min.
     Musical
     md: George Cates
     Welk and cast feature Crosby's songs.

V223. Dec 1   Bing Crosby's White Christmas CBS 60 min.
     Musical special Taped in Jul in England.
          d, p: Norman Campbell; ep: Frank Konigsberg;
     m: Peter Knight; w Herbert Baker; art Ken Wheatley
          Host: Bing Crosby. Guests: Kathryn, Mary, Harry,
Nathaniel Crosby, Jackie Gleason, Bernadette Peters

V224. Dec 3   The Joe Franklin Show WOR-TV, New York
     Late-night talk show
          Host: Joe Franklin. Guests: Bing Crosby, Kathryn
Crosby, Steve Mason, Arthur Tracy

V225. Dec 6   Today NBC 2hrs. Morning talk show
     Bing Crosby was interviewed.

V226. Dec 7   Bing with Pat: A Look at a Legend WCBS, New
     York
          Pat [Collins] interviews Bing.

V227. Dec   Bing on Broadway WCBS, New York 2 hrs.
     Bing is interviewed by Jack O'Brien, in relation
to Bing's New York concert.

V228. Dec 10   A.M. America   ABC   2 hrs.   Morning talk show
        Bing is interviewed.

V229. Dec 12   Tonight: With Johnny Carson   NBC   90 min.
      Late-night variety show   Rerun of Mar 5 (V214).

V230. Dec 17   A.M. America   ABC   2 hrs.   Morning talk show
        Bing is interviewed.

V231. Dec 25   New York, New York (West Germany)   NDR
        Werner Baecker interviews Bing in his suite at the
      Waldorf-Astoria, New York.   Bing sings, including a
      duet of "Silent Night" in German with Kathryn.

1977
V232. Jan 12   International Pro-Celebrity Golf (England)
      BBC-2
        USA vs. UK for the Bing Crosby Cup.   Bing serves
      as the USA captain and plays with Johnny Miller in the
      first match against Sean Connery and Tony Jacklin.
      Bing has also appeared in other programs of the series.

V233. Mar 20   Bing! A 50th Anniversary Gala   CBS   90 min.
      Musical special
        d: Marty Pasetta; ep: Frank Konigsberg; p: Paset-
      ta; w: Buz Kohan; m: Nick Perito; art: Roy Christopher
        Host: Bing Crosby.   Guests: Bob Hope, Paul Anka,
      Pearl Bailey, Rosemary Clooney, Kathryn Crosby, Harry
      Crosby, Mary Crosby, Nathaniel Crosby, Sandy Duncan,
      Donald O'Connor, Debbie Reynolds, Martha Raye, Bette
      Midler, Anson Williams, the Mills Brothers
        NOTE: It was taped and edited from three hours at
      the Ambassador Auditorium on Thursday, Mar 3, at the
      end of which he fell 20 feet into the orchestra pit,
      seriously injuring his back.   The program followed the
      general format of his recent international concerts.

V234. Mar 26   All You Need Is Love (England)   ITV   Documen-
      tary
        Includes a brief interview with Bing on his early
      career as part of a documentary on popular music.

V235. Apr 25   The Paul Anka Show   Unknown   Variety special
        Bing is a guest and sings a few lines of "My Way."

V236. May 31   The Barbara Walter's Special   ABC   60 min.
      Talk show
        d: John Desmond, Don Mischer; ep: Don Mischer;
      p: Lucy Jarvis and others
        Barbara Walters, in her third special, interviews
      Bob Hope, Bing Crosby, Redd Foxx
        Bing discusses drugs, premarital sex, wealth, and
      a possible epitaph.   At the Hillsborough home, he walks
      in his yard singing "Singin' in the Rain" in a drizzle.

V237. Aug 28   Bing in Norway (Norway)   Live musical special
      broadcast only on the Continent.   It was an open-air
      concert at Mysen, Norway, celebrating a century of
      recorded sound.   Taped Aug 27.

Bing Crosby, Harry Crosby, and others
Following the broadcast Bing sang three encores amidst receiving several special recognitions. He chose to sing "The Way We Were," "Cuando caliente el sol," and "Dinah."

V238. Sep 21   Tonight (England) BBC-2
Bing is interviewed, taped in the Palladium bar.

V239. Sep 29   Nationwide (England) BBC-1
Frank Bough interviews Bing in his dressing room of the Palladium, taped Sep 28.

V240. Oct 9   60 Minutes CBS 60 min. Investigative reporting
Mike Wallace interviews Bing about imitator Jack Harris, who had impersonated Bing in some commercials and was stopped by a Crosby lawsuit, taped Oct 8.

Bing Crosby dies Oct 14 in Spain.

V241. Oct 28   On the Road with Bing: A Special Tribute to Bing Crosby NBC 2 hrs.
A special by Bob Hope, replacing at the last minute his scheduled two-hour show titled "Bob Hope's Road to Hollywood," which aired Mar 2, 1983.
Host: Bob Hope.

V242. Nov 30   Bing Crosby's Merrie Olde Christmas CBS 60 min. Christmas variety special
d: Dwight Hemion; ep: Frank Konigsberg; p: Gary Smith, Hemion; w: Buz Kohan; m: Ian Frazer
Hosts: Bing Crosby and Kathryn, Mary, Harry, Nathaniel Crosby. Guests: Twiggy, Ron Moody, Stanley Baxter, David Bowie
NOTE: The program was aired posthumously. It was Bing's 42nd Christmas special.

1978
V243. May 25   Bing Crosby: His Life and Legend ABC 2 hrs. Documentary
Host: William Holden. Guests: Rosemary Clooney, Danny Kaye, Princess Grace of Monaco, Dinah Shore, Twiggy, Ella Fitzgerald, and others

V244. Dec 2   Bing Crosby: The Christmas Years CBS 60 min.
A review of Bing's Christmas music and specials.

1979
V245. Dec 6   A Bing Crosby Christmas--Just Like the Ones We Used to Know CBS 60 min. Musical special
Host: Kathryn Crosby.
A review of Bing's TV Christmas specials from 1962 to 1977.

NOTE: Bing Crosby specials continue to appear, like the 1987 "Remembering Bing" (PBS, see p. 69) and the 1992 "The Magic of Bing Crosby" (V273 and V273A).

1989
V245A. Dec 6   The Secret Files of J. Edgar Hoover Syndi-
cated, Eric Lieber Productions, 1989 2 hrs. Viewed on
WFTV, Channel 9, Orlando, Florida.
    d: Jerry Kupcinet; ep: Ron Glazer, Western Inter-
national Syndication; w: Bruce Cohn; e: Ned Weisman;
a: Don Morrow.
    Host: Mike Connors. Commentators: Jack Anderson,
Thayer Walker, Wendy Gordon.
    Surveys the secret FBI files on such celebrities
as John Wayne, Marilyn Monroe, Elvis Presley, John
Lennon, Bing Crosby, Grace Kelly, Rock Hudson, Errol
Flynn, and John F. Kennedy.
    States that Bing was thought a "hard-drinking
playboy" in the 1930s, paid $10,000 in extortion in
1937, was in an illegal casino in 1947, and invited a
mobster to his Elko, Nevada, ranch.

1991
V245B.   Stars and Stripes: Hollywood and World War II
American Movie Classics 64 min.
    w, p: Marcia Ely ep: Sandy Shapiro, Bradley J.
Siegel
        Narrator: Tony Randall. Guests: Maxene
Andrews, Eddie Bracken, Douglas Fairbanks, Jr., Bob
Hope, Anne Jeffreys, Frances Langford, Dorothy Lamour,
Roddy McDowall, Sherwood Schwartz, Esther Williams
    Clips of many performances by celebrities at
military camps and selling War Bonds. Bing appears
singing "Buy, Buy Bonds," in a jeep in a bond drive,
singing "Mairzy Doats and Doazy Doats" with Bob Hope at
a USO show, and in the special Command Performance on
Dick Tracy (see R69) starring Bing and others.

    Nearly every January, Bing Crosby appeared for a
day or two on the annual televised Bing Crosby National
Pro-Am Golf Tournament, staged at Pebble Beach, CA. It
was first televised in 1958.

    Crosby also appeared each year since about 1965 on
about four "The American Sportsman" half-hour programs
for ABC-TV, usually hunting or fishing, sometimes in
Africa or England, and sometimes promoting conservation. The series began Jan 31, 1965, hosted by Curt
Gowdy with Roone Arledge the executive producer.

    Kathryn Crosby appeared on Bob Hope's 75th birth-
day special May 29, 1978 (three hours); on his Christmas special Dec 13, 1979; on his 80th birthday special,
May 23, 1983; and other shows.

SAMPLE OF BOB HOPE'S TV COMMENTS ON BING CROSBY

V246.   Bob Hope was the guest on "The Jack Benny Show" on
CBS-TV, May 23, 1954. Having taken Benny's pants to
begin the show with a monologue, Hope says, "CBS,
that's Crosby's and Benny's Strongbox." He adds, "This
is where Bing did his last show, and I think they've

done very nicely. They've gotten most of it out of the
curtains. He's up in Nevada now looking over Boulder
Dam--his piggy bank is filled. He's loaded, you know.
He uses Howard Hughes for a bellboy." (Hope's reference to a Crosby show is to V9.) Benny's sketch was
called "On the Road to Nairobi," in which Hope and
Benny rest after bagging a tiger, and a gorilla dressed
like Bing, carrying a golf club, wearing a golf cap and
loud sportshirt, ambles past with a chimpanzee caddy.
The show had other guest appearances when cannibals
can't start the fire to cook Hope and Benny: Dean
Martin and Jerry Lewis run down through the audience to
provide the matches.

SELECTED HOME VIDEOS (VHS Format)
        Note: HV means Home Video.

V247. The Bells of St. Mary's. 126 min. Republic Pictures
V248. Bing Crosby Festival. 60 min. Shorts of Billboard
      Girl, Blue of the Night, and I Surrender Dear. Dis-
      count Video.
V249. Bing Crosby: Hollywood's Greatest Entertainer. bw,
      col 105 min. Goodtimes Home Video. p Paul Harris,
      Sandy Oliveri; narrated by Murray Roberts. 1991.
V250. Bing Crosby Show. 60 min. Two episodes of the 1964-
      65 series. Discount Video.
V251. Bing Crosby Special. 45 min. An early TV special
      with Bing, Dean Martin, Frank Sinatra, Bob Hope.
      Discount Video.
V252. Bob Hope: Thanks for the Memories. bw, col 58 min.
      Includes shots of Bing on the golf course, in Road to
      Morocco, on the Danny Thomas Show with Hope, and Hope
      visiting a Crosby TV program. Goodtimes 8090, 1991.
V253. Cancel My Reservation. 99 min. Hope's 1972 film.
      Columbia HV.
V253A. Check and Double Check. bw 71 min. The 1930 film.
      Video Yesteryear.
V254. Combat/Action Collection: 4. 61 min. Bing sings a
      war-bonds song. Video Yesteryear.
V255. Comedy Special: 2. 60 min. Outtakes with Bing, Hope,
      the Ritz Brothers. Video Communications.
V256. A Connecticut Yankee in King Arthur's Court. 108 min.
      MCA/Universal HV.
V257. Country Girl. 104 min. Paramount HV.
V258. Dammed Forever. Narrator. 28 min. 1975 documentary
      on dams in the Northwest. TV Sports Scene.
V259. The Edsel Show. 30 min. 1957 TV show with Sinatra,
      Louis Armstrong, Bing Crosby, Rosemary Clooney. Dis-
      count Videotape. See V21, V292.
V260. Ford Star Jubilee Salute to Cole Porter. 60 min. A
      1956 TV show with Bing, Gordon MacRae, Louis Armstrong,
      Shirley Jones. Discount Video. See V18.
V261. The Funniest Men of Comedy, Plus Jack Benny Comedy
      Hour. bw 87 min. Includes Bing Crosby's Billboard
      Girl, Sennett short of 1931. Goodtimes, VGT-8809,
      1986. Another version with the same Crosby short: 60
      min. Goodtimes, VGT-5098, 1985.
V262. Going My Way. bw 2hrs., 6 min. MCA Home Video, VHS-

55038, 1986; MCA/Universal. A Hi-Fi copy of the 1944 film.
V263. Here Comes the Groom. 114 min. The 1951 film. Paramount HV.
V264. High Society. 107 min. The 1956 film. MGM/UA HV.
V265. Holiday Inn. Alternate: Irving Berlin's Holiday Inn. bw 1 hr., 41 min. MCA Home Video, VHS-55039, 1986. Hi-Fi
V266. Hollywood Goes to War. 41 min. Five shorts, including Bing in All Star Bond Rally. Video Yesteryear.
V267. Hollywood Palace Finale. 52 min. The 1970 TV show. Video Dimensions. See V161.
V268. Jack Benny. 110 min. Three shows from 1953 to 1965. Shokus Video.
V269. Jack Benny Show. 60 min. Final episodes of shows of 1951 and 1953. Discount Video Tapes.
V270. King of Jazz. 93 min. The 1930 movie. MCA/Universal.
V271. The Legend of Sleepy Hollow, Plus Two Disney Cartoons. col 49 min. Walt Disney, No. 075-2, 1962, 1983. The Washington Irving tale narrated and sung by Crosby in 1949.
V272. Let's Make Love. 118 min. The 1960 film with Bing's cameo role. CBS/Fox HV.
V273. The Magic of Bing Crosby: Part One, 55 min. A*Vision Entertainment Production, NBD Pictures Ltd. ep Lori Weitraub; p, d Bryan Johnson; w, e Barnett Kiel Many of Bing's TV and film scenes and interviews with friends. V-27286, 1992.
V273A. The Magic of Bing Crosby [extended version] 84 min. Reader's Digest. This includes all of V273 and adds about 30 min. in lieu of producing a Part Two. 1992
V274. Missing Halves Special. 60 min. First half of "Here Come the Stars" with Bing (V150) and the second half of "Cavalcade of Stars" with Jackie Gleason and Victor Borge (V154?). Discount Video Tapes.
V275. Music of Man. 60 min. 1979. Time/Live HV.
V276. My Favorite Brunette. 85 min. Hope's 1947 film with Bing's cameo appearance. Kartes Video Communications.
V277. 1940s. 60 min. 1988. Includes Bing Crosby, Winston Churchill. Kultur.
V278. Old Globe: A Theatre Reborn. 30 min. 1984. With Bob Hope and Bing. San Diego State Univ.
V279. The Princess and the Pirate. 94 min. Hope's 1944 film with a cameo by Bing. Nelson Entertainment.
V280. Reaching for the Moon. 62 min. The 1931 film with a brief appearance by Bing. Kartes Communications.
V281. Revenge of the TV Bloopers. 50 min. Includes Bing in the 1960s. Video Dimensions.
V282. Road to Bali. 90 min. The 1953 film. Unicorn Video.
V283. Road to Hollywood. 70 min. Shorts of Bing issued in 1942. Discount Video Tapes.
V284. The Road to Hong Kong. 91 min. The 1962 film. Baker and Taylor Video.
V285. Road to Lebanon. 50 min. The 1966 Danny Thomas TV special with Bing, Hope, Hugh Downs, Claudine Auger, Sheldon Leonard. Discount Video Tapes. See V109.
V286. Road to Rio. 100 min. The 1947 film. RCA/Columbia HV.
V287. Road to Utopia. 90 min. The 1946 film. MCA/Univer-

sal HV.
V288. Robin and the 7 Hoods. 124 min. The 1964 film.
Warner HV.
V289. Strictly G.I. 45 min. <u>All Star Bond Rally</u> and other
1944 shorts. Discount Video Tapes.
V290. That's Entertainment. 132 min. The 1974 film.
MGM/UA HV.
V291. That's Entertainment, Part II. 133 min. The 1976
film. MGM/UA HV.
V292. TV Variety: 8. 115 min. Four early TV kinescopes,
including Bing on Sinatra's 1959 TV show (V32) and on
"The Edsel Show" of 1957 (V21). Shokus.
V293. Vintage Commercials: 5. 60 min. TV commercials of
1950-1970, some with Bing. Shokus.
V294. Vintage Sitcoms: 8. 110 min. Includes the pilot for
a Bing Crosby Show of 19[64]. Shokus. See V62.
V295. White Christmas. 120 min. The 1954 film. Paramount
HV.
V296. World War II: The Music Video, Vol. 1. 60 min. With
Bing Crosby, the Andrews Sisters, Kate Smith, Benny
Goodman, Bob Hope. Congress Video Group.
V297. Young Bing Crosby. 39 min. The early shorts of
<u>Crooner's Holiday</u>, <u>Blue of the Night</u>, <u>Sing, Bing, Sing</u>.
Video Yesteryear.

Bing Crosby appeared on about 300 television
programs, including 127 of his own specials and series.

Bibliography

MAJOR BOOKS

B1.   Barnes, Ken. <u>The Crosby Years</u>. New York: St. Mar-
       tin's, 1980. 216 pages; chronological discography
       and filmography; illustrated, bibliography. Useful
       brief insider's account since 1974.

B2.   Bassett, John, and others. <u>The Bing Crosby LP-ogra-
       phy</u>. 1973; rev. 1977. On Bing's albums.

B3.   Bauer, Barbara. <u>Bing Crosby</u>. A Pyramid Illustrated
       History of the Movies. New York: Pyramid, 1977. 153
       pages; indexed. Good brief study; illustrated; bibli-
       ography.

B4.   <u>Bing Crosby: A Pictorial Tribute</u>. New York: Dell,
       1977.

B5.   "Bing Crosby on Broadway." <u>Playbill: Uris Theatre</u>.
       New York: Dec. 1976. 64 pages, illustrated.

B6.   Bishop, Bert, and John Bassett. <u>Bing: Just for the
       Record</u>. Private, 1980. A discography of Bing's commer-
       cial recordings; 122 pp.

B7.   Bookbinder, Robert. <u>The Films of Bing Crosby</u>. Secau-
       cus, NJ: Citadel, 1977. 254 pages; fair detail on 55
       feature films, 17 cameo appearances, 1 television
       movie, 2 narrations, and an anthology; illustrated.

B8.   Carpozi, George, Jr. <u>The Fabulous Life of Bing Cros-
       by</u>. New York: Manor, 1977. 217 pages; paperback,
       illustrated; convenient but occasionally careless.

B9.   Crosby, Bing, as told to Pete Martin. <u>Call Me Lucky</u>.
       New York: Simon and Schuster, 1953. 333 pages and
       index; illustrated. Serialized in <u>The Saturday Evening
       Post</u> (Feb. 14, 21, 28, Mar. 7, 14, 21, 28, April 4,
       1953) and a <u>Reader's Digest Condensed Book</u>. Candid and
       breezy on personalities more than career.

B10. Crosby, Gary, and Ross Firestone. Going My Own Way.
Garden City: Doubleday, 1983. 304 pages; illustrated.
The story of the eldest Crosby son, with an emphasis on
Bing's harsh treatment of him.

B11. Crosby, Kathryn. Bing and Other Things. New York:
Meredith, 1967. 214 pages; illustrated; no index. An
impressionistic account of her own life but primarily
with Bing.

B12. ---. My Life with Bing. Wheeling, IL: Collage, 1983.
355 pages. Personal views up to 1965; lavishly illustrated. Oversize pages. Candid, but some tales vary
from her earlier book.

B13. Crosby, Ted, and Larry Crosby. Bing. 1937; revised
by Ted Crosby, The Story of Bing Crosby, Cleveland:
World, 1946. The 1946 revision has 226 pages, a page
listing Bing's films through 1945, and 11-page discography of Brunswick and Decca Records; illustrated; no
index; Foreword by Bob Hope dated 1945; some names and
places are changed.

B14. A Guy Called Bing. World Distributors, Manchester,
England: 1977. A tribute.

B15. Hope, Bob, and Bob Thomas. The Road to Hollywood: My
40-year Love Affair with the Movies. New York: Doubleday, 1977. 271 pp., oversize, illustrated. Comments
on Hope's films, including those with Bing; casts,
credits and synopses of Hope's films.

B16. Hope, Bob, with Melville Shavelson. Don't Shoot, It's
Only Me: Bob Hope's Comedy History of the United
States. New York: Putnam, 1990. 315 pp., illustrated.
Many stories of Hope's experiences with Bing.

B17. Koenig, Joseph L. Bing. New York: Dell, 1977. A
brief biography.

B18. Martin, George V. The Bells of St. Mary's. New York:
Grosset & Dunlap, 1946.

B19. Mello, Edward J., and Tom McBride. Bing Crosby Discography. San Francisco, Jan. 31, 1947. 79 pages.

B20. Mize, J. T. H. Bing Crosby and the Bing Crosby Style:
Crosbyana Thru Biography-Photography-Discography.
Chicago: Who Is Who in Music, Inc., 1946, revised 1948.
175 pages for 1948; alphabetized discography through
1947; lists Brunswick masters released on many other
labels and three pages of 35 album sets. The book is
informative and candid by an erudite, eccentric musi-
cologist.

B21. Morgereth, Timothy A. Bing Crosby: A Discography,
Radio Program List and Filmography. Jefferson, NC:
McFarland, 1987. 502 pages and index; chronological
list of records to 1957, radio shows to 1954 (some

places of broadcast are erroneous), and films; extensive detail with a few errors. Illustrated.

B21. Netland, Dwayne. The Crosby: Greatest Show in Golf. New York: Doubleday, 1975.

B22. O'Connell, Sheldon, with Gordon Atkinson. Bing: A Voice for All Seasons. Private, 1984. 244 pages of discography, plus index.

B23. Paradissis, A.G. The Bing Book of Verse. Melbourne, Australia: Globe, 1983.

B24. Pleasants, Henry. The Great American Popular Singers. New York: Simon and Schuster, 1974. Perceptive chapters on individual popular singers and musicians, with an especially good one on Crosby.

B25. Pugh, Colin. Alternate Bing Crosby. Bristol, England: 1988. Lists alternate recording takes of Bing's songs.

B26. Reynolds, Fred. Road to Hollywood: The Bing Crosby Films Book. Rev. Gateshead, Tyne & Wear, England: John Joyce and Son, 1986. A Foreword by Bing Crosby for the first edition. Copious notes on all of Bing's films; 331 pp. Indexed and illustrated.

B27. ---. The Crosby Collection: Part One, 1926-34. England: John Joyce & Son, 1991. Notes on Bing's early records; 244 pp.

B28. Rosenbaum, Linda. Bing Crosby Album. Lorelei: 1977.

B29. Shepherd, Donald, and Robert F. Slatzer. Bing Crosby: The Hollow Man. New York: St. Martin's, 1981; rpt. New York: Pinnacle, 1982. 387 pages in paperback, including a 100-item filmography and 10 films of Dixie Lee; indexed. A hostile view of Bing's life. The book is recommended by the National Enquirer. Slatzer claims to have been married to Marilyn Monroe for a few days in the 1950s.

B30. Thomas, Bob. The One and Only Bing. New York: Grosset & Dunlap, 1977.

B31. Thompson, Charles. Bing: An Authorized Biography. London: W.H. Allen, 1975 [New York: David McKay, 1976]. 240 pp.; 4-page Postscript of views of Bing by Sammy Davis, Jr., Douglas Fairbanks, Jr., Stephanie Powers, Frank Capra, and 14 others; illustrated; index. Excerpts were printed in eight weekly issues of National Enquirer, March 2 to April 20, 1976; illustrated. Revised as The Complete Crosby.

B32. Ulanov, Barry. The Incredible Crosby. New York: Whittlesey House (McGraw-Hill), 1948. 321 pp. with discography; illustrated; index. The author was the editor of Metronome. Kathryn Crosby writes that this "is a very good book. Bing's career is outlined with accuracy."

B33. Zwisohn, Laurence J.   Bing Crosby: A Lifetime of Music.   Los Angeles: Palm Tree Library, 1978.   148 pp.; lists the recordings alphabetically; a tribute to Crosby in the Foreword by James Van Heusen. Includes a 12-page biographical sketch; other pages on aspects of Crosby's singing career, and three pages comparing Bing and Elvis Presley, listing 31 songs both recorded. Includes four-page "Record Label Index."

ARTICLES AND BRIEF ACCOUNTS

NOTE: See also film reviews listed in the Filmography.

B34. Achorn, Robert C. "Bing: The Entertainer." Worcester, Mass., Evening Gazette, Nov. 2, 1977: 23. A survey of Bing's career, one of hundreds after Bing's death, by the newspaper's editor. It defends Bing against the charge by Bosley Crowther, critic of the New York Times, that Bing in the 1950s was "aloof and patronizing toward black performers."

B35. "All Night Stand." Time, June 30, 1952: 45. Brief but glowing review of Bing and Bob Hope on a telethon for the U.S. Olympic team over 14.5 hours.

B36. Archerd, Army. Daily Variety. Oct. 21, 1957. His column reported that Kathryn Grant saw Bing at the Edsel exhibition in Los Angeles and began to cry.

B37. Arnold, Maxine. "Cowboy Crosby." Photoplay, March 1946: 50+. On Bing as a simple rancher in Nevada; illustrated.

B38. ---. "Man at the Top." Photoplay, March 1947: 32+.

B39. ---. "The Christmas Gift." Photoplay, Dec. 1947: 36+.

B40. ---. "Bing-Goes That Crosby Myth." Photoplay, June 1955: 56+. States that Bing "destroyed" the Crosby myth that he was merely a crooner by superb acting in Country Girl; illustrated.

B41. Austin, J. "Mr. Bing, God Bless Him!" American Home, Feb. 1956: 43+.

B42. B.A.A. Review of the Morrissey Revue in San Diego about June 1926, unnamed newspaper. Qtd. in Shepherd and Slatzer 70-71.

B43. "Back on Broadway." Worcester, Mass., Evening Gazette, Oct. 1, 1976: 1. Associated Press report that Bing planned two weeks on Broadway in Dec.

B44. Baker, Russell. "Bing and Elvis." New York Times,

rpt. Worcester, Mass., <u>Evening Gazette</u>, Oct. 20, 1977:
16; and J. Roger Osterholm, <u>The Riddle Reader and
Rhetoric</u> (Needham Heights, Mass.,: Ginn, 1988) 122-23.
Compares Crosby as soothing to a troubled generation
and Presley as energetic to a laid-back generation.

B45. Balliett, Whitney. "Mr. Boo-doop-a-doop." <u>Saturday
Review</u>, June 27, 1953: 17-18. A review of <u>Call Me
Lucky</u> that states the book is "a bagful of anecdotes"
and that Bing is "something more than just an entertainment idol or Hollywood star" to the world; he is
the "ideal American male," "one of the first of the
Universal Common Men."

B46. Barnes, Clive. "Stage: Bing Is June in December."
New York <u>Times</u>, Dec. 9, 1976. A review of <u>Bing Crosby
on Broadway</u> in superlatives.

B47. Barnes, Ken. <u>Sinatra and the Great Song Stylists</u>.
London: Ian Allen, 1972.

B48. Barnett, Lincoln. "Bing, Inc." <u>Life</u>, June 18, 1945,
86-95. Abridged in <u>The Reader's Digest</u>, Sept. 1945:
30+. A review of Bing's career, fortune, lack of
vanity, fine intellect, and the new "sober self-
assurance" he gained from Europe in 1944.

B49. Baskette, Kirtley. <u>Modern Screen</u>, July 1, 1945, 84.
Calls Bing the most popular living American, basic to
the American culture.

B50. "Bathroom Baritone, Inc." <u>Time</u>, July 13, 1953: 98-
102. A favorable review of <u>Call Me Lucky</u> and calls
Bing "something like a public utility in the entertainment business. . . . Now at last the utility has issued
a report to the stockholders."

B51. Bige. [Joe Bigelow]. "New Acts." <u>Variety</u>, Nov. 10,
1931, 37. Notice that Crosby led "the current flock
of popular baritones" and deserved "stage headlining"
at the Paramount.

B52. <u>Bing</u>. 30- to 40-page publication three times a year
from the International Crosby Circle. Editor Malcolm
Macfarlane, 16 Bracey Rise, West Bridgford, Nottingham
NG2 7AX (England), replaced Ken Crossland in 1993.
First published under other titles since 1950, the
100th edition appeared April 1992. See the ICC below.

B53. "Bing and His Boys." <u>Newsweek</u>, June 25, 1951: 42.

B54. "Bing Crosby and Grace Kelly Try for an Academy
Award." <u>Look</u>, Dec. 14, 1954: 163+. Review of <u>Country
Girl</u>.

B55. "Bing Crosby Click May Lead to More Sennetts." <u>The
Hollywood Reporter</u>, June 16, 1931. Report that Sennett
was enthusiastic over Bing in <u>I Surrender, Dear</u> before
its release, labeling Bing "the actor-singer."

B56. "Bing Crosby Goes Columbia Network." The Hollywood Reporter, Aug. 25, 1931. A note on the end of the blacklisting and on the contract "closed" by Roger Marchetti for an unsponsored show on CBS. Qtd. in Shepherd and Slatzer 175-76.

B57. Bing Crosby: His Life and Legend. 2 hours. ABC-TV, May 25, 1978. A documentary and tribute narrated by William Holden.

B58. "Bing Crosby Lives Here." House Beautiful, Aug. 1949: 46+.

B59. "Bing Crosby's Biggest Gamble." TV Guide, May 8, 1953: 6. On the early TV shows.

B60. "Bing Crosby's Father Dies." New York Times, Oct. 5, 1950: 31.

B61. "Bing Crosby's Son Gary." Look, Aug. 10, 1954: 40+.

B62. "Bing Crosby Tumbles from Stage." Worcester, Mass., Evening Gazette, March 4, 1977: 26. Associated Press reported from Pasadena, CA, that Bing fell March 3 after taping a special TV program (March 20) and seemed in fair condition "and in good spirits."

B63. "Bing on Binge." Life, Dec. 6, 1954: 106. A review of Country Girl applauding Bing's performance.

B64. Bing Pictorial. A quarterly photocopied magazine of the New Bing Crosby Colour Photo Club, Wallsend, England, published in eight issues, about 40 pages each, from Sept. 1987 to June 1989. Frank Murphy editor.

B65. "Bing Sing." Newsweek, Sept. 13, 1954: 68. A review of an early Bing Crosby television special.

B66. "Bing Sure Started Something." Variety, Nov. 17, 1954. A survey of responses by disc jockeys over Bing criticism in Look the week before that D.J.'s were not reliable in creating hits.

B67. "Bing Tags a Marlin." Field and Stream, Dec. 1962: 31+.

B68. BINGANG. A semiannual, 24-page magazine from Club Crosby, Kirkwood, MO. Begun about 1937 in Maine.

B69. "Bing-Come-Lately: The Bing Crosby Show." Life, Jan. 11, 1954: 57. Approving Crosby's serious entrance into television; calls Bing "certainly the most enduring popular singer of his time."

B70. "Bingle Jr." Time, June 21, 1954: 55.

B71. "Bing's Back." Newsweek, Jan. 24, 1966: 78.

B72. "Bing's Boys on Their Own." Life, Sept. 15, 1958: 85-

88. The boys' development and Bing's assistance on "Thanks," a record by Philip. Cover photo.

B73   <u>Bing's Friends & Collectors Newsletter</u>. Published six times a year in Sonoma, CA.

B73A. "Bing's Party." <u>Time</u>, Jan. 19, 1948: 52+.

B74. "Bing's Second Family." <u>Look</u>, July 17, 1962: 16+.

B75. "Bing's Secret Weapons." <u>American Magazine</u>, Dec. 1943: 28+. See similar article, <u>American Magazine</u>, July 1945, 32+.

B76. "Bing's Son Says It." <u>Newsweek</u>, Dec. 1, 1958: 90.

B77. <u>BINGTALKS</u>. 36-page quarterly of BINGthings Society, Tacoma, WA, and Lake Havasu, AZ.

B77A. Binyon, C. "Close-up of the Groaner." <u>Photoplay</u>, Feb. 22, 1939, 62+.

B78. Boone, A.R. "The Crosby Research Foundation." <u>Nation's Business</u>, Feb. 1943: 22.

B79. "Canned Crosby." <u>Newsweek</u>, Aug. 26, 1946: 56+. On the transcribed radio program.

B80. Carroll, Carroll. <u>None of Your Business: Or, My Life with J. Walter Thompson</u>. New York: Cowles, 1970. Includes a chapter titled "Hail KMH [Kraft Music Hall]" with Bing on radio.

B81. Clooney, Rosemary, with Raymond Strait. <u>This for Remembrance</u>. Chicago: Playboy, 1977; rpt. 1979, 256 pp. London: Robson, 1978. A Foreword by Bing dated Sept. 1977 and many comments on him.

B82. Conrad, Barnaby. "The Good New Life of Bing Crosby." <u>Good Housekeeping</u>, May 1966: 88+. The painter spent 12 months completing portraits of Bing and Kathryn and summarizes Bing's and his family's life that year.

B83. "Country Girl." <u>N.Y. Times Magazine</u>, Nov. 14, 1954: 39+. A film review.

B84. Crosby, Bing. "Introduction," 2 pp. <u>They Got Me Covered</u> by Bob Hope. Hollywood, CA: Bob Hope, 1941. 95 pp; illustrated. The introduction is two pages of gags, claiming to have met Bob on a golf course and emphasizing Hope's "This could be a nose, I thought." The book is Hope's early autobiography.

B85. ---. "Christmas 1944." <u>Photoplay</u>, Jan. 1945: 21+.

B86. ---. "I Got Plenty of Mousetraps." <u>American Magazine</u>, July 1945: 32+. Crosby writes about his research foundation and its work for the war effort. An interim account appears as "Guiding Investors," <u>Business Week</u>,

Aug 8, 1942.

B87.   ---. Advice on musical phrasing, in Nick Kenny's <u>How to Write, Sing and Sell Popular Songs</u> (New York: Hermitage, 1946), 198. Bing explains the importance of variety, clarity, and surprises in phrasing.

B88.   ---. "I Like Frank Sinatra." <u>Disc Digest</u> (Columbia Records publication), rpt. <u>Swank</u>, Sept. 1, 1946: 86. A respectful view of Crosby's competitor with humor.

B89.   ---. "How I Got My Goat." <u>The Saturday Evening Post</u>, Oct. 16, 1948: 20+.

B90.   ---. "That's My Boy." <u>Newsweek</u>, June 21, 1954: 55. Bing waxes proud at the successes of son Gary.

B91.   ---. "My Four Sons--and Me." <u>McCalls</u>, Oct. 1954: 74+. A long personal review of his life two years after Dixie's death and the hopes he had for raising decent children, giving Dixie most of the credit.

B92.   ---. "I Never Had to Scream." <u>Look</u>, Nov. 2, 1954. Asserts that some new music was a "nuisance" and some disc jockeys had untoward influence in creating hits.

B93.   ---. "Bing Scans His Elgin." N.Y. <u>Times</u>, Dec. 12, 1954: II, 7. Bing states his reluctance to play Frank Elgin in <u>Country Girl</u> and his immersion in the role.

B94.   ---. "My Competition Has a Crew Cut." <u>Coronet</u>, Sept. 1955: 24+. Bing writes about son Gary.

B95.   ---. Letter to columnist Hy Gardner. New York <u>Herald-Tribune</u>, Nov. 4, 1955. On Bing's dream of singing occasionally with a band in a nightclub.

B96.   ---. "The First Time I Sang 'Silent Night.'" <u>Good Housekeeping</u>, Dec. 1955: 42, 128. Account of Crosby's experiences singing and recording "Silent Night," on radio in 1936, and the charities helped by the record.

B97.   ---. "The Crosby Family Album." <u>McCalls</u>, Dec. 1956: 50-60. A selection of 36 personal photographs and other memorabilia, with candid comments by the author.

B98.   ---. "How I Want to Bring Up My Daughter," ed. B. Willett. <u>Ladies Home Journal</u>, Oct. 1960: 80+.

B99.   ---. "My Second Family." <u>Ladies Home Journal</u>, May 1966: 81+.

B100. Crosby, Bob. "I Hated Being Bing's Brother: As Told to M. Abramson." <u>Look</u>, July 22, 1958: 57+.

B101. "A Crosby Fishing-and-Tall Story Expedition." <u>TV Guide</u>, Aug. 30, 1969: 25.

B102. "Crosby Gives First Concert." Worcester, MA, <u>Evening</u>

Gazette, March 18, 1976: 29. Associated Press report
that Bing sang well on St. Patrick's Day and his "demi-
centennial in show business" at the Music Center in Los
Angeles.

B103. Crosby, Harry Lillis Sr. "He's My Boy." _Photoplay_,
May 1948, 60+. Bing's father (actually Harry Lowe
Crosby) reminisces on Bing's industrious and mischie-
vous childhood, his cavalier treatment of money, and an
Oklahoma newspaper that labeled him the "voice of the
people"; illustrated. This issue also includes articles on Bing by Bob Hope, Bill Morrow, Louella Parsons
interviewing Dixie Lee, and F.R. Sammes.

B104. Crosby, Kathryn Grant. "Bing and I." _Good Housekeep-
ing_, March 1963: 86+. A candid article on her recent
life with Bing and family picnics with Bing's sons.

B105. "Crosby Meets Court." _Newsweek_, Jan. 14, 1946: 78+.

B106. "Crosby Understudy Radio Sensation." _The Hollywood
Reporter_, Oct. 7, 1931. Account that Russ Columbo,
Bing's "former understudy" in California, was "cutting
his wide swath" as "Crosby has begun to fade."

B107. "Crosby-Philco Pact Stirs Pix Names to Reappraise Wax;
Promise of $$ Ahead." _Billboard_, Sept. 7, 1946, 8.
Report that Crosby's contract that allows transcrip-
tions for radio will appeal to stars and studios.

B108. "Crosby's Contract." _Business Week_, Jan. 26, 1946:
87. On transcribing the new radio show.

B109. Davidson, B. "The Crosbys of Hollywood." _Look_, June
7, 1960: 34+.

B110. ---. "Old Dad Has a Long Way to Slide." _Saturday
Evening Post_, April 9, 1966: 28+.

B111. Davidson, Muriel. "Kitchen for Bing and Kathy."
Ladies Home Journal, Sept. 1958: 70+.

B112. ---. "Gary Crosby: A Man's Victory Over Alcohol."
Good Housekeeping, Sept. 1967: 93+. Gary is candid on
his feelings of inferiority, Bing's perceptiveness, and
Gary's recovery from alcoholism in 1961.

B113. Davidson, Muriel, and Janet Rale. "Bing Crosby and
His New Movie: _Stagecoach_." _Saturday Evening Post_,
April 9, 1966: 30+. An inside view of filming _Stage-
coach_.

B114. Defresne, F. "Bing Would Rather Go Fishing." _Field
and Stream_, Dec. 1961: 48+.

B115. Delehanty, T. "Going Bing's Way." _Photoplay_, Jan.
1945: 47+.

B116. Dexter, Dave Jr. _Playback_. New York: Billboard Publications, 1976. On Bing's 1976 Broadway concert.

B117. Duncan, G. "Bing Crosby and His Four Sons." _Coronet_,
Nov. 1949: 43+.

B118. Durslag, M. "The Sweet Life." _TV Guide_, Jan. 21,
1967: 24.

B119. Edwards, Ralph. "Play Truth or Consequences with Bing
Crosby." _Photoplay_, April 1948: 46+. A radio contest
host interviews the crooner.

B120. Endres, Stacey, and Robert Cushman. _Hollywood at Your
Feet: The Story of the World-Famous Chinese Theatre_.
Los Angeles, Pomegranate, 1992. Includes an account of
Bing's cement square at the theater, set in 1936.

B121. Fisher, Alan. The Los Angeles _Times_, Dec. 10, 1978.
Crosby's butler reveals Bing was not stern at home.

B122. Fisher, John. _Call Them Irreplaceable_. New York:
Stein & Day, 1976. Bing is surveyed pp. 117-133.

B123. Follen, V. "With a Song in His Heart." _Photoplay_,
May 1945: 30+.

B124. Friedwald, Will. _Jazz Singing_. New York: Collier-
Macmillan, 1992. Indexed and illustrated; 493 pp.
Fifteen chapters, one on Louis Armstrong and Crosby; a
glowing tribute to Bing as the preeminent jazz singer.

B125. "Gary Crosby Turns Into a Second Groaner." _Life_, July
30, 1951: 37-40. On Gary's recordings, radio appear-
ances, and his chores. Cover photo.

B126. "Going His Way Is a Nation's Habit After Twenty Years
of Crosby's Song." _Newsweek_, Jan. 28, 1946: 66+.

B126A. "Good News: Bing Crosby Plays Santa." _Quick_, Dec 25,
1950. Bing as honoray chairman of "Tide of Toys"
program for European children; illustrated.

B127. Gordon, Stanley, John Hunt, and Herb Kamm. "Bing
Talks." _Look_, May 13, 1958: 46-52. An interview with
Bing and Kathryn Crosby on Bing's thoughts of retire-
ment and Kathryn's future in the movies; illustrated.

B128. ---. "Meet Mrs. Crosby and Little Bing." _Look_, Jan.
20, 1959: 25+. An update on the life and plans of
Bing's wife and the birth of Harry III.

B129. Gottfried, Martin. "Bing Crosby Brings Back the
Past." New York _Post_, Dec. 11, 1976: 22, 44. On Bing
and his Broadway show; while partial to the Sinatra of
the new "hedonistic, pragmatic" '50s, he states that in
High Society, "Crosby outwitted and outclassed Sinatra,
hung him out to dry."

B130. Gottlieb, Bill. _Downbeat_, Aug. 12, 1946, 13. An-

nounced that Robert Weil of New York advertised his
complete collection of Crosbyana recordings for
$18,000.

B131. Gourse, Leslie. Louis' Children: American Jazz Singers. New York: Quill, 1984. Bing is surveyed in Chap
ter 4.

B132. Grapevine: Bing Crosby Newsletter. Quarterly published in Teddington, Middlesex, England TW11 OQD.

B133. "The Great Throat: Bing Crosby, First in Films, First
on the Air, and First on the Phonographs of His Coun-
trymen." Fortune, Jan. 1947: 128+. A staff-written
survey of Bing's development, lifestyle, and status in
1946, with a focus on his income. Well illustrated.

B133A. "The Groaner." Time, April 7, 1941: 92+.

B134. Gwynne, Helen. Rev. of College Humor. The Hollywood
Reporter, June 30, 1933. Qtd. in S&S 208.

B135. Haller, Scot, and Maria Wilhelm. "The Sad Ballad of
Bing and His Boys." People Weekly, March 21, 1983: 88-
94. Cover story, a review of Gary's book with opposing
views of Philip Crosby, Kathryn Crosby, Bob Crosby, and
Phil Harris, and a description of the lives of the four
older sons.

B136. Hamburger, Philip. "Notes for a Gazeteer: XLIII--
Spokane, Wash." The New Yorker, Oct. 26, 1963: 198-
204. Describes Crosby mementos in the Crosbyana Room,
Bing Crosby Library of Gonzaga University.

B137. Harris, S. "Bing Crosby Inc. Unlimited." Photoplay,
Sept. 21, 1936, 3+.

B138. Harper, Mr. "After Hours." Harper, Aug. 1949: 99.

B139. ---. "One of Bing's Things." Harper, June 1952: 94.

B140. Haymes, Marguerite. The Haymes Way. New York: Publication Research Associates, 1945. The mother of two
popular singers, the author notes that in one song
Bing's versatile voice could produce softness, stacca-
to, and depth (p. 48).

B141. Hemming, Roy, and David Hajdu. Discovering Great
Singers of Classic Pop. New York: Newmarket, 1991.
Indexed and illustrated; 296 pp. A brief on Crosby's
career and of 37 others; selected discographies and
videographies. Notes Bing's supreme musical achievements, including that he introduced more Top Ten songs
than anyone else.

B142. Hobson, Wilder. "Bu-bu-bu-bu Bing." New York Times
Book Review, June 28, 1953: 3+. A review of Bing's
autobiography, delighting in the many anecdotes.

B143. ---. "The Amen Corner: Crosby and Christmas and
Such." <u>Saturday Review</u>, Nov. 26, 1955: 62-63. A
record review that emphasizes 36 sides of Crosby's
songs in the "Old Masters" album from Decca (DX-152).

B144. Hoffman, I. "Bing's Big Break." <u>Coronet</u>, April 1952:
133+.

B145. Hollywood <u>Citizen News</u>, Oct. 30, 1952. On Bing's
reason (Dixie's doctors' advice) for going to France
while Dixie was gravely ill.

B146. "Hollywood Kids in Hell." <u>The Joan Rivers Show</u>,
Syndicated, WFTV, Ch. 9, Orlando, FL, Sept. 19, 1991,
10 a.m. Gary Crosby is featured with Christina Crawford and B. D. Hyman (daughter of Bette Davis); Gary
said Bing beat him until he became 18 but that Bing was
not abusive, but the program implies otherwise.

B147. "Home on the Range?" <u>Time</u>, Aug. 7, 1950: 45. Focuses
on son Gary's summers at the Nevada ranch.

B147A. "Honeymoon Lane." <u>The Hollywood Reporter</u>. Sept. 30,
1930. Brief announcement of the marriage of Bing and
Dixie, qtd. in S&S 155.

B148. "Hooked Hollywood." <u>Geraldo</u>, Syndicated, WFTV, Ch. 9,
Orlando, FL, July 9, 1992. Gary Crosby discusses his
addiction to chocolates and alcohol.

B149. Hope, Bob. <u>Modern Screen</u>, July 1, 1945, 46. Hope
wrote an admiring piece on Crosby, saying he was much
like the priest he played on film.

B150. ---. "I and Hope." <u>Photoplay</u>, May 1948, 58+. Hope
wrote three pages, reviewing his association with Bing
and experiences at the studio and on War Bond tours.

B151. ---. "Bob Tells on Bing." <u>Music Journal</u>, Sept. 1962:
27+.

B152. ---. <u>The Road to Hollywood</u>. New York: Doubleday,
1977. 271 pp. Hope explains his career and humor,
noting he makes fun of what he cares about, like Presi-
dents, golf, and Bing Crosby.

B153. ---. <u>Confessions of a Hooker!: My Lifetime Affair
with Golf</u>. New York: Doubleday, 1985. Chapter 8 is
devoted to Bing.

B154. Hopper, Hedda. "Dixie." <u>Photoplay</u>, Feb. 1953: 44+.
The gossip columnist's tribute to Dixie Lee Crosby and
the mutual love between her and Bing; illustrated.

B155. ---. "A Tribute to Dixie Lee." Ms. given the Academy
of Motion Picture Arts and Sciences library in 1953, a
few months after Dixie's death. 16 pp. typescript;
seems to be the manuscript of the Feb. 1953 <u>Photoplay</u>
article, which mainly defends Bing.

B156. Hume, R. "Hollywood's Bing." Films & Filming, Oct. 1962: 64.

B157. Hunt, J. "Bing Walks Alone." Photoplay, Feb. 1954: 48.

B158. Hyams, Joe. "How Bing Crosby 'Failed' His Four Sons." Letter by Bing Crosby to Hyams of the Associated Press, March 30-31, 1959. A two-part column in which Bing expresses disappointment with his first four sons and blames himself for being too severe.

B159. Jacobs, Jody. Los Angeles Times. Dec. 10, 1978. Interview with Alan Fisher, who explains why he took the "lowly" position with the Crosbys in late 1961.

B160. Keen, Harold. "Race Track Production Line." Flying Magazine, May 1944: 67+. On the Del Mar Turf Club 1941 to 1944 and its aircraft subassemblies.

B161. "Keeping His Hand In." TV Guide, Feb. 28, 1959: 14.

B162. Kelley, Kitty. His Way: The Unauthorized Biography of Frank Sinatra. 545 pp.; index and illustrations. Documents Sinatra's continuing admiration for Bing (26, 32-33, 88) and Sinatra's anger over President Kennedy's decision to stay twice at Bing's Palm Spring's home and avoid Sinatra's (301-03, 328).

B163. Kurnitz, H. "Crosby Moves in High Society." Holiday, Sept. 1956: 69+. A film review.

B164. Lardner, John. "The Air: Synthetic Fun." The New Yorker, Nov. 2, 1957: 106-09. On Crosby's and Sinatra's recent television specials, that these and other singers are good but the comedy is vacuous. Only Crosby offers the authentic nonchalance and timing of a "personality" to please, but his "ersatz humor" is mere cheerfulness. Sinatra and Perry Como are worse.

B165. LaRocque, Ray. "Crosby Leads Some Old Names in New Issues." Worcester, Mass., Sunday Telegram, Feb. 20, 1977: C14. A local music reviewer praises ten of a dozen songs recorded in summer 1976 in London for the British album Feels Good, Feels Right (PS-679).

B166. Levine, Janet Hirst. "Letter from Bing Crosby." Modern Maturity, Dec.-Jan. 1975-76: 66-68. Survey of Bing's life since "retiring" in 1969 at age 65. It includes a two-page letter dated April 14, 1975.

B167. Little, S. "Decorating Ideas from Bing Crosby's House." House Beautiful, Sept. 1956: 114+.

B168. Los Angeles Examiner, March 5, 1931. Account of Dixie's reported amicable separation from Bing.

B169. ---, May 10, 1950. Report that Dixie said there was no serious trouble in the marriage, and the rumor probably was based on financial discussion.

B170. Los Angeles *Times*, May 9, 1950. Report that John O'Melveny and Larry Crosby announced "strained relations" in Bing's marriage.

B171. ---, May 10, 1950. Report that Dixie's attorney, Brenton L. Metzler, was unaware of Dixie's statement that there was no serious problem in the marriage. Excerpt in S&S 255.

B172. "Lucky Bing." *Newsweek*, June 29, 1953: 92. A favorable review of Bing's autobiography.

B173. McFadden, Robert D. "Crosby Will Be Buried Tuesday; His Songs, in Tribute, Aired Anew." New York *Times*, Oct. 16, 1977: 42. Report of funeral arrangements, tributes from the world, and memorial services.

B174. Marill. A.H. "Bing Crosby, Inc., Filmography." *Films in Review*, June-July 1968: 321.

B175. Martin, Mary. "I Sing for Bing." *American Magazine*, April 1943: 44+. Digested in *Reader's Digest*, June 1943: 34+.

B176. Martin, Pete. "I Call on Bing Crosby." *Saturday Evening Post*, May 11, 1957: 38+. Martin notes Crosby's thoughts on Presley, Ed Sullivan, and television exposure. Martin edited Bing's autobiography.

B177. ---. "I Call on Kathy Grant Crosby." *Saturday Evening Post*, April 5, 1958: 28+. On Kathryn's life, career, the Holmby Hills home, but little on Bing.

B178. Maxwell, E. "Bing's My Dish." *Photoplay*, Aug. 1948: 44+.

B179. Mercer, Johnny. *Metronome*, Oct. 1, 1944, 37. The songwriter expresses his admiration for Bing.

B180. "Minute Maid's Man." *Time*, Oct. 18, 1948: 91.

B181. Monroe, Vaughn. *Band Leaders*, March 1, 1945, 18. The popular band leader and singer states that Bing is best in interpretations and technique in singing.

B182. Morrow, Bill. "Checked Shirt and Trails." *Photoplay*, May 1948: 59-60. Brief account of the unflappable Bing fishing with the author several places but angry when Morrow's camera disturbed Bing's golf swing.

B183. Murphy, Father Robert. "My Friend Bing Crosby." *American Classic Screen*, Jan.-Feb. 1984: 29-32. A priest describes Bing and a house visit Jan. 1, 1969.

B184. Murray, William. *Del Mar: Its Life & Good Times*. Del Mar, CA.: Del Mar Thoroughbred Club, 1988. 49 pp.; many illustrations. History stressing Bing's participation; the track's name was altered in 1970.

B185. Muir, Florabel. Account of Bing's strained marriage.
Syndicated. May 9, 1950. Qtd. in S&S 253-54.

B186. Nass, Herbert E., Esq. Wills of the Rich and Famous.
New York: Warner, 1991. An explanation and excerpts of
Bing's 1977 will, pp. 75-77.

B187. "New Millionaires." Time, Dec. 27, 1954: 64-65. A
survey of several new millionaires, including Crosby.

B188. "New Sennett Shorts Click in Big Style." Rev. of I
Surrender, Dear. The Hollywood Reporter, June 25,
1931. Qtd. in S&S 166-67.

B189. "New Stars for CBS." Newsweek, Jan. 31, 1949: 49.

B190. Nolan, Martin F. "Crosby Symbolized Irish-American
Success Dream." Boston Globe, Oct. 16, 1977: 71-72. A
survey of Bing's career.

B191. Norman, Barry. The Film Greats. London: Future,
1985.

B192. Nugent, Frank S. "At Home with the Crosby Team."
N.Y. Times Magazine, March 4, 1946: 16+. A profile
especially of the Crosby sons; illustrated.

B193. O'Hara, J. "Bing Crosby's Phonograph Recording of
Ballad for Americans." Newsweek, Sept. 16, 1940: 62+.

B194. O'Flaherty, Terrence. San Francisco Chronicle, May
25, 1978. A reporter friend explains that Bing's
aloofness was not coldness and Bing admired Upstairs,
Downstairs, the British televised masterpiece.

B195. "On Wax." New Yorker June 14, 1947: 20.

B196. Osterholm, J. Roger. "The Groaner's Alive, Well and
Singing." Worcester, Mass., Evening Gazette, Dec. 15,
1976: 38. A review of Bing Crosby on Broadway at the
Uris Theater, New York.

B197. ---. "The Legacy of Bing Crosby in Perspective Fifteen Years After His Death." Avion (Embry-Riddle
Aeronautical University, Daytona Beach, Florida), Oct.
14, 1992: B4, B7. Contrasts Bing's generation and
values to those since the 1960s and asserts that "Al
Rinker invented the nasty Crosby" and that son Gary
helped invent the sadistic Crosby.

B198. ---. "The Bing Crosby Baseball Stadium in Virginia."
Bing, 102 (Dec. 1992): 7-8. An account of Front Royal,
VA, for the premiere of Riding High in 1950.

B199. Parsons, Louella O. "Bing--As I Know Him." Photoplay, Dec. 1944: 32+. Personal praise by a gossip
columnist on an interview in August 1944; illustrated.

B200. ---. "My Bing: Dixie Crosby Talks." <u>Photoplay</u>, May
1948: 56. One of Dixie's rare interviews; she expresses her love of Bing, determination to discipline her
sons, and the loss of an intimate Hollywood.

B201. ---. Syndicated. International News Service, publ.
New York <u>Herald-Tribune</u>, Nov. 5, 1955. Asserts that
Bing wants to retire from TV and films and perhaps even
recordings; retracted July 29, 1956.

B202. "Philco Signs Bing." <u>Business Week</u>, Aug. 31, 1946:
40.

B203. Pleasants, Henry. "A Bel Canto Baritone Named Bing
Crosby." New York <u>Times</u>, Dec. 5, 1976: II: 1,18.
Notes that Bing's 1975 recordings reveal a "richer and
warmer" voice, that Crosby is not truly a crooner, and
that he is "the most important and influential transi-
tional figure in the history of American popular singing," primarily because of "his identification with
jazz, his predilection for an oratorical approach to
song now generally recognized as Afro-American."

B204. Posner, C. "Why Bing and Kathy Need This Baby So
Much." <u>Photoplay</u>, Sept. 1958: 51+.

B205. Prescott, Orville. Review of <u>Call Me Lucky</u>. New York
<u>Times</u>, June 29, 1953. Finds strength in Crosby as "a
thoroughly nice person" and weakness a lack of facts.

B206. Proctor, K. "Play Truth or Consequences with Bing
Crosby." <u>Photoplay</u>, June 1943: 48.

B207. Pryor, Thomas M. "Dr. Crosby's Remedy." <u>N.Y. Times
Magazine</u>, May 4, 1952: 18+. Bing recommends relaxation
and fun for a "pressure age." Illustrated.

B208. "The Reluctant Dragon." <u>TV Guide</u>, Jan. 1, 1954: 5.

B209. Reynolds, Quentin. "Kid from Spokane." <u>Collier's</u>,
Apr. 27, 1935: 20+. An early view of Crosby.

B210. Review of <u>Bing Crosby and Friends</u> at London's Palladium. <u>Variety</u>. Ca. Sept. 27, 1977. Bing's last review,
qtd. in S&S 305.

B211. Review of Aug. 9, 1927, performance of the Rhythm Boys
at Keith's 81st St. Theatre, New York. <u>Billboard</u>.
Qtd. in S&S 99.

B212. "The Rhythm Boys." <u>Time</u>, July 19, 1943: 70. On the
Rhythm Boys reunion July 4, 1943, with Paul Whiteman.

B213. "Rita, Marlene and the Farmer's Daughter." <u>Life</u>, Aug.
3, 1953: 65-68. On <u>Little Boy Lost</u> and Nicole Maurey
as, to Bing, Hayworth, Deitrich, and the "daughter."

B214. Rockwell, John. "Crosby Set Style for an Older Age
and Led Way for Rock." New York <u>Times</u>, Oct. 15, 1977.

An appreciation of Bing's music, endorsing Pleasant's views on his voice, and is close on most dates.

B215. ---. "An Homage to the 'Classical' Crooners." New York Times, Oct. 29, 1982. A comparison of Bing and Sinatra in recent re-releases, suggesting rock and roll resulted from poor popular songs of the 1950s.

B216. "Romp for Two Ageless Troubadours." Life, March 10, 1961: 77-81. A review of Crosby's TV show (V38) with Maurice Chevalier and Carol Lawrence; cover photo.

B217. Ryan, D. "The Secret of Bing Crosby's Greatness." Photoplay, Oct. 1935: 52+.

B218. Sammes, Fred R. "Million-dollar Minstrel." Photoplay, May 1948: 55. The introduction by the publisher to "Crosby Cavalcade," articles by Bob Hope, Bill Morrow, Bing's father, and Louella Parsons' interview with Dixie on the occasion of Bing's fourth Gold Medal from the magazine as the year's "favorite movie star."

B219. Scott, Walter. "Walter Scott's Personality Parade." Parade, Feb. 25, 1990: 2. Explains that Lindsay, an alcoholic, shot himself when his inheritance from his mother expired and money from Bing would not commence until age 65.

B220. Seldes, Gilbert. "The Incomparable Bing." Esquire, Feb. 1, 1944, 38. A noted critic writes that Bing "is the unchallenged top man," of whom one does not tire and is the "best example" of "the kind of thing America can produce."

B221. Shales, Tom. Legends: Remembering America's Greatest Stars. New York: Random House, 1989. Includes a section titled "Easy Going: Bing Crosby."

B222. Shanley, J.P. "Television: Special Program on Behalf of the Edsel Car." America, Oct. 26, 1957: 118.

B223. Shearer, E. "Gary Crosby and Friend." Collier's, Jan. 6, 1951: 12+.

B224. Shearer, Lloyd. "Bing the Generous." Parade, Aug. 1, 1976: 6. Bing to perform at the Palladium if tickets cost only £5 ($9) and receipts given to charities.

B225. Sher, J. "Bing and His Pirates." Photoplay, Oct. 1948: 38.

B226. "Show Business: Old Master." Time, Oct. 13, 1958: 53. Note that Bing agreed to $2 million to perform two TV specials for five years and produce another ten programs, and his recent special was "topnotch," revealing Bing as "the master entertainer."

B227. Simon, George. Metronome, Oct. 1, 1944, 38. The co-editor of the magazine notes Bing's sincerity and unaffected manner, which have improved popular music.

B228. Slater, L. "Crisis for the Crosbys: What's Bothering Bing's Boys." McCalls, May 1959: 58+.

B229. Smith, Edward J. The Musical Digest, July 1, 1946: 37. The associate editor estimates Crosby's vast dominance of the nation's recorded radio music, the audience of his radio program (25 million), and viewers of each film (250 million), noting his appeal to people of every race and condition in the world.

B230. Smith, H. Allen. "Bing Crosby--King of the Groaners." The Saturday Evening Post, Oct. 31, Nov. 7, 1942. Abridged in The Reader's Digest, July 1943: 74+. An article noting Bing's phase of sowing wild oats to becoming "America's No. 1 Minstrel," whose voice is heard every minute somewhere in the world, and Army camps demand Crosby on the Hit Parade, forcing Kraft to relax its exclusive hold on him.

B231. Swift, Pamela. "Keeping up . . . with Youth." Parade, Feb. 29, 1976: 18. Article on Nathaniel, 14, as showing great promise as a golfer.

B232. "Talk with the Stars." Newsweek, July 8, 1957: 89.

B233. Thomas, B. "The Crosby Myth." Photoplay, June 1950, 52.

B234. Thomas, Bob. "The Afterwaves of Daddy Dearest." Daytona Beach, FL, Evening Journal, April 14, 1983. The Associated Press article on the "blood feud" between Gary and brother Philip.

B235. Tubert, Jack. "Area Hits High C--Como and Channing for Class." Worcester, Mass., Sunday Telegram, Aug. 21, 1977: A29. Como heaps "praise on the dean of crooners, Bing Crosby. 'If it had not been for Bing we [Como, Sinatra, Bennett] would all be doing our respective jobs--bricklaying or cutting hair. Not enough credit has been given this man [Bing Crosby].'"

B236. "Two Misters Play Sisters." Collier's, Oct. 15, 1954: 74+. An article on the film White Christmas.

B237. Ulanov, Barry. Metronome, Oct. 10, 1944, 17. The co-editor discusses Bing's boys and notes Bing's legendary stature as a "good man" and "the great figure" in entertainment.

B238. Vandervoort, Paul II. "Uncle Sam Sans Whiskers." Band Leaders, Jan. 1, 1946, 31. States that Crosby is Uncle Sam without whiskers and that he has made a friend of the world as the king of popular music.

B239. Venables, Ralph. Vocal Jazz. London: Jazz Tempo Publications, 1945. 23 pages. "Can Bing Crosby Sing Jazz?" (3-6) is a survey of 12 British music critics,

in which 11 stated that Bing was the best white jazz
singer around. Excerpted in Mize 170-72.

B240. Weinman, M. "High Jinks in High Society." Collier's,
June 8, 1956: 32+. A review of High Society.

B241. Westmore, Wally. "Make Mine Crosby Style." Photoplay, Feb. 1949, 43+. Experiences of a make-up man
with Bing at Paramount and elsewhere.

B242. Whitburn, Joel. Joel Whitburn's Pop Memories, 1890-
1954. Record Research, Inc., Wisconsin: 1986. A list
of Bing's hit records.

B243. Wilkie, Jane. "Unsentimental Gentleman." Modern
Screen, Feb. 1947.

B244. Williams, M. "Columbia, Epic and Crosby." Saturday
Review, June 29, 1968: 56+.

B245. Winchell, Walter. "Story of a Song." Birmingham
Post, Feb. 2, 1945, 6. An account of how Johnny Burke
thought of the song "Swinging on a Star" while lectur-
ing Gary Crosby at the Crosby home in March 1943.

B246. Wilkerson, W.R. "Billy." "Tradeviews" and "The Low
Down" columns. The Hollywood Reporter. ca. Jan. 1932
on Bing's income and ca. June 1933 on Bing buying back
Roger Marchetti's interest. Qtd. in S&S 176.

B247. "With $15,000,000 Bing Wants to Slowly Bow Out."
Newsweek, Jan. 4, 1954: 38.

B248. Wood, Thomas. "Bing Crosby, Mousetrap Builder." New
York Times Magazine, June 6, 1948: 17+. Survey of
Bing's life and style.

B249. "Youth: Who's the New Champ? She's Bing's Girl."
Life, March 2, 1962: 43-44. Pictures of Mary Frances,
age 2, as the youngest Red Cross Beginner's Swimmer,
witnessed by 26 newsmen, "Kathryn Grant," and Johnny
Weissmuller.

OTHER SOURCES THAT TOUCH ON CROSBY AND HIS INTERESTS

B250. Balliett, Whitney. American Singers: 27 Portraits in
Song. Oxford. Mainly profiles from The New Yorker.
244 pp.

B251. Brumer, Andy. "Land, Sea and Golf: They Meet at
Pebble Beach, Open Site." 1992 United States Open,
Advertising Supplement to The Wall Street Journal,
[June 17, 1992]:14+. On the Crosby Pro-Am Tournament.

B252. Burns, George. Gracie: A Love Story. New York: G. P.
Putnam's Sons, 1988. 319 pp.; illustrated; no index.
Includes information on early days of radio (92-108,
161-74) and films, some with Crosby.

B253. Cahn, Sammy. I Should Care: The Sammy Cahn Story.
New York: Arbor House, 1975.

B254. Carter, Claire. "Our Love Was Strong." Parade, Feb.
16, 1992: 4-7. Tony Bennett mentions Bing's encouragement in calling him "the best singer I ever heard," and
a Hirschfeld cartoon of Bing, Bennett, and four other
singers as "A Group of America's Great Artists."

B255. Collier, James Lincoln. Benny Goodman and the Swing
Era. Oxford. Focuses on the music of the 1920s and
1930s. 404 pp.; illustrated.

B256. Davis, Sammy Jr., with Jane and Burt Boyar. Why Me?
FSG. 374 pp.

B257. Eckhouse, M., and C. Mastrocola. This Date in Pittsburgh Pirates History. Scarborough. 272 pp.

B258. Faith, William Robert. Bob Hope: A Life in Comedy.
New York: Putnam's Sons, 1982. 400 pp. plus index,
Illustrations, documentation. Many references to Bing.

B259. Fordham, John. The Sound of Jazz. Hamlyn. The
evolution of musicians and vocalists; illustrated. 158
pp.

B260. Goldman, Herbert G. Jolson: The Legend Comes to Life.
Oxford. 411 pp.

B261. Goldstein, Norman. The History of Television. Portland: Associated Press. 299 pp.

B262. Hirschhorn, Clive. The Hollywood Musical. Portland.
Covers films from 1927 to 1990; illustrated. 480 pp.

B263. Hopper, Hedda, with James Brough. The Whole Truth and
Nothing But. New York: Doubleday, 1963.

B264. Hutchinson, Tom. Niven's Hollywood. Salem House.
Photographs by David Niven. 192 pp.

B265. Jones, Max. Talking Jazz. Norton. Interviews since
1950 by the editor of Jazz Music. 293 pp.

B266. Lamour, Dorothy, with Dick McInnes. My Side of the
Road. Englewood Cliffs, NJ: Prentice-Hall, 1980. 226
pp. plus filmography and index; illustrated. Ch. 14 is
titled "Produced by Hope and Crosby."

B267. Lee, Peggy. Miss Peggy Lee: An Autobiography. New
York: Donald I. Fine, 1989. 170 pp. and index; illustrated. Favorable comments on working with Bing.

B268. Leonard, Neil. Jazz: Myth and Religion. Oxford.
221pp. A survey of the early resistance and gradual
acceptance of jazz.

B269. Levin, Martin, ed. Hollywood and the Great Fan Magazines. Selections of the 1930s from <u>Photoplay</u>, <u>Motion Picture</u>, and others. Harrison House. 224 pp.

B270. Sanford, Herb. <u>Tommy and Jimmy: The Dorsey Years</u>. New Rochelle, NY: Arlington House, 1972.

B271. Shipman, David. <u>Judy Garland: The Secret Life of an American Legend</u>. New York: Hyperion, 1992. Many references to Bing.

B272. Silvers, Phil, with Robert Saffron. <u>This Laugh Is on Me</u>. Englewood Cliffs, NJ: Prentice-Hall, 1973.

B273. Spada, James. <u>Grace: The Secret Lives of a Princess</u>. Garden City: Dolphin-Doubleday, 1987. 275 pp. plus notes and an index. States that Grace Kelly and Bing dated often.

B274. Sudhalter, Richard M., Philip R. Evans, and Dean Myatt. <u>Bix: Man and Legend</u>. New York: Shirmer, 1974. 478 pp. plus indexes dealing with Bix Beiderbecke, including early radio and recording work with Bing.

B275. Swindell, Larry. <u>The Last Hero: A Biography of Gary Cooper</u>. Garden City: Doubleday, 1980. 328 pp. plus index, illustrations. A few references to Bing in the 1930s and later.

B276. Tosches, Nick. <u>Dino: Living High in the Dirty Business of Dreams</u>. Garden City: Doubleday, 1992. 548 pp. plus index; filmography, discography, bibliography; illustrated. Several references to Bing Crosby as Dean Martin's early model for singing.

B277. Torme, Mel. <u>It Wasn't All Velvet</u>. New York: Viking 1988.   373 pages, including discography; indexed, illustrations. Idolizing Crosby's music, and respect for Crosby as a person (p. 82).

B278. Walker, Leo. <u>The Wonderful Era of the Great Dance Bands</u>. Includes anecdotes of Crosby.

B279. ---. <u>The Big Band Almanac</u>. Revised. New York: Da Capo, 1989. Illustrated and indexed; 466 pp. Orig. publ. 1978 in Hollywood. Some on Crosby and a photo of him with Gus Arnheim's band about 1930 (15).

REFERENCES

B280. Allen, Frederick Lewis. <u>Only Yesterday</u>. 1931. New York: Bantam, 1946. See Ch. 5, "The Revolution in Manners and Morals," and Chs. 12-14 on the Depression for an insightful eye-witness account of the 1920s.

B281. Apel, Willi, and Ralph T. Daniel. <u>The Harvard Brief Dictionary of Music</u>. 1960; New York: Pocket Books, 1961. A reliable guide to musical terms and styles.

B282. Cowley, Robert. "Invasion Jitters, 1942." MHQ: The Quarterly Journal of Military History. 4 (Spring 1992): 24-27.

B283. Earley, Steven C. An Introduction to American Movies. New York: New American Library-Mentor, 1978. A scholarly history of many aspects of films from 1890 to 1977.

B284. Fedler, Fred. Reporting for the Print Media. 4th ed. New York: Harcourt Brace Jovanovich, 1989. Mentions the ploy of two writers for the National Enquirer impersonating priests at Bing's funeral as an "obviously unethical" attempt for an exclusive story (270).

B285. Handbook of American Popular Culture, ed. M. Thomas Inge. 2d ed. 3 vols. New York: Greenwood Press, 1989. Articles on "Jazz" by William Howland Kenney III and Bill Bennett and "Records and the Recording Industry" by James Von Schilling.

B286. Maltin, Leonard, ed. Leonard Maltin's TV Movies and Video Guide. New York: New American, 1989. 1222 pp.

B287. McDonough, John. "Hear It Now: Pearl Harbor Day Radio." The Wall Street Journal, Dec. 6, 1991: A13. A summary of radio reports of Dec. 7, 1941, and how radio treated sponsored programs.

B288. Medved, Michael. "Does Hollywood Hate Religion?" The Reader's Digest, July 1990: 99-103. Notes Hollywood's obsessive antagonism to religion, unlike Crosby's time.

B289. Milward, John. "Rock 'n' Roll Has Crow's Feet, Love Handles." Daytona Beach, FL, News-Journal, March 7, 1992: 1D-2D. A NY Times News Service article stating that rock and roll has been dull "for decades" and will be forgotten by 2010.

B290. The Motion Picture Guide, ed. Jay Robert Nash and Stanley Ralph Ross. 12 vols. Chicago: Cinebooks, 1986. Annual updates followed.

B291. Murrells, Joseph. Million Selling Records from the 1900s to the 1980s. New York: Arco, 1984. 508 pp.; index, illustrated.

B292. Peterson, Karen S. "Are Parents the New Scapegoats?" USA Today, Oct. 31, 1991: 1D-2D. States that children unfairly blame their parents for failings, based on views of psychiatrist Steven Wolin and many others.

B293. Pitts, Michael R., and Louis H. Harrison. Hollywood on Record: The Film Stars' Discography. Metuchen, N.J.: Scarecrow, 1978. 410 pp.

B294. Rust, Brian. The Complete Entertainment Discography. New York: Arlington House, 1972.

B295. ---. <u>Jazz Records, 1897-1942</u>. 2 vols. 4th ed. New Rochelle: Arlington House, 1978.

B296. Siegel, Joel. <u>Good Morning America</u>. ABC-TV. WFTV, Orlando, FL. June 27, 1990. The Entertainment Editor reported that, with adjustments for inflation and only first releases, <u>White Christmas</u> (1954) placed as the 32nd all-time grossing film at an adjusted $245 million in receipts. He stated that Disney's <u>Snow White</u> (1937 and $188 million) and <u>Gone with the Wind</u> (1939 and $396 million) were 58th and 6th, respectively.

B297. <u>A Thirty-Year History of Programs Carried on National Radio Networks in the United States, 1926-56</u>, ed. Harrison B. Summers. New York: Arno-N.Y. Times, 1971. 228pp.

B298. Widick, Kathy. Interview. Daytona Beach, FL, March 19, 1992. A member of the Communications Department of the Ladies Professional Golf Association explained the 1974-75 dates of the Bing Crosby International Classic Golf Tournament, Guadalajara, Mexico.

B299. <u>World War II: A 50th Anniversary History by the Writers and Photographers of the Associated Press</u>. New York: Holt, 1989. Mentions Bing Crosby's bond rallies and the importance of "White Christmas."

BING CROSBY CLUBS

        These are listed in many sources, including Randy Skretvedt and Jordan R. Young, <u>The Nostalgia Entertainment Sourcebook</u>, Beverly Hills: Moonstone, 1991.

B300. Bing Crosby Historical Society [disbanded in 1993], President Ken Twiss, P.O. Box 216, Tacoma, WA 98401. All holdings were transferred June 2, 1993, to the Foley Center Library, Gonzaga University, 502 East Boone Avenue, Spokane, WA 99258. Their Crosby Collection has 24,000 items, including monogrammed pajamas, socks, an old T-shirt, hairpieces, and a Stretch to Health device endorsed by Bing. Displays are at the Crosby Student Center, formerly the Library.

B301. Bing Crosby Library, Gonzaga University, Spokane, WA. See the above entry, B300.

B302. Bing Crosby Newsletter, Editor John C. Marshall, 30 Kings Road, Teddington, Middlesex, TW11 OQD, England. Annual dues are $8. See <u>Grapevine</u>, B132.

B303. Bing's Friends and Collectors Society, 236 Andrieux Street, Sonoma, CA 95476-6909. Annual dues are $10.50. See their <u>Newsletter</u>, B73.

B304. BINGthings Society, President Bob Lundberg, 5021 57th Avenue Court West, Tacoma, WA 98467-4802. The society was founded in 1988. Annual dues are $10 a year, $15 overseas. See <u>BINGTALKS</u>, B77.

B305. Club Crosby, President Mark Scrimger, P.O. Box 3849,
Kirkwood, MO 63122. Founded in 1936 in North Vassal-
boro, ME; in 1978 it was the only Crosby fan club in
the United States. Annual dues are $12. See <u>Bingang</u>,
B68.

B306. International Crosby Circle, Michael Crampton, Secre-
tary-Treasurer, 19 Carrholm Crescent, Chapel Allerton,
Leeds LS7 2NL, England. The United States representative is F.B. "Wig" Wiggins, 5608 North 34th St., Arlington, VA 22207. Annual dues in America are $20; £7
in the United Kingdom. See <u>Bing</u> periodical, B52.

B307. Queensland Bing Crosby Society, 17 Thurecht Parade,
Scarborough, Queensland, Australia.

B308. Victorian Bing Crosby Society, P.O. Box 422, South
Melbourne, Victoria 3205, Australia.

Index

Recordings, films, directors, actors, radio and TV programs, and major topics and other people are included, like major songwriters and many crew members. Many orchestras and vocal groups are listed under the leaders' first names. Dates are given for selected people. The series designators, like D for discs, indicate whether an entry is a recording, film, radio or TV show, or publication, but when ambiguity exists the type is stated.

"Carnegie Hall V-Disc Session," R55
Carol (Ladd), Sue, 13-14, 23, 40, D207, F4
"Carol Burnett Show, The," V156, V184
"Carolina in the Morning," D1802
Caron, Leslie, R105
Carpenella, Paul Sr., xiii
Carpenter, Ken, 20-21, 33, 38, 41-43, F58-59, R37 passim to R118, V6
Carpozi, George Jr., 16, 18, 42, 45, R54, B8
Carr, Mary, F50
Carr, Vikki (b. 1941), V82, V119
Carradine, John, F149
Carrol, Dixie, see Crosby, Dixie Lee
Carroll, Carroll, 20, 23, 33, D503, D658, F81, 317, R18, 318, R20 passim to R77, B80
Carroll, Alma, V175
Carroll, Leo G., 342
Caroll, Diahann, V99, V130
Caroll, Joan, F87, R78, R82, R89
Caroll, Madeleine (b. 1906), F63, F140
"Carry Me Back to Old Virginny," D131, D1231, D1478, D1422, D2467, F54, F95
Carson, Jack (1910-63), F73, F75, R30
Carson, Johnny, F155, V214, V229
Carter, Ann, F100
Carter, Claire, B254
Carter, President Jimmy (James Earl), 66
"Casey Jones," D1478, D2422
Cash, Johnny, V162
Casino Theatre, 6
Cass, Maurice, F31
Cass County Boys, D1086-87, D1134-35
"Cassidy, Hopalong" (William Boyd), 270
Castellano, Richard, V179
Catalina Island, CA, 18, 76, F26
Catlett, Walter (1889-1960), F67, F111
Caulfield, Joan (b. 1922), 33, F90, F92, F94, F181, R72
"Cavalcade of America, The," R121
"Cavalcade of Stars," with Jackie Gleason, V274
Cavallaro, Carmen (b. 1913),

D730-31, D845-46, D939-40, F83, R67, R73
Cavett, Frank, 33, F72, F117
CBC (Canada), V105, V108
CBS (Columbia Broadcasting Company), 15-17, 19, 31, 36, 39, 42, 43, 45, 47, 49-50, 52, 66-67, 75-76, 79-80, 82-83, 86, 89-90
"CBS News Special: Sinatra," V98A
"Cecilia," D1603
"Cela m'est égal," D1110, F123
Celebrating V Disc 50th Anniversay (CD), D2579
Chakiris, George, F125, V18
Champion, Marge and Gower, F110
"Chances Are," D2183
Chandler, Chick, R35
Chaney, Lon, F91
Chang, Sue, F144
"Change Partners," D1853
"Changes," D28
"Changing Partners" (song), D1135, V6
"Channel 9 Kaleidescope," V112
"Chapel in the Valley," D523
Chaplin, Charlie (1899-1977), 18, 28, F119
Chapman, Jack, x
Charioteers, The, R79
Charisse, Cyd, V120
Charles, Ray, V182-83
Chase, Barrie, F125
"Chattanoogie Shoe Shine Boy," D969
Check and Double Check (film), 13, 74, F4, V253A
"Cheek to Cheek," D1303, F90
Cherbourg, France, 29, 37, 80, 82
Cherry, Don, V126
Chesterfield Cigarettes radio shows, 16-17, 40, 75, 82-83, R14-15, R96 passim to R107
Chesterfield Show, The (album), D2308
Chevalier, Maurice (1888-1972), F132, F142, R80, V38, B216
Chicago, 9, 11-13, 17, 24, 45, 51, 53, 58, 60, 70, 73
"Chicago Style," D1090, F120
"Chicago," D1341
Chicago's South Side, 11
Chief Yellow Horse, F149
"Children," D1861
"Chim Chim Charee," D1742
"Chinatown, My Chinatown,"

"Conversations 1967-68," V129
Converse, Frank, F154
Conway, Tim (b. 1933), V97
Coogan, Jackie (1914-84), F134
Cool of the Evening (album), D2321
"Cool Water," D1094
Suzanne Somers 61
Cooper, Gary (1901-61), 13, 17-18, 21, 25, 30, 34, 54, 80, F11, F27-28, F32, F72, F94, F98, F136, 297, F163, R15, R83, R105, B275
Cooper, Jackie (b. 1921), F17, R34
"Copacabana," D1030
"Coquette," D100, D1718
Corbett, Harry H., V94
Cord, Alex, F149
Corey, Wendell, F136, R105
Corkery, Francis, 4-5
"Cornbelt Symphony," D1144
Cornell, Lillian, F58
Corrado, Gino, F47
Corregidor, 25
Correll, Charles V. (Andy), F4
Corrigan, Lloyd, F118, F131
"Corrine Corrina," D304
Cosbey, Ronnie, F61
Coslow, Sam, D165 passim to D1902, F2, F16, F20, F38, F45, F84
Cosmopolitan-M-G-M, 18, F21
Cossart, Ernest, F31
Costa, Mary, V160, V182
Costello, John, F101
Cotsworth, Staats, F154
Cotton Club, The, Harlem, 10
Cotton Club, The, Los Angeles, 14
Cottrell, Jimmy, 3, 22, 30, 72, F87
Count and Countess of Segonzac, 37
Count Basie Orchestra, see Basie, Count
"Count Your Blessings Instead of Sheep," D1196, D2137, 197, F125
Counter-culture, The, 60
Country Crosby (album), D2322
Country Girl, The (flim), 42-44, 46, 83-84, F126, F163, V257, B54; reviews, B63, B83
"Country Style," D808, F92
Country Style (album), D2323
"Couple of Song and Dance Men, A," D793, D1846, F90, V208
Couple of Song and Dance Men,

A (album), 63, D1842-53, D2324
Court Jester (film), 45
Cowan, Jerome, F50
Cowboy Songs (album), D2325
Cowley, Robert, B282
Cox Broadcasting Corp., 60, 88, 253, 352
Craig, Catherine, F81
Craig, Yvonne, F141
Crain, Jeanne (b. 1925), 197, F82, F85, F134
Crampton, Michael, B306
Cranbourne Court, England, 54
Crane, Bob (1928-78), V101
Crane, Jimmy, F87
Crawford, Gwen, F81
Crawford, Joan (1908-77), 32
"Crazy Arms," D1671
"Crazy Rhythm," D2170
"Cremo Singer, The," 15, 75, R12-13
Crews, Laura Hope (1880-1942), F47, F51
Crinoline Choir, The, D281-82
Crockett, Dick, F141
Cronyn, Hume (b. 1911), F101
"Crooner, The" (early title for F12), 16
Crooner, The (album), D2326
Crooners, The (CD), D2593
Crooners Originals (CD), D2594
Crooner's Holiday (film), F9, F33, V297
Crooning, 6, 10, 13, 17, 19, 21, 25, 29-31, 33, 39-40, 45, 53, 68, 75, F26, F37, F84
"Crosby and Rinker, Two Boys with a Piano," 7
Crosby, Bing (Harry Lillis Crosby, 1903-77), Academy Awards and Nominations, 315-16; acting style, F99; Aircraft Division, 27; "All-time boxoffice championship," 81; and a bullfighter, 59; arrested, see jailed; autobiography reviews, B81, B142, B172, B205; baldness/hairpieces, 5, 19-20, 25, 30, F27, F30, V3, B300; banks owned, 88; baptism, 1-2; Bible readings, V203; B.C. Day, 37, 82, F108, R98; Binglin Breeding Stables, 22, 77, 262; Bing's Things, 81; Bingsday, 32; birth, 1; Black Forest (horse), 19; blackface, F48, F64, F81; blacklisting, 15, 35, 75,

Dallas, TX, 42
"Dammed Forever," V258
Damone, Vic (b. 1928), V43
Damrosch, Walter, F51
Dance bands, B278-79
"Dance with a Dolly," D1763, see "Buffalo Gals"
Dancer's Big Band Hall of Fame, Davenport, IA, 66, 90
"Dancing in the Dark," D163
"Dancing Shadows," D52
"Dancing Under the Stars," D352
Dandridge, Dorothy, V18
Daniel, Ralph T., B281
Daniels, Bebe (1901-71), F5
Daniels, Larry, F88
Danner, Blythe, F154
"Danny Boy," D547
"Danny Thomas Hour, The," V131
"Danny Thomas Show, The: The Road to Lebanon," V109
"Dardanella," D1469
Darin, Bobby (1936-73), 48, F142
"Daring Young Man, The," D1609, D1882
"Dark Eyes," D1886
Dark Moon (album), D2330
"Dark Town Strutter's Ball," D1595, F123
"Darling je vous aime beau- coup," D555
"Darling Nellie Gray," D378
Darnell, Linda, F82
Darrell, Jean, 29
Darro, Frankie, F108
Darrow, Henry, F155
DaSilva, Howard, F86, F94
"Daughter of Molly Malone," D1705
Dauphin, Claude, F123
Davenport, Harry, F108
Davenport Hotel, Spokane, 6, 73
David, Michael, F140
Davidson, B., B109-111
Davidson, Muriel, F149, B112- 13
Davies, Marion (1897-1961), 18, 26, F21
Davis, Freeman "Bones," F108
Davis, Gail, F136
Davis, Jim, F136
Davis, Joan, V5
Davis, Mac, V194
Davis, Rufe, F47
Davis, Sammy Jr. (1925-90), 56, D1685-86, F142, F147, B256
D'Avril, Yola, F2, F123
Dawson, Hal K., F126

Day, Dennis, R91, V83
"Day After Forever, The," D641, F72
"Day by Day," D749
"Day Dreaming," D554
Day Dreaming (album), D2331
"Day You Came Along, The," D238, D1179, F20
Daytona Beach (FL) News- Journal (periodical), B289
DeCarlo, Yvonne (b. 1922), F66, F81
De Corday, Paul, F99
De Cordova, Arturo, F86
De Cordova, Fred, V6
De Cordova, Pedro, R70
De La Brosse, Marcel, F125
De Rita, Joe, 29
De Segonzal, Gladys, F123
De Zulueta, Cesar, 66
Dean, Barney, 23, 34, F54
Dean, Jimmy, V61
Dean, Julie, F99
"Dean Martin Show, The," V27, V30, V126, V141, V158, V179
"Dean Martin-Jerry Lewis Show, The," R95
"Dear Evelina," D1478, D2422
"Dear Friend," D669
"Dear Hearts and Gentle People," 38, D954, 196 No. 20
"Dear Little Boy of Mine," D545
"Dear Old Donegal," D757
"Dear Old Girl," D328
Dearing, Edgar, F44, F67, F88, F94
"Dearly Beloved," D653
Debussy, Claude (1862-1918), D396
Decade of Bad Manners (1920s), 60
Decca Records, 19-20, 24-25, 27, 36, 38-39, 43, 45, 53, 61, 77, 83-84, 88, 91
Decca White Label Special Pressing, D282-85
"Deck the Halls," D932, D1000, D1257
"'Deed I Do," D1291, D2188
"Deep in the Heart of Texas," D564
"Deep Purple," D422
Deering, Ed, F3
Defresne, F., B114
DeHaven, Gloria (b. 1925), F70, F112, R53
Deitz, Howard, D896, F159
"Deja vu," D1946
Dekker, Albert, F67
Del Mar Track and Turf Club, 21, 22, 32, 77, 78, 81,

197
"Domino," D1063
Don Clarke Biltmore Hotel
Orchestra, 73, D1-2
Don Rose and his Rag Doll
Dancers, F2
Doncaster, England, 63
Donlevy, Brian (1889-1972),
F61, F86, R36
Donnelly, Ruth, F87
"Donovans, The," D945, F101
"Don't Be a Do Badder," 87,
D1687, F147
"Don't Be That Way," D375
"Don't Blame Me," D2190
"Don't Break the Spell," D544
"Don't Ever Be Afraid to Go
Home," D1076
"Don't Fence Me In," 28, 31-
32, 79-80, D670, D1897, 195
No. 11, F75A
Don't Fence Me In (album),
D2337
"Don't Get Around Much Any-
more," 65, D1954, F173
Don't Hook Now (film), 22,
78, F46
"Don't Hook Now" (song), see
"Tomorrow's My Lucky Day"
"Don't Let a Good Thing Get
Away," D1731A
"Don't Let That Moon Get
Away," D383, D390, F48
"Don't Sit Under the Apple
Tree," D1607
"Don't Somebody Need Some-
body," D2
"Don't Take Your Love from
Me," D2167
"Don't Worry About Tomorrow"
(theme song), R117
"Doodle Do Do," D1416
Doodletown Pipers, The, V169
Dooley, Billy, F37
Doonican, Val, V213
"Door Will Open, A," D745
Doran, Ann (b. 1914), F81,
F91, F94
Dorian, Bob, F67
D'Orsay, Fifi, F21
Dorsey, Jimmy (1904-57), x-
xi, 10, 20, D337-41, D382,
D744-45, 320, R20 passim to
R24, R53
Dorsey, Tommy (1905-56), x,
22, 24, 28, F130, R14-15,
R29, R39, R53, R55, R101
Dorsey Brothers, The (Tommy
and Jimmy), 12, F61, 292,
R53, F61, B270
Dorsey Brothers, The (CD),
D2598
Dorsey Brothers, The--Harlem

Lullaby (CD), D2599
Dorsey Brothers Orchestra,
The, D96-98, D219-20, D286-
91, D2598, D2632
Dorziat, Gabrielle, F123
Double or Nothing (film), 22,
26, 77-78, F45
"Double Dozen Double-Damask
Dinner Napkins, The,"
(routine), F47
Douglas, Gordon, F147, F149
Douglas, Katya, F144
Douglas, Mike, V202, V207
Douglas, Paul (1907-59),
F113, F115, R14-15
Dowling, Doris, F99
"Down Among the Sheltering
Palms," D1326
"Down Argentine Way," D1456
"Down By the Old Mill
Stream," D421
"Down By the River," D279,
F30
"Down By the Riverside,"
D1133
"Down in the Valley," D1478,
D2422
Down Memory Lane (film), 36,
F104
Down Memory Lane (album),
D2338
"Down the Old Ox Road," D236,
D1177, F16-17, V160
"Down Where the Trade Winds
Play" (song), F74
Downbeat (periodical), 28,
37, 79, poll 82, B130
Downey, Morton, F11-12, R15,
R88
Downriver Golf Course, Spo-
kane, 6
Downs, Hugh (b. 1921), V109,
V135
Doylestown, PA, 60
Dr. Cook's Garden (TV film),
61, 88, F154, V171
Dr. Rhythm (film), see Doctor
Rhythm
Drake, Alfred, V1A
Drake, Doña (b. 1920), F66-
67, F83
Draper, Paul, F90
"Dream a Little Dream of Me,"
D1324-24A, D2294
"Dream Girl of Pi K. A.,"
D539
Dream House (film), 15, F9,
F33, F146
"Dream House" (song), F9
Drew, Ellen (b. 1915), F48
"Drifting and Dreaming," D816
Drifing and Dreaming (album),
D2339

"Flores Negras," see "You're the Moment of a Lifetime"
Florida, 4, 5, 86
"Flow Gently Sweet Afton," D1478, D2422
"Fly by Night" (film project), 223
"Flying Trapeze," see "The Daring Young Man"
Flynn, Joe, V176
Folger, Abigail, 54
"Folks Who Live on the Hill, The," D357
Follen, V., B123
Fonda, Henry (1905-83), 297, R30
Fontaine, Frank (1920-78), F111, F122
Fontaine, Jacqueline, F126
Fontaine, Joan (b. 1917), F99, V83
"Fool Me Some More," D142
"For He's a Jolly Good Fellow," D1478, D2422
"For Love Alone," D325
"For Want of a Nail," D1364
"For You," F10, F34
Forbes Field, Pittsburgh, 84
Ford Motors, 5, 12, 47, 50
Ford, John (1895-1973), F149
Ford, Tennessee Ernie (1919-91), V117
"Ford Radio Show, The," 85, R117
"Ford Star Jubilee Salute to Cole Porter," V18, V26
"Ford Star Jubilee: High Tor," V16, see High Tor
"Ford V-8 Review," R22
Fordham, John, B259
Fordham Preparatory School, 64, 90
Foreman Avenue, Spokane, 17, 76
Forever (album), D2353
"Forever and Ever," D1612
"Forevermore (Lei Aloha, Lei Makamae)," D1655
Fornebu, Norway, 65
Forrest, Sally, V18
"Forsaking All Others," D1040
Fort Ord, CA, R112
'40s Hits" (CD), D2602
Fortune (periodical), B133
"Forty-five Minutes from Broadway," D1478, D2422
Foulk, Robert, F147
Fountain, Pete, V48
"Fountain in the Park," see "While Strolling Through the Park"
Four Aces, The, R114
Four Lads, The, 48

Four Preps, The, V21
Four Tops, The, V153
"Four Walls," D1668
"Four Winds and the Seven Seas, The," D939
Fourcade, Christian (b. 1944), F123
Fourcade, Christiane, F123
Foursome, The, D460
Fowley, Douglas, F31
Fox Film Corp., 13-14, 16, 74, 82, F1, F7-10, F15, F85, F100, see 20th Century-Fox
Fox, Sonny, V164
Fox Movietone Follies of 1929, 13
Foxx, Redd (1922-91), V236
Foy, Eddie Jr. (1905-83), F69
France, 29, 39-40, 48, 55, 59, 82, 87
Frances (film), F169
Franchi, Sergio, V160
Franciosa, Tony, V61
"Frangipani Blossom," D1658
Frank, Abe, 13, 15, 75
Frank, Mel, 54
Frank De Vol Orchestra, D1389-92
"Frank Sinatra Timex Show, The," V32
Franklin, Joe, V224
Frawley, William (1887-1966), F28, F45, F58, F72, R24
"Fred Allen Show, The," R86
Fred Waring and his Pennsylvanians, D941-42, D1102-03, D1680-84
Fred Waring Glee Club, The, D847-48, D941-42
Frederickson, Barbara, 52
Freed, Arthur, D128, D132, F159
"Freedom Train, The," D844
Freeman, Mona (b. 1926), 41, F81, F94, F117
Freeman, Y. Frank, 26, F67
"Freemont, Y. Frank" (character), F67
Freleng, I., F40
French golf championship, 85
"Frenesi," D1841, R41
"Frère Jacques," D1877, F123
Friars Club, The, 17, 41, 75
Friday, Pat, R33
Friedenwald, Will, 19, B124
"Friend of Yours, A," D664
"Friendly Islands, The," D993
"Friendly Mountains," D817, F99
"Friendly Persuasion," D1760
Friendly Persuasion (film), 263

Hollywood, 21, 77, F38, F72
Graves, Teresa, V174
Gray, Colleen (b. 1922), F108
Gray, Dolores (b. 1924), V18
Gray, Lita, 18
Grayson, Kathryn (b. 1922), F97, F127
Great Country Hits (album), D2361
"Great Day," D125, D1824
Great Depression, The, 16-17, 68, F158, B280, see 1930s
Great Entertainers, The, Vol. 2, (CD) D2609
Great John L, The (film), 32, 80, 247
Great Songs! Great Bands! In a Sentimental Mood: I, (CD) D2610
Great St. Bernard, The (film project), 308
Great Standards (album), 162, D2362
Great Victor Duets (CD), D2611
Greatest Christmas Show, The (album), D2363
Greatest Hits of Bing Crosby The (album), D2364
Greatest Show on Earth, The (film), 40, 83, F117
Green, Eddie, F86
Green, Harry, F20
"Green Eyes," D1855
"Green Grow the Lilacs," D1405
Green Mill, The, Chicago, 11
Greene, Richard, 22
Greenock, Scotland, 29
Greenwood Press, xiv, 91, B285
Greer, Ethel, F59
Greig, Robert, F39
Grey, Joel, V215
Grey, Lynda, F64
Greystoke, Cumberland, England, 59
Grieg, Edvard (1843-1907), D688, D692
Grier, Jimmy, 14, R17, see Jimmy Grier Orchestra
"Grieving," D54
Griffin, Merv (b. 1925), V212
Griffith, James, F129
Griffith, Julia, F7
Grillo, Basil, 32, 36, 60, 66, 80
Grimes, Karolyn, F90
Grimes, Tammy, V107
Groaner, The Old (nickname), 22, 52, 58, 60, 63, 65
Grofe, Ferde, F2
Gruber, Franz, see "Silent

Night"
Grumpy Old Men (film), F179
Guadalajara, Mexico, 62, 88
Guardsmen Quartet, The, D296, D311-12
Guest, Raymond R., 37
"Guest Star Time," R110
Guild Hall, Preston, England, 90
Guinness Book of World Records, 68
Guldahl, Ralph, F46
"Gulf Screen Guild Show, The: Revue," R32
"Gulf Screen Guild Theatre: Altar Bound," R41; "Mr. Jinx Goes to Sea," R35; "Too Many Husbands," R44
"Gumtree Canoe," see "Tom Bigbee River"
Gus Arnheim Cocoanut Grove Orchestra, D142-50, D153-54
"Gus Edwards' Medley," D452-54, D455
Guthrie, Woody (1912-67), D1681
Gutmacher, Glenn, xiii
Guy Called Bing, A, B14
Guy Lombardo Royal Canadians, D216-18, D1152-53, D2326
Guy Lombardo: 16 Most Requested Songs (CD), D2612
Guys and Dolls (film), 45, 280
Guys and Dolls (CD), D2613
Gwynne, Helen, B134
"Gypsy in My Soul, The" (song), V18A
"Gypsy Love Song," D405
G-Man, 17
"G.I. Journal" (radio), R126

Haads, William, F67
Hagen, Earle, F137
Hagen, Walter, F53
"Hail, Alma Mater," F72
Haines, Connie, R57
Hajdu, David, B141
Hal Roach Studios, 37
Hale, Barbara (b. 1922), F70, F102
Haley, Jack (1899-1979), F70
Haley, Jack Jr., F157
Hall, Thurston (1883-1958), F51, F92
"Hall of Fame Awards," V148
Haller, Scot, B135
Hall-Johnson Negro Choir, F61
Halo Shampoo, D1318
Hamburger, Philip, B136
Hamilton, John, F47
Hamilton, Mahlon, F30
Hamilton, Margaret (1902-85),

75
Jack Teagarden Orchestra,
D532-33, see Teagarden, Jack
"Jackie Gleason Show, The,"
48, V134, "The Honeymooners
in Hollywood" V154
Jacklin, Tony, V232
Jackson, Eddie, 295
Jackson, Mahalia (1911-72),
50, V26
Jacobs, Jody, B159
Jagger, Dean (1903-91), F125
Jaglom, Henry, F161
Jamaica, 53, 86
"Jamboree Jones," D971
James, Claire, F88
James, Harry (1916-83), 24,
56, F73, F82, R91
James, Margot, 42
Jamison, Bud, F14, F64
Janssen, David, V61
Jascha Heifetz--The Decca
Masters (CD), D2626
Jasper National Park, Canada,
34, F99; Invitational Golf
Tournament, 81
Jazz, ix, xi, 4-5, 7-10, 13,
19, 23, 33, 38, 47, 54, 60,
63, 66, 70, 74, 89, B239,
B259, B265, B268, B285
Jazz on CD and Cassette
(periodical), 70
Jazzin' Bing Crosby, The
(album), D2387
Jazzin' Bing Crosby, 1927-
1940 (CD), D2627
"Jealous Heart," D1667
Jean, Gloria, F57
Jeanmaire, Zizi (Renée) (b.
1924), 45, D1233, F129
"Jeepers Creepers," D1289
Jeff Alexander Chorus, D922
passim to D1006
Jello Pudding, R27
Jenkins, Allen, F147
"Jennie Jenkins," D1406
Jenks, Franky (1902-62), F60
Jens, Salome, F135
Jerome Kern Songs (album),
D2388
Jerome Kern--A Fine Romance
(CD), D2628
Jessel, George (1898-1981),
F51, R28, V150
"Jim, Johnny and Jonas,"
D1229
Jimmy Dorsey Orchestra, D313-
15, D322-24, D330-31, D337-
41, D740-41, D796, see
Dorsey, Jimmy, and the
Dorsey Brothers
Jimmy Durante and Bing Crosby
(CD), D2629

"Jimmy Durante Story" (film
project), 295
Jimmy Grier Orchestra, D26-
40, D254-57, R17
"Jimmy Valentine," D453
"Jingle Bells," 26-27, 43,
D633, D2408, D2680, 195 No
8, F6, F170
"Joan Rivers Show, The," B146
Joe Bushkin Celebrates 100
Years of Recorded Sound
(album), D2389
Joe Bushkin Quartet, 66,
D1871, D1825
Joe Bushkin Trio, 63, 89, see
Bushkin, Joe
"Joe Franklin Show, The,"
V224
Joe Venuti Orchestra, D456-
57, D864-65, see Venuti,
Joe
"Joey Bishop Show, The,"
V131A
Johannessen, Grant, V90
"John Barleycorn," 84, D1262,
D1265, F131
John Scott Trotter's Frying
Pan Five, D460, D1073
John Scott Trotter Orchestra,
D348 passim to D1228
"John Wayne TV Special,
The--Swing Out, Sweet
Land," V169
"Johnnny Appleseed," D1354
Johnson, Arte, V176
Johnson, Dwight "Spike," ix,
5-6
Johnson, Eddie, F67
Johnson, Rita (1912-65), 336
Johnston, Arthur, D96, D156,
D165, D226 passim to D441,
D1163 passim to D1214,
D1441, D1898, 196, F16,
F20, F41, F45
Johnston, Johnnie, F67
Johnston, Mary, D1660
Johnston, Pat, D656
Join Bing and Sing Along
(album), D1410-37, D2390
Join Bing and Sing Along: 51
Good Time Songs (album),
D2391
Join Bing in a Gang Song Sing
Along (album), D2392
Joker Is Wild, The (book) 11,
film F134
Jolson, Al (1886-1950), xiii,
4, 14, 17, 21, 34, 72, 81,
D829-30, D1337, D1598,
D1698, D2217, D2233, D2530,
196 No. 16, F39, F56, F65,
F74, R17, R24, R31, R80,
R83, R92, R96-97, R99, B260

Jolson Sings Again, F102
Jonay, Roberta, F81, F99
Jones, Anissa "Buffy," V149
Jones, Jacqueline, F144
Jones, Jane, F50
Jones, Jennifer (b. 1919),
  42, F126
Jones, Max, B265
Jones, Paul, 25, 270
Jones, Shirley (b. 1934),
  F142, V18, V217
Jones, Spike (1911-65), R43,
  R65, R77, R79
Jonson, Ben (1572-1637),
  D1478
"Joobalai," D400, F49
Joplin, Scott (1868-1917),
  D1847
Joseph Lilley Orchestra, D674
  passim to D710, D1089-90,
  D1158-60A, D1195-96, D1217-
  19, D1224-27, D1231-33,
  D1260-66, D1272-73, D1371-
  71A, see Lilley, Joseph J.
"Joshua Fit de Battle of
  Jericho," D1478, D2422, V33
Joslin, Howard, F126
Joslyn, Allyn (1905-81), F57
"Joy to the World," D1252
"Joyful Hour, The," V18D
Jud Conlon Choir, D1039-41,
  D1220-21; Singers, D957-59;
  Conlon's Rhythmaires,
  ?D948-52, D968-69, D982,
  D987-90, see the Rhyth-
  maires
Judy and Bing Together
  (album), D2393
Judy Garland--Changing My
  Tune (CD), D2630
Juicy Seven, The, 4-5, 72
Juke Box Saturday Night (CD),
  D2631
Juliette, V108
Julius Caesar (play), 3
"June Comes Around Every
  Year," D689, F84
"June in January," 19, D271,
  D1185, D1956, F28, F134
"June Is Bustin' Out All
  Over," D1962
"Just a Gigolo," D150
"Just a Kid Named Joe," D412
"Just a Little Lovin'," D1080
"Just a Prayer Away," D666
Just an Echo (film), 19, 76,
  F23
"Just an Echo in the Valley"
  (theme song), D210, D1167,
  F16, F21, F23, 317
"Just an Old Romance" (song),
  F48
"Just Around the Corner,"
  D2194
"Just A-Wearyin' for You,"
  D263, D715
Just Breezin' Along (album),
  D2394, (CD) D2632
Just for Fun (album), D2395
"Just for Tonight," D1768E
Just for You (film), 36, 39,
  82-83, F119
"Just for You" (song), D1069,
  F119
Just for You (album ST),
  D2396
"Just My Luck," D772
"Just One More Chance," 13,
  15, 74-75, D156, D165,
  D441, D1163, D1902, F6, F8,
  F16, F93, F156
Just One More Chance (film),
  see One More Chance
"Just One of Those Things,"
  D695
"Just One Word of Consola-
  tion," D329
"Just Plain Lonesome," D594
"Just What I Wanted for
  Christmas," D1392
"Just You, Just Me," D2135
"J'attendrai," D759

Kabibble, Ish (Mervyn Bogue,
  1909-94), F108
Kahn, Gus (lyricist, 1886-
  1941), D83, D87, D166
  passim to D275, D443 passim
  to D554, D807 passim to
  D882, D1072 passim to
  D1215, D1328 passim to
  D1437, D1718 passim to
  D1866, D2130, D2170, D2193
Kahn, Madeline, F156
"Kaigoon" (song), F54
Kaiser, Henry J. (1882-1967),
  F16
Kamm, Herb, B127-28
Kane, Margie "Babe," F10, F14
Kapp, Dave ("Mickey Leader"),
  D666, D712, D879, D1763,
  178
Kapp, Jack, 15, 19-20, 28,
  79, D241/43
Karloff, Boris (1887-1969),
  F87
Karlson, Phil, F104
Kasznar, Kurt (1913-79), F129
Katchenaro, Pete, F66
"Kathryn Crosby Show, The,"
  V193
"Katrina" (song), D888, D950,
  F103
Kauai, Hawaii, 55
Kay Thompson Reviews, The
  (album), D2397

F135, F142
KPTV, Portland, OR, 48
Kraft Choral Society, R65
"Kraft Music Hall" (radio)
   19, 21, 32, 52, 77, 79, 81,
   86, 90, R20-21, R23-25, R27
   passim to R77, (TV) 350,
   B80
Kraft Music Hall (album),
   D2399
Kristofferson, Kris, F149
Kruger, Otto, 247
Kuhl, Cal, 20, 320, R20
   passim to R77
"Kukuberra Sits in the Old
   Gum Tree, A," D1878
Kulp, Nancy, V176
Kurnitz, H., B163
Kyser, Kay (1897-1985), F182,
   R71

"La borracita," D1859
"La Golondrina (The
   Swallow)," D58
"La mer," D1116
La Moraleja Golf Club, Spain,
   66, 90
"La Paloma," D57
"La Piñata" (song), V75
"La Seine," D1118
"La vie en rose," D990, D1121
Ladd, Alan (1913-64), 23, 44,
   F67, F83, F86, F91, F94
Ladd, Cheryl (Stoppelmoore,
   b. 1951), F163
Ladd, Diane (b. 1932), F163
Ladd, Sue Carol, see Carol
   (Ladd), Sue
Ladies Professional Golf
   Association, 62, B298
"Lady Esther Screen Guild
   Players": "Going My Way,"
   R68; "Holiday Inn," R47;
   "The Bells of St. Mary's,"
   R78; "The Birth of the
   Blues," R51
"Lady Is a Tramp, The," D2186
Lady Lonsdale, 59
Laemmle, Carl, F2
Lafayette Cafe, Hollywood, 7,
   73
Lahr, Bert (1895-1967), F94,
   F146, R31
Laine, Frankie (b. 1913), 37,
   48, D953, D2168, R83
Lake, Veronica (1919-73),
   F67, F84, F86, F94
Lake Saratoga, NY, 19
Lakeside Golf Club, Holly-
   wood, 12, 15, 17, 21, 77
Lamarr, Hedy (b. 1913), F182,
   R44
Lamb, Gil (b. 1906), F67

Lamour, Dorothy (b. 1914), x,
   17, 23, 25, 34, 40, 64, 66,
   78, F54, F59, F66-67, F69,
   F86, F88, F91, F94-95,
   F111, F117, F120, F144,
   F180, R45, R52, R106, V3,
   V119, V131A, V144, V150,
   B266
"Lamplighter's Serenade,
   The," D576
Lancaster, Burt (b. 1913),
   280, F94, F132
"Land Around Us, The," D1224,
   F126
"Land of the Midnight Sun,
   The" (song), V163
Landon, Michael (1936-91),
   V191
Lane, Charles (b. 1899), F58,
   F108
Lane, Ken, V179
Lane, Muriel, D557-60
Lane (Mullican), Priscilla
   (b. 1917), F28, R40, see
   the Lane Sisters
Lane, Robbie, and the Disci-
   ples, V108
Lane Sisters, The (Lola,
   Rosemary and Priscilla),
   F28, F51
Lanfield, Sidney, F63
Lang, Eddie (1900-33), x-xi,
   12, 15-17, 19, 40, 58, 74-
   76, F12, R11-15
Lang, Kitty (Kitty Lang
   Good), 17
Lang, Walter, F85
Langdon, Harry (1884-1944),
   F19, F146
Langford, Frances (b. 1914),
   D330-31, D405-06, V127,
   V245B
Lani, Prince Lei, F42
Lani McIntire Hawaiians,
   D335-36, D352-55
Lansky, Meyer, 50
Lantz, Walter (1900-94), F2
Lardner, John, 33, B164
Lareida's Dance Pavilion,
   Spokane, 6, 73
LaRocca, Nick, D1475, D2158,
   F61, see the Original
   Dixieland Jazz Band
LaRocque, Ray, B165
"Laroo Laroo Lilli Bolero,"
   D876
LaRue, Grace, F57
LaRue, Jack (1903-84), F88,
   F91, F147
Las Cruces, Mexico, 50, 54-
   58, 86-87
Las Vegas, NV, 49-51, 56, 68,
   85

Mears, Martha, F64
Medford, Kay, V179
Medved, Michael, B288
Meek, Donald (1880-1946),
  F41, F85
Meeker, George, F95
"Meet Me in St. Louis," D1419
"Meet Me Tonight in Dream-
  land," D2191
"Meet the Sun Half Way,"
  D473, F57
Megaphone, 5-6
Mel Torme Mel Tones and
  Instrumental Trio, D749-51,
  see Torme, Mel
"Melancholie," D1582
"Melancholy Baby" (song), F61
Melchior, Lauritz (1890-
  1973), R64
"Mele Kalikimaka," D1011,
  F176
Melesh, Alex, F49
Mello, Edward J., B19
Mellomen, The, D1027, D1089-
  92, D1235
Melody in Spring (film), 18
Melotone Records, 91
"Memories," D870
"Memories Are Made of This,"
  D1277
Memories of You (CD), D2636
Memphis Five, The, x
Menjou, Adolphe (1890-1963),
  F70
Menzies, William Cameron, F5
Mercer, Johnny (lyricist,
  1909-76), 26, 63, 89, D315,
  D340, D361, D384-86, D394
  passim to D691, D966-67
  passim to D1308, D1473-75,
  D1746, D1783, D1794, D1799-
  1800A passim to D2169,
  D2411, 196-97, F38, F61,
  F67, F81, F84, F111, F119,
  R30, R36, R51, R67, R91,
  V36, V111, V221, B179
Merkel, Una (1903-86), F59,
  F114
Merman, Ethel (1908-84), 20,
  (CD) D2530, F6, F26, F35,
  F37, F94, R80, R91, V142A,
  V161
"Merrily We Roll Along"
  (song), F9
"Merry Christmas, Fred, from
  the Crosbys" (TV), 64, V208
Merry Christmas (album), 34,
  38, D820-21, D2408, (CD)
  D2639-40, 195 No. 3
Merry Christmas (CD), D2637-
  38,
Merry Christmas--All Time
  Christmas Hits (CD), D2641

Merry Macs, The, D500, D521-
  22, F110
"Merry-Go-Runaround," D1092,
  F120
"Merv Griffin Show, The,"
  V212
Metro-Goldwyn-Mayer Studios,
  17, 46, 48, 76, 79, 84, 89,
  F21 passim to F32, F62, F97
  passim to F130, F133 passim
  to F159, 316 No. 30
"Metropolis," D45
Metropolitan Studios, Holly-
  wood, 8, 73, F22
Metropolitan Theatre, Los
  Angeles, 7, 73
Metrotone News, F62
"Mexicali Rose," D393, D1206
Mexican Ballet, The, F119
Mexico, 62, 63, 75, 88
Meyers, Vic, x, 5-6
Microphone, 8, 13-14, 16, 34,
  49, 75
Midji Minstrels, The, 22
Midler, Bette (b. 1945), V233
Midwest, 11
"Mighty Lak' a Rose," D752
"Mike Douglas Show, The,"
  V202, V207
"Milady," D981, F110
Milestone, Lewis, F37
Military, U.S., 26-27, 78-79
Miljan, John (1893-1960),
  F18, F30
Milland, Raymond (1905-86),
  32, F26, F67, F94
Millbrae, CA, 90
Miller, Ann (b. 1919), F112
Miller, David, F101
Miller, David Humphreys, F149
Miller, Dennis, x
Miller, Glenn (1904-44), 29,
  F72
Miller, John "Skins," F101
Miller, Johnny, V232
Miller, Julia Rinker, 60
Miller, Lisa, V151
Miller, Roger, V132
Millican, James, F67
Milligan, Spike (Ahmednagar,
  b. 1918), V94
Millionaire for Christy, A,
  F114
Millionairess (British,
  1960), F144
Mills Brothers, The, x, 8,
  18-19, 63, 76, 89, D176,
  D219-20, F12, F79, R17,
  R88, R96, R107, V121, V233
"Mills Brothers Charity Show,
  The" (TV), 63, 89
Mills Brothers, Chronological
  (CD), D2642

"Riders in the Sky," see
"Ghost Riders"
Riders of the Purple Sage,
The, R66
Riding High (film), 37, 82,
F108, B198
"Ridin' Around in the Rain,"
D257, medley F26
"Ridin' Down the Canyon,"
D550
Rigoletto (opera), F111
Riley, Jeannie C., V143
Ring, Blanche, F57
Ringling Brothers and Barnum
& Bailey Circus, 51, F117
"Rings on My Fingers" (song),
F50
Rinker, Alton "Al" (1907-82),
3, 5-6, 9, 27, 60, 69, 73,
79, D850, F2-4, F6, F61,
B211-12, see the Rhythm
Boys and Bailey, Mildred
Rinker, Miles (Al's brother),
5
"Rip Van Winkle," D1314
Rip Van Winkle (album), D2443
Ripley, Clements, 257
Ripstitch the Tailor (film),
13, 74, F1
Rising River Ranch, CA, 47,
68, 84
Riss, Dan, F133
"River, The," D1157
River Derwent, Cockermouth,
England, 60, V116A
"River Stay Away from My
Door," D1747
Rivers, Joan (b. 1933), 69
Riviera, The, 54
Riviera Country Club, The,
Los Angeles, F72
RKO, 13, 74
RKO-Pathe, F3
Roach, Hal, 75
Road Begins, The (album),
D2444
Road to Bali (film), 40, 83,
F120, V282
"Road to Bali, The," D1095,
F120, V282
Road to Bali, The (album),
D2445
"Road to Bombay" (film
project), 303
"Road to Brooklyn" (film
project), 257
"Road to Calcutta" (film
project), 303
"Road to Christmas" (film
project), 309
"Road to Glory, The" (misno-
mer), F73
Road to Hollywood (film), 32,

F93, V283
Road to Hong Kong, The
(film), 54, 55, 86, D1591-
93, F54, F144, V49, V284
Road to Hong Kong, The
(album), D2446
"Road to Hong Kong, The,"
D1593, F144
"Road to India" (film
project), 303
"Road to Lebanon, The" (TV)
V109, V285
"Road to Mandalay, The" (film
project), 23
Road to Morocco (film), 25-
26, 79, F66, version R48
"Road to Morocco, The," D615,
D687, F66, F162, R48, V21
Road to Peace, The (film),
F107
Road to Rio, 34, 81, F54,
F95, V286
Road to Singapore (film), 23,
78, F54
"Road to the Fountain of
Youth" (film project), 64,
90, 312
"Road to the Moon" (film
project), 283
"Road to Tomorrow" (film
project), 64, 311
Road to Utopia (film), 28,
32, 79, 81, F88, F94, F181,
V287
Road to Utopia (album), D2710
Road to Victory, The (film),
28, 79, F75
Road to Zanzibar (film), 23-
24, 78, F59
"Roamin' in the Gloamin',"
D1696
Robards, Jason Jr. (b. 1922),
297
Robert Mitchell Boys' Choir,
F72
Roberti, Lyda (1910-38), F35
Roberts, Murray, V249
Robertson, Ralph, F12
Robeson, Paul (1898-1976),
35, R40, R42
Robin and the 7 Hoods (film),
57, 87, D1685-87, F147,
V288
Robin and the 7 Hoods
(album), D2447
Robin, Leo (lyricist, 1900-
73), D104, D108, D200,
D202, D258 passim to D400,
D502, D775-76, D778-79,
D1068-69, D1077-79, D1156
passim to D1285, D1899,
D1910, D1956, D2185, 196-
97, F12, F27-28, F35, F37-

"TV Variety: 8," V292
Twain, Mark (Samuel L. Clemens, 1825-1910), F100, V168, see Tom Sawyer
"Twelve Days of Christmas, The," D926
Twelve Songs of Christmas (album), D1688-92, D2490
20th Anniversary in Show Business (album), D2491
Twentieth Century-Fox Film Corp., 9, 20, 31, 50, 80, 85, see William Fox Film Corp.
20 Beautiful Christmas Songs (CD), D2687
20 Golden Greats (CD), D2688
20 Golden Memories (CD), D2689
Twiggy (Leslie Hornby, b. 1946), V242-43
"Twilight on the Trail," D301
Twilight on the Trail (album), D2492
Twiss, Ken (1912-93), xiii, 4, B300
"Twixt Myself and Me," F100
"Two Boys and a Piano--Singing Songs Their Own Way" (billing), 7-8, 73
"Two Cigarettes in the Dark," D268
Two for the Seesaw (film), 297
"Two for Tonight," D289, F31
Two for Tonight (film), 19, 77, F31
Two Plus Fours (film), 13, 74, F3
"Two Shadows on the Sand," D1589
"Two Shillelagh O'Sullivan," D1074
Two Tickets to Broadway (film), F112
"Two Tickets to Georgia" (song), F23
Tyler, Dickie, F87
Tyler, Leon, F119

Uggams, Leslie (b. 1943), V111
Ulanov, Barry, 24, 31, B32, B237
"Umh-Hum," see "All She'd Say Was 'Umh-Hum'"
"Unchained Melody," D2132
"Uncle Sam Sans Whiskers" (article), B238
"Under Paris Skies," D1580
Under Western Skies (album), D2713
United Artists of England, 63

United Nations, The, D1471, 161
U.N. International Children's Choir, V132
United Service Organization (USO), 28-29, V245B
"USO Christmas Show," V28
U.S. Department of State, 61
U.S. Olympic Fund, F126
U.S. Olympic Team, V3
U.S. Senate, 53, Commerce Committee 48, 85
U.S.S. Nathaniel Crosby, 29
U.S. War Department, see Department of War
Universal Studios, 12, 23, 78
University of California at Berkeley, 8
"Until You've Played the Palace" (song), V161
"Up, Up and Away," D1740
"Up a Lazy River," D1471
Uris Theater, N.Y., 64, 90, B5, B196, see "Bing on Broadway"
Usher Hall, Edinburgh, 64

Vacuum Foods Corp., 35, 46
Vagabond King, The (film), F127
Valens, Ricky, 48
Valente, Caterina (b. 1931), V54, V97
Valentine, Hobart, 2
Valentine, Karen, V194
Valentino, Rudolph (1895-1926), 8
Vallee, Rudy (Hubert Vallée, 1901-86), x-xi, 23, D847, D1883, F4, F6, F11-13, R10, R13, R19, R21, R24, R67, R77, R80, R91, R131, V142A
Van, Bobby (1930-80), V59
Van Heusen, James "Jimmy" (Edward Chester Babcock, 1913-90) 24-26, 48, 68, 79, D382, D507, D517-20, D557 passim to D1732, D1894, D1904, D2144, 196-97, F46, F59, F66, F69, F72, 247, F86-88, F92, F94-95, F99-101, F108, F110, F113, F120, F123, F129, F134, F137, F140-41, F144, F147, V29, V32, V41, V62, B33
Van Horne, Harriet, 51
Vancouver, B.C., 39, 52, R88
Vandervoort, Paul II, B238
Vanoff, Nick, V52, V54, V59-60, V159, see "The Hollywood Palace"
Variety (periodical), B66
Variety Clubs International,

About the Author

J. ROGER OSTERHOLM is a Professor in the Humanities Department at Embry-Riddle Aeronautical University, Daytona Beach, Florida, where he teaches courses in cultural history, aviation literature, and writing. A native of Worcester, Massachusetts, he has degrees from Upsala College, the City College of New York, and the University of Massachusetts at Amherst. He also attended Texas Tech University, Clark University, and Worcester State College. He has taught at several colleges in Massachusetts and Florida.

ISBN 0-313-27726-5

90000>

HARDCOVER BAR CODE